THIS

HOLY BIBLE

IS PRESENTED TO

BY

ON

THY WORD IS A LAMP UNTO MY FEET,
AND A LIGHT UNTO MY PATH.

PSALM 119:105

KING JAMES VERSION

New Testament

THOMAS NELSON
KJV

THOMAS NELSON
Since 1798

www.ThomasNelson.com

KJV Personal Size New Testament

Published in Nashville, TN, by Thomas Nelson. Thomas Nelson is a registered trademark of HarperCollins Christian Publishing, Inc.

Library of Congress Control Number: 2025931445

A Note Regarding the Type

This Bible was set in the Thomas Nelson KJV Typeface, commissioned by Thomas Nelson Publishers and designed in Aarhus by Klaus Krogh and Heidi Rand Sørensen of 2K/DENMARK. The design takes inspiration from a distinctive typeface found in an early Thomas Nelson Novum Testamentum, printed in 1844 in Edinburgh—a type that in turn reflects several Scotch Roman fonts created by the celebrated English punchcutter Richard Austin for the type foundry of William Miller, circa 1808–1813. The designers of the Thomas Nelson KJV Typeface sought to reflect Thomas Nelson's rich, 200-year tradition of stewarding the KJV, while also embodying the best advancements in modern Bible typography. The result is a distinctive new Bible typeface that is uncompromisingly beautiful, bold and readable at any size, and perfectly suited to the King James Version.

Printed in India

25 26 27 28 29 30 31 32 33 /BPI/ 15 14 13 12 11 10 9 8 7 6 5 4 3 2 1

CONTENTS

THE NEW TESTAMENT

The Gospel According to
MATTHEW

The Genealogy of Christ

The book of the generation of Jesus Christ, the son of David, the son of Abraham.

2 Abraham begat Isaac; and Isaac begat Jacob; and Jacob begat Judas and his brethren;

3 And Judas begat Phares and Zara of Thamar; and Phares begat Esrom; and Esrom begat Aram;

4 And Aram begat Aminadab; and Aminadab begat Naasson; and Naasson begat Salmon;

5 And Salmon begat Booz of Rachab; and Booz begat Obed of Ruth; and Obed begat Jesse;

6 And Jesse begat David the king; and David the king begat Solomon of her *that had been the wife* of Urias;

7 And Solomon begat Roboam; and Roboam begat Abia; and Abia begat Asa;

8 And Asa begat Josaphat; and Josaphat begat Joram; and Joram begat Ozias;

9 And Ozias begat Joatham; and Joatham begat Achaz; and Achaz begat Ezekias;

10 And Ezekias begat Manasses; and Manasses begat Amon; and Amon begat Josias;

11 And Josias begat Jechonias and his brethren, about the time they were carried away to Babylon:

12 And after they were brought to Babylon, Jechonias begat Salathiel; and Salathiel begat Zorobabel;

13 And Zorobabel begat Abiud; and Abiud begat Eliakim; and Eliakim begat Azor;

14 And Azor begat Sadoc; and Sadoc begat Achim; and Achim begat Eliud;

15 And Eliud begat Eleazar; and Eleazar begat Matthan; and Matthan begat Jacob;

16 And Jacob begat Joseph the husband of Mary, of whom was born Jesus, who is called Christ.

17 So all the generations from Abraham to David *are* fourteen generations; and from David until the carrying away into Babylon *are* fourteen generations; and from the carrying away into Babylon unto Christ *are* fourteen generations.

The Birth of Christ

18 Now the birth of Jesus Christ was on this wise: When as his mother Mary was espoused to Joseph, before they came together, she was found with child of the Holy Ghost.

19 Then Joseph her husband, being a just *man,* and not willing to make her a publick example, was minded to put her away privily.

20 But while he thought on these things, behold, the angel of the Lord appeared unto him in a dream, saying, Joseph, thou son of David, fear not to take unto thee Mary thy wife: for that which is conceived in her is of the Holy Ghost.

21 And she shall bring forth a son, and thou shalt call his name JESUS: for he shall save his people from their sins.

22 Now all this was done, that it might be fulfilled which was spoken of the Lord by the prophet, saying,

23 Behold, a virgin shall be with child, and shall bring forth a son, and they shall call his name Emmanuel, which being interpreted is, God with us.

24 Then Joseph being raised from sleep did as the angel of the Lord had bidden him, and took unto him his wife:

25 And knew her not till she had brought forth her firstborn son: and he called his name JESUS.

The Magi's Visit

2 Now when Jesus was born in Bethlehem of Judaea in the days of Herod the king, behold, there came wise men from the east to Jerusalem,

2 Saying, Where is he that is born King of the Jews? for we have seen his star in the east, and are come to worship him.

3 When Herod the king had heard *these things,* he was troubled, and all Jerusalem with him.

4 And when he had gathered all the chief priests and scribes of the people together, he demanded of them where Christ should be born.

5 And they said unto him, In Bethlehem of Judaea: for thus it is written by the prophet,

6 And thou Bethlehem, *in* the land of Juda, art not the least among the princes of Juda: for out of thee shall come a Governor, that shall rule my people Israel.

7 Then Herod, when he had privily called the wise men, enquired of them diligently what time the star appeared.

8 And he sent them to Bethlehem, and said, Go and search diligently for the young child; and when ye have found *him,* bring me word again, that I may come and worship him also.

9 When they had heard the king, they departed; and, lo, the star, which they saw in the east, went before them, till it came and stood over where the young child was.

10 When they saw the star, they rejoiced with exceeding great joy.

11 And when they were come into the house, they saw the young child with Mary his mother, and fell down, and worshipped him: and when they had opened their treasures, they presented unto him gifts; gold, and frankincense, and myrrh.

12 And being warned of God in a dream that they should not return to Herod, they departed into their own country another way.

The Flight to Egypt

13 And when they were departed, behold, the angel of the Lord appeareth to Joseph in a dream, saying, Arise, and take the young child and his mother, and flee into Egypt, and be thou there until I bring thee word: for Herod will seek the young child to destroy him.

14 When he arose, he took the young child and his mother by night, and departed into Egypt:

15 And was there until the death of Herod: that it might be fulfilled which was spoken of the Lord by the prophet, saying, Out of Egypt have I called my son.

16 Then Herod, when he saw that he was mocked of the wise men, was exceeding wroth, and sent forth, and slew all the children that were in Bethlehem, and in all the coasts thereof, from two years old and under, according to the time which he had diligently enquired of the wise men.

17 Then was fulfilled that which was spoken by Jeremy the prophet, saying,

18 In Rama was there a voice heard, lamentation, and weeping, and great mourning, Rachel weeping *for* her children, and would not be comforted, because they are not.

The Return to Nazareth

19 But when Herod was dead, behold, an angel of the Lord appeareth in a dream to Joseph in Egypt,

20 Saying, Arise, and take the young child and his mother, and go into the land of Israel: for they are dead which sought the young child's life.

21 And he arose, and took the young child and his mother, and came into the land of Israel.

22 But when he heard that Archelaus did reign in Judaea in the room of his father Herod, he was afraid to go thither: notwithstanding, being warned of God in a dream, he turned aside into the parts of Galilee:

23 And he came and dwelt in a city called Nazareth: that it might be fulfilled which was spoken by the prophets, He shall be called a Nazarene.

John the Baptist's Ministry

3 In those days came John the Baptist, preaching in the wilderness of Judaea,

2 And saying, Repent ye: for the kingdom of heaven is at hand.

3 For this is he that was spoken of by the prophet Esaias, saying, The voice of one crying in the wilderness, Prepare ye the way of the Lord, make his paths straight.

4 And the same John had his raiment of camel's hair, and a leathern girdle about his loins; and his meat was locusts and wild honey.

5 Then went out to him Jerusalem, and all Judaea, and all the region round about Jordan,

6 And were baptized of him in Jordan, confessing their sins.

7 But when he saw many of the Pharisees and Sadducees come to his baptism, he said unto them, O generation of vipers, who hath warned you to flee from the wrath to come?

8 Bring forth therefore fruits meet for repentance:

9 And think not to say within yourselves, We have Abraham to *our* father: for I say unto you, that God is able of these stones to raise up children unto Abraham.

10 And now also the axe is laid unto the root of the trees: therefore every tree which bringeth not forth good fruit is hewn down, and cast into the fire.

11 I indeed baptize you with water unto repentance: but he that cometh after me is mightier than I, whose shoes I am not worthy to bear: he shall baptize you with the Holy Ghost, and *with* fire:

12 Whose fan *is* in his hand, and he will throughly purge his floor, and gather his wheat into the garner; but he will burn up the chaff with unquenchable fire.

The Baptism of the Beloved Son

13 Then cometh Jesus from Galilee to Jordan unto John, to be baptized of him.

14 But John forbad him, saying, I have need to be baptized of thee, and comest thou to me?

15 And Jesus answering said unto him, Suffer *it to be so* now: for thus it becometh us to fulfil all righteousness. Then he suffered him.

16 And Jesus, when he was baptized, went up straightway out of the water: and, lo, the heavens were opened unto him, and he saw the Spirit of God descending like a dove, and lighting upon him:

17 And lo a voice from heaven, saying, This is my beloved Son, in whom I am well pleased.

The Three Temptations of Jesus

4 Then was Jesus led up of the Spirit into the wilderness to be tempted of the devil.

2 And when he had fasted forty
days and forty nights, he was after-
ward an hungred.
3 And when the tempter came to
him, he said, If thou be the Son of
God, command that these stones
be made bread.
4 But he answered and said, It is
written, Man shall not live by bread
alone, but by every word that pro-
ceedeth out of the mouth of God.
5 Then the devil taketh him up
into the holy city, and setteth him
on a pinnacle of the temple,
6 And saith unto him, If thou be
the Son of God, cast thyself down:
for it is written, He shall give his
angels charge concerning thee: and
in *their* hands they shall bear thee
up, lest at any time thou dash thy
foot against a stone.
7 Jesus said unto him, It is writ-
ten again, Thou shalt not tempt the
Lord thy God.
8 Again, the devil taketh him up
into an exceeding high mountain,
and sheweth him all the kingdoms
of the world, and the glory of them;
9 And saith unto him, All these
things will I give thee, if thou wilt
fall down and worship me.
10 Then saith Jesus unto him, Get
thee hence, Satan: for it is written,
Thou shalt worship the Lord thy
God, and him only shalt thou serve.
11 Then the devil leaveth him, and,
behold, angels came and ministered
unto him.

The Preaching Ministry of Jesus

12 Now when Jesus had heard
that John was cast into prison, he
departed into Galilee;
13 And leaving Nazareth, he came
and dwelt in Capernaum, which is
upon the sea coast, in the borders
of Zabulon and Nephthalim:
14 That it might be fulfilled which
was spoken by Esaias the prophet,
saying,
15 The land of Zabulon, and the
land of Nephthalim, *by* the way of
the sea, beyond Jordan, Galilee of
the Gentiles;
16 The people which sat in dark-
ness saw great light; and to them
which sat in the region and shadow
of death light is sprung up.
17 From that time Jesus began to
preach, and to say, Repent: for the
kingdom of heaven is at hand.

The Calling of the First Four Disciples

18 And Jesus, walking by the
sea of Galilee, saw two brethren,
Simon called Peter, and Andrew his
brother, casting a net into the sea:
for they were fishers.
19 And he saith unto them, Follow
me, and I will make you fishers of
men.
20 And they straightway left *their*
nets, and followed him.
21 And going on from thence,
he saw other two brethren, James
the son of Zebedee, and John his
brother, in a ship with Zebedee their
father, mending their nets; and he
called them.
22 And they immediately left the
ship and their father, and followed
him.

The Healing Ministry of Jesus

23 And Jesus went about all Gal-
ilee, teaching in their synagogues,
and preaching the gospel of the
kingdom, and healing all manner
of sickness and all manner of disease
among the people.
24 And his fame went throughout
all Syria: and they brought unto him
all sick people that were taken with
divers diseases and torments, and
those which were possessed with
devils, and those which were luna-
tick, and those that had the palsy;
and he healed them.
25 And there followed him great
multitudes of people from Galilee,

and *from* Decapolis, and *from* Jeru-
salem, and *from* Judaea, and *from*
beyond Jordan.

The Beatitudes

5 And seeing the multitudes, he
went up into a mountain: and
when he was set, his disciples came
unto him:
2 And he opened his mouth, and
taught them, saying,
3 Blessed *are* the poor in spirit:
for theirs is the kingdom of heaven.
4 Blessed *are* they that mourn: for
they shall be comforted.
5 Blessed *are* the meek: for they
shall inherit the earth.
6 Blessed *are* they which do hun-
ger and thirst after righteousness:
for they shall be filled.
7 Blessed *are* the merciful: for they
shall obtain mercy.
8 Blessed *are* the pure in heart:
for they shall see God.
9 Blessed *are* the peacemakers:
for they shall be called the children
of God.
10 Blessed *are* they which are per-
secuted for righteousness' sake: for
theirs is the kingdom of heaven.
11 Blessed are ye, when *men* shall
revile you, and persecute *you,* and
shall say all manner of evil against
you falsely, for my sake.
12 Rejoice, and be exceeding glad:
for great *is* your reward in heaven:
for so persecuted they the prophets
which were before you.

The Salt of the Earth

13 Ye are the salt of the earth:
but if the salt have lost his savour,
wherewith shall it be salted? it is
thenceforth good for nothing, but
to be cast out, and to be trodden
under foot of men.
14 Ye are the light of the world. A
city that is set on an hill cannot be
hid.
15 Neither do men light a candle,
and put it under a bushel, but on a
candlestick; and it giveth light unto
all that are in the house.
16 Let your light so shine before
men, that they may see your good
works, and glorify your Father
which is in heaven.
17 Think not that I am come to
destroy the law, or the prophets: I
am not come to destroy, but to fulfil.
18 For verily I say unto you, Till
heaven and earth pass, one jot or
one tittle shall in no wise pass from
the law, till all be fulfilled.
19 Whosoever therefore shall
break one of these least command-
ments, and shall teach men so, he
shall be called the least in the king-
dom of heaven: but whosoever shall
do and teach *them,* the same shall
be called great in the kingdom of
heaven.
20 For I say unto you, That except
your righteousness shall exceed *the
righteousness* of the scribes and
Pharisees, ye shall in no case enter
into the kingdom of heaven.

Teachings on Murder and Anger

21 Ye have heard that it was said
by them of old time, Thou shalt not
kill; and whosoever shall kill shall be
in danger of the judgment:
22 But I say unto you, That who-
soever is angry with his brother
without a cause shall be in danger
of the judgment: and whosoever
shall say to his brother, Raca, shall
be in danger of the council: but who-
soever shall say, Thou fool, shall be
in danger of hell fire.
23 Therefore if thou bring thy gift
to the altar, and there rememberest
that thy brother hath ought against
thee;
24 Leave there thy gift before the
altar, and go thy way; first be recon-
ciled to thy brother, and then come
and offer thy gift.
25 Agree with thine adversary
quickly, whiles thou art in the way

with him; lest at any time the adver-
sary deliver thee to the judge, and
the judge deliver thee to the officer,
and thou be cast into prison.
26 Verily I say unto thee, Thou
shalt by no means come out thence,
till thou hast paid the uttermost
farthing.

Teachings on Temptation

27 Ye have heard that it was said
by them of old time, Thou shalt not
commit adultery:
28 But I say unto you, That who-
soever looketh on a woman to lust
after her hath committed adultery
with her already in his heart.
29 And if thy right eye offend thee,
pluck it out, and cast *it* from thee:
for it is profitable for thee that one
of thy members should perish, and
not *that* thy whole body should be
cast into hell.
30 And if thy right hand offend
thee, cut it off, and cast *it* from thee:
for it is profitable for thee that one
of thy members should perish, and
not *that* thy whole body should be
cast into hell.

Teachings on Divorce

31 It hath been said, Whosoever
shall put away his wife, let him give
her a writing of divorcement:
32 But I say unto you, That whoso-
ever shall put away his wife, saving
for the cause of fornication, causeth
her to commit adultery: and whoso-
ever shall marry her that is divorced
committeth adultery.

Teachings on Oaths

33 Again, ye have heard that it
hath been said by them of old time,
Thou shalt not forswear thyself, but
shalt perform unto the Lord thine
oaths:
34 But I say unto you, Swear not at
all; neither by heaven; for it is God's
throne:
35 Nor by the earth; for it is his
footstool: neither by Jerusalem; for
it is the city of the great King.
36 Neither shalt thou swear by thy
head, because thou canst not make
one hair white or black.
37 But let your communication
be, Yea, yea; Nay, nay: for whatso-
ever is more than these cometh of
evil.

Teachings on Forgiveness

38 Ye have heard that it hath been
said, An eye for an eye, and a tooth
for a tooth:
39 But I say unto you, That ye re-
sist not evil: but whosoever shall
smite thee on thy right cheek, turn
to him the other also.
40 And if any man will sue thee at
the law, and take away thy coat, let
him have *thy* cloke also.
41 And whosoever shall compel
thee to go a mile, go with him twain.
42 Give to him that asketh thee,
and from him that would borrow
of thee turn not thou away.

Teachings on Loving One's Enemies

43 Ye have heard that it hath been
said, Thou shalt love thy neighbour,
and hate thine enemy.
44 But I say unto you, Love your
enemies, bless them that curse you,
do good to them that hate you, and
pray for them which despitefully use
you, and persecute you;
45 That ye may be the children of
your Father which is in heaven: for
he maketh his sun to rise on the evil
and on the good, and sendeth rain
on the just and on the unjust.
46 For if ye love them which love
you, what reward have ye? do not
even the publicans the same?
47 And if ye salute your brethren
only, what do ye more *than others?*
do not even the publicans so?
48 Be ye therefore perfect, even
as your Father which is in heaven
is perfect.

Teachings on Giving

6 Take heed that ye do not your
alms before men, to be seen of
them: otherwise ye have no reward
of your Father which is in heaven.
2 Therefore when thou doest
thine alms, do not sound a trum-
pet before thee, as the hypocrites
do in the synagogues and in the
streets, that they may have glory
of men. Verily I say unto you, They
have their reward.
3 But when thou doest alms, let
not thy left hand know what thy
right hand doeth:
4 That thine alms may be in secret:
and thy Father which seeth in secret
himself shall reward thee openly.

Teachings on Prayer

5 And when thou prayest, thou
shalt not be as the hypocrites *are:*
for they love to pray standing in the
synagogues and in the corners of
the streets, that they may be seen
of men. Verily I say unto you, They
have their reward.
6 But thou, when thou prayest,
enter into thy closet, and when
thou hast shut thy door, pray to thy
Father which is in secret; and thy
Father which seeth in secret shall
reward thee openly.
7 But when ye pray, use not vain
repetitions, as the heathen *do:* for
they think that they shall be heard
for their much speaking.
8 Be not ye therefore like unto
them: for your Father knoweth what
things ye have need of, before ye ask
him.
9 After this manner therefore pray
ye: Our Father which art in heaven,
Hallowed be thy name.
10 Thy kingdom come. Thy will be
done in earth, as *it is* in heaven.
11 Give us this day our daily bread.
12 And forgive us our debts, as we
forgive our debtors.
13 And lead us not into tempta-
tion, but deliver us from evil: For
thine is the kingdom, and the power,
and the glory, for ever. Amen.
14 For if ye forgive men their tres-
passes, your heavenly Father will
also forgive you:
15 But if ye forgive not men their
trespasses, neither will your Father
forgive your trespasses.

Teachings on Fasting

16 Moreover when ye fast, be not,
as the hypocrites, of a sad counte-
nance: for they disfigure their faces,
that they may appear unto men to
fast. Verily I say unto you, They have
their reward.
17 But thou, when thou fastest,
anoint thine head, and wash thy
face;
18 That thou appear not unto men
to fast, but unto thy Father which
is in secret: and thy Father, which
seeth in secret, shall reward thee
openly.

Teachings on Treasures in Heaven

19 Lay not up for yourselves trea-
sures upon earth, where moth and
rust doth corrupt, and where thieves
break through and steal:
20 But lay up for yourselves trea-
sures in heaven, where neither moth
nor rust doth corrupt, and where
thieves do not break through nor
steal:
21 For where your treasure is,
there will your heart be also.
22 The light of the body is the eye:
if therefore thine eye be single, thy
whole body shall be full of light.
23 But if thine eye be evil, thy
whole body shall be full of dark-
ness. If therefore the light that is in
thee be darkness, how great *is* that
darkness!
24 No man can serve two masters:
for either he will hate the one, and
love the other; or else he will hold
to the one, and despise the other. Ye
cannot serve God and mammon.

Teachings on Worry

25 Therefore I say unto you, Take
no thought for your life, what ye
shall eat, or what ye shall drink; nor
yet for your body, what ye shall put
on. Is not the life more than meat,
and the body than raiment?
26 Behold the fowls of the air: for
they sow not, neither do they reap,
nor gather into barns; yet your heav-
enly Father feedeth them. Are ye not
much better than they?
27 Which of you by taking thought
can add one cubit unto his stature?
28 And why take ye thought for
raiment? Consider the lilies of the
field, how they grow; they toil not,
neither do they spin:
29 And yet I say unto you, That
even Solomon in all his glory was
not arrayed like one of these.
30 Wherefore, if God so clothe the
grass of the field, which to day is,
and to morrow is cast into the oven,
shall he not much more *clothe* you,
O ye of little faith?
31 Therefore take no thought, say-
ing, What shall we eat? or, What shall
we drink? or, Wherewithal shall we
be clothed?
32 (For after all these things do
the Gentiles seek:) for your heavenly
Father knoweth that ye have need
of all these things.
33 But seek ye first the kingdom
of God, and his righteousness; and
all these things shall be added unto
you.
34 Take therefore no thought for
the morrow: for the morrow shall
take thought for the things of itself.
Sufficient unto the day *is* the evil
thereof.

Judging and Being Judged

7 Judge not, that ye be not judged.
2 For with what judgment ye
judge, ye shall be judged: and with
what measure ye mete, it shall be
measured to you again.
3 And why beholdest thou the
mote that is in thy brother's eye,
but considerest not the beam that
is in thine own eye?
4 Or how wilt thou say to thy
brother, Let me pull out the mote
out of thine eye; and, behold, a beam
is in thine own eye?
5 Thou hypocrite, first cast out
the beam out of thine own eye; and
then shalt thou see clearly to cast
out the mote out of thy brother's
eye.
6 Give not that which is holy
unto the dogs, neither cast ye your
pearls before swine, lest they tram-
ple them under their feet, and turn
again and rend you.

Asking and Receiving

7 Ask, and it shall be given you;
seek, and ye shall find; knock, and
it shall be opened unto you:
8 For every one that asketh re-
ceiveth; and he that seeketh findeth;
and to him that knocketh it shall be
opened.
9 Or what man is there of you,
whom if his son ask bread, will he
give him a stone?
10 Or if he ask a fish, will he give
him a serpent?
11 If ye then, being evil, know how
to give good gifts unto your children,
how much more shall your Father
which is in heaven give good things
to them that ask him?
12 Therefore all things whatsoever
ye would that men should do to you,
do ye even so to them: for this is the
law and the prophets.

The Strait and Wide Gates

13 Enter ye in at the strait gate:
for wide *is* the gate, and broad *is*
the way, that leadeth to destruc-
tion, and many there be which go
in thereat:
14 Because strait *is* the gate, and
narrow *is* the way, which leadeth
unto life, and few there be that
find it.

False Prophets

15 Beware of false prophets, which come to you in sheep's clothing, but inwardly they are ravening wolves.

16 Ye shall know them by their fruits. Do men gather grapes of thorns, or figs of thistles?

17 Even so every good tree bringeth forth good fruit; but a corrupt tree bringeth forth evil fruit.

18 A good tree cannot bring forth evil fruit, neither *can* a corrupt tree bring forth good fruit.

19 Every tree that bringeth not forth good fruit is hewn down, and cast into the fire.

20 Wherefore by their fruits ye shall know them.

21 Not every one that saith unto me, Lord, Lord, shall enter into the kingdom of heaven; but he that doeth the will of my Father which is in heaven.

22 Many will say to me in that day, Lord, Lord, have we not prophesied in thy name? and in thy name have cast out devils? and in thy name done many wonderful works?

23 And then will I profess unto them, I never knew you: depart from me, ye that work iniquity.

Rock or Sand Foundations

24 Therefore whosoever heareth these sayings of mine, and doeth them, I will liken him unto a wise man, which built his house upon a rock:

25 And the rain descended, and the floods came, and the winds blew, and beat upon that house; and it fell not: for it was founded upon a rock.

26 And every one that heareth these sayings of mine, and doeth them not, shall be likened unto a foolish man, which built his house upon the sand:

27 And the rain descended, and the floods came, and the winds blew, and beat upon that house; and it fell: and great was the fall of it.

28 And it came to pass, when Jesus had ended these sayings, the people were astonished at his doctrine:

29 For he taught them as *one* having authority, and not as the scribes.

Jesus Heals a Leper

8 When he was come down from the mountain, great multitudes followed him.

2 And, behold, there came a leper and worshipped him, saying, Lord, if thou wilt, thou canst make me clean.

3 And Jesus put forth *his* hand, and touched him, saying, I will; be thou clean. And immediately his leprosy was cleansed.

4 And Jesus saith unto him, See thou tell no man; but go thy way, shew thyself to the priest, and offer the gift that Moses commanded, for a testimony unto them.

A Centurion's Faith

5 And when Jesus was entered into Capernaum, there came unto him a centurion, beseeching him,

6 And saying, Lord, my servant lieth at home sick of the palsy, grievously tormented.

7 And Jesus saith unto him, I will come and heal him.

8 The centurion answered and said, Lord, I am not worthy that thou shouldest come under my roof: but speak the word only, and my servant shall be healed.

9 For I am a man under authority, having soldiers under me: and I say to this *man,* Go, and he goeth; and to another, Come, and he cometh; and to my servant, Do this, and he doeth *it.*

10 When Jesus heard *it,* he marvelled, and said to them that followed, Verily I say unto you, I have not found so great faith, no, not in Israel.

11 And I say unto you, That many shall come from the east and west, and shall sit down with Abraham, and Isaac, and Jacob, in the kingdom of heaven.

12 But the children of the kingdom shall be cast out into outer darkness: there shall be weeping and gnashing of teeth.

13 And Jesus said unto the centurion, Go thy way; and as thou hast believed, *so* be it done unto thee. And his servant was healed in the selfsame hour.

Jesus Heals Peter's Mother-in-Law

14 And when Jesus was come into Peter's house, he saw his wife's mother laid, and sick of a fever.

15 And he touched her hand, and the fever left her: and she arose, and ministered unto them.

16 When the even was come, they brought unto him many that were possessed with devils: and he cast out the spirits with *his* word, and healed all that were sick:

17 That it might be fulfilled which was spoken by Esaias the prophet, saying, Himself took our infirmities, and bare *our* sicknesses.

The Cost of Discipleship

18 Now when Jesus saw great multitudes about him, he gave commandment to depart unto the other side.

19 And a certain scribe came, and said unto him, Master, I will follow thee whithersoever thou goest.

20 And Jesus saith unto him, The foxes have holes, and the birds of the air *have* nests; but the Son of man hath not where to lay *his* head.

21 And another of his disciples said unto him, Lord, suffer me first to go and bury my father.

22 But Jesus said unto him, Follow me; and let the dead bury their dead.

Jesus Calms the Winds and the Sea

23 And when he was entered into a ship, his disciples followed him.

24 And, behold, there arose a great tempest in the sea, insomuch that the ship was covered with the waves: but he was asleep.

25 And his disciples came to *him,* and awoke him, saying, Lord, save us: we perish.

26 And he saith unto them, Why are ye fearful, O ye of little faith? Then he arose, and rebuked the winds and the sea; and there was a great calm.

27 But the men marvelled, saying, What manner of man is this, that even the winds and the sea obey him!

Healing of Devil-Possessed Men

28 And when he was come to the other side into the country of the Gergesenes, there met him two possessed with devils, coming out of the tombs, exceeding fierce, so that no man might pass by that way.

29 And, behold, they cried out, saying, What have we to do with thee, Jesus, thou Son of God? art thou come hither to torment us before the time?

30 And there was a good way off from them an herd of many swine feeding.

31 So the devils besought him, saying, If thou cast us out, suffer us to go away into the herd of swine.

32 And he said unto them, Go. And when they were come out, they went into the herd of swine: and, behold, the whole herd of swine ran violently down a steep place into the sea, and perished in the waters.

33 And they that kept them fled, and went their ways into the city, and told every thing, and what was befallen to the possessed of the devils.

34 And, behold, the whole city
came out to meet Jesus: and when
they saw him, they besought *him*
that he would depart out of their
coasts.

Healing a Man with Palsy

9 And he entered into a ship, and
passed over, and came into his
own city.
2 And, behold, they brought to
him a man sick of the palsy, lying on
a bed: and Jesus seeing their faith
said unto the sick of the palsy; Son,
be of good cheer; thy sins be for-
given thee.
3 And, behold, certain of the
scribes said within themselves, This
man blasphemeth.
4 And Jesus knowing their
thoughts said, Wherefore think ye
evil in your hearts?
5 For whether is easier, to say, *Thy*
sins be forgiven thee; or to say, Arise,
and walk?
6 But that ye may know that the
Son of man hath power on earth to
forgive sins, (then saith he to the
sick of the palsy,) Arise, take up thy
bed, and go unto thine house.
7 And he arose, and departed to
his house.
8 But when the multitudes saw *it,*
they marvelled, and glorified God,
which had given such power unto
men.

Matthew Follows Jesus

9 And as Jesus passed forth from
thence, he saw a man, named Mat-
thew, sitting at the receipt of cus-
tom: and he saith unto him, Follow
me. And he arose, and followed him.
10 And it came to pass, as Jesus sat
at meat in the house, behold, many
publicans and sinners came and sat
down with him and his disciples.
11 And when the Pharisees saw
it, they said unto his disciples, Why
eateth your Master with publicans
and sinners?
12 But when Jesus heard *that,* he
said unto them, They that be whole
need not a physician, but they that
are sick.
13 But go ye and learn what *that*
meaneth, I will have mercy, and not
sacrifice: for I am not come to call
the righteous, but sinners to repen-
tance.

Questions About Fasting

14 Then came to him the disciples
of John, saying, Why do we and the
Pharisees fast oft, but thy disciples
fast not?
15 And Jesus said unto them, Can
the children of the bridechamber
mourn, as long as the bridegroom is
with them? but the days will come,
when the bridegroom shall be taken
from them, and then shall they fast.
16 No man putteth a piece of new
cloth unto an old garment, for that
which is put in to fill it up taketh
from the garment, and the rent is
made worse.
17 Neither do men put new wine
into old bottles: else the bottles
break, and the wine runneth out,
and the bottles perish: but they put
new wine into new bottles, and both
are preserved.

The Healing of a Ruler's Daughter

18 While he spake these things
unto them, behold, there came a
certain ruler, and worshipped him,
saying, My daughter is even now
dead: but come and lay thy hand
upon her, and she shall live.
19 And Jesus arose, and followed
him, and *so did* his disciples.
20 And, behold, a woman, which
was diseased with an issue of blood
twelve years, came behind *him,* and
touched the hem of his garment:
21 For she said within herself, If I
may but touch his garment, I shall
be whole.
22 But Jesus turned him about,

and when he saw her, he said,
Daughter, be of good comfort; thy
faith hath made thee whole. And the
woman was made whole from that
hour.
23 And when Jesus came into the
ruler's house, and saw the minstrels
and the people making a noise,
24 He said unto them, Give
place: for the maid is not dead, but
sleepeth. And they laughed him to
scorn.
25 But when the people were put
forth, he went in, and took her by
the hand, and the maid arose.
26 And the fame hereof went
abroad into all that land.

Sight and Speech Restored

27 And when Jesus departed
thence, two blind men followed
him, crying, and saying, *Thou* son
of David, have mercy on us.
28 And when he was come into the
house, the blind men came to him:
and Jesus saith unto them, Believe
ye that I am able to do this? They
said unto him, Yea, Lord.
29 Then touched he their eyes,
saying, According to your faith be
it unto you.
30 And their eyes were opened;
and Jesus straitly charged them,
saying, See *that* no man know *it.*
31 But they, when they were de-
parted, spread abroad his fame in
all that country.
32 As they went out, behold, they
brought to him a dumb man pos-
sessed with a devil.
33 And when the devil was cast
out, the dumb spake: and the mul-
titudes marvelled, saying, It was
never so seen in Israel.
34 But the Pharisees said, He
casteth out devils through the
prince of the devils.

Labourers for the Harvest

35 And Jesus went about all the
cities and villages, teaching in their
synagogues, and preaching the gos-
pel of the kingdom, and healing
every sickness and every disease
among the people.
36 But when he saw the multi-
tudes, he was moved with compas-
sion on them, because they fainted,
and were scattered abroad, as sheep
having no shepherd.
37 Then saith he unto his disci-
ples, The harvest truly *is* plenteous,
but the labourers *are* few;
38 Pray ye therefore the Lord of
the harvest, that he will send forth
labourers into his harvest.

Instructions to the Disciples

10 And when he had called unto
him his twelve disciples, he
gave them power *against* unclean
spirits, to cast them out, and to heal
all manner of sickness and all man-
ner of disease.
2 Now the names of the twelve
apostles are these; The first, Simon,
who is called Peter, and Andrew his
brother; James *the son* of Zebedee,
and John his brother;
3 Philip, and Bartholomew;
Thomas, and Matthew the pub-
lican; James *the son* of Alphaeus,
and Lebbaeus, whose surname was
Thaddaeus;
4 Simon the Canaanite, and Judas
Iscariot, who also betrayed him.
5 These twelve Jesus sent forth,
and commanded them, saying, Go
not into the way of the Gentiles, and
into *any* city of the Samaritans enter
ye not:
6 But go rather to the lost sheep
of the house of Israel.
7 And as ye go, preach, saying, The
kingdom of heaven is at hand.
8 Heal the sick, cleanse the lepers,
raise the dead, cast out devils: freely
ye have received, freely give.
9 Provide neither gold, nor silver,
nor brass in your purses,
10 Nor scrip for *your* journey,
neither two coats, neither shoes,

nor yet staves: for the workman is
worthy of his meat.
11 And into whatsoever city or
town ye shall enter, enquire who
in it is worthy; and there abide till
ye go thence.
12 And when ye come into an
house, salute it.
13 And if the house be worthy, let
your peace come upon it: but if it be
not worthy, let your peace return to
you.
14 And whosoever shall not receive
you, nor hear your words, when ye
depart out of that house or city,
shake off the dust of your feet.
15 Verily I say unto you, It shall
be more tolerable for the land of
Sodom and Gomorrha in the day of
judgment, than for that city.

Sheep Among Wolves

16 Behold, I send you forth as
sheep in the midst of wolves: be
ye therefore wise as serpents, and
harmless as doves.
17 But beware of men: for they
will deliver you up to the councils,
and they will scourge you in their
synagogues;
18 And ye shall be brought before
governors and kings for my sake,
for a testimony against them and
the Gentiles.
19 But when they deliver you
up, take no thought how or what
ye shall speak: for it shall be given
you in that same hour what ye shall
speak.
20 For it is not ye that speak, but
the Spirit of your Father which
speaketh in you.
21 And the brother shall deliver up
the brother to death, and the father
the child: and the children shall rise
up against *their* parents, and cause
them to be put to death.
22 And ye shall be hated of all *men*
for my name's sake: but he that en-
dureth to the end shall be saved.
23 But when they persecute you
in this city, flee ye into another: for
verily I say unto you, Ye shall not
have gone over the cities of Israel,
till the Son of man be come.
24 The disciple is not above *his*
master, nor the servant above his
lord.
25 It is enough for the disciple that
he be as his master, and the servant
as his lord. If they have called the
master of the house Beelzebub, how
much more *shall they call* them of
his household?
26 Fear them not therefore: for
there is nothing covered, that shall
not be revealed; and hid, that shall
not be known.
27 What I tell you in darkness, *that*
speak ye in light: and what ye hear
in the ear, *that* preach ye upon the
housetops.
28 And fear not them which kill
the body, but are not able to kill the
soul: but rather fear him which is
able to destroy both soul and body
in hell.
29 Are not two sparrows sold for
a farthing? and one of them shall
not fall on the ground without your
Father.
30 But the very hairs of your head
are all numbered.
31 Fear ye not therefore, ye are of
more value than many sparrows.
32 Whosoever therefore shall
confess me before men, him will I
confess also before my Father which
is in heaven.
33 But whosoever shall deny me
before men, him will I also deny
before my Father which is in heaven.
34 Think not that I am come to
send peace on earth: I came not to
send peace, but a sword.
35 For I am come to set a man
at variance against his father, and
the daughter against her mother,
and the daughter in law against her
mother in law.
36 And a man's foes *shall be* they
of his own household.

37 He that loveth father or mother
more than me is not worthy of me:
and he that loveth son or daughter
more than me is not worthy of me.
38 And he that taketh not his
cross, and followeth after me, is
not worthy of me.
39 He that findeth his life shall
lose it: and he that loseth his life for
my sake shall find it.
40 He that receiveth you receiveth
me, and he that receiveth me re-
ceiveth him that sent me.
41 He that receiveth a prophet in
the name of a prophet shall receive
a prophet's reward; and he that re-
ceiveth a righteous man in the name
of a righteous man shall receive a
righteous man's reward.
42 And whosoever shall give to
drink unto one of these little ones a
cup of cold *water* only in the name
of a disciple, verily I say unto you,
he shall in no wise lose his reward.

John's Questions for Jesus

11 And it came to pass, when Jesus
had made an end of command-
ing his twelve disciples, he departed
thence to teach and to preach in
their cities.
2 Now when John had heard in
the prison the works of Christ, he
sent two of his disciples,
3 And said unto him, Art thou he
that should come, or do we look for
another?
4 Jesus answered and said unto
them, Go and shew John again
those things which ye do hear and
see:
5 The blind receive their sight,
and the lame walk, the lepers are
cleansed, and the deaf hear, the dead
are raised up, and the poor have the
gospel preached to them.
6 And blessed is *he,* whosoever
shall not be offended in me.
7 And as they departed, Jesus
began to say unto the multitudes
concerning John, What went ye out
into the wilderness to see? A reed
shaken with the wind?
8 But what went ye out for to see?
A man clothed in soft raiment? be-
hold, they that wear soft *clothing*
are in kings' houses.
9 But what went ye out for to see?
A prophet? yea, I say unto you, and
more than a prophet.
10 For this is *he,* of whom it is writ-
ten, Behold, I send my messenger
before thy face, which shall prepare
thy way before thee.
11 Verily I say unto you, Among
them that are born of women there
hath not risen a greater than John
the Baptist: notwithstanding he that
is least in the kingdom of heaven is
greater than he.
12 And from the days of John the
Baptist until now the kingdom of
heaven suffereth violence, and the
violent take it by force.
13 For all the prophets and the law
prophesied until John.
14 And if ye will receive *it,* this is
Elias, which was for to come.
15 He that hath ears to hear, let
him hear.
16 But whereunto shall I liken this
generation? It is like unto children
sitting in the markets, and calling
unto their fellows,
17 And saying, We have piped unto
you, and ye have not danced; we
have mourned unto you, and ye
have not lamented.
18 For John came neither eating
nor drinking, and they say, He hath
a devil.
19 The Son of man came eating
and drinking, and they say, Behold a
man gluttonous, and a winebibber, a
friend of publicans and sinners. But
wisdom is justified of her children.

Unrepentant Cities

20 Then began he to upbraid the
cities wherein most of his mighty
works were done, because they re-
pented not:

21 Woe unto thee, Chorazin! woe unto thee, Bethsaida! for if the mighty works, which were done in you, had been done in Tyre and Sidon, they would have repented long ago in sackcloth and ashes.

22 But I say unto you, It shall be more tolerable for Tyre and Sidon at the day of judgment, than for you.

23 And thou, Capernaum, which art exalted unto heaven, shalt be brought down to hell: for if the mighty works, which have been done in thee, had been done in Sodom, it would have remained until this day.

24 But I say unto you, That it shall be more tolerable for the land of Sodom in the day of judgment, than for thee.

Rest for the Heavy Laden

25 At that time Jesus answered and said, I thank thee, O Father, Lord of heaven and earth, because thou hast hid these things from the wise and prudent, and hast revealed them unto babes.

26 Even so, Father: for so it seemed good in thy sight.

27 All things are delivered unto me of my Father: and no man knoweth the Son, but the Father; neither knoweth any man the Father, save the Son, and *he* to whomsoever the Son will reveal *him*.

28 Come unto me, all *ye* that labour and are heavy laden, and I will give you rest.

29 Take my yoke upon you, and learn of me; for I am meek and lowly in heart: and ye shall find rest unto your souls.

30 For my yoke *is* easy, and my burden is light.

The Son of Man Is Lord of the Sabbath

12 At that time Jesus went on the sabbath day through the corn; and his disciples were an hungred, and began to pluck the ears of corn, and to eat.

2 But when the Pharisees saw *it*, they said unto him, Behold, thy disciples do that which is not lawful to do upon the sabbath day.

3 But he said unto them, Have ye not read what David did, when he was an hungred, and they that were with him;

4 How he entered into the house of God, and did eat the shewbread, which was not lawful for him to eat, neither for them which were with him, but only for the priests?

5 Or have ye not read in the law, how that on the sabbath days the priests in the temple profane the sabbath, and are blameless?

6 But I say unto you, That in this place is *one* greater than the temple.

7 But if ye had known what *this* meaneth, I will have mercy, and not sacrifice, ye would not have condemned the guiltless.

8 For the Son of man is Lord even of the sabbath day.

9 And when he was departed thence, he went into their synagogue:

10 And, behold, there was a man which had *his* hand withered. And they asked him, saying, Is it lawful to heal on the sabbath days? that they might accuse him.

11 And he said unto them, What man shall there be among you, that shall have one sheep, and if it fall into a pit on the sabbath day, will he not lay hold on it, and lift *it* out?

12 How much then is a man better than a sheep? Wherefore it is lawful to do well on the sabbath days.

13 Then saith he to the man, Stretch forth thine hand. And he stretched *it* forth; and it was restored whole, like as the other.

14 Then the Pharisees went out, and held a council against him, how they might destroy him.

God's Beloved Servant

15 But when Jesus knew *it,* he
withdrew himself from thence: and
great multitudes followed him, and
he healed them all;
16 And charged them that they
should not make him known:
17 That it might be fulfilled which
was spoken by Esaias the prophet,
saying,
18 Behold my servant, whom I
have chosen; my beloved, in whom
my soul is well pleased: I will put my
spirit upon him, and he shall shew
judgment to the Gentiles.
19 He shall not strive, nor cry; nei-
ther shall any man hear his voice in
the streets.
20 A bruised reed shall he not
break, and smoking flax shall he not
quench, till he send forth judgment
unto victory.
21 And in his name shall the Gen-
tiles trust.

Of Beelzebub or God?

22 Then was brought unto him
one possessed with a devil, blind,
and dumb: and he healed him, in-
somuch that the blind and dumb
both spake and saw.
23 And all the people were
amazed, and said, Is not this the
son of David?
24 But when the Pharisees heard
it, they said, This *fellow* doth not
cast out devils, but by Beelzebub
the prince of the devils.
25 And Jesus knew their thoughts,
and said unto them, Every kingdom
divided against itself is brought to
desolation; and every city or house
divided against itself shall not stand:
26 And if Satan cast out Satan, he
is divided against himself; how shall
then his kingdom stand?
27 And if I by Beelzebub cast out
devils, by whom do your children
cast *them* out? therefore they shall
be your judges.
28 But if I cast out devils by the
Spirit of God, then the kingdom of
God is come unto you.
29 Or else how can one enter into
a strong man's house, and spoil
his goods, except he first bind the
strong man? and then he will spoil
his house.
30 He that is not with me is
against me; and he that gathereth
not with me scattereth abroad.
31 Wherefore I say unto you, All
manner of sin and blasphemy shall
be forgiven unto men: but the blas-
phemy *against* the *Holy* Ghost shall
not be forgiven unto men.
32 And whosoever speaketh a
word against the Son of man, it shall
be forgiven him: but whosoever
speaketh against the Holy Ghost, it
shall not be forgiven him, neither
in this world, neither in the *world*
to come.
33 Either make the tree good, and
his fruit good; or else make the tree
corrupt, and his fruit corrupt: for
the tree is known by *his* fruit.
34 O generation of vipers, how can
ye, being evil, speak good things? for
out of the abundance of the heart
the mouth speaketh.
35 A good man out of the good
treasure of the heart bringeth forth
good things: and an evil man out of
the evil treasure bringeth forth evil
things.
36 But I say unto you, That every
idle word that men shall speak, they
shall give account thereof in the day
of judgment.
37 For by thy words thou shalt
be justified, and by thy words thou
shalt be condemned.

The Sign of the Prophet

38 Then certain of the scribes and
of the Pharisees answered, saying,
Master, we would see a sign from
thee.
39 But he answered and said unto
them, An evil and adulterous gener-
ation seeketh after a sign; and there

shall no sign be given to it, but the
sign of the prophet Jonas:
40 For as Jonas was three days and
three nights in the whale's belly; so
shall the Son of man be three days
and three nights in the heart of the
earth.
41 The men of Nineveh shall rise
in judgment with this generation,
and shall condemn it: because they
repented at the preaching of Jonas;
and, behold, a greater than Jonas *is*
here.
42 The queen of the south shall
rise up in the judgment with this
generation, and shall condemn it:
for she came from the uttermost
parts of the earth to hear the wis-
dom of Solomon; and, behold, a
greater than Solomon *is* here.
43 When the unclean spirit is gone
out of a man, he walketh through
dry places, seeking rest, and findeth
none.
44 Then he saith, I will return into
my house from whence I came out;
and when he is come, he findeth *it*
empty, swept, and garnished.
45 Then goeth he, and taketh with
himself seven other spirits more
wicked than himself, and they enter
in and dwell there: and the last *state*
of that man is worse than the first.
Even so shall it be also unto this
wicked generation.

The Family of Jesus

46 While he yet talked to the
people, behold, *his* mother and his
brethren stood without, desiring to
speak with him.
47 Then one said unto him, Be-
hold, thy mother and thy brethren
stand without, desiring to speak
with thee.
48 But he answered and said
unto him that told him, Who is my
mother? and who are my brethren?
49 And he stretched forth his hand
toward his disciples, and said, Be-
hold my mother and my brethren!
50 For whosoever shall do the will
of my Father which is in heaven, the
same is my brother, and sister, and
mother.

The Sower and the Seed

13 The same day went Jesus out
of the house, and sat by the
sea side.
2 And great multitudes were
gathered together unto him, so
that he went into a ship, and sat;
and the whole multitude stood on
the shore.
3 And he spake many things unto
them in parables, saying, Behold, a
sower went forth to sow;
4 And when he sowed, some *seeds*
fell by the way side, and the fowls
came and devoured them up:
5 Some fell upon stony places,
where they had not much earth: and
forthwith they sprung up, because
they had no deepness of earth:
6 And when the sun was up, they
were scorched; and because they
had no root, they withered away.
7 And some fell among thorns;
and the thorns sprung up, and
choked them:
8 But other fell into good ground,
and brought forth fruit, some an
hundredfold, some sixtyfold, some
thirtyfold.
9 Who hath ears to hear, let him
hear.
10 And the disciples came, and
said unto him, Why speakest thou
unto them in parables?
11 He answered and said unto
them, Because it is given unto you
to know the mysteries of the king-
dom of heaven, but to them it is not
given.
12 For whosoever hath, to him
shall be given, and he shall have
more abundance: but whosoever
hath not, from him shall be taken
away even that he hath.
13 Therefore speak I to them in
parables: because they seeing see

not; and hearing they hear not, nei-
ther do they understand.
14 And in them is fulfilled the
prophecy of Esaias, which saith,
By hearing ye shall hear, and shall
not understand; and seeing ye shall
see, and shall not perceive:
15 For this people's heart is waxed
gross, and *their* ears are dull of hear-
ing, and their eyes they have closed;
lest at any time they should see with
their eyes, and hear with *their* ears,
and should understand with *their*
heart, and should be converted, and
I should heal them.
16 But blessed *are* your eyes, for
they see: and your ears, for they
hear.
17 For verily I say unto you, That
many prophets and righteous *men*
have desired to see *those things*
which ye see, and have not seen
them; and to hear *those things* which
ye hear, and have not heard *them.*
18 Hear ye therefore the parable
of the sower.
19 When any one heareth the word
of the kingdom, and understandeth
it not, then cometh the wicked *one,*
and catcheth away that which was
sown in his heart. This is he which
received seed by the way side.
20 But he that received the seed
into stony places, the same is he that
heareth the word, and anon with joy
receiveth it;
21 Yet hath he not root in him-
self, but dureth for a while: for when
tribulation or persecution ariseth
because of the word, by and by he
is offended.
22 He also that received seed
among the thorns is he that heareth
the word; and the care of this world,
and the deceitfulness of riches,
choke the word, and he becometh
unfruitful.
23 But he that received seed into
the good ground is he that heareth
the word, and understandeth *it;*
which also beareth fruit, and bring-
eth forth, some an hundredfold,
some sixty, some thirty.

The Wheat and the Tares

24 Another parable put he forth
unto them, saying, The kingdom of
heaven is likened unto a man which
sowed good seed in his field:
25 But while men slept, his enemy
came and sowed tares among the
wheat, and went his way.
26 But when the blade was sprung
up, and brought forth fruit, then
appeared the tares also.
27 So the servants of the house-
holder came and said unto him,
Sir, didst not thou sow good seed
in thy field? from whence then hath
it tares?
28 He said unto them, An enemy
hath done this. The servants said
unto him, Wilt thou then that we
go and gather them up?
29 But he said, Nay; lest while ye
gather up the tares, ye root up also
the wheat with them.
30 Let both grow together until
the harvest: and in the time of har-
vest I will say to the reapers, Gather
ye together first the tares, and bind
them in bundles to burn them: but
gather the wheat into my barn.

The Mustard Seed and the Leaven

31 Another parable put he forth
unto them, saying, The kingdom of
heaven is like to a grain of mustard
seed, which a man took, and sowed
in his field:
32 Which indeed is the least of all
seeds: but when it is grown, it is the
greatest among herbs, and becom-
eth a tree, so that the birds of the
air come and lodge in the branches
thereof.
33 Another parable spake he unto
them; The kingdom of heaven is like
unto leaven, which a woman took,
and hid in three measures of meal,
till the whole was leavened.

34 All these things spake Jesus
unto the multitude in parables; and
without a parable spake he not unto
them:
35 That it might be fulfilled which
was spoken by the prophet, saying,
I will open my mouth in parables;
I will utter things which have been
kept secret from the foundation of
the world.

The Tares Explained

36 Then Jesus sent the multitude
away, and went into the house: and
his disciples came unto him, saying,
Declare unto us the parable of the
tares of the field.
37 He answered and said unto
them, He that soweth the good seed
is the Son of man;
38 The field is the world; the good
seed are the children of the king-
dom; but the tares are the children
of the wicked *one;*
39 The enemy that sowed them is
the devil; the harvest is the end of
the world; and the reapers are the
angels.
40 As therefore the tares are gath-
ered and burned in the fire; so shall
it be in the end of this world.
41 The Son of man shall send forth
his angels, and they shall gather out
of his kingdom all things that of-
fend, and them which do iniquity;
42 And shall cast them into a fur-
nace of fire: there shall be wailing
and gnashing of teeth.
43 Then shall the righteous shine
forth as the sun in the kingdom of
their Father. Who hath ears to hear,
let him hear.

The Treasure and the Goodly Pearl

44 Again, the kingdom of heaven
is like unto treasure hid in a field;
the which when a man hath found,
he hideth, and for joy thereof goeth
and selleth all that he hath, and buy-
eth that field.
45 Again, the kingdom of heaven
is like unto a merchant man, seeking
goodly pearls:
46 Who, when he had found one
pearl of great price, went and sold
all that he had, and bought it.

The Full Net

47 Again, the kingdom of heaven
is like unto a net, that was cast into
the sea, and gathered of every kind:
48 Which, when it was full, they
drew to shore, and sat down, and
gathered the good into vessels, but
cast the bad away.
49 So shall it be at the end of the
world: the angels shall come forth,
and sever the wicked from among
the just,
50 And shall cast them into the
furnace of fire: there shall be wailing
and gnashing of teeth.
51 Jesus saith unto them, Have ye
understood all these things? They
say unto him, Yea, Lord.
52 Then said he unto them, There-
fore every scribe *which is* instructed
unto the kingdom of heaven is like
unto a man *that is* an householder,
which bringeth forth out of his trea-
sure *things* new and old.

Without Honour in His Own Country

53 And it came to pass, *that* when
Jesus had finished these parables,
he departed thence.
54 And when he was come into
his own country, he taught them
in their synagogue, insomuch that
they were astonished, and said,
Whence hath this *man* this wisdom,
and *these* mighty works?
55 Is not this the carpenter's son?
is not his mother called Mary? and
his brethren, James, and Joses, and
Simon, and Judas?
56 And his sisters, are they not
all with us? Whence then hath this
man all these things?
57 And they were offended in him.

But Jesus said unto them, A prophet is not without honour, save in his own country, and in his own house.

58 And he did not many mighty works there because of their unbelief.

The Death of John the Baptist

14 At that time Herod the tetrarch heard of the fame of Jesus,

2 And said unto his servants, This is John the Baptist; he is risen from the dead; and therefore mighty works do shew forth themselves in him.

3 For Herod had laid hold on John, and bound him, and put *him* in prison for Herodias' sake, his brother Philip's wife.

4 For John said unto him, It is not lawful for thee to have her.

5 And when he would have put him to death, he feared the multitude, because they counted him as a prophet.

6 But when Herod's birthday was kept, the daughter of Herodias danced before them, and pleased Herod.

7 Whereupon he promised with an oath to give her whatsoever she would ask.

8 And she, being before instructed of her mother, said, Give me here John Baptist's head in a charger.

9 And the king was sorry: nevertheless for the oath's sake, and them which sat with him at meat, he commanded *it* to be given *her.*

10 And he sent, and beheaded John in the prison.

11 And his head was brought in a charger, and given to the damsel: and she brought *it* to her mother.

12 And his disciples came, and took up the body, and buried it, and went and told Jesus.

Five Thousand Fed

13 When Jesus heard *of it,* he departed thence by ship into a desert place apart: and when the people had heard *thereof,* they followed him on foot out of the cities.

14 And Jesus went forth, and saw a great multitude, and was moved with compassion toward them, and he healed their sick.

15 And when it was evening, his disciples came to him, saying, This is a desert place, and the time is now past; send the multitude away, that they may go into the villages, and buy themselves victuals.

16 But Jesus said unto them, They need not depart; give ye them to eat.

17 And they say unto him, We have here but five loaves, and two fishes.

18 He said, Bring them hither to me.

19 And he commanded the multitude to sit down on the grass, and took the five loaves, and the two fishes, and looking up to heaven, he blessed, and brake, and gave the loaves to *his* disciples, and the disciples to the multitude.

20 And they did all eat, and were filled: and they took up of the fragments that remained twelve baskets full.

21 And they that had eaten were about five thousand men, beside women and children.

Jesus Walks on the Sea

22 And straightway Jesus constrained his disciples to get into a ship, and to go before him unto the other side, while he sent the multitudes away.

23 And when he had sent the multitudes away, he went up into a mountain apart to pray: and when the evening was come, he was there alone.

24 But the ship was now in the midst of the sea, tossed with waves: for the wind was contrary.

25 And in the fourth watch of the night Jesus went unto them, walking on the sea.

26 And when the disciples saw him walking on the sea, they were troubled, saying, It is a spirit; and they cried out for fear.

27 But straightway Jesus spake unto them, saying, Be of good cheer; it is I; be not afraid.

28 And Peter answered him and said, Lord, if it be thou, bid me come unto thee on the water.

29 And he said, Come. And when Peter was come down out of the ship, he walked on the water, to go to Jesus.

30 But when he saw the wind boisterous, he was afraid; and beginning to sink, he cried, saying, Lord, save me.

31 And immediately Jesus stretched forth *his* hand, and caught him, and said unto him, O thou of little faith, wherefore didst thou doubt?

32 And when they were come into the ship, the wind ceased.

33 Then they that were in the ship came and worshipped him, saying, Of a truth thou art the Son of God.

34 And when they were gone over, they came into the land of Gennesaret.

35 And when the men of that place had knowledge of him, they sent out into all that country round about, and brought unto him all that were diseased;

36 And besought him that they might only touch the hem of his garment: and as many as touched were made perfectly whole.

Defilement Comes from Within

15 Then came to Jesus scribes and Pharisees, which were of Jerusalem, saying,

2 Why do thy disciples transgress the tradition of the elders? for they wash not their hands when they eat bread.

3 But he answered and said unto them, Why do ye also transgress the commandment of God by your tradition?

4 For God commanded, saying, Honour thy father and mother: and, He that curseth father or mother, let him die the death.

5 But ye say, Whosoever shall say to *his* father or *his* mother, *It is* a gift, by whatsoever thou mightest be profited by me;

6 And honour not his father or his mother, *he shall be free.* Thus have ye made the commandment of God of none effect by your tradition.

7 *Ye* hypocrites, well did Esaias prophesy of you, saying,

8 This people draweth nigh unto me with their mouth, and honoureth me with *their* lips; but their heart is far from me.

9 But in vain they do worship me, teaching *for* doctrines the commandments of men.

10 And he called the multitude, and said unto them, Hear, and understand:

11 Not that which goeth into the mouth defileth a man; but that which cometh out of the mouth, this defileth a man.

12 Then came his disciples, and said unto him, Knowest thou that the Pharisees were offended, after they heard this saying?

13 But he answered and said, Every plant, which my heavenly Father hath not planted, shall be rooted up.

14 Let them alone: they be blind leaders of the blind. And if the blind lead the blind, both shall fall into the ditch.

15 Then answered Peter and said unto him, Declare unto us this parable.

16 And Jesus said, Are ye also yet without understanding?

17 Do not ye yet understand, that whatsoever entereth in at the mouth goeth into the belly, and is cast out into the draught?

18 But those things which proceed
out of the mouth come forth from
the heart; and they defile the man.
19 For out of the heart proceed
evil thoughts, murders, adulteries,
fornications, thefts, false witness,
blasphemies:
20 These are *the things* which de-
file a man: but to eat with unwashen
hands defileth not a man.

A Canaanite Woman's Faith

21 Then Jesus went thence, and
departed into the coasts of Tyre and
Sidon.
22 And, behold, a woman of Ca-
naan came out of the same coasts,
and cried unto him, saying, Have
mercy on me, O Lord, *thou* son of
David; my daughter is grievously
vexed with a devil.
23 But he answered her not a
word. And his disciples came and
besought him, saying, Send her
away; for she crieth after us.
24 But he answered and said, I am
not sent but unto the lost sheep of
the house of Israel.
25 Then came she and worshipped
him, saying, Lord, help me.
26 But he answered and said, It
is not meet to take the children's
bread, and to cast *it* to dogs.
27 And she said, Truth, Lord: yet
the dogs eat of the crumbs which
fall from their masters' table.
28 Then Jesus answered and said
unto her, O woman, great *is* thy
faith: be it unto thee even as thou
wilt. And her daughter was made
whole from that very hour.

Four Thousand Fed

29 And Jesus departed from
thence, and came nigh unto the
sea of Galilee; and went up into a
mountain, and sat down there.
30 And great multitudes came
unto him, having with them *those*
that were lame, blind, dumb,
maimed, and many others, and cast
them down at Jesus' feet; and he
healed them:
31 Insomuch that the multitude
wondered, when they saw the dumb
to speak, the maimed to be whole,
the lame to walk, and the blind to
see: and they glorified the God of
Israel.
32 Then Jesus called his disciples
unto him, and said, I have compas-
sion on the multitude, because they
continue with me now three days,
and have nothing to eat: and I will
not send them away fasting, lest
they faint in the way.
33 And his disciples say unto him,
Whence should we have so much
bread in the wilderness, as to fill so
great a multitude?
34 And Jesus saith unto them,
How many loaves have ye? And they
said, Seven, and a few little fishes.
35 And he commanded the mul-
titude to sit down on the ground.
36 And he took the seven loaves
and the fishes, and gave thanks, and
brake *them,* and gave to his disciples,
and the disciples to the multitude.
37 And they did all eat, and were
filled: and they took up of the broken
meat that was left seven baskets full.
38 And they that did eat were four
thousand men, beside women and
children.
39 And he sent away the multi-
tude, and took ship, and came into
the coasts of Magdala.

The Request for a Sign from Heaven

16 The Pharisees also with the
Sadducees came, and tempt-
ing desired him that he would shew
them a sign from heaven.
2 He answered and said unto
them, When it is evening, ye say,
It will be fair weather: for the sky is
red.
3 And in the morning, *It will be*
foul weather to day: for the sky is
red and lowring. O *ye* hypocrites,

ye can discern the face of the sky;
but can ye not *discern* the signs of
the times?
4 A wicked and adulterous gener-
ation seeketh after a sign; and there
shall no sign be given unto it, but
the sign of the prophet Jonas. And
he left them, and departed.

The Pharisees' and Sadducees' Leaven

5 And when his disciples were
come to the other side, they had
forgotten to take bread.
6 Then Jesus said unto them, Take
heed and beware of the leaven of the
Pharisees and of the Sadducees.
7 And they reasoned among them-
selves, saying, *It is* because we have
taken no bread.
8 *Which* when Jesus perceived, he
said unto them, O ye of little faith,
why reason ye among yourselves,
because ye have brought no bread?
9 Do ye not yet understand, nei-
ther remember the five loaves of
the five thousand, and how many
baskets ye took up?
10 Neither the seven loaves of the
four thousand, and how many bas-
kets ye took up?
11 How is it that ye do not under-
stand that I spake *it* not to you
concerning bread, that ye should
beware of the leaven of the Phari-
sees and of the Sadducees?
12 Then understood they how
that he bade *them* not beware of the
leaven of bread, but of the doctrine
of the Pharisees and of the Saddu-
cees.

The Confession of Simon Peter

13 When Jesus came into the
coasts of Caesarea Philippi, he asked
his disciples, saying, Whom do men
say that I the Son of man am?
14 And they said, Some *say that
thou art* John the Baptist: some,
Elias; and others, Jeremias, or one
of the prophets.
15 He saith unto them, But whom
say ye that I am?
16 And Simon Peter answered and
said, Thou art the Christ, the Son of
the living God.
17 And Jesus answered and said
unto him, Blessed art thou, Simon
Bar-jona: for flesh and blood hath
not revealed *it* unto thee, but my
Father which is in heaven.
18 And I say also unto thee, That
thou art Peter, and upon this rock I
will build my church; and the gates
of hell shall not prevail against it.
19 And I will give unto thee the
keys of the kingdom of heaven:
and whatsoever thou shalt bind
on earth shall be bound in heaven:
and whatsoever thou shalt loose on
earth shall be loosed in heaven.
20 Then charged he his disciples
that they should tell no man that he
was Jesus the Christ.

Jesus Prepares His Disciples

21 From that time forth began
Jesus to shew unto his disciples,
how that he must go unto Jerusa-
lem, and suffer many things of the
elders and chief priests and scribes,
and be killed, and be raised again
the third day.
22 Then Peter took him, and began
to rebuke him, saying, Be it far from
thee, Lord: this shall not be unto thee.
23 But he turned, and said unto
Peter, Get thee behind me, Satan:
thou art an offence unto me: for
thou savourest not the things that
be of God, but those that be of men.
24 Then said Jesus unto his dis-
ciples, If any *man* will come after
me, let him deny himself, and take
up his cross, and follow me.
25 For whosoever will save his life
shall lose it: and whosoever will lose
his life for my sake shall find it.
26 For what is a man profited, if
he shall gain the whole world, and
lose his own soul? or what shall a
man give in exchange for his soul?

27 For the Son of man shall come
in the glory of his Father with his
angels; and then he shall reward
every man according to his works.
28 Verily I say unto you, There be
some standing here, which shall not
taste of death, till they see the Son
of man coming in his kingdom.

The Transfiguration of Jesus

17 And after six days Jesus tak-
eth Peter, James, and John his
brother, and bringeth them up into
an high mountain apart,
2 And was transfigured before
them: and his face did shine as the
sun, and his raiment was white as
the light.
3 And, behold, there appeared
unto them Moses and Elias talking
with him.
4 Then answered Peter, and said
unto Jesus, Lord, it is good for us to
be here: if thou wilt, let us make here
three tabernacles; one for thee, and
one for Moses, and one for Elias.
5 While he yet spake, behold, a
bright cloud overshadowed them:
and behold a voice out of the cloud,
which said, This is my beloved Son,
in whom I am well pleased; hear ye
him.
6 And when the disciples heard
it, they fell on their face, and were
sore afraid.
7 And Jesus came and touched
them, and said, Arise, and be not
afraid.
8 And when they had lifted up
their eyes, they saw no man, save
Jesus only.
9 And as they came down from
the mountain, Jesus charged them,
saying, Tell the vision to no man,
until the Son of man be risen again
from the dead.
10 And his disciples asked him,
saying, Why then say the scribes
that Elias must first come?
11 And Jesus answered and said
unto them, Elias truly shall first
come, and restore all things.
12 But I say unto you, That Elias
is come already, and they knew him
not, but have done unto him what-
soever they listed. Likewise shall
also the Son of man suffer of them.
13 Then the disciples understood
that he spake unto them of John the
Baptist.

The Healing of a Devil-Possessed Boy

14 And when they were come to
the multitude, there came to him a
certain man, kneeling down to him,
and saying,
15 Lord, have mercy on my son:
for he is lunatick, and sore vexed:
for ofttimes he falleth into the fire,
and oft into the water.
16 And I brought him to thy disci-
ples, and they could not cure him.
17 Then Jesus answered and said,
O faithless and perverse generation,
how long shall I be with you? how
long shall I suffer you? bring him
hither to me.
18 And Jesus rebuked the devil;
and he departed out of him: and
the child was cured from that very
hour.
19 Then came the disciples to
Jesus apart, and said, Why could
not we cast him out?
20 And Jesus said unto them, Be-
cause of your unbelief: for verily
I say unto you, If ye have faith as
a grain of mustard seed, ye shall
say unto this mountain, Remove
hence to yonder place; and it shall
remove; and nothing shall be im-
possible unto you.
21 Howbeit this kind goeth not
out but by prayer and fasting.
22 And while they abode in Gali-
lee, Jesus said unto them, The Son
of man shall be betrayed into the
hands of men:
23 And they shall kill him, and the
third day he shall be raised again.
And they were exceeding sorry.

The Question of Paying Tribute

24 And when they were come to
Capernaum, they that received trib-
ute *money* came to Peter, and said,
Doth not your master pay tribute?
25 He saith, Yes. And when he was
come into the house, Jesus pre-
vented him, saying, What thinkest
thou, Simon? of whom do the kings
of the earth take custom or tribute?
of their own children, or of strangers?
26 Peter saith unto him, Of strang-
ers. Jesus saith unto him, Then are
the children free.
27 Notwithstanding, lest we
should offend them, go thou to the
sea, and cast an hook, and take up
the fish that first cometh up; and
when thou hast opened his mouth,
thou shalt find a piece of money:
that take, and give unto them for
me and thee.

The Least Is the Greatest

18 At the same time came the
disciples unto Jesus, saying,
Who is the greatest in the kingdom
of heaven?
2 And Jesus called a little child
unto him, and set him in the midst
of them,
3 And said, Verily I say unto you,
Except ye be converted, and become
as little children, ye shall not enter
into the kingdom of heaven.
4 Whosoever therefore shall hum-
ble himself as this little child, the
same is greatest in the kingdom of
heaven.
5 And whoso shall receive one
such little child in my name re-
ceiveth me.
6 But whoso shall offend one of
these little ones which believe in
me, it were better for him that a
millstone were hanged about his
neck, and *that* he were drowned in
the depth of the sea.
7 Woe unto the world because of
offences! for it must needs be that
offences come; but woe to that man
by whom the offence cometh!
8 Wherefore if thy hand or thy foot
offend thee, cut them off, and cast
them from thee: it is better for thee
to enter into life halt or maimed,
rather than having two hands or
two feet to be cast into everlasting
fire.
9 And if thine eye offend thee,
pluck it out, and cast *it* from thee:
it is better for thee to enter into life
with one eye, rather than having
two eyes to be cast into hell fire.
10 Take heed that ye despise not
one of these little ones; for I say unto
you, That in heaven their angels do
always behold the face of my Father
which is in heaven.
11 For the Son of man is come to
save that which was lost.

A Lost Sheep

12 How think ye? if a man have an
hundred sheep, and one of them be
gone astray, doth he not leave the
ninety and nine, and goeth into the
mountains, and seeketh that which
is gone astray?
13 And if so be that he find it, verily
I say unto you, he rejoiceth more of
that *sheep,* than of the ninety and
nine which went not astray.
14 Even so it is not the will of your
Father which is in heaven, that one
of these little ones should perish.

A Trespassing Brother

15 Moreover if thy brother shall
trespass against thee, go and tell
him his fault between thee and him
alone: if he shall hear thee, thou hast
gained thy brother.
16 But if he will not hear *thee, then*
take with thee one or two more, that
in the mouth of two or three wit-
nesses every word may be estab-
lished.
17 And if he shall neglect to hear
them, tell *it* unto the church: but if
he neglect to hear the church, let

him be unto thee as an heathen man
and a publican.
18 Verily I say unto you, Whatso-
ever ye shall bind on earth shall be
bound in heaven: and whatsoever ye
shall loose on earth shall be loosed
in heaven.
19 Again I say unto you, That if
two of you shall agree on earth as
touching any thing that they shall
ask, it shall be done for them of my
Father which is in heaven.
20 For where two or three are
gathered together in my name, there
am I in the midst of them.
21 Then came Peter to him, and
said, Lord, how oft shall my brother
sin against me, and I forgive him?
till seven times?
22 Jesus saith unto him, I say not
unto thee, Until seven times: but,
Until seventy times seven.

An Unforgiving Servant

23 Therefore is the kingdom of
heaven likened unto a certain king,
which would take account of his
servants.
24 And when he had begun to
reckon, one was brought unto him,
which owed him ten thousand tal-
ents.
25 But forasmuch as he had not
to pay, his lord commanded him to
be sold, and his wife, and children,
and all that he had, and payment to
be made.
26 The servant therefore fell
down, and worshipped him, saying,
Lord, have patience with me, and I
will pay thee all.
27 Then the lord of that servant
was moved with compassion, and
loosed him, and forgave him the
debt.
28 But the same servant went out,
and found one of his fellowservants,
which owed him an hundred pence:
and he laid hands on him, and took
him by the throat, saying, Pay me
that thou owest.
29 And his fellowservant fell down
at his feet, and besought him, say-
ing, Have patience with me, and I
will pay thee all.
30 And he would not: but went
and cast him into prison, till he
should pay the debt.
31 So when his fellowservants
saw what was done, they were very
sorry, and came and told unto their
lord all that was done.
32 Then his lord, after that he had
called him, said unto him, O thou
wicked servant, I forgave thee all that
debt, because thou desiredst me:
33 Shouldest not thou also have
had compassion on thy fellowser-
vant, even as I had pity on thee?
34 And his lord was wroth, and
delivered him to the tormentors,
till he should pay all that was due
unto him.
35 So likewise shall my heavenly
Father do also unto you, if ye from
your hearts forgive not every one
his brother their trespasses.

Teachings on Divorce

19 And it came to pass, *that* when
Jesus had finished these say-
ings, he departed from Galilee, and
came into the coasts of Judaea be-
yond Jordan;
2 And great multitudes followed
him; and he healed them there.
3 The Pharisees also came unto
him, tempting him, and saying unto
him, Is it lawful for a man to put
away his wife for every cause?
4 And he answered and said unto
them, Have ye not read, that he
which made *them* at the beginning
made them male and female,
5 And said, For this cause shall a
man leave father and mother, and
shall cleave to his wife: and they
twain shall be one flesh?
6 Wherefore they are no more
twain, but one flesh. What there-
fore God hath joined together, let
not man put asunder.

7 They say unto him, Why did
Moses then command to give a
writing of divorcement, and to put
her away?
8 He saith unto them, Moses be-
cause of the hardness of your hearts
suffered you to put away your wives:
but from the beginning it was not so.
9 And I say unto you, Whosoever
shall put away his wife, except *it
be* for fornication, and shall marry
another, committeth adultery: and
whoso marrieth her which is put
away doth commit adultery.
10 His disciples say unto him, If
the case of the man be so with *his*
wife, it is not good to marry.
11 But he said unto them, All *men*
cannot receive this saying, save *they*
to whom it is given.
12 For there are some eunuchs,
which were so born from *their*
mother's womb: and there are
some eunuchs, which were made
eunuchs of men: and there be eu-
nuchs, which have made themselves
eunuchs for the kingdom of heav-
en's sake. He that is able to receive
it, let him receive *it.*

Little Children Brought to Jesus

13 Then were there brought unto
him little children, that he should
put *his* hands on them, and pray:
and the disciples rebuked them.
14 But Jesus said, Suffer little chil-
dren, and forbid them not, to come
unto me: for of such is the kingdom
of heaven.
15 And he laid *his* hands on them,
and departed thence.

The Rich Young Man

16 And, behold, one came and said
unto him, Good Master, what good
thing shall I do, that I may have eter-
nal life?
17 And he said unto him, Why
callest thou me good? *there is* none
good but one, *that is,* God: but if
thou wilt enter into life, keep the
commandments.
18 He saith unto him, Which? Jesus
said, Thou shalt do no murder, Thou
shalt not commit adultery, Thou
shalt not steal, Thou shalt not bear
false witness,
19 Honour thy father and *thy*
mother: and, Thou shalt love thy
neighbour as thyself.
20 The young man saith unto him,
All these things have I kept from my
youth up: what lack I yet?
21 Jesus said unto him, If thou
wilt be perfect, go *and* sell that thou
hast, and give to the poor, and thou
shalt have treasure in heaven: and
come *and* follow me.
22 But when the young man heard
that saying, he went away sorrow-
ful: for he had great possessions.
23 Then said Jesus unto his dis-
ciples, Verily I say unto you, That a
rich man shall hardly enter into the
kingdom of heaven.
24 And again I say unto you, It is
easier for a camel to go through the
eye of a needle, than for a rich man
to enter into the kingdom of God.
25 When his disciples heard *it,*
they were exceedingly amazed, say-
ing, Who then can be saved?
26 But Jesus beheld *them,* and
said unto them, With men this is
impossible; but with God all things
are possible.
27 Then answered Peter and said
unto him, Behold, we have forsaken
all, and followed thee; what shall we
have therefore?
28 And Jesus said unto them, Ver-
ily I say unto you, That ye which
have followed me, in the regenera-
tion when the Son of man shall sit in
the throne of his glory, ye also shall
sit upon twelve thrones, judging the
twelve tribes of Israel.
29 And every one that hath for-
saken houses, or brethren, or sis-
ters, or father, or mother, or wife,
or children, or lands, for my name's

sake, shall receive an hundredfold, and shall inherit everlasting life.

30 But many *that are* first shall be last; and the last *shall be* first.

The Parable of the Hired Labourers

20 For the kingdom of heaven is like unto a man *that is* an householder, which went out early in the morning to hire labourers into his vineyard.

2 And when he had agreed with the labourers for a penny a day, he sent them into his vineyard.

3 And he went out about the third hour, and saw others standing idle in the marketplace,

4 And said unto them; Go ye also into the vineyard, and whatsoever is right I will give you. And they went their way.

5 Again he went out about the sixth and ninth hour, and did likewise.

6 And about the eleventh hour he went out, and found others standing idle, and saith unto them, Why stand ye here all the day idle?

7 They say unto him, Because no man hath hired us. He saith unto them, Go ye also into the vineyard; and whatsoever is right, *that* shall ye receive.

8 So when even was come, the lord of the vineyard saith unto his steward, Call the labourers, and give them *their* hire, beginning from the last unto the first.

9 And when they came that *were hired* about the eleventh hour, they received every man a penny.

10 But when the first came, they supposed that they should have received more; and they likewise received every man a penny.

11 And when they had received *it,* they murmured against the goodman of the house,

12 Saying, These last have wrought *but* one hour, and thou hast made them equal unto us, which have borne the burden and heat of the day.

13 But he answered one of them, and said, Friend, I do thee no wrong: didst not thou agree with me for a penny?

14 Take *that* thine *is,* and go thy way: I will give unto this last, even as unto thee.

15 Is it not lawful for me to do what I will with mine own? Is thine eye evil, because I am good?

16 So the last shall be first, and the first last: for many be called, but few chosen.

Jesus Predicts His Death

17 And Jesus going up to Jerusalem took the twelve disciples apart in the way, and said unto them,

18 Behold, we go up to Jerusalem; and the Son of man shall be betrayed unto the chief priests and unto the scribes, and they shall condemn him to death,

19 And shall deliver him to the Gentiles to mock, and to scourge, and to crucify *him:* and the third day he shall rise again.

The Request of James and John's Mother

20 Then came to him the mother of Zebedee's children with her sons, worshipping *him,* and desiring a certain thing of him.

21 And he said unto her, What wilt thou? She saith unto him, Grant that these my two sons may sit, the one on thy right hand, and the other on the left, in thy kingdom.

22 But Jesus answered and said, Ye know not what ye ask. Are ye able to drink of the cup that I shall drink of, and to be baptized with the baptism that I am baptized with? They say unto him, We are able.

23 And he saith unto them, Ye shall drink indeed of my cup, and be baptized with the baptism that

I am baptized with: but to sit on my
right hand, and on my left, is not
mine to give, but *it shall be given to
them* for whom it is prepared of my
Father.
24 And when the ten heard *it,*
they were moved with indignation
against the two brethren.
25 But Jesus called them *unto him,*
and said, Ye know that the princes
of the Gentiles exercise dominion
over them, and they that are great
exercise authority upon them.
26 But it shall not be so among
you: but whosoever will be great
among you, let him be your minister;
27 And whosoever will be chief
among you, let him be your servant:
28 Even as the Son of man came
not to be ministered unto, but to
minister, and to give his life a ran-
som for many.

Jesus' Compassion for Two Blind Men

29 And as they departed from Jeri-
cho, a great multitude followed him.
30 And, behold, two blind men
sitting by the way side, when they
heard that Jesus passed by, cried
out, saying, Have mercy on us,
O Lord, *thou* son of David.
31 And the multitude rebuked
them, because they should hold
their peace: but they cried the more,
saying, Have mercy on us, O Lord,
thou son of David.
32 And Jesus stood still, and called
them, and said, What will ye that I
shall do unto you?
33 They say unto him, Lord, that
our eyes may be opened.
34 So Jesus had compassion *on
them,* and touched their eyes: and
immediately their eyes received
sight, and they followed him.

Jesus' Triumphal Entry

21 And when they drew nigh
unto Jerusalem, and were
come to Bethphage, unto the mount
of Olives, then sent Jesus two dis-
ciples,
2 Saying unto them, Go into
the village over against you, and
straightway ye shall find an ass tied,
and a colt with her: loose *them,* and
bring *them* unto me.
3 And if any *man* say ought unto
you, ye shall say, The Lord hath need
of them; and straightway he will
send them.
4 All this was done, that it might
be fulfilled which was spoken by the
prophet, saying,
5 Tell ye the daughter of Sion, Be-
hold, thy King cometh unto thee,
meek, and sitting upon an ass, and
a colt the foal of an ass.
6 And the disciples went, and did
as Jesus commanded them,
7 And brought the ass, and the
colt, and put on them their clothes,
and they set *him* thereon.
8 And a very great multitude
spread their garments in the way;
others cut down branches from the
trees, and strawed *them* in the way.
9 And the multitudes that went
before, and that followed, cried,
saying, Hosanna to the son of Da-
vid: Blessed *is* he that cometh in the
name of the Lord; Hosanna in the
highest.
10 And when he was come into
Jerusalem, all the city was moved,
saying, Who is this?
11 And the multitude said, This
is Jesus the prophet of Nazareth of
Galilee.

Jesus Cleanses the Temple

12 And Jesus went into the temple
of God, and cast out all them that
sold and bought in the temple, and
overthrew the tables of the money-
changers, and the seats of them that
sold doves,
13 And said unto them, It is writ-
ten, My house shall be called the
house of prayer; but ye have made
it a den of thieves.

14 And the blind and the lame came to him in the temple; and he healed them.

15 And when the chief priests and scribes saw the wonderful things that he did, and the children crying in the temple, and saying, Hosanna to the son of David; they were sore displeased,

16 And said unto him, Hearest thou what these say? And Jesus saith unto them, Yea; have ye never read, Out of the mouth of babes and sucklings thou hast perfected praise?

17 And he left them, and went out of the city into Bethany; and he lodged there.

The Withered Fig Tree

18 Now in the morning as he returned into the city, he hungered.

19 And when he saw a fig tree in the way, he came to it, and found nothing thereon, but leaves only, and said unto it, Let no fruit grow on thee henceforward for ever. And presently the fig tree withered away.

20 And when the disciples saw *it,* they marvelled, saying, How soon is the fig tree withered away!

21 Jesus answered and said unto them, Verily I say unto you, If ye have faith, and doubt not, ye shall not only do this *which is done* to the fig tree, but also if ye shall say unto this mountain, Be thou removed, and be thou cast into the sea; it shall be done.

22 And all things, whatsoever ye shall ask in prayer, believing, ye shall receive.

23 And when he was come into the temple, the chief priests and the elders of the people came unto him as he was teaching, and said, By what authority doest thou these things? and who gave thee this authority?

24 And Jesus answered and said unto them, I also will ask you one thing, which if ye tell me, I in like wise will tell you by what authority I do these things.

25 The baptism of John, whence was it? from heaven, or of men? And they reasoned with themselves, saying, If we shall say, From heaven; he will say unto us, Why did ye not then believe him?

26 But if we shall say, Of men; we fear the people; for all hold John as a prophet.

27 And they answered Jesus, and said, We cannot tell. And he said unto them, Neither tell I you by what authority I do these things.

The Parable of Two Sons

28 But what think ye? A *certain* man had two sons; and he came to the first, and said, Son, go work to day in my vineyard.

29 He answered and said, I will not: but afterward he repented, and went.

30 And he came to the second, and said likewise. And he answered and said, I *go,* sir: and went not.

31 Whether of them twain did the will of *his* father? They say unto him, The first. Jesus saith unto them, Verily I say unto you, That the publicans and the harlots go into the kingdom of God before you.

32 For John came unto you in the way of righteousness, and ye believed him not: but the publicans and the harlots believed him: and ye, when ye had seen *it,* repented not afterward, that ye might believe him.

The Parable of the Vineyard

33 Hear another parable: There was a certain householder, which planted a vineyard, and hedged it round about, and digged a winepress in it, and built a tower, and let it out to husbandmen, and went into a far country:

34 And when the time of the fruit
drew near, he sent his servants to
the husbandmen, that they might
receive the fruits of it.
35 And the husbandmen took his
servants, and beat one, and killed
another, and stoned another.
36 Again, he sent other servants
more than the first: and they did
unto them likewise.
37 But last of all he sent unto them
his son, saying, They will reverence
my son.
38 But when the husbandmen
saw the son, they said among them-
selves, This is the heir; come, let
us kill him, and let us seize on his
inheritance.
39 And they caught him, and cast
him out of the vineyard, and slew
him.
40 When the lord therefore of the
vineyard cometh, what will he do
unto those husbandmen?
41 They say unto him, He will mis-
erably destroy those wicked men,
and will let out *his* vineyard unto
other husbandmen, which shall ren-
der him the fruits in their seasons.
42 Jesus saith unto them, Did ye
never read in the scriptures, The
stone which the builders rejected,
the same is become the head of the
corner: this is the Lord's doing, and
it is marvellous in our eyes?
43 Therefore say I unto you, The
kingdom of God shall be taken from
you, and given to a nation bringing
forth the fruits thereof.
44 And whosoever shall fall on
this stone shall be broken: but on
whomsoever it shall fall, it will grind
him to powder.
45 And when the chief priests and
Pharisees had heard his parables,
they perceived that he spake of
them.
46 But when they sought to lay
hands on him, they feared the mul-
titude, because they took him for a
prophet.

The Parable of the Wedding Banquet

22 And Jesus answered and
spake unto them again by
parables, and said,
2 The kingdom of heaven is like
unto a certain king, which made a
marriage for his son,
3 And sent forth his servants to
call them that were bidden to the
wedding: and they would not come.
4 Again, he sent forth other ser-
vants, saying, Tell them which are
bidden, Behold, I have prepared my
dinner: my oxen and *my* fatlings *are*
killed, and all things *are* ready: come
unto the marriage.
5 But they made light of *it,* and
went their ways, one to his farm,
another to his merchandise:
6 And the remnant took his ser-
vants, and intreated *them* spitefully,
and slew *them.*
7 But when the king heard *thereof,*
he was wroth: and he sent forth his
armies, and destroyed those mur-
derers, and burned up their city.
8 Then saith he to his servants,
The wedding is ready, but they
which were bidden were not worthy.
9 Go ye therefore into the high-
ways, and as many as ye shall find,
bid to the marriage.
10 So those servants went out into
the highways, and gathered together
all as many as they found, both bad
and good: and the wedding was fur-
nished with guests.
11 And when the king came in to
see the guests, he saw there a man
which had not on a wedding gar-
ment:
12 And he saith unto him, Friend,
how camest thou in hither not hav-
ing a wedding garment? And he was
speechless.
13 Then said the king to the ser-
vants, Bind him hand and foot, and
take him away, and cast *him* into
outer darkness; there shall be weep-
ing and gnashing of teeth.

14 For many are called, but few *are*
chosen.

Render Tribute to Caesar and to God

15 Then went the Pharisees, and
took counsel how they might en-
tangle him in *his* talk.
16 And they sent out unto him
their disciples with the Herodians,
saying, Master, we know that thou
art true, and teachest the way of
God in truth, neither carest thou for
any *man:* for thou regardest not the
person of men.
17 Tell us therefore, What thinkest
thou? Is it lawful to give tribute unto
Caesar, or not?
18 But Jesus perceived their wick-
edness, and said, Why tempt ye me,
ye hypocrites?
19 Shew me the tribute money.
And they brought unto him a penny.
20 And he saith unto them, Whose
is this image and superscription?
21 They say unto him, Caesar's.
Then saith he unto them, Render
therefore unto Caesar the things
which are Caesar's; and unto God
the things that are God's.
22 When they had heard *these*
words, they marvelled, and left him,
and went their way.

Teachings on the Resurrection

23 The same day came to him the
Sadducees, which say that there is
no resurrection, and asked him,
24 Saying, Master, Moses said, If
a man die, having no children, his
brother shall marry his wife, and
raise up seed unto his brother.
25 Now there were with us seven
brethren: and the first, when he had
married a wife, deceased, and, hav-
ing no issue, left his wife unto his
brother:
26 Likewise the second also, and
the third, unto the seventh.
27 And last of all the woman died
also.
28 Therefore in the resurrection
whose wife shall she be of the seven?
for they all had her.
29 Jesus answered and said unto
them, Ye do err, not knowing the
scriptures, nor the power of God.
30 For in the resurrection they
neither marry, nor are given in mar-
riage, but are as the angels of God
in heaven.
31 But as touching the resurrec-
tion of the dead, have ye not read
that which was spoken unto you by
God, saying,
32 I am the God of Abraham, and
the God of Isaac, and the God of Ja-
cob? God is not the God of the dead,
but of the living.
33 And when the multitude heard
this, they were astonished at his
doctrine.

The First and Great Commandment

34 But when the Pharisees had
heard that he had put the Saddu-
cees to silence, they were gathered
together.
35 Then one of them, *which was* a
lawyer, asked *him a question,* tempt-
ing him, and saying,
36 Master, which *is* the great com-
mandment in the law?
37 Jesus said unto him, Thou shalt
love the Lord thy God with all thy
heart, and with all thy soul, and with
all thy mind.
38 This is the first and great com-
mandment.
39 And the second *is* like unto it,
Thou shalt love thy neighbour as
thyself.
40 On these two commandments
hang all the law and the prophets.

Pharisees Questioned

41 While the Pharisees were gath-
ered together, Jesus asked them,
42 Saying, What think ye of Christ?
whose son is he? They say unto him,
The son of David.

43 He saith unto them, How then
doth David in spirit call him Lord,
saying,
44 The LORD said unto my Lord,
Sit thou on my right hand, till I make
thine enemies thy footstool?
45 If David then call him Lord,
how is he his son?
46 And no man was able to an-
swer him a word, neither durst any
man from that day forth ask him any
more *questions.*

The Scribes and Pharisees

23 Then spake Jesus to the mul-
titude, and to his disciples,
2 Saying, The scribes and the
Pharisees sit in Moses' seat:
3 All therefore whatsoever they
bid you observe, *that* observe and
do; but do not ye after their works:
for they say, and do not.
4 For they bind heavy burdens
and grievous to be borne, and lay
them on men's shoulders; but they
themselves will not move them with
one of their fingers.

Hypocrisy Denounced

5 But all their works they do for
to be seen of men: they make broad
their phylacteries, and enlarge the
borders of their garments,
6 And love the uppermost rooms
at feasts, and the chief seats in the
synagogues,
7 And greetings in the markets,
and to be called of men, Rabbi,
Rabbi.
8 But be not ye called Rabbi: for
one is your Master, *even* Christ; and
all ye are brethren.
9 And call no *man* your father
upon the earth: for one is your Fa-
ther, which is in heaven.
10 Neither be ye called masters:
for one is your Master, *even* Christ.
11 But he that is greatest among
you shall be your servant.
12 And whosoever shall exalt
himself shall be abased; and he
that shall humble himself shall be
exalted.
13 But woe unto you, scribes and
Pharisees, hypocrites! for ye shut
up the kingdom of heaven against
men: for ye neither go in *yourselves,*
neither suffer ye them that are en-
tering to go in.
14 Woe unto you, scribes and
Pharisees, hypocrites! for ye devour
widows' houses, and for a pretence
make long prayer: therefore ye shall
receive the greater damnation.
15 Woe unto you, scribes and
Pharisees, hypocrites! for ye com-
pass sea and land to make one pros-
elyte, and when he is made, ye make
him twofold more the child of hell
than yourselves.

Woe on Scribes and Pharisees

16 Woe unto you, *ye* blind guides,
which say, Whosoever shall swear by
the temple, it is nothing; but who-
soever shall swear by the gold of the
temple, he is a debtor!
17 *Ye* fools and blind: for whether
is greater, the gold, or the temple
that sanctifieth the gold?
18 And, Whosoever shall swear
by the altar, it is nothing; but who-
soever sweareth by the gift that is
upon it, he is guilty.
19 *Ye* fools and blind: for whether
is greater, the gift, or the altar that
sanctifieth the gift?
20 Whoso therefore shall swear
by the altar, sweareth by it, and by
all things thereon.
21 And whoso shall swear by the
temple, sweareth by it, and by him
that dwelleth therein.
22 And he that shall swear by
heaven, sweareth by the throne
of God, and by him that sitteth
thereon.
23 Woe unto you, scribes and
Pharisees, hypocrites! for ye pay
tithe of mint and anise and cum-
min, and have omitted the weightier
matters of the law, judgment, mercy,

and faith: these ought ye to have
done, and not to leave the other
undone.
24 *Ye* blind guides, which strain
at a gnat, and swallow a camel.
25 Woe unto you, scribes and
Pharisees, hypocrites! for ye make
clean the outside of the cup and of
the platter, but within they are full
of extortion and excess.
26 *Thou* blind Pharisee, cleanse
first that *which is* within the cup
and platter, that the outside of them
may be clean also.
27 Woe unto you, scribes and
Pharisees, hypocrites! for ye are like
unto whited sepulchres, which in-
deed appear beautiful outward, but
are within full of dead *men's* bones,
and of all uncleanness.
28 Even so ye also outwardly ap-
pear righteous unto men, but within
ye are full of hypocrisy and iniquity.
29 Woe unto you, scribes and
Pharisees, hypocrites! because ye
build the tombs of the prophets,
and garnish the sepulchres of the
righteous,
30 And say, If we had been in the
days of our fathers, we would not
have been partakers with them in
the blood of the prophets.
31 Wherefore ye be witnesses unto
yourselves, that ye are the children
of them which killed the prophets.
32 Fill ye up then the measure of
your fathers.
33 *Ye* serpents, *ye* generation of
vipers, how can ye escape the dam-
nation of hell?
34 Wherefore, behold, I send unto
you prophets, and wise men, and
scribes: and *some* of them ye shall
kill and crucify; and *some* of them
shall ye scourge in your synagogues,
and persecute *them* from city to city:
35 That upon you may come all
the righteous blood shed upon the
earth, from the blood of righteous
Abel unto the blood of Zacharias
son of Barachias, whom ye slew
between the temple and the altar.
36 Verily I say unto you, All these
things shall come upon this gener-
ation.
37 O Jerusalem, Jerusalem, *thou*
that killest the prophets, and ston-
est them which are sent unto thee,
how often would I have gathered
thy children together, even as a hen
gathereth her chickens under *her*
wings, and ye would not!
38 Behold, your house is left unto
you desolate.
39 For I say unto you, Ye shall not
see me henceforth, till ye shall say,
Blessed *is* he that cometh in the
name of the Lord.

Signs of the End

24 And Jesus went out, and de-
parted from the temple: and
his disciples came to *him* for to shew
him the buildings of the temple.
2 And Jesus said unto them, See
ye not all these things? verily I say
unto you, There shall not be left here
one stone upon another, that shall
not be thrown down.
3 And as he sat upon the mount of
Olives, the disciples came unto him
privately, saying, Tell us, when shall
these things be? and what *shall be*
the sign of thy coming, and of the
end of the world?
4 And Jesus answered and said
unto them, Take heed that no man
deceive you.
5 For many shall come in my
name, saying, I am Christ; and shall
deceive many.
6 And ye shall hear of wars and
rumours of wars: see that ye be not
troubled: for all *these things* must
come to pass, but the end is not yet.
7 For nation shall rise against na-
tion, and kingdom against kingdom:
and there shall be famines, and pes-
tilences, and earthquakes, in divers
places.
8 All these *are* the beginning of
sorrows.

9 Then shall they deliver you up to
be afflicted, and shall kill you: and
ye shall be hated of all nations for
my name's sake.
10 And then shall many be offended, and shall betray one another, and shall hate one another.
11 And many false prophets shall
rise, and shall deceive many.
12 And because iniquity shall
abound, the love of many shall wax
cold.
13 But he that shall endure unto
the end, the same shall be saved.
14 And this gospel of the kingdom
shall be preached in all the world for
a witness unto all nations; and then
shall the end come.

The Coming of the Son of Man

15 When ye therefore shall see the
abomination of desolation, spoken
of by Daniel the prophet, stand in
the holy place, (whoso readeth, let
him understand:)
16 Then let them which be in Judaea flee into the mountains:
17 Let him which is on the housetop not come down to take any thing
out of his house:
18 Neither let him which is in the
field return back to take his clothes.
19 And woe unto them that are
with child, and to them that give
suck in those days!
20 But pray ye that your flight be
not in the winter, neither on the
sabbath day:
21 For then shall be great tribulation, such as was not since the
beginning of the world to this time,
no, nor ever shall be.
22 And except those days should
be shortened, there should no flesh
be saved: but for the elect's sake
those days shall be shortened.
23 Then if any man shall say unto
you, Lo, here *is* Christ, or there; believe *it* not.
24 For there shall arise false
Christs, and false prophets, and
shall shew great signs and wonders;
insomuch that, if *it were* possible,
they shall deceive the very elect.
25 Behold, I have told you before.
26 Wherefore if they shall say unto
you, Behold, he is in the desert; go
not forth: behold, *he is* in the secret
chambers; believe *it* not.
27 For as the lightning cometh out
of the east, and shineth even unto
the west; so shall also the coming
of the Son of man be.
28 For wheresoever the carcase
is, there will the eagles be gathered
together.
29 Immediately after the tribulation of those days shall the sun be
darkened, and the moon shall not
give her light, and the stars shall fall
from heaven, and the powers of the
heavens shall be shaken:
30 And then shall appear the sign
of the Son of man in heaven: and
then shall all the tribes of the earth
mourn, and they shall see the Son of
man coming in the clouds of heaven
with power and great glory.
31 And he shall send his angels
with a great sound of a trumpet, and
they shall gather together his elect
from the four winds, from one end
of heaven to the other.
32 Now learn a parable of the fig
tree; When his branch is yet tender,
and putteth forth leaves, ye know
that summer *is* nigh:
33 So likewise ye, when ye shall
see all these things, know that it is
near, *even* at the doors.
34 Verily I say unto you, This generation shall not pass, till all these
things be fulfilled.
35 Heaven and earth shall pass
away, but my words shall not pass
away.

God Knows the Day and Hour

36 But of that day and hour
knoweth no *man,* no, not the angels
of heaven, but my Father only.
37 But as the days of Noe *were,* so

shall also the coming of the Son of
man be.
38 For as in the days that were
before the flood they were eating
and drinking, marrying and giving
in marriage, until the day that Noe
entered into the ark,
39 And knew not until the flood
came, and took them all away; so
shall also the coming of the Son of
man be.
40 Then shall two be in the field;
the one shall be taken, and the other
left.
41 Two *women shall be* grinding
at the mill; the one shall be taken,
and the other left.
42 Watch therefore: for ye know
not what hour your Lord doth
come.
43 But know this, that if the good-
man of the house had known in
what watch the thief would come,
he would have watched, and would
not have suffered his house to be
broken up.
44 Therefore be ye also ready: for
in such an hour as ye think not the
Son of man cometh.
45 Who then is a faithful and wise
servant, whom his lord hath made
ruler over his household, to give
them meat in due season?
46 Blessed *is* that servant, whom
his lord when he cometh shall find
so doing.
47 Verily I say unto you, That he
shall make him ruler over all his
goods.
48 But and if that evil servant shall
say in his heart, My lord delayeth his
coming;
49 And shall begin to smite *his*
fellowservants, and to eat and drink
with the drunken;
50 The lord of that servant shall
come in a day when he looketh not
for *him,* and in an hour that he is
not aware of,
51 And shall cut him asunder, and
appoint *him* his portion with the
hypocrites: there shall be weeping
and gnashing of teeth.

Readiness and Stewardship

25 Then shall the kingdom of
heaven be likened unto ten
virgins, which took their lamps, and
went forth to meet the bridegroom.
2 And five of them were wise, and
five *were* foolish.
3 They that *were* foolish took their
lamps, and took no oil with them:
4 But the wise took oil in their
vessels with their lamps.
5 While the bridegroom tarried,
they all slumbered and slept.
6 And at midnight there was a
cry made, Behold, the bridegroom
cometh; go ye out to meet him.
7 Then all those virgins arose, and
trimmed their lamps.
8 And the foolish said unto the
wise, Give us of your oil; for our
lamps are gone out.
9 But the wise answered, saying,
Not so; lest there be not enough for
us and you: but go ye rather to them
that sell, and buy for yourselves.
10 And while they went to buy, the
bridegroom came; and they that
were ready went in with him to the
marriage: and the door was shut.
11 Afterward came also the other
virgins, saying, Lord, Lord, open
to us.
12 But he answered and said, Ver-
ily I say unto you, I know you not.
13 Watch therefore, for ye know
neither the day nor the hour wherein
the Son of man cometh.
14 For *the kingdom of heaven is* as
a man travelling into a far country,
who called his own servants, and
delivered unto them his goods.
15 And unto one he gave five tal-
ents, to another two, and to another
one; to every man according to his
several ability; and straightway took
his journey.
16 Then he that had received the
five talents went and traded with

the same, and made *them* other five talents.

17 And likewise he that *had received* two, he also gained other two.

18 But he that had received one went and digged in the earth, and hid his lord's money.

19 After a long time the lord of those servants cometh, and reckoneth with them.

20 And so he that had received five talents came and brought other five talents, saying, Lord, thou deliveredst unto me five talents: behold, I have gained beside them five talents more.

21 His lord said unto him, Well done, *thou* good and faithful servant: thou hast been faithful over a few things, I will make thee ruler over many things: enter thou into the joy of thy lord.

22 He also that had received two talents came and said, Lord, thou deliveredst unto me two talents: behold, I have gained two other talents beside them.

23 His lord said unto him, Well done, good and faithful servant; thou hast been faithful over a few things, I will make thee ruler over many things: enter thou into the joy of thy lord.

24 Then he which had received the one talent came and said, Lord, I knew thee that thou art an hard man, reaping where thou hast not sown, and gathering where thou hast not strawed:

25 And I was afraid, and went and hid thy talent in the earth: lo, *there* thou hast *that is* thine.

26 His lord answered and said unto him, *Thou* wicked and slothful servant, thou knewest that I reap where I sowed not, and gather where I have not strawed:

27 Thou oughtest therefore to have put my money to the exchangers, and *then* at my coming I should have received mine own with usury.

28 Take therefore the talent from him, and give *it* unto him which hath ten talents.

29 For unto every one that hath shall be given, and he shall have abundance: but from him that hath not shall be taken away even that which he hath.

30 And cast ye the unprofitable servant into outer darkness: there shall be weeping and gnashing of teeth.

The Separation of Sheep and Goats

31 When the Son of man shall come in his glory, and all the holy angels with him, then shall he sit upon the throne of his glory:

32 And before him shall be gathered all nations: and he shall separate them one from another, as a shepherd divideth *his* sheep from the goats:

33 And he shall set the sheep on his right hand, but the goats on the left.

34 Then shall the King say unto them on his right hand, Come, ye blessed of my Father, inherit the kingdom prepared for you from the foundation of the world:

35 For I was an hungred, and ye gave me meat: I was thirsty, and ye gave me drink: I was a stranger, and ye took me in:

36 Naked, and ye clothed me: I was sick, and ye visited me: I was in prison, and ye came unto me.

37 Then shall the righteous answer him, saying, Lord, when saw we thee an hungred, and fed *thee?* or thirsty, and gave *thee* drink?

38 When saw we thee a stranger, and took *thee* in? or naked, and clothed *thee?*

39 Or when saw we thee sick, or in prison, and came unto thee?

40 And the King shall answer and say unto them, Verily I say unto you, Inasmuch as ye have done *it* unto

one of the least of these my brethren, ye have done *it* unto me.
41 Then shall he say also unto
them on the left hand, Depart from
me, ye cursed, into everlasting fire,
prepared for the devil and his angels:
42 For I was an hungred, and ye
gave me no meat: I was thirsty, and
ye gave me no drink:
43 I was a stranger, and ye took
me not in: naked, and ye clothed
me not: sick, and in prison, and ye
visited me not.
44 Then shall they also answer
him, saying, Lord, when saw we thee
an hungred, or athirst, or a stranger,
or naked, or sick, or in prison, and
did not minister unto thee?
45 Then shall he answer them,
saying, Verily I say unto you, Inasmuch as ye did *it* not to one of the
least of these, ye did *it* not to me.
46 And these shall go away into
everlasting punishment: but the
righteous into life eternal.

The Religious Leaders' Plan to Kill Jesus

26 And it came to pass, when
Jesus had finished all these
sayings, he said unto his disciples,
2 Ye know that after two days is
the feast of the passover, and the Son
of man is betrayed to be crucified.
3 Then assembled together the
chief priests, and the scribes, and
the elders of the people, unto the
palace of the high priest, who was
called Caiaphas,
4 And consulted that they might
take Jesus by subtilty, and kill *him.*
5 But they said, Not on the feast
day, lest there be an uproar among
the people.

Precious Ointment

6 Now when Jesus was in Bethany,
in the house of Simon the leper,
7 There came unto him a woman
having an alabaster box of very precious ointment, and poured it on his
head, as he sat *at meat.*
8 But when his disciples saw *it,*
they had indignation, saying, To
what purpose *is* this waste?
9 For this ointment might have
been sold for much, and given to
the poor.
10 When Jesus understood *it,* he
said unto them, Why trouble ye
the woman? for she hath wrought
a good work upon me.
11 For ye have the poor always
with you; but me ye have not always.
12 For in that she hath poured this
ointment on my body, she did *it* for
my burial.
13 Verily I say unto you, Wheresoever this gospel shall be preached
in the whole world, *there* shall also
this, that this woman hath done, be
told for a memorial of her.

Judas Agrees to Betray Jesus

14 Then one of the twelve, called
Judas Iscariot, went unto the chief
priests,
15 And said *unto them,* What will
ye give me, and I will deliver him
unto you? And they covenanted with
him for thirty pieces of silver.
16 And from that time he sought
opportunity to betray him.

The Passover Meal

17 Now the first *day* of the *feast
of* unleavened bread the disciples
came to Jesus, saying unto him,
Where wilt thou that we prepare
for thee to eat the passover?
18 And he said, Go into the city to
such a man, and say unto him, The
Master saith, My time is at hand; I
will keep the passover at thy house
with my disciples.
19 And the disciples did as Jesus
had appointed them; and they made
ready the passover.
20 Now when the even was come,
he sat down with the twelve.

21 And as they did eat, he said,
Verily I say unto you, that one of
you shall betray me.
22 And they were exceeding sor-
rowful, and began every one of them
to say unto him, Lord, is it I?
23 And he answered and said, He
that dippeth *his* hand with me in the
dish, the same shall betray me.
24 The Son of man goeth as it is
written of him: but woe unto that
man by whom the Son of man is
betrayed! it had been good for that
man if he had not been born.
25 Then Judas, which betrayed
him, answered and said, Master,
is it I? He said unto him, Thou hast
said.
26 And as they were eating, Jesus
took bread, and blessed *it,* and brake
it, and gave *it* to the disciples, and
said, Take, eat; this is my body.
27 And he took the cup, and gave
thanks, and gave *it* to them, saying,
Drink ye all of it;
28 For this is my blood of the new
testament, which is shed for many
for the remission of sins.
29 But I say unto you, I will not
drink henceforth of this fruit of the
vine, until that day when I drink it
new with you in my Father's king-
dom.
30 And when they had sung an
hymn, they went out into the mount
of Olives.

Peter's Vow of Loyalty

31 Then saith Jesus unto them,
All ye shall be offended because
of me this night: for it is written,
I will smite the shepherd, and the
sheep of the flock shall be scattered
abroad.
32 But after I am risen again, I will
go before you into Galilee.
33 Peter answered and said unto
him, Though all *men* shall be of-
fended because of thee, *yet* will I
never be offended.
34 Jesus said unto him, Verily I say
unto thee, That this night, before
the cock crow, thou shalt deny me
thrice.
35 Peter said unto him, Though I
should die with thee, yet will I not
deny thee. Likewise also said all the
disciples.

Jesus' Prayer in Gethsemane

36 Then cometh Jesus with them
unto a place called Gethsemane, and
saith unto the disciples, Sit ye here,
while I go and pray yonder.
37 And he took with him Peter and
the two sons of Zebedee, and began
to be sorrowful and very heavy.
38 Then saith he unto them, My
soul is exceeding sorrowful, even
unto death: tarry ye here, and watch
with me.
39 And he went a little farther, and
fell on his face, and prayed, saying,
O my Father, if it be possible, let this
cup pass from me: nevertheless not
as I will, but as thou *wilt.*
40 And he cometh unto the disci-
ples, and findeth them asleep, and
saith unto Peter, What, could ye not
watch with me one hour?
41 Watch and pray, that ye enter
not into temptation: the spirit in-
deed *is* willing, but the flesh *is* weak.
42 He went away again the second
time, and prayed, saying, O my Fa-
ther, if this cup may not pass away
from me, except I drink it, thy will
be done.
43 And he came and found them
asleep again: for their eyes were
heavy.
44 And he left them, and went
away again, and prayed the third
time, saying the same words.
45 Then cometh he to his disci-
ples, and saith unto them, Sleep on
now, and take *your* rest: behold, the
hour is at hand, and the Son of man
is betrayed into the hands of sin-
ners.
46 Rise, let us be going: behold,
he is at hand that doth betray me.

Jesus' Betrayal and Arrest

47 And while he yet spake, lo, Judas, one of the twelve, came, and with him a great multitude with swords and staves, from the chief priests and elders of the people.

48 Now he that betrayed him gave them a sign, saying, Whomsoever I shall kiss, that same is he: hold him fast.

49 And forthwith he came to Jesus, and said, Hail, master; and kissed him.

50 And Jesus said unto him, Friend, wherefore art thou come? Then came they, and laid hands on Jesus, and took him.

51 And, behold, one of them which were with Jesus stretched out *his* hand, and drew his sword, and struck a servant of the high priest's, and smote off his ear.

52 Then said Jesus unto him, Put up again thy sword into his place: for all they that take the sword shall perish with the sword.

53 Thinkest thou that I cannot now pray to my Father, and he shall presently give me more than twelve legions of angels?

54 But how then shall the scriptures be fulfilled, that thus it must be?

55 In that same hour said Jesus to the multitudes, Are ye come out as against a thief with swords and staves for to take me? I sat daily with you teaching in the temple, and ye laid no hold on me.

56 But all this was done, that the scriptures of the prophets might be fulfilled. Then all the disciples forsook him, and fled.

Jesus Before Caiaphas

57 And they that had laid hold on Jesus led *him* away to Caiaphas the high priest, where the scribes and the elders were assembled.

58 But Peter followed him afar off unto the high priest's palace, and went in, and sat with the servants, to see the end.

59 Now the chief priests, and elders, and all the council, sought false witness against Jesus, to put him to death;

60 But found none: yea, though many false witnesses came, *yet* found they none. At the last came two false witnesses,

61 And said, This *fellow* said, I am able to destroy the temple of God, and to build it in three days.

62 And the high priest arose, and said unto him, Answerest thou nothing? what *is it which* these witness against thee?

63 But Jesus held his peace, And the high priest answered and said unto him, I adjure thee by the living God, that thou tell us whether thou be the Christ, the Son of God.

64 Jesus saith unto him, Thou hast said: nevertheless I say unto you, Hereafter shall ye see the Son of man sitting on the right hand of power, and coming in the clouds of heaven.

65 Then the high priest rent his clothes, saying, He hath spoken blasphemy; what further need have we of witnesses? behold, now ye have heard his blasphemy.

66 What think ye? They answered and said, He is guilty of death.

67 Then did they spit in his face, and buffeted him; and others smote *him* with the palms of their hands,

68 Saying, Prophesy unto us, thou Christ, Who is he that smote thee?

Peter's Denial of Jesus

69 Now Peter sat without in the palace: and a damsel came unto him, saying, Thou also wast with Jesus of Galilee.

70 But he denied before *them* all, saying, I know not what thou sayest.

71 And when he was gone out into the porch, another *maid* saw him, and said unto them that were there,

This *fellow* was also with Jesus of
Nazareth.
72 And again he denied with an
oath, I do not know the man.
73 And after a while came unto
him they that stood by, and said
to Peter, Surely thou also art *one*
of them; for thy speech bewrayeth
thee.
74 Then began he to curse and to
swear, *saying,* I know not the man.
And immediately the cock crew.
75 And Peter remembered the
word of Jesus, which said unto him,
Before the cock crow, thou shalt
deny me thrice. And he went out,
and wept bitterly.

The Remorse and Death of Judas

27 When the morning was come,
all the chief priests and elders
of the people took counsel against
Jesus to put him to death:
2 And when they had bound him,
they led *him* away, and delivered
him to Pontius Pilate the governor.
3 Then Judas, which had betrayed
him, when he saw that he was con-
demned, repented himself, and
brought again the thirty pieces of
silver to the chief priests and elders,
4 Saying, I have sinned in that I
have betrayed the innocent blood.
And they said, What *is that* to us?
see thou *to that.*
5 And he cast down the pieces of
silver in the temple, and departed,
and went and hanged himself.
6 And the chief priests took the sil-
ver pieces, and said, It is not lawful
for to put them into the treasury,
because it is the price of blood.
7 And they took counsel, and
bought with them the potter's field,
to bury strangers in.
8 Wherefore that field was called,
The field of blood, unto this day.
9 Then was fulfilled that which
was spoken by Jeremy the prophet,
saying, And they took the thirty
pieces of silver, the price of him
that was valued, whom they of the
children of Israel did value;
10 And gave them for the potter's
field, as the Lord appointed me.

Jesus Appears Before Pilate

11 And Jesus stood before the
governor: and the governor asked
him, saying, Art thou the King of
the Jews? And Jesus said unto him,
Thou sayest.
12 And when he was accused of
the chief priests and elders, he an-
swered nothing.
13 Then said Pilate unto him,
Hearest thou not how many things
they witness against thee?
14 And he answered him to never
a word; insomuch that the governor
marvelled greatly.
15 Now at *that* feast the governor
was wont to release unto the people
a prisoner, whom they would.
16 And they had then a notable
prisoner, called Barabbas.
17 Therefore when they were gath-
ered together, Pilate said unto them,
Whom will ye that I release unto
you? Barabbas, or Jesus which is
called Christ?
18 For he knew that for envy they
had delivered him.
19 When he was set down on the
judgment seat, his wife sent unto
him, saying, Have thou nothing to
do with that just man: for I have
suffered many things this day in a
dream because of him.
20 But the chief priests and elders
persuaded the multitude that they
should ask Barabbas, and destroy
Jesus.
21 The governor answered and
said unto them, Whether of the
twain will ye that I release unto
you? They said, Barabbas.
22 Pilate saith unto them, What
shall I do then with Jesus which is
called Christ? *They* all say unto him,
Let him be crucified.

23 And the governor said, Why, what evil hath he done? But they cried out the more, saying, Let him be crucified.

24 When Pilate saw that he could prevail nothing, but *that* rather a tumult was made, he took water, and washed *his* hands before the multitude, saying, I am innocent of the blood of this just person: see ye *to it.*

25 Then answered all the people, and said, His blood *be* on us, and on our children.

26 Then released he Barabbas unto them: and when he had scourged Jesus, he delivered *him* to be crucified.

27 Then the soldiers of the governor took Jesus into the common hall, and gathered unto him the whole band *of soldiers.*

28 And they stripped him, and put on him a scarlet robe.

29 And when they had platted a crown of thorns, they put *it* upon his head, and a reed in his right hand: and they bowed the knee before him, and mocked him, saying, Hail, King of the Jews!

30 And they spit upon him, and took the reed, and smote him on the head.

31 And after that they had mocked him, they took the robe off from him, and put his own raiment on him, and led him away to crucify *him.*

The Crucifixion of Jesus

32 And as they came out, they found a man of Cyrene, Simon by name: him they compelled to bear his cross.

33 And when they were come unto a place called Golgotha, that is to say, a place of a skull,

34 They gave him vinegar to drink mingled with gall: and when he had tasted *thereof,* he would not drink.

35 And they crucified him, and parted his garments, casting lots: that it might be fulfilled which was spoken by the prophet, They parted my garments among them, and upon my vesture did they cast lots.

36 And sitting down they watched him there;

37 And set up over his head his accusation written, THIS IS JESUS THE KING OF THE JEWS.

38 Then were there two thieves crucified with him, one on the right hand, and another on the left.

39 And they that passed by reviled him, wagging their heads,

40 And saying, Thou that destroyest the temple, and buildest *it* in three days, save thyself. If thou be the Son of God, come down from the cross.

41 Likewise also the chief priests mocking *him,* with the scribes and elders, said,

42 He saved others; himself he cannot save. If he be the King of Israel, let him now come down from the cross, and we will believe him.

43 He trusted in God; let him deliver him now, if he will have him: for he said, I am the Son of God.

44 The thieves also, which were crucified with him, cast the same in his teeth.

Jesus' Death on the Cross

45 Now from the sixth hour there was darkness over all the land unto the ninth hour.

46 And about the ninth hour Jesus cried with a loud voice, saying, Eli, Eli, lama sabachthani? that is to say, My God, my God, why hast thou forsaken me?

47 Some of them that stood there, when they heard *that,* said, This *man* calleth for Elias.

48 And straightway one of them ran, and took a spunge, and filled *it* with vinegar, and put *it* on a reed, and gave him to drink.

49 The rest said, Let be, let us see whether Elias will come to save him.

50 Jesus, when he had cried again
with a loud voice, yielded up the
ghost.
51 And, behold, the veil of the
temple was rent in twain from the
top to the bottom; and the earth did
quake, and the rocks rent;
52 And the graves were opened;
and many bodies of the saints which
slept arose,
53 And came out of the graves after
his resurrection, and went into the
holy city, and appeared unto many.
54 Now when the centurion, and
they that were with him, watching
Jesus, saw the earthquake, and
those things that were done, they
feared greatly, saying, Truly this was
the Son of God.
55 And many women were there
beholding afar off, which followed
Jesus from Galilee, ministering unto
him:
56 Among which was Mary Magdalene,
and Mary the mother of
James and Joses, and the mother
of Zebedee's children.

Jesus Buried in Joseph's Tomb

57 When the even was come, there
came a rich man of Arimathaea,
named Joseph, who also himself
was Jesus' disciple:
58 He went to Pilate, and begged
the body of Jesus. Then Pilate commanded
the body to be delivered.
59 And when Joseph had taken
the body, he wrapped it in a clean
linen cloth,
60 And laid it in his own new
tomb, which he had hewn out in
the rock: and he rolled a great stone
to the door of the sepulchre, and
departed.
61 And there was Mary Magdalene,
and the other Mary, sitting over
against the sepulchre.

Setting a Watch

62 Now the next day, that followed
the day of the preparation, the chief
priests and Pharisees came together
unto Pilate,
63 Saying, Sir, we remember that
that deceiver said, while he was
yet alive, After three days I will rise
again.
64 Command therefore that the
sepulchre be made sure until the
third day, lest his disciples come by
night, and steal him away, and say
unto the people, He is risen from
the dead: so the last error shall be
worse than the first.
65 Pilate said unto them, Ye have a
watch: go your way, make *it* as sure
as ye can.
66 So they went, and made the
sepulchre sure, sealing the stone,
and setting a watch.

The Risen Christ

28 In the end of the sabbath, as
it began to dawn toward the
first *day* of the week, came Mary
Magdalene and the other Mary to
see the sepulchre.
2 And, behold, there was a great
earthquake: for the angel of the Lord
descended from heaven, and came
and rolled back the stone from the
door, and sat upon it.
3 His countenance was like lightning,
and his raiment white as snow:
4 And for fear of him the keepers
did shake, and became as dead *men*.
5 And the angel answered and said
unto the women, Fear not ye: for I
know that ye seek Jesus, which was
crucified.
6 He is not here: for he is risen, as
he said. Come, see the place where
the Lord lay.
7 And go quickly, and tell his disciples
that he is risen from the dead;
and, behold, he goeth before you
into Galilee; there shall ye see him:
lo, I have told you.
8 And they departed quickly from
the sepulchre with fear and great
joy; and did run to bring his disciples
word.

9 And as they went to tell his dis-
ciples, behold, Jesus met them, say-
ing, All hail. And they came and held
him by the feet, and worshipped
him.
10 Then said Jesus unto them, Be
not afraid: go tell my brethren that
they go into Galilee, and there shall
they see me.
11 Now when they were going, be-
hold, some of the watch came into
the city, and shewed unto the chief
priests all the things that were done.
12 And when they were assembled
with the elders, and had taken coun-
sel, they gave large money unto the
soldiers,
13 Saying, Say ye, His disciples
came by night, and stole him *away*
while we slept.
14 And if this come to the gover-
nor's ears, we will persuade him,
and secure you.
15 So they took the money, and did
as they were taught: and this saying
is commonly reported among the
Jews until this day.

Jesus' Commission

16 Then the eleven disciples went
away into Galilee, into a mountain
where Jesus had appointed them.
17 And when they saw him, they
worshipped him: but some doubted.
18 And Jesus came and spake unto
them, saying, All power is given unto
me in heaven and in earth.
19 Go ye therefore, and teach all
nations, baptizing them in the name
of the Father, and of the Son, and of
the Holy Ghost:
20 Teaching them to observe all
things whatsoever I have com-
manded you: and, lo, I am with
you alway, *even* unto the end of the
world. Amen.

The Gospel According to

MARK

John's Message of Repentance

The beginning of the gospel of
Jesus Christ, the Son of God;
2 As it is written in the prophets,
Behold, I send my messenger before
thy face, which shall prepare thy
way before thee.
3 The voice of one crying in the
wilderness, Prepare ye the way of
the Lord, make his paths straight.
4 John did baptize in the wilder-
ness, and preach the baptism of re-
pentance for the remission of sins.
5 And there went out unto him all
the land of Judaea, and they of Jeru-
salem, and were all baptized of him
in the river of Jordan, confessing
their sins.
6 And John was clothed with
camel's hair, and with a girdle of a
skin about his loins; and he did eat
locusts and wild honey;
7 And preached, saying, There
cometh one mightier than I after
me, the latchet of whose shoes I
am not worthy to stoop down and
unloose.
8 I indeed have baptized you with
water: but he shall baptize you with
the Holy Ghost.

Jesus' Baptism and Temptations

9 And it came to pass in those
days, that Jesus came from Naza-
reth of Galilee, and was baptized of
John in Jordan.
10 And straightway coming up out
of the water, he saw the heavens
opened, and the Spirit like a dove
descending upon him:
11 And there came a voice from
heaven, *saying,* Thou art my beloved
Son, in whom I am well pleased.
12 And immediately the Spirit
driveth him into the wilderness.
13 And he was there in the wilder-
ness forty days, tempted of Satan;
and was with the wild beasts; and
the angels ministered unto him.

Peter, Andrew, James, and John Called

14 Now after that John was put
in prison, Jesus came into Galilee,
preaching the gospel of the kingdom
of God,
15 And saying, The time is fulfilled,
and the kingdom of God is at hand:
repent ye, and believe the gospel.
16 Now as he walked by the sea of
Galilee, he saw Simon and Andrew
his brother casting a net into the
sea: for they were fishers.
17 And Jesus said unto them,
Come ye after me, and I will make
you to become fishers of men.
18 And straightway they forsook
their nets, and followed him.
19 And when he had gone a little
farther thence, he saw James the *son*
of Zebedee, and John his brother,
who also were in the ship mending
their nets.
20 And straightway he called
them: and they left their father
Zebedee in the ship with the hired
servants, and went after him.

An Unclean Spirit Rebuked

21 And they went into Caper-
naum; and straightway on the

sabbath day he entered into the synagogue, and taught.

22 And they were astonished at his doctrine: for he taught them as one that had authority, and not as the scribes.

23 And there was in their synagogue a man with an unclean spirit; and he cried out,

24 Saying, Let *us* alone; what have we to do with thee, thou Jesus of Nazareth? art thou come to destroy us? I know thee who thou art, the Holy One of God.

25 And Jesus rebuked him, saying, Hold thy peace, and come out of him.

26 And when the unclean spirit had torn him, and cried with a loud voice, he came out of him.

27 And they were all amazed, insomuch that they questioned among themselves, saying, What thing is this? what new doctrine *is* this? for with authority commandeth he even the unclean spirits, and they do obey him.

28 And immediately his fame spread abroad throughout all the region round about Galilee.

Many Diseased and Possessed Are Helped

29 And forthwith, when they were come out of the synagogue, they entered into the house of Simon and Andrew, with James and John.

30 But Simon's wife's mother lay sick of a fever, and anon they tell him of her.

31 And he came and took her by the hand, and lifted her up; and immediately the fever left her, and she ministered unto them.

32 And at even, when the sun did set, they brought unto him all that were diseased, and them that were possessed with devils.

33 And all the city was gathered together at the door.

34 And he healed many that were sick of divers diseases, and cast out many devils; and suffered not the devils to speak, because they knew him.

35 And in the morning, rising up a great while before day, he went out, and departed into a solitary place, and there prayed.

36 And Simon and they that were with him followed after him.

37 And when they had found him, they said unto him, All *men* seek for thee.

38 And he said unto them, Let us go into the next towns, that I may preach there also: for therefore came I forth.

39 And he preached in their synagogues throughout all Galilee, and cast out devils.

A Leper Is Healed

40 And there came a leper to him, beseeching him, and kneeling down to him, and saying unto him, If thou wilt, thou canst make me clean.

41 And Jesus, moved with compassion, put forth *his* hand, and touched him, and saith unto him, I will; be thou clean.

42 And as soon as he had spoken, immediately the leprosy departed from him, and he was cleansed.

43 And he straitly charged him, and forthwith sent him away;

44 And saith unto him, See thou say nothing to any man: but go thy way, shew thyself to the priest, and offer for thy cleansing those things which Moses commanded, for a testimony unto them.

45 But he went out, and began to publish *it* much, and to blaze abroad the matter, insomuch that Jesus could no more openly enter into the city, but was without in desert places: and they came to him from every quarter.

Jesus Heals a Man with Palsy

2 And again he entered into Capernaum after *some* days; and it was noised that he was in the house.

2 And straightway many were
gathered together, insomuch that
there was no room to receive *them,*
no, not so much as about the door:
and he preached the word unto
them.
3 And they come unto him, bring-
ing one sick of the palsy, which was
borne of four.
4 And when they could not come
nigh unto him for the press, they
uncovered the roof where he was:
and when they had broken *it* up,
they let down the bed wherein the
sick of the palsy lay.
5 When Jesus saw their faith, he
said unto the sick of the palsy, Son,
thy sins be forgiven thee.
6 But there were certain of the
scribes sitting there, and reasoning
in their hearts,
7 Why doth this *man* thus speak
blasphemies? who can forgive sins
but God only?
8 And immediately when Jesus
perceived in his spirit that they so
reasoned within themselves, he said
unto them, Why reason ye these
things in your hearts?
9 Whether is it easier to say to the
sick of the palsy, *Thy* sins be forgiven
thee; or to say, Arise, and take up thy
bed, and walk?
10 But that ye may know that the
Son of man hath power on earth to
forgive sins, (he saith to the sick of
the palsy,)
11 I say unto thee, Arise, and take
up thy bed, and go thy way into
thine house.
12 And immediately he arose, took
up the bed, and went forth before
them all; insomuch that they were
all amazed, and glorified God, say-
ing, We never saw it on this fashion.

The Calling of Levi

13 And he went forth again by
the sea side; and all the multitude
resorted unto him, and he taught
them.
14 And as he passed by, he saw
Levi the *son* of Alphaeus sitting at
the receipt of custom, and said unto
him, Follow me. And he arose and
followed him.
15 And it came to pass, that, as
Jesus sat at meat in his house, many
publicans and sinners sat also to-
gether with Jesus and his disciples:
for there were many, and they fol-
lowed him.
16 And when the scribes and Phari-
sees saw him eat with publicans and
sinners, they said unto his disciples,
How is it that he eateth and drinketh
with publicans and sinners?
17 When Jesus heard *it,* he saith
unto them, They that are whole have
no need of the physician, but they
that are sick: I came not to call the
righteous, but sinners to repentance.
18 And the disciples of John and
of the Pharisees used to fast: and
they come and say unto him, Why
do the disciples of John and of the
Pharisees fast, but thy disciples fast
not?
19 And Jesus said unto them, Can
the children of the bridechamber
fast, while the bridegroom is with
them? as long as they have the bride-
groom with them, they cannot fast.
20 But the days will come, when
the bridegroom shall be taken away
from them, and then shall they fast
in those days.
21 No man also seweth a piece of
new cloth on an old garment: else
the new piece that filled it up taketh
away from the old, and the rent is
made worse.
22 And no man putteth new wine
into old bottles: else the new wine
doth burst the bottles, and the wine
is spilled, and the bottles will be
marred: but new wine must be put
into new bottles.

The Sabbath Made for Man

23 And it came to pass, that he
went through the corn fields on

the sabbath day; and his disciples began, as they went, to pluck the ears of corn.

24 And the Pharisees said unto him, Behold, why do they on the sabbath day that which is not lawful?

25 And he said unto them, Have ye never read what David did, when he had need, and was an hungered, he, and they that were with him?

26 How he went into the house of God in the days of Abiathar the high priest, and did eat the shewbread, which is not lawful to eat but for the priests, and gave also to them which were with him?

27 And he said unto them, The sabbath was made for man, and not man for the sabbath:

28 Therefore the Son of man is Lord also of the sabbath.

Jesus Heals a Withered Hand

3 And he entered again into the synagogue; and there was a man there which had a withered hand.

2 And they watched him, whether he would heal him on the sabbath day; that they might accuse him.

3 And he saith unto the man which had the withered hand, Stand forth.

4 And he saith unto them, Is it lawful to do good on the sabbath days, or to do evil? to save life, or to kill? But they held their peace.

5 And when he had looked round about on them with anger, being grieved for the hardness of their hearts, he saith unto the man, Stretch forth thine hand. And he stretched *it* out: and his hand was restored whole as the other.

6 And the Pharisees went forth, and straightway took counsel with the Herodians against him, how they might destroy him.

The Multitude Follow Jesus

7 But Jesus withdrew himself with his disciples to the sea: and a great multitude from Galilee followed him, and from Judaea,

8 And from Jerusalem, and from Idumaea, and *from* beyond Jordan; and they about Tyre and Sidon, a great multitude, when they had heard what great things he did, came unto him.

9 And he spake to his disciples, that a small ship should wait on him because of the multitude, lest they should throng him.

10 For he had healed many; insomuch that they pressed upon him for to touch him, as many as had plagues.

11 And unclean spirits, when they saw him, fell down before him, and cried, saying, Thou art the Son of God.

12 And he straitly charged them that they should not make him known.

Jesus Ordains Twelve Disciples

13 And he goeth up into a mountain, and calleth *unto him* whom he would: and they came unto him.

14 And he ordained twelve, that they should be with him, and that he might send them forth to preach,

15 And to have power to heal sicknesses, and to cast out devils:

16 And Simon he surnamed Peter;

17 And James the *son* of Zebedee, and John the brother of James; and he surnamed them Boanerges, which is, The sons of thunder:

18 And Andrew, and Philip, and Bartholomew, and Matthew, and Thomas, and James the *son* of Alphaeus, and Thaddaeus, and Simon the Canaanite,

19 And Judas Iscariot, which also betrayed him: and they went into an house.

A Divided Kingdom

20 And the multitude cometh together again, so that they could not so much as eat bread.

21 And when his friends heard *of*
it, they went out to lay hold on him:
for they said, He is beside himself.
22 And the scribes which came
down from Jerusalem said, He hath
Beelzebub, and by the prince of the
devils casteth he out devils.
23 And he called them *unto him,*
and said unto them in parables, How
can Satan cast out Satan?
24 And if a kingdom be divided
against itself, that kingdom cannot
stand.
25 And if a house be divided
against itself, that house cannot
stand.
26 And if Satan rise up against
himself, and be divided, he cannot
stand, but hath an end.
27 No man can enter into a strong
man's house, and spoil his goods,
except he will first bind the strong
man; and then he will spoil his
house.
28 Verily I say unto you, All sins
shall be forgiven unto the sons of
men, and blasphemies wherewith
soever they shall blaspheme:
29 But he that shall blaspheme
against the Holy Ghost hath never
forgiveness, but is in danger of eter-
nal damnation:
30 Because they said, He hath an
unclean spirit.

Jesus' Family

31 There came then his brethren
and his mother, and, standing with-
out, sent unto him, calling him.
32 And the multitude sat about
him, and they said unto him, Be-
hold, thy mother and thy brethren
without seek for thee.
33 And he answered them, saying,
Who is my mother, or my brethren?
34 And he looked round about on
them which sat about him, and said,
Behold my mother and my brethren!
35 For whosoever shall do the will
of God, the same is my brother, and
my sister, and mother.

The Sower's Seed

4 And he began again to teach
by the sea side: and there was
gathered unto him a great multi-
tude, so that he entered into a ship,
and sat in the sea; and the whole
multitude was by the sea on the
land.
2 And he taught them many things
by parables, and said unto them in
his doctrine,
3 Hearken; Behold, there went out
a sower to sow:
4 And it came to pass, as he sowed,
some fell by the way side, and the
fowls of the air came and devoured
it up.
5 And some fell on stony ground,
where it had not much earth; and
immediately it sprang up, because
it had no depth of earth:
6 But when the sun was up, it
was scorched; and because it had
no root, it withered away.
7 And some fell among thorns,
and the thorns grew up, and choked
it, and it yielded no fruit.
8 And other fell on good ground,
and did yield fruit that sprang up
and increased; and brought forth,
some thirty, and some sixty, and
some an hundred.
9 And he said unto them, He that
hath ears to hear, let him hear.
10 And when he was alone, they
that were about him with the twelve
asked of him the parable.
11 And he said unto them, Unto
you it is given to know the mystery
of the kingdom of God: but unto
them that are without, all *these*
things are done in parables:
12 That seeing they may see, and
not perceive; and hearing they may
hear, and not understand; lest at any
time they should be converted, and
their sins should be forgiven them.
13 And he said unto them, Know
ye not this parable? and how then
will ye know all parables?
14 The sower soweth the word.

15 And these are they by the way side, where the word is sown; but when they have heard, Satan cometh immediately, and taketh away the word that was sown in their hearts.

16 And these are they likewise which are sown on stony ground; who, when they have heard the word, immediately receive it with gladness;

17 And have no root in themselves, and so endure but for a time: afterward, when affliction or persecution ariseth for the word's sake, immediately they are offended.

18 And these are they which are sown among thorns; such as hear the word,

19 And the cares of this world, and the deceitfulness of riches, and the lusts of other things entering in, choke the word, and it becometh unfruitful.

20 And these are they which are sown on good ground; such as hear the word, and receive *it,* and bring forth fruit, some thirtyfold, some sixty, and some an hundred.

Set Your Candle on a Candlestick

21 And he said unto them, Is a candle brought to be put under a bushel, or under a bed? and not to be set on a candlestick?

22 For there is nothing hid, which shall not be manifested; neither was any thing kept secret, but that it should come abroad.

23 If any man have ears to hear, let him hear.

24 And he said unto them, Take heed what ye hear: with what measure ye mete, it shall be measured to you: and unto you that hear shall more be given.

25 For he that hath, to him shall be given: and he that hath not, from him shall be taken even that which he hath.

The Growing Seed

26 And he said, So is the kingdom of God, as if a man should cast seed into the ground;

27 And should sleep, and rise night and day, and the seed should spring and grow up, he knoweth not how.

28 For the earth bringeth forth fruit of herself; first the blade, then the ear, after that the full corn in the ear.

29 But when the fruit is brought forth, immediately he putteth in the sickle, because the harvest is come.

The Grain of Mustard Seed

30 And he said, Whereunto shall we liken the kingdom of God? or with what comparison shall we compare it?

31 *It is* like a grain of mustard seed, which, when it is sown in the earth, is less than all the seeds that be in the earth:

32 But when it is sown, it groweth up, and becometh greater than all herbs, and shooteth out great branches; so that the fowls of the air may lodge under the shadow of it.

33 And with many such parables spake he the word unto them, as they were able to hear *it.*

34 But without a parable spake he not unto them: and when they were alone, he expounded all things to his disciples.

Jesus Rebukes the Wind

35 And the same day, when the even was come, he saith unto them, Let us pass over unto the other side.

36 And when they had sent away the multitude, they took him even as he was in the ship. And there were also with him other little ships.

37 And there arose a great storm of wind, and the waves beat into the ship, so that it was now full.

38 And he was in the hinder part of the ship, asleep on a pillow: and they awake him, and say unto him,

Master, carest thou not that we perish?
39 And he arose, and rebuked the
wind, and said unto the sea, Peace,
be still. And the wind ceased, and
there was a great calm.
40 And he said unto them, Why
are ye so fearful? how is it that ye
have no faith?
41 And they feared exceedingly,
and said one to another, What
manner of man is this, that even
the wind and the sea obey him?

A Man with an Unclean Spirit

5 And they came over unto the
other side of the sea, into the
country of the Gadarenes.
2 And when he was come out of
the ship, immediately there met
him out of the tombs a man with
an unclean spirit,
3 Who had *his* dwelling among
the tombs; and no man could bind
him, no, not with chains:
4 Because that he had been often
bound with fetters and chains, and
the chains had been plucked asunder by him, and the fetters broken
in pieces: neither could any *man*
tame him.
5 And always, night and day, he
was in the mountains, and in the
tombs, crying, and cutting himself
with stones.
6 But when he saw Jesus afar off,
he ran and worshipped him,
7 And cried with a loud voice, and
said, What have I to do with thee,
Jesus, *thou* Son of the most high
God? I adjure thee by God, that thou
torment me not.
8 For he said unto him, Come out
of the man, *thou* unclean spirit.
9 And he asked him, What *is* thy
name? And he answered, saying, My
name *is* Legion: for we are many.
10 And he besought him much that
he would not send them away out
of the country.
11 Now there was there nigh unto
the mountains a great herd of swine
feeding.
12 And all the devils besought him,
saying, Send us into the swine, that
we may enter into them.
13 And forthwith Jesus gave them
leave. And the unclean spirits went
out, and entered into the swine: and
the herd ran violently down a steep
place into the sea, (they were about
two thousand;) and were choked in
the sea.
14 And they that fed the swine
fled, and told *it* in the city, and in
the country. And they went out to
see what it was that was done.
15 And they come to Jesus, and
see him that was possessed with
the devil, and had the legion, sitting,
and clothed, and in his right mind:
and they were afraid.
16 And they that saw *it* told them
how it befell to him that was possessed with the devil, and *also* concerning the swine.
17 And they began to pray him to
depart out of their coasts.
18 And when he was come into the
ship, he that had been possessed
with the devil prayed him that he
might be with him.
19 Howbeit Jesus suffered him not,
but saith unto him, Go home to thy
friends, and tell them how great
things the Lord hath done for thee,
and hath had compassion on thee.
20 And he departed, and began
to publish in Decapolis how great
things Jesus had done for him: and
all *men* did marvel.

Jairus's Daughter Is Raised to Life

21 And when Jesus was passed
over again by ship unto the other
side, much people gathered unto
him: and he was nigh unto the sea.
22 And, behold, there cometh one
of the rulers of the synagogue, Jairus by name; and when he saw him,
he fell at his feet,

23 And besought him greatly, saying, My little daughter lieth at the point of death: *I pray thee,* come and lay thy hands on her, that she may be healed; and she shall live.

24 And *Jesus* went with him; and much people followed him, and thronged him.

25 And a certain woman, which had an issue of blood twelve years,

26 And had suffered many things of many physicians, and had spent all that she had, and was nothing bettered, but rather grew worse,

27 When she had heard of Jesus, came in the press behind, and touched his garment.

28 For she said, If I may touch but his clothes, I shall be whole.

29 And straightway the fountain of her blood was dried up; and she felt in *her* body that she was healed of that plague.

30 And Jesus, immediately knowing in himself that virtue had gone out of him, turned him about in the press, and said, Who touched my clothes?

31 And his disciples said unto him, Thou seest the multitude thronging thee, and sayest thou, Who touched me?

32 And he looked round about to see her that had done this thing.

33 But the woman fearing and trembling, knowing what was done in her, came and fell down before him, and told him all the truth.

34 And he said unto her, Daughter, thy faith hath made thee whole; go in peace, and be whole of thy plague.

35 While he yet spake, there came from the ruler of the synagogue's *house certain* which said, Thy daughter is dead: why troublest thou the Master any further?

36 As soon as Jesus heard the word that was spoken, he saith unto the ruler of the synagogue, Be not afraid, only believe.

37 And he suffered no man to follow him, save Peter, and James, and John the brother of James.

38 And he cometh to the house of the ruler of the synagogue, and seeth the tumult, and them that wept and wailed greatly.

39 And when he was come in, he saith unto them, Why make ye this ado, and weep? the damsel is not dead, but sleepeth.

40 And they laughed him to scorn. But when he had put them all out, he taketh the father and the mother of the damsel, and them that were with him, and entereth in where the damsel was lying.

41 And he took the damsel by the hand, and said unto her, Talitha cumi; which is, being interpreted, Damsel, I say unto thee, arise.

42 And straightway the damsel arose, and walked; for she was *of the age* of twelve years. And they were astonished with a great astonishment.

43 And he charged them straitly that no man should know it; and commanded that something should be given her to eat.

Jesus Is Rejected in Nazareth

6 And he went out from thence, and came into his own country; and his disciples follow him.

2 And when the sabbath day was come, he began to teach in the synagogue: and many hearing *him* were astonished, saying, From whence hath this *man* these things? and what wisdom *is* this which is given unto him, that even such mighty works are wrought by his hands?

3 Is not this the carpenter, the son of Mary, the brother of James, and Joses, and of Juda, and Simon? and are not his sisters here with us? And they were offended at him.

4 But Jesus said unto them, A prophet is not without honour, but in his own country, and among his

own kin, and in his own house.
5 And he could there do no mighty
work, save that he laid his hands
upon a few sick folk, and healed
them.
6 And he marvelled because of
their unbelief. And he went round
about the villages, teaching.

The Disciples Sent Forth

7 And he called *unto him* the
twelve, and began to send them
forth by two and two; and gave them
power over unclean spirits;
8 And commanded them that they
should take nothing for *their* jour-
ney, save a staff only; no scrip, no
bread, no money in *their* purse:
9 But *be* shod with sandals; and
not put on two coats.
10 And he said unto them, In what
place soever ye enter into an house,
there abide till ye depart from that
place.
11 And whosoever shall not receive
you, nor hear you, when ye depart
thence, shake off the dust under
your feet for a testimony against
them. Verily I say unto you, It shall
be more tolerable for Sodom and
Gomorrha in the day of judgment,
than for that city.
12 And they went out, and
preached that men should repent.
13 And they cast out many devils,
and anointed with oil many that
were sick, and healed *them.*

Herod's Fear of John the Baptist

14 And king Herod heard *of him;*
(for his name was spread abroad:)
and he said, That John the Baptist
was risen from the dead, and there-
fore mighty works do shew forth
themselves in him.
15 Others said, That it is Elias. And
others said, That it is a prophet, or
as one of the prophets.
16 But when Herod heard *thereof,*
he said, It is John, whom I be-
headed: he is risen from the dead.
17 For Herod himself had sent
forth and laid hold upon John, and
bound him in prison for Herodias'
sake, his brother Philip's wife: for
he had married her.
18 For John had said unto Herod,
It is not lawful for thee to have thy
brother's wife.
19 Therefore Herodias had a quar-
rel against him, and would have
killed him; but she could not:
20 For Herod feared John, know-
ing that he was a just man and an
holy, and observed him; and when
he heard him, he did many things,
and heard him gladly.
21 And when a convenient day
was come, that Herod on his birth-
day made a supper to his lords,
high captains, and chief *estates* of
Galilee;
22 And when the daughter of the
said Herodias came in, and danced,
and pleased Herod and them that
sat with him, the king said unto the
damsel, Ask of me whatsoever thou
wilt, and I will give *it* thee.
23 And he sware unto her, What-
soever thou shalt ask of me, I will
give *it* thee, unto the half of my
kingdom.
24 And she went forth, and said
unto her mother, What shall I ask?
And she said, The head of John the
Baptist.
25 And she came in straightway
with haste unto the king, and asked,
saying, I will that thou give me by
and by in a charger the head of John
the Baptist.
26 And the king was exceeding
sorry; *yet* for his oath's sake, and
for their sakes which sat with him,
he would not reject her.
27 And immediately the king sent
an executioner, and commanded his
head to be brought: and he went and
beheaded him in the prison,
28 And brought his head in a charg-
er, and gave it to the damsel: and

the damsel gave it to her mother.

29 And when his disciples heard *of it,* they came and took up his corpse, and laid it in a tomb.

Feeding the Five Thousand

30 And the apostles gathered themselves together unto Jesus, and told him all things, both what they had done, and what they had taught.

31 And he said unto them, Come ye yourselves apart into a desert place, and rest a while: for there were many coming and going, and they had no leisure so much as to eat.

32 And they departed into a desert place by ship privately.

33 And the people saw them departing, and many knew him, and ran afoot thither out of all cities, and outwent them, and came together unto him.

34 And Jesus, when he came out, saw much people, and was moved with compassion toward them, because they were as sheep not having a shepherd: and he began to teach them many things.

35 And when the day was now far spent, his disciples came unto him, and said, This is a desert place, and now the time *is* far passed:

36 Send them away, that they may go into the country round about, and into the villages, and buy themselves bread: for they have nothing to eat.

37 He answered and said unto them, Give ye them to eat. And they say unto him, Shall we go and buy two hundred pennyworth of bread, and give them to eat?

38 He saith unto them, How many loaves have ye? go and see. And when they knew, they say, Five, and two fishes.

39 And he commanded them to make all sit down by companies upon the green grass.

40 And they sat down in ranks, by hundreds, and by fifties.

41 And when he had taken the five loaves and the two fishes, he looked up to heaven, and blessed, and brake the loaves, and gave *them* to his disciples to set before them; and the two fishes divided he among them all.

42 And they did all eat, and were filled.

43 And they took up twelve baskets full of the fragments, and of the fishes.

44 And they that did eat of the loaves were about five thousand men.

Jesus Walks on the Sea

45 And straightway he constrained his disciples to get into the ship, and to go to the other side before unto Bethsaida, while he sent away the people.

46 And when he had sent them away, he departed into a mountain to pray.

47 And when even was come, the ship was in the midst of the sea, and he alone on the land.

48 And he saw them toiling in rowing; for the wind was contrary unto them: and about the fourth watch of the night he cometh unto them, walking upon the sea, and would have passed by them.

49 But when they saw him walking upon the sea, they supposed it had been a spirit, and cried out:

50 For they all saw him, and were troubled. And immediately he talked with them, and saith unto them, Be of good cheer: it is I; be not afraid.

51 And he went up unto them into the ship; and the wind ceased: and they were sore amazed in themselves beyond measure, and wondered.

52 For they considered not *the miracle* of the loaves: for their heart was hardened.

Those Who Touch Jesus
Are Made Well

53 And when they had passed
over, they came into the land of
Gennesaret, and drew to the shore.
54 And when they were come out
of the ship, straightway they knew
him,
55 And ran through that whole
region round about, and began to
carry about in beds those that were
sick, where they heard he was.
56 And whithersoever he entered,
into villages, or cities, or country,
they laid the sick in the streets, and
besought him that they might touch
if it were but the border of his gar-
ment: and as many as touched him
were made whole.

The Pharisees Rebuked

7 Then came together unto him
the Pharisees, and certain of
the scribes, which came from Je-
rusalem.
2 And when they saw some of his
disciples eat bread with defiled, that
is to say, with unwashen, hands,
they found fault.
3 For the Pharisees, and all the
Jews, except they wash *their* hands
oft, eat not, holding the tradition of
the elders.
4 And *when they come* from the
market, except they wash, they eat
not. And many other things there be,
which they have received to hold,
as the washing of cups, and pots,
brasen vessels, and of tables.
5 Then the Pharisees and scribes
asked him, Why walk not thy disci-
ples according to the tradition of the
elders, but eat bread with unwashen
hands?
6 He answered and said unto
them, Well hath Esaias prophesied
of you hypocrites, as it is written,
This people honoureth me with
their lips, but their heart is far
from me.
7 Howbeit in vain do they wor-
ship me, teaching *for* doctrines the
commandments of men.
8 For laying aside the command-
ment of God, ye hold the tradition
of men, *as* the washing of pots and
cups: and many other such like
things ye do.
9 And he said unto them, Full well
ye reject the commandment of God,
that ye may keep your own tradition.
10 For Moses said, Honour thy fa-
ther and thy mother; and, Whoso
curseth father or mother, let him
die the death:
11 But ye say, If a man shall say to
his father or mother, *It is* Corban,
that is to say, a gift, by whatsoever
thou mightest be profited by me;
he shall be free.
12 And ye suffer him no more to do
ought for his father or his mother;
13 Making the word of God of none
effect through your tradition, which
ye have delivered: and many such
like things do ye.

Things from Within Defile

14 And when he had called all the
people *unto him,* he said unto them,
Hearken unto me every one *of you,*
and understand:
15 There is nothing from without a
man, that entering into him can de-
file him: but the things which come
out of him, those are they that defile
the man.
16 If any man have ears to hear, let
him hear.
17 And when he was entered into
the house from the people, his dis-
ciples asked him concerning the
parable.
18 And he saith unto them, Are ye
so without understanding also? Do
ye not perceive, that whatsoever
thing from without entereth into
the man, *it* cannot defile him;
19 Because it entereth not into his
heart, but into the belly, and goeth
out into the draught, purging all
meats?

20 And he said, That which com-
eth out of the man, that defileth the
man.
21 For from within, out of the
heart of men, proceed evil thoughts,
adulteries, fornications, murders,
22 Thefts, covetousness, wicked-
ness, deceit, lasciviousness, an evil
eye, blasphemy, pride, foolishness:
23 All these evil things come from
within, and defile the man.

A Girl Delivered and a Deaf Man Healed

24 And from thence he arose, and
went into the borders of Tyre and
Sidon, and entered into an house,
and would have no man know *it:*
but he could not be hid.
25 For a *certain* woman, whose
young daughter had an unclean
spirit, heard of him, and came and
fell at his feet:
26 The woman was a Greek, a
Syrophenician by nation; and she
besought him that he would cast
forth the devil out of her daughter.
27 But Jesus said unto her, Let the
children first be filled: for it is not
meet to take the children's bread,
and to cast *it* unto the dogs.
28 And she answered and said
unto him, Yes, Lord: yet the dogs
under the table eat of the children's
crumbs.
29 And he said unto her, For this
saying go thy way; the devil is gone
out of thy daughter.
30 And when she was come to her
house, she found the devil gone out,
and her daughter laid upon the bed.
31 And again, departing from the
coasts of Tyre and Sidon, he came
unto the sea of Galilee, through the
midst of the coasts of Decapolis.
32 And they bring unto him one
that was deaf, and had an imped-
iment in his speech; and they be-
seech him to put his hand upon him.
33 And he took him aside from the
multitude, and put his fingers into
his ears, and he spit, and touched
his tongue;
34 And looking up to heaven, he
sighed, and saith unto him, Eph-
phatha, that is, Be opened.
35 And straightway his ears were
opened, and the string of his tongue
was loosed, and he spake plain.
36 And he charged them that they
should tell no man: but the more he
charged them, so much the more a
great deal they published *it;*
37 And were beyond measure as-
tonished, saying, He hath done all
things well: he maketh both the deaf
to hear, and the dumb to speak.

Feeding the Multitude

8 In those days the multitude be-
ing very great, and having noth-
ing to eat, Jesus called his disciples
unto him, and saith unto them,
2 I have compassion on the mul-
titude, because they have now been
with me three days, and have noth-
ing to eat:
3 And if I send them away fasting
to their own houses, they will faint
by the way: for divers of them came
from far.
4 And his disciples answered him,
From whence can a man satisfy
these *men* with bread here in the
wilderness?
5 And he asked them, How many
loaves have ye? And they said, Seven.
6 And he commanded the peo-
ple to sit down on the ground: and
he took the seven loaves, and gave
thanks, and brake, and gave to his
disciples to set before *them;* and
they did set *them* before the people.
7 And they had a few small fishes:
and he blessed, and commanded to
set them also before *them.*
8 So they did eat, and were filled:
and they took up of the broken *meat*
that was left seven baskets.
9 And they that had eaten were
about four thousand: and he sent
them away.

10 And straightway he entered into a ship with his disciples, and came into the parts of Dalmanutha.

11 And the Pharisees came forth, and began to question with him, seeking of him a sign from heaven, tempting him.

12 And he sighed deeply in his spirit, and saith, Why doth this generation seek after a sign? verily I say unto you, There shall no sign be given unto this generation.

13 And he left them, and entering into the ship again departed to the other side.

The Leaven of the Pharisees

14 Now *the disciples* had forgotten to take bread, neither had they in the ship with them more than one loaf.

15 And he charged them, saying, Take heed, beware of the leaven of the Pharisees, and *of* the leaven of Herod.

16 And they reasoned among themselves, saying, *It is* because we have no bread.

17 And when Jesus knew *it,* he saith unto them, Why reason ye, because ye have no bread? perceive ye not yet, neither understand? have ye your heart yet hardened?

18 Having eyes, see ye not? and having ears, hear ye not? and do ye not remember?

19 When I brake the five loaves among five thousand, how many baskets full of fragments took ye up? They say unto him, Twelve.

20 And when the seven among four thousand, how many baskets full of fragments took ye up? And they said, Seven.

21 And he said unto them, How is it that ye do not understand?

Jesus Heals a Blind Man at Bethsaida

22 And he cometh to Bethsaida; and they bring a blind man unto him, and besought him to touch him.

23 And he took the blind man by the hand, and led him out of the town; and when he had spit on his eyes, and put his hands upon him, he asked him if he saw ought.

24 And he looked up, and said, I see men as trees, walking.

25 After that he put *his* hands again upon his eyes, and made him look up: and he was restored, and saw every man clearly.

26 And he sent him away to his house, saying, Neither go into the town, nor tell *it* to any in the town.

27 And Jesus went out, and his disciples, into the towns of Caesarea Philippi: and by the way he asked his disciples, saying unto them, Whom do men say that I am?

28 And they answered, John the Baptist: but some *say,* Elias; and others, One of the prophets.

29 And he saith unto them, But whom say ye that I am? And Peter answereth and saith unto him, Thou art the Christ.

30 And he charged them that they should tell no man of him.

Jesus' Coming Death

31 And he began to teach them, that the Son of man must suffer many things, and be rejected of the elders, and *of* the chief priests, and scribes, and be killed, and after three days rise again.

32 And he spake that saying openly. And Peter took him, and began to rebuke him.

33 But when he had turned about and looked on his disciples, he rebuked Peter, saying, Get thee behind me, Satan: for thou savourest not the things that be of God, but the things that be of men.

Follow Me

34 And when he had called the people *unto him* with his disciples

also, he said unto them, Whosoever
will come after me, let him deny
himself, and take up his cross, and
follow me.
35 For whosoever will save his life
shall lose it; but whosoever shall
lose his life for my sake and the gos-
pel's, the same shall save it.
36 For what shall it profit a man,
if he shall gain the whole world, and
lose his own soul?
37 Or what shall a man give in ex-
change for his soul?
38 Whosoever therefore shall be
ashamed of me and of my words in
this adulterous and sinful gener-
ation; of him also shall the Son of
man be ashamed, when he cometh
in the glory of his Father with the
holy angels.

Jesus' Transfiguration

9 And he said unto them, Verily
I say unto you, That there be
some of them that stand here, which
shall not taste of death, till they have
seen the kingdom of God come with
power.
2 And after six days Jesus taketh
with him Peter, and James, and
John, and leadeth them up into an
high mountain apart by themselves:
and he was transfigured before
them.
3 And his raiment became shining,
exceeding white as snow; so as no
fuller on earth can white them.
4 And there appeared unto them
Elias with Moses: and they were
talking with Jesus.
5 And Peter answered and said
to Jesus, Master, it is good for us
to be here: and let us make three
tabernacles; one for thee, and one
for Moses, and one for Elias.
6 For he wist not what to say; for
they were sore afraid.
7 And there was a cloud that over-
shadowed them: and a voice came
out of the cloud, saying, This is my
beloved Son: hear him.
8 And suddenly, when they had
looked round about, they saw no
man any more, save Jesus only with
themselves.
9 And as they came down from
the mountain, he charged them that
they should tell no man what things
they had seen, till the Son of man
were risen from the dead.
10 And they kept that saying with
themselves, questioning one with
another what the rising from the
dead should mean.
11 And they asked him, saying,
Why say the scribes that Elias must
first come?
12 And he answered and told
them, Elias verily cometh first, and
restoreth all things; and how it is
written of the Son of man, that he
must suffer many things, and be set
at nought.
13 But I say unto you, That Elias
is indeed come, and they have done
unto him whatsoever they listed, as
it is written of him.

A Dumb and Deaf Spirit Cast Out

14 And when he came to *his* disci-
ples, he saw a great multitude about
them, and the scribes questioning
with them.
15 And straightway all the people,
when they beheld him, were greatly
amazed, and running to *him* saluted
him.
16 And he asked the scribes, What
question ye with them?
17 And one of the multitude an-
swered and said, Master, I have
brought unto thee my son, which
hath a dumb spirit;
18 And wheresoever he taketh him,
he teareth him: and he foameth, and
gnasheth with his teeth, and pineth
away: and I spake to thy disciples
that they should cast him out; and
they could not.
19 He answereth him, and saith,
O faithless generation, how long

shall I be with you? how long shall I suffer you? bring him unto me.

20 And they brought him unto him: and when he saw him, straightway the spirit tare him; and he fell on the ground, and wallowed foaming.

21 And he asked his father, How long is it ago since this came unto him? And he said, Of a child.

22 And ofttimes it hath cast him into the fire, and into the waters, to destroy him: but if thou canst do any thing, have compassion on us, and help us.

23 Jesus said unto him, If thou canst believe, all things *are* possible to him that believeth.

24 And straightway the father of the child cried out, and said with tears, Lord, I believe; help thou mine unbelief.

25 When Jesus saw that the people came running together, he rebuked the foul spirit, saying unto him, *Thou* dumb and deaf spirit, I charge thee, come out of him, and enter no more into him.

26 And *the spirit* cried, and rent him sore, and came out of him: and he was as one dead; insomuch that many said, He is dead.

27 But Jesus took him by the hand, and lifted him up; and he arose.

28 And when he was come into the house, his disciples asked him privately, Why could not we cast him out?

29 And he said unto them, This kind can come forth by nothing, but by prayer and fasting.

30 And they departed thence, and passed through Galilee; and he would not that any man should know *it*.

31 For he taught his disciples, and said unto them, The Son of man is delivered into the hands of men, and they shall kill him; and after that he is killed, he shall rise the third day.

32 But they understood not that saying, and were afraid to ask him.

The Disciples' Dispute

33 And he came to Capernaum: and being in the house he asked them, What was it that ye disputed among yourselves by the way?

34 But they held their peace: for by the way they had disputed among themselves, who *should be* the greatest.

35 And he sat down, and called the twelve, and saith unto them, If any man desire to be first, *the same* shall be last of all, and servant of all.

36 And he took a child, and set him in the midst of them: and when he had taken him in his arms, he said unto them,

37 Whosoever shall receive one of such children in my name, receiveth me: and whosoever shall receive me, receiveth not me, but him that sent me.

Miracles in Jesus' Name

38 And John answered him, saying, Master, we saw one casting out devils in thy name, and he followeth not us: and we forbad him, because he followeth not us.

39 But Jesus said, Forbid him not: for there is no man which shall do a miracle in my name, that can lightly speak evil of me.

40 For he that is not against us is on our part.

41 For whosoever shall give you a cup of water to drink in my name, because ye belong to Christ, verily I say unto you, he shall not lose his reward.

Offend Not the Little Ones

42 And whosoever shall offend one of *these* little ones that believe in me, it is better for him that a millstone were hanged about his neck, and he were cast into the sea.

43 And if thy hand offend thee, cut it off: it is better for thee to enter into life maimed, than having two hands to go into hell, into the

fire that never shall be quenched:
44 Where their worm dieth not,
and the fire is not quenched.
45 And if thy foot offend thee, cut
it off: it is better for thee to enter
halt into life, than having two feet
to be cast into hell, into the fire that
never shall be quenched:
46 Where their worm dieth not,
and the fire is not quenched.
47 And if thine eye offend thee,
pluck it out: it is better for thee to
enter into the kingdom of God with
one eye, than having two eyes to be
cast into hell fire:
48 Where their worm dieth not,
and the fire is not quenched.

Have Salt in Yourselves

49 For every one shall be salted
with fire, and every sacrifice shall
be salted with salt.
50 Salt *is* good: but if the salt have
lost his saltness, wherewith will ye
season it? Have salt in yourselves,
and have peace one with another.

Marriage and Divorce

10 And he arose from thence,
and cometh into the coasts
of Judaea by the farther side of Jordan: and the people resort unto
him again; and, as he was wont, he
taught them again.
2 And the Pharisees came to him,
and asked him, Is it lawful for a
man to put away *his* wife? tempting
him.
3 And he answered and said unto
them, What did Moses command
you?
4 And they said, Moses suffered
to write a bill of divorcement, and
to put *her* away.
5 And Jesus answered and said
unto them, For the hardness of your
heart he wrote you this precept.
6 But from the beginning of the
creation God made them male and
female.
7 For this cause shall a man leave
his father and mother, and cleave to
his wife;
8 And they twain shall be one
flesh: so then they are no more
twain, but one flesh.
9 What therefore God hath joined
together, let not man put asunder.
10 And in the house his disciples
asked him again of the same *matter*.
11 And he saith unto them, Whosoever shall put away his wife, and
marry another, committeth adultery
against her.
12 And if a woman shall put away
her husband, and be married to another, she committeth adultery.

Jesus Blesses the Children

13 And they brought young children to him, that he should touch
them: and *his* disciples rebuked
those that brought *them*.
14 But when Jesus saw *it*, he was
much displeased, and said unto
them, Suffer the little children to
come unto me, and forbid them
not: for of such is the kingdom
of God.
15 Verily I say unto you, Whosoever shall not receive the kingdom
of God as a little child, he shall not
enter therein.
16 And he took them up in his
arms, put *his* hands upon them,
and blessed them.

The Rich Young Man

17 And when he was gone forth
into the way, there came one running, and kneeled to him, and asked
him, Good Master, what shall I do
that I may inherit eternal life?
18 And Jesus said unto him, Why
callest thou me good? *there is* none
good but one, *that is*, God.
19 Thou knowest the commandments, Do not commit adultery, Do
not kill, Do not steal, Do not bear
false witness, Defraud not, Honour
thy father and mother.
20 And he answered and said

unto him, Master, all these have I observed from my youth.
21 Then Jesus beholding him
loved him, and said unto him, One thing thou lackest: go thy way, sell whatsoever thou hast, and give to the poor, and thou shalt have treasure in heaven: and come, take up the cross, and follow me.
22 And he was sad at that saying,
and went away grieved: for he had great possessions.

All Things Are Possible with God

23 And Jesus looked round about,
and saith unto his disciples, How hardly shall they that have riches enter into the kingdom of God!
24 And the disciples were aston-
ished at his words. But Jesus answereth again, and saith unto them, Children, how hard is it for them that trust in riches to enter into the kingdom of God!
25 It is easier for a camel to go
through the eye of a needle, than for a rich man to enter into the kingdom of God.
26 And they were astonished out
of measure, saying among themselves, Who then can be saved?
27 And Jesus looking upon them
saith, With men *it is* impossible, but not with God: for with God all things are possible.
28 Then Peter began to say unto
him, Lo, we have left all, and have followed thee.
29 And Jesus answered and said,
Verily I say unto you, There is no man that hath left house, or brethren, or sisters, or father, or mother, or wife, or children, or lands, for my sake, and the gospel's,
30 But he shall receive an
hundredfold now in this time, houses, and brethren, and sisters, and mothers, and children, and lands, with persecutions; and in the world to come eternal life.
31 But many *that are* first shall be
last; and the last first.

The Disciples Prepared for Jesus' Death

32 And they were in the way
going up to Jerusalem; and Jesus went before them: and they were amazed; and as they followed, they were afraid. And he took again the twelve, and began to tell them what things should happen unto him,
33 *Saying,* Behold, we go up to
Jerusalem; and the Son of man shall be delivered unto the chief priests, and unto the scribes; and they shall condemn him to death, and shall deliver him to the Gentiles:
34 And they shall mock him, and
shall scourge him, and shall spit upon him, and shall kill him: and the third day he shall rise again.

James and John's Request

35 And James and John, the sons
of Zebedee, come unto him, saying, Master, we would that thou shouldest do for us whatsoever we shall desire.
36 And he said unto them, What
would ye that I should do for you?
37 They said unto him, Grant unto
us that we may sit, one on thy right hand, and the other on thy left hand, in thy glory.
38 But Jesus said unto them, Ye
know not what ye ask: can ye drink of the cup that I drink of? and be baptized with the baptism that I am baptized with?
39 And they said unto him, We
can. And Jesus said unto them, Ye shall indeed drink of the cup that I drink of; and with the baptism that I am baptized withal shall ye be baptized:
40 But to sit on my right hand
and on my left hand is not mine to give; but *it shall be given to them* for whom it is prepared.

41 And when the ten heard *it,* they began to be much displeased with James and John.

42 But Jesus called them *to him,* and saith unto them, Ye know that they which are accounted to rule over the Gentiles exercise lordship over them; and their great ones exercise authority upon them.

43 But so shall it not be among you: but whosoever will be great among you, shall be your minister:

44 And whosoever of you will be the chiefest, shall be servant of all.

45 For even the Son of man came not to be ministered unto, but to minister, and to give his life a ransom for many.

Jesus Heals Bartimaeus

46 And they came to Jericho: and as he went out of Jericho with his disciples and a great number of people, blind Bartimaeus, the son of Timaeus, sat by the highway side begging.

47 And when he heard that it was Jesus of Nazareth, he began to cry out, and say, Jesus, *thou* son of David, have mercy on me.

48 And many charged him that he should hold his peace: but he cried the more a great deal, *Thou* son of David, have mercy on me.

49 And Jesus stood still, and commanded him to be called. And they call the blind man, saying unto him, Be of good comfort, rise; he calleth thee.

50 And he, casting away his garment, rose, and came to Jesus.

51 And Jesus answered and said unto him, What wilt thou that I should do unto thee? The blind man said unto him, Lord, that I might receive my sight.

52 And Jesus said unto him, Go thy way; thy faith hath made thee whole. And immediately he received his sight, and followed Jesus in the way.

Jesus Enters Jerusalem

11 And when they came nigh to Jerusalem, unto Bethphage and Bethany, at the mount of Olives, he sendeth forth two of his disciples,

2 And saith unto them, Go your way into the village over against you: and as soon as ye be entered into it, ye shall find a colt tied, whereon never man sat; loose him, and bring *him.*

3 And if any man say unto you, Why do ye this? say ye that the Lord hath need of him; and straightway he will send him hither.

4 And they went their way, and found the colt tied by the door without in a place where two ways met; and they loose him.

5 And certain of them that stood there said unto them, What do ye, loosing the colt?

6 And they said unto them even as Jesus had commanded: and they let them go.

7 And they brought the colt to Jesus, and cast their garments on him; and he sat upon him.

8 And many spread their garments in the way: and others cut down branches off the trees, and strawed *them* in the way.

9 And they that went before, and they that followed, cried, saying, Hosanna; Blessed *is* he that cometh in the name of the Lord:

10 Blessed *be* the kingdom of our father David, that cometh in the name of the Lord: Hosanna in the highest.

A Fig Tree Rebuked

11 And Jesus entered into Jerusalem, and into the temple: and when he had looked round about upon all things, and now the eventide was come, he went out unto Bethany with the twelve.

12 And on the morrow, when they were come from Bethany, he was hungry:

13 And seeing a fig tree afar off having leaves, he came, if haply he might find any thing thereon: and when he came to it, he found nothing but leaves; for the time of figs was not *yet.*

14 And Jesus answered and said unto it, No man eat fruit of thee hereafter for ever. And his disciples heard *it.*

Moneychangers Evicted

15 And they come to Jerusalem: and Jesus went into the temple, and began to cast out them that sold and bought in the temple, and overthrew the tables of the moneychangers, and the seats of them that sold doves;

16 And would not suffer that any man should carry *any* vessel through the temple.

17 And he taught, saying unto them, Is it not written, My house shall be called of all nations the house of prayer? but ye have made it a den of thieves.

18 And the scribes and chief priests heard *it,* and sought how they might destroy him: for they feared him, because all the people was astonished at his doctrine.

19 And when even was come, he went out of the city.

The Lesson of the Fig Tree

20 And in the morning, as they passed by, they saw the fig tree dried up from the roots.

21 And Peter calling to remembrance saith unto him, Master, behold, the fig tree which thou cursedst is withered away.

22 And Jesus answering saith unto them, Have faith in God.

23 For verily I say unto you, That whosoever shall say unto this mountain, Be thou removed, and be thou cast into the sea; and shall not doubt in his heart, but shall believe that those things which he saith shall come to pass; he shall have whatsoever he saith.

24 Therefore I say unto you, What things soever ye desire, when ye pray, believe that ye receive *them,* and ye shall have *them.*

25 And when ye stand praying, forgive, if ye have ought against any: that your Father also which is in heaven may forgive you your trespasses.

26 But if ye do not forgive, neither will your Father which is in heaven forgive your trespasses.

Jesus' Authority Questioned

27 And they come again to Jerusalem: and as he was walking in the temple, there come to him the chief priests, and the scribes, and the elders,

28 And say unto him, By what authority doest thou these things? and who gave thee this authority to do these things?

29 And Jesus answered and said unto them, I will also ask of you one question, and answer me, and I will tell you by what authority I do these things.

30 The baptism of John, was *it* from heaven, or of men? answer me.

31 And they reasoned with themselves, saying, If we shall say, From heaven; he will say, Why then did ye not believe him?

32 But if we shall say, Of men; they feared the people: for all *men* counted John, that he was a prophet indeed.

33 And they answered and said unto Jesus, We cannot tell. And Jesus answering saith unto them, Neither do I tell you by what authority I do these things.

The Parable of the Vineyard

12 And he began to speak unto them by parables. A *certain* man planted a vineyard, and set an hedge about *it,* and digged *a place*

for the winefat, and built a tower,
and let it out to husbandmen, and
went into a far country.
2 And at the season he sent to
the husbandmen a servant, that he
might receive from the husband-
men of the fruit of the vineyard.
3 And they caught *him,* and beat
him, and sent *him* away empty.
4 And again he sent unto them
another servant; and at him they
cast stones, and wounded *him* in the
head, and sent *him* away shamefully
handled.
5 And again he sent another; and
him they killed, and many others;
beating some, and killing some.
6 Having yet therefore one son,
his wellbeloved, he sent him also
last unto them, saying, They will
reverence my son.
7 But those husbandmen said
among themselves, This is the heir;
come, let us kill him, and the inher-
itance shall be ours.
8 And they took him, and killed
him, and cast *him* out of the vine-
yard.
9 What shall therefore the lord of
the vineyard do? he will come and
destroy the husbandmen, and will
give the vineyard unto others.
10 And have ye not read this scrip-
ture; The stone which the builders
rejected is become the head of the
corner:
11 This was the Lord's doing, and
it is marvellous in our eyes?
12 And they sought to lay hold on
him, but feared the people: for they
knew that he had spoken the parable
against them: and they left him, and
went their way.

Paying Tribute

13 And they send unto him certain
of the Pharisees and of the Herodi-
ans, to catch him in *his* words.
14 And when they were come, they
say unto him, Master, we know that
thou art true, and carest for no man:
for thou regardest not the person of
men, but teachest the way of God in
truth: Is it lawful to give tribute to
Caesar, or not?
15 Shall we give, or shall we not
give? But he, knowing their hypoc-
risy, said unto them, Why tempt ye
me? bring me a penny, that I may
see *it.*
16 And they brought *it.* And he
saith unto them, Whose *is* this im-
age and superscription? And they
said unto him, Caesar's.
17 And Jesus answering said unto
them, Render to Caesar the things
that are Caesar's, and to God the
things that are God's. And they mar-
velled at him.

Resurrection Questions

18 Then come unto him the Sad-
ducees, which say there is no resur-
rection; and they asked him, saying,
19 Master, Moses wrote unto us,
If a man's brother die, and leave *his*
wife *behind him,* and leave no chil-
dren, that his brother should take
his wife, and raise up seed unto his
brother.
20 Now there were seven breth-
ren: and the first took a wife, and
dying left no seed.
21 And the second took her, and
died, neither left he any seed: and
the third likewise.
22 And the seven had her, and left
no seed: last of all the woman died
also.
23 In the resurrection therefore,
when they shall rise, whose wife
shall she be of them? for the seven
had her to wife.
24 And Jesus answering said unto
them, Do ye not therefore err, be-
cause ye know not the scriptures,
neither the power of God?
25 For when they shall rise from
the dead, they neither marry, nor
are given in marriage; but are as the
angels which are in heaven.
26 And as touching the dead, that

they rise: have ye not read in the
book of Moses, how in the bush
God spake unto him, saying, I *am*
the God of Abraham, and the God
of Isaac, and the God of Jacob?
27 He is not the God of the dead,
but the God of the living: ye there-
fore do greatly err.

The Scribes and the Commandments

28 And one of the scribes came,
and having heard them reasoning
together, and perceiving that he had
answered them well, asked him,
Which is the first commandment
of all?
29 And Jesus answered him, The
first of all the commandments *is,*
Hear, O Israel; The Lord our God is
one Lord:
30 And thou shalt love the Lord
thy God with all thy heart, and with
all thy soul, and with all thy mind,
and with all thy strength: this *is* the
first commandment.
31 And the second *is* like, *namely*
this, Thou shalt love thy neighbour
as thyself. There is none other com-
mandment greater than these.
32 And the scribe said unto him,
Well, Master, thou hast said the
truth: for there is one God; and there
is none other but he:
33 And to love him with all the
heart, and with all the understand-
ing, and with all the soul, and with
all the strength, and to love *his*
neighbour as himself, is more than
all whole burnt offerings and sacri-
fices.
34 And when Jesus saw that he
answered discreetly, he said unto
him, Thou art not far from the king-
dom of God. And no man after that
durst ask him *any question.*
35 And Jesus answered and said,
while he taught in the temple, How
say the scribes that Christ is the son
of David?
36 For David himself said by the
Holy Ghost, The LORD said to my
Lord, Sit thou on my right hand, till
I make thine enemies thy footstool.
37 David therefore himself calleth
him Lord; and whence is he *then* his
son? And the common people heard
him gladly.
38 And he said unto them in his
doctrine, Beware of the scribes,
which love to go in long clothing,
and *love* salutations in the market-
places,
39 And the chief seats in the syn-
agogues, and the uppermost rooms
at feasts:
40 Which devour widows' houses,
and for a pretence make long
prayers: these shall receive greater
damnation.

The Widow's Offering of Two Mites

41 And Jesus sat over against the
treasury, and beheld how the peo-
ple cast money into the treasury:
and many that were rich cast in
much.
42 And there came a certain poor
widow, and she threw in two mites,
which make a farthing.
43 And he called *unto him* his dis-
ciples, and saith unto them, Verily I
say unto you, That this poor widow
hath cast more in, than all they
which have cast into the treasury:
44 For all *they* did cast in of their
abundance; but she of her want did
cast in all that she had, *even* all her
living.

Signs of the End Times

13 And as he went out of the
temple, one of his disciples
saith unto him, Master, see what
manner of stones and what build-
ings *are here!*
2 And Jesus answering said unto
him, Seest thou these great build-
ings? there shall not be left one
stone upon another, that shall not
be thrown down.

3 And as he sat upon the mount
of Olives over against the temple,
Peter and James and John and An-
drew asked him privately,
4 Tell us, when shall these things
be? and what *shall be* the sign when
all these things shall be fulfilled?

Wars and Rumours of Wars

5 And Jesus answering them be-
gan to say, Take heed lest any *man*
deceive you:
6 For many shall come in my
name, saying, I am *Christ;* and shall
deceive many.
7 And when ye shall hear of wars
and rumours of wars, be ye not trou-
bled: for *such things* must needs be;
but the end *shall* not *be* yet.
8 For nation shall rise against na-
tion, and kingdom against kingdom:
and there shall be earthquakes in
divers places, and there shall be
famines and troubles: these *are* the
beginnings of sorrows.
9 But take heed to yourselves: for
they shall deliver you up to coun-
cils; and in the synagogues ye shall
be beaten: and ye shall be brought
before rulers and kings for my sake,
for a testimony against them.
10 And the gospel must first be
published among all nations.
11 But when they shall lead *you,*
and deliver you up, take no thought
beforehand what ye shall speak, nei-
ther do ye premeditate: but whatso-
ever shall be given you in that hour,
that speak ye: for it is not ye that
speak, but the Holy Ghost.

Brother Shall Betray Brother

12 Now the brother shall betray
the brother to death, and the fa-
ther the son; and children shall rise
up against *their* parents, and shall
cause them to be put to death.
13 And ye shall be hated of all *men*
for my name's sake: but he that shall
endure unto the end, the same shall
be saved.

Days of Affliction

14 But when ye shall see the abom-
ination of desolation, spoken of by
Daniel the prophet, standing where
it ought not, (let him that readeth
understand,) then let them that be
in Judaea flee to the mountains:
15 And let him that is on the
housetop not go down into the
house, neither enter *therein,* to take
any thing out of his house:
16 And let him that is in the field
not turn back again for to take up
his garment.
17 But woe to them that are with
child, and to them that give suck in
those days!
18 And pray ye that your flight be
not in the winter.
19 For *in* those days shall be af-
fliction, such as was not from the
beginning of the creation which
God created unto this time, neither
shall be.
20 And except that the Lord had
shortened those days, no flesh
should be saved: but for the elect's
sake, whom he hath chosen, he hath
shortened the days.
21 And then if any man shall say
to you, Lo, here *is* Christ; or, lo, *he*
is there; believe *him* not:
22 For false Christs and false
prophets shall rise, and shall shew
signs and wonders, to seduce, if *it*
were possible, even the elect.
23 But take ye heed: behold, I have
foretold you all things.
24 But in those days, after that trib-
ulation, the sun shall be darkened,
and the moon shall not give her light,
25 And the stars of heaven shall
fall, and the powers that are in
heaven shall be shaken.

The Son of Man's Coming

26 And then shall they see the Son
of man coming in the clouds with
great power and glory.
27 And then shall he send his an-
gels, and shall gather together his

elect from the four winds, from the
uttermost part of the earth to the
uttermost part of heaven.
28 Now learn a parable of the fig
tree; When her branch is yet tender,
and putteth forth leaves, ye know
that summer is near:
29 So ye in like manner, when
ye shall see these things come to
pass, know that it is nigh, *even* at
the doors.
30 Verily I say unto you, that this
generation shall not pass, till all
these things be done.
31 Heaven and earth shall pass
away: but my words shall not pass
away.

Watch and Pray

32 But of that day and *that* hour
knoweth no man, no, not the angels
which are in heaven, neither the
Son, but the Father.
33 Take ye heed, watch and pray:
for ye know not when the time is.
34 *For the Son of man is* as a man
taking a far journey, who left his
house, and gave authority to his
servants, and to every man his
work, and commanded the porter
to watch.
35 Watch ye therefore: for ye know
not when the master of the house
cometh, at even, or at midnight, or
at the cockcrowing, or in the morn-
ing:
36 Lest coming suddenly he find
you sleeping.
37 And what I say unto you I say
unto all, Watch.

A Woman Anoints Jesus

14 After two days was *the feast of*
the passover, and of unleav-
ened bread: and the chief priests
and the scribes sought how they
might take him by craft, and put
him to death.
2 But they said, Not on the feast
day, lest there be an uproar of the
people.
3 And being in Bethany in the
house of Simon the leper, as he sat
at meat, there came a woman hav-
ing an alabaster box of ointment of
spikenard very precious; and she
brake the box, and poured *it* on his
head.
4 And there were some that had
indignation within themselves, and
said, Why was this waste of the oint-
ment made?
5 For it might have been sold for
more than three hundred pence,
and have been given to the poor.
And they murmured against her.
6 And Jesus said, Let her alone;
why trouble ye her? she hath
wrought a good work on me.
7 For ye have the poor with you
always, and whensoever ye will ye
may do them good: but me ye have
not always.
8 She hath done what she could:
she is come aforehand to anoint my
body to the burying.
9 Verily I say unto you, Whereso-
ever this gospel shall be preached
throughout the whole world, *this*
also that she hath done shall be spo-
ken of for a memorial of her.
10 And Judas Iscariot, one of the
twelve, went unto the chief priests,
to betray him unto them.
11 And when they heard *it,* they
were glad, and promised to give him
money. And he sought how he might
conveniently betray him.

The Passover Prepared

12 And the first day of unleavened
bread, when they killed the pass-
over, his disciples said unto him,
Where wilt thou that we go and
prepare that thou mayest eat the
passover?
13 And he sendeth forth two of
his disciples, and saith unto them,
Go ye into the city, and there shall
meet you a man bearing a pitcher
of water: follow him.
14 And wheresoever he shall go

in, say ye to the goodman of the house, The Master saith, Where is the guestchamber, where I shall eat the passover with my disciples?

15 And he will shew you a large upper room furnished *and* prepared: there make ready for us.

16 And his disciples went forth, and came into the city, and found as he had said unto them: and they made ready the passover.

17 And in the evening he cometh with the twelve.

18 And as they sat and did eat, Jesus said, Verily I say unto you, One of you which eateth with me shall betray me.

19 And they began to be sorrowful, and to say unto him one by one, *Is* it I? and another *said, Is* it I?

20 And he answered and said unto them, *It is* one of the twelve, that dippeth with me in the dish.

21 The Son of man indeed goeth, as it is written of him: but woe to that man by whom the Son of man is betrayed! good were it for that man if he had never been born.

The Lord's Supper

22 And as they did eat, Jesus took bread, and blessed, and brake *it,* and gave to them, and said, Take, eat: this is my body.

23 And he took the cup, and when he had given thanks, he gave *it* to them: and they all drank of it.

24 And he said unto them, This is my blood of the new testament, which is shed for many.

25 Verily I say unto you, I will drink no more of the fruit of the vine, until that day that I drink it new in the kingdom of God.

26 And when they had sung an hymn, they went out into the mount of Olives.

Peter Asserts His Loyalty

27 And Jesus saith unto them, All ye shall be offended because of me this night: for it is written, I will smite the shepherd, and the sheep shall be scattered.

28 But after that I am risen, I will go before you into Galilee.

29 But Peter said unto him, Although all shall be offended, yet *will* not I.

30 And Jesus saith unto him, Verily I say unto thee, That this day, *even* in this night, before the cock crow twice, thou shalt deny me thrice.

31 But he spake the more vehemently, If I should die with thee, I will not deny thee in any wise. Likewise also said they all.

Prayer in the Garden

32 And they came to a place which was named Gethsemane: and he saith to his disciples, Sit ye here, while I shall pray.

33 And he taketh with him Peter and James and John, and began to be sore amazed, and to be very heavy;

34 And saith unto them, My soul is exceeding sorrowful unto death: tarry ye here, and watch.

35 And he went forward a little, and fell on the ground, and prayed that, if it were possible, the hour might pass from him.

36 And he said, Abba, Father, all things *are* possible unto thee; take away this cup from me: nevertheless not what I will, but what thou wilt.

37 And he cometh, and findeth them sleeping, and saith unto Peter, Simon, sleepest thou? couldest not thou watch one hour?

38 Watch ye and pray, lest ye enter into temptation. The spirit truly *is* ready, but the flesh *is* weak.

39 And again he went away, and prayed, and spake the same words.

40 And when he returned, he found them asleep again, (for their eyes were heavy,) neither wist they what to answer him.

41 And he cometh the third time,

and saith unto them, Sleep on now, and take *your* rest: it is enough, the hour is come; behold, the Son of man is betrayed into the hands of sinners.

42 Rise up, let us go; lo, he that betrayeth me is at hand.

Jesus' Arrest

43 And immediately, while he yet spake, cometh Judas, one of the twelve, and with him a great multitude with swords and staves, from the chief priests and the scribes and the elders.

44 And he that betrayed him had given them a token, saying, Whomsoever I shall kiss, that same is he; take him, and lead *him* away safely.

45 And as soon as he was come, he goeth straightway to him, and saith, Master, master; and kissed him.

46 And they laid their hands on him, and took him.

47 And one of them that stood by drew a sword, and smote a servant of the high priest, and cut off his ear.

48 And Jesus answered and said unto them, Are ye come out, as against a thief, with swords and *with* staves to take me?

49 I was daily with you in the temple teaching, and ye took me not: but the scriptures must be fulfilled.

50 And they all forsook him, and fled.

51 And there followed him a certain young man, having a linen cloth cast about *his* naked *body;* and the young men laid hold on him:

52 And he left the linen cloth, and fled from them naked.

Condemnation by the High Priest

53 And they led Jesus away to the high priest: and with him were assembled all the chief priests and the elders and the scribes.

54 And Peter followed him afar off, even into the palace of the high priest: and he sat with the servants, and warmed himself at the fire.

55 And the chief priests and all the council sought for witness against Jesus to put him to death; and found none.

56 For many bare false witness against him, but their witness agreed not together.

57 And there arose certain, and bare false witness against him, saying,

58 We heard him say, I will destroy this temple that is made with hands, and within three days I will build another made without hands.

59 But neither so did their witness agree together.

60 And the high priest stood up in the midst, and asked Jesus, saying, Answerest thou nothing? what *is it which* these witness against thee?

61 But he held his peace, and answered nothing. Again the high priest asked him, and said unto him, Art thou the Christ, the Son of the Blessed?

62 And Jesus said, I am: and ye shall see the Son of man sitting on the right hand of power, and coming in the clouds of heaven.

63 Then the high priest rent his clothes, and saith, What need we any further witnesses?

64 Ye have heard the blasphemy: what think ye? And they all condemned him to be guilty of death.

65 And some began to spit on him, and to cover his face, and to buffet him, and to say unto him, Prophesy: and the servants did strike him with the palms of their hands.

Peter's Denial of Jesus

66 And as Peter was beneath in the palace, there cometh one of the maids of the high priest:

67 And when she saw Peter warming himself, she looked upon him, and said, And thou also wast with Jesus of Nazareth.

68 But he denied, saying, I know
not, neither understand I what thou
sayest. And he went out into the
porch; and the cock crew.
69 And a maid saw him again, and
began to say to them that stood by,
This is *one* of them.
70 And he denied it again. And a
little after, they that stood by said
again to Peter, Surely thou art *one*
of them: for thou art a Galilaean,
and thy speech agreeth *thereto*.
71 But he began to curse and to
swear, *saying,* I know not this man
of whom ye speak.
72 And the second time the cock
crew. And Peter called to mind the
word that Jesus said unto him,
Before the cock crow twice, thou
shalt deny me thrice. And when he
thought thereon, he wept.

Jesus' Trial Before Pilate

15 And straightway in the morn-
ing the chief priests held a
consultation with the elders and
scribes and the whole council, and
bound Jesus, and carried *him* away,
and delivered *him* to Pilate.
2 And Pilate asked him, Art thou
the King of the Jews? And he an-
swering said unto him, Thou say-
est *it*.
3 And the chief priests accused
him of many things: but he an-
swered nothing.
4 And Pilate asked him again,
saying, Answerest thou nothing?
behold how many things they wit-
ness against thee.
5 But Jesus yet answered nothing;
so that Pilate marvelled.
6 Now at *that* feast he released
unto them one prisoner, whomso-
ever they desired.
7 And there was *one* named Bar-
abbas, *which lay* bound with them
that had made insurrection with
him, who had committed murder
in the insurrection.
8 And the multitude crying aloud
began to desire *him to do* as he had
ever done unto them.
9 But Pilate answered them, say-
ing, Will ye that I release unto you
the King of the Jews?
10 For he knew that the chief
priests had delivered him for envy.
11 But the chief priests moved the
people, that he should rather release
Barabbas unto them.
12 And Pilate answered and said
again unto them, What will ye then
that I shall do *unto him* whom ye
call the King of the Jews?
13 And they cried out again, Cru-
cify him.
14 Then Pilate said unto them,
Why, what evil hath he done? And
they cried out the more exceedingly,
Crucify him.
15 And *so* Pilate, willing to content
the people, released Barabbas unto
them, and delivered Jesus, when he
had scourged *him,* to be crucified.
16 And the soldiers led him away
into the hall, called Praetorium; and
they call together the whole band.
17 And they clothed him with pur-
ple, and platted a crown of thorns,
and put it about his *head,*
18 And began to salute him, Hail,
King of the Jews!
19 And they smote him on the
head with a reed, and did spit upon
him, and bowing *their* knees wor-
shipped him.
20 And when they had mocked
him, they took off the purple from
him, and put his own clothes on
him, and led him out to crucify him.

Jesus Is Crucified at Golgotha

21 And they compel one Simon
a Cyrenian, who passed by, com-
ing out of the country, the father
of Alexander and Rufus, to bear his
cross.
22 And they bring him unto the
place Golgotha, which is, being in-
terpreted, The place of a skull.
23 And they gave him to drink

wine mingled with myrrh: but he
received *it* not.
24 And when they had crucified
him, they parted his garments, cast-
ing lots upon them, what every man
should take.
25 And it was the third hour, and
they crucified him.
26 And the superscription of his
accusation was written over, THE
KING OF THE JEWS.
27 And with him they crucify two
thieves; the one on his right hand,
and the other on his left.
28 And the scripture was fulfilled,
which saith, And he was numbered
with the transgressors.
29 And they that passed by railed
on him, wagging their heads, and
saying, Ah, thou that destroyest the
temple, and buildest *it* in three days,
30 Save thyself, and come down
from the cross.
31 Likewise also the chief priests
mocking said among themselves
with the scribes, He saved others;
himself he cannot save.
32 Let Christ the King of Israel de-
scend now from the cross, that we
may see and believe. And they that
were crucified with him reviled him.

Jesus Dies on the Cross

33 And when the sixth hour was
come, there was darkness over the
whole land until the ninth hour.
34 And at the ninth hour Jesus
cried with a loud voice, saying, Eloi,
Eloi, lama sabachthani? which is,
being interpreted, My God, my God,
why hast thou forsaken me?
35 And some of them that stood
by, when they heard *it,* said, Behold,
he calleth Elias.
36 And one ran and filled a spunge
full of vinegar, and put *it* on a reed,
and gave him to drink, saying, Let
alone; let us see whether Elias will
come to take him down.
37 And Jesus cried with a loud
voice, and gave up the ghost.
38 And the veil of the temple was
rent in twain from the top to the
bottom.
39 And when the centurion, which
stood over against him, saw that he
so cried out, and gave up the ghost,
he said, Truly this man was the Son
of God.
40 There were also women look-
ing on afar off: among whom was
Mary Magdalene, and Mary the
mother of James the less and of
Joses, and Salome;
41 (Who also, when he was in Gal-
ilee, followed him, and ministered
unto him;) and many other women
which came up with him unto Je-
rusalem.
42 And now when the even was
come, because it was the prepa-
ration, that is, the day before the
sabbath,
43 Joseph of Arimathaea, an
honourable counsellor, which also
waited for the kingdom of God,
came, and went in boldly unto Pi-
late, and craved the body of Jesus.
44 And Pilate marvelled if he were
already dead: and calling *unto him*
the centurion, he asked him whether
he had been any while dead.
45 And when he knew *it* of the
centurion, he gave the body to Jo-
seph.
46 And he bought fine linen, and
took him down, and wrapped him in
the linen, and laid him in a sepulchre
which was hewn out of a rock, and
rolled a stone unto the door of the
sepulchre.
47 And Mary Magdalene and Mary
the mother of Joses beheld where he
was laid.

The Resurrected Christ

16 And when the sabbath was
past, Mary Magdalene, and
Mary the *mother* of James, and Sa-
lome, had bought sweet spices, that
they might come and anoint him.
2 And very early in the morning

the first *day* of the week, they came unto the sepulchre at the rising of the sun.
3 And they said among themselves, Who shall roll us away the stone from the door of the sepulchre?
4 And when they looked, they saw that the stone was rolled away: for it was very great.
5 And entering into the sepulchre, they saw a young man sitting on the right side, clothed in a long white garment; and they were affrighted.
6 And he saith unto them, Be not affrighted: Ye seek Jesus of Nazareth, which was crucified: he is risen; he is not here: behold the place where they laid him.
7 But go your way, tell his disciples and Peter that he goeth before you into Galilee: there shall ye see him, as he said unto you.
8 And they went out quickly, and fled from the sepulchre; for they trembled and were amazed: neither said they any thing to any *man;* for they were afraid.

Jesus' First Appearance

9 Now when *Jesus* was risen early the first *day* of the week, he appeared first to Mary Magdalene, out of whom he had cast seven devils.
10 *And* she went and told them that had been with him, as they mourned and wept.
11 And they, when they had heard that he was alive, and had been seen of her, believed not.
12 After that he appeared in another form unto two of them, as they walked, and went into the country.
13 And they went and told *it* unto the residue: neither believed they them.

Jesus' Commission of the Eleven

14 Afterward he appeared unto the eleven as they sat at meat, and upbraided them with their unbelief and hardness of heart, because they believed not them which had seen him after he was risen.
15 And he said unto them, Go ye into all the world, and preach the gospel to every creature.
16 He that believeth and is baptized shall be saved; but he that believeth not shall be damned.
17 And these signs shall follow them that believe; In my name shall they cast out devils; they shall speak with new tongues;
18 They shall take up serpents; and if they drink any deadly thing, it shall not hurt them; they shall lay hands on the sick, and they shall recover.

Jesus Ascends to Heaven

19 So then after the Lord had spoken unto them, he was received up into heaven, and sat on the right hand of God.
20 And they went forth, and preached every where, the Lord working with *them,* and confirming the word with signs following. Amen.

The Gospel According to
LUKE

Luke's Letter to Theophilus

Forasmuch as many have taken
in hand to set forth in order a
declaration of those things which
are most surely believed among us,
2 Even as they delivered them
unto us, which from the beginning
were eyewitnesses, and ministers
of the word;
3 It seemed good to me also, hav-
ing had perfect understanding of all
things from the very first, to write
unto thee in order, most excellent
Theophilus,
4 That thou mightest know the
certainty of those things, wherein
thou hast been instructed.

*An Angel Foretells
John's Birth*

5 There was in the days of Herod,
the king of Judaea, a certain priest
named Zacharias, of the course of
Abia: and his wife *was* of the daugh-
ters of Aaron, and her name *was*
Elisabeth.
6 And they were both righteous
before God, walking in all the com-
mandments and ordinances of the
Lord blameless.
7 And they had no child, because
that Elisabeth was barren, and
they both were *now* well stricken
in years.
8 And it came to pass, that while
he executed the priest's office before
God in the order of his course,
9 According to the custom of the
priest's office, his lot was to burn
incense when he went into the tem-
ple of the Lord.
10 And the whole multitude of the
people were praying without at the
time of incense.
11 And there appeared unto him
an angel of the Lord standing on the
right side of the altar of incense.
12 And when Zacharias saw *him,*
he was troubled, and fear fell upon
him.
13 But the angel said unto him,
Fear not, Zacharias: for thy prayer is
heard; and thy wife Elisabeth shall
bear thee a son, and thou shalt call
his name John.
14 And thou shalt have joy and
gladness; and many shall rejoice at
his birth.
15 For he shall be great in the sight
of the Lord, and shall drink neither
wine nor strong drink; and he shall
be filled with the Holy Ghost, even
from his mother's womb.
16 And many of the children of Is-
rael shall he turn to the Lord their
God.
17 And he shall go before him in
the spirit and power of Elias, to turn
the hearts of the fathers to the chil-
dren, and the disobedient to the
wisdom of the just; to make ready
a people prepared for the Lord.
18 And Zacharias said unto the
angel, Whereby shall I know this?
for I am an old man, and my wife
well stricken in years.
19 And the angel answering said
unto him, I am Gabriel, that stand in
the presence of God; and am sent to
speak unto thee, and to shew thee
these glad tidings.
20 And, behold, thou shalt be

dumb, and not able to speak, until
the day that these things shall be
performed, because thou believest
not my words, which shall be ful-
filled in their season.
21 And the people waited for
Zacharias, and marvelled that he
tarried so long in the temple.
22 And when he came out, he
could not speak unto them: and
they perceived that he had seen a
vision in the temple: for he beck-
oned unto them, and remained
speechless.
23 And it came to pass, that, as
soon as the days of his ministration
were accomplished, he departed to
his own house.
24 And after those days his wife
Elisabeth conceived, and hid herself
five months, saying,
25 Thus hath the Lord dealt with
me in the days wherein he looked
on *me,* to take away my reproach
among men.

An Angel Foretells Jesus' Birth

26 And in the sixth month the an-
gel Gabriel was sent from God unto
a city of Galilee, named Nazareth,
27 To a virgin espoused to a man
whose name was Joseph, of the
house of David; and the virgin's
name *was* Mary.
28 And the angel came in unto her,
and said, Hail, *thou that art* highly
favoured, the Lord *is* with thee:
blessed *art* thou among women.
29 And when she saw *him,* she was
troubled at his saying, and cast in
her mind what manner of salutation
this should be.
30 And the angel said unto her,
Fear not, Mary: for thou hast found
favour with God.
31 And, behold, thou shalt con-
ceive in thy womb, and bring forth
a son, and shalt call his name JESUS.
32 He shall be great, and shall
be called the Son of the Highest:
and the Lord God shall give unto
him the throne of his father David:
33 And he shall reign over the
house of Jacob for ever; and of his
kingdom there shall be no end.
34 Then said Mary unto the angel,
How shall this be, seeing I know not
a man?
35 And the angel answered and
said unto her, The Holy Ghost shall
come upon thee, and the power of
the Highest shall overshadow thee:
therefore also that holy thing which
shall be born of thee shall be called
the Son of God.
36 And, behold, thy cousin Elisa-
beth, she hath also conceived a son
in her old age: and this is the sixth
month with her, who was called
barren.
37 For with God nothing shall be
impossible.
38 And Mary said, Behold the
handmaid of the Lord; be it unto
me according to thy word. And the
angel departed from her.

Elisabeth's Joy

39 And Mary arose in those days,
and went into the hill country with
haste, into a city of Juda;
40 And entered into the house of
Zacharias, and saluted Elisabeth.
41 And it came to pass, that, when
Elisabeth heard the salutation of
Mary, the babe leaped in her womb;
and Elisabeth was filled with the
Holy Ghost:
42 And she spake out with a loud
voice, and said, Blessed *art* thou
among women, and blessed *is* the
fruit of thy womb.
43 And whence *is* this to me, that
the mother of my Lord should come
to me?
44 For, lo, as soon as the voice of
thy salutation sounded in mine ears,
the babe leaped in my womb for joy.
45 And blessed *is* she that be-
lieved: for there shall be a perfor-
mance of those things which were
told her from the Lord.

Mary's Joyful Song

46 And Mary said, My soul doth magnify the Lord,

47 And my spirit hath rejoiced in God my Saviour.

48 For he hath regarded the low estate of his handmaiden: for, behold, from henceforth all generations shall call me blessed.

49 For he that is mighty hath done to me great things; and holy *is* his name.

50 And his mercy *is* on them that fear him from generation to generation.

51 He hath shewed strength with his arm; he hath scattered the proud in the imagination of their hearts.

52 He hath put down the mighty from *their* seats, and exalted them of low degree.

53 He hath filled the hungry with good things; and the rich he hath sent empty away.

54 He hath holpen his servant Israel, in remembrance of *his* mercy;

55 As he spake to our fathers, to Abraham, and to his seed for ever.

56 And Mary abode with her about three months, and returned to her own house.

John the Baptist's Birth

57 Now Elisabeth's full time came that she should be delivered; and she brought forth a son.

58 And her neighbours and her cousins heard how the Lord had shewed great mercy upon her; and they rejoiced with her.

59 And it came to pass, that on the eighth day they came to circumcise the child; and they called him Zacharias, after the name of his father.

60 And his mother answered and said, Not *so;* but he shall be called John.

61 And they said unto her, There is none of thy kindred that is called by this name.

62 And they made signs to his father, how he would have him called.

63 And he asked for a writing table, and wrote, saying, His name is John. And they marvelled all.

64 And his mouth was opened immediately, and his tongue *loosed,* and he spake, and praised God.

65 And fear came on all that dwelt round about them: and all these sayings were noised abroad throughout all the hill country of Judaea.

66 And all they that heard *them* laid *them* up in their hearts, saying, What manner of child shall this be! And the hand of the Lord was with him.

67 And his father Zacharias was filled with the Holy Ghost, and prophesied, saying,

68 Blessed *be* the Lord God of Israel; for he hath visited and redeemed his people,

69 And hath raised up an horn of salvation for us in the house of his servant David;

70 As he spake by the mouth of his holy prophets, which have been since the world began:

71 That we should be saved from our enemies, and from the hand of all that hate us;

72 To perform the mercy *promised* to our fathers, and to remember his holy covenant;

73 The oath which he sware to our father Abraham,

74 That he would grant unto us, that we being delivered out of the hand of our enemies might serve him without fear,

75 In holiness and righteousness before him, all the days of our life.

76 And thou, child, shalt be called the prophet of the Highest: for thou shalt go before the face of the Lord to prepare his ways;

77 To give knowledge of salvation unto his people by the remission of their sins,

78 Through the tender mercy of

our God; whereby the dayspring
from on high hath visited us,
79 To give light to them that sit
in darkness and *in* the shadow of
death, to guide our feet into the way
of peace.
80 And the child grew, and waxed
strong in spirit, and was in the deserts till the day of his shewing unto
Israel.

Jesus' Birth in Bethlehem

2 And it came to pass in those
days, that there went out a decree from Caesar Augustus, that all
the world should be taxed.
2 (*And* this taxing was first made
when Cyrenius was governor of
Syria.)
3 And all went to be taxed, every
one into his own city.
4 And Joseph also went up from
Galilee, out of the city of Nazareth,
into Judaea, unto the city of David,
which is called Bethlehem; (because
he was of the house and lineage of
David:)
5 To be taxed with Mary his espoused wife, being great with child.
6 And so it was, that, while they
were there, the days were accomplished that she should be delivered.
7 And she brought forth her
firstborn son, and wrapped him in
swaddling clothes, and laid him in a
manger; because there was no room
for them in the inn.

Tidings of Great Joy

8 And there were in the same
country shepherds abiding in the
field, keeping watch over their flock
by night.
9 And, lo, the angel of the Lord
came upon them, and the glory of
the Lord shone round about them:
and they were sore afraid.
10 And the angel said unto them,
Fear not: for, behold, I bring you
good tidings of great joy, which shall
be to all people.
11 For unto you is born this day in
the city of David a Saviour, which is
Christ the Lord.
12 And this *shall be* a sign unto
you; Ye shall find the babe wrapped
in swaddling clothes, lying in a manger.
13 And suddenly there was with
the angel a multitude of the heavenly host praising God, and saying,
14 Glory to God in the highest, and
on earth peace, good will toward
men.
15 And it came to pass, as the angels were gone away from them into
heaven, the shepherds said one to
another, Let us now go even unto
Bethlehem, and see this thing which
is come to pass, which the Lord hath
made known unto us.
16 And they came with haste, and
found Mary, and Joseph, and the
babe lying in a manger.
17 And when they had seen *it*, they
made known abroad the saying
which was told them concerning
this child.
18 And all they that heard *it* wondered at those things which were
told them by the shepherds.
19 But Mary kept all these things,
and pondered *them* in her heart.
20 And the shepherds returned,
glorifying and praising God for all
the things that they had heard and
seen, as it was told unto them.

Naming and Presentation

21 And when eight days were accomplished for the circumcising
of the child, his name was called
JESUS, which was so named of the
angel before he was conceived in
the womb.
22 And when the days of her purification according to the law of
Moses were accomplished, they
brought him to Jerusalem, to present *him* to the Lord;
23 (As it is written in the law of
the Lord, Every male that openeth

the womb shall be called holy to the
Lord;)
24 And to offer a sacrifice accord-
ing to that which is said in the law
of the Lord, A pair of turtledoves, or
two young pigeons.

Simeon Beholds God's Salvation

25 And, behold, there was a man
in Jerusalem, whose name *was* Sim-
eon; and the same man *was* just and
devout, waiting for the consolation
of Israel: and the Holy Ghost was
upon him.
26 And it was revealed unto him
by the Holy Ghost, that he should
not see death, before he had seen
the Lord's Christ.
27 And he came by the Spirit into
the temple: and when the parents
brought in the child Jesus, to do for
him after the custom of the law,
28 Then took he him up in his
arms, and blessed God, and said,
29 Lord, now lettest thou thy ser-
vant depart in peace, according to
thy word:
30 For mine eyes have seen thy
salvation,
31 Which thou hast prepared be-
fore the face of all people;
32 A light to lighten the Gentiles,
and the glory of thy people Israel.
33 And Joseph and his mother
marvelled at those things which
were spoken of him.
34 And Simeon blessed them, and
said unto Mary his mother, Behold,
this *child* is set for the fall and rising
again of many in Israel; and for a
sign which shall be spoken against;
35 (Yea, a sword shall pierce
through thy own soul also,) that
the thoughts of many hearts may
be revealed.

Anna Gives Thanks

36 And there was one Anna, a
prophetess, the daughter of Pha-
nuel, of the tribe of Aser: she was
of a great age, and had lived with
an husband seven years from her
virginity;
37 And she *was* a widow of about
fourscore and four years, which
departed not from the temple,
but served *God* with fastings and
prayers night and day.
38 And she coming in that instant
gave thanks likewise unto the Lord,
and spake of him to all them that
looked for redemption in Jerusalem.
39 And when they had performed
all things according to the law of the
Lord, they returned into Galilee, to
their own city Nazareth.
40 And the child grew, and waxed
strong in spirit, filled with wisdom:
and the grace of God was upon him.

Jesus Converses with Teachers

41 Now his parents went to Jeru-
salem every year at the feast of the
passover.
42 And when he was twelve years
old, they went up to Jerusalem after
the custom of the feast.
43 And when they had fulfilled
the days, as they returned, the child
Jesus tarried behind in Jerusalem;
and Joseph and his mother knew
not *of it*.
44 But they, supposing him to
have been in the company, went a
day's journey; and they sought him
among *their* kinsfolk and acquain-
tance.
45 And when they found him not,
they turned back again to Jerusa-
lem, seeking him.
46 And it came to pass, that after
three days they found him in the
temple, sitting in the midst of the
doctors, both hearing them, and
asking them questions.
47 And all that heard him were
astonished at his understanding
and answers.
48 And when they saw him, they
were amazed: and his mother said
unto him, Son, why hast thou thus

dealt with us? behold, thy father and
I have sought thee sorrowing.
49 And he said unto them, How
is it that ye sought me? wist ye not
that I must be about my Father's
business?
50 And they understood not the
saying which he spake unto them.
51 And he went down with them,
and came to Nazareth, and was sub-
ject unto them: but his mother kept
all these sayings in her heart.
52 And Jesus increased in wisdom
and stature, and in favour with God
and man.

John Preaches Repentance

3 Now in the fifteenth year of the
reign of Tiberius Caesar, Pontius
Pilate being governor of Judaea, and
Herod being tetrarch of Galilee, and
his brother Philip tetrarch of Ituraea
and of the region of Trachonitis, and
Lysanias the tetrarch of Abilene,
2 Annas and Caiaphas being the
high priests, the word of God came
unto John the son of Zacharias in
the wilderness.
3 And he came into all the country
about Jordan, preaching the bap-
tism of repentance for the remission
of sins;
4 As it is written in the book of
the words of Esaias the prophet,
saying, The voice of one crying in
the wilderness, Prepare ye the way
of the Lord, make his paths straight.
5 Every valley shall be filled, and
every mountain and hill shall be
brought low; and the crooked shall
be made straight, and the rough
ways *shall be* made smooth;
6 And all flesh shall see the salva-
tion of God.

John Addresses the Multitude

7 Then said he to the multitude
that came forth to be baptized of
him, O generation of vipers, who
hath warned you to flee from the
wrath to come?
8 Bring forth therefore fruits wor-
thy of repentance, and begin not
to say within yourselves, We have
Abraham to *our* father: for I say unto
you, That God is able of these stones
to raise up children unto Abraham.
9 And now also the axe is laid
unto the root of the trees: every tree
therefore which bringeth not forth
good fruit is hewn down, and cast
into the fire.
10 And the people asked him, say-
ing, What shall we do then?
11 He answereth and saith unto
them, He that hath two coats, let
him impart to him that hath none;
and he that hath meat, let him do
likewise.
12 Then came also publicans to be
baptized, and said unto him, Master,
what shall we do?
13 And he said unto them, Exact
no more than that which is ap-
pointed you.
14 And the soldiers likewise de-
manded of him, saying, And what
shall we do? And he said unto them,
Do violence to no man, neither ac-
cuse *any* falsely; and be content
with your wages.
15 And as the people were in ex-
pectation, and all men mused in
their hearts of John, whether he
were the Christ, or not;
16 John answered, saying unto
them all, I indeed baptize you with
water; but one mightier than I com-
eth, the latchet of whose shoes I
am not worthy to unloose: he shall
baptize you with the Holy Ghost and
with fire:
17 Whose fan *is* in his hand, and
he will throughly purge his floor,
and will gather the wheat into his
garner; but the chaff he will burn
with fire unquenchable.
18 And many other things in his
exhortation preached he unto the
people.
19 But Herod the tetrarch, being
reproved by him for Herodias his

brother Philip's wife, and for all the evils which Herod had done,

20 Added yet this above all, that he shut up John in prison.

John's Baptism of Jesus

21 Now when all the people were baptized, it came to pass, that Jesus also being baptized, and praying, the heaven was opened,

22 And the Holy Ghost descended in a bodily shape like a dove upon him, and a voice came from heaven, which said, Thou art my beloved Son; in thee I am well pleased.

The Genealogy of Jesus

23 And Jesus himself began to be about thirty years of age, being (as was supposed) the son of Joseph, which was *the son* of Heli,

24 Which was *the son* of Matthat, which was *the son* of Levi, which was *the son* of Melchi, which was *the son* of Janna, which was *the son* of Joseph,

25 Which was *the son* of Mattathias, which was *the son* of Amos, which was *the son* of Naum, which was *the son* of Esli, which was *the son* of Nagge,

26 Which was *the son* of Maath, which was *the son* of Mattathias, which was *the son* of Semei, which was *the son* of Joseph, which was *the son* of Juda,

27 Which was *the son* of Joanna, which was *the son* of Rhesa, which was *the son* of Zorobabel, which was *the son* of Salathiel, which was *the son* of Neri,

28 Which was *the son* of Melchi, which was *the son* of Addi, which was *the son* of Cosam, which was *the son* of Elmodam, which was *the son* of Er,

29 Which was *the son* of Jose, which was *the son* of Eliezer, which was *the son* of Jorim, which was *the son* of Matthat, which was *the son* of Levi,

30 Which was *the son* of Simeon, which was *the son* of Juda, which was *the son* of Joseph, which was *the son* of Jonan, which was *the son* of Eliakim,

31 Which was *the son* of Melea, which was *the son* of Menan, which was *the son* of Mattatha, which was *the son* of Nathan, which was *the son* of David,

32 Which was *the son* of Jesse, which was *the son* of Obed, which was *the son* of Booz, which was *the son* of Salmon, which was *the son* of Naasson,

33 Which was *the son* of Aminadab, which was *the son* of Aram, which was *the son* of Esrom, which was *the son* of Phares, which was *the son* of Juda,

34 Which was *the son* of Jacob, which was *the son* of Isaac, which was *the son* of Abraham, which was *the son* of Thara, which was *the son* of Nachor,

35 Which was *the son* of Saruch, which was *the son* of Ragau, which was *the son* of Phalec, which was *the son* of Heber, which was *the son* of Sala,

36 Which was *the son* of Cainan, which was *the son* of Arphaxad, which was *the son* of Sem, which was *the son* of Noe, which was *the son* of Lamech,

37 Which was *the son* of Mathusala, which was *the son* of Enoch, which was *the son* of Jared, which was *the son* of Maleleel, which was *the son* of Cainan,

38 Which was *the son* of Enos, which was *the son* of Seth, which was *the son* of Adam, which was *the son* of God.

The Temptation of Jesus

4 And Jesus being full of the Holy Ghost returned from Jordan, and was led by the Spirit into the wilderness,

2 Being forty days tempted of the

devil. And in those days he did eat
nothing: and when they were ended,
he afterward hungered.
3 And the devil said unto him, If
thou be the Son of God, command
this stone that it be made bread.
4 And Jesus answered him, say-
ing, It is written, That man shall not
live by bread alone, but by every
word of God.
5 And the devil, taking him up into
an high mountain, shewed unto him
all the kingdoms of the world in a
moment of time.
6 And the devil said unto him, All
this power will I give thee, and the
glory of them: for that is delivered
unto me; and to whomsoever I will
I give it.
7 If thou therefore wilt worship
me, all shall be thine.
8 And Jesus answered and said
unto him, Get thee behind me,
Satan: for it is written, Thou shalt
worship the Lord thy God, and him
only shalt thou serve.
9 And he brought him to Jerusa-
lem, and set him on a pinnacle of
the temple, and said unto him, If
thou be the Son of God, cast thyself
down from hence:
10 For it is written, He shall give his
angels charge over thee, to keep thee:
11 And in *their* hands they shall
bear thee up, lest at any time thou
dash thy foot against a stone.
12 And Jesus answering said unto
him, It is said, Thou shalt not tempt
the Lord thy God.
13 And when the devil had ended
all the temptation, he departed from
him for a season.

Jesus Preaches in Nazareth

14 And Jesus returned in the
power of the Spirit into Galilee:
and there went out a fame of him
through all the region round about.
15 And he taught in their syna-
gogues, being glorified of all.
16 And he came to Nazareth,
where he had been brought up: and,
as his custom was, he went into the
synagogue on the sabbath day, and
stood up for to read.
17 And there was delivered unto
him the book of the prophet Esai-
as. And when he had opened the
book, he found the place where it
was written,
18 The Spirit of the Lord *is* upon
me, because he hath anointed me
to preach the gospel to the poor; he
hath sent me to heal the broken-
hearted, to preach deliverance to the
captives, and recovering of sight to
the blind, to set at liberty them that
are bruised,
19 To preach the acceptable year
of the Lord.
20 And he closed the book, and
he gave *it* again to the minister, and
sat down. And the eyes of all them
that were in the synagogue were
fastened on him.
21 And he began to say unto them,
This day is this scripture fulfilled in
your ears.
22 And all bare him witness, and
wondered at the gracious words
which proceeded out of his mouth.
And they said, Is not this Joseph's
son?
23 And he said unto them, Ye will
surely say unto me this proverb,
Physician, heal thyself: whatsoever
we have heard done in Capernaum,
do also here in thy country.
24 And he said, Verily I say unto
you, No prophet is accepted in his
own country.
25 But I tell you of a truth, many
widows were in Israel in the days of
Elias, when the heaven was shut up
three years and six months, when
great famine was throughout all the
land;
26 But unto none of them was
Elias sent, save unto Sarepta, *a city*
of Sidon, unto a woman *that was* a
widow.
27 And many lepers were in Israel

in the time of Eliseus the prophet; and none of them was cleansed, saving Naaman the Syrian.
28 And all they in the synagogue, when they heard these things, were filled with wrath,
29 And rose up, and thrust him out of the city, and led him unto the brow of the hill whereon their city was built, that they might cast him down headlong.
30 But he passing through the midst of them went his way,

A Spirit of an Unclean Devil

31 And came down to Capernaum, a city of Galilee, and taught them on the sabbath days.
32 And they were astonished at his doctrine: for his word was with power.
33 And in the synagogue there was a man, which had a spirit of an unclean devil, and cried out with a loud voice,
34 Saying, Let *us* alone; what have we to do with thee, *thou* Jesus of Nazareth? art thou come to destroy us? I know thee who thou art; the Holy One of God.
35 And Jesus rebuked him, saying, Hold thy peace, and come out of him. And when the devil had thrown him in the midst, he came out of him, and hurt him not.
36 And they were all amazed, and spake among themselves, saying, What a word *is* this! for with authority and power he commandeth the unclean spirits, and they come out.
37 And the fame of him went out into every place of the country round about.

Jesus' Healing Ministry

38 And he arose out of the synagogue, and entered into Simon's house. And Simon's wife's mother was taken with a great fever; and they besought him for her.
39 And he stood over her, and rebuked the fever; and it left her: and immediately she arose and ministered unto them.
40 Now when the sun was setting, all they that had any sick with divers diseases brought them unto him; and he laid his hands on every one of them, and healed them.
41 And devils also came out of many, crying out, and saying, Thou art Christ the Son of God. And he rebuking *them* suffered them not to speak: for they knew that he was Christ.
42 And when it was day, he departed and went into a desert place: and the people sought him, and came unto him, and stayed him, that he should not depart from them.
43 And he said unto them, I must preach the kingdom of God to other cities also: for therefore am I sent.
44 And he preached in the synagogues of Galilee.

Fishermen Follow Jesus

5 And it came to pass, that, as the people pressed upon him to hear the word of God, he stood by the lake of Gennesaret,
2 And saw two ships standing by the lake: but the fishermen were gone out of them, and were washing *their* nets.
3 And he entered into one of the ships, which was Simon's, and prayed him that he would thrust out a little from the land. And he sat down, and taught the people out of the ship.
4 Now when he had left speaking, he said unto Simon, Launch out into the deep, and let down your nets for a draught.
5 And Simon answering said unto him, Master, we have toiled all the night, and have taken nothing: nevertheless at thy word I will let down the net.
6 And when they had this done, they inclosed a great multitude of fishes: and their net brake.

7 And they beckoned unto *their*
partners, which were in the other
ship, that they should come and help
them. And they came, and filled both
the ships, so that they began to sink.
8 When Simon Peter saw *it,* he
fell down at Jesus' knees, saying,
Depart from me; for I am a sinful
man, O Lord.
9 For he was astonished, and all
that were with him, at the draught
of the fishes which they had taken:
10 And so *was* also James, and
John, the sons of Zebedee, which
were partners with Simon. And
Jesus said unto Simon, Fear not;
from henceforth thou shalt catch
men.
11 And when they had brought
their ships to land, they forsook all,
and followed him.

Jesus Heals a Leper

12 And it came to pass, when he
was in a certain city, behold a man
full of leprosy: who seeing Jesus
fell on *his* face, and besought him,
saying, Lord, if thou wilt, thou canst
make me clean.
13 And he put forth *his* hand, and
touched him, saying, I will: be thou
clean. And immediately the leprosy
departed from him.
14 And he charged him to tell no
man: but go, and shew thyself to the
priest, and offer for thy cleansing,
according as Moses commanded,
for a testimony unto them.
15 But so much the more went
there a fame abroad of him: and
great multitudes came together
to hear, and to be healed by him of
their infirmities.
16 And he withdrew himself into
the wilderness, and prayed.

Jesus Heals a Man Taken with Palsy

17 And it came to pass on a certain
day, as he was teaching, that there
were Pharisees and doctors of the
law sitting by, which were come out
of every town of Galilee, and Judaea,
and Jerusalem: and the power of the
Lord was *present* to heal them.
18 And, behold, men brought in
a bed a man which was taken with
a palsy: and they sought *means* to
bring him in, and to lay *him* before
him.
19 And when they could not find
by what *way* they might bring him
in because of the multitude, they
went upon the housetop, and let
him down through the tiling with *his*
couch into the midst before Jesus.
20 And when he saw their faith,
he said unto him, Man, thy sins are
forgiven thee.
21 And the scribes and the Phar-
isees began to reason, saying, Who
is this which speaketh blasphemies?
Who can forgive sins, but God alone?
22 But when Jesus perceived
their thoughts, he answering said
unto them, What reason ye in your
hearts?
23 Whether is easier, to say, Thy
sins be forgiven thee; or to say, Rise
up and walk?
24 But that ye may know that the
Son of man hath power upon earth
to forgive sins, (he said unto the sick
of the palsy,) I say unto thee, Arise,
and take up thy couch, and go into
thine house.
25 And immediately he rose up
before them, and took up that
whereon he lay, and departed to
his own house, glorifying God.
26 And they were all amazed, and
they glorified God, and were filled
with fear, saying, We have seen
strange things to day.

Levi Follows Jesus

27 And after these things he went
forth, and saw a publican, named
Levi, sitting at the receipt of custom:
and he said unto him, Follow me.
28 And he left all, rose up, and
followed him.

29 And Levi made him a great feast in his own house: and there was a great company of publicans and of others that sat down with them.

30 But their scribes and Pharisees murmured against his disciples, saying, Why do ye eat and drink with publicans and sinners?

31 And Jesus answering said unto them, They that are whole need not a physician; but they that are sick.

32 I came not to call the righteous, but sinners to repentance.

Fasting Customs Addressed

33 And they said unto him, Why do the disciples of John fast often, and make prayers, and likewise *the disciples* of the Pharisees; but thine eat and drink?

34 And he said unto them, Can ye make the children of the bridechamber fast, while the bridegroom is with them?

35 But the days will come, when the bridegroom shall be taken away from them, and then shall they fast in those days.

36 And he spake also a parable unto them; No man putteth a piece of a new garment upon an old; if otherwise, then both the new maketh a rent, and the piece that was *taken* out of the new agreeth not with the old.

37 And no man putteth new wine into old bottles; else the new wine will burst the bottles, and be spilled, and the bottles shall perish.

38 But new wine must be put into new bottles; and both are preserved.

39 No man also having drunk old *wine* straightway desireth new: for he saith, The old is better.

Behavior on the Sabbath

6 And it came to pass on the second sabbath after the first, that he went through the corn fields; and his disciples plucked the ears of corn, and did eat, rubbing *them* in *their* hands.

2 And certain of the Pharisees said unto them, Why do ye that which is not lawful to do on the sabbath days?

3 And Jesus answering them said, Have ye not read so much as this, what David did, when himself was an hungred, and they which were with him;

4 How he went into the house of God, and did take and eat the shewbread, and gave also to them that were with him; which it is not lawful to eat but for the priests alone?

5 And he said unto them, That the Son of man is Lord also of the sabbath.

6 And it came to pass also on another sabbath, that he entered into the synagogue and taught: and there was a man whose right hand was withered.

7 And the scribes and Pharisees watched him, whether he would heal on the sabbath day; that they might find an accusation against him.

8 But he knew their thoughts, and said to the man which had the withered hand, Rise up, and stand forth in the midst. And he arose and stood forth.

9 Then said Jesus unto them, I will ask you one thing; Is it lawful on the sabbath days to do good, or to do evil? to save life, or to destroy *it?*

10 And looking round about upon them all, he said unto the man, Stretch forth thy hand. And he did so: and his hand was restored whole as the other.

11 And they were filled with madness; and communed one with another what they might do to Jesus.

Twelve Apostles Chosen

12 And it came to pass in those days, that he went out into a mountain to pray, and continued all night in prayer to God.

13 And when it was day, he called
unto him his disciples: and of them
he chose twelve, whom also he
named apostles;
14 Simon, (whom he also named
Peter,) and Andrew his brother,
James and John, Philip and Bar-
tholomew,
15 Matthew and Thomas, James
the *son* of Alphaeus, and Simon
called Zelotes,
16 And Judas *the brother* of James,
and Judas Iscariot, which also was
the traitor.

Words of Blessing and Woe

17 And he came down with them,
and stood in the plain, and the com-
pany of his disciples, and a great
multitude of people out of all Ju-
daea and Jerusalem, and from the
sea coast of Tyre and Sidon, which
came to hear him, and to be healed
of their diseases;
18 And they that were vexed with
unclean spirits: and they were
healed.
19 And the whole multitude
sought to touch him: for there went
virtue out of him, and healed *them*
all.
20 And he lifted up his eyes on
his disciples, and said, Blessed *be*
ye poor: for yours is the kingdom
of God.
21 Blessed *are ye* that hunger
now: for ye shall be filled. Blessed
are ye that weep now: for ye shall
laugh.
22 Blessed are ye, when men shall
hate you, and when they shall sep-
arate you *from their company,* and
shall reproach *you,* and cast out your
name as evil, for the Son of man's
sake.
23 Rejoice ye in that day, and leap
for joy: for, behold, your reward *is*
great in heaven: for in the like man-
ner did their fathers unto the proph-
ets.
24 But woe unto you that are rich!
for ye have received your consola-
tion.
25 Woe unto you that are full! for
ye shall hunger. Woe unto you that
laugh now! for ye shall mourn and
weep.
26 Woe unto you, when all men
shall speak well of you! for so did
their fathers to the false prophets.

Teachings on Treatment of Others

27 But I say unto you which hear,
Love your enemies, do good to them
which hate you,
28 Bless them that curse you, and
pray for them which despitefully use
you.
29 And unto him that smiteth thee
on the *one* cheek offer also the other;
and him that taketh away thy cloak
forbid not *to take thy* coat also.
30 Give to every man that asketh
of thee; and of him that taketh away
thy goods ask *them* not again.
31 And as ye would that men
should do to you, do ye also to them
likewise.
32 For if ye love them which love
you, what thank have ye? for sinners
also love those that love them.
33 And if ye do good to them
which do good to you, what thank
have ye? for sinners also do even the
same.
34 And if ye lend *to them* of whom
ye hope to receive, what thank have
ye? for sinners also lend to sinners,
to receive as much again.
35 But love ye your enemies, and
do good, and lend, hoping for noth-
ing again; and your reward shall be
great, and ye shall be the children
of the Highest: for he is kind unto
the unthankful and *to* the evil.
36 Be ye therefore merciful, as
your Father also is merciful.

Teachings on Judging Others

37 Judge not, and ye shall not be
judged: condemn not, and ye shall

not be condemned: forgive, and ye
shall be forgiven:
38 Give, and it shall be given
unto you; good measure, pressed
down, and shaken together, and
running over, shall men give into
your bosom. For with the same measure
that ye mete withal it shall be
measured to you again.
39 And he spake a parable unto
them, Can the blind lead the blind?
shall they not both fall into the
ditch?
40 The disciple is not above his
master: but every one that is perfect
shall be as his master.
41 And why beholdest thou the
mote that is in thy brother's eye,
but perceivest not the beam that is
in thine own eye?
42 Either how canst thou say to
thy brother, Brother, let me pull out
the mote that is in thine eye, when
thou thyself beholdest not the beam
that is in thine own eye? Thou hypocrite,
cast out first the beam out of
thine own eye, and then shalt thou
see clearly to pull out the mote that
is in thy brother's eye.

Good and Bad Fruit

43 For a good tree bringeth not
forth corrupt fruit; neither doth a
corrupt tree bring forth good fruit.
44 For every tree is known by his
own fruit. For of thorns men do not
gather figs, nor of a bramble bush
gather they grapes.
45 A good man out of the good
treasure of his heart bringeth forth
that which is good; and an evil man
out of the evil treasure of his heart
bringeth forth that which is evil: for
of the abundance of the heart his
mouth speaketh.

Building on a Firm Foundation

46 And why call ye me, Lord, Lord,
and do not the things which I say?
47 Whosoever cometh to me,
and heareth my sayings, and doeth
them, I will shew you to whom he
is like:
48 He is like a man which built an
house, and digged deep, and laid the
foundation on a rock: and when the
flood arose, the stream beat vehemently
upon that house, and could
not shake it: for it was founded upon
a rock.
49 But he that heareth, and doeth
not, is like a man that without a
foundation built an house upon the
earth; against which the stream did
beat vehemently, and immediately
it fell; and the ruin of that house was
great.

A Centurion's Faith

7 Now when he had ended all his
sayings in the audience of the
people, he entered into Capernaum.
2 And a certain centurion's servant,
who was dear unto him, was
sick, and ready to die.
3 And when he heard of Jesus, he
sent unto him the elders of the Jews,
beseeching him that he would come
and heal his servant.
4 And when they came to Jesus,
they besought him instantly, saying,
That he was worthy for whom he
should do this:
5 For he loveth our nation, and he
hath built us a synagogue.
6 Then Jesus went with them. And
when he was now not far from the
house, the centurion sent friends to
him, saying unto him, Lord, trouble
not thyself: for I am not worthy that
thou shouldest enter under my roof:
7 Wherefore neither thought I
myself worthy to come unto thee:
but say in a word, and my servant
shall be healed.
8 For I also am a man set under
authority, having under me soldiers,
and I say unto one, Go, and he goeth;
and to another, Come, and he cometh;
and to my servant, Do this, and
he doeth *it*.

9 When Jesus heard these things, he marvelled at him, and turned him about, and said unto the people that followed him, I say unto you, I have not found so great faith, no, not in Israel.

10 And they that were sent, returning to the house, found the servant whole that had been sick.

Jesus Raises a Dead Man

11 And it came to pass the day after, that he went into a city called Nain; and many of his disciples went with him, and much people.

12 Now when he came nigh to the gate of the city, behold, there was a dead man carried out, the only son of his mother, and she was a widow: and much people of the city was with her.

13 And when the Lord saw her, he had compassion on her, and said unto her, Weep not.

14 And he came and touched the bier: and they that bare *him* stood still. And he said, Young man, I say unto thee, Arise.

15 And he that was dead sat up, and began to speak. And he delivered him to his mother.

16 And there came a fear on all: and they glorified God, saying, That a great prophet is risen up among us; and, That God hath visited his people.

17 And this rumour of him went forth throughout all Judaea, and throughout all the region round about.

John's Disciples

18 And the disciples of John shewed him of all these things.

19 And John calling *unto him* two of his disciples sent *them* to Jesus, saying, Art thou he that should come? or look we for another?

20 When the men were come unto him, they said, John Baptist hath sent us unto thee, saying, Art thou he that should come? or look we for another?

21 And in that same hour he cured many of *their* infirmities and plagues, and of evil spirits; and unto many *that were* blind he gave sight.

22 Then Jesus answering said unto them, Go your way, and tell John what things ye have seen and heard; how that the blind see, the lame walk, the lepers are cleansed, the deaf hear, the dead are raised, to the poor the gospel is preached.

23 And blessed is *he,* whosoever shall not be offended in me.

24 And when the messengers of John were departed, he began to speak unto the people concerning John, What went ye out into the wilderness for to see? A reed shaken with the wind?

25 But what went ye out for to see? A man clothed in soft raiment? Behold, they which are gorgeously apparelled, and live delicately, are in kings' courts.

26 But what went ye out for to see? A prophet? Yea, I say unto you, and much more than a prophet.

27 This is *he,* of whom it is written, Behold, I send my messenger before thy face, which shall prepare thy way before thee.

28 For I say unto you, Among those that are born of women there is not a greater prophet than John the Baptist: but he that is least in the kingdom of God is greater than he.

29 And all the people that heard *him,* and the publicans, justified God, being baptized with the baptism of John.

30 But the Pharisees and lawyers rejected the counsel of God against themselves, being not baptized of him.

31 And the Lord said, Whereunto then shall I liken the men of this generation? and to what are they like?

32 They are like unto children sitting in the marketplace, and calling

one to another, and saying, We have
piped unto you, and ye have not
danced; we have mourned to you,
and ye have not wept.
33 For John the Baptist came neither eating bread nor drinking wine;
and ye say, He hath a devil.
34 The Son of man is come eating
and drinking; and ye say, Behold a
gluttonous man, and a winebibber,
a friend of publicans and sinners!
35 But wisdom is justified of all
her children.

Jesus' Feet Washed with Tears

36 And one of the Pharisees desired him that he would eat with
him. And he went into the Pharisee's
house, and sat down to meat.
37 And, behold, a woman in the
city, which was a sinner, when she
knew that *Jesus* sat at meat in the
Pharisee's house, brought an alabaster box of ointment,
38 And stood at his feet behind
him weeping, and began to wash
his feet with tears, and did wipe
them with the hairs of her head, and
kissed his feet, and anointed *them*
with the ointment.
39 Now when the Pharisee which
had bidden him saw *it,* he spake
within himself, saying, This man,
if he were a prophet, would have
known who and what manner of
woman *this is* that toucheth him:
for she is a sinner.
40 And Jesus answering said unto
him, Simon, I have somewhat to
say unto thee. And he saith, Master,
say on.
41 There was a certain creditor
which had two debtors: the one
owed five hundred pence, and the
other fifty.
42 And when they had nothing to
pay, he frankly forgave them both.
Tell me therefore, which of them
will love him most?
43 Simon answered and said, I
suppose that *he,* to whom he forgave most. And he said unto him,
Thou hast rightly judged.
44 And he turned to the woman,
and said unto Simon, Seest thou this
woman? I entered into thine house,
thou gavest me no water for my feet:
but she hath washed my feet with
tears, and wiped *them* with the hairs
of her head.
45 Thou gavest me no kiss: but
this woman since the time I came
in hath not ceased to kiss my feet.
46 My head with oil thou didst
not anoint: but this woman hath
anointed my feet with ointment.
47 Wherefore I say unto thee, Her
sins, which are many, are forgiven;
for she loved much: but to whom little is forgiven, *the same* loveth little.
48 And he said unto her, Thy sins
are forgiven.
49 And they that sat at meat with
him began to say within themselves,
Who is this that forgiveth sins also?
50 And he said to the woman, Thy
faith hath saved thee; go in peace.

Throughout Every City

8 And it came to pass afterward,
that he went throughout every city and village, preaching and
shewing the glad tidings of the kingdom of God: and the twelve *were*
with him,
2 And certain women, which had
been healed of evil spirits and infirmities, Mary called Magdalene, out
of whom went seven devils,
3 And Joanna the wife of Chuza
Herod's steward, and Susanna, and
many others, which ministered unto
him of their substance.
4 And when much people were
gathered together, and were come
to him out of every city, he spake by
a parable:

The Parable of the Sower

5 A sower went out to sow his
seed: and as he sowed, some fell
by the way side; and it was trodden

down, and the fowls of the air de-
voured it.
6 And some fell upon a rock; and as
soon as it was sprung up, it withered
away, because it lacked moisture.
7 And some fell among thorns;
and the thorns sprang up with it,
and choked it.
8 And other fell on good ground,
and sprang up, and bare fruit an
hundredfold. And when he had said
these things, he cried, He that hath
ears to hear, let him hear.
9 And his disciples asked him,
saying, What might this parable be?
10 And he said, Unto you it is
given to know the mysteries of the
kingdom of God: but to others in
parables; that seeing they might
not see, and hearing they might not
understand.
11 Now the parable is this: The
seed is the word of God.
12 Those by the way side are they
that hear; then cometh the devil,
and taketh away the word out of
their hearts, lest they should believe
and be saved.
13 They on the rock *are they,*
which, when they hear, receive the
word with joy; and these have no
root, which for a while believe, and
in time of temptation fall away.
14 And that which fell among
thorns are they, which, when they
have heard, go forth, and are choked
with cares and riches and pleasures
of *this* life, and bring no fruit to per-
fection.
15 But that on the good ground
are they, which in an honest and
good heart, having heard the word,
keep *it,* and bring forth fruit with
patience.

The Candle's Light

16 No man, when he hath lighted a
candle, covereth it with a vessel, or
putteth *it* under a bed; but setteth
it on a candlestick, that they which
enter in may see the light.
17 For nothing is secret, that shall
not be made manifest; neither *any
thing* hid, that shall not be known
and come abroad.
18 Take heed therefore how ye
hear: for whosoever hath, to him
shall be given; and whosoever hath
not, from him shall be taken even
that which he seemeth to have.

The Family of Jesus

19 Then came to him *his* mother
and his brethren, and could not
come at him for the press.
20 And it was told him *by certain*
which said, Thy mother and thy
brethren stand without, desiring
to see thee.
21 And he answered and said unto
them, My mother and my brethren
are these which hear the word of
God, and do it.

Jesus Calms the Waters

22 Now it came to pass on a certain
day, that he went into a ship with his
disciples: and he said unto them, Let
us go over unto the other side of the
lake. And they launched forth.
23 But as they sailed he fell asleep:
and there came down a storm of
wind on the lake; and they were
filled *with water,* and were in jeop-
ardy.
24 And they came to him, and
awoke him, saying, Master, mas-
ter, we perish. Then he arose, and
rebuked the wind and the raging
of the water: and they ceased, and
there was a calm.
25 And he said unto them, Where
is your faith? And they being afraid
wondered, saying one to another,
What manner of man is this! for he
commandeth even the winds and
water, and they obey him.

A Man Possessed with Devils

26 And they arrived at the coun-
try of the Gadarenes, which is over
against Galilee.

27 And when he went forth to land, there met him out of the city a certain man, which had devils long time, and ware no clothes, neither abode in *any* house, but in the tombs.

28 When he saw Jesus, he cried out, and fell down before him, and with a loud voice said, What have I to do with thee, Jesus, *thou* Son of God most high? I beseech thee, torment me not.

29 (For he had commanded the unclean spirit to come out of the man. For oftentimes it had caught him: and he was kept bound with chains and in fetters; and he brake the bands, and was driven of the devil into the wilderness.)

30 And Jesus asked him, saying, What is thy name? And he said, Legion: because many devils were entered into him.

31 And they besought him that he would not command them to go out into the deep.

32 And there was there an herd of many swine feeding on the mountain: and they besought him that he would suffer them to enter into them. And he suffered them.

33 Then went the devils out of the man, and entered into the swine: and the herd ran violently down a steep place into the lake, and were choked.

34 When they that fed *them* saw what was done, they fled, and went and told *it* in the city and in the country.

35 Then they went out to see what was done; and came to Jesus, and found the man, out of whom the devils were departed, sitting at the feet of Jesus, clothed, and in his right mind: and they were afraid.

36 They also which saw *it* told them by what means he that was possessed of the devils was healed.

37 Then the whole multitude of the country of the Gadarenes round about besought him to depart from them; for they were taken with great fear: and he went up into the ship, and returned back again.

38 Now the man out of whom the devils were departed besought him that he might be with him: but Jesus sent him away, saying,

39 Return to thine own house, and shew how great things God hath done unto thee. And he went his way, and published throughout the whole city how great things Jesus had done unto him.

Jairus's Daughter

40 And it came to pass, that, when Jesus was returned, the people *gladly* received him: for they were all waiting for him.

41 And, behold, there came a man named Jairus, and he was a ruler of the synagogue: and he fell down at Jesus' feet, and besought him that he would come into his house:

42 For he had one only daughter, about twelve years of age, and she lay a dying. But as he went the people thronged him.

43 And a woman having an issue of blood twelve years, which had spent all her living upon physicians, neither could be healed of any,

44 Came behind *him,* and touched the border of his garment: and immediately her issue of blood stanched.

45 And Jesus said, Who touched me? When all denied, Peter and they that were with him said, Master, the multitude throng thee and press *thee,* and sayest thou, Who touched me?

46 And Jesus said, Somebody hath touched me: for I perceive that virtue is gone out of me.

47 And when the woman saw that she was not hid, she came trembling, and falling down before him, she declared unto him before all the people for what cause she had

touched him, and how she was
healed immediately.
48 And he said unto her, Daughter,
be of good comfort: thy faith hath
made thee whole; go in peace.
49 While he yet spake, there cometh
one from the ruler of the synagogue's
house, saying to him, Thy daughter is
dead; trouble not the Master.
50 But when Jesus heard *it,* he an-
swered him, saying, Fear not: believe
only, and she shall be made whole.
51 And when he came into the
house, he suffered no man to go
in, save Peter, and James, and John,
and the father and the mother of the
maiden.
52 And all wept, and bewailed her:
but he said, Weep not; she is not
dead, but sleepeth.
53 And they laughed him to scorn,
knowing that she was dead.
54 And he put them all out, and
took her by the hand, and called,
saying, Maid, arise.
55 And her spirit came again, and
she arose straightway: and he com-
manded to give her meat.
56 And her parents were aston-
ished: but he charged them that they
should tell no man what was done.

The Twelve Sent to Preach and Heal

9 Then he called his twelve dis-
ciples together, and gave them
power and authority over all devils,
and to cure diseases.
2 And he sent them to preach the
kingdom of God, and to heal the sick.
3 And he said unto them, Take
nothing for *your* journey, neither
staves, nor scrip, neither bread, nei-
ther money; neither have two coats
apiece.
4 And whatsoever house ye enter
into, there abide, and thence depart.
5 And whosoever will not receive
you, when ye go out of that city,
shake off the very dust from your
feet for a testimony against them.
6 And they departed, and went
through the towns, preaching the
gospel, and healing every where.
7 Now Herod the tetrarch heard
of all that was done by him: and he
was perplexed, because that it was
said of some, that John was risen
from the dead;
8 And of some, that Elias had ap-
peared; and of others, that one of
the old prophets was risen again.
9 And Herod said, John have I be-
headed: but who is this, of whom I
hear such things? And he desired to
see him.

Feeding the Five Thousand

10 And the apostles, when they
were returned, told him all that they
had done. And he took them, and
went aside privately into a desert
place belonging to the city called
Bethsaida.
11 And the people, when they
knew *it,* followed him: and he re-
ceived them, and spake unto them
of the kingdom of God, and healed
them that had need of healing.
12 And when the day began to
wear away, then came the twelve,
and said unto him, Send the mul-
titude away, that they may go into
the towns and country round about,
and lodge, and get victuals: for we
are here in a desert place.
13 But he said unto them, Give ye
them to eat. And they said, We have
no more but five loaves and two
fishes; except we should go and buy
meat for all this people.
14 For they were about five thou-
sand men. And he said to his disci-
ples, Make them sit down by fifties
in a company.
15 And they did so, and made them
all sit down.
16 Then he took the five loaves
and the two fishes, and looking up
to heaven, he blessed them, and
brake, and gave to the disciples to
set before the multitude.

17 And they did eat, and were all filled: and there was taken up of fragments that remained to them twelve baskets.

18 And it came to pass, as he was alone praying, his disciples were with him: and he asked them, saying, Whom say the people that I am?

19 They answering said, John the Baptist; but some *say,* Elias; and others *say,* that one of the old prophets is risen again.

20 He said unto them, But whom say ye that I am? Peter answering said, The Christ of God.

21 And he straitly charged them, and commanded *them* to tell no man that thing;

22 Saying, The Son of man must suffer many things, and be rejected of the elders and chief priests and scribes, and be slain, and be raised the third day.

Follow Me

23 And he said to *them* all, If any *man* will come after me, let him deny himself, and take up his cross daily, and follow me.

24 For whosoever will save his life shall lose it: but whosoever will lose his life for my sake, the same shall save it.

25 For what is a man advantaged, if he gain the whole world, and lose himself, or be cast away?

26 For whosoever shall be ashamed of me and of my words, of him shall the Son of man be ashamed, when he shall come in his own glory, and *in his* Father's, and of the holy angels.

27 But I tell you of a truth, there be some standing here, which shall not taste of death, till they see the kingdom of God.

Jesus' Transfiguration

28 And it came to pass about an eight days after these sayings, he took Peter and John and James, and went up into a mountain to pray.

29 And as he prayed, the fashion of his countenance was altered, and his raiment *was* white *and* glistering.

30 And, behold, there talked with him two men, which were Moses and Elias:

31 Who appeared in glory, and spake of his decease which he should accomplish at Jerusalem.

32 But Peter and they that were with him were heavy with sleep: and when they were awake, they saw his glory, and the two men that stood with him.

33 And it came to pass, as they departed from him, Peter said unto Jesus, Master, it is good for us to be here: and let us make three tabernacles; one for thee, and one for Moses, and one for Elias: not knowing what he said.

34 While he thus spake, there came a cloud, and overshadowed them: and they feared as they entered into the cloud.

35 And there came a voice out of the cloud, saying, This is my beloved Son: hear him.

36 And when the voice was past, Jesus was found alone. And they kept *it* close, and told no man in those days any of those things which they had seen.

Jesus Heals a Possessed Boy

37 And it came to pass, that on the next day, when they were come down from the hill, much people met him.

38 And, behold, a man of the company cried out, saying, Master, I beseech thee, look upon my son: for he is mine only child.

39 And, lo, a spirit taketh him, and he suddenly crieth out; and it teareth him that he foameth again, and bruising him hardly departeth from him.

40 And I besought thy disciples to cast him out; and they could not.

41 And Jesus answering said,
O faithless and perverse generation,
how long shall I be with you, and
suffer you? Bring thy son hither.
42 And as he was yet a coming,
the devil threw him down, and tare
him. And Jesus rebuked the unclean
spirit, and healed the child, and de-
livered him again to his father.

Jesus Again Predicts His Death

43 And they were all amazed at the
mighty power of God. But while they
wondered every one at all things
which Jesus did, he said unto his
disciples,
44 Let these sayings sink down
into your ears: for the Son of man
shall be delivered into the hands of
men.
45 But they understood not this
saying, and it was hid from them,
that they perceived it not: and they
feared to ask him of that saying.

The Least to Be the Greatest

46 Then there arose a reasoning
among them, which of them should
be greatest.
47 And Jesus, perceiving the
thought of their heart, took a child,
and set him by him,
48 And said unto them, Whoso-
ever shall receive this child in my
name receiveth me: and whosoever
shall receive me receiveth him that
sent me: for he that is least among
you all, the same shall be great.
49 And John answered and said,
Master, we saw one casting out dev-
ils in thy name; and we forbad him,
because he followeth not with us.
50 And Jesus said unto him, For-
bid *him* not: for he that is not against
us is for us.

Samaritans' Rejection of Jesus

51 And it came to pass, when the
time was come that he should be
received up, he stedfastly set his
face to go to Jerusalem,
52 And sent messengers before
his face: and they went, and entered
into a village of the Samaritans, to
make ready for him.
53 And they did not receive him,
because his face was as though he
would go to Jerusalem.
54 And when his disciples James
and John saw *this,* they said, Lord,
wilt thou that we command fire to
come down from heaven, and con-
sume them, even as Elias did?
55 But he turned, and rebuked
them, and said, Ye know not what
manner of spirit ye are of.
56 For the Son of man is not come
to destroy men's lives, but to save
them. And they went to another vil-
lage.

The High Cost of Discipleship

57 And it came to pass, that, as
they went in the way, a certain *man*
said unto him, Lord, I will follow
thee whithersoever thou goest.
58 And Jesus said unto him, Foxes
have holes, and birds of the air *have*
nests; but the Son of man hath not
where to lay *his* head.
59 And he said unto another, Fol-
low me. But he said, Lord, suffer me
first to go and bury my father.
60 Jesus said unto him, Let the
dead bury their dead: but go thou
and preach the kingdom of God.
61 And another also said, Lord,
I will follow thee; but let me first
go bid them farewell, which are at
home at my house.
62 And Jesus said unto him, No
man, having put his hand to the
plough, and looking back, is fit for
the kingdom of God.

Seventy Labourers Sent Forth

10 After these things the Lord
appointed other seventy also,
and sent them two and two before
his face into every city and place,
whither he himself would come.
2 Therefore said he unto them, The

harvest truly *is* great, but the labourers *are* few: pray ye therefore the Lord of the harvest, that he would send forth labourers into his harvest.

3 Go your ways: behold, I send you forth as lambs among wolves.

4 Carry neither purse, nor scrip, nor shoes: and salute no man by the way.

5 And into whatsoever house ye enter, first say, Peace *be* to this house.

6 And if the son of peace be there, your peace shall rest upon it: if not, it shall turn to you again.

7 And in the same house remain, eating and drinking such things as they give: for the labourer is worthy of his hire. Go not from house to house.

8 And into whatsoever city ye enter, and they receive you, eat such things as are set before you:

9 And heal the sick that are therein, and say unto them, The kingdom of God is come nigh unto you.

10 But into whatsoever city ye enter, and they receive you not, go your ways out into the streets of the same, and say,

11 Even the very dust of your city, which cleaveth on us, we do wipe off against you: notwithstanding be ye sure of this, that the kingdom of God is come nigh unto you.

12 But I say unto you, that it shall be more tolerable in that day for Sodom, than for that city.

13 Woe unto thee, Chorazin! woe unto thee, Bethsaida! for if the mighty works had been done in Tyre and Sidon, which have been done in you, they had a great while ago repented, sitting in sackcloth and ashes.

14 But it shall be more tolerable for Tyre and Sidon at the judgment, than for you.

15 And thou, Capernaum, which art exalted to heaven, shalt be thrust down to hell.

16 He that heareth you heareth me; and he that despiseth you despiseth me; and he that despiseth me despiseth him that sent me.

The Labourers' Joyful Return

17 And the seventy returned again with joy, saying, Lord, even the devils are subject unto us through thy name.

18 And he said unto them, I beheld Satan as lightning fall from heaven.

19 Behold, I give unto you power to tread on serpents and scorpions, and over all the power of the enemy: and nothing shall by any means hurt you.

20 Notwithstanding in this rejoice not, that the spirits are subject unto you; but rather rejoice, because your names are written in heaven.

Jesus Rejoices in the Spirit

21 In that hour Jesus rejoiced in spirit, and said, I thank thee, O Father, Lord of heaven and earth, that thou hast hid these things from the wise and prudent, and hast revealed them unto babes: even so, Father; for so it seemed good in thy sight.

22 All things are delivered to me of my Father: and no man knoweth who the Son is, but the Father; and who the Father is, but the Son, and *he* to whom the Son will reveal *him.*

23 And he turned him unto *his* disciples, and said privately, Blessed *are* the eyes which see the things that ye see:

24 For I tell you, that many prophets and kings have desired to see those things which ye see, and have not seen *them;* and to hear those things which ye hear, and have not heard *them.*

The Parable of the Good Samaritan

25 And, behold, a certain lawyer stood up, and tempted him, saying, Master, what shall I do to inherit eternal life?

26 He said unto him, What is writ-
ten in the law? how readest thou?
27 And he answering said, Thou
shalt love the Lord thy God with all
thy heart, and with all thy soul, and
with all thy strength, and with all thy
mind; and thy neighbour as thyself.
28 And he said unto him, Thou
hast answered right: this do, and
thou shalt live.
29 But he, willing to justify him-
self, said unto Jesus, And who is my
neighbour?
30 And Jesus answering said, A
certain *man* went down from Je-
rusalem to Jericho, and fell among
thieves, which stripped him of his
raiment, and wounded *him,* and
departed, leaving *him* half dead.
31 And by chance there came
down a certain priest that way: and
when he saw him, he passed by on
the other side.
32 And likewise a Levite, when he
was at the place, came and looked *on*
him, and passed by on the other side.
33 But a certain Samaritan, as he
journeyed, came where he was: and
when he saw him, he had compas-
sion *on him,*
34 And went to *him,* and bound
up his wounds, pouring in oil and
wine, and set him on his own beast,
and brought him to an inn, and took
care of him.
35 And on the morrow when he
departed, he took out two pence,
and gave *them* to the host, and said
unto him, Take care of him; and
whatsoever thou spendest more,
when I come again, I will repay thee.
36 Which now of these three,
thinkest thou, was neighbour unto
him that fell among the thieves?
37 And he said, He that shewed
mercy on him. Then said Jesus unto
him, Go, and do thou likewise.

Martha and Mary

38 Now it came to pass, as they
went, that he entered into a certain
village: and a certain woman named
Martha received him into her house.
39 And she had a sister called
Mary, which also sat at Jesus' feet,
and heard his word.
40 But Martha was cumbered
about much serving, and came to
him, and said, Lord, dost thou not
care that my sister hath left me to
serve alone? bid her therefore that
she help me.
41 And Jesus answered and said
unto her, Martha, Martha, thou art
careful and troubled about many
things:
42 But one thing is needful: and
Mary hath chosen that good part,
which shall not be taken away from
her.

The Model Prayer

11 And it came to pass, that, as
he was praying in a certain
place, when he ceased, one of his
disciples said unto him, Lord, teach
us to pray, as John also taught his
disciples.
2 And he said unto them, When
ye pray, say, Our Father which art in
heaven, Hallowed be thy name. Thy
kingdom come. Thy will be done, as
in heaven, so in earth.
3 Give us day by day our daily
bread.
4 And forgive us our sins; for we
also forgive every one that is in-
debted to us. And lead us not into
temptation; but deliver us from evil.
5 And he said unto them, Which of
you shall have a friend, and shall go
unto him at midnight, and say unto
him, Friend, lend me three loaves;
6 For a friend of mine in his jour-
ney is come to me, and I have noth-
ing to set before him?
7 And he from within shall answer
and say, Trouble me not: the door
is now shut, and my children are
with me in bed; I cannot rise and
give thee.
8 I say unto you, Though he will

not rise and give him, because he
is his friend, yet because of his im-
portunity he will rise and give him
as many as he needeth.
9 And I say unto you, Ask, and it
shall be given you; seek, and ye shall
find; knock, and it shall be opened
unto you.
10 For every one that asketh re-
ceiveth; and he that seeketh findeth;
and to him that knocketh it shall be
opened.
11 If a son shall ask bread of any
of you that is a father, will he give
him a stone? or if *he ask* a fish, will
he for a fish give him a serpent?
12 Or if he shall ask an egg, will he
offer him a scorpion?
13 If ye then, being evil, know how
to give good gifts unto your chil-
dren: how much more shall *your*
heavenly Father give the Holy Spirit
to them that ask him?

Jesus Accused of Evil

14 And he was casting out a devil,
and it was dumb. And it came to
pass, when the devil was gone out,
the dumb spake; and the people
wondered.
15 But some of them said, He
casteth out devils through Beelze-
bub the chief of the devils.
16 And others, tempting *him,*
sought of him a sign from heaven.

A House Divided Cannot Stand

17 But he, knowing their thoughts,
said unto them, Every kingdom di-
vided against itself is brought to
desolation; and a house *divided*
against a house falleth.
18 If Satan also be divided against
himself, how shall his kingdom
stand? because ye say that I cast
out devils through Beelzebub.
19 And if I by Beelzebub cast out
devils, by whom do your sons cast
them out? therefore shall they be
your judges.
20 But if I with the finger of God
cast out devils, no doubt the king-
dom of God is come upon you.
21 When a strong man armed
keepeth his palace, his goods are
in peace:
22 But when a stronger than he
shall come upon him, and over-
come him, he taketh from him all
his armour wherein he trusted, and
divideth his spoils.
23 He that is not with me is
against me: and he that gathereth
not with me scattereth.
24 When the unclean spirit is gone
out of a man, he walketh through
dry places, seeking rest; and finding
none, he saith, I will return unto my
house whence I came out.
25 And when he cometh, he find-
eth *it* swept and garnished.
26 Then goeth he, and taketh *to
him* seven other spirits more wicked
than himself; and they enter in, and
dwell there: and the last *state* of that
man is worse than the first.
27 And it came to pass, as he spake
these things, a certain woman of the
company lifted up her voice, and
said unto him, Blessed *is* the womb
that bare thee, and the paps which
thou hast sucked.
28 But he said, Yea rather, blessed
are they that hear the word of God,
and keep it.

Jonas and the Son of Man

29 And when the people were
gathered thick together, he began
to say, This is an evil generation:
they seek a sign; and there shall no
sign be given it, but the sign of Jonas
the prophet.
30 For as Jonas was a sign unto
the Ninevites, so shall also the Son
of man be to this generation.
31 The queen of the south shall
rise up in the judgment with the
men of this generation, and con-
demn them: for she came from the
utmost parts of the earth to hear the

wisdom of Solomon; and, behold, a greater than Solomon *is* here.

32 The men of Nineve shall rise up in the judgment with this generation, and shall condemn it: for they repented at the preaching of Jonas; and, behold, a greater than Jonas *is* here.

The Light of the Body

33 No man, when he hath lighted a candle, putteth *it* in a secret place, neither under a bushel, but on a candlestick, that they which come in may see the light.

34 The light of the body is the eye: therefore when thine eye is single, thy whole body also is full of light; but when *thine eye* is evil, thy body also *is* full of darkness.

35 Take heed therefore that the light which is in thee be not darkness.

36 If thy whole body therefore *be* full of light, having no part dark, the whole shall be full of light, as when the bright shining of a candle doth give thee light.

Jesus Rebukes the Pharisees

37 And as he spake, a certain Pharisee besought him to dine with him: and he went in, and sat down to meat.

38 And when the Pharisee saw *it,* he marvelled that he had not first washed before dinner.

39 And the Lord said unto him, Now do ye Pharisees make clean the outside of the cup and the platter; but your inward part is full of ravening and wickedness.

40 *Ye* fools, did not he that made that which is without make that which is within also?

41 But rather give alms of such things as ye have; and, behold, all things are clean unto you.

42 But woe unto you, Pharisees! for ye tithe mint and rue and all manner of herbs, and pass over judgment and the love of God: these ought ye to have done, and not to leave the other undone.

43 Woe unto you, Pharisees! for ye love the uppermost seats in the synagogues, and greetings in the markets.

44 Woe unto you, scribes and Pharisees, hypocrites! for ye are as graves which appear not, and the men that walk over *them* are not aware *of them.*

Jesus Rebukes Lawyers

45 Then answered one of the lawyers, and said unto him, Master, thus saying thou reproachest us also.

46 And he said, Woe unto you also, *ye* lawyers! for ye lade men with burdens grievous to be borne, and ye yourselves touch not the burdens with one of your fingers.

47 Woe unto you! for ye build the sepulchres of the prophets, and your fathers killed them.

48 Truly ye bear witness that ye allow the deeds of your fathers: for they indeed killed them, and ye build their sepulchres.

49 Therefore also said the wisdom of God, I will send them prophets and apostles, and *some* of them they shall slay and persecute:

50 That the blood of all the prophets, which was shed from the foundation of the world, may be required of this generation;

51 From the blood of Abel unto the blood of Zacharias, which perished between the altar and the temple: verily I say unto you, It shall be required of this generation.

52 Woe unto you, lawyers! for ye have taken away the key of knowledge: ye entered not in yourselves, and them that were entering in ye hindered.

53 And as he said these things unto them, the scribes and the Pharisees began to urge *him* vehemently, and to provoke him to speak of many things:

54 Laying wait for him, and seek-
ing to catch something out of his
mouth, that they might accuse him.

Beware of Hypocrisy

12 In the mean time, when there
were gathered together an
innumerable multitude of people,
insomuch that they trode one upon
another, he began to say unto his
disciples first of all, Beware ye of
the leaven of the Pharisees, which
is hypocrisy.
2 For there is nothing covered,
that shall not be revealed; neither
hid, that shall not be known.
3 Therefore whatsoever ye have
spoken in darkness shall be heard
in the light; and that which ye have
spoken in the ear in closets shall be
proclaimed upon the housetops.

Fear the Power of God

4 And I say unto you my friends,
Be not afraid of them that kill the
body, and after that have no more
that they can do.
5 But I will forewarn you whom ye
shall fear: Fear him, which after he
hath killed hath power to cast into
hell; yea, I say unto you, Fear him.
6 Are not five sparrows sold for
two farthings, and not one of them
is forgotten before God?
7 But even the very hairs of your
head are all numbered. Fear not
therefore: ye are of more value than
many sparrows.
8 Also I say unto you, Whosoever
shall confess me before men, him
shall the Son of man also confess
before the angels of God:
9 But he that denieth me before
men shall be denied before the an-
gels of God.
10 And whosoever shall speak a
word against the Son of man, it shall
be forgiven him: but unto him that
blasphemeth against the Holy Ghost
it shall not be forgiven.
11 And when they bring you unto
the synagogues, and *unto* mag-
istrates, and powers, take ye no
thought how or what thing ye shall
answer, or what ye shall say:
12 For the Holy Ghost shall teach
you in the same hour what ye ought
to say.

Beware of Covetousness

13 And one of the company said
unto him, Master, speak to my
brother, that he divide the inheri-
tance with me.
14 And he said unto him, Man, who
made me a judge or a divider over
you?
15 And he said unto them, Take
heed, and beware of covetousness:
for a man's life consisteth not in the
abundance of the things which he
possesseth.
16 And he spake a parable unto
them, saying, The ground of a certain
rich man brought forth plentifully:
17 And he thought within himself,
saying, What shall I do, because I
have no room where to bestow my
fruits?
18 And he said, This will I do: I
will pull down my barns, and build
greater; and there will I bestow all
my fruits and my goods.
19 And I will say to my soul, Soul,
thou hast much goods laid up for
many years; take thine ease, eat,
drink, *and* be merry.
20 But God said unto him, *Thou*
fool, this night thy soul shall be
required of thee: then whose shall
those things be, which thou hast
provided?
21 So *is* he that layeth up treasure
for himself, and is not rich toward
God.

Do Not Worry or Be Fearful

22 And he said unto his disciples,
Therefore I say unto you, Take no
thought for your life, what ye shall
eat; neither for the body, what ye
shall put on.

23 The life is more than meat, and the body *is more* than raiment.

24 Consider the ravens: for they neither sow nor reap; which neither have storehouse nor barn; and God feedeth them: how much more are ye better than the fowls?

25 And which of you with taking thought can add to his stature one cubit?

26 If ye then be not able to do that thing which is least, why take ye thought for the rest?

27 Consider the lilies how they grow: they toil not, they spin not; and yet I say unto you, that Solomon in all his glory was not arrayed like one of these.

28 If then God so clothe the grass, which is to day in the field, and to morrow is cast into the oven; how much more *will he clothe* you, O ye of little faith?

29 And seek not ye what ye shall eat, or what ye shall drink, neither be ye of doubtful mind.

30 For all these things do the nations of the world seek after: and your Father knoweth that ye have need of these things.

31 But rather seek ye the kingdom of God; and all these things shall be added unto you.

32 Fear not, little flock; for it is your Father's good pleasure to give you the kingdom.

33 Sell that ye have, and give alms; provide yourselves bags which wax not old, a treasure in the heavens that faileth not, where no thief approacheth, neither moth corrupteth.

34 For where your treasure is, there will your heart be also.

Be Watchful

35 Let your loins be girded about, and *your* lights burning;

36 And ye yourselves like unto men that wait for their lord, when he will return from the wedding; that when he cometh and knocketh, they may open unto him immediately.

37 Blessed *are* those servants, whom the lord when he cometh shall find watching: verily I say unto you, that he shall gird himself, and make them to sit down to meat, and will come forth and serve them.

38 And if he shall come in the second watch, or come in the third watch, and find *them* so, blessed are those servants.

39 And this know, that if the goodman of the house had known what hour the thief would come, he would have watched, and not have suffered his house to be broken through.

40 Be ye therefore ready also: for the Son of man cometh at an hour when ye think not.

41 Then Peter said unto him, Lord, speakest thou this parable unto us, or even to all?

42 And the Lord said, Who then is that faithful and wise steward, whom *his* lord shall make ruler over his household, to give *them their* portion of meat in due season?

43 Blessed *is* that servant, whom his lord when he cometh shall find so doing.

44 Of a truth I say unto you, that he will make him ruler over all that he hath.

45 But and if that servant say in his heart, My lord delayeth his coming; and shall begin to beat the menservants and maidens, and to eat and drink, and to be drunken;

46 The lord of that servant will come in a day when he looketh not for *him,* and at an hour when he is not aware, and will cut him in sunder, and will appoint him his portion with the unbelievers.

47 And that servant, which knew his lord's will, and prepared not *himself,* neither did according to his will, shall be beaten with many *stripes.*

48 But he that knew not, and did

commit things worthy of stripes, shall be beaten with few *stripes.* For unto whomsoever much is given, of him shall be much required: and to whom men have committed much, of him they will ask the more.

49 I am come to send fire on the earth; and what will I, if it be already kindled?

50 But I have a baptism to be baptized with; and how am I straitened till it be accomplished!

51 Suppose ye that I am come to give peace on earth? I tell you, Nay; but rather division:

52 For from henceforth there shall be five in one house divided, three against two, and two against three.

53 The father shall be divided against the son, and the son against the father; the mother against the daughter, and the daughter against the mother; the mother in law against her daughter in law, and the daughter in law against her mother in law.

Discerning the Times

54 And he said also to the people, When ye see a cloud rise out of the west, straightway ye say, There cometh a shower; and so it is.

55 And when *ye see* the south wind blow, ye say, There will be heat; and it cometh to pass.

56 *Ye* hypocrites, ye can discern the face of the sky and of the earth; but how is it that ye do not discern this time?

57 Yea, and why even of yourselves judge ye not what is right?

58 When thou goest with thine adversary to the magistrate, *as thou art* in the way, give diligence that thou mayest be delivered from him; lest he hale thee to the judge, and the judge deliver thee to the officer, and the officer cast thee into prison.

59 I tell thee, thou shalt not depart thence, till thou hast paid the very last mite.

Repent or Perish

13 There were present at that season some that told him of the Galilaeans, whose blood Pilate had mingled with their sacrifices.

2 And Jesus answering said unto them, Suppose ye that these Galilaeans were sinners above all the Galilaeans, because they suffered such things?

3 I tell you, Nay: but, except ye repent, ye shall all likewise perish.

4 Or those eighteen, upon whom the tower in Siloam fell, and slew them, think ye that they were sinners above all men that dwelt in Jerusalem?

5 I tell you, Nay: but, except ye repent, ye shall all likewise perish.

6 He spake also this parable; A certain *man* had a fig tree planted in his vineyard; and he came and sought fruit thereon, and found none.

7 Then said he unto the dresser of his vineyard, Behold, these three years I come seeking fruit on this fig tree, and find none: cut it down; why cumbereth it the ground?

8 And he answering said unto him, Lord, let it alone this year also, till I shall dig about it, and dung *it:*

9 And if it bear fruit, *well:* and if not, *then* after that thou shalt cut it down.

A Woman with Infirmity Healed

10 And he was teaching in one of the synagogues on the sabbath.

11 And, behold, there was a woman which had a spirit of infirmity eighteen years, and was bowed together, and could in no wise lift up *herself.*

12 And when Jesus saw her, he called *her to him,* and said unto her, Woman, thou art loosed from thine infirmity.

13 And he laid *his* hands on her: and immediately she was made straight, and glorified God.

14 And the ruler of the synagogue
answered with indignation, because
that Jesus had healed on the sab-
bath day, and said unto the people,
There are six days in which men
ought to work: in them therefore
come and be healed, and not on the
sabbath day.
15 The Lord then answered him,
and said, *Thou* hypocrite, doth not
each one of you on the sabbath loose
his ox or *his* ass from the stall, and
lead *him* away to watering?
16 And ought not this woman, be-
ing a daughter of Abraham, whom
Satan hath bound, lo, these eighteen
years, be loosed from this bond on
the sabbath day?
17 And when he had said these
things, all his adversaries were
ashamed: and all the people rejoiced
for all the glorious things that were
done by him.

The Kingdom of God

18 Then said he, Unto what is the
kingdom of God like? and where-
unto shall I resemble it?
19 It is like a grain of mustard seed,
which a man took, and cast into his
garden; and it grew, and waxed a
great tree; and the fowls of the air
lodged in the branches of it.
20 And again he said, Whereunto
shall I liken the kingdom of God?
21 It is like leaven, which a woman
took and hid in three measures of
meal, till the whole was leavened.

The Strait Gate

22 And he went through the cities
and villages, teaching, and journey-
ing toward Jerusalem.
23 Then said one unto him, Lord,
are there few that be saved? And he
said unto them,
24 Strive to enter in at the strait
gate: for many, I say unto you, will
seek to enter in, and shall not be
able.
25 When once the master of the
house is risen up, and hath shut
to the door, and ye begin to stand
without, and to knock at the door,
saying, Lord, Lord, open unto us;
and he shall answer and say unto
you, I know you not whence ye are:
26 Then shall ye begin to say, We
have eaten and drunk in thy pres-
ence, and thou hast taught in our
streets.
27 But he shall say, I tell you, I
know you not whence ye are; depart
from me, all *ye* workers of iniquity.
28 There shall be weeping and
gnashing of teeth, when ye shall see
Abraham, and Isaac, and Jacob, and
all the prophets, in the kingdom of
God, and you *yourselves* thrust out.
29 And they shall come from the
east, and *from* the west, and from
the north, and *from* the south, and
shall sit down in the kingdom of
God.
30 And, behold, there are last
which shall be first, and there are
first which shall be last.

Jerusalem's Desolate House

31 The same day there came cer-
tain of the Pharisees, saying unto
him, Get thee out, and depart hence:
for Herod will kill thee.
32 And he said unto them, Go ye,
and tell that fox, Behold, I cast out
devils, and I do cures to day and to
morrow, and the third *day* I shall
be perfected.
33 Nevertheless I must walk to
day, and to morrow, and the *day*
following: for it cannot be that a
prophet perish out of Jerusalem.
34 O Jerusalem, Jerusalem, which
killest the prophets, and stonest
them that are sent unto thee; how
often would I have gathered thy
children together, as a hen *doth*
gather her brood under *her* wings,
and ye would not!
35 Behold, your house is left
unto you desolate: and verily I say
unto you, Ye shall not see me, until

the time come when ye shall say, Blessed *is* he that cometh in the name of the Lord.

Teachings on Humility

14 And it came to pass, as he went
into the house of one of the
chief Pharisees to eat bread on the
sabbath day, that they watched him.
2 And, behold, there was a cer-
tain man before him which had the
dropsy.
3 And Jesus answering spake unto
the lawyers and Pharisees, saying, Is
it lawful to heal on the sabbath day?
4 And they held their peace. And
he took *him,* and healed him, and
let him go;
5 And answered them, saying,
Which of you shall have an ass or
an ox fallen into a pit, and will not
straightway pull him out on the sab-
bath day?
6 And they could not answer him
again to these things.
7 And he put forth a parable to
those which were bidden, when he
marked how they chose out the chief
rooms; saying unto them,
8 When thou art bidden of any
man to a wedding, sit not down in
the highest room; lest a more hon-
ourable man than thou be bidden
of him;
9 And he that bade thee and him
come and say to thee, Give this man
place; and thou begin with shame
to take the lowest room.
10 But when thou art bidden, go
and sit down in the lowest room;
that when he that bade thee com-
eth, he may say unto thee, Friend,
go up higher: then shalt thou have
worship in the presence of them
that sit at meat with thee.
11 For whosoever exalteth himself
shall be abased; and he that hum-
bleth himself shall be exalted.
12 Then said he also to him that
bade him, When thou makest a din-
ner or a supper, call not thy friends,
nor thy brethren, neither thy kins-
men, nor *thy* rich neighbours; lest
they also bid thee again, and a rec-
ompence be made thee.
13 But when thou makest a feast,
call the poor, the maimed, the lame,
the blind:
14 And thou shalt be blessed; for
they cannot recompense thee: for
thou shalt be recompensed at the
resurrection of the just.

A Great Supper

15 And when one of them that sat
at meat with him heard these things,
he said unto him, Blessed *is* he that
shall eat bread in the kingdom of
God.
16 Then said he unto him, A certain
man made a great supper, and bade
many:
17 And sent his servant at supper
time to say to them that were bid-
den, Come; for all things are now
ready.
18 And they all with one *consent*
began to make excuse. The first said
unto him, I have bought a piece of
ground, and I must needs go and
see it: I pray thee have me excused.
19 And another said, I have bought
five yoke of oxen, and I go to prove
them: I pray thee have me excused.
20 And another said, I have mar-
ried a wife, and therefore I cannot
come.
21 So that servant came, and
shewed his lord these things. Then
the master of the house being angry
said to his servant, Go out quickly
into the streets and lanes of the city,
and bring in hither the poor, and the
maimed, and the halt, and the blind.
22 And the servant said, Lord, it
is done as thou hast commanded,
and yet there is room.
23 And the lord said unto the ser-
vant, Go out into the highways and
hedges, and compel *them* to come
in, that my house may be filled.
24 For I say unto you, That none

of those men which were bidden
shall taste of my supper.

The Cost of Discipleship

25 And there went great multi-
tudes with him: and he turned, and
said unto them,
26 If any *man* come to me, and
hate not his father, and mother, and
wife, and children, and brethren,
and sisters, yea, and his own life
also, he cannot be my disciple.
27 And whosoever doth not bear
his cross, and come after me, cannot
be my disciple.
28 For which of you, intending to
build a tower, sitteth not down first,
and counteth the cost, whether he
have *sufficient* to finish *it?*
29 Lest haply, after he hath laid
the foundation, and is not able to
finish *it,* all that behold *it* begin to
mock him,
30 Saying, This man began to
build, and was not able to finish.
31 Or what king, going to make
war against another king, sitteth not
down first, and consulteth whether
he be able with ten thousand to
meet him that cometh against him
with twenty thousand?
32 Or else, while the other is yet
a great way off, he sendeth an am-
bassage, and desireth conditions of
peace.
33 So likewise, whosoever he be
of you that forsaketh not all that he
hath, he cannot be my disciple.
34 Salt *is* good: but if the salt have
lost his savour, wherewith shall it
be seasoned?
35 It is neither fit for the land, nor
yet for the dunghill; *but* men cast
it out. He that hath ears to hear, let
him hear.

A Lost Sheep, a Lost Coin, and a Lost Son

15 Then drew near unto him all
the publicans and sinners for
to hear him.
2 And the Pharisees and scribes
murmured, saying, This man re-
ceiveth sinners, and eateth with
them.
3 And he spake this parable unto
them, saying,
4 What man of you, having an
hundred sheep, if he lose one of
them, doth not leave the ninety and
nine in the wilderness, and go after
that which is lost, until he find it?
5 And when he hath found *it,* he
layeth *it* on his shoulders, rejoicing.
6 And when he cometh home,
he calleth together *his* friends and
neighbours, saying unto them, Re-
joice with me; for I have found my
sheep which was lost.
7 I say unto you, that likewise joy
shall be in heaven over one sinner
that repenteth, more than over
ninety and nine just persons, which
need no repentance.
8 Either what woman having ten
pieces of silver, if she lose one piece,
doth not light a candle, and sweep
the house, and seek diligently till
she find *it?*
9 And when she hath found *it,* she
calleth *her* friends and *her* neigh-
bours together, saying, Rejoice with
me; for I have found the piece which
I had lost.
10 Likewise, I say unto you, there
is joy in the presence of the angels of
God over one sinner that repenteth.
11 And he said, A certain man had
two sons:
12 And the younger of them said
to *his* father, Father, give me the
portion of goods that falleth *to me.*
And he divided unto them *his* living.
13 And not many days after the
younger son gathered all together,
and took his journey into a far coun-
try, and there wasted his substance
with riotous living.
14 And when he had spent all,
there arose a mighty famine in that
land; and he began to be in want.
15 And he went and joined him-

self to a citizen of that country; and
he sent him into his fields to feed
swine.
16 And he would fain have filled
his belly with the husks that the
swine did eat: and no man gave
unto him.
17 And when he came to himself,
he said, How many hired servants of
my father's have bread enough and
to spare, and I perish with hunger!
18 I will arise and go to my father,
and will say unto him, Father, I have
sinned against heaven, and before
thee,
19 And am no more worthy to be
called thy son: make me as one of
thy hired servants.
20 And he arose, and came to his
father. But when he was yet a great
way off, his father saw him, and had
compassion, and ran, and fell on his
neck, and kissed him.
21 And the son said unto him, Father,
I have sinned against heaven,
and in thy sight, and am no more
worthy to be called thy son.
22 But the father said to his servants,
Bring forth the best robe, and
put *it* on him; and put a ring on his
hand, and shoes on *his* feet:
23 And bring hither the fatted
calf, and kill *it;* and let us eat, and
be merry:
24 For this my son was dead, and
is alive again; he was lost, and is
found. And they began to be merry.
25 Now his elder son was in the
field: and as he came and drew nigh
to the house, he heard musick and
dancing.
26 And he called one of the servants,
and asked what these things
meant.
27 And he said unto him, Thy
brother is come; and thy father hath
killed the fatted calf, because he
hath received him safe and sound.
28 And he was angry, and would
not go in: therefore came his father
out, and intreated him.
29 And he answering said to *his*
father, Lo, these many years do I
serve thee, neither transgressed I
at any time thy commandment: and
yet thou never gavest me a kid, that I
might make merry with my friends:
30 But as soon as this thy son was
come, which hath devoured thy living
with harlots, thou hast killed for
him the fatted calf.
31 And he said unto him, Son,
thou art ever with me, and all that
I have is thine.
32 It was meet that we should
make merry, and be glad: for this
thy brother was dead, and is alive
again; and was lost, and is found.

An Unjust Steward

16 And he said also unto his disciples,
There was a certain rich
man, which had a steward; and the
same was accused unto him that he
had wasted his goods.
2 And he called him, and said
unto him, How is it that I hear this
of thee? give an account of thy stewardship;
for thou mayest be no longer
steward.
3 Then the steward said within
himself, What shall I do? for my
lord taketh away from me the stewardship:
I cannot dig; to beg I am
ashamed.
4 I am resolved what to do, that,
when I am put out of the stewardship,
they may receive me into their
houses.
5 So he called every one of his
lord's debtors *unto him,* and said
unto the first, How much owest
thou unto my lord?
6 And he said, An hundred measures
of oil. And he said unto him,
Take thy bill, and sit down quickly,
and write fifty.
7 Then said he to another, And
how much owest thou? And he said,
An hundred measures of wheat. And
he said unto him, Take thy bill, and
write fourscore.

8 And the lord commended the unjust steward, because he had done wisely: for the children of this world are in their generation wiser than the children of light.

9 And I say unto you, Make to yourselves friends of the mammon of unrighteousness; that, when ye fail, they may receive you into everlasting habitations.

10 He that is faithful in that which is least is faithful also in much: and he that is unjust in the least is unjust also in much.

11 If therefore ye have not been faithful in the unrighteous mammon, who will commit to your trust the true *riches?*

12 And if ye have not been faithful in that which is another man's, who shall give you that which is your own?

13 No servant can serve two masters: for either he will hate the one, and love the other; or else he will hold to the one, and despise the other. Ye cannot serve God and mammon.

God Knows the Heart

14 And the Pharisees also, who were covetous, heard all these things: and they derided him.

15 And he said unto them, Ye are they which justify yourselves before men; but God knoweth your hearts: for that which is highly esteemed among men is abomination in the sight of God.

16 The law and the prophets *were* until John: since that time the kingdom of God is preached, and every man presseth into it.

17 And it is easier for heaven and earth to pass, than one tittle of the law to fail.

18 Whosoever putteth away his wife, and marrieth another, committeth adultery: and whosoever marrieth her that is put away from *her* husband committeth adultery.

The Rich Man and the Beggar

19 There was a certain rich man, which was clothed in purple and fine linen, and fared sumptuously every day:

20 And there was a certain beggar named Lazarus, which was laid at his gate, full of sores,

21 And desiring to be fed with the crumbs which fell from the rich man's table: moreover the dogs came and licked his sores.

22 And it came to pass, that the beggar died, and was carried by the angels into Abraham's bosom: the rich man also died, and was buried;

23 And in hell he lift up his eyes, being in torments, and seeth Abraham afar off, and Lazarus in his bosom.

24 And he cried and said, Father Abraham, have mercy on me, and send Lazarus, that he may dip the tip of his finger in water, and cool my tongue; for I am tormented in this flame.

25 But Abraham said, Son, remember that thou in thy lifetime receivedst thy good things, and likewise Lazarus evil things: but now he is comforted, and thou art tormented.

26 And beside all this, between us and you there is a great gulf fixed: so that they which would pass from hence to you cannot; neither can they pass to us, that *would come* from thence.

27 Then he said, I pray thee therefore, father, that thou wouldest send him to my father's house:

28 For I have five brethren; that he may testify unto them, lest they also come into this place of torment.

29 Abraham saith unto him, They have Moses and the prophets; let them hear them.

30 And he said, Nay, father Abraham: but if one went unto them from the dead, they will repent.

31 And he said unto him, If they hear not Moses and the prophets, neither will they be persuaded, though one rose from the dead.

Offences Will Come

17 Then said he unto the disciples, It is impossible but that offences will come: but woe *unto him,* through whom they come!

2 It were better for him that a millstone were hanged about his neck, and he cast into the sea, than that he should offend one of these little ones.

3 Take heed to yourselves: If thy brother trespass against thee, rebuke him; and if he repent, forgive him.

4 And if he trespass against thee seven times in a day, and seven times in a day turn again to thee, saying, I repent; thou shalt forgive him.

5 And the apostles said unto the Lord, Increase our faith.

6 And the Lord said, If ye had faith as a grain of mustard seed, ye might say unto this sycamine tree, Be thou plucked up by the root, and be thou planted in the sea; and it should obey you.

7 But which of you, having a servant plowing or feeding cattle, will say unto him by and by, when he is come from the field, Go and sit down to meat?

8 And will not rather say unto him, Make ready wherewith I may sup, and gird thyself, and serve me, till I have eaten and drunken; and afterward thou shalt eat and drink?

9 Doth he thank that servant because he did the things that were commanded him? I trow not.

10 So likewise ye, when ye shall have done all those things which are commanded you, say, We are unprofitable servants: we have done that which was our duty to do.

Jesus Heals Ten Lepers

11 And it came to pass, as he went to Jerusalem, that he passed through the midst of Samaria and Galilee.

12 And as he entered into a certain village, there met him ten men that were lepers, which stood afar off:

13 And they lifted up *their* voices, and said, Jesus, Master, have mercy on us.

14 And when he saw *them,* he said unto them, Go shew yourselves unto the priests. And it came to pass, that, as they went, they were cleansed.

15 And one of them, when he saw that he was healed, turned back, and with a loud voice glorified God,

16 And fell down on *his* face at his feet, giving him thanks: and he was a Samaritan.

17 And Jesus answering said, Were there not ten cleansed? but where *are* the nine?

18 There are not found that returned to give glory to God, save this stranger.

19 And he said unto him, Arise, go thy way: thy faith hath made thee whole.

Teachings on God's Kingdom

20 And when he was demanded of the Pharisees, when the kingdom of God should come, he answered them and said, The kingdom of God cometh not with observation:

21 Neither shall they say, Lo here! or, lo there! for, behold, the kingdom of God is within you.

22 And he said unto the disciples, The days will come, when ye shall desire to see one of the days of the Son of man, and ye shall not see *it.*

23 And they shall say to you, See here; or, see there: go not after *them,* nor follow *them.*

24 For as the lightning, that lighteneth out of the one *part* under heaven, shineth unto the other *part* under heaven; so shall also the Son of man be in his day.

25 But first must he suffer many
things, and be rejected of this gen-
eration.
26 And as it was in the days of Noe,
so shall it be also in the days of the
Son of man.
27 They did eat, they drank, they
married wives, they were given in
marriage, until the day that Noe
entered into the ark, and the flood
came, and destroyed them all.
28 Likewise also as it was in the
days of Lot; they did eat, they drank,
they bought, they sold, they planted,
they builded;
29 But the same day that Lot went
out of Sodom it rained fire and brim-
stone from heaven, and destroyed
them all.
30 Even thus shall it be in the day
when the Son of man is revealed.
31 In that day, he which shall be
upon the housetop, and his stuff in
the house, let him not come down
to take it away: and he that is in the
field, let him likewise not return back.
32 Remember Lot's wife.
33 Whosoever shall seek to save
his life shall lose it; and whosoever
shall lose his life shall preserve it.
34 I tell you, in that night there
shall be two *men* in one bed; the
one shall be taken, and the other
shall be left.
35 Two *women* shall be grinding
together; the one shall be taken, and
the other left.
36 Two *men* shall be in the field;
the one shall be taken, and the other
left.
37 And they answered and said
unto him, Where, Lord? And he said
unto them, Wheresoever the body *is,*
thither will the eagles be gathered
together.

God Avenges His Own

18 And he spake a parable unto
them *to this end,* that men
ought always to pray, and not to
faint;
2 Saying, There was in a city a
judge, which feared not God, nei-
ther regarded man:
3 And there was a widow in that
city; and she came unto him, saying,
Avenge me of mine adversary.
4 And he would not for a while:
but afterward he said within him-
self, Though I fear not God, nor re-
gard man;
5 Yet because this widow trou-
bleth me, I will avenge her, lest by
her continual coming she weary me.
6 And the Lord said, Hear what
the unjust judge saith.
7 And shall not God avenge his
own elect, which cry day and night
unto him, though he bear long with
them?
8 I tell you that he will avenge
them speedily. Nevertheless when
the Son of man cometh, shall he find
faith on the earth?

The Pharisee and the Publican

9 And he spake this parable unto
certain which trusted in themselves
that they were righteous, and de-
spised others:
10 Two men went up into the tem-
ple to pray; the one a Pharisee, and
the other a publican.
11 The Pharisee stood and prayed
thus with himself, God, I thank thee,
that I am not as other men *are,* ex-
tortioners, unjust, adulterers, or
even as this publican.
12 I fast twice in the week, I give
tithes of all that I possess.
13 And the publican, standing afar
off, would not lift up so much as *his*
eyes unto heaven, but smote upon
his breast, saying, God be merciful
to me a sinner.
14 I tell you, this man went down
to his house justified *rather* than
the other: for every one that ex-
alteth himself shall be abased; and
he that humbleth himself shall be
exalted.

Let the Children Come

15 And they brought unto him also infants, that he would touch them: but when *his* disciples saw *it,* they rebuked them.

16 But Jesus called them *unto him,* and said, Suffer little children to come unto me, and forbid them not: for of such is the kingdom of God.

17 Verily I say unto you, Whosoever shall not receive the kingdom of God as a little child shall in no wise enter therein.

A Ruler's Love of Money

18 And a certain ruler asked him, saying, Good Master, what shall I do to inherit eternal life?

19 And Jesus said unto him, Why callest thou me good? none *is* good, save one, *that is,* God.

20 Thou knowest the commandments, Do not commit adultery, Do not kill, Do not steal, Do not bear false witness, Honour thy father and thy mother.

21 And he said, All these have I kept from my youth up.

22 Now when Jesus heard these things, he said unto him, Yet lackest thou one thing: sell all that thou hast, and distribute unto the poor, and thou shalt have treasure in heaven: and come, follow me.

23 And when he heard this, he was very sorrowful: for he was very rich.

24 And when Jesus saw that he was very sorrowful, he said, How hardly shall they that have riches enter into the kingdom of God!

25 For it is easier for a camel to go through a needle's eye, than for a rich man to enter into the kingdom of God.

26 And they that heard *it* said, Who then can be saved?

27 And he said, The things which are impossible with men are possible with God.

28 Then Peter said, Lo, we have left all, and followed thee.

29 And he said unto them, Verily I say unto you, There is no man that hath left house, or parents, or brethren, or wife, or children, for the kingdom of God's sake,

30 Who shall not receive manifold more in this present time, and in the world to come life everlasting.

Jesus' Coming Death

31 Then he took *unto him* the twelve, and said unto them, Behold, we go up to Jerusalem, and all things that are written by the prophets concerning the Son of man shall be accomplished.

32 For he shall be delivered unto the Gentiles, and shall be mocked, and spitefully entreated, and spitted on:

33 And they shall scourge *him,* and put him to death: and the third day he shall rise again.

34 And they understood none of these things: and this saying was hid from them, neither knew they the things which were spoken.

Jesus Heals a Blind Man

35 And it came to pass, that as he was come nigh unto Jericho, a certain blind man sat by the way side begging:

36 And hearing the multitude pass by, he asked what it meant.

37 And they told him, that Jesus of Nazareth passeth by.

38 And he cried, saying, Jesus, *thou* son of David, have mercy on me.

39 And they which went before rebuked him, that he should hold his peace: but he cried so much the more, *Thou* son of David, have mercy on me.

40 And Jesus stood, and commanded him to be brought unto him: and when he was come near, he asked him,

41 Saying, What wilt thou that I shall do unto thee? And he said, Lord, that I may receive my sight.

42 And Jesus said unto him, Re-
ceive thy sight: thy faith hath saved
thee.
43 And immediately he received
his sight, and followed him, glori-
fying God: and all the people, when
they saw *it,* gave praise unto God.

Jesus' Encounter with Zacchaeus

19 And *Jesus* entered and passed
through Jericho.
2 And, behold, *there was* a man
named Zacchaeus, which was the
chief among the publicans, and he
was rich.
3 And he sought to see Jesus who
he was; and could not for the press,
because he was little of stature.
4 And he ran before, and climbed
up into a sycomore tree to see him:
for he was to pass that *way.*
5 And when Jesus came to the
place, he looked up, and saw him,
and said unto him, Zacchaeus, make
haste, and come down; for to day I
must abide at thy house.
6 And he made haste, and came
down, and received him joyfully.
7 And when they saw *it,* they all
murmured, saying, That he was
gone to be guest with a man that is
a sinner.
8 And Zacchaeus stood, and said
unto the Lord; Behold, Lord, the half
of my goods I give to the poor; and
if I have taken any thing from any
man by false accusation, I restore
him fourfold.
9 And Jesus said unto him, This
day is salvation come to this house,
forsomuch as he also is a son of
Abraham.
10 For the Son of man is come to
seek and to save that which was lost.

A Nobleman's Ten Pounds

11 And as they heard these things,
he added and spake a parable, be-
cause he was nigh to Jerusalem,
and because they thought that the
kingdom of God should immediately
appear.
12 He said therefore, A certain no-
bleman went into a far country to
receive for himself a kingdom, and
to return.
13 And he called his ten servants,
and delivered them ten pounds, and
said unto them, Occupy till I come.
14 But his citizens hated him, and
sent a message after him, saying,
We will not have this *man* to reign
over us.
15 And it came to pass, that when
he was returned, having received
the kingdom, then he commanded
these servants to be called unto him,
to whom he had given the money,
that he might know how much every
man had gained by trading.
16 Then came the first, saying,
Lord, thy pound hath gained ten
pounds.
17 And he said unto him, Well,
thou good servant: because thou
hast been faithful in a very little,
have thou authority over ten cities.
18 And the second came, saying,
Lord, thy pound hath gained five
pounds.
19 And he said likewise to him, Be
thou also over five cities.
20 And another came, saying,
Lord, behold, *here is* thy pound,
which I have kept laid up in a nap-
kin:
21 For I feared thee, because thou
art an austere man: thou takest up
that thou layedst not down, and
reapest that thou didst not sow.
22 And he saith unto him, Out of
thine own mouth will I judge thee,
thou wicked servant. Thou knewest
that I was an austere man, taking up
that I laid not down, and reaping
that I did not sow:
23 Wherefore then gavest not
thou my money into the bank, that
at my coming I might have required
mine own with usury?
24 And he said unto them that

stood by, Take from him the pound,
and give *it* to him that hath ten
pounds.
25 (And they said unto him, Lord,
he hath ten pounds.)
26 For I say unto you, That unto
every one which hath shall be given;
and from him that hath not, even
that he hath shall be taken away
from him.
27 But those mine enemies, which
would not that I should reign over
them, bring hither, and slay *them*
before me.

The Entry into Jerusalem

28 And when he had thus spoken,
he went before, ascending up to Jerusalem.
29 And it came to pass, when he
was come nigh to Bethphage and
Bethany, at the mount called *the
mount* of Olives, he sent two of his
disciples,
30 Saying, Go ye into the village
over against *you;* in the which at
your entering ye shall find a colt
tied, whereon yet never man sat:
loose him, and bring *him hither.*
31 And if any man ask you, Why
do ye loose *him?* thus shall ye say
unto him, Because the Lord hath
need of him.
32 And they that were sent went
their way, and found even as he had
said unto them.
33 And as they were loosing the
colt, the owners thereof said unto
them, Why loose ye the colt?
34 And they said, The Lord hath
need of him.
35 And they brought him to Jesus:
and they cast their garments upon
the colt, and they set Jesus thereon.
36 And as he went, they spread
their clothes in the way.
37 And when he was come nigh,
even now at the descent of the
mount of Olives, the whole multitude of the disciples began to rejoice
and praise God with a loud voice for
all the mighty works that they had
seen;
38 Saying, Blessed *be* the King that
cometh in the name of the Lord:
peace in heaven, and glory in the
highest.
39 And some of the Pharisees
from among the multitude said
unto him, Master, rebuke thy disciples.
40 And he answered and said unto
them, I tell you that, if these should
hold their peace, the stones would
immediately cry out.
41 And when he was come near,
he beheld the city, and wept over it,
42 Saying, If thou hadst known,
even thou, at least in this thy day,
the things *which belong* unto thy
peace! but now they are hid from
thine eyes.
43 For the days shall come upon
thee, that thine enemies shall cast
a trench about thee, and compass
thee round, and keep thee in on every side,
44 And shall lay thee even with
the ground, and thy children within
thee; and they shall not leave in thee
one stone upon another; because
thou knewest not the time of thy
visitation.
45 And he went into the temple,
and began to cast out them that sold
therein, and them that bought;
46 Saying unto them, It is written,
My house is the house of prayer: but
ye have made it a den of thieves.
47 And he taught daily in the temple. But the chief priests and the
scribes and the chief of the people
sought to destroy him,
48 And could not find what they
might do: for all the people were
very attentive to hear him.

Jesus' Authority Questioned

20 And it came to pass, *that*
on one of those days, as he
taught the people in the temple,
and preached the gospel, the chief

priests and the scribes came upon
him with the elders,
2 And spake unto him, saying, Tell
us, by what authority doest thou
these things? or who is he that gave
thee this authority?
3 And he answered and said unto
them, I will also ask you one thing;
and answer me:
4 The baptism of John, was it from
heaven, or of men?
5 And they reasoned with themselves,
saying, If we shall say, From
heaven; he will say, Why then believed
ye him not?
6 But and if we say, Of men; all
the people will stone us: for they be
persuaded that John was a prophet.
7 And they answered, that they
could not tell whence *it was.*
8 And Jesus said unto them, Neither
tell I you by what authority I
do these things.

The Lord of the Vineyard

9 Then began he to speak to the
people this parable; A certain man
planted a vineyard, and let it forth
to husbandmen, and went into a far
country for a long time.
10 And at the season he sent a servant
to the husbandmen, that they
should give him of the fruit of the
vineyard: but the husbandmen beat
him, and sent *him* away empty.
11 And again he sent another servant:
and they beat him also, and
entreated *him* shamefully, and sent
him away empty.
12 And again he sent a third: and
they wounded him also, and cast
him out.
13 Then said the lord of the vineyard,
What shall I do? I will send
my beloved son: it may be they will
reverence *him* when they see him.
14 But when the husbandmen saw
him, they reasoned among themselves,
saying, This is the heir: come,
let us kill him, that the inheritance
may be ours.
15 So they cast him out of the vineyard,
and killed *him.* What therefore
shall the lord of the vineyard do unto
them?
16 He shall come and destroy these
husbandmen, and shall give the
vineyard to others. And when they
heard *it,* they said, God forbid.
17 And he beheld them, and said,
What is this then that is written, The
stone which the builders rejected,
the same is become the head of the
corner?
18 Whosoever shall fall upon that
stone shall be broken; but on whomsoever
it shall fall, it will grind him
to powder.
19 And the chief priests and the
scribes the same hour sought to
lay hands on him; and they feared
the people: for they perceived that
he had spoken this parable against
them.

Paying Tribute to Caesar

20 And they watched *him,* and
sent forth spies, which should feign
themselves just men, that they
might take hold of his words, that
so they might deliver him unto the
power and authority of the governor.
21 And they asked him, saying,
Master, we know that thou sayest
and teachest rightly, neither acceptest
thou the person *of any,* but
teachest the way of God truly:
22 Is it lawful for us to give tribute
unto Caesar, or no?
23 But he perceived their craftiness,
and said unto them, Why
tempt ye me?
24 Shew me a penny. Whose image
and superscription hath it? They
answered and said, Caesar's.
25 And he said unto them, Render
therefore unto Caesar the things
which be Caesar's, and unto God
the things which be God's.
26 And they could not take hold
of his words before the people: and

they marvelled at his answer, and
held their peace.

Children of the Resurrection

27 Then came to *him* certain of the
Sadducees, which deny that there
is any resurrection; and they asked
him,
28 Saying, Master, Moses wrote
unto us, If any man's brother die,
having a wife, and he die without
children, that his brother should
take his wife, and raise up seed unto
his brother.
29 There were therefore seven
brethren: and the first took a wife,
and died without children.
30 And the second took her to
wife, and he died childless.
31 And the third took her; and in
like manner the seven also: and they
left no children, and died.
32 Last of all the woman died also.
33 Therefore in the resurrection
whose wife of them is she? for seven
had her to wife.
34 And Jesus answering said unto
them, The children of this world
marry, and are given in marriage:
35 But they which shall be ac-
counted worthy to obtain that
world, and the resurrection from
the dead, neither marry, nor are
given in marriage:
36 Neither can they die any more:
for they are equal unto the angels;
and are the children of God, being
the children of the resurrection.
37 Now that the dead are raised,
even Moses shewed at the bush,
when he calleth the Lord the God
of Abraham, and the God of Isaac,
and the God of Jacob.
38 For he is not a God of the dead,
but of the living: for all live unto
him.
39 Then certain of the scribes an-
swering said, Master, thou hast well
said.
40 And after that they durst not
ask him any *question at all.*

David's Son and Lord

41 And he said unto them, How
say they that Christ is David's son?
42 And David himself saith in the
book of Psalms, The LORD said unto
my Lord, Sit thou on my right hand,
43 Till I make thine enemies thy
footstool.
44 David therefore calleth him
Lord, how is he then his son?
45 Then in the audience of all the
people he said unto his disciples,
46 Beware of the scribes, which
desire to walk in long robes, and
love greetings in the markets,
and the highest seats in the syn-
agogues, and the chief rooms at
feasts;
47 Which devour widows' houses,
and for a shew make long prayers:
the same shall receive greater dam-
nation.

A Widow's Sacrificial Offering

21 And he looked up, and saw the
rich men casting their gifts
into the treasury.
2 And he saw also a certain poor
widow casting in thither two mites.
3 And he said, Of a truth I say unto
you, that this poor widow hath cast
in more than they all:
4 For all these have of their abun-
dance cast in unto the offerings of
God: but she of her penury hath cast
in all the living that she had.

Not One Stone Left on Another

5 And as some spake of the tem-
ple, how it was adorned with goodly
stones and gifts, he said,
6 *As for* these things which ye
behold, the days will come, in the
which there shall not be left one
stone upon another, that shall not
be thrown down.
7 And they asked him, saying,
Master, but when shall these things
be? and what sign *will there be* when
these things shall come to pass?

Deceivers, Wars, and Disasters

8 And he said, Take heed that ye be
not deceived: for many shall come
in my name, saying, I am *Christ;* and
the time draweth near: go ye not
therefore after them.
9 But when ye shall hear of wars
and commotions, be not terrified:
for these things must first come to
pass; but the end *is* not by and by.
10 Then said he unto them, Nation
shall rise against nation, and king-
dom against kingdom:
11 And great earthquakes shall
be in divers places, and famines,
and pestilences; and fearful sights
and great signs shall there be from
heaven.

Persecution Will Come

12 But before all these, they shall
lay their hands on you, and perse-
cute *you,* delivering *you* up to the
synagogues, and into prisons, being
brought before kings and rulers for
my name's sake.
13 And it shall turn to you for a
testimony.
14 Settle *it* therefore in your
hearts, not to meditate before what
ye shall answer:
15 For I will give you a mouth and
wisdom, which all your adversaries
shall not be able to gainsay nor re-
sist.
16 And ye shall be betrayed both
by parents, and brethren, and kins-
folks, and friends; and *some* of you
shall they cause to be put to death.
17 And ye shall be hated of all *men*
for my name's sake.
18 But there shall not an hair of
your head perish.
19 In your patience possess ye
your souls.

Take Heed and Watch

20 And when ye shall see Jerusalem
compassed with armies, then know
that the desolation thereof is nigh.
21 Then let them which are in
Judaea flee to the mountains; and
let them which are in the midst of
it depart out; and let not them that
are in the countries enter thereinto.
22 For these be the days of ven-
geance, that all things which are
written may be fulfilled.
23 But woe unto them that are
with child, and to them that give
suck, in those days! for there shall
be great distress in the land, and
wrath upon this people.
24 And they shall fall by the edge
of the sword, and shall be led away
captive into all nations: and Jeru-
salem shall be trodden down of the
Gentiles, until the times of the Gen-
tiles be fulfilled.
25 And there shall be signs in the
sun, and in the moon, and in the
stars; and upon the earth distress
of nations, with perplexity; the sea
and the waves roaring;
26 Men's hearts failing them for
fear, and for looking after those
things which are coming on the
earth: for the powers of heaven shall
be shaken.
27 And then shall they see the
Son of man coming in a cloud with
power and great glory.
28 And when these things begin to
come to pass, then look up, and lift
up your heads; for your redemption
draweth nigh.
29 And he spake to them a parable;
Behold the fig tree, and all the trees;
30 When they now shoot forth,
ye see and know of your own selves
that summer is now nigh at hand.
31 So likewise ye, when ye see
these things come to pass, know
ye that the kingdom of God is nigh
at hand.
32 Verily I say unto you, This gen-
eration shall not pass away, till all
be fulfilled.
33 Heaven and earth shall pass
away: but my words shall not pass
away.

34 And take heed to yourselves,
lest at any time your hearts be over-
charged with surfeiting, and drunk-
enness, and cares of this life, and *so*
that day come upon you unawares.
35 For as a snare shall it come on
all them that dwell on the face of
the whole earth.
36 Watch ye therefore, and pray
always, that ye may be accounted
worthy to escape all these things
that shall come to pass, and to stand
before the Son of man.
37 And in the day time he was
teaching in the temple; and at night
he went out, and abode in the mount
that is called *the mount* of Olives.
38 And all the people came early
in the morning to him in the temple,
for to hear him.

Judas Agrees to Betray Jesus

22 Now the feast of unleavened
bread drew nigh, which is
called the Passover.
2 And the chief priests and scribes
sought how they might kill him; for
they feared the people.
3 Then entered Satan into Judas
surnamed Iscariot, being of the
number of the twelve.
4 And he went his way, and com-
muned with the chief priests and
captains, how he might betray him
unto them.
5 And they were glad, and cov-
enanted to give him money.
6 And he promised, and sought
opportunity to betray him unto
them in the absence of the multi-
tude.

Passover Preparations

7 Then came the day of unleav-
ened bread, when the passover must
be killed.
8 And he sent Peter and John, say-
ing, Go and prepare us the passover,
that we may eat.
9 And they said unto him, Where
wilt thou that we prepare?
10 And he said unto them, Behold,
when ye are entered into the city,
there shall a man meet you, bearing
a pitcher of water; follow him into
the house where he entereth in.
11 And ye shall say unto the good-
man of the house, The Master saith
unto thee, Where is the guestcham-
ber, where I shall eat the passover
with my disciples?
12 And he shall shew you a large
upper room furnished: there make
ready.
13 And they went, and found as he
had said unto them: and they made
ready the passover.

The Lord's Supper

14 And when the hour was come,
he sat down, and the twelve apostles
with him.
15 And he said unto them, With
desire I have desired to eat this pass-
over with you before I suffer:
16 For I say unto you, I will not any
more eat thereof, until it be fulfilled
in the kingdom of God.
17 And he took the cup, and gave
thanks, and said, Take this, and di-
vide *it* among yourselves:
18 For I say unto you, I will not
drink of the fruit of the vine, until
the kingdom of God shall come.
19 And he took bread, and gave
thanks, and brake *it,* and gave unto
them, saying, This is my body which
is given for you: this do in remem-
brance of me.
20 Likewise also the cup after
supper, saying, This cup *is* the new
testament in my blood, which is
shed for you.
21 But, behold, the hand of him
that betrayeth me *is* with me on the
table.
22 And truly the Son of man goeth,
as it was determined: but woe unto
that man by whom he is betrayed!
23 And they began to enquire
among themselves, which of them
it was that should do this thing.

24 And there was also a strife
among them, which of them should
be accounted the greatest.
25 And he said unto them, The
kings of the Gentiles exercise lord-
ship over them; and they that exer-
cise authority upon them are called
benefactors.
26 But ye *shall* not *be* so: but he
that is greatest among you, let him
be as the younger; and he that is
chief, as he that doth serve.
27 For whether *is* greater, he that
sitteth at meat, or he that serveth?
is not he that sitteth at meat? but I
am among you as he that serveth.
28 Ye are they which have contin-
ued with me in my temptations.
29 And I appoint unto you a king-
dom, as my Father hath appointed
unto me;
30 That ye may eat and drink at
my table in my kingdom, and sit on
thrones judging the twelve tribes of
Israel.

Advice for the Disciples

31 And the Lord said, Simon,
Simon, behold, Satan hath desired
to have you, that he may sift *you* as
wheat:
32 But I have prayed for thee, that
thy faith fail not: and when thou art
converted, strengthen thy brethren.
33 And he said unto him, Lord, I
am ready to go with thee, both into
prison, and to death.
34 And he said, I tell thee, Peter,
the cock shall not crow this day, be-
fore that thou shalt thrice deny that
thou knowest me.
35 And he said unto them, When
I sent you without purse, and scrip,
and shoes, lacked ye any thing? And
they said, Nothing.
36 Then said he unto them, But
now, he that hath a purse, let him
take *it,* and likewise *his* scrip: and
he that hath no sword, let him sell
his garment, and buy one.
37 For I say unto you, that this
that is written must yet be accom-
plished in me, And he was reckoned
among the transgressors: for the
things concerning me have an end.
38 And they said, Lord, behold,
here *are* two swords. And he said
unto them, It is enough.

Jesus' Agony in Prayer

39 And he came out, and went,
as he was wont, to the mount of
Olives; and his disciples also fol-
lowed him.
40 And when he was at the place,
he said unto them, Pray that ye enter
not into temptation.
41 And he was withdrawn from
them about a stone's cast, and
kneeled down, and prayed,
42 Saying, Father, if thou be will-
ing, remove this cup from me: nev-
ertheless not my will, but thine, be
done.
43 And there appeared an angel
unto him from heaven, strength-
ening him.
44 And being in an agony he
prayed more earnestly: and his
sweat was as it were great drops of
blood falling down to the ground.
45 And when he rose up from
prayer, and was come to his dis-
ciples, he found them sleeping for
sorrow,
46 And said unto them, Why sleep
ye? rise and pray, lest ye enter into
temptation.

Judas's Betrayal of Jesus

47 And while he yet spake, behold
a multitude, and he that was called
Judas, one of the twelve, went be-
fore them, and drew near unto Jesus
to kiss him.
48 But Jesus said unto him, Judas,
betrayest thou the Son of man with
a kiss?
49 When they which were about
him saw what would follow, they
said unto him, Lord, shall we smite
with the sword?

50 And one of them smote the servant of the high priest, and cut off his right ear.

51 And Jesus answered and said, Suffer ye thus far. And he touched his ear, and healed him.

52 Then Jesus said unto the chief priests, and captains of the temple, and the elders, which were come to him, Be ye come out, as against a thief, with swords and staves?

53 When I was daily with you in the temple, ye stretched forth no hands against me: but this is your hour, and the power of darkness.

Peter's Denial of Jesus

54 Then took they him, and led *him,* and brought him into the high priest's house. And Peter followed afar off.

55 And when they had kindled a fire in the midst of the hall, and were set down together, Peter sat down among them.

56 But a certain maid beheld him as he sat by the fire, and earnestly looked upon him, and said, This man was also with him.

57 And he denied him, saying, Woman, I know him not.

58 And after a little while another saw him, and said, Thou art also of them. And Peter said, Man, I am not.

59 And about the space of one hour after another confidently affirmed, saying, Of a truth this *fellow* also was with him: for he is a Galilaean.

60 And Peter said, Man, I know not what thou sayest. And immediately, while he yet spake, the cock crew.

61 And the Lord turned, and looked upon Peter. And Peter remembered the word of the Lord, how he had said unto him, Before the cock crow, thou shalt deny me thrice.

62 And Peter went out, and wept bitterly.

Jesus Mocked and Smitten

63 And the men that held Jesus mocked him, and smote *him.*

64 And when they had blindfolded him, they struck him on the face, and asked him, saying, Prophesy, who is it that smote thee?

65 And many other things blasphemously spake they against him.

Jesus Before the Council

66 And as soon as it was day, the elders of the people and the chief priests and the scribes came together, and led him into their council, saying,

67 Art thou the Christ? tell us. And he said unto them, If I tell you, ye will not believe:

68 And if I also ask *you,* ye will not answer me, nor let *me* go.

69 Hereafter shall the Son of man sit on the right hand of the power of God.

70 Then said they all, Art thou then the Son of God? And he said unto them, Ye say that I am.

71 And they said, What need we any further witness? for we ourselves have heard of his own mouth.

Pilate Finds No Fault in Jesus

23 And the whole multitude of them arose, and led him unto Pilate.

2 And they began to accuse him, saying, We found this *fellow* perverting the nation, and forbidding to give tribute to Caesar, saying that he himself is Christ a King.

3 And Pilate asked him, saying, Art thou the King of the Jews? And he answered him and said, Thou sayest *it.*

4 Then said Pilate to the chief priests and *to* the people, I find no fault in this man.

5 And they were the more fierce, saying, He stirreth up the people, teaching throughout all Jewry, beginning from Galilee to this place.

6 When Pilate heard of Galilee,
he asked whether the man were a
Galilaean.

Jesus Sent to Herod

7 And as soon as he knew that he
belonged unto Herod's jurisdiction,
he sent him to Herod, who himself
also was at Jerusalem at that time.
8 And when Herod saw Jesus, he
was exceeding glad: for he was de-
sirous to see him of a long *season*,
because he had heard many things
of him; and he hoped to have seen
some miracle done by him.
9 Then he questioned with him in
many words; but he answered him
nothing.
10 And the chief priests and scribes
stood and vehemently accused him.
11 And Herod with his men of war
set him at nought, and mocked *him*,
and arrayed him in a gorgeous robe,
and sent him again to Pilate.
12 And the same day Pilate and
Herod were made friends together:
for before they were at enmity be-
tween themselves.

Pilate Seeks to Release Jesus

13 And Pilate, when he had called
together the chief priests and the
rulers and the people,
14 Said unto them, Ye have
brought this man unto me, as one
that perverteth the people: and, be-
hold, I, having examined *him* before
you, have found no fault in this man
touching those things whereof ye
accuse him:
15 No, nor yet Herod: for I sent you
to him; and, lo, nothing worthy of
death is done unto him.
16 I will therefore chastise him,
and release *him*.
17 (For of necessity he must re-
lease one unto them at the feast.)
18 And they cried out all at once,
saying, Away with this *man*, and
release unto us Barabbas:
19 (Who for a certain sedition
made in the city, and for murder,
was cast into prison.)
20 Pilate therefore, willing to re-
lease Jesus, spake again to them.
21 But they cried, saying, Crucify
him, crucify him.
22 And he said unto them the third
time, Why, what evil hath he done?
I have found no cause of death in
him: I will therefore chastise him,
and let *him* go.
23 And they were instant with
loud voices, requiring that he might
be crucified. And the voices of them
and of the chief priests prevailed.
24 And Pilate gave sentence that
it should be as they required.
25 And he released unto them him
that for sedition and murder was
cast into prison, whom they had
desired; but he delivered Jesus to
their will.

Jesus Crucified at Calvary

26 And as they led him away, they
laid hold upon one Simon, a Cyre-
nian, coming out of the country, and
on him they laid the cross, that he
might bear *it* after Jesus.
27 And there followed him a great
company of people, and of women,
which also bewailed and lamented
him.
28 But Jesus turning unto them
said, Daughters of Jerusalem, weep
not for me, but weep for yourselves,
and for your children.
29 For, behold, the days are com-
ing, in the which they shall say,
Blessed *are* the barren, and the
wombs that never bare, and the
paps which never gave suck.
30 Then shall they begin to say to
the mountains, Fall on us; and to
the hills, Cover us.
31 For if they do these things in
a green tree, what shall be done in
the dry?
32 And there were also two other,
malefactors, led with him to be put
to death.

33 And when they were come to the place, which is called Calvary, there they crucified him, and the malefactors, one on the right hand, and the other on the left.

34 Then said Jesus, Father, forgive them; for they know not what they do. And they parted his raiment, and cast lots.

35 And the people stood beholding. And the rulers also with them derided *him,* saying, He saved others; let him save himself, if he be Christ, the chosen of God.

36 And the soldiers also mocked him, coming to him, and offering him vinegar,

37 And saying, If thou be the king of the Jews, save thyself.

38 And a superscription also was written over him in letters of Greek, and Latin, and Hebrew, THIS IS THE KING OF THE JEWS.

39 And one of the malefactors which were hanged railed on him, saying, If thou be Christ, save thyself and us.

40 But the other answering rebuked him, saying, Dost not thou fear God, seeing thou art in the same condemnation?

41 And we indeed justly; for we receive the due reward of our deeds: but this man hath done nothing amiss.

42 And he said unto Jesus, Lord, remember me when thou comest into thy kingdom.

43 And Jesus said unto him, Verily I say unto thee, To day shalt thou be with me in paradise.

Jesus Commends His Spirit to God

44 And it was about the sixth hour, and there was a darkness over all the earth until the ninth hour.

45 And the sun was darkened, and the veil of the temple was rent in the midst.

46 And when Jesus had cried with a loud voice, he said, Father, into thy hands I commend my spirit: and having said thus, he gave up the ghost.

47 Now when the centurion saw what was done, he glorified God, saying, Certainly this was a righteous man.

48 And all the people that came together to that sight, beholding the things which were done, smote their breasts, and returned.

49 And all his acquaintance, and the women that followed him from Galilee, stood afar off, beholding these things.

Joseph Buries the Body of Jesus

50 And, behold, *there was* a man named Joseph, a counsellor; *and he was* a good man, and a just:

51 (The same had not consented to the counsel and deed of them;) *he was* of Arimathaea, a city of the Jews: who also himself waited for the kingdom of God.

52 This *man* went unto Pilate, and begged the body of Jesus.

53 And he took it down, and wrapped it in linen, and laid it in a sepulchre that was hewn in stone, wherein never man before was laid.

54 And that day was the preparation, and the sabbath drew on.

55 And the women also, which came with him from Galilee, followed after, and beheld the sepulchre, and how his body was laid.

56 And they returned, and prepared spices and ointments; and rested the sabbath day according to the commandment.

The Resurrection of Jesus

24 Now upon the first *day* of the week, very early in the morning, they came unto the sepulchre, bringing the spices which they had prepared, and certain *others* with them.

2 And they found the stone rolled
away from the sepulchre.
3 And they entered in, and found
not the body of the Lord Jesus.
4 And it came to pass, as they were
much perplexed thereabout, behold,
two men stood by them in shining
garments:
5 And as they were afraid, and
bowed down *their* faces to the earth,
they said unto them, Why seek ye
the living among the dead?
6 He is not here, but is risen: re-
member how he spake unto you
when he was yet in Galilee,
7 Saying, The Son of man must be
delivered into the hands of sinful
men, and be crucified, and the third
day rise again.
8 And they remembered his words,
9 And returned from the sepul-
chre, and told all these things unto
the eleven, and to all the rest.
10 It was Mary Magdalene, and Jo-
anna, and Mary *the mother* of James,
and other *women that were* with
them, which told these things unto
the apostles.
11 And their words seemed to
them as idle tales, and they believed
them not.
12 Then arose Peter, and ran unto
the sepulchre; and stooping down,
he beheld the linen clothes laid by
themselves, and departed, won-
dering in himself at that which was
come to pass.

The Emmaus Road

13 And, behold, two of them went
that same day to a village called Em-
maus, which was from Jerusalem
about threescore furlongs.
14 And they talked together of all
these things which had happened.
15 And it came to pass, that, while
they communed *together* and rea-
soned, Jesus himself drew near, and
went with them.
16 But their eyes were holden that
they should not know him.
17 And he said unto them, What
manner of communications *are*
these that ye have one to another,
as ye walk, and are sad?
18 And the one of them, whose
name was Cleopas, answering said
unto him, Art thou only a stranger
in Jerusalem, and hast not known
the things which are come to pass
there in these days?
19 And he said unto them, What
things? And they said unto him, Con-
cerning Jesus of Nazareth, which
was a prophet mighty in deed and
word before God and all the people:
20 And how the chief priests and
our rulers delivered him to be con-
demned to death, and have crucified
him.
21 But we trusted that it had been
he which should have redeemed
Israel: and beside all this, to day is
the third day since these things were
done.
22 Yea, and certain women also of
our company made us astonished,
which were early at the sepulchre;
23 And when they found not his
body, they came, saying, that they
had also seen a vision of angels,
which said that he was alive.
24 And certain of them which
were with us went to the sepulchre,
and found *it* even so as the women
had said: but him they saw not.
25 Then he said unto them,
O fools, and slow of heart to believe
all that the prophets have spoken:
26 Ought not Christ to have suf-
fered these things, and to enter into
his glory?
27 And beginning at Moses and all
the prophets, he expounded unto
them in all the scriptures the things
concerning himself.
28 And they drew nigh unto the
village, whither they went: and he
made as though he would have gone
further.
29 But they constrained him, say-
ing, Abide with us: for it is toward

evening, and the day is far spent.
And he went in to tarry with them.
30 And it came to pass, as he sat
at meat with them, he took bread,
and blessed *it,* and brake, and gave
to them.
31 And their eyes were opened,
and they knew him; and he vanished
out of their sight.
32 And they said one to another,
Did not our heart burn within us,
while he talked with us by the way,
and while he opened to us the scrip-
tures?
33 And they rose up the same
hour, and returned to Jerusalem,
and found the eleven gathered to-
gether, and them that were with
them,
34 Saying, The Lord is risen in-
deed, and hath appeared to Simon.
35 And they told what things *were*
done in the way, and how he was
known of them in breaking of bread.

Jesus' Appearance

36 And as they thus spake, Jesus
himself stood in the midst of them,
and saith unto them, Peace *be* unto
you.
37 But they were terrified and
affrighted, and supposed that they
had seen a spirit.
38 And he said unto them, Why are
ye troubled? and why do thoughts
arise in your hearts?
39 Behold my hands and my feet,
that it is I myself: handle me, and
see; for a spirit hath not flesh and
bones, as ye see me have.
40 And when he had thus spoken,
he shewed them *his* hands and *his*
feet.
41 And while they yet believed not
for joy, and wondered, he said unto
them, Have ye here any meat?
42 And they gave him a piece of a
broiled fish, and of an honeycomb.
43 And he took *it,* and did eat be-
fore them.

The Scriptures Fulfilled

44 And he said unto them, These
are the words which I spake unto
you, while I was yet with you, that
all things must be fulfilled, which
were written in the law of Moses,
and *in* the prophets, and *in* the
psalms, concerning me.
45 Then opened he their under-
standing, that they might under-
stand the scriptures,
46 And said unto them, Thus it is
written, and thus it behoved Christ
to suffer, and to rise from the dead
the third day:
47 And that repentance and re-
mission of sins should be preached
in his name among all nations, be-
ginning at Jerusalem.
48 And ye are witnesses of these
things.
49 And, behold, I send the promise
of my Father upon you: but tarry ye
in the city of Jerusalem, until ye be
endued with power from on high.

Jesus' Ascension

50 And he led them out as far as to
Bethany, and he lifted up his hands,
and blessed them.
51 And it came to pass, while he
blessed them, he was parted from
them, and carried up into heaven.
52 And they worshipped him, and
returned to Jerusalem with great
joy:
53 And were continually in the
temple, praising and blessing God.
Amen.

The Gospel According to
JOHN

The Word Was God

In the beginning was the Word,
and the Word was with God, and
the Word was God.
2 The same was in the beginning
with God.
3 All things were made by him;
and without him was not any thing
made that was made.
4 In him was life; and the life was
the light of men.
5 And the light shineth in dark-
ness; and the darkness compre-
hended it not.
6 There was a man sent from God,
whose name *was* John.
7 The same came for a witness,
to bear witness of the Light, that all
men through him might believe.
8 He was not that Light, but *was*
sent to bear witness of that Light.
9 *That* was the true Light, which
lighteth every man that cometh into
the world.
10 He was in the world, and the
world was made by him, and the
world knew him not.
11 He came unto his own, and his
own received him not.
12 But as many as received him,
to them gave he power to become
the sons of God, *even* to them that
believe on his name:
13 Which were born, not of blood,
nor of the will of the flesh, nor of the
will of man, but of God.
14 And the Word was made flesh,
and dwelt among us, (and we beheld
his glory, the glory as of the only
begotten of the Father,) full of grace
and truth.

John's Witness of Christ

15 John bare witness of him, and
cried, saying, This was he of whom
I spake, He that cometh after me
is preferred before me: for he was
before me.
16 And of his fulness have all we
received, and grace for grace.
17 For the law was given by Moses,
but grace and truth came by Jesus
Christ.
18 No man hath seen God at any
time; the only begotten Son, which
is in the bosom of the Father, he
hath declared *him*.

John's Denial That He Was the Christ

19 And this is the record of John,
when the Jews sent priests and Le-
vites from Jerusalem to ask him,
Who art thou?
20 And he confessed, and denied
not; but confessed, I am not the
Christ.
21 And they asked him, What
then? Art thou Elias? And he saith,
I am not. Art thou that prophet? And
he answered, No.
22 Then said they unto him, Who
art thou? that we may give an an-
swer to them that sent us. What
sayest thou of thyself?
23 He said, I *am* the voice of one
crying in the wilderness, Make
straight the way of the Lord, as said
the prophet Esaias.
24 And they which were sent were
of the Pharisees.
25 And they asked him, and said
unto him, Why baptizest thou then,

if thou be not that Christ, nor Elias, neither that prophet?

26 John answered them, saying, I baptize with water: but there standeth one among you, whom ye know not;

27 He it is, who coming after me is preferred before me, whose shoe's latchet I am not worthy to unloose.

28 These things were done in Bethabara beyond Jordan, where John was baptizing.

Behold the Lamb of God

29 The next day John seeth Jesus coming unto him, and saith, Behold the Lamb of God, which taketh away the sin of the world.

30 This is he of whom I said, After me cometh a man which is preferred before me: for he was before me.

31 And I knew him not: but that he should be made manifest to Israel, therefore am I come baptizing with water.

32 And John bare record, saying, I saw the Spirit descending from heaven like a dove, and it abode upon him.

33 And I knew him not: but he that sent me to baptize with water, the same said unto me, Upon whom thou shalt see the Spirit descending, and remaining on him, the same is he which baptizeth with the Holy Ghost.

34 And I saw, and bare record that this is the Son of God.

Two of John's Disciples Follow Jesus

35 Again the next day after John stood, and two of his disciples;

36 And looking upon Jesus as he walked, he saith, Behold the Lamb of God!

37 And the two disciples heard him speak, and they followed Jesus.

38 Then Jesus turned, and saw them following, and saith unto them, What seek ye? They said unto him, Rabbi, (which is to say, being interpreted, Master,) where dwellest thou?

39 He saith unto them, Come and see. They came and saw where he dwelt, and abode with him that day: for it was about the tenth hour.

40 One of the two which heard John *speak,* and followed him, was Andrew, Simon Peter's brother.

41 He first findeth his own brother Simon, and saith unto him, We have found the Messias, which is, being interpreted, the Christ.

42 And he brought him to Jesus. And when Jesus beheld him, he said, Thou art Simon the son of Jona: thou shalt be called Cephas, which is by interpretation, A stone.

The Calling of Philip and Nathanael

43 The day following Jesus would go forth into Galilee, and findeth Philip, and saith unto him, Follow me.

44 Now Philip was of Bethsaida, the city of Andrew and Peter.

45 Philip findeth Nathanael, and saith unto him, We have found him, of whom Moses in the law, and the prophets, did write, Jesus of Nazareth, the son of Joseph.

46 And Nathanael said unto him, Can there any good thing come out of Nazareth? Philip saith unto him, Come and see.

47 Jesus saw Nathanael coming to him, and saith of him, Behold an Israelite indeed, in whom is no guile!

48 Nathanael saith unto him, Whence knowest thou me? Jesus answered and said unto him, Before that Philip called thee, when thou wast under the fig tree, I saw thee.

49 Nathanael answered and saith unto him, Rabbi, thou art the Son of God; thou art the King of Israel.

50 Jesus answered and said unto him, Because I said unto thee, I saw

thee under the fig tree, believest thou? thou shalt see greater things than these.

51 And he saith unto him, Verily, verily, I say unto you, Hereafter ye shall see heaven open, and the angels of God ascending and descending upon the Son of man.

Jesus Turns Water into Wine

2 And the third day there was a marriage in Cana of Galilee; and the mother of Jesus was there:

2 And both Jesus was called, and his disciples, to the marriage.

3 And when they wanted wine, the mother of Jesus saith unto him, They have no wine.

4 Jesus saith unto her, Woman, what have I to do with thee? mine hour is not yet come.

5 His mother saith unto the servants, Whatsoever he saith unto you, do *it*.

6 And there were set there six waterpots of stone, after the manner of the purifying of the Jews, containing two or three firkins apiece.

7 Jesus saith unto them, Fill the waterpots with water. And they filled them up to the brim.

8 And he saith unto them, Draw out now, and bear unto the governor of the feast. And they bare *it*.

9 When the ruler of the feast had tasted the water that was made wine, and knew not whence it was: (but the servants which drew the water knew;) the governor of the feast called the bridegroom,

10 And saith unto him, Every man at the beginning doth set forth good wine; and when men have well drunk, then that which is worse: *but* thou hast kept the good wine until now.

11 This beginning of miracles did Jesus in Cana of Galilee, and manifested forth his glory; and his disciples believed on him.

Jesus Cleanses the Temple

12 After this he went down to Capernaum, he, and his mother, and his brethren, and his disciples: and they continued there not many days.

13 And the Jews' passover was at hand, and Jesus went up to Jerusalem,

14 And found in the temple those that sold oxen and sheep and doves, and the changers of money sitting:

15 And when he had made a scourge of small cords, he drove them all out of the temple, and the sheep, and the oxen; and poured out the changers' money, and overthrew the tables;

16 And said unto them that sold doves, Take these things hence; make not my Father's house an house of merchandise.

17 And his disciples remembered that it was written, The zeal of thine house hath eaten me up.

18 Then answered the Jews and said unto him, What sign shewest thou unto us, seeing that thou doest these things?

19 Jesus answered and said unto them, Destroy this temple, and in three days I will raise it up.

20 Then said the Jews, Forty and six years was this temple in building, and wilt thou rear it up in three days?

21 But he spake of the temple of his body.

22 When therefore he was risen from the dead, his disciples remembered that he had said this unto them; and they believed the scripture, and the word which Jesus had said.

23 Now when he was in Jerusalem at the passover, in the feast *day*, many believed in his name, when they saw the miracles which he did.

24 But Jesus did not commit himself unto them, because he knew all *men*,

25 And needed not that any should

testify of man: for he knew what was
in man.

Nicodemus Questions Jesus

3 There was a man of the Phari-
sees, named Nicodemus, a ruler
of the Jews:
2 The same came to Jesus by
night, and said unto him, Rabbi, we
know that thou art a teacher come
from God: for no man can do these
miracles that thou doest, except God
be with him.
3 Jesus answered and said unto
him, Verily, verily, I say unto thee,
Except a man be born again, he can-
not see the kingdom of God.
4 Nicodemus saith unto him, How
can a man be born when he is old?
can he enter the second time into
his mother's womb, and be born?
5 Jesus answered, Verily, verily, I
say unto thee, Except a man be born
of water and *of* the Spirit, he cannot
enter into the kingdom of God.
6 That which is born of the flesh
is flesh; and that which is born of
the Spirit is spirit.
7 Marvel not that I said unto thee,
Ye must be born again.
8 The wind bloweth where it
listeth, and thou hearest the sound
thereof, but canst not tell whence it
cometh, and whither it goeth: so is
every one that is born of the Spirit.
9 Nicodemus answered and said
unto him, How can these things be?
10 Jesus answered and said unto
him, Art thou a master of Israel, and
knowest not these things?
11 Verily, verily, I say unto thee, We
speak that we do know, and testify
that we have seen; and ye receive
not our witness.

God So Loved the World

12 If I have told you earthly things,
and ye believe not, how shall ye be-
lieve, if I tell you *of* heavenly things?
13 And no man hath ascended up
to heaven, but he that came down
from heaven, *even* the Son of man
which is in heaven.
14 And as Moses lifted up the ser-
pent in the wilderness, even so must
the Son of man be lifted up:
15 That whosoever believeth in
him should not perish, but have
eternal life.
16 For God so loved the world, that
he gave his only begotten Son, that
whosoever believeth in him should
not perish, but have everlasting life.
17 For God sent not his Son into
the world to condemn the world;
but that the world through him
might be saved.
18 He that believeth on him is not
condemned: but he that believeth
not is condemned already, because
he hath not believed in the name of
the only begotten Son of God.
19 And this is the condemnation,
that light is come into the world,
and men loved darkness rather than
light, because their deeds were evil.
20 For every one that doeth evil
hateth the light, neither cometh to
the light, lest his deeds should be
reproved.
21 But he that doeth truth com-
eth to the light, that his deeds may
be made manifest, that they are
wrought in God.

John's Testimony About Jesus

22 After these things came Jesus
and his disciples into the land of
Judaea; and there he tarried with
them, and baptized.
23 And John also was baptizing in
Aenon near to Salim, because there
was much water there: and they
came, and were baptized.
24 For John was not yet cast into
prison.
25 Then there arose a question
between *some* of John's disciples
and the Jews about purifying.
26 And they came unto John, and
said unto him, Rabbi, he that was
with thee beyond Jordan, to whom

thou barest witness, behold, the same baptizeth, and all *men* come to him.

27 John answered and said, A man can receive nothing, except it be given him from heaven.

28 Ye yourselves bear me witness, that I said, I am not the Christ, but that I am sent before him.

29 He that hath the bride is the bridegroom: but the friend of the bridegroom, which standeth and heareth him, rejoiceth greatly because of the bridegroom's voice: this my joy therefore is fulfilled.

30 He must increase, but I *must* decrease.

31 He that cometh from above is above all: he that is of the earth is earthly, and speaketh of the earth: he that cometh from heaven is above all.

32 And what he hath seen and heard, that he testifieth; and no man receiveth his testimony.

33 He that hath received his testimony hath set to his seal that God is true.

34 For he whom God hath sent speaketh the words of God: for God giveth not the Spirit by measure *unto him.*

35 The Father loveth the Son, and hath given all things into his hand.

36 He that believeth on the Son hath everlasting life: and he that believeth not the Son shall not see life; but the wrath of God abideth on him.

The Woman at Jacob's Well

4 When therefore the Lord knew how the Pharisees had heard that Jesus made and baptized more disciples than John,

2 (Though Jesus himself baptized not, but his disciples,)

3 He left Judaea, and departed again into Galilee.

4 And he must needs go through Samaria.

5 Then cometh he to a city of Samaria, which is called Sychar, near to the parcel of ground that Jacob gave to his son Joseph.

6 Now Jacob's well was there. Jesus therefore, being wearied with *his* journey, sat thus on the well: *and* it was about the sixth hour.

7 There cometh a woman of Samaria to draw water: Jesus saith unto her, Give me to drink.

8 (For his disciples were gone away unto the city to buy meat.)

9 Then saith the woman of Samaria unto him, How is it that thou, being a Jew, askest drink of me, which am a woman of Samaria? for the Jews have no dealings with the Samaritans.

10 Jesus answered and said unto her, If thou knewest the gift of God, and who it is that saith to thee, Give me to drink; thou wouldest have asked of him, and he would have given thee living water.

11 The woman saith unto him, Sir, thou hast nothing to draw with, and the well is deep: from whence then hast thou that living water?

12 Art thou greater than our father Jacob, which gave us the well, and drank thereof himself, and his children, and his cattle?

13 Jesus answered and said unto her, Whosoever drinketh of this water shall thirst again:

14 But whosoever drinketh of the water that I shall give him shall never thirst; but the water that I shall give him shall be in him a well of water springing up into everlasting life.

15 The woman saith unto him, Sir, give me this water, that I thirst not, neither come hither to draw.

16 Jesus saith unto her, Go, call thy husband, and come hither.

17 The woman answered and said, I have no husband. Jesus said unto her, Thou hast well said, I have no husband:

18 For thou hast had five husbands; and he whom thou now hast is not thy husband: in that saidst thou truly.

19 The woman saith unto him, Sir, I perceive that thou art a prophet.

20 Our fathers worshipped in this mountain; and ye say, that in Jerusalem is the place where men ought to worship.

21 Jesus saith unto her, Woman, believe me, the hour cometh, when ye shall neither in this mountain, nor yet at Jerusalem, worship the Father.

22 Ye worship ye know not what: we know what we worship: for salvation is of the Jews.

23 But the hour cometh, and now is, when the true worshippers shall worship the Father in spirit and in truth: for the Father seeketh such to worship him.

24 God *is* a Spirit: and they that worship him must worship *him* in spirit and in truth.

25 The woman saith unto him, I know that Messias cometh, which is called Christ: when he is come, he will tell us all things.

26 Jesus saith unto her, I that speak unto thee am *he*.

Fields Are White to Harvest

27 And upon this came his disciples, and marvelled that he talked with the woman: yet no man said, What seekest thou? or, Why talkest thou with her?

28 The woman then left her waterpot, and went her way into the city, and saith to the men,

29 Come, see a man, which told me all things that ever I did: is not this the Christ?

30 Then they went out of the city, and came unto him.

31 In the mean while his disciples prayed him, saying, Master, eat.

32 But he said unto them, I have meat to eat that ye know not of.

33 Therefore said the disciples one to another, Hath any man brought him *ought* to eat?

34 Jesus saith unto them, My meat is to do the will of him that sent me, and to finish his work.

35 Say not ye, There are yet four months, and *then* cometh harvest? behold, I say unto you, Lift up your eyes, and look on the fields; for they are white already to harvest.

36 And he that reapeth receiveth wages, and gathereth fruit unto life eternal: that both he that soweth and he that reapeth may rejoice together.

37 And herein is that saying true, One soweth, and another reapeth.

38 I sent you to reap that whereon ye bestowed no labour: other men laboured, and ye are entered into their labours.

The Belief of the Samaritans

39 And many of the Samaritans of that city believed on him for the saying of the woman, which testified, He told me all that ever I did.

40 So when the Samaritans were come unto him, they besought him that he would tarry with them: and he abode there two days.

41 And many more believed because of his own word;

42 And said unto the woman, Now we believe, not because of thy saying: for we have heard *him* ourselves, and know that this is indeed the Christ, the Saviour of the world.

Jesus Heals a Nobleman's Son

43 Now after two days he departed thence, and went into Galilee.

44 For Jesus himself testified, that a prophet hath no honour in his own country.

45 Then when he was come into Galilee, the Galilaeans received him, having seen all the things that he did at Jerusalem at the feast: for they also went unto the feast.

46 So Jesus came again into Cana of Galilee, where he made the water wine. And there was a certain nobleman, whose son was sick at Capernaum.

47 When he heard that Jesus was come out of Judaea into Galilee, he went unto him, and besought him that he would come down, and heal his son: for he was at the point of death.

48 Then said Jesus unto him, Except ye see signs and wonders, ye will not believe.

49 The nobleman saith unto him, Sir, come down ere my child die.

50 Jesus saith unto him, Go thy way; thy son liveth. And the man believed the word that Jesus had spoken unto him, and he went his way.

51 And as he was now going down, his servants met him, and told *him,* saying, Thy son liveth.

52 Then enquired he of them the hour when he began to amend. And they said unto him, Yesterday at the seventh hour the fever left him.

53 So the father knew that *it was* at the same hour, in the which Jesus said unto him, Thy son liveth: and himself believed, and his whole house.

54 This *is* again the second miracle *that* Jesus did, when he was come out of Judaea into Galilee.

A Healing at the Pool of Bethesda

5 After this there was a feast of the Jews; and Jesus went up to Jerusalem.

2 Now there is at Jerusalem by the sheep *market* a pool, which is called in the Hebrew tongue Bethesda, having five porches.

3 In these lay a great multitude of impotent folk, of blind, halt, withered, waiting for the moving of the water.

4 For an angel went down at a certain season into the pool, and troubled the water: whosoever then first after the troubling of the water stepped in was made whole of whatsoever disease he had.

5 And a certain man was there, which had an infirmity thirty and eight years.

6 When Jesus saw him lie, and knew that he had been now a long time *in that case,* he saith unto him, Wilt thou be made whole?

7 The impotent man answered him, Sir, I have no man, when the water is troubled, to put me into the pool: but while I am coming, another steppeth down before me.

8 Jesus saith unto him, Rise, take up thy bed, and walk.

9 And immediately the man was made whole, and took up his bed, and walked: and on the same day was the sabbath.

10 The Jews therefore said unto him that was cured, It is the sabbath day: it is not lawful for thee to carry *thy* bed.

11 He answered them, He that made me whole, the same said unto me, Take up thy bed, and walk.

12 Then asked they him, What man is that which said unto thee, Take up thy bed, and walk?

13 And he that was healed wist not who it was: for Jesus had conveyed himself away, a multitude being in *that* place.

14 Afterward Jesus findeth him in the temple, and said unto him, Behold, thou art made whole: sin no more, lest a worse thing come unto thee.

15 The man departed, and told the Jews that it was Jesus, which had made him whole.

16 And therefore did the Jews persecute Jesus, and sought to slay him, because he had done these things on the sabbath day.

17 But Jesus answered them, My Father worketh hitherto, and I work.

18 Therefore the Jews sought the
more to kill him, because he not
only had broken the sabbath, but
said also that God was his Father,
making himself equal with God.

All Judgment Given to Jesus

19 Then answered Jesus and said
unto them, Verily, verily, I say unto
you, The Son can do nothing of him-
self, but what he seeth the Father
do: for what things soever he doeth,
these also doeth the Son likewise.
20 For the Father loveth the Son,
and sheweth him all things that
himself doeth: and he will shew
him greater works than these, that
ye may marvel.
21 For as the Father raiseth up the
dead, and quickeneth *them;* even so
the Son quickeneth whom he will.
22 For the Father judgeth no man,
but hath committed all judgment
unto the Son:
23 That all *men* should honour
the Son, even as they honour the
Father. He that honoureth not the
Son honoureth not the Father which
hath sent him.
24 Verily, verily, I say unto you,
He that heareth my word, and be-
lieveth on him that sent me, hath
everlasting life, and shall not come
into condemnation; but is passed
from death unto life.
25 Verily, verily, I say unto you,
The hour is coming, and now is,
when the dead shall hear the voice
of the Son of God: and they that hear
shall live.
26 For as the Father hath life in
himself; so hath he given to the Son
to have life in himself;
27 And hath given him authority
to execute judgment also, because
he is the Son of man.
28 Marvel not at this: for the hour
is coming, in the which all that are
in the graves shall hear his voice,
29 And shall come forth; they that
have done good, unto the resurrec-
tion of life; and they that have done
evil, unto the resurrection of dam-
nation.
30 I can of mine own self do
nothing: as I hear, I judge: and my
judgment is just; because I seek not
mine own will, but the will of the
Father which hath sent me.

Bearing Witness of Jesus

31 If I bear witness of myself, my
witness is not true.
32 There is another that beareth
witness of me; and I know that the
witness which he witnesseth of me
is true.
33 Ye sent unto John, and he bare
witness unto the truth.
34 But I receive not testimony
from man: but these things I say,
that ye might be saved.
35 He was a burning and a shin-
ing light: and ye were willing for a
season to rejoice in his light.
36 But I have greater witness than
that of John: for the works which the
Father hath given me to finish, the
same works that I do, bear witness
of me, that the Father hath sent me.
37 And the Father himself, which
hath sent me, hath borne witness of
me. Ye have neither heard his voice
at any time, nor seen his shape.
38 And ye have not his word abid-
ing in you: for whom he hath sent,
him ye believe not.
39 Search the scriptures; for in
them ye think ye have eternal life:
and they are they which testify
of me.
40 And ye will not come to me,
that ye might have life.
41 I receive not honour from men.
42 But I know you, that ye have
not the love of God in you.
43 I am come in my Father's
name, and ye receive me not: if an-
other shall come in his own name,
him ye will receive.
44 How can ye believe, which re-
ceive honour one of another, and

seek not the honour that *cometh* from God only?

45 Do not think that I will accuse you to the Father: there is *one* that accuseth you, *even* Moses, in whom ye trust.

46 For had ye believed Moses, ye would have believed me: for he wrote of me.

47 But if ye believe not his writings, how shall ye believe my words?

Five Loaves and Two Fishes

6 After these things Jesus went over the sea of Galilee, which is *the sea* of Tiberias.

2 And a great multitude followed him, because they saw his miracles which he did on them that were diseased.

3 And Jesus went up into a mountain, and there he sat with his disciples.

4 And the passover, a feast of the Jews, was nigh.

5 When Jesus then lifted up *his* eyes, and saw a great company come unto him, he saith unto Philip, Whence shall we buy bread, that these may eat?

6 And this he said to prove him: for he himself knew what he would do.

7 Philip answered him, Two hundred pennyworth of bread is not sufficient for them, that every one of them may take a little.

8 One of his disciples, Andrew, Simon Peter's brother, saith unto him,

9 There is a lad here, which hath five barley loaves, and two small fishes: but what are they among so many?

10 And Jesus said, Make the men sit down. Now there was much grass in the place. So the men sat down, in number about five thousand.

11 And Jesus took the loaves; and when he had given thanks, he distributed to the disciples, and the disciples to them that were set down; and likewise of the fishes as much as they would.

12 When they were filled, he said unto his disciples, Gather up the fragments that remain, that nothing be lost.

13 Therefore they gathered *them* together, and filled twelve baskets with the fragments of the five barley loaves, which remained over and above unto them that had eaten.

14 Then those men, when they had seen the miracle that Jesus did, said, This is of a truth that prophet that should come into the world.

15 When Jesus therefore perceived that they would come and take him by force, to make him a king, he departed again into a mountain himself alone.

Jesus Walks on the Sea

16 And when even was *now* come, his disciples went down unto the sea,

17 And entered into a ship, and went over the sea toward Capernaum. And it was now dark, and Jesus was not come to them.

18 And the sea arose by reason of a great wind that blew.

19 So when they had rowed about five and twenty or thirty furlongs, they see Jesus walking on the sea, and drawing nigh unto the ship: and they were afraid.

20 But he saith unto them, It is I; be not afraid.

21 Then they willingly received him into the ship: and immediately the ship was at the land whither they went.

22 The day following, when the people which stood on the other side of the sea saw that there was none other boat there, save that one whereinto his disciples were entered, and that Jesus went not with his disciples into the boat, but *that* his disciples were gone away alone;

23 (Howbeit there came other

boats from Tiberias nigh unto the place where they did eat bread, after that the Lord had given thanks:)

24 When the people therefore saw that Jesus was not there, neither his disciples, they also took shipping, and came to Capernaum, seeking for Jesus.

Jesus Is the True Bread from Heaven

25 And when they had found him on the other side of the sea, they said unto him, Rabbi, when camest thou hither?

26 Jesus answered them and said, Verily, verily, I say unto you, Ye seek me, not because ye saw the miracles, but because ye did eat of the loaves, and were filled.

27 Labour not for the meat which perisheth, but for that meat which endureth unto everlasting life, which the Son of man shall give unto you: for him hath God the Father sealed.

28 Then said they unto him, What shall we do, that we might work the works of God?

29 Jesus answered and said unto them, This is the work of God, that ye believe on him whom he hath sent.

30 They said therefore unto him, What sign shewest thou then, that we may see, and believe thee? what dost thou work?

31 Our fathers did eat manna in the desert; as it is written, He gave them bread from heaven to eat.

32 Then Jesus said unto them, Verily, verily, I say unto you, Moses gave you not that bread from heaven; but my Father giveth you the true bread from heaven.

33 For the bread of God is he which cometh down from heaven, and giveth life unto the world.

34 Then said they unto him, Lord, evermore give us this bread.

35 And Jesus said unto them, I am the bread of life: he that cometh to me shall never hunger; and he that believeth on me shall never thirst.

36 But I said unto you, That ye also have seen me, and believe not.

37 All that the Father giveth me shall come to me; and him that cometh to me I will in no wise cast out.

38 For I came down from heaven, not to do mine own will, but the will of him that sent me.

39 And this is the Father's will which hath sent me, that of all which he hath given me I should lose nothing, but should raise it up again at the last day.

40 And this is the will of him that sent me, that every one which seeth the Son, and believeth on him, may have everlasting life: and I will raise him up at the last day.

The Murmuring of the Jews

41 The Jews then murmured at him, because he said, I am the bread which came down from heaven.

42 And they said, Is not this Jesus, the son of Joseph, whose father and mother we know? how is it then that he saith, I came down from heaven?

43 Jesus therefore answered and said unto them, Murmur not among yourselves.

44 No man can come to me, except the Father which hath sent me draw him: and I will raise him up at the last day.

45 It is written in the prophets, And they shall be all taught of God. Every man therefore that hath heard, and hath learned of the Father, cometh unto me.

46 Not that any man hath seen the Father, save he which is of God, he hath seen the Father.

47 Verily, verily, I say unto you, He that believeth on me hath everlasting life.

48 I am that bread of life.

49 Your fathers did eat manna in the wilderness, and are dead.

50 This is the bread which cometh
down from heaven, that a man may
eat thereof, and not die.
51 I am the living bread which
came down from heaven: if any man
eat of this bread, he shall live for
ever: and the bread that I will give
is my flesh, which I will give for the
life of the world.
52 The Jews therefore strove
among themselves, saying, How
can this man give us *his* flesh to eat?
53 Then Jesus said unto them,
Verily, verily, I say unto you, Except
ye eat the flesh of the Son of man,
and drink his blood, ye have no life
in you.
54 Whoso eateth my flesh, and
drinketh my blood, hath eternal life;
and I will raise him up at the last
day.
55 For my flesh is meat indeed,
and my blood is drink indeed.
56 He that eateth my flesh, and
drinketh my blood, dwelleth in me,
and I in him.
57 As the living Father hath sent
me, and I live by the Father: so he
that eateth me, even he shall live
by me.
58 This is that bread which came
down from heaven: not as your fa-
thers did eat manna, and are dead:
he that eateth of this bread shall live
for ever.
59 These things said he in the syn-
agogue, as he taught in Capernaum.

Many Disciples Fall Away

60 Many therefore of his disciples,
when they had heard *this,* said, This
is an hard saying; who can hear it?
61 When Jesus knew in himself
that his disciples murmured at it,
he said unto them, Doth this offend
you?
62 *What* and if ye shall see the Son
of man ascend up where he was be-
fore?
63 It is the spirit that quickeneth;
the flesh profiteth nothing: the
words that I speak unto you, *they*
are spirit, and *they* are life.
64 But there are some of you that
believe not. For Jesus knew from
the beginning who they were that
believed not, and who should betray
him.
65 And he said, Therefore said I
unto you, that no man can come
unto me, except it were given unto
him of my Father.
66 From that *time* many of his dis-
ciples went back, and walked no
more with him.
67 Then said Jesus unto the
twelve, Will ye also go away?
68 Then Simon Peter answered
him, Lord, to whom shall we go?
thou hast the words of eternal life.
69 And we believe and are sure
that thou art that Christ, the Son of
the living God.
70 Jesus answered them, Have
not I chosen you twelve, and one
of you is a devil?
71 He spake of Judas Iscariot
the son of Simon: for he it was that
should betray him, being one of the
twelve.

The Disbelief of Jesus' Brothers

7 After these things Jesus walked
in Galilee: for he would not walk
in Jewry, because the Jews sought
to kill him.
2 Now the Jews' feast of taberna-
cles was at hand.
3 His brethren therefore said unto
him, Depart hence, and go into Ju-
daea, that thy disciples also may see
the works that thou doest.
4 For *there is* no man *that* doeth
any thing in secret, and he himself
seeketh to be known openly. If thou
do these things, shew thyself to the
world.
5 For neither did his brethren be-
lieve in him.
6 Then Jesus said unto them, My
time is not yet come: but your time
is alway ready.

7 The world cannot hate you; but me it hateth, because I testify of it, that the works thereof are evil.

8 Go ye up unto this feast: I go not up yet unto this feast; for my time is not yet full come.

9 When he had said these words unto them, he abode *still* in Galilee.

10 But when his brethren were gone up, then went he also up unto the feast, not openly, but as it were in secret.

11 Then the Jews sought him at the feast, and said, Where is he?

12 And there was much murmuring among the people concerning him: for some said, He is a good man: others said, Nay; but he deceiveth the people.

13 Howbeit no man spake openly of him for fear of the Jews.

The Jews Marvel at Jesus' Teaching

14 Now about the midst of the feast Jesus went up into the temple, and taught.

15 And the Jews marvelled, saying, How knoweth this man letters, having never learned?

16 Jesus answered them, and said, My doctrine is not mine, but his that sent me.

17 If any man will do his will, he shall know of the doctrine, whether it be of God, or *whether* I speak of myself.

18 He that speaketh of himself seeketh his own glory: but he that seeketh his glory that sent him, the same is true, and no unrighteousness is in him.

19 Did not Moses give you the law, and *yet* none of you keepeth the law? Why go ye about to kill me?

20 The people answered and said, Thou hast a devil: who goeth about to kill thee?

21 Jesus answered and said unto them, I have done one work, and ye all marvel.

22 Moses therefore gave unto you circumcision; (not because it is of Moses, but of the fathers;) and ye on the sabbath day circumcise a man.

23 If a man on the sabbath day receive circumcision, that the law of Moses should not be broken; are ye angry at me, because I have made a man every whit whole on the sabbath day?

24 Judge not according to the appearance, but judge righteous judgment.

A Division Among the People

25 Then said some of them of Jerusalem, Is not this he, whom they seek to kill?

26 But, lo, he speaketh boldly, and they say nothing unto him. Do the rulers know indeed that this is the very Christ?

27 Howbeit we know this man whence he is: but when Christ cometh, no man knoweth whence he is.

28 Then cried Jesus in the temple as he taught, saying, Ye both know me, and ye know whence I am: and I am not come of myself, but he that sent me is true, whom ye know not.

29 But I know him: for I am from him, and he hath sent me.

30 Then they sought to take him: but no man laid hands on him, because his hour was not yet come.

31 And many of the people believed on him, and said, When Christ cometh, will he do more miracles than these which this *man* hath done?

32 The Pharisees heard that the people murmured such things concerning him; and the Pharisees and the chief priests sent officers to take him.

33 Then said Jesus unto them, Yet a little while am I with you, and *then* I go unto him that sent me.

34 Ye shall seek me, and shall not find *me:* and where I am, *thither* ye cannot come.

35 Then said the Jews among
themselves, Whither will he go,
that we shall not find him? will he
go unto the dispersed among the
Gentiles, and teach the Gentiles?
36 What *manner of* saying is this
that he said, Ye shall seek me, and
shall not find *me:* and where I am,
thither ye cannot come?
37 In the last day, that great *day*
of the feast, Jesus stood and cried,
saying, If any man thirst, let him
come unto me, and drink.
38 He that believeth on me, as the
scripture hath said, out of his belly
shall flow rivers of living water.
39 (But this spake he of the Spirit,
which they that believe on him
should receive: for the Holy Ghost
was not yet *given;* because that
Jesus was not yet glorified.)
40 Many of the people therefore,
when they heard this saying, said,
Of a truth this is the Prophet.
41 Others said, This is the Christ.
But some said, Shall Christ come
out of Galilee?
42 Hath not the scripture said,
That Christ cometh of the seed of
David, and out of the town of Beth-
lehem, where David was?
43 So there was a division among
the people because of him.
44 And some of them would have
taken him; but no man laid hands
on him.

The Pharisees' Unbelief

45 Then came the officers to the
chief priests and Pharisees; and they
said unto them, Why have ye not
brought him?
46 The officers answered, Never
man spake like this man.
47 Then answered them the Phar-
isees, Are ye also deceived?
48 Have any of the rulers or of the
Pharisees believed on him?
49 But this people who knoweth
not the law are cursed.
50 Nicodemus saith unto them,
(he that came to Jesus by night, be-
ing one of them,)
51 Doth our law judge *any* man,
before it hear him, and know what
he doeth?
52 They answered and said unto
him, Art thou also of Galilee? Search,
and look: for out of Galilee ariseth
no prophet.
53 And every man went unto his
own house.

Jesus Forgives an Adulterous Woman

8 Jesus went unto the mount of
Olives.
2 And early in the morning he
came again into the temple, and
all the people came unto him; and
he sat down, and taught them.
3 And the scribes and Pharisees
brought unto him a woman taken
in adultery; and when they had set
her in the midst,
4 They say unto him, Master, this
woman was taken in adultery, in the
very act.
5 Now Moses in the law com-
manded us, that such should be
stoned: but what sayest thou?
6 This they said, tempting him,
that they might have to accuse him.
But Jesus stooped down, and with
his finger wrote on the ground, *as
though he heard them not.*
7 So when they continued asking
him, he lifted up himself, and said
unto them, He that is without sin
among you, let him first cast a stone
at her.
8 And again he stooped down, and
wrote on the ground.
9 And they which heard *it,* being
convicted by *their own* conscience,
went out one by one, beginning at
the eldest, *even* unto the last: and
Jesus was left alone, and the woman
standing in the midst.
10 When Jesus had lifted up him-
self, and saw none but the woman,
he said unto her, Woman, where are

those thine accusers? hath no man
condemned thee?
11 She said, No man, Lord. And
Jesus said unto her, Neither do I
condemn thee: go, and sin no more.

The Light of the World

12 Then spake Jesus again unto
them, saying, I am the light of the
world: he that followeth me shall
not walk in darkness, but shall have
the light of life.
13 The Pharisees therefore said
unto him, Thou bearest record of
thyself; thy record is not true.
14 Jesus answered and said unto
them, Though I bear record of my-
self, *yet* my record is true: for I know
whence I came, and whither I go;
but ye cannot tell whence I come,
and whither I go.
15 Ye judge after the flesh; I judge
no man.
16 And yet if I judge, my judgment
is true: for I am not alone, but I and
the Father that sent me.
17 It is also written in your law, that
the testimony of two men is true.
18 I am one that bear witness of
myself, and the Father that sent me
beareth witness of me.
19 Then said they unto him, Where
is thy Father? Jesus answered, Ye
neither know me, nor my Father: if
ye had known me, ye should have
known my Father also.
20 These words spake Jesus in the
treasury, as he taught in the temple:
and no man laid hands on him; for
his hour was not yet come.
21 Then said Jesus again unto
them, I go my way, and ye shall
seek me, and shall die in your sins:
whither I go, ye cannot come.
22 Then said the Jews, Will he kill
himself? because he saith, Whither
I go, ye cannot come.

Jesus Speaks for the Father

23 And he said unto them, Ye are
from beneath; I am from above: ye
are of this world; I am not of this
world.
24 I said therefore unto you, that
ye shall die in your sins: for if ye be-
lieve not that I am *he,* ye shall die in
your sins.
25 Then said they unto him, Who
art thou? And Jesus saith unto
them, Even *the same* that I said
unto you from the beginning.
26 I have many things to say and
to judge of you: but he that sent
me is true; and I speak to the world
those things which I have heard of
him.
27 They understood not that he
spake to them of the Father.
28 Then said Jesus unto them,
When ye have lifted up the Son of
man, then shall ye know that I am
he, and *that* I do nothing of myself;
but as my Father hath taught me, I
speak these things.
29 And he that sent me is with me:
the Father hath not left me alone;
for I do always those things that
please him.
30 As he spake these words, many
believed on him.

Abraham's Seed

31 Then said Jesus to those Jews
which believed on him, If ye con-
tinue in my word, *then* are ye my
disciples indeed;
32 And ye shall know the truth,
and the truth shall make you free.
33 They answered him, We be
Abraham's seed, and were never
in bondage to any man: how sayest
thou, Ye shall be made free?
34 Jesus answered them, Verily,
verily, I say unto you, Whosoever
committeth sin is the servant of
sin.
35 And the servant abideth not
in the house for ever: *but* the Son
abideth ever.
36 If the Son therefore shall make
you free, ye shall be free indeed.
37 I know that ye are Abraham's

seed; but ye seek to kill me, because my word hath no place in you.

38 I speak that which I have seen with my Father: and ye do that which ye have seen with your father.

39 They answered and said unto him, Abraham is our father. Jesus saith unto them, If ye were Abraham's children, ye would do the works of Abraham.

40 But now ye seek to kill me, a man that hath told you the truth, which I have heard of God: this did not Abraham.

41 Ye do the deeds of your father. Then said they to him, We be not born of fornication; we have one Father, *even* God.

42 Jesus said unto them, If God were your Father, ye would love me: for I proceeded forth and came from God; neither came I of myself, but he sent me.

43 Why do ye not understand my speech? *even* because ye cannot hear my word.

The Devil's Children

44 Ye are of *your* father the devil, and the lusts of your father ye will do. He was a murderer from the beginning, and abode not in the truth, because there is no truth in him. When he speaketh a lie, he speaketh of his own: for he is a liar, and the father of it.

45 And because I tell *you* the truth, ye believe me not.

46 Which of you convinceth me of sin? And if I say the truth, why do ye not believe me?

47 He that is of God heareth God's words: ye therefore hear *them* not, because ye are not of God.

Honoured by the Father

48 Then answered the Jews, and said unto him, Say we not well that thou art a Samaritan, and hast a devil?

49 Jesus answered, I have not a devil; but I honour my Father, and ye do dishonour me.

50 And I seek not mine own glory: there is one that seeketh and judgeth.

51 Verily, verily, I say unto you, If a man keep my saying, he shall never see death.

52 Then said the Jews unto him, Now we know that thou hast a devil. Abraham is dead, and the prophets; and thou sayest, If a man keep my saying, he shall never taste of death.

53 Art thou greater than our father Abraham, which is dead? and the prophets are dead: whom makest thou thyself?

54 Jesus answered, If I honour myself, my honour is nothing: it is my Father that honoureth me; of whom ye say, that he is your God:

55 Yet ye have not known him; but I know him: and if I should say, I know him not, I shall be a liar like unto you: but I know him, and keep his saying.

56 Your father Abraham rejoiced to see my day: and he saw *it,* and was glad.

57 Then said the Jews unto him, Thou art not yet fifty years old, and hast thou seen Abraham?

58 Jesus said unto them, Verily, verily, I say unto you, Before Abraham was, I am.

59 Then took they up stones to cast at him: but Jesus hid himself, and went out of the temple, going through the midst of them, and so passed by.

Jesus Heals a Man Blind from Birth

9 And as *Jesus* passed by, he saw a man which was blind from *his* birth.

2 And his disciples asked him, saying, Master, who did sin, this man, or his parents, that he was born blind?

3 Jesus answered, Neither hath this man sinned, nor his parents: but that the works of God should be made manifest in him.

4 I must work the works of him that sent me, while it is day: the night cometh, when no man can work.

5 As long as I am in the world, I am the light of the world.

6 When he had thus spoken, he spat on the ground, and made clay of the spittle, and he anointed the eyes of the blind man with the clay,

7 And said unto him, Go, wash in the pool of Siloam, (which is by interpretation, Sent.) He went his way therefore, and washed, and came seeing.

8 The neighbours therefore, and they which before had seen him that he was blind, said, Is not this he that sat and begged?

9 Some said, This is he: others *said,* He is like him: *but* he said, I am *he.*

10 Therefore said they unto him, How were thine eyes opened?

11 He answered and said, A man that is called Jesus made clay, and anointed mine eyes, and said unto me, Go to the pool of Siloam, and wash: and I went and washed, and I received sight.

12 Then said they unto him, Where is he? He said, I know not.

The Pharisees Question the Healing

13 They brought to the Pharisees him that aforetime was blind.

14 And it was the sabbath day when Jesus made the clay, and opened his eyes.

15 Then again the Pharisees also asked him how he had received his sight. He said unto them, He put clay upon mine eyes, and I washed, and do see.

16 Therefore said some of the Pharisees, This man is not of God, because he keepeth not the sabbath day. Others said, How can a man that is a sinner do such miracles? And there was a division among them.

17 They say unto the blind man again, What sayest thou of him, that he hath opened thine eyes? He said, He is a prophet.

18 But the Jews did not believe concerning him, that he had been blind, and received his sight, until they called the parents of him that had received his sight.

19 And they asked them, saying, Is this your son, who ye say was born blind? how then doth he now see?

20 His parents answered them and said, We know that this is our son, and that he was born blind:

21 But by what means he now seeth, we know not; or who hath opened his eyes, we know not: he is of age; ask him: he shall speak for himself.

22 These *words* spake his parents, because they feared the Jews: for the Jews had agreed already, that if any man did confess that he was Christ, he should be put out of the synagogue.

23 Therefore said his parents, He is of age; ask him.

24 Then again called they the man that was blind, and said unto him, Give God the praise: we know that this man is a sinner.

25 He answered and said, Whether he be a sinner *or no,* I know not: one thing I know, that, whereas I was blind, now I see.

26 Then said they to him again, What did he to thee? how opened he thine eyes?

27 He answered them, I have told you already, and ye did not hear: wherefore would ye hear *it* again? will ye also be his disciples?

28 Then they reviled him, and said, Thou art his disciple; but we are Moses' disciples.

29 We know that God spake unto

Moses: *as for* this *fellow,* we know
not from whence he is.
30 The man answered and said
unto them, Why herein is a marvellous thing, that ye know not
from whence he is, and *yet* he hath
opened mine eyes.
31 Now we know that God heareth
not sinners: but if any man be a worshipper of God, and doeth his will,
him he heareth.
32 Since the world began was it
not heard that any man opened the
eyes of one that was born blind.
33 If this man were not of God, he
could do nothing.
34 They answered and said unto
him, Thou wast altogether born in
sins, and dost thou teach us? And
they cast him out.

The Healed Man's Belief

35 Jesus heard that they had cast
him out; and when he had found
him, he said unto him, Dost thou
believe on the Son of God?
36 He answered and said, Who
is he, Lord, that I might believe on
him?
37 And Jesus said unto him, Thou
hast both seen him, and it is he that
talketh with thee.
38 And he said, Lord, I believe.
And he worshipped him.
39 And Jesus said, For judgment I
am come into this world, that they
which see not might see; and that
they which see might be made blind.
40 And *some* of the Pharisees
which were with him heard these
words, and said unto him, Are we
blind also?
41 Jesus said unto them, If ye
were blind, ye should have no sin:
but now ye say, We see; therefore
your sin remaineth.

The Good Shepherd

10 Verily, verily, I say unto you,
He that entereth not by
the door into the sheepfold, but
climbeth up some other way, the
same is a thief and a robber.
2 But he that entereth in by the
door is the shepherd of the sheep.
3 To him the porter openeth; and
the sheep hear his voice: and he calleth his own sheep by name, and
leadeth them out.
4 And when he putteth forth his
own sheep, he goeth before them,
and the sheep follow him: for they
know his voice.
5 And a stranger will they not follow, but will flee from him: for they
know not the voice of strangers.
6 This parable spake Jesus unto
them: but they understood not what
things they were which he spake
unto them.
7 Then said Jesus unto them
again, Verily, verily, I say unto you,
I am the door of the sheep.
8 All that ever came before me are
thieves and robbers: but the sheep
did not hear them.
9 I am the door: by me if any man
enter in, he shall be saved, and shall
go in and out, and find pasture.
10 The thief cometh not, but for
to steal, and to kill, and to destroy:
I am come that they might have life,
and that they might have *it* more
abundantly.
11 I am the good shepherd: the
good shepherd giveth his life for
the sheep.
12 But he that is an hireling, and
not the shepherd, whose own the
sheep are not, seeth the wolf coming, and leaveth the sheep, and
fleeth: and the wolf catcheth them,
and scattereth the sheep.
13 The hireling fleeth, because he
is an hireling, and careth not for the
sheep.
14 I am the good shepherd, and
know my *sheep,* and am known of
mine.
15 As the Father knoweth me, even
so know I the Father: and I lay down
my life for the sheep.

16 And other sheep I have, which are not of this fold: them also I must bring, and they shall hear my voice; and there shall be one fold, *and* one shepherd.
17 Therefore doth my Father love me, because I lay down my life, that I might take it again.
18 No man taketh it from me, but I lay it down of myself. I have power to lay it down, and I have power to take it again. This commandment have I received of my Father.
19 There was a division therefore again among the Jews for these sayings.
20 And many of them said, He hath a devil, and is mad; why hear ye him?
21 Others said, These are not the words of him that hath a devil. Can a devil open the eyes of the blind?

Jesus Charged with Blasphemy

22 And it was at Jerusalem the feast of the dedication, and it was winter.
23 And Jesus walked in the temple in Solomon's porch.
24 Then came the Jews round about him, and said unto him, How long dost thou make us to doubt? If thou be the Christ, tell us plainly.
25 Jesus answered them, I told you, and ye believed not: the works that I do in my Father's name, they bear witness of me.
26 But ye believe not, because ye are not of my sheep, as I said unto you.
27 My sheep hear my voice, and I know them, and they follow me:
28 And I give unto them eternal life; and they shall never perish, neither shall any *man* pluck them out of my hand.
29 My Father, which gave *them* me, is greater than all; and no *man* is able to pluck *them* out of my Father's hand.
30 I and *my* Father are one.
31 Then the Jews took up stones again to stone him.
32 Jesus answered them, Many good works have I shewed you from my Father; for which of those works do ye stone me?
33 The Jews answered him, saying, For a good work we stone thee not; but for blasphemy; and because that thou, being a man, makest thyself God.
34 Jesus answered them, Is it not written in your law, I said, Ye are gods?
35 If he called them gods, unto whom the word of God came, and the scripture cannot be broken;
36 Say ye of him, whom the Father hath sanctified, and sent into the world, Thou blasphemest; because I said, I am the Son of God?
37 If I do not the works of my Father, believe me not.
38 But if I do, though ye believe not me, believe the works: that ye may know, and believe, that the Father *is* in me, and I in him.
39 Therefore they sought again to take him: but he escaped out of their hand,
40 And went away again beyond Jordan into the place where John at first baptized; and there he abode.
41 And many resorted unto him, and said, John did no miracle: but all things that John spake of this man were true.
42 And many believed on him there.

Jesus' Friend Lazarus Dies

11 Now a certain *man* was sick, *named* Lazarus, of Bethany, the town of Mary and her sister Martha.
2 (It was *that* Mary which anointed the Lord with ointment, and wiped his feet with her hair, whose brother Lazarus was sick.)
3 Therefore his sisters sent unto him, saying, Lord, behold, he whom thou lovest is sick.

4 When Jesus heard *that,* he said,
This sickness is not unto death, but
for the glory of God, that the Son of
God might be glorified thereby.
5 Now Jesus loved Martha, and
her sister, and Lazarus.
6 When he had heard therefore
that he was sick, he abode two days
still in the same place where he was.
7 Then after that saith he to *his*
disciples, Let us go into Judaea
again.
8 *His* disciples say unto him, Mas-
ter, the Jews of late sought to stone
thee; and goest thou thither again?
9 Jesus answered, Are there not
twelve hours in the day? If any man
walk in the day, he stumbleth not,
because he seeth the light of this
world.
10 But if a man walk in the night,
he stumbleth, because there is no
light in him.
11 These things said he: and after
that he saith unto them, Our friend
Lazarus sleepeth; but I go, that I
may awake him out of sleep.
12 Then said his disciples, Lord, if
he sleep, he shall do well.
13 Howbeit Jesus spake of his
death: but they thought that he had
spoken of taking of rest in sleep.
14 Then said Jesus unto them
plainly, Lazarus is dead.
15 And I am glad for your sakes
that I was not there, to the intent
ye may believe; nevertheless let us
go unto him.
16 Then said Thomas, which is
called Didymus, unto his fellow-
disciples, Let us also go, that we
may die with him.

Martha's Assurance of the Resurrection

17 Then when Jesus came, he
found that he had *lain* in the grave
four days already.
18 Now Bethany was nigh unto
Jerusalem, about fifteen furlongs
off:
19 And many of the Jews came to
Martha and Mary, to comfort them
concerning their brother.
20 Then Martha, as soon as she
heard that Jesus was coming, went
and met him: but Mary sat *still* in
the house.
21 Then said Martha unto Jesus,
Lord, if thou hadst been here, my
brother had not died.
22 But I know, that even now,
whatsoever thou wilt ask of God,
God will give *it* thee.
23 Jesus saith unto her, Thy
brother shall rise again.
24 Martha saith unto him, I know
that he shall rise again in the resur-
rection at the last day.
25 Jesus said unto her, I am the
resurrection, and the life: he that
believeth in me, though he were
dead, yet shall he live:
26 And whosoever liveth and be-
lieveth in me shall never die. Be-
lievest thou this?
27 She saith unto him, Yea, Lord: I
believe that thou art the Christ, the
Son of God, which should come into
the world.
28 And when she had so said, she
went her way, and called Mary her
sister secretly, saying, The Master
is come, and calleth for thee.
29 As soon as she heard *that,* she
arose quickly, and came unto him.
30 Now Jesus was not yet come
into the town, but was in that place
where Martha met him.
31 The Jews then which were with
her in the house, and comforted her,
when they saw Mary, that she rose
up hastily and went out, followed
her, saying, She goeth unto the grave
to weep there.

Jesus Weeps

32 Then when Mary was come
where Jesus was, and saw him, she
fell down at his feet, saying unto
him, Lord, if thou hadst been here,
my brother had not died.

33 When Jesus therefore saw her
weeping, and the Jews also weeping
which came with her, he groaned in
the spirit, and was troubled,
34 And said, Where have ye laid
him? They said unto him, Lord,
come and see.
35 Jesus wept.
36 Then said the Jews, Behold
how he loved him!
37 And some of them said, Could
not this man, which opened the eyes
of the blind, have caused that even
this man should not have died?

Jesus Raises Lazarus

38 Jesus therefore again groaning
in himself cometh to the grave. It
was a cave, and a stone lay upon it.
39 Jesus said, Take ye away the
stone. Martha, the sister of him that
was dead, saith unto him, Lord, by
this time he stinketh: for he hath
been *dead* four days.
40 Jesus saith unto her, Said I not
unto thee, that, if thou wouldest
believe, thou shouldest see the glory
of God?
41 Then they took away the stone
from the place where the dead was
laid. And Jesus lifted up *his* eyes,
and said, Father, I thank thee that
thou hast heard me.
42 And I knew that thou hear-
est me always: but because of the
people which stand by I said *it,* that
they may believe that thou hast
sent me.
43 And when he thus had spoken,
he cried with a loud voice, Lazarus,
come forth.
44 And he that was dead came
forth, bound hand and foot with
graveclothes: and his face was
bound about with a napkin. Jesus
saith unto them, Loose him, and let
him go.

The Plan to Kill Jesus

45 Then many of the Jews which
came to Mary, and had seen the
things which Jesus did, believed
on him.
46 But some of them went their
ways to the Pharisees, and told
them what things Jesus had done.
47 Then gathered the chief priests
and the Pharisees a council, and
said, What do we? for this man doeth
many miracles.
48 If we let him thus alone, all *men*
will believe on him: and the Romans
shall come and take away both our
place and nation.
49 And one of them, *named* Ca-
iaphas, being the high priest that
same year, said unto them, Ye know
nothing at all,
50 Nor consider that it is expedi-
ent for us, that one man should die
for the people, and that the whole
nation perish not.
51 And this spake he not of him-
self: but being high priest that year,
he prophesied that Jesus should die
for that nation;
52 And not for that nation only,
but that also he should gather to-
gether in one the children of God
that were scattered abroad.
53 Then from that day forth they
took counsel together for to put him
to death.
54 Jesus therefore walked no
more openly among the Jews; but
went thence unto a country near
to the wilderness, into a city called
Ephraim, and there continued with
his disciples.
55 And the Jews' passover was
nigh at hand: and many went out of
the country up to Jerusalem before
the passover, to purify themselves.
56 Then sought they for Jesus, and
spake among themselves, as they
stood in the temple, What think ye,
that he will not come to the feast?
57 Now both the chief priests and
the Pharisees had given a com-
mandment, that, if any man knew
where he were, he should shew *it,*
that they might take him.

Mary Anoints the Feet of Jesus

12 Then Jesus six days before
the passover came to Beth-
any, where Lazarus was which had
been dead, whom he raised from
the dead.
2 There they made him a supper;
and Martha served: but Lazarus was
one of them that sat at the table with
him.
3 Then took Mary a pound of
ointment of spikenard, very costly,
and anointed the feet of Jesus, and
wiped his feet with her hair: and the
house was filled with the odour of
the ointment.
4 Then saith one of his disciples,
Judas Iscariot, Simon's *son,* which
should betray him,
5 Why was not this ointment sold
for three hundred pence, and given
to the poor?
6 This he said, not that he cared
for the poor; but because he was
a thief, and had the bag, and bare
what was put therein.
7 Then said Jesus, Let her alone:
against the day of my burying hath
she kept this.
8 For the poor always ye have with
you; but me ye have not always.
9 Much people of the Jews there-
fore knew that he was there: and
they came not for Jesus' sake only,
but that they might see Lazarus also,
whom he had raised from the dead.
10 But the chief priests consulted
that they might put Lazarus also to
death;
11 Because that by reason of him
many of the Jews went away, and
believed on Jesus.

Jesus Enters Jerusalem

12 On the next day much people
that were come to the feast, when
they heard that Jesus was coming
to Jerusalem,
13 Took branches of palm trees,
and went forth to meet him, and
cried, Hosanna: Blessed *is* the King
of Israel that cometh in the name of
the Lord.
14 And Jesus, when he had found a
young ass, sat thereon; as it is writ-
ten,
15 Fear not, daughter of Sion: be-
hold, thy King cometh, sitting on an
ass's colt.
16 These things understood not
his disciples at the first: but when
Jesus was glorified, then remem-
bered they that these things were
written of him, and *that* they had
done these things unto him.
17 The people therefore that was
with him when he called Lazarus
out of his grave, and raised him from
the dead, bare record.
18 For this cause the people also
met him, for that they heard that he
had done this miracle.
19 The Pharisees therefore said
among themselves, Perceive ye
how ye prevail nothing? behold,
the world is gone after him.

The Son of Man to Be Glorified

20 And there were certain Greeks
among them that came up to wor-
ship at the feast:
21 The same came therefore to
Philip, which was of Bethsaida of
Galilee, and desired him, saying,
Sir, we would see Jesus.
22 Philip cometh and telleth An-
drew: and again Andrew and Philip
tell Jesus.
23 And Jesus answered them, say-
ing, The hour is come, that the Son
of man should be glorified.
24 Verily, verily, I say unto you,
Except a corn of wheat fall into the
ground and die, it abideth alone:
but if it die, it bringeth forth much
fruit.
25 He that loveth his life shall lose
it; and he that hateth his life in this
world shall keep it unto life eternal.
26 If any man serve me, let him
follow me; and where I am, there

shall also my servant be: if any man
serve me, him will *my* Father hon-
our.
27 Now is my soul troubled; and
what shall I say? Father, save me
from this hour: but for this cause
came I unto this hour.
28 Father, glorify thy name. Then
came there a voice from heaven,
saying, I have both glorified *it,* and
will glorify *it* again.
29 The people therefore, that
stood by, and heard *it,* said that it
thundered: others said, An angel
spake to him.
30 Jesus answered and said, This
voice came not because of me, but
for your sakes.
31 Now is the judgment of this
world: now shall the prince of this
world be cast out.
32 And I, if I be lifted up from the
earth, will draw all *men* unto me.
33 This he said, signifying what
death he should die.
34 The people answered him, We
have heard out of the law that Christ
abideth for ever: and how sayest
thou, The Son of man must be lifted
up? who is this Son of man?
35 Then Jesus said unto them,
Yet a little while is the light with
you. Walk while ye have the light,
lest darkness come upon you: for he
that walketh in darkness knoweth
not whither he goeth.
36 While ye have light, believe in
the light, that ye may be the children
of light. These things spake Jesus,
and departed, and did hide himself
from them.

Refusal to Confess Jesus

37 But though he had done so
many miracles before them, yet
they believed not on him:
38 That the saying of Esaias the
prophet might be fulfilled, which
he spake, Lord, who hath believed
our report? and to whom hath the
arm of the Lord been revealed?
39 Therefore they could not be-
lieve, because that Esaias said again,
40 He hath blinded their eyes,
and hardened their heart; that they
should not see with *their* eyes, nor
understand with *their* heart, and be
converted, and I should heal them.
41 These things said Esaias, when
he saw his glory, and spake of him.
42 Nevertheless among the chief
rulers also many believed on him;
but because of the Pharisees they
did not confess *him,* lest they should
be put out of the synagogue:
43 For they loved the praise of
men more than the praise of God.
44 Jesus cried and said, He that
believeth on me, believeth not on
me, but on him that sent me.
45 And he that seeth me seeth him
that sent me.
46 I am come a light into the
world, that whosoever believeth
on me should not abide in darkness.
47 And if any man hear my words,
and believe not, I judge him not: for
I came not to judge the world, but
to save the world.
48 He that rejecteth me, and re-
ceiveth not my words, hath one that
judgeth him: the word that I have
spoken, the same shall judge him
in the last day.
49 For I have not spoken of myself;
but the Father which sent me, he
gave me a commandment, what I
should say, and what I should speak.
50 And I know that his command-
ment is life everlasting: whatsoever
I speak therefore, even as the Father
said unto me, so I speak.

Jesus Washes the Feet of the Disciples

13 Now before the feast of the
passover, when Jesus knew
that his hour was come that he
should depart out of this world unto
the Father, having loved his own
which were in the world, he loved
them unto the end.

2 And supper being ended, the
devil having now put into the heart
of Judas Iscariot, Simon's *son,* to
betray him;
3 Jesus knowing that the Father
had given all things into his hands,
and that he was come from God,
and went to God;
4 He riseth from supper, and
laid aside his garments; and took a
towel, and girded himself.
5 After that he poureth water into
a bason, and began to wash the
disciples' feet, and to wipe *them*
with the towel wherewith he was
girded.
6 Then cometh he to Simon Peter:
and Peter saith unto him, Lord, dost
thou wash my feet?
7 Jesus answered and said unto
him, What I do thou knowest not
now; but thou shalt know hereafter.
8 Peter saith unto him, Thou shalt
never wash my feet. Jesus answered
him, If I wash thee not, thou hast no
part with me.
9 Simon Peter saith unto him,
Lord, not my feet only, but also *my*
hands and *my* head.
10 Jesus saith to him, He that is
washed needeth not save to wash
his feet, but is clean every whit: and
ye are clean, but not all.
11 For he knew who should betray
him; therefore said he, Ye are not all
clean.
12 So after he had washed their
feet, and had taken his garments,
and was set down again, he said
unto them, Know ye what I have
done to you?
13 Ye call me Master and Lord: and
ye say well; for *so* I am.
14 If I then, *your* Lord and Master,
have washed your feet; ye also ought
to wash one another's feet.
15 For I have given you an exam-
ple, that ye should do as I have done
to you.
16 Verily, verily, I say unto you, The
servant is not greater than his lord;
neither he that is sent greater than
he that sent him.
17 If ye know these things, happy
are ye if ye do them.

Preparing for His Betrayal

18 I speak not of you all: I know
whom I have chosen: but that the
scripture may be fulfilled, He that
eateth bread with me hath lifted up
his heel against me.
19 Now I tell you before it come,
that, when it is come to pass, ye may
believe that I am *he.*
20 Verily, verily, I say unto you, He
that receiveth whomsoever I send
receiveth me; and he that receiveth
me receiveth him that sent me.
21 When Jesus had thus said, he
was troubled in spirit, and testified,
and said, Verily, verily, I say unto
you, that one of you shall betray me.
22 Then the disciples looked one
on another, doubting of whom he
spake.
23 Now there was leaning on
Jesus' bosom one of his disciples,
whom Jesus loved.
24 Simon Peter therefore beck-
oned to him, that he should ask who
it should be of whom he spake.
25 He then lying on Jesus' breast
saith unto him, Lord, who is it?
26 Jesus answered, He it is, to
whom I shall give a sop, when I have
dipped *it.* And when he had dipped
the sop, he gave *it* to Judas Iscariot,
the son of Simon.
27 And after the sop Satan entered
into him. Then said Jesus unto him,
That thou doest, do quickly.
28 Now no man at the table knew
for what intent he spake this unto
him.
29 For some *of them* thought, be-
cause Judas had the bag, that Jesus
had said unto him, Buy *those things*
that we have need of against the
feast; or, that he should give some-
thing to the poor.
30 He then having received the

sop went immediately out: and it
was night.

Peter to Deny Jesus

31 Therefore, when he was gone
out, Jesus said, Now is the Son of
man glorified, and God is glorified
in him.
32 If God be glorified in him, God
shall also glorify him in himself, and
shall straightway glorify him.
33 Little children, yet a little while
I am with you. Ye shall seek me: and
as I said unto the Jews, Whither I
go, ye cannot come; so now I say
to you.
34 A new commandment I give
unto you, That ye love one another;
as I have loved you, that ye also love
one another.
35 By this shall all *men* know that
ye are my disciples, if ye have love
one to another.
36 Simon Peter said unto him,
Lord, whither goest thou? Jesus
answered him, Whither I go, thou
canst not follow me now; but thou
shalt follow me afterwards.
37 Peter said unto him, Lord, why
cannot I follow thee now? I will lay
down my life for thy sake.
38 Jesus answered him, Wilt thou
lay down thy life for my sake? Verily,
verily, I say unto thee, The cock shall
not crow, till thou hast denied me
thrice.

A House of Many Mansions

14 Let not your heart be troubled:
ye believe in God, believe also
in me.
2 In my Father's house are many
mansions: if *it were* not *so,* I would
have told you. I go to prepare a place
for you.
3 And if I go and prepare a place
for you, I will come again, and re-
ceive you unto myself; that where
I am, *there* ye may be also.
4 And whither I go ye know, and
the way ye know.

Jesus Is the Way, the Truth, and the Life

5 Thomas saith unto him, Lord,
we know not whither thou goest;
and how can we know the way?
6 Jesus saith unto him, I am the
way, the truth, and the life: no man
cometh unto the Father, but by me.
7 If ye had known me, ye should
have known my Father also: and
from henceforth ye know him, and
have seen him.
8 Philip saith unto him, Lord, shew
us the Father, and it sufficeth us.
9 Jesus saith unto him, Have I
been so long time with you, and yet
hast thou not known me, Philip?
he that hath seen me hath seen the
Father; and how sayest thou *then,*
Shew us the Father?
10 Believest thou not that I am in
the Father, and the Father in me?
the words that I speak unto you I
speak not of myself: but the Father
that dwelleth in me, he doeth the
works.
11 Believe me that I *am* in the Fa-
ther, and the Father in me: or else
believe me for the very works' sake.
12 Verily, verily, I say unto you, He
that believeth on me, the works that
I do shall he do also; and greater
works than these shall he do; be-
cause I go unto my Father.
13 And whatsoever ye shall ask
in my name, that will I do, that the
Father may be glorified in the Son.
14 If ye shall ask any thing in my
name, I will do *it.*

A Comforter Will Come

15 If ye love me, keep my com-
mandments.
16 And I will pray the Father, and
he shall give you another Comforter,
that he may abide with you for ever;
17 *Even* the Spirit of truth; whom
the world cannot receive, because it
seeth him not, neither knoweth him:
but ye know him; for he dwelleth
with you, and shall be in you.

18 I will not leave you comfortless:
I will come to you.
19 Yet a little while, and the world
seeth me no more; but ye see me:
because I live, ye shall live also.
20 At that day ye shall know that I
am in my Father, and ye in me, and
I in you.
21 He that hath my command-
ments, and keepeth them, he it is
that loveth me: and he that loveth
me shall be loved of my Father, and
I will love him, and will manifest
myself to him.
22 Judas saith unto him, not Is-
cariot, Lord, how is it that thou wilt
manifest thyself unto us, and not
unto the world?
23 Jesus answered and said unto
him, If a man love me, he will keep
my words: and my Father will love
him, and we will come unto him,
and make our abode with him.
24 He that loveth me not keepeth
not my sayings: and the word which
ye hear is not mine, but the Father's
which sent me.
25 These things have I spoken
unto you, being *yet* present with
you.
26 But the Comforter, *which is* the
Holy Ghost, whom the Father will
send in my name, he shall teach you
all things, and bring all things to
your remembrance, whatsoever I
have said unto you.
27 Peace I leave with you, my
peace I give unto you: not as the
world giveth, give I unto you. Let
not your heart be troubled, neither
let it be afraid.
28 Ye have heard how I said unto
you, I go away, and come *again* unto
you. If ye loved me, ye would rejoice,
because I said, I go unto the Father:
for my Father is greater than I.
29 And now I have told you before
it come to pass, that, when it is come
to pass, ye might believe.
30 Hereafter I will not talk much
with you: for the prince of this world
cometh, and hath nothing in me.
31 But that the world may know
that I love the Father; and as the Fa-
ther gave me commandment, even
so I do. Arise, let us go hence.

The True Vine

15 I am the true vine, and my Fa-
ther is the husbandman.
2 Every branch in me that beareth
not fruit he taketh away: and every
branch that beareth fruit, he purg-
eth it, that it may bring forth more
fruit.
3 Now ye are clean through the
word which I have spoken unto you.
4 Abide in me, and I in you. As the
branch cannot bear fruit of itself,
except it abide in the vine; no more
can ye, except ye abide in me.
5 I am the vine, ye *are* the
branches: He that abideth in me,
and I in him, the same bringeth
forth much fruit: for without me
ye can do nothing.
6 If a man abide not in me, he is
cast forth as a branch, and is with-
ered; and men gather them, and
cast *them* into the fire, and they are
burned.
7 If ye abide in me, and my words
abide in you, ye shall ask what ye
will, and it shall be done unto you.
8 Herein is my Father glorified,
that ye bear much fruit; so shall ye
be my disciples.
9 As the Father hath loved me, so
have I loved you: continue ye in my
love.
10 If ye keep my commandments,
ye shall abide in my love; even as I
have kept my Father's command-
ments, and abide in his love.
11 These things have I spoken
unto you, that my joy might remain
in you, and *that* your joy might be
full.
12 This is my commandment, That
ye love one another, as I have loved
you.
13 Greater love hath no man than

this, that a man lay down his life for
his friends.
14 Ye are my friends, if ye do what-
soever I command you.
15 Henceforth I call you not ser-
vants; for the servant knoweth
not what his lord doeth: but I have
called you friends; for all things that
I have heard of my Father I have
made known unto you.
16 Ye have not chosen me, but I
have chosen you, and ordained you,
that ye should go and bring forth
fruit, and *that* your fruit should re-
main: that whatsoever ye shall ask
of the Father in my name, he may
give it you.
17 These things I command you,
that ye love one another.

The World Will Hate Jesus' Followers

18 If the world hate you, ye know
that it hated me before *it hated* you.
19 If ye were of the world, the
world would love his own: but be-
cause ye are not of the world, but I
have chosen you out of the world,
therefore the world hateth you.
20 Remember the word that I said
unto you, The servant is not greater
than his lord. If they have perse-
cuted me, they will also persecute
you; if they have kept my saying,
they will keep yours also.
21 But all these things will they
do unto you for my name's sake,
because they know not him that
sent me.
22 If I had not come and spoken
unto them, they had not had sin: but
now they have no cloke for their sin.
23 He that hateth me hateth my
Father also.
24 If I had not done among them
the works which none other man
did, they had not had sin: but now
have they both seen and hated both
me and my Father.
25 But *this cometh to pass,* that
the word might be fulfilled that is
written in their law, They hated me
without a cause.
26 But when the Comforter is
come, whom I will send unto you
from the Father, *even* the Spirit of
truth, which proceedeth from the
Father, he shall testify of me:
27 And ye also shall bear witness,
because ye have been with me from
the beginning.

Words of Warning

16 These things have I spoken
unto you, that ye should not
be offended.
2 They shall put you out of the
synagogues: yea, the time cometh,
that whosoever killeth you will think
that he doeth God service.
3 And these things will they do
unto you, because they have not
known the Father, nor me.
4 But these things have I told you,
that when the time shall come, ye
may remember that I told you of
them. And these things I said not
unto you at the beginning, because
I was with you.
5 But now I go my way to him that
sent me; and none of you asketh me,
Whither goest thou?
6 But because I have said these
things unto you, sorrow hath filled
your heart.
7 Nevertheless I tell you the
truth; It is expedient for you that
I go away: for if I go not away, the
Comforter will not come unto you;
but if I depart, I will send him unto
you.
8 And when he is come, he will
reprove the world of sin, and of righ-
teousness, and of judgment:
9 Of sin, because they believe not
on me;
10 Of righteousness, because I
go to my Father, and ye see me no
more;
11 Of judgment, because the
prince of this world is judged.
12 I have yet many things to say

unto you, but ye cannot bear them
now.
13 Howbeit when he, the Spirit
of truth, is come, he will guide you
into all truth: for he shall not speak
of himself; but whatsoever he shall
hear, *that* shall he speak: and he will
shew you things to come.
14 He shall glorify me: for he shall
receive of mine, and shall shew *it*
unto you.
15 All things that the Father hath
are mine: therefore said I, that he
shall take of mine, and shall shew
it unto you.
16 A little while, and ye shall not
see me: and again, a little while, and
ye shall see me, because I go to the
Father.

Your Sorrow Will Turn to Joy

17 Then said *some* of his disciples
among themselves, What is this that
he saith unto us, A little while, and
ye shall not see me: and again, a
little while, and ye shall see me: and,
Because I go to the Father?
18 They said therefore, What is
this that he saith, A little while? we
cannot tell what he saith.
19 Now Jesus knew that they were
desirous to ask him, and said unto
them, Do ye enquire among your-
selves of that I said, A little while,
and ye shall not see me: and again,
a little while, and ye shall see me?
20 Verily, verily, I say unto you,
That ye shall weep and lament, but
the world shall rejoice: and ye shall
be sorrowful, but your sorrow shall
be turned into joy.
21 A woman when she is in travail
hath sorrow, because her hour is
come: but as soon as she is delivered
of the child, she remembereth no
more the anguish, for joy that a man
is born into the world.
22 And ye now therefore have sor-
row: but I will see you again, and
your heart shall rejoice, and your
joy no man taketh from you.
23 And in that day ye shall ask me
nothing. Verily, verily, I say unto you,
Whatsoever ye shall ask the Father
in my name, he will give *it* you.
24 Hitherto have ye asked noth-
ing in my name: ask, and ye shall
receive, that your joy may be full.
25 These things have I spoken
unto you in proverbs: but the time
cometh, when I shall no more speak
unto you in proverbs, but I shall
shew you plainly of the Father.
26 At that day ye shall ask in my
name: and I say not unto you, that
I will pray the Father for you:
27 For the Father himself loveth
you, because ye have loved me, and
have believed that I came out from
God.
28 I came forth from the Father,
and am come into the world: again,
I leave the world, and go to the Fa-
ther.
29 His disciples said unto him,
Lo, now speakest thou plainly, and
speakest no proverb.
30 Now are we sure that thou
knowest all things, and needest
not that any man should ask thee:
by this we believe that thou camest
forth from God.
31 Jesus answered them, Do ye
now believe?
32 Behold, the hour cometh, yea,
is now come, that ye shall be scat-
tered, every man to his own, and
shall leave me alone: and yet I am
not alone, because the Father is
with me.
33 These things I have spoken
unto you, that in me ye might have
peace. In the world ye shall have
tribulation: but be of good cheer; I
have overcome the world.

Jesus' Prayer for Himself

17 These words spake Jesus, and
lifted up his eyes to heaven,
and said, Father, the hour is come;
glorify thy Son, that thy Son also
may glorify thee:

2 As thou hast given him power
over all flesh, that he should give
eternal life to as many as thou hast
given him.
3 And this is life eternal, that they
might know thee the only true God,
and Jesus Christ, whom thou hast
sent.
4 I have glorified thee on the earth:
I have finished the work which thou
gavest me to do.
5 And now, O Father, glorify thou
me with thine own self with the
glory which I had with thee before
the world was.

Jesus' Prayer for His Disciples

6 I have manifested thy name unto
the men which thou gavest me out
of the world: thine they were, and
thou gavest them me; and they have
kept thy word.
7 Now they have known that all
things whatsoever thou hast given
me are of thee.
8 For I have given unto them the
words which thou gavest me; and
they have received *them,* and have
known surely that I came out from
thee, and they have believed that
thou didst send me.
9 I pray for them: I pray not for
the world, but for them which thou
hast given me; for they are thine.
10 And all mine are thine, and
thine are mine; and I am glorified
in them.
11 And now I am no more in the
world, but these are in the world,
and I come to thee. Holy Father,
keep through thine own name those
whom thou hast given me, that they
may be one, as we *are.*
12 While I was with them in the
world, I kept them in thy name:
those that thou gavest me I have
kept, and none of them is lost, but
the son of perdition; that the scrip-
ture might be fulfilled.
13 And now come I to thee; and
these things I speak in the world,
that they might have my joy fulfilled
in themselves.
14 I have given them thy word; and
the world hath hated them, because
they are not of the world, even as I
am not of the world.
15 I pray not that thou shouldest
take them out of the world, but that
thou shouldest keep them from the
evil.
16 They are not of the world, even
as I am not of the world.
17 Sanctify them through thy
truth: thy word is truth.
18 As thou hast sent me into the
world, even so have I also sent them
into the world.
19 And for their sakes I sanctify
myself, that they also might be sanc-
tified through the truth.

Jesus' Prayer for Believers

20 Neither pray I for these alone,
but for them also which shall believe
on me through their word;
21 That they all may be one; as
thou, Father, *art* in me, and I in thee,
that they also may be one in us: that
the world may believe that thou hast
sent me.
22 And the glory which thou gav-
est me I have given them; that they
may be one, even as we are one:
23 I in them, and thou in me, that
they may be made perfect in one;
and that the world may know that
thou hast sent me, and hast loved
them, as thou hast loved me.
24 Father, I will that they also,
whom thou hast given me, be with
me where I am; that they may be-
hold my glory, which thou hast
given me: for thou lovedst me before
the foundation of the world.
25 O righteous Father, the world
hath not known thee: but I have
known thee, and these have known
that thou hast sent me.
26 And I have declared unto them
thy name, and will declare *it:* that

the love wherewith thou hast loved me may be in them, and I in them.

Betrayal in the Garden

18 When Jesus had spoken these words, he went forth with his disciples over the brook Cedron, where was a garden, into the which he entered, and his disciples.

2 And Judas also, which betrayed him, knew the place: for Jesus ofttimes resorted thither with his disciples.

3 Judas then, having received a band *of men* and officers from the chief priests and Pharisees, cometh thither with lanterns and torches and weapons.

4 Jesus therefore, knowing all things that should come upon him, went forth, and said unto them, Whom seek ye?

5 They answered him, Jesus of Nazareth. Jesus saith unto them, I am *he*. And Judas also, which betrayed him, stood with them.

6 As soon then as he had said unto them, I am *he,* they went backward, and fell to the ground.

7 Then asked he them again, Whom seek ye? And they said, Jesus of Nazareth.

8 Jesus answered, I have told you that I am *he:* if therefore ye seek me, let these go their way:

9 That the saying might be fulfilled, which he spake, Of them which thou gavest me have I lost none.

10 Then Simon Peter having a sword drew it, and smote the high priest's servant, and cut off his right ear. The servant's name was Malchus.

11 Then said Jesus unto Peter, Put up thy sword into the sheath: the cup which my Father hath given me, shall I not drink it?

Jesus Appears Before Annas

12 Then the band and the captain and officers of the Jews took Jesus, and bound him,

13 And led him away to Annas first; for he was father in law to Caiaphas, which was the high priest that same year.

14 Now Caiaphas was he, which gave counsel to the Jews, that it was expedient that one man should die for the people.

Peter Denies Jesus

15 And Simon Peter followed Jesus, and *so did* another disciple: that disciple was known unto the high priest, and went in with Jesus into the palace of the high priest.

16 But Peter stood at the door without. Then went out that other disciple, which was known unto the high priest, and spake unto her that kept the door, and brought in Peter.

17 Then saith the damsel that kept the door unto Peter, Art not thou also *one* of this man's disciples? He saith, I am not.

18 And the servants and officers stood there, who had made a fire of coals; for it was cold: and they warmed themselves: and Peter stood with them, and warmed himself.

Jesus Is Questioned About His Doctrine

19 The high priest then asked Jesus of his disciples, and of his doctrine.

20 Jesus answered him, I spake openly to the world; I ever taught in the synagogue, and in the temple, whither the Jews always resort; and in secret have I said nothing.

21 Why askest thou me? ask them which heard me, what I have said unto them: behold, they know what I said.

22 And when he had thus spoken, one of the officers which stood by struck Jesus with the palm of his hand, saying, Answerest thou the high priest so?

23 Jesus answered him, If I have spoken evil, bear witness of the evil: but if well, why smitest thou me?

24 Now Annas had sent him bound unto Caiaphas the high priest.

Peter Twice Again Denies Jesus

25 And Simon Peter stood and warmed himself. They said therefore unto him, Art not thou also *one* of his disciples? He denied *it,* and said, I am not.

26 One of the servants of the high priest, being *his* kinsman whose ear Peter cut off, saith, Did not I see thee in the garden with him?

27 Peter then denied again: and immediately the cock crew.

Jesus Is Brought Before Pilate

28 Then led they Jesus from Caiaphas unto the hall of judgment: and it was early; and they themselves went not into the judgment hall, lest they should be defiled; but that they might eat the passover.

29 Pilate then went out unto them, and said, What accusation bring ye against this man?

30 They answered and said unto him, If he were not a malefactor, we would not have delivered him up unto thee.

31 Then said Pilate unto them, Take ye him, and judge him according to your law. The Jews therefore said unto him, It is not lawful for us to put any man to death:

32 That the saying of Jesus might be fulfilled, which he spake, signifying what death he should die.

33 Then Pilate entered into the judgment hall again, and called Jesus, and said unto him, Art thou the King of the Jews?

34 Jesus answered him, Sayest thou this thing of thyself, or did others tell it thee of me?

35 Pilate answered, Am I a Jew? Thine own nation and the chief priests have delivered thee unto me: what hast thou done?

36 Jesus answered, My kingdom is not of this world: if my kingdom were of this world, then would my servants fight, that I should not be delivered to the Jews: but now is my kingdom not from hence.

37 Pilate therefore said unto him, Art thou a king then? Jesus answered, Thou sayest that I am a king. To this end was I born, and for this cause came I into the world, that I should bear witness unto the truth. Every one that is of the truth heareth my voice.

38 Pilate saith unto him, What is truth? And when he had said this, he went out again unto the Jews, and saith unto them, I find in him no fault *at all.*

39 But ye have a custom, that I should release unto you one at the passover: will ye therefore that I release unto you the King of the Jews?

40 Then cried they all again, saying, Not this man, but Barabbas. Now Barabbas was a robber.

Jesus Is Scourged and Mocked

19 Then Pilate therefore took Jesus, and scourged *him.*

2 And the soldiers platted a crown of thorns, and put *it* on his head, and they put on him a purple robe,

3 And said, Hail, King of the Jews! and they smote him with their hands.

4 Pilate therefore went forth again, and saith unto them, Behold, I bring him forth to you, that ye may know that I find no fault in him.

5 Then came Jesus forth, wearing the crown of thorns, and the purple robe. And *Pilate* saith unto them, Behold the man!

6 When the chief priests therefore and officers saw him, they cried out, saying, Crucify *him,* crucify *him.* Pilate saith unto them, Take ye him, and crucify *him:* for I find no fault in him.

7 The Jews answered him, We have a law, and by our law he ought to die, because he made himself the Son of God.

8 When Pilate therefore heard that saying, he was the more afraid;

9 And went again into the judgment hall, and saith unto Jesus, Whence art thou? But Jesus gave him no answer.

10 Then saith Pilate unto him, Speakest thou not unto me? knowest thou not that I have power to crucify thee, and have power to release thee?

11 Jesus answered, Thou couldest have no power *at all* against me, except it were given thee from above: therefore he that delivered me unto thee hath the greater sin.

12 And from thenceforth Pilate sought to release him: but the Jews cried out, saying, If thou let this man go, thou art not Caesar's friend: whosoever maketh himself a king speaketh against Caesar.

13 When Pilate therefore heard that saying, he brought Jesus forth, and sat down in the judgment seat in a place that is called the Pavement, but in the Hebrew, Gabbatha.

14 And it was the preparation of the passover, and about the sixth hour: and he saith unto the Jews, Behold your King!

15 But they cried out, Away with *him,* away with *him,* crucify him. Pilate saith unto them, Shall I crucify your King? The chief priests answered, We have no king but Caesar.

16 Then delivered he him therefore unto them to be crucified. And they took Jesus, and led *him* away.

Jesus Is Crucified at Golgotha

17 And he bearing his cross went forth into a place called *the place* of a skull, which is called in the Hebrew Golgotha:

18 Where they crucified him, and two other with him, on either side one, and Jesus in the midst.

19 And Pilate wrote a title, and put *it* on the cross. And the writing was, JESUS OF NAZARETH THE KING OF THE JEWS.

20 This title then read many of the Jews: for the place where Jesus was crucified was nigh to the city: and it was written in Hebrew, *and* Greek, *and* Latin.

21 Then said the chief priests of the Jews to Pilate, Write not, The King of the Jews; but that he said, I am King of the Jews.

22 Pilate answered, What I have written I have written.

23 Then the soldiers, when they had crucified Jesus, took his garments, and made four parts, to every soldier a part; and also *his* coat: now the coat was without seam, woven from the top throughout.

24 They said therefore among themselves, Let us not rend it, but cast lots for it, whose it shall be: that the scripture might be fulfilled, which saith, They parted my raiment among them, and for my vesture they did cast lots. These things therefore the soldiers did.

25 Now there stood by the cross of Jesus his mother, and his mother's sister, Mary the *wife* of Cleophas, and Mary Magdalene.

26 When Jesus therefore saw his mother, and the disciple standing by, whom he loved, he saith unto his mother, Woman, behold thy son!

27 Then saith he to the disciple, Behold thy mother! And from that hour that disciple took her unto his own *home.*

Jesus Dies on the Cross

28 After this, Jesus knowing that all things were now accomplished, that the scripture might be fulfilled, saith, I thirst.

29 Now there was set a vessel full of vinegar: and they filled a spunge with vinegar, and put *it* upon hyssop, and put *it* to his mouth.

30 When Jesus therefore had received the vinegar, he said, It is finished: and he bowed his head, and gave up the ghost.

31 The Jews therefore, because it was the preparation, that the bodies should not remain upon the cross on the sabbath day, (for that sabbath day was an high day,) besought Pilate that their legs might be broken, and *that* they might be taken away.

32 Then came the soldiers, and brake the legs of the first, and of the other which was crucified with him.

33 But when they came to Jesus, and saw that he was dead already, they brake not his legs:

34 But one of the soldiers with a spear pierced his side, and forthwith came there out blood and water.

35 And he that saw *it* bare record, and his record is true: and he knoweth that he saith true, that ye might believe.

36 For these things were done, that the scripture should be fulfilled, A bone of him shall not be broken.

37 And again another scripture saith, They shall look on him whom they pierced.

Joseph and Nicodemus Bury Jesus

38 And after this Joseph of Arimathaea, being a disciple of Jesus, but secretly for fear of the Jews, besought Pilate that he might take away the body of Jesus: and Pilate gave *him* leave. He came therefore, and took the body of Jesus.

39 And there came also Nicodemus, which at the first came to Jesus by night, and brought a mixture of myrrh and aloes, about an hundred pound *weight.*

40 Then took they the body of Jesus, and wound it in linen clothes with the spices, as the manner of the Jews is to bury.

41 Now in the place where he was crucified there was a garden; and in the garden a new sepulchre, wherein was never man yet laid.

42 There laid they Jesus therefore because of the Jews' preparation *day;* for the sepulchre was nigh at hand.

An Empty Tomb

20 The first *day* of the week cometh Mary Magdalene early, when it was yet dark, unto the sepulchre, and seeth the stone taken away from the sepulchre.

2 Then she runneth, and cometh to Simon Peter, and to the other disciple, whom Jesus loved, and saith unto them, They have taken away the Lord out of the sepulchre, and we know not where they have laid him.

3 Peter therefore went forth, and that other disciple, and came to the sepulchre.

4 So they ran both together: and the other disciple did outrun Peter, and came first to the sepulchre.

5 And he stooping down, *and looking in,* saw the linen clothes lying; yet went he not in.

6 Then cometh Simon Peter following him, and went into the sepulchre, and seeth the linen clothes lie,

7 And the napkin, that was about his head, not lying with the linen clothes, but wrapped together in a place by itself.

8 Then went in also that other disciple, which came first to the sepulchre, and he saw, and believed.

9 For as yet they knew not the scripture, that he must rise again from the dead.

10 Then the disciples went away again unto their own home.

Mary Magdalene Sees Jesus

11 But Mary stood without at the sepulchre weeping: and as she wept, she stooped down, *and looked* into the sepulchre,

12 And seeth two angels in white
sitting, the one at the head, and the
other at the feet, where the body of
Jesus had lain.
13 And they say unto her, Woman,
why weepest thou? She saith unto
them, Because they have taken away
my Lord, and I know not where they
have laid him.
14 And when she had thus said,
she turned herself back, and saw
Jesus standing, and knew not that
it was Jesus.
15 Jesus saith unto her, Woman,
why weepest thou? whom seekest
thou? She, supposing him to be
the gardener, saith unto him, Sir,
if thou have borne him hence, tell
me where thou hast laid him, and I
will take him away.
16 Jesus saith unto her, Mary. She
turned herself, and saith unto him,
Rabboni; which is to say, Master.
17 Jesus saith unto her, Touch me
not; for I am not yet ascended to my
Father: but go to my brethren, and
say unto them, I ascend unto my
Father, and your Father; and *to* my
God, and your God.
18 Mary Magdalene came and told
the disciples that she had seen the
Lord, and *that* he had spoken these
things unto her.

The Disciples See Jesus

19 Then the same day at evening,
being the first *day* of the week,
when the doors were shut where
the disciples were assembled for
fear of the Jews, came Jesus and
stood in the midst, and saith unto
them, Peace *be* unto you.
20 And when he had so said, he
shewed unto them *his* hands and
his side. Then were the disciples
glad, when they saw the Lord.
21 Then said Jesus to them again,
Peace *be* unto you: as *my* Father
hath sent me, even so send I you.
22 And when he had said this, he
breathed on *them*, and saith unto
them, Receive ye the Holy Ghost:
23 Whose soever sins ye remit,
they are remitted unto them; *and*
whose soever *sins* ye retain, they
are retained.

Thomas Sees Jesus

24 But Thomas, one of the twelve,
called Didymus, was not with them
when Jesus came.
25 The other disciples therefore
said unto him, We have seen the
Lord. But he said unto them, Except
I shall see in his hands the print of
the nails, and put my finger into
the print of the nails, and thrust my
hand into his side, I will not believe.
26 And after eight days again his
disciples were within, and Thomas
with them: *then* came Jesus, the
doors being shut, and stood in the
midst, and said, Peace *be* unto you.
27 Then saith he to Thomas,
Reach hither thy finger, and be-
hold my hands; and reach hither
thy hand, and thrust *it* into my side:
and be not faithless, but believing.
28 And Thomas answered and
said unto him, My Lord and my God.
29 Jesus saith unto him, Thomas,
because thou hast seen me, thou
hast believed: blessed *are* they
that have not seen, and *yet* have
believed.
30 And many other signs truly did
Jesus in the presence of his disci-
ples, which are not written in this
book:
31 But these are written, that
ye might believe that Jesus is the
Christ, the Son of God; and that be-
lieving ye might have life through
his name.

Jesus' Appearance by the Sea

21 After these things Jesus
shewed himself again to the
disciples at the sea of Tiberias; and
on this wise shewed he *himself.*
2 There were together Simon
Peter, and Thomas called Didymus,

and Nathanael of Cana in Galilee, and the *sons* of Zebedee, and two other of his disciples.

3 Simon Peter saith unto them, I go a fishing. They say unto him, We also go with thee. They went forth, and entered into a ship immediately; and that night they caught nothing.

4 But when the morning was now come, Jesus stood on the shore: but the disciples knew not that it was Jesus.

5 Then Jesus saith unto them, Children, have ye any meat? They answered him, No.

6 And he said unto them, Cast the net on the right side of the ship, and ye shall find. They cast therefore, and now they were not able to draw it for the multitude of fishes.

7 Therefore that disciple whom Jesus loved saith unto Peter, It is the Lord. Now when Simon Peter heard that it was the Lord, he girt *his* fisher's coat *unto him,* (for he was naked,) and did cast himself into the sea.

8 And the other disciples came in a little ship; (for they were not far from land, but as it were two hundred cubits,) dragging the net with fishes.

9 As soon then as they were come to land, they saw a fire of coals there, and fish laid thereon, and bread.

10 Jesus saith unto them, Bring of the fish which ye have now caught.

11 Simon Peter went up, and drew the net to land full of great fishes, an hundred and fifty and three: and for all there were so many, yet was not the net broken.

12 Jesus saith unto them, Come *and* dine. And none of the disciples durst ask him, Who art thou? knowing that it was the Lord.

13 Jesus then cometh, and taketh bread, and giveth them, and fish likewise.

14 This is now the third time that Jesus shewed himself to his disciples, after that he was risen from the dead.

Jesus Challenges Peter

15 So when they had dined, Jesus saith to Simon Peter, Simon, *son* of Jonas, lovest thou me more than these? He saith unto him, Yea, Lord; thou knowest that I love thee. He saith unto him, Feed my lambs.

16 He saith to him again the second time, Simon, *son* of Jonas, lovest thou me? He saith unto him, Yea, Lord; thou knowest that I love thee. He saith unto him, Feed my sheep.

17 He saith unto him the third time, Simon, *son* of Jonas, lovest thou me? Peter was grieved because he said unto him the third time, Lovest thou me? And he said unto him, Lord, thou knowest all things; thou knowest that I love thee. Jesus saith unto him, Feed my sheep.

18 Verily, verily, I say unto thee, When thou wast young, thou girdedst thyself, and walkedst whither thou wouldest: but when thou shalt be old, thou shalt stretch forth thy hands, and another shall gird thee, and carry *thee* whither thou wouldest not.

19 This spake he, signifying by what death he should glorify God. And when he had spoken this, he saith unto him, Follow me.

20 Then Peter, turning about, seeth the disciple whom Jesus loved following; which also leaned on his breast at supper, and said, Lord, which is he that betrayeth thee?

21 Peter seeing him saith to Jesus, Lord, and what *shall* this man *do?*

22 Jesus saith unto him, If I will that he tarry till I come, what *is that* to thee? follow thou me.

23 Then went this saying abroad among the brethren, that that disciple should not die: yet Jesus said not unto him, He shall not die; but,

If I will that he tarry till I come, what
is that to thee?
24 This is the disciple which tes-
tifieth of these things, and wrote
these things: and we know that his
testimony is true.

25 And there are also many other
things which Jesus did, the which,
if they should be written every one,
I suppose that even the world itself
could not contain the books that
should be written. Amen.

The ACTS of the Apostles

Prologue

The former treatise have I made, O Theophilus, of all that Jesus began both to do and teach,

2 Until the day in which he was taken up, after that he through the Holy Ghost had given commandments unto the apostles whom he had chosen:

3 To whom also he shewed himself alive after his passion by many infallible proofs, being seen of them forty days, and speaking of the things pertaining to the kingdom of God:

Wait for the Promise of the Father

4 And, being assembled together with *them,* commanded them that they should not depart from Jerusalem, but wait for the promise of the Father, which, *saith he,* ye have heard of me.

5 For John truly baptized with water; but ye shall be baptized with the Holy Ghost not many days hence.

6 When they therefore were come together, they asked of him, saying, Lord, wilt thou at this time restore again the kingdom to Israel?

7 And he said unto them, It is not for you to know the times or the seasons, which the Father hath put in his own power.

8 But ye shall receive power, after that the Holy Ghost is come upon you: and ye shall be witnesses unto me both in Jerusalem, and in all Judaea, and in Samaria, and unto the uttermost part of the earth.

Jesus' Ascension into Heaven

9 And when he had spoken these things, while they beheld, he was taken up; and a cloud received him out of their sight.

10 And while they looked stedfastly toward heaven as he went up, behold, two men stood by them in white apparel;

11 Which also said, Ye men of Galilee, why stand ye gazing up into heaven? this same Jesus, which is taken up from you into heaven, shall so come in like manner as ye have seen him go into heaven.

The Upper Room

12 Then returned they unto Jerusalem from the mount called Olivet, which is from Jerusalem a sabbath day's journey.

13 And when they were come in, they went up into an upper room, where abode both Peter, and James, and John, and Andrew, Philip, and Thomas, Bartholomew, and Matthew, James *the son* of Alphaeus, and Simon Zelotes, and Judas *the brother* of James.

14 These all continued with one accord in prayer and supplication, with the women, and Mary the mother of Jesus, and with his brethren.

Judas Is Replaced by Matthias

15 And in those days Peter stood up in the midst of the disciples, and said, (the number of names together were about an hundred and twenty,)

16 Men *and* brethren, this scripture must needs have been fulfilled, which the Holy Ghost by the mouth of David spake before concerning Judas, which was guide to them that took Jesus.

17 For he was numbered with us, and had obtained part of this ministry.

18 Now this man purchased a field with the reward of iniquity; and falling headlong, he burst asunder in the midst, and all his bowels gushed out.

19 And it was known unto all the dwellers at Jerusalem; insomuch as that field is called in their proper tongue, Aceldama, that is to say, The field of blood.

20 For it is written in the book of Psalms, Let his habitation be desolate, and let no man dwell therein: and his bishoprick let another take.

21 Wherefore of these men which have companied with us all the time that the Lord Jesus went in and out among us,

22 Beginning from the baptism of John, unto that same day that he was taken up from us, must one be ordained to be a witness with us of his resurrection.

23 And they appointed two, Joseph called Barsabas, who was surnamed Justus, and Matthias.

24 And they prayed, and said, Thou, Lord, which knowest the hearts of all *men,* shew whether of these two thou hast chosen,

25 That he may take part of this ministry and apostleship, from which Judas by transgression fell, that he might go to his own place.

26 And they gave forth their lots; and the lot fell upon Matthias; and he was numbered with the eleven apostles.

The Day of Pentecost

2 And when the day of Pentecost was fully come, they were all with one accord in one place.

2 And suddenly there came a sound from heaven as of a rushing mighty wind, and it filled all the house where they were sitting.

3 And there appeared unto them cloven tongues like as of fire, and it sat upon each of them.

4 And they were all filled with the Holy Ghost, and began to speak with other tongues, as the Spirit gave them utterance.

5 And there were dwelling at Jerusalem Jews, devout men, out of every nation under heaven.

6 Now when this was noised abroad, the multitude came together, and were confounded, because that every man heard them speak in his own language.

7 And they were all amazed and marvelled, saying one to another, Behold, are not all these which speak Galilaeans?

8 And how hear we every man in our own tongue, wherein we were born?

9 Parthians, and Medes, and Elamites, and the dwellers in Mesopotamia, and in Judaea, and Cappadocia, in Pontus, and Asia,

10 Phrygia, and Pamphylia, in Egypt, and in the parts of Libya about Cyrene, and strangers of Rome, Jews and proselytes,

11 Cretes and Arabians, we do hear them speak in our tongues the wonderful works of God.

12 And they were all amazed, and were in doubt, saying one to another, What meaneth this?

13 Others mocking said, These men are full of new wine.

Peter Addresses the Crowd

14 But Peter, standing up with the eleven, lifted up his voice, and said unto them, Ye men of Judaea, and all *ye* that dwell at Jerusalem, be this known unto you, and hearken to my words:

15 For these are not drunken, as

ye suppose, seeing it is *but* the third
hour of the day.
16 But this is that which was spo-
ken by the prophet Joel;
17 And it shall come to pass in
the last days, saith God, I will pour
out of my Spirit upon all flesh: and
your sons and your daughters shall
prophesy, and your young men shall
see visions, and your old men shall
dream dreams:
18 And on my servants and on
my handmaidens I will pour out in
those days of my Spirit; and they
shall prophesy:
19 And I will shew wonders in
heaven above, and signs in the earth
beneath; blood, and fire, and vapour
of smoke:
20 The sun shall be turned into
darkness, and the moon into blood,
before that great and notable day of
the Lord come:
21 And it shall come to pass, *that*
whosoever shall call on the name
of the Lord shall be saved.
22 Ye men of Israel, hear these
words; Jesus of Nazareth, a man
approved of God among you by mir-
acles and wonders and signs, which
God did by him in the midst of you,
as ye yourselves also know:
23 Him, being delivered by the de-
terminate counsel and foreknowl-
edge of God, ye have taken, and by
wicked hands have crucified and
slain:
24 Whom God hath raised up,
having loosed the pains of death:
because it was not possible that he
should be holden of it.
25 For David speaketh concern-
ing him, I foresaw the Lord always
before my face, for he is on my right
hand, that I should not be moved:
26 Therefore did my heart rejoice,
and my tongue was glad; moreover
also my flesh shall rest in hope:
27 Because thou wilt not leave my
soul in hell, neither wilt thou suffer
thine Holy One to see corruption.
28 Thou hast made known to me
the ways of life; thou shalt make me
full of joy with thy countenance.
29 Men *and* brethren, let me freely
speak unto you of the patriarch Da-
vid, that he is both dead and buried,
and his sepulchre is with us unto
this day.
30 Therefore being a prophet, and
knowing that God had sworn with
an oath to him, that of the fruit of
his loins, according to the flesh, he
would raise up Christ to sit on his
throne;
31 He seeing this before spake of
the resurrection of Christ, that his
soul was not left in hell, neither his
flesh did see corruption.
32 This Jesus hath God raised up,
whereof we all are witnesses.
33 Therefore being by the right
hand of God exalted, and having
received of the Father the promise
of the Holy Ghost, he hath shed forth
this, which ye now see and hear.
34 For David is not ascended into
the heavens: but he saith himself,
The LORD said unto my Lord, Sit
thou on my right hand,
35 Until I make thy foes thy foot-
stool.
36 Therefore let all the house of
Israel know assuredly, that God hath
made that same Jesus, whom ye
have crucified, both Lord and Christ.

The Crowd's Response

37 Now when they heard *this,*
they were pricked in their heart,
and said unto Peter and to the rest
of the apostles, Men *and* brethren,
what shall we do?
38 Then Peter said unto them, Re-
pent, and be baptized every one of
you in the name of Jesus Christ for
the remission of sins, and ye shall
receive the gift of the Holy Ghost.
39 For the promise is unto you,
and to your children, and to all that
are afar off, *even* as many as the Lord
our God shall call.

40 And with many other words
did he testify and exhort, saying,
Save yourselves from this untoward
generation.
41 Then they that gladly received
his word were baptized: and the
same day there were added *unto*
them about three thousand souls.
42 And they continued stedfastly
in the apostles' doctrine and fellow-
ship, and in breaking of bread, and
in prayers.
43 And fear came upon every soul:
and many wonders and signs were
done by the apostles.
44 And all that believed were to-
gether, and had all things common;
45 And sold their possessions and
goods, and parted them to all *men,*
as every man had need.
46 And they, continuing daily with
one accord in the temple, and break-
ing bread from house to house, did
eat their meat with gladness and
singleness of heart,
47 Praising God, and having fa-
vour with all the people. And the
Lord added to the church daily such
as should be saved.

A Lame Man Healed

3 Now Peter and John went up
together into the temple at the
hour of prayer, *being* the ninth *hour.*
2 And a certain man lame from his
mother's womb was carried, whom
they laid daily at the gate of the tem-
ple which is called Beautiful, to ask
alms of them that entered into the
temple;
3 Who seeing Peter and John about
to go into the temple asked an alms.
4 And Peter, fastening his eyes
upon him with John, said, Look
on us.
5 And he gave heed unto them,
expecting to receive something of
them.
6 Then Peter said, Silver and gold
have I none; but such as I have give
I thee: In the name of Jesus Christ
of Nazareth rise up and walk.
7 And he took him by the right
hand, and lifted *him* up: and im-
mediately his feet and ankle bones
received strength.
8 And he leaping up stood, and
walked, and entered with them into
the temple, walking, and leaping,
and praising God.
9 And all the people saw him walk-
ing and praising God:
10 And they knew that it was he
which sat for alms at the Beautiful
gate of the temple: and they were
filled with wonder and amazement
at that which had happened unto
him.

Peter Admonishes the Onlookers

11 And as the lame man which was
healed held Peter and John, all the
people ran together unto them in
the porch that is called Solomon's,
greatly wondering.
12 And when Peter saw *it,* he an-
swered unto the people, Ye men of
Israel, why marvel ye at this? or why
look ye so earnestly on us, as though
by our own power or holiness we
had made this man to walk?
13 The God of Abraham, and of
Isaac, and of Jacob, the God of our
fathers, hath glorified his Son Jesus;
whom ye delivered up, and denied
him in the presence of Pilate, when
he was determined to let *him* go.
14 But ye denied the Holy One and
the Just, and desired a murderer to
be granted unto you;
15 And killed the Prince of life,
whom God hath raised from the
dead; whereof we are witnesses.
16 And his name through faith
in his name hath made this man
strong, whom ye see and know: yea,
the faith which is by him hath given
him this perfect soundness in the
presence of you all.
17 And now, brethren, I wot that
through ignorance ye did *it,* as *did*
also your rulers.

18 But those things, which God before had shewed by the mouth of all his prophets, that Christ should suffer, he hath so fulfilled.

19 Repent ye therefore, and be converted, that your sins may be blotted out, when the times of refreshing shall come from the presence of the Lord;

20 And he shall send Jesus Christ, which before was preached unto you:

21 Whom the heaven must receive until the times of restitution of all things, which God hath spoken by the mouth of all his holy prophets since the world began.

22 For Moses truly said unto the fathers, A prophet shall the Lord your God raise up unto you of your brethren, like unto me; him shall ye hear in all things whatsoever he shall say unto you.

23 And it shall come to pass, *that* every soul, which will not hear that prophet, shall be destroyed from among the people.

24 Yea, and all the prophets from Samuel and those that follow after, as many as have spoken, have likewise foretold of these days.

25 Ye are the children of the prophets, and of the covenant which God made with our fathers, saying unto Abraham, And in thy seed shall all the kindreds of the earth be blessed.

26 Unto you first God, having raised up his Son Jesus, sent him to bless you, in turning away every one of you from his iniquities.

Peter and John Are Arrested

4 And as they spake unto the people, the priests, and the captain of the temple, and the Sadducees, came upon them,

2 Being grieved that they taught the people, and preached through Jesus the resurrection from the dead.

3 And they laid hands on them, and put *them* in hold unto the next day: for it was now eventide.

4 Howbeit many of them which heard the word believed; and the number of the men was about five thousand.

Peter's Sermon to the Council

5 And it came to pass on the morrow, that their rulers, and elders, and scribes,

6 And Annas the high priest, and Caiaphas, and John, and Alexander, and as many as were of the kindred of the high priest, were gathered together at Jerusalem.

7 And when they had set them in the midst, they asked, By what power, or by what name, have ye done this?

8 Then Peter, filled with the Holy Ghost, said unto them, Ye rulers of the people, and elders of Israel,

9 If we this day be examined of the good deed done to the impotent man, by what means he is made whole;

10 Be it known unto you all, and to all the people of Israel, that by the name of Jesus Christ of Nazareth, whom ye crucified, whom God raised from the dead, *even* by him doth this man stand here before you whole.

11 This is the stone which was set at nought of you builders, which is become the head of the corner.

12 Neither is there salvation in any other: for there is none other name under heaven given among men, whereby we must be saved.

13 Now when they saw the boldness of Peter and John, and perceived that they were unlearned and ignorant men, they marvelled; and they took knowledge of them, that they had been with Jesus.

14 And beholding the man which was healed standing with them, they could say nothing against it.

15 But when they had commanded them to go aside out of the council, they conferred among themselves,

16 Saying, What shall we do to these men? for that indeed a notable miracle hath been done by them *is* manifest to all them that dwell in Jerusalem; and we cannot deny *it*.

17 But that it spread no further among the people, let us straitly threaten them, that they speak henceforth to no man in this name.

Peter and John Must Speak

18 And they called them, and commanded them not to speak at all nor teach in the name of Jesus.

19 But Peter and John answered and said unto them, Whether it be right in the sight of God to hearken unto you more than unto God, judge ye.

20 For we cannot but speak the things which we have seen and heard.

21 So when they had further threatened them, they let them go, finding nothing how they might punish them, because of the people: for all *men* glorified God for that which was done.

22 For the man was above forty years old, on whom this miracle of healing was shewed.

A Prayer for Boldness

23 And being let go, they went to their own company, and reported all that the chief priests and elders had said unto them.

24 And when they heard that, they lifted up their voice to God with one accord, and said, Lord, thou *art* God, which hast made heaven, and earth, and the sea, and all that in them is:

25 Who by the mouth of thy servant David hast said, Why did the heathen rage, and the people imagine vain things?

26 The kings of the earth stood up, and the rulers were gathered together against the Lord, and against his Christ.

27 For of a truth against thy holy child Jesus, whom thou hast anointed, both Herod, and Pontius Pilate, with the Gentiles, and the people of Israel, were gathered together,

28 For to do whatsoever thy hand and thy counsel determined before to be done.

29 And now, Lord, behold their threatenings: and grant unto thy servants, that with all boldness they may speak thy word,

30 By stretching forth thine hand to heal; and that signs and wonders may be done by the name of thy holy child Jesus.

31 And when they had prayed, the place was shaken where they were assembled together; and they were all filled with the Holy Ghost, and they spake the word of God with boldness.

Distribution of Possessions

32 And the multitude of them that believed were of one heart and of one soul: neither said any *of them* that ought of the things which he possessed was his own; but they had all things common.

33 And with great power gave the apostles witness of the resurrection of the Lord Jesus: and great grace was upon them all.

34 Neither was there any among them that lacked: for as many as were possessors of lands or houses sold them, and brought the prices of the things that were sold,

35 And laid *them* down at the apostles' feet: and distribution was made unto every man according as he had need.

36 And Joses, who by the apostles was surnamed Barnabas, (which is, being interpreted, The son of consolation,) a Levite, *and* of the country of Cyprus,

37 Having land, sold *it,* and brought the money, and laid *it* at the apostles' feet.

Ananias and Sapphira

5 But a certain man named Ananias, with Sapphira his wife, sold a possession,

2 And kept back *part* of the price, his wife also being privy *to it,* and brought a certain part, and laid *it* at the apostles' feet.

3 But Peter said, Ananias, why hath Satan filled thine heart to lie to the Holy Ghost, and to keep back *part* of the price of the land?

4 Whiles it remained, was it not thine own? and after it was sold, was it not in thine own power? why hast thou conceived this thing in thine heart? thou hast not lied unto men, but unto God.

5 And Ananias hearing these words fell down, and gave up the ghost: and great fear came on all them that heard these things.

6 And the young men arose, wound him up, and carried *him* out, and buried *him.*

7 And it was about the space of three hours after, when his wife, not knowing what was done, came in.

8 And Peter answered unto her, Tell me whether ye sold the land for so much? And she said, Yea, for so much.

9 Then Peter said unto her, How is it that ye have agreed together to tempt the Spirit of the Lord? behold, the feet of them which have buried thy husband *are* at the door, and shall carry thee out.

10 Then fell she down straightway at his feet, and yielded up the ghost: and the young men came in, and found her dead, and, carrying *her* forth, buried *her* by her husband.

11 And great fear came upon all the church, and upon as many as heard these things.

Many Signs and Wonders

12 And by the hands of the apostles were many signs and wonders wrought among the people; (and they were all with one accord in Solomon's porch.

13 And of the rest durst no man join himself to them: but the people magnified them.

14 And believers were the more added to the Lord, multitudes both of men and women.)

15 Insomuch that they brought forth the sick into the streets, and laid *them* on beds and couches, that at the least the shadow of Peter passing by might overshadow some of them.

16 There came also a multitude *out* of the cities round about unto Jerusalem, bringing sick folks, and them which were vexed with unclean spirits: and they were healed every one.

The Apostles Suffer Persecution

17 Then the high priest rose up, and all they that were with him, (which is the sect of the Sadducees,) and were filled with indignation,

18 And laid their hands on the apostles, and put them in the common prison.

19 But the angel of the Lord by night opened the prison doors, and brought them forth, and said,

20 Go, stand and speak in the temple to the people all the words of this life.

21 And when they heard *that,* they entered into the temple early in the morning, and taught. But the high priest came, and they that were with him, and called the council together, and all the senate of the children of Israel, and sent to the prison to have them brought.

22 But when the officers came, and found them not in the prison, they returned, and told,

23 Saying, The prison truly found
we shut with all safety, and the
keepers standing without before
the doors: but when we had opened,
we found no man within.
24 Now when the high priest and
the captain of the temple and the
chief priests heard these things, they
doubted of them whereunto this
would grow.
25 Then came one and told them,
saying, Behold, the men whom ye
put in prison are standing in the
temple, and teaching the people.
26 Then went the captain with the
officers, and brought them without
violence: for they feared the people,
lest they should have been stoned.
27 And when they had brought
them, they set *them* before the
council: and the high priest asked
them,
28 Saying, Did not we straitly
command you that ye should not
teach in this name? and, behold,
ye have filled Jerusalem with your
doctrine, and intend to bring this
man's blood upon us.
29 Then Peter and the *other* apos-
tles answered and said, We ought to
obey God rather than men.
30 The God of our fathers raised
up Jesus, whom ye slew and hanged
on a tree.
31 Him hath God exalted with his
right hand *to be* a Prince and a Sav-
iour, for to give repentance to Israel,
and forgiveness of sins.
32 And we are his witnesses of
these things; and *so is* also the Holy
Ghost, whom God hath given to
them that obey him.

Gamaliel's Counsel

33 When they heard *that,* they
were cut *to the heart,* and took coun-
sel to slay them.
34 Then stood there up one in
the council, a Pharisee, named Ga-
maliel, a doctor of the law, had in
reputation among all the people,
and commanded to put the apostles
forth a little space;
35 And said unto them, Ye men of
Israel, take heed to yourselves what
ye intend to do as touching these
men.
36 For before these days rose up
Theudas, boasting himself to be
somebody; to whom a number of
men, about four hundred, joined
themselves: who was slain; and all,
as many as obeyed him, were scat-
tered, and brought to nought.
37 After this man rose up Judas
of Galilee in the days of the taxing,
and drew away much people after
him: he also perished; and all, *even*
as many as obeyed him, were dis-
persed.
38 And now I say unto you, Re-
frain from these men, and let them
alone: for if this counsel or this work
be of men, it will come to nought:
39 But if it be of God, ye cannot
overthrow it; lest haply ye be found
even to fight against God.
40 And to him they agreed: and
when they had called the apostles,
and beaten *them,* they commanded
that they should not speak in the
name of Jesus, and let them go.
41 And they departed from the
presence of the council, rejoicing
that they were counted worthy to
suffer shame for his name.
42 And daily in the temple, and
in every house, they ceased not to
teach and preach Jesus Christ.

Seven Spirit-Filled Men

6 And in those days, when the
number of the disciples was
multiplied, there arose a murmur-
ing of the Grecians against the He-
brews, because their widows were
neglected in the daily ministration.
2 Then the twelve called the mul-
titude of the disciples *unto them,*
and said, It is not reason that we
should leave the word of God, and
serve tables.

3 Wherefore, brethren, look ye out
among you seven men of honest
report, full of the Holy Ghost and
wisdom, whom we may appoint
over this business.
4 But we will give ourselves con-
tinually to prayer, and to the min-
istry of the word.
5 And the saying pleased the
whole multitude: and they chose
Stephen, a man full of faith and
of the Holy Ghost, and Philip, and
Prochorus, and Nicanor, and Timon,
and Parmenas, and Nicolas a pros-
elyte of Antioch:
6 Whom they set before the apos-
tles: and when they had prayed, they
laid *their* hands on them.
7 And the word of God increased;
and the number of the disciples
multiplied in Jerusalem greatly;
and a great company of the priests
were obedient to the faith.

Stephen Charged with Blasphemy

8 And Stephen, full of faith and
power, did great wonders and mir-
acles among the people.
9 Then there arose certain of
the synagogue, which is called *the
synagogue* of the Libertines, and
Cyrenians, and Alexandrians, and of
them of Cilicia and of Asia, disputing
with Stephen.
10 And they were not able to resist
the wisdom and the spirit by which
he spake.
11 Then they suborned men,
which said, We have heard him
speak blasphemous words against
Moses, and *against* God.
12 And they stirred up the people,
and the elders, and the scribes, and
came upon *him*, and caught him,
and brought *him* to the council,
13 And set up false witnesses,
which said, This man ceaseth not to
speak blasphemous words against
this holy place, and the law:
14 For we have heard him say, that
this Jesus of Nazareth shall destroy
this place, and shall change the cus-
toms which Moses delivered us.
15 And all that sat in the council,
looking stedfastly on him, saw his
face as it had been the face of an
angel.

Stephen's Council Speech

7 Then said the high priest, Are
these things so?
2 And he said, Men, brethren, and
fathers, hearken; The God of glory
appeared unto our father Abraham,
when he was in Mesopotamia, be-
fore he dwelt in Charran,
3 And said unto him, Get thee out
of thy country, and from thy kin-
dred, and come into the land which
I shall shew thee.
4 Then came he out of the land of
the Chaldeans, and dwelt in Charran:
and from thence, when his father
was dead, he removed him into this
land, wherein ye now dwell.
5 And he gave him none inheri-
tance in it, no, not *so much as* to set
his foot on: yet he promised that
he would give it to him for a pos-
session, and to his seed after him,
when *as yet* he had no child.
6 And God spake on this wise, That
his seed should sojourn in a strange
land; and that they should bring
them into bondage, and entreat
them evil four hundred years.
7 And the nation to whom they
shall be in bondage will I judge, said
God: and after that shall they come
forth, and serve me in this place.
8 And he gave him the covenant
of circumcision: and so *Abraham*
begat Isaac, and circumcised him
the eighth day; and Isaac *begat* Ja-
cob; and Jacob *begat* the twelve
patriarchs.

Joseph Sold by the Patriarchs

9 And the patriarchs, moved with
envy, sold Joseph into Egypt: but
God was with him,

10 And delivered him out of all his
afflictions, and gave him favour and
wisdom in the sight of Pharaoh king
of Egypt; and he made him governor
over Egypt and all his house.
11 Now there came a dearth over
all the land of Egypt and Chanaan,
and great affliction: and our fathers
found no sustenance.
12 But when Jacob heard that
there was corn in Egypt, he sent
out our fathers first.
13 And at the second *time* Joseph
was made known to his brethren;
and Joseph's kindred was made
known unto Pharaoh.
14 Then sent Joseph, and called his
father Jacob to *him,* and all his kin-
dred, threescore and fifteen souls.
15 So Jacob went down into Egypt,
and died, he, and our fathers,
16 And were carried over into Sy-
chem, and laid in the sepulchre that
Abraham bought for a sum of money
of the sons of Emmor *the father* of
Sychem.
17 But when the time of the prom-
ise drew nigh, which God had sworn
to Abraham, the people grew and
multiplied in Egypt,
18 Till another king arose, which
knew not Joseph.
19 The same dealt subtilly with
our kindred, and evil entreated our
fathers, so that they cast out their
young children, to the end they
might not live.

Through Moses God Delivered Israel

20 In which time Moses was born,
and was exceeding fair, and nour-
ished up in his father's house three
months:
21 And when he was cast out,
Pharaoh's daughter took him up,
and nourished him for her own son.
22 And Moses was learned in all
the wisdom of the Egyptians, and
was mighty in words and in deeds.
23 And when he was full forty
years old, it came into his heart to
visit his brethren the children of
Israel.
24 And seeing one *of them* suf-
fer wrong, he defended *him,* and
avenged him that was oppressed,
and smote the Egyptian:
25 For he supposed his brethren
would have understood how that
God by his hand would deliver them:
but they understood not.
26 And the next day he shewed
himself unto them as they strove,
and would have set them at one
again, saying, Sirs, ye are brethren;
why do ye wrong one to another?
27 But he that did his neighbour
wrong thrust him away, saying,
Who made thee a ruler and a judge
over us?
28 Wilt thou kill me, as thou did-
dest the Egyptian yesterday?
29 Then fled Moses at this saying,
and was a stranger in the land of
Madian, where he begat two sons.
30 And when forty years were ex-
pired, there appeared to him in the
wilderness of mount Sina an angel
of the Lord in a flame of fire in a
bush.
31 When Moses saw *it,* he won-
dered at the sight: and as he drew
near to behold *it,* the voice of the
Lord came unto him,
32 *Saying,* I *am* the God of thy fa-
thers, the God of Abraham, and the
God of Isaac, and the God of Jacob.
Then Moses trembled, and durst
not behold.
33 Then said the Lord to him, Put
off thy shoes from thy feet: for the
place where thou standest is holy
ground.
34 I have seen, I have seen the
affliction of my people which is in
Egypt, and I have heard their groan-
ing, and am come down to deliver
them. And now come, I will send
thee into Egypt.
35 This Moses whom they refused,
saying, Who made thee a ruler and a

judge? the same did God send *to be*
a ruler and a deliverer by the hand
of the angel which appeared to him
in the bush.
36 He brought them out, after
that he had shewed wonders and
signs in the land of Egypt, and in
the Red sea, and in the wilderness
forty years.

Raising Up a Prophet

37 This is that Moses, which
said unto the children of Israel, A
prophet shall the Lord your God
raise up unto you of your brethren,
like unto me; him shall ye hear.
38 This is he, that was in the
church in the wilderness with the
angel which spake to him in the
mount Sina, and *with* our fathers:
who received the lively oracles to
give unto us:
39 To whom our fathers would
not obey, but thrust *him* from them,
and in their hearts turned back again
into Egypt,
40 Saying unto Aaron, Make us
gods to go before us: for *as for* this
Moses, which brought us out of the
land of Egypt, we wot not what is
become of him.
41 And they made a calf in those
days, and offered sacrifice unto the
idol, and rejoiced in the works of
their own hands.
42 Then God turned, and gave
them up to worship the host of
heaven; as it is written in the book
of the prophets, O ye house of Israel,
have ye offered to me slain beasts
and sacrifices *by the space of* forty
years in the wilderness?
43 Yea, ye took up the tabernacle
of Moloch, and the star of your god
Remphan, figures which ye made to
worship them: and I will carry you
away beyond Babylon.
44 Our fathers had the taberna-
cle of witness in the wilderness, as
he had appointed, speaking unto
Moses, that he should make it ac-
cording to the fashion that he had
seen.
45 Which also our fathers that
came after brought in with Jesus
into the possession of the Gentiles,
whom God drave out before the face
of our fathers, unto the days of Da-
vid;
46 Who found favour before God,
and desired to find a tabernacle for
the God of Jacob.
47 But Solomon built him an
house.
48 Howbeit the most High dwell-
eth not in temples made with hands;
as saith the prophet,
49 Heaven *is* my throne, and earth
is my footstool: what house will ye
build me? saith the Lord: or what *is*
the place of my rest?
50 Hath not my hand made all
these things?

Stephen Accuses His Accusers

51 Ye stiffnecked and uncircum-
cised in heart and ears, ye do always
resist the Holy Ghost: as your fathers
did, so *do* ye.
52 Which of the prophets have
not your fathers persecuted? and
they have slain them which shewed
before of the coming of the Just One;
of whom ye have been now the be-
trayers and murderers:
53 Who have received the law by
the disposition of angels, and have
not kept *it.*

The Stoning of Stephen

54 When they heard these things,
they were cut to the heart, and they
gnashed on him with *their* teeth.
55 But he, being full of the Holy
Ghost, looked up stedfastly into
heaven, and saw the glory of God,
and Jesus standing on the right
hand of God,
56 And said, Behold, I see the
heavens opened, and the Son of
man standing on the right hand of
God.

57 Then they cried out with a loud
voice, and stopped their ears, and
ran upon him with one accord,
58 And cast *him* out of the city,
and stoned *him:* and the witnesses
laid down their clothes at a young
man's feet, whose name was Saul.
59 And they stoned Stephen,
calling upon *God,* and saying, Lord
Jesus, receive my spirit.
60 And he kneeled down, and
cried with a loud voice, Lord, lay
not this sin to their charge. And
when he had said this, he fell
asleep.

Persecution of the Church

8 And Saul was consenting
unto his death. And at that
time there was a great persecu-
tion against the church which was
at Jerusalem; and they were all
scattered abroad throughout the
regions of Judaea and Samaria,
except the apostles.
2 And devout men carried Ste-
phen *to his burial,* and made great
lamentation over him.
3 As for Saul, he made havock
of the church, entering into every
house, and haling men and women
committed *them* to prison.

Philip Preaches in Samaria

4 Therefore they that were scat-
tered abroad went every where
preaching the word.
5 Then Philip went down to the
city of Samaria, and preached Christ
unto them.
6 And the people with one accord
gave heed unto those things which
Philip spake, hearing and seeing the
miracles which he did.
7 For unclean spirits, crying with
loud voice, came out of many that
were possessed *with them:* and
many taken with palsies, and that
were lame, were healed.
8 And there was great joy in that
city.

Simon's Attempted Purchase

9 But there was a certain man,
called Simon, which beforetime
in the same city used sorcery, and
bewitched the people of Samaria,
giving out that himself was some
great one:
10 To whom they all gave heed,
from the least to the greatest, say-
ing, This man is the great power of
God.
11 And to him they had regard,
because that of long time he had
bewitched them with sorceries.
12 But when they believed Philip
preaching the things concerning
the kingdom of God, and the name
of Jesus Christ, they were baptized,
both men and women.
13 Then Simon himself believed
also: and when he was baptized,
he continued with Philip, and won-
dered, beholding the miracles and
signs which were done.
14 Now when the apostles which
were at Jerusalem heard that Sa-
maria had received the word of God,
they sent unto them Peter and John:
15 Who, when they were come
down, prayed for them, that they
might receive the Holy Ghost:
16 (For as yet he was fallen upon
none of them: only they were bap-
tized in the name of the Lord Jesus.)
17 Then laid they *their* hands on
them, and they received the Holy
Ghost.
18 And when Simon saw that
through laying on of the apostles'
hands the Holy Ghost was given,
he offered them money,
19 Saying, Give me also this power,
that on whomsoever I lay hands, he
may receive the Holy Ghost.
20 But Peter said unto him, Thy
money perish with thee, because
thou hast thought that the gift of
God may be purchased with money.
21 Thou hast neither part nor lot
in this matter: for thy heart is not
right in the sight of God.

22 Repent therefore of this thy
wickedness, and pray God, if perhaps the thought of thine heart may
be forgiven thee.
23 For I perceive that thou art
in the gall of bitterness, and *in* the
bond of iniquity.
24 Then answered Simon, and
said, Pray ye to the Lord for me, that
none of these things which ye have
spoken come upon me.
25 And they, when they had testified and preached the word of the
Lord, returned to Jerusalem, and
preached the gospel in many villages
of the Samaritans.

The Ethiopian Eunuch's Baptism

26 And the angel of the Lord spake
unto Philip, saying, Arise, and go
toward the south unto the way that
goeth down from Jerusalem unto
Gaza, which is desert.
27 And he arose and went: and,
behold, a man of Ethiopia, an eunuch of great authority under Candace queen of the Ethiopians, who
had the charge of all her treasure,
and had come to Jerusalem for to
worship,
28 Was returning, and sitting in
his chariot read Esaias the prophet.
29 Then the Spirit said unto Philip,
Go near, and join thyself to this chariot.
30 And Philip ran thither to *him,*
and heard him read the prophet
Esaias, and said, Understandest
thou what thou readest?
31 And he said, How can I, except
some man should guide me? And he
desired Philip that he would come
up and sit with him.
32 The place of the scripture
which he read was this, He was led
as a sheep to the slaughter; and like
a lamb dumb before his shearer, so
opened he not his mouth:
33 In his humiliation his judgment
was taken away: and who shall declare his generation? for his life is
taken from the earth.
34 And the eunuch answered
Philip, and said, I pray thee, of
whom speaketh the prophet this?
of himself, or of some other man?
35 Then Philip opened his mouth,
and began at the same scripture,
and preached unto him Jesus.
36 And as they went on *their* way,
they came unto a certain water: and
the eunuch said, See, *here is* water;
what doth hinder me to be baptized?
37 And Philip said, If thou believest with all thine heart, thou
mayest. And he answered and said,
I believe that Jesus Christ is the Son
of God.
38 And he commanded the chariot
to stand still: and they went down
both into the water, both Philip and
the eunuch; and he baptized him.
39 And when they were come up
out of the water, the Spirit of the
Lord caught away Philip, that the
eunuch saw him no more: and he
went on his way rejoicing.
40 But Philip was found at Azotus:
and passing through he preached in
all the cities, till he came to Caesarea.

Saul's Conversion

9 And Saul, yet breathing out
threatenings and slaughter
against the disciples of the Lord,
went unto the high priest,
2 And desired of him letters to Damascus to the synagogues, that if
he found any of this way, whether
they were men or women, he might
bring them bound unto Jerusalem.
3 And as he journeyed, he came
near Damascus: and suddenly there
shined round about him a light from
heaven:
4 And he fell to the earth, and
heard a voice saying unto him, Saul,
Saul, why persecutest thou me?
5 And he said, Who art thou, Lord?
And the Lord said, I am Jesus whom

thou persecutest: *it is* hard for thee
to kick against the pricks.
6 And he trembling and astonished said, Lord, what wilt thou have me to do? And the Lord *said* unto him, Arise, and go into the city, and it shall be told thee what thou must do.
7 And the men which journeyed with him stood speechless, hearing a voice, but seeing no man.
8 And Saul arose from the earth; and when his eyes were opened, he saw no man: but they led him by the hand, and brought *him* into Damascus.
9 And he was three days without sight, and neither did eat nor drink.

Ananias and Saul

10 And there was a certain disciple at Damascus, named Ananias; and to him said the Lord in a vision, Ananias. And he said, Behold, I *am here,* Lord.
11 And the Lord *said* unto him, Arise, and go into the street which is called Straight, and enquire in the house of Judas for *one* called Saul, of Tarsus: for, behold, he prayeth,
12 And hath seen in a vision a man named Ananias coming in, and putting *his* hand on him, that he might receive his sight.
13 Then Ananias answered, Lord, I have heard by many of this man, how much evil he hath done to thy saints at Jerusalem:
14 And here he hath authority from the chief priests to bind all that call on thy name.
15 But the Lord said unto him, Go thy way: for he is a chosen vessel unto me, to bear my name before the Gentiles, and kings, and the children of Israel:
16 For I will shew him how great things he must suffer for my name's sake.
17 And Ananias went his way, and entered into the house; and putting his hands on him said, Brother Saul, the Lord, *even* Jesus, that appeared unto thee in the way as thou camest, hath sent me, that thou mightest receive thy sight, and be filled with the Holy Ghost.
18 And immediately there fell from his eyes as it had been scales: and he received sight forthwith, and arose, and was baptized.

Saul in Damascus

19 And when he had received meat, he was strengthened. Then was Saul certain days with the disciples which were at Damascus.
20 And straightway he preached Christ in the synagogues, that he is the Son of God.
21 But all that heard *him* were amazed, and said; Is not this he that destroyed them which called on this name in Jerusalem, and came hither for that intent, that he might bring them bound unto the chief priests?
22 But Saul increased the more in strength, and confounded the Jews which dwelt at Damascus, proving that this is very Christ.

The Disciples Save Saul from Death

23 And after that many days were fulfilled, the Jews took counsel to kill him:
24 But their laying await was known of Saul. And they watched the gates day and night to kill him.
25 Then the disciples took him by night, and let *him* down by the wall in a basket.

Saul in Jerusalem

26 And when Saul was come to Jerusalem, he assayed to join himself to the disciples: but they were all afraid of him, and believed not that he was a disciple.
27 But Barnabas took him, and brought *him* to the apostles, and declared unto them how he had

seen the Lord in the way, and that he had spoken to him, and how he had preached boldly at Damascus in the name of Jesus.

28 And he was with them coming in and going out at Jerusalem.

29 And he spake boldly in the name of the Lord Jesus, and disputed against the Grecians: but they went about to slay him.

30 *Which* when the brethren knew, they brought him down to Caesarea, and sent him forth to Tarsus.

31 Then had the churches rest throughout all Judaea and Galilee and Samaria, and were edified; and walking in the fear of the Lord, and in the comfort of the Holy Ghost, were multiplied.

Aeneas Healed by Peter

32 And it came to pass, as Peter passed throughout all *quarters,* he came down also to the saints which dwelt at Lydda.

33 And there he found a certain man named Aeneas, which had kept his bed eight years, and was sick of the palsy.

34 And Peter said unto him, Aeneas, Jesus Christ maketh thee whole: arise, and make thy bed. And he arose immediately.

35 And all that dwelt at Lydda and Saron saw him, and turned to the Lord.

Dorcas Raised from Death

36 Now there was at Joppa a certain disciple named Tabitha, which by interpretation is called Dorcas: this woman was full of good works and almsdeeds which she did.

37 And it came to pass in those days, that she was sick, and died: whom when they had washed, they laid *her* in an upper chamber.

38 And forasmuch as Lydda was nigh to Joppa, and the disciples had heard that Peter was there, they sent unto him two men, desiring *him* that he would not delay to come to them.

39 Then Peter arose and went with them. When he was come, they brought him into the upper chamber: and all the widows stood by him weeping, and shewing the coats and garments which Dorcas made, while she was with them.

40 But Peter put them all forth, and kneeled down, and prayed; and turning *him* to the body said, Tabitha, arise. And she opened her eyes: and when she saw Peter, she sat up.

41 And he gave her *his* hand, and lifted her up, and when he had called the saints and widows, presented her alive.

42 And it was known throughout all Joppa; and many believed in the Lord.

43 And it came to pass, that he tarried many days in Joppa with one Simon a tanner.

Cornelius's Vision

10 There was a certain man in Caesarea called Cornelius, a centurion of the band called the Italian *band,*

2 A devout *man,* and one that feared God with all his house, which gave much alms to the people, and prayed to God alway.

3 He saw in a vision evidently about the ninth hour of the day an angel of God coming in to him, and saying unto him, Cornelius.

4 And when he looked on him, he was afraid, and said, What is it, Lord? And he said unto him, Thy prayers and thine alms are come up for a memorial before God.

5 And now send men to Joppa, and call for *one* Simon, whose surname is Peter:

6 He lodgeth with one Simon a tanner, whose house is by the sea side: he shall tell thee what thou oughtest to do.

7 And when the angel which spake
unto Cornelius was departed, he
called two of his household ser-
vants, and a devout soldier of them
that waited on him continually;
8 And when he had declared all
these things unto them, he sent
them to Joppa.

Peter's Trance and Vision

9 On the morrow, as they went on
their journey, and drew nigh unto
the city, Peter went up upon the
housetop to pray about the sixth
hour:
10 And he became very hungry, and
would have eaten: but while they
made ready, he fell into a trance,
11 And saw heaven opened, and a
certain vessel descending unto him,
as it had been a great sheet knit at
the four corners, and let down to
the earth:
12 Wherein were all manner of
fourfooted beasts of the earth, and
wild beasts, and creeping things,
and fowls of the air.
13 And there came a voice to him,
Rise, Peter; kill, and eat.
14 But Peter said, Not so, Lord; for
I have never eaten any thing that is
common or unclean.
15 And the voice *spake* unto him
again the second time, What God
hath cleansed, *that* call not thou
common.
16 This was done thrice: and the
vessel was received up again into
heaven.
17 Now while Peter doubted in
himself what this vision which he
had seen should mean, behold, the
men which were sent from Cornel-
ius had made enquiry for Simon's
house, and stood before the gate,
18 And called, and asked whether
Simon, which was surnamed Peter,
were lodged there.
19 While Peter thought on the vi-
sion, the Spirit said unto him, Be-
hold, three men seek thee.
20 Arise therefore, and get thee
down, and go with them, doubting
nothing: for I have sent them.
21 Then Peter went down to the
men which were sent unto him from
Cornelius; and said, Behold, I am he
whom ye seek: what *is* the cause
wherefore ye are come?
22 And they said, Cornelius the
centurion, a just man, and one that
feareth God, and of good report
among all the nation of the Jews,
was warned from God by an holy
angel to send for thee into his house,
and to hear words of thee.

Peter Visits Cornelius

23 Then called he them in, and
lodged *them*. And on the morrow
Peter went away with them, and
certain brethren from Joppa accom-
panied him.
24 And the morrow after they en-
tered into Caesarea. And Cornelius
waited for them, and had called to-
gether his kinsmen and near friends.
25 And as Peter was coming in,
Cornelius met him, and fell down
at his feet, and worshipped *him*.
26 But Peter took him up, saying,
Stand up; I myself also am a man.
27 And as he talked with him, he
went in, and found many that were
come together.
28 And he said unto them, Ye
know how that it is an unlawful
thing for a man that is a Jew to keep
company, or come unto one of an-
other nation; but God hath shewed
me that I should not call any man
common or unclean.
29 Therefore came I *unto you*
without gainsaying, as soon as I was
sent for: I ask therefore for what
intent ye have sent for me?
30 And Cornelius said, Four days
ago I was fasting until this hour;
and at the ninth hour I prayed in
my house, and, behold, a man stood
before me in bright clothing,
31 And said, Cornelius, thy prayer

is heard, and thine alms are had in
remembrance in the sight of God.
32 Send therefore to Joppa, and
call hither Simon, whose surname
is Peter; he is lodged in the house of
one Simon a tanner by the sea side:
who, when he cometh, shall speak
unto thee.
33 Immediately therefore I sent to
thee; and thou hast well done that
thou art come. Now therefore are
we all here present before God, to
hear all things that are commanded
thee of God.

Preaching to Cornelius

34 Then Peter opened *his* mouth,
and said, Of a truth I perceive that
God is no respecter of persons:
35 But in every nation he that
feareth him, and worketh righteous-
ness, is accepted with him.
36 The word which *God* sent unto
the children of Israel, preaching
peace by Jesus Christ: (he is Lord
of all:)
37 That word, *I say,* ye know,
which was published throughout
all Judaea, and began from Gali-
lee, after the baptism which John
preached;
38 How God anointed Jesus of
Nazareth with the Holy Ghost and
with power: who went about do-
ing good, and healing all that were
oppressed of the devil; for God was
with him.
39 And we are witnesses of all
things which he did both in the
land of the Jews, and in Jerusalem;
whom they slew and hanged on a
tree:
40 Him God raised up the third
day, and shewed him openly;
41 Not to all the people, but unto
witnesses chosen before of God,
even to us, who did eat and drink
with him after he rose from the
dead.
42 And he commanded us to
preach unto the people, and to tes-
tify that it is he which was ordained
of God *to be* the Judge of quick and
dead.
43 To him give all the prophets
witness, that through his name
whosoever believeth in him shall
receive remission of sins.

Gentiles Receive the Holy Spirit

44 While Peter yet spake these
words, the Holy Ghost fell on all
them which heard the word.
45 And they of the circumcision
which believed were astonished, as
many as came with Peter, because
that on the Gentiles also was poured
out the gift of the Holy Ghost.
46 For they heard them speak with
tongues, and magnify God. Then
answered Peter,
47 Can any man forbid water, that
these should not be baptized, which
have received the Holy Ghost as well
as we?
48 And he commanded them to
be baptized in the name of the Lord.
Then prayed they him to tarry cer-
tain days.

Jewish Believers Challenge Peter

11 And the apostles and brethren
that were in Judaea heard that
the Gentiles had also received the
word of God.
2 And when Peter was come up
to Jerusalem, they that were of the
circumcision contended with him,
3 Saying, Thou wentest in to men
uncircumcised, and didst eat with
them.
4 But Peter rehearsed *the matter*
from the beginning, and expounded
it by order unto them, saying,
5 I was in the city of Joppa pray-
ing: and in a trance I saw a vision,
A certain vessel descend, as it had
been a great sheet, let down from
heaven by four corners; and it came
even to me:

6 Upon the which when I had fastened mine eyes, I considered, and saw fourfooted beasts of the earth, and wild beasts, and creeping things, and fowls of the air.

7 And I heard a voice saying unto me, Arise, Peter; slay and eat.

8 But I said, Not so, Lord: for nothing common or unclean hath at any time entered into my mouth.

9 But the voice answered me again from heaven, What God hath cleansed, *that* call not thou common.

10 And this was done three times: and all were drawn up again into heaven.

11 And, behold, immediately there were three men already come unto the house where I was, sent from Caesarea unto me.

12 And the Spirit bade me go with them, nothing doubting. Moreover these six brethren accompanied me, and we entered into the man's house:

13 And he shewed us how he had seen an angel in his house, which stood and said unto him, Send men to Joppa, and call for Simon, whose surname is Peter;

14 Who shall tell thee words, whereby thou and all thy house shall be saved.

15 And as I began to speak, the Holy Ghost fell on them, as on us at the beginning.

16 Then remembered I the word of the Lord, how that he said, John indeed baptized with water; but ye shall be baptized with the Holy Ghost.

17 Forasmuch then as God gave them the like gift as *he did* unto us, who believed on the Lord Jesus Christ; what was I, that I could withstand God?

18 When they heard these things, they held their peace, and glorified God, saying, Then hath God also to the Gentiles granted repentance unto life.

Barnabas Sent to Antioch

19 Now they which were scattered abroad upon the persecution that arose about Stephen travelled as far as Phenice, and Cyprus, and Antioch, preaching the word to none but unto the Jews only.

20 And some of them were men of Cyprus and Cyrene, which, when they were come to Antioch, spake unto the Grecians, preaching the Lord Jesus.

21 And the hand of the Lord was with them: and a great number believed, and turned unto the Lord.

22 Then tidings of these things came unto the ears of the church which was in Jerusalem: and they sent forth Barnabas, that he should go as far as Antioch.

23 Who, when he came, and had seen the grace of God, was glad, and exhorted them all, that with purpose of heart they would cleave unto the Lord.

24 For he was a good man, and full of the Holy Ghost and of faith: and much people was added unto the Lord.

25 Then departed Barnabas to Tarsus, for to seek Saul:

26 And when he had found him, he brought him unto Antioch. And it came to pass, that a whole year they assembled themselves with the church, and taught much people. And the disciples were called Christians first in Antioch.

Relief for Judaea

27 And in these days came prophets from Jerusalem unto Antioch.

28 And there stood up one of them named Agabus, and signified by the Spirit that there should be great dearth throughout all the world: which came to pass in the days of Claudius Caesar.

29 Then the disciples, every man according to his ability, determined

to send relief unto the brethren which dwelt in Judaea:

30 Which also they did, and sent it to the elders by the hands of Barnabas and Saul.

Persecution by Herod

12 Now about that time Herod the king stretched forth *his* hands to vex certain of the church.

2 And he killed James the brother of John with the sword.

3 And because he saw it pleased the Jews, he proceeded further to take Peter also. (Then were the days of unleavened bread.)

4 And when he had apprehended him, he put *him* in prison, and delivered *him* to four quaternions of soldiers to keep him; intending after Easter to bring him forth to the people.

5 Peter therefore was kept in prison: but prayer was made without ceasing of the church unto God for him.

6 And when Herod would have brought him forth, the same night Peter was sleeping between two soldiers, bound with two chains: and the keepers before the door kept the prison.

The Angel of the Lord Frees Peter

7 And, behold, the angel of the Lord came upon *him,* and a light shined in the prison: and he smote Peter on the side, and raised him up, saying, Arise up quickly. And his chains fell off from *his* hands.

8 And the angel said unto him, Gird thyself, and bind on thy sandals. And so he did. And he saith unto him, Cast thy garment about thee, and follow me.

9 And he went out, and followed him; and wist not that it was true which was done by the angel; but thought he saw a vision.

10 When they were past the first and the second ward, they came unto the iron gate that leadeth unto the city; which opened to them of his own accord: and they went out, and passed on through one street; and forthwith the angel departed from him.

11 And when Peter was come to himself, he said, Now I know of a surety, that the Lord hath sent his angel, and hath delivered me out of the hand of Herod, and *from* all the expectation of the people of the Jews.

12 And when he had considered *the thing,* he came to the house of Mary the mother of John, whose surname was Mark; where many were gathered together praying.

13 And as Peter knocked at the door of the gate, a damsel came to hearken, named Rhoda.

14 And when she knew Peter's voice, she opened not the gate for gladness, but ran in, and told how Peter stood before the gate.

15 And they said unto her, Thou art mad. But she constantly affirmed that it was even so. Then said they, It is his angel.

16 But Peter continued knocking: and when they had opened *the door,* and saw him, they were astonished.

17 But he, beckoning unto them with the hand to hold their peace, declared unto them how the Lord had brought him out of the prison. And he said, Go shew these things unto James, and to the brethren. And he departed, and went into another place.

18 Now as soon as it was day, there was no small stir among the soldiers, what was become of Peter.

19 And when Herod had sought for him, and found him not, he examined the keepers, and commanded that *they* should be put to death. And he went down from Judaea to Caesarea, and *there* abode.

God Smites Herod

20 And Herod was highly dis-
pleased with them of Tyre and
Sidon: but they came with one
accord to him, and, having made
Blastus the king's chamberlain their
friend, desired peace; because their
country was nourished by the king's
country.
21 And upon a set day Herod, ar-
rayed in royal apparel, sat upon his
throne, and made an oration unto
them.
22 And the people gave a shout,
saying, It is the voice of a god, and
not of a man.
23 And immediately the angel of
the Lord smote him, because he
gave not God the glory: and he was
eaten of worms, and gave up the
ghost.
24 But the word of God grew and
multiplied.
25 And Barnabas and Saul re-
turned from Jerusalem, when they
had fulfilled *their* ministry, and took
with them John, whose surname
was Mark.

Saul and Barnabas
Sail to Cyprus

13 Now there were in the church
that was at Antioch certain
prophets and teachers; as Barnabas,
and Simeon that was called Niger,
and Lucius of Cyrene, and Manaen,
which had been brought up with
Herod the tetrarch, and Saul.
2 As they ministered to the Lord,
and fasted, the Holy Ghost said, Sep-
arate me Barnabas and Saul for the
work whereunto I have called them.
3 And when they had fasted and
prayed, and laid *their* hands on
them, they sent *them* away.
4 So they, being sent forth by the
Holy Ghost, departed unto Seleu-
cia; and from thence they sailed to
Cyprus.
5 And when they were at Salamis,
they preached the word of God in
the synagogues of the Jews: and
they had also John to *their* minister.
6 And when they had gone
through the isle unto Paphos, they
found a certain sorcerer, a false
prophet, a Jew, whose name *was*
Bar-jesus:
7 Which was with the deputy of
the country, Sergius Paulus, a pru-
dent man; who called for Barnabas
and Saul, and desired to hear the
word of God.
8 But Elymas the sorcerer (for so
is his name by interpretation) with-
stood them, seeking to turn away
the deputy from the faith.
9 Then Saul, (who also *is called*
Paul,) filled with the Holy Ghost,
set his eyes on him,
10 And said, O full of all subtilty
and all mischief, *thou* child of the
devil, *thou* enemy of all righteous-
ness, wilt thou not cease to pervert
the right ways of the Lord?
11 And now, behold, the hand of
the Lord *is* upon thee, and thou shalt
be blind, not seeing the sun for a
season. And immediately there fell
on him a mist and a darkness; and
he went about seeking some to lead
him by the hand.
12 Then the deputy, when he saw
what was done, believed, being as-
tonished at the doctrine of the Lord.

Paul and Barnabas in Antioch

13 Now when Paul and his com-
pany loosed from Paphos, they
came to Perga in Pamphylia: and
John departing from them returned
to Jerusalem.
14 But when they departed from
Perga, they came to Antioch in Pi-
sidia, and went into the synagogue
on the sabbath day, and sat down.
15 And after the reading of the law
and the prophets the rulers of the
synagogue sent unto them, saying,
Ye men *and* brethren, if ye have any
word of exhortation for the people,
say on.

16 Then Paul stood up, and beck-
oning with *his* hand said, Men of
Israel, and ye that fear God, give
audience.
17 The God of this people of Israel
chose our fathers, and exalted the
people when they dwelt as strangers
in the land of Egypt, and with an
high arm brought he them out of it.
18 And about the time of forty
years suffered he their manners in
the wilderness.
19 And when he had destroyed
seven nations in the land of Cha-
naan, he divided their land to them
by lot.
20 And after that he gave *unto
them* judges about the space of four
hundred and fifty years, until Sam-
uel the prophet.
21 And afterward they desired a
king: and God gave unto them Saul
the son of Cis, a man of the tribe
of Benjamin, by the space of forty
years.
22 And when he had removed him,
he raised up unto them David to be
their king; to whom also he gave
testimony, and said, I have found
David the *son* of Jesse, a man after
mine own heart, which shall fulfil
all my will.
23 Of this man's seed hath God
according to *his* promise raised unto
Israel a Saviour, Jesus:
24 When John had first preached
before his coming the baptism of
repentance to all the people of Israel.
25 And as John fulfilled his course,
he said, Whom think ye that I am? I
am not *he*. But, behold, there com-
eth one after me, whose shoes of
his feet I am not worthy to loose.
26 Men *and* brethren, children of
the stock of Abraham, and whoso-
ever among you feareth God, to you
is the word of this salvation sent.
27 For they that dwell at Jerusa-
lem, and their rulers, because they
knew him not, nor yet the voices of
the prophets which are read every
sabbath day, they have fulfilled *them*
in condemning *him*.
28 And though they found no
cause of death *in him*, yet desired
they Pilate that he should be slain.
29 And when they had fulfilled all
that was written of him, they took
him down from the tree, and laid
him in a sepulchre.
30 But God raised him from the
dead:
31 And he was seen many days
of them which came up with him
from Galilee to Jerusalem, who are
his witnesses unto the people.
32 And we declare unto you glad
tidings, how that the promise which
was made unto the fathers,
33 God hath fulfilled the same
unto us their children, in that he
hath raised up Jesus again; as it is
also written in the second psalm,
Thou art my Son, this day have I
begotten thee.
34 And as concerning that he
raised him up from the dead, *now*
no more to return to corruption, he
said on this wise, I will give you the
sure mercies of David.
35 Wherefore he saith also in an-
other *psalm*, Thou shalt not suffer
thine Holy One to see corruption.
36 For David, after he had served
his own generation by the will of
God, fell on sleep, and was laid unto
his fathers, and saw corruption:
37 But he, whom God raised again,
saw no corruption.
38 Be it known unto you therefore,
men *and* brethren, that through this
man is preached unto you the for-
giveness of sins:
39 And by him all that believe are
justified from all things, from which
ye could not be justified by the law
of Moses.
40 Beware therefore, lest that
come upon you, which is spoken
of in the prophets;
41 Behold, ye despisers, and won-
der, and perish: for I work a work

in your days, a work which ye shall
in no wise believe, though a man
declare it unto you.
42 And when the Jews were gone
out of the synagogue, the Gentiles
besought that these words might be
preached to them the next sabbath.
43 Now when the congregation
was broken up, many of the Jews
and religious proselytes followed
Paul and Barnabas: who, speaking
to them, persuaded them to con-
tinue in the grace of God.
44 And the next sabbath day came
almost the whole city together to
hear the word of God.
45 But when the Jews saw the
multitudes, they were filled with
envy, and spake against those things
which were spoken by Paul, contra-
dicting and blaspheming.
46 Then Paul and Barnabas waxed
bold, and said, It was necessary that
the word of God should first have
been spoken to you: but seeing ye
put it from you, and judge your-
selves unworthy of everlasting life,
lo, we turn to the Gentiles.
47 For so hath the Lord com-
manded us, *saying,* I have set thee
to be a light of the Gentiles, that
thou shouldest be for salvation unto
the ends of the earth.
48 And when the Gentiles heard
this, they were glad, and glorified
the word of the Lord: and as many
as were ordained to eternal life be-
lieved.
49 And the word of the Lord was
published throughout all the region.
50 But the Jews stirred up the de-
vout and honourable women, and
the chief men of the city, and raised
persecution against Paul and Barna-
bas, and expelled them out of their
coasts.
51 But they shook off the dust of
their feet against them, and came
unto Iconium.
52 And the disciples were filled
with joy, and with the Holy Ghost.

Paul and Barnabas at Iconium

14 And it came to pass in Ico-
nium, that they went both
together into the synagogue of the
Jews, and so spake, that a great mul-
titude both of the Jews and also of
the Greeks believed.
2 But the unbelieving Jews stirred
up the Gentiles, and made their
minds evil affected against the
brethren.
3 Long time therefore abode they
speaking boldly in the Lord, which
gave testimony unto the word of his
grace, and granted signs and won-
ders to be done by their hands.
4 But the multitude of the city
was divided: and part held with the
Jews, and part with the apostles.
5 And when there was an assault
made both of the Gentiles, and also
of the Jews with their rulers, to use
them despitefully, and to stone them,
6 They were ware of *it,* and fled
unto Lystra and Derbe, cities of Lyc-
aonia, and unto the region that lieth
round about:
7 And there they preached the
gospel.

Ministry in Lystra

8 And there sat a certain man at
Lystra, impotent in his feet, being
a cripple from his mother's womb,
who never had walked:
9 The same heard Paul speak:
who stedfastly beholding him, and
perceiving that he had faith to be
healed,
10 Said with a loud voice, Stand
upright on thy feet. And he leaped
and walked.
11 And when the people saw what
Paul had done, they lifted up their
voices, saying in the speech of Lyc-
aonia, The gods are come down to
us in the likeness of men.
12 And they called Barnabas, Ju-
piter; and Paul, Mercurius, because
he was the chief speaker.

13 Then the priest of Jupiter,
which was before their city, brought
oxen and garlands unto the gates,
and would have done sacrifice with
the people.
14 *Which* when the apostles, Bar-
nabas and Paul, heard *of,* they rent
their clothes, and ran in among the
people, crying out,
15 And saying, Sirs, why do ye
these things? We also are men of like
passions with you, and preach unto
you that ye should turn from these
vanities unto the living God, which
made heaven, and earth, and the
sea, and all things that are therein:
16 Who in times past suffered all
nations to walk in their own ways.
17 Nevertheless he left not himself
without witness, in that he did good,
and gave us rain from heaven, and
fruitful seasons, filling our hearts
with food and gladness.
18 And with these sayings scarce
restrained they the people, that they
had not done sacrifice unto them.

Paul Stoned and Left for Dead

19 And there came thither *certain*
Jews from Antioch and Iconium,
who persuaded the people, and,
having stoned Paul, drew *him* out
of the city, supposing he had been
dead.
20 Howbeit, as the disciples stood
round about him, he rose up, and
came into the city: and the next day
he departed with Barnabas to Derbe.

The Return to Antioch

21 And when they had preached
the gospel to that city, and had
taught many, they returned again
to Lystra, and *to* Iconium, and An-
tioch,
22 Confirming the souls of the
disciples, *and* exhorting them to
continue in the faith, and that we
must through much tribulation en-
ter into the kingdom of God.
23 And when they had ordained
them elders in every church, and
had prayed with fasting, they com-
mended them to the Lord, on whom
they believed.
24 And after they had passed
throughout Pisidia, they came to
Pamphylia.
25 And when they had preached
the word in Perga, they went down
into Attalia:
26 And thence sailed to Antioch,
from whence they had been recom-
mended to the grace of God for the
work which they fulfilled.
27 And when they were come, and
had gathered the church together,
they rehearsed all that God had done
with them, and how he had opened
the door of faith unto the Gentiles.
28 And there they abode long time
with the disciples.

A Dispute over Circumcision

15 And certain men which came
down from Judaea taught the
brethren, *and said,* Except ye be
circumcised after the manner of
Moses, ye cannot be saved.
2 When therefore Paul and Bar-
nabas had no small dissension and
disputation with them, they deter-
mined that Paul and Barnabas, and
certain other of them, should go up
to Jerusalem unto the apostles and
elders about this question.
3 And being brought on their way
by the church, they passed through
Phenice and Samaria, declaring the
conversion of the Gentiles: and they
caused great joy unto all the breth-
ren.
4 And when they were come to
Jerusalem, they were received of
the church, and *of* the apostles and
elders, and they declared all things
that God had done with them.
5 But there rose up certain of the
sect of the Pharisees which believed,
saying, That it was needful to cir-
cumcise them, and to command
them to keep the law of Moses.

6 And the apostles and elders
came together for to consider of
this matter.
7 And when there had been much
disputing, Peter rose up, and said
unto them, Men *and* brethren, ye
know how that a good while ago
God made choice among us, that the
Gentiles by my mouth should hear
the word of the gospel, and believe.
8 And God, which knoweth the
hearts, bare them witness, giving
them the Holy Ghost, even as *he did*
unto us;
9 And put no difference between
us and them, purifying their hearts
by faith.
10 Now therefore why tempt ye
God, to put a yoke upon the neck
of the disciples, which neither our
fathers nor we were able to bear?
11 But we believe that through the
grace of the Lord Jesus Christ we
shall be saved, even as they.
12 Then all the multitude kept
silence, and gave audience to Barnabas and Paul, declaring what miracles and wonders God had wrought
among the Gentiles by them.
13 And after they had held their
peace, James answered, saying, Men
and brethren, hearken unto me:
14 Simeon hath declared how God
at the first did visit the Gentiles, to
take out of them a people for his
name.
15 And to this agree the words of
the prophets; as it is written,
16 After this I will return, and will
build again the tabernacle of David,
which is fallen down; and I will build
again the ruins thereof, and I will
set it up:
17 That the residue of men might
seek after the Lord, and all the Gentiles, upon whom my name is called,
saith the Lord, who doeth all these
things.
18 Known unto God are all his
works from the beginning of the
world.
19 Wherefore my sentence is, that
we trouble not them, which from
among the Gentiles are turned to
God:
20 But that we write unto them,
that they abstain from pollutions of
idols, and *from* fornication, and *from*
things strangled, and *from* blood.
21 For Moses of old time hath in
every city them that preach him,
being read in the synagogues every
sabbath day.

Letters to the Gentile Believers

22 Then pleased it the apostles
and elders, with the whole church,
to send chosen men of their own
company to Antioch with Paul and
Barnabas; *namely,* Judas surnamed
Barsabas, and Silas, chief men
among the brethren:
23 And they wrote *letters* by them
after this manner; The apostles and
elders and brethren *send* greeting
unto the brethren which are of the
Gentiles in Antioch and Syria and
Cilicia:
24 Forasmuch as we have heard,
that certain which went out from
us have troubled you with words,
subverting your souls, saying, *Ye
must* be circumcised, and keep the
law: to whom we gave no *such* commandment:
25 It seemed good unto us, being
assembled with one accord, to send
chosen men unto you with our beloved Barnabas and Paul,
26 Men that have hazarded their
lives for the name of our Lord Jesus
Christ.
27 We have sent therefore Judas
and Silas, who shall also tell *you* the
same things by mouth.
28 For it seemed good to the Holy
Ghost, and to us, to lay upon you no
greater burden than these necessary
things;
29 That ye abstain from meats
offered to idols, and from blood,
and from things strangled, and from

fornication: from which if ye keep yourselves, ye shall do well. Fare ye well.

30 So when they were dismissed, they came to Antioch: and when they had gathered the multitude together, they delivered the epistle:

31 *Which* when they had read, they rejoiced for the consolation.

32 And Judas and Silas, being prophets also themselves, exhorted the brethren with many words, and confirmed *them*.

33 And after they had tarried *there* a space, they were let go in peace from the brethren unto the apostles.

34 Notwithstanding it pleased Silas to abide there still.

35 Paul also and Barnabas continued in Antioch, teaching and preaching the word of the Lord, with many others also.

Paul and Barnabas Disagree

36 And some days after Paul said unto Barnabas, Let us go again and visit our brethren in every city where we have preached the word of the Lord, *and see* how they do.

37 And Barnabas determined to take with them John, whose surname was Mark.

38 But Paul thought not good to take him with them, who departed from them from Pamphylia, and went not with them to the work.

39 And the contention was so sharp between them, that they departed asunder one from the other: and so Barnabas took Mark, and sailed unto Cyprus;

40 And Paul chose Silas, and departed, being recommended by the brethren unto the grace of God.

41 And he went through Syria and Cilicia, confirming the churches.

Timothy Joins Paul and Silas

16 Then came he to Derbe and Lystra: and, behold, a certain disciple was there, named Timotheus, the son of a certain woman, which was a Jewess, and believed; but his father *was* a Greek:

2 Which was well reported of by the brethren that were at Lystra and Iconium.

3 Him would Paul have to go forth with him; and took and circumcised him because of the Jews which were in those quarters: for they knew all that his father was a Greek.

4 And as they went through the cities, they delivered them the decrees for to keep, that were ordained of the apostles and elders which were at Jerusalem.

5 And so were the churches established in the faith, and increased in number daily.

Paul's Macedonian Vision

6 Now when they had gone throughout Phrygia and the region of Galatia, and were forbidden of the Holy Ghost to preach the word in Asia,

7 After they were come to Mysia, they assayed to go into Bithynia: but the Spirit suffered them not.

8 And they passing by Mysia came down to Troas.

9 And a vision appeared to Paul in the night; There stood a man of Macedonia, and prayed him, saying, Come over into Macedonia, and help us.

10 And after he had seen the vision, immediately we endeavoured to go into Macedonia, assuredly gathering that the Lord had called us for to preach the gospel unto them.

Lydia Is Converted and Baptized

11 Therefore loosing from Troas, we came with a straight course to Samothracia, and the next *day* to Neapolis;

12 And from thence to Philippi, which is the chief city of that part of Macedonia, *and* a colony: and

we were in that city abiding certain days.

13 And on the sabbath we went out of the city by a river side, where prayer was wont to be made; and we sat down, and spake unto the women which resorted *thither.*

14 And a certain woman named Lydia, a seller of purple, of the city of Thyatira, which worshipped God, heard *us:* whose heart the Lord opened, that she attended unto the things which were spoken of Paul.

15 And when she was baptized, and her household, she besought *us,* saying, If ye have judged me to be faithful to the Lord, come into my house, and abide *there.* And she constrained us.

16 And it came to pass, as we went to prayer, a certain damsel possessed with a spirit of divination met us, which brought her masters much gain by soothsaying:

17 The same followed Paul and us, and cried, saying, These men are the servants of the most high God, which shew unto us the way of salvation.

18 And this did she many days. But Paul, being grieved, turned and said to the spirit, I command thee in the name of Jesus Christ to come out of her. And he came out the same hour.

19 And when her masters saw that the hope of their gains was gone, they caught Paul and Silas, and drew *them* into the marketplace unto the rulers,

Paul and Silas Are Beaten and Jailed

20 And brought them to the magistrates, saying, These men, being Jews, do exceedingly trouble our city,

21 And teach customs, which are not lawful for us to receive, neither to observe, being Romans.

22 And the multitude rose up together against them: and the magistrates rent off their clothes, and commanded to beat *them.*

23 And when they had laid many stripes upon them, they cast *them* into prison, charging the jailor to keep them safely:

24 Who, having received such a charge, thrust them into the inner prison, and made their feet fast in the stocks.

25 And at midnight Paul and Silas prayed, and sang praises unto God: and the prisoners heard them.

Conversion of the Prison Keeper

26 And suddenly there was a great earthquake, so that the foundations of the prison were shaken: and immediately all the doors were opened, and every one's bands were loosed.

27 And the keeper of the prison awaking out of his sleep, and seeing the prison doors open, he drew out his sword, and would have killed himself, supposing that the prisoners had been fled.

28 But Paul cried with a loud voice, saying, Do thyself no harm: for we are all here.

29 Then he called for a light, and sprang in, and came trembling, and fell down before Paul and Silas,

30 And brought them out, and said, Sirs, what must I do to be saved?

31 And they said, Believe on the Lord Jesus Christ, and thou shalt be saved, and thy house.

32 And they spake unto him the word of the Lord, and to all that were in his house.

33 And he took them the same hour of the night, and washed *their* stripes; and was baptized, he and all his, straightway.

34 And when he had brought them into his house, he set meat before them, and rejoiced, believing in God with all his house.

35 And when it was day, the mag-
istrates sent the serjeants, saying,
Let those men go.
36 And the keeper of the prison
told this saying to Paul, The magis-
trates have sent to let you go: now
therefore depart, and go in peace.
37 But Paul said unto them, They
have beaten us openly uncon-
demned, being Romans, and have
cast *us* into prison; and now do they
thrust us out privily? nay verily; but
let them come themselves and fetch
us out.
38 And the serjeants told these
words unto the magistrates: and
they feared, when they heard that
they were Romans.
39 And they came and besought
them, and brought *them* out, and
desired *them* to depart out of the
city.
40 And they went out of the
prison, and entered into *the house
of* Lydia: and when they had seen
the brethren, they comforted them,
and departed.

Preaching at Thessalonica

17 Now when they had passed
through Amphipolis and Ap-
ollonia, they came to Thessalonica,
where was a synagogue of the Jews:
2 And Paul, as his manner was,
went in unto them, and three sab-
bath days reasoned with them out
of the scriptures,
3 Opening and alleging, that Christ
must needs have suffered, and risen
again from the dead; and that this
Jesus, whom I preach unto you, is
Christ.
4 And some of them believed, and
consorted with Paul and Silas; and
of the devout Greeks a great multi-
tude, and of the chief women not a
few.

Jason's House Assaulted

5 But the Jews which believed not,
moved with envy, took unto them
certain lewd fellows of the baser
sort, and gathered a company, and
set all the city on an uproar, and
assaulted the house of Jason, and
sought to bring them out to the
people.
6 And when they found them not,
they drew Jason and certain breth-
ren unto the rulers of the city, crying,
These that have turned the world
upside down are come hither also;
7 Whom Jason hath received: and
these all do contrary to the decrees
of Caesar, saying that there is an-
other king, *one* Jesus.
8 And they troubled the people
and the rulers of the city, when they
heard these things.
9 And when they had taken secu-
rity of Jason, and of the other, they
let them go.

The Night Journey to Berea

10 And the brethren immediately
sent away Paul and Silas by night
unto Berea: who coming *thither*
went into the synagogue of the
Jews.
11 These were more noble than
those in Thessalonica, in that they
received the word with all readiness
of mind, and searched the scriptures
daily, whether those things were so.
12 Therefore many of them be-
lieved; also of honourable women
which were Greeks, and of men, not
a few.
13 But when the Jews of Thessalo-
nica had knowledge that the word of
God was preached of Paul at Berea,
they came thither also, and stirred
up the people.
14 And then immediately the
brethren sent away Paul to go as it
were to the sea: but Silas and Timo-
theus abode there still.
15 And they that conducted Paul
brought him unto Athens: and re-
ceiving a commandment unto Silas
and Timotheus for to come to him
with all speed, they departed.

Paul Waits in Athens

16 Now while Paul waited for them at Athens, his spirit was stirred in him, when he saw the city wholly given to idolatry.

17 Therefore disputed he in the synagogue with the Jews, and with the devout persons, and in the market daily with them that met with him.

18 Then certain philosophers of the Epicureans, and of the Stoicks, encountered him. And some said, What will this babbler say? other some, He seemeth to be a setter forth of strange gods: because he preached unto them Jesus, and the resurrection.

19 And they took him, and brought him unto Areopagus, saying, May we know what this new doctrine, whereof thou speakest, *is?*

20 For thou bringest certain strange things to our ears: we would know therefore what these things mean.

21 (For all the Athenians and strangers which were there spent their time in nothing else, but either to tell, or to hear some new thing.)

Paul Addresses the Men of Athens

22 Then Paul stood in the midst of Mars' hill, and said, *Ye* men of Athens, I perceive that in all things ye are too superstitious.

23 For as I passed by, and beheld your devotions, I found an altar with this inscription, TO THE UNKNOWN GOD. Whom therefore ye ignorantly worship, him declare I unto you.

24 God that made the world and all things therein, seeing that he is Lord of heaven and earth, dwelleth not in temples made with hands;

25 Neither is worshipped with men's hands, as though he needed any thing, seeing he giveth to all life, and breath, and all things;

26 And hath made of one blood all nations of men for to dwell on all the face of the earth, and hath determined the times before appointed, and the bounds of their habitation;

27 That they should seek the Lord, if haply they might feel after him, and find him, though he be not far from every one of us:

28 For in him we live, and move, and have our being; as certain also of your own poets have said, For we are also his offspring.

29 Forasmuch then as we are the offspring of God, we ought not to think that the Godhead is like unto gold, or silver, or stone, graven by art and man's device.

30 And the times of this ignorance God winked at; but now commandeth all men every where to repent:

31 Because he hath appointed a day, in the which he will judge the world in righteousness by *that* man whom he hath ordained; *whereof* he hath given assurance unto all *men,* in that he hath raised him from the dead.

32 And when they heard of the resurrection of the dead, some mocked: and others said, We will hear thee again of this *matter.*

33 So Paul departed from among them.

34 Howbeit certain men clave unto him, and believed: among the which *was* Dionysius the Areopagite, and a woman named Damaris, and others with them.

Paul Completes His Journey

18 After these things Paul departed from Athens, and came to Corinth;

2 And found a certain Jew named Aquila, born in Pontus, lately come from Italy, with his wife Priscilla; (because that Claudius had commanded all Jews to depart from Rome:) and came unto them.

3 And because he was of the same craft, he abode with them, and

wrought: for by their occupation they were tentmakers.

4 And he reasoned in the synagogue every sabbath, and persuaded the Jews and the Greeks.

5 And when Silas and Timotheus were come from Macedonia, Paul was pressed in the spirit, and testified to the Jews *that* Jesus *was* Christ.

6 And when they opposed themselves, and blasphemed, he shook *his* raiment, and said unto them, Your blood *be* upon your own heads; I *am* clean: from henceforth I will go unto the Gentiles.

7 And he departed thence, and entered into a certain *man's* house, named Justus, *one* that worshipped God, whose house joined hard to the synagogue.

8 And Crispus, the chief ruler of the synagogue, believed on the Lord with all his house; and many of the Corinthians hearing believed, and were baptized.

9 Then spake the Lord to Paul in the night by a vision, Be not afraid, but speak, and hold not thy peace:

10 For I am with thee, and no man shall set on thee to hurt thee: for I have much people in this city.

11 And he continued *there* a year and six months, teaching the word of God among them.

12 And when Gallio was the deputy of Achaia, the Jews made insurrection with one accord against Paul, and brought him to the judgment seat,

13 Saying, This *fellow* persuadeth men to worship God contrary to the law.

14 And when Paul was now about to open *his* mouth, Gallio said unto the Jews, If it were a matter of wrong or wicked lewdness, O *ye* Jews, reason would that I should bear with you:

15 But if it be a question of words and names, and *of* your law, look ye *to it;* for I will be no judge of such *matters.*

16 And he drave them from the judgment seat.

17 Then all the Greeks took Sosthenes, the chief ruler of the synagogue, and beat *him* before the judgment seat. And Gallio cared for none of those things.

18 And Paul *after this* tarried *there* yet a good while, and then took his leave of the brethren, and sailed thence into Syria, and with him Priscilla and Aquila; having shorn *his* head in Cenchrea: for he had a vow.

19 And he came to Ephesus, and left them there: but he himself entered into the synagogue, and reasoned with the Jews.

20 When they desired *him* to tarry longer time with them, he consented not;

21 But bade them farewell, saying, I must by all means keep this feast that cometh in Jerusalem: but I will return again unto you, if God will. And he sailed from Ephesus.

22 And when he had landed at Caesarea, and gone up, and saluted the church, he went down to Antioch.

23 And after he had spent some time *there,* he departed, and went over *all* the country of Galatia and Phrygia in order, strengthening all the disciples.

Apollos Speaks in the Synagogue

24 And a certain Jew named Apollos, born at Alexandria, an eloquent man, *and* mighty in the scriptures, came to Ephesus.

25 This man was instructed in the way of the Lord; and being fervent in the spirit, he spake and taught diligently the things of the Lord, knowing only the baptism of John.

26 And he began to speak boldly in the synagogue: whom when Aquila

and Priscilla had heard, they took him unto *them,* and expounded unto him the way of God more perfectly.

27 And when he was disposed to pass into Achaia, the brethren wrote, exhorting the disciples to receive him: who, when he was come, helped them much which had believed through grace:

28 For he mightily convinced the Jews, *and that* publickly, shewing by the scriptures that Jesus was Christ.

The Baptism of John's Disciples

19 And it came to pass, that, while Apollos was at Corinth, Paul having passed through the upper coasts came to Ephesus: and finding certain disciples,

2 He said unto them, Have ye received the Holy Ghost since ye believed? And they said unto him, We have not so much as heard whether there be any Holy Ghost.

3 And he said unto them, Unto what then were ye baptized? And they said, Unto John's baptism.

4 Then said Paul, John verily baptized with the baptism of repentance, saying unto the people, that they should believe on him which should come after him, that is, on Christ Jesus.

5 When they heard *this,* they were baptized in the name of the Lord Jesus.

6 And when Paul had laid *his* hands upon them, the Holy Ghost came on them; and they spake with tongues, and prophesied.

7 And all the men were about twelve.

8 And he went into the synagogue, and spake boldly for the space of three months, disputing and persuading the things concerning the kingdom of God.

9 But when divers were hardened, and believed not, but spake evil of that way before the multitude, he departed from them, and separated the disciples, disputing daily in the school of one Tyrannus.

10 And this continued by the space of two years; so that all they which dwelt in Asia heard the word of the Lord Jesus, both Jews and Greeks.

God's Miracles Through Paul

11 And God wrought special miracles by the hands of Paul:

12 So that from his body were brought unto the sick handkerchiefs or aprons, and the diseases departed from them, and the evil spirits went out of them.

13 Then certain of the vagabond Jews, exorcists, took upon them to call over them which had evil spirits the name of the Lord Jesus, saying, We adjure you by Jesus whom Paul preacheth.

14 And there were seven sons of *one* Sceva, a Jew, *and* chief of the priests, which did so.

15 And the evil spirit answered and said, Jesus I know, and Paul I know; but who are ye?

16 And the man in whom the evil spirit was leaped on them, and overcame them, and prevailed against them, so that they fled out of that house naked and wounded.

17 And this was known to all the Jews and Greeks also dwelling at Ephesus; and fear fell on them all, and the name of the Lord Jesus was magnified.

18 And many that believed came, and confessed, and shewed their deeds.

19 Many of them also which used curious arts brought their books together, and burned them before all *men:* and they counted the price of them, and found *it* fifty thousand *pieces* of silver.

20 So mightily grew the word of God and prevailed.

21 After these things were ended,

Paul purposed in the spirit, when he had passed through Macedonia and Achaia, to go to Jerusalem, saying, After I have been there, I must also see Rome.

22 So he sent into Macedonia two of them that ministered unto him, Timotheus and Erastus; but he himself stayed in Asia for a season.

Confusion in Ephesus

23 And the same time there arose no small stir about that way.

24 For a certain *man* named Demetrius, a silversmith, which made silver shrines for Diana, brought no small gain unto the craftsmen;

25 Whom he called together with the workmen of like occupation, and said, Sirs, ye know that by this craft we have our wealth.

26 Moreover ye see and hear, that not alone at Ephesus, but almost throughout all Asia, this Paul hath persuaded and turned away much people, saying that they be no gods, which are made with hands:

27 So that not only this our craft is in danger to be set at nought; but also that the temple of the great goddess Diana should be despised, and her magnificence should be destroyed, whom all Asia and the world worshippeth.

28 And when they heard *these sayings,* they were full of wrath, and cried out, saying, Great *is* Diana of the Ephesians.

29 And the whole city was filled with confusion: and having caught Gaius and Aristarchus, men of Macedonia, Paul's companions in travel, they rushed with one accord into the theatre.

30 And when Paul would have entered in unto the people, the disciples suffered him not.

31 And certain of the chief of Asia, which were his friends, sent unto him, desiring *him* that he would not adventure himself into the theatre.

32 Some therefore cried one thing, and some another: for the assembly was confused; and the more part knew not wherefore they were come together.

33 And they drew Alexander out of the multitude, the Jews putting him forward. And Alexander beckoned with the hand, and would have made his defence unto the people.

34 But when they knew that he was a Jew, all with one voice about the space of two hours cried out, Great *is* Diana of the Ephesians.

35 And when the townclerk had appeased the people, he said, *Ye* men of Ephesus, what man is there that knoweth not how that the city of the Ephesians is a worshipper of the great goddess Diana, and of the *image* which fell down from Jupiter?

36 Seeing then that these things cannot be spoken against, ye ought to be quiet, and to do nothing rashly.

37 For ye have brought hither these men, which are neither robbers of churches, nor yet blasphemers of your goddess.

38 Wherefore if Demetrius, and the craftsmen which are with him, have a matter against any man, the law is open, and there are deputies: let them implead one another.

39 But if ye enquire any thing concerning other matters, it shall be determined in a lawful assembly.

40 For we are in danger to be called in question for this day's uproar, there being no cause whereby we may give an account of this concourse.

41 And when he had thus spoken, he dismissed the assembly.

Paul Visits Macedonia and Greece

20 And after the uproar was ceased, Paul called unto *him* the disciples, and embraced *them,* and departed for to go into Macedonia.

2 And when he had gone over
those parts, and had given them
much exhortation, he came into
Greece,
3 And *there* abode three months.
And when the Jews laid wait for him,
as he was about to sail into Syria, he
purposed to return through Mace-
donia.
4 And there accompanied him
into Asia Sopater of Berea; and of
the Thessalonians, Aristarchus and
Secundus; and Gaius of Derbe, and
Timotheus; and of Asia, Tychicus
and Trophimus.
5 These going before tarried for
us at Troas.
6 And we sailed away from Philippi
after the days of unleavened bread,
and came unto them to Troas in five
days; where we abode seven days.

Eutychus Is Raised from the Dead

7 And upon the first *day* of the
week, when the disciples came to-
gether to break bread, Paul preached
unto them, ready to depart on the
morrow; and continued his speech
until midnight.
8 And there were many lights in
the upper chamber, where they were
gathered together.
9 And there sat in a window a
certain young man named Euty-
chus, being fallen into a deep sleep:
and as Paul was long preaching, he
sunk down with sleep, and fell down
from the third loft, and was taken
up dead.
10 And Paul went down, and fell
on him, and embracing *him* said,
Trouble not yourselves; for his life
is in him.
11 When he therefore was come
up again, and had broken bread, and
eaten, and talked a long while, even
till break of day, so he departed.
12 And they brought the young
man alive, and were not a little com-
forted.

Paul Calls the Ephesian Elders

13 And we went before to ship, and
sailed unto Assos, there intending to
take in Paul: for so had he appointed,
minding himself to go afoot.
14 And when he met with us at
Assos, we took him in, and came to
Mitylene.
15 And we sailed thence, and came
the next *day* over against Chios; and
the next *day* we arrived at Samos,
and tarried at Trogyllium; and the
next *day* we came to Miletus.
16 For Paul had determined to
sail by Ephesus, because he would
not spend the time in Asia: for he
hasted, if it were possible for him,
to be at Jerusalem the day of Pen-
tecost.
17 And from Miletus he sent to
Ephesus, and called the elders of
the church.
18 And when they were come to
him, he said unto them, Ye know,
from the first day that I came into
Asia, after what manner I have been
with you at all seasons,
19 Serving the Lord with all humil-
ity of mind, and with many tears,
and temptations, which befell me
by the lying in wait of the Jews:
20 *And* how I kept back nothing
that was profitable *unto you,* but
have shewed you, and have taught
you publickly, and from house to
house,
21 Testifying both to the Jews,
and also to the Greeks, repentance
toward God, and faith toward our
Lord Jesus Christ.
22 And now, behold, I go bound
in the spirit unto Jerusalem, not
knowing the things that shall befall
me there:
23 Save that the Holy Ghost wit-
nesseth in every city, saying that
bonds and afflictions abide me.
24 But none of these things move
me, neither count I my life dear unto
myself, so that I might finish my

course with joy, and the ministry, which I have received of the Lord Jesus, to testify the gospel of the grace of God.

25 And now, behold, I know that ye all, among whom I have gone preaching the kingdom of God, shall see my face no more.

26 Wherefore I take you to record this day, that I *am* pure from the blood of all *men*.

27 For I have not shunned to declare unto you all the counsel of God.

28 Take heed therefore unto yourselves, and to all the flock, over the which the Holy Ghost hath made you overseers, to feed the church of God, which he hath purchased with his own blood.

29 For I know this, that after my departing shall grievous wolves enter in among you, not sparing the flock.

30 Also of your own selves shall men arise, speaking perverse things, to draw away disciples after them.

31 Therefore watch, and remember, that by the space of three years I ceased not to warn every one night and day with tears.

32 And now, brethren, I commend you to God, and to the word of his grace, which is able to build you up, and to give you an inheritance among all them which are sanctified.

33 I have coveted no man's silver, or gold, or apparel.

34 Yea, ye yourselves know, that these hands have ministered unto my necessities, and to them that were with me.

35 I have shewed you all things, how that so labouring ye ought to support the weak, and to remember the words of the Lord Jesus, how he said, It is more blessed to give than to receive.

36 And when he had thus spoken, he kneeled down, and prayed with them all.

37 And they all wept sore, and fell on Paul's neck, and kissed him,

38 Sorrowing most of all for the words which he spake, that they should see his face no more. And they accompanied him unto the ship.

Danger in Jerusalem

21 And it came to pass, that after we were gotten from them, and had launched, we came with a straight course unto Coos, and the *day* following unto Rhodes, and from thence unto Patara:

2 And finding a ship sailing over unto Phenicia, we went aboard, and set forth.

3 Now when we had discovered Cyprus, we left it on the left hand, and sailed into Syria, and landed at Tyre: for there the ship was to unlade her burden.

4 And finding disciples, we tarried there seven days: who said to Paul through the Spirit, that he should not go up to Jerusalem.

5 And when we had accomplished those days, we departed and went our way; and they all brought us on our way, with wives and children, till *we were* out of the city: and we kneeled down on the shore, and prayed.

6 And when we had taken our leave one of another, we took ship; and they returned home again.

7 And when we had finished *our* course from Tyre, we came to Ptolemais, and saluted the brethren, and abode with them one day.

8 And the next *day* we that were of Paul's company departed, and came unto Caesarea: and we entered into the house of Philip the evangelist, which was *one* of the seven; and abode with him.

9 And the same man had four daughters, virgins, which did prophesy.

10 And as we tarried *there* many

days, there came down from Judaea
a certain prophet, named Agabus.
11 And when he was come unto
us, he took Paul's girdle, and bound
his own hands and feet, and said,
Thus saith the Holy Ghost, So shall
the Jews at Jerusalem bind the man
that owneth this girdle, and shall
deliver *him* into the hands of the
Gentiles.
12 And when we heard these
things, both we, and they of that
place, besought him not to go up
to Jerusalem.
13 Then Paul answered, What
mean ye to weep and to break
mine heart? for I am ready not to
be bound only, but also to die at Je-
rusalem for the name of the Lord
Jesus.
14 And when he would not be per-
suaded, we ceased, saying, The will
of the Lord be done.
15 And after those days we took
up our carriages, and went up to
Jerusalem.
16 There went with us also *cer-
tain* of the disciples of Caesarea, and
brought with them one Mnason of
Cyprus, an old disciple, with whom
we should lodge.

Paul Is Arrested and Bound

17 And when we were come to Je-
rusalem, the brethren received us
gladly.
18 And the *day* following Paul
went in with us unto James; and
all the elders were present.
19 And when he had saluted them,
he declared particularly what things
God had wrought among the Gen-
tiles by his ministry.
20 And when they heard *it,* they
glorified the Lord, and said unto
him, Thou seest, brother, how many
thousands of Jews there are which
believe; and they are all zealous of
the law:
21 And they are informed of
thee, that thou teachest all the
Jews which are among the Gen-
tiles to forsake Moses, saying that
they ought not to circumcise *their*
children, neither to walk after the
customs.
22 What is it therefore? the multi-
tude must needs come together: for
they will hear that thou art come.
23 Do therefore this that we say
to thee: We have four men which
have a vow on them;
24 Them take, and purify thy-
self with them, and be at charges
with them, that they may shave
their heads: and all may know
that those things, whereof they
were informed concerning thee,
are nothing; but *that* thou thyself
also walkest orderly, and keepest
the law.
25 As touching the Gentiles which
believe, we have written *and* con-
cluded that they observe no such
thing, save only that they keep
themselves from *things* offered to
idols, and from blood, and from
strangled, and from fornication.
26 Then Paul took the men, and
the next day purifying himself with
them entered into the temple, to
signify the accomplishment of the
days of purification, until that an
offering should be offered for every
one of them.
27 And when the seven days were
almost ended, the Jews which were
of Asia, when they saw him in the
temple, stirred up all the people,
and laid hands on him,
28 Crying out, Men of Israel, help:
This is the man, that teacheth all
men every where against the peo-
ple, and the law, and this place: and
further brought Greeks also into the
temple, and hath polluted this holy
place.
29 (For they had seen before with
him in the city Trophimus an Ephe-
sian, whom they supposed that Paul
had brought into the temple.)
30 And all the city was moved, and

the people ran together: and they took Paul, and drew him out of the temple: and forthwith the doors were shut.

31 And as they went about to kill him, tidings came unto the chief captain of the band, that all Jerusalem was in an uproar.

32 Who immediately took soldiers and centurions, and ran down unto them: and when they saw the chief captain and the soldiers, they left beating of Paul.

33 Then the chief captain came near, and took him, and commanded *him* to be bound with two chains; and demanded who he was, and what he had done.

34 And some cried one thing, some another, among the multitude: and when he could not know the certainty for the tumult, he commanded him to be carried into the castle.

35 And when he came upon the stairs, so it was, that he was borne of the soldiers for the violence of the people.

36 For the multitude of the people followed after, crying, Away with him.

37 And as Paul was to be led into the castle, he said unto the chief captain, May I speak unto thee? Who said, Canst thou speak Greek?

38 Art not thou that Egyptian, which before these days madest an uproar, and leddest out into the wilderness four thousand men that were murderers?

39 But Paul said, I am a man *which am* a Jew of Tarsus, *a city* in Cilicia, a citizen of no mean city: and, I beseech thee, suffer me to speak unto the people.

40 And when he had given him licence, Paul stood on the stairs, and beckoned with the hand unto the people. And when there was made a great silence, he spake unto *them* in the Hebrew tongue, saying,

Paul's Testimony

22 Men, brethren, and fathers, hear ye my defence *which I make* now unto you.

2 (And when they heard that he spake in the Hebrew tongue to them, they kept the more silence: and he saith,)

3 I am verily a man *which am* a Jew, born in Tarsus, *a city* in Cilicia, yet brought up in this city at the feet of Gamaliel, *and* taught according to the perfect manner of the law of the fathers, and was zealous toward God, as ye all are this day.

4 And I persecuted this way unto the death, binding and delivering into prisons both men and women.

5 As also the high priest doth bear me witness, and all the estate of the elders: from whom also I received letters unto the brethren, and went to Damascus, to bring them which were there bound unto Jerusalem, for to be punished.

Saul Meets the Lord

6 And it came to pass, that, as I made my journey, and was come nigh unto Damascus about noon, suddenly there shone from heaven a great light round about me.

7 And I fell unto the ground, and heard a voice saying unto me, Saul, Saul, why persecutest thou me?

8 And I answered, Who art thou, Lord? And he said unto me, I am Jesus of Nazareth, whom thou persecutest.

9 And they that were with me saw indeed the light, and were afraid; but they heard not the voice of him that spake to me.

10 And I said, What shall I do, Lord? And the Lord said unto me, Arise, and go into Damascus; and there it shall be told thee of all things which are appointed for thee to do.

11 And when I could not see for the glory of that light, being led by the

hand of them that were with me, I
came into Damascus.
12 And one Ananias, a devout man
according to the law, having a good
report of all the Jews which dwelt
there,
13 Came unto me, and stood, and
said unto me, Brother Saul, receive
thy sight. And the same hour I
looked up upon him.

God's Choice of a Witness

14 And he said, The God of our fa-
thers hath chosen thee, that thou
shouldest know his will, and see
that Just One, and shouldest hear
the voice of his mouth.
15 For thou shalt be his witness
unto all men of what thou hast seen
and heard.
16 And now why tarriest thou?
arise, and be baptized, and wash
away thy sins, calling on the name
of the Lord.
17 And it came to pass, that, when
I was come again to Jerusalem, even
while I prayed in the temple, I was
in a trance;
18 And saw him saying unto me,
Make haste, and get thee quickly out
of Jerusalem: for they will not re-
ceive thy testimony concerning me.
19 And I said, Lord, they know that
I imprisoned and beat in every syn-
agogue them that believed on thee:
20 And when the blood of thy mar-
tyr Stephen was shed, I also was
standing by, and consenting unto
his death, and kept the raiment of
them that slew him.
21 And he said unto me, Depart:
for I will send thee far hence unto
the Gentiles.

Paul's Citizenship

22 And they gave him audience
unto this word, and *then* lifted up
their voices, and said, Away with
such a *fellow* from the earth: for it
is not fit that he should live.
23 And as they cried out, and cast
off *their* clothes, and threw dust into
the air,
24 The chief captain commanded
him to be brought into the castle,
and bade that he should be exam-
ined by scourging; that he might
know wherefore they cried so
against him.
25 And as they bound him with
thongs, Paul said unto the centurion
that stood by, Is it lawful for you to
scourge a man that is a Roman, and
uncondemned?
26 When the centurion heard *that,*
he went and told the chief captain,
saying, Take heed what thou doest:
for this man is a Roman.
27 Then the chief captain came,
and said unto him, Tell me, art thou
a Roman? He said, Yea.
28 And the chief captain an-
swered, With a great sum obtained
I this freedom. And Paul said, But I
was *free* born.
29 Then straightway they de-
parted from him which should have
examined him: and the chief captain
also was afraid, after he knew that
he was a Roman, and because he
had bound him.
30 On the morrow, because he
would have known the certainty
wherefore he was accused of the
Jews, he loosed him from *his* bands,
and commanded the chief priests
and all their council to appear, and
brought Paul down, and set him
before them.

Paul Addresses the Council

23 And Paul, earnestly behold-
ing the council, said, Men
and brethren, I have lived in all
good conscience before God until
this day.
2 And the high priest Ananias
commanded them that stood by
him to smite him on the mouth.
3 Then said Paul unto him, God
shall smite thee, *thou* whited wall:
for sittest thou to judge me after

the law, and commandest me to be
smitten contrary to the law?
4 And they that stood by said, Re-
vilest thou God's high priest?
5 Then said Paul, I wist not, breth-
ren, that he was the high priest: for
it is written, Thou shalt not speak
evil of the ruler of thy people.
6 But when Paul perceived that
the one part were Sadducees, and
the other Pharisees, he cried out in
the council, Men *and* brethren, I am
a Pharisee, the son of a Pharisee:
of the hope and resurrection of the
dead I am called in question.
7 And when he had so said, there
arose a dissension between the
Pharisees and the Sadducees: and
the multitude was divided.
8 For the Sadducees say that there
is no resurrection, neither angel,
nor spirit: but the Pharisees confess
both.
9 And there arose a great cry: and
the scribes *that were* of the Phari-
sees' part arose, and strove, saying,
We find no evil in this man: but if
a spirit or an angel hath spoken to
him, let us not fight against God.
10 And when there arose a great
dissension, the chief captain, fearing
lest Paul should have been pulled
in pieces of them, commanded the
soldiers to go down, and to take him
by force from among them, and to
bring *him* into the castle.
11 And the night following the
Lord stood by him, and said, Be
of good cheer, Paul: for as thou
hast testified of me in Jerusalem,
so must thou bear witness also at
Rome.

A Conspiracy to Kill Paul

12 And when it was day, certain
of the Jews banded together, and
bound themselves under a curse,
saying that they would neither eat
nor drink till they had killed Paul.
13 And they were more than forty
which had made this conspiracy.
14 And they came to the chief
priests and elders, and said, We
have bound ourselves under a great
curse, that we will eat nothing until
we have slain Paul.
15 Now therefore ye with the
council signify to the chief captain
that he bring him down unto you
to morrow, as though ye would
enquire something more perfectly
concerning him: and we, or ever he
come near, are ready to kill him.
16 And when Paul's sister's son
heard of their lying in wait, he went
and entered into the castle, and told
Paul.
17 Then Paul called one of the cen-
turions unto *him,* and said, Bring
this young man unto the chief cap-
tain: for he hath a certain thing to
tell him.
18 So he took him, and brought
him to the chief captain, and said,
Paul the prisoner called me unto
him, and prayed me to bring this
young man unto thee, who hath
something to say unto thee.
19 Then the chief captain took
him by the hand, and went *with him*
aside privately, and asked *him,* What
is that thou hast to tell me?
20 And he said, The Jews have
agreed to desire thee that thou
wouldest bring down Paul to mor-
row into the council, as though they
would enquire somewhat of him
more perfectly.
21 But do not thou yield unto
them: for there lie in wait for him
of them more than forty men, which
have bound themselves with an
oath, that they will neither eat nor
drink till they have killed him: and
now are they ready, looking for a
promise from thee.
22 So the chief captain *then* let
the young man depart, and charged

him, See thou tell no man that thou
hast shewed these things to me.

Paul Taken to Caesarea

23 And he called unto *him* two
centurions, saying, Make ready two
hundred soldiers to go to Caesarea,
and horsemen threescore and ten,
and spearmen two hundred, at the
third hour of the night;
24 And provide *them* beasts, that
they may set Paul on, and bring *him*
safe unto Felix the governor.
25 And he wrote a letter after this
manner:
26 Claudius Lysias unto the most
excellent governor Felix *sendeth*
greeting.
27 This man was taken of the
Jews, and should have been killed of
them: then came I with an army, and
rescued him, having understood
that he was a Roman.
28 And when I would have known
the cause wherefore they accused
him, I brought him forth into their
council:
29 Whom I perceived to be ac-
cused of questions of their law, but
to have nothing laid to his charge
worthy of death or of bonds.
30 And when it was told me how
that the Jews laid wait for the man,
I sent straightway to thee, and gave
commandment to his accusers also
to say before thee what *they had*
against him. Farewell.
31 Then the soldiers, as it was
commanded them, took Paul, and
brought *him* by night to Antipatris.
32 On the morrow they left the
horsemen to go with him, and re-
turned to the castle:
33 Who, when they came to Caes-
area, and delivered the epistle to
the governor, presented Paul also
before him.
34 And when the governor had
read *the letter,* he asked of what
province he was. And when he
understood that *he was* of Cilicia;
35 I will hear thee, said he, when
thine accusers are also come. And
he commanded him to be kept in
Herod's judgment hall.

Paul Speaks Before Felix

24 And after five days Ananias
the high priest descended
with the elders, and *with* a certain
orator *named* Tertullus, who in-
formed the governor against Paul.
2 And when he was called forth,
Tertullus began to accuse *him,* say-
ing, Seeing that by thee we enjoy
great quietness, and that very wor-
thy deeds are done unto this nation
by thy providence,
3 We accept *it* always, and in all
places, most noble Felix, with all
thankfulness.
4 Notwithstanding, that I be not
further tedious unto thee, I pray
thee that thou wouldest hear us of
thy clemency a few words.
5 For we have found this man *a*
pestilent *fellow,* and a mover of sedi-
tion among all the Jews throughout
the world, and a ringleader of the
sect of the Nazarenes:
6 Who also hath gone about to
profane the temple: whom we took,
and would have judged according to
our law.
7 But the chief captain Lysias came
upon us, and with great violence
took *him* away out of our hands,
8 Commanding his accusers to
come unto thee: by examining of
whom thyself mayest take knowl-
edge of all these things, whereof we
accuse him.
9 And the Jews also assented, say-
ing that these things were so.

Paul's Defense Before Felix

10 Then Paul, after that the gov-
ernor had beckoned unto him to

speak, answered, Forasmuch as I
know that thou hast been of many
years a judge unto this nation, I do
the more cheerfully answer for my-
self:
11 Because that thou mayest
understand, that there are yet but
twelve days since I went up to Je-
rusalem for to worship.
12 And they neither found me in
the temple disputing with any man,
neither raising up the people, nei-
ther in the synagogues, nor in the
city:
13 Neither can they prove the
things whereof they now accuse me.
14 But this I confess unto thee,
that after the way which they call
heresy, so worship I the God of my
fathers, believing all things which
are written in the law and in the
prophets:
15 And have hope toward God,
which they themselves also allow,
that there shall be a resurrection of
the dead, both of the just and unjust.
16 And herein do I exercise myself,
to have always a conscience void
of offence toward God, and *toward*
men.
17 Now after many years I came to
bring alms to my nation, and offer-
ings.
18 Whereupon certain Jews from
Asia found me purified in the tem-
ple, neither with multitude, nor with
tumult.
19 Who ought to have been here
before thee, and object, if they had
ought against me.
20 Or else let these same *here* say,
if they have found any evil doing in
me, while I stood before the council,
21 Except it be for this one voice,
that I cried standing among them,
Touching the resurrection of the
dead I am called in question by you
this day.
22 And when Felix heard these
things, having more perfect knowl-
edge of *that* way, he deferred them,
and said, When Lysias the chief cap-
tain shall come down, I will know
the uttermost of your matter.
23 And he commanded a centu-
rion to keep Paul, and to let *him*
have liberty, and that he should
forbid none of his acquaintance to
minister or come unto him.
24 And after certain days, when
Felix came with his wife Drusilla,
which was a Jewess, he sent for
Paul, and heard him concerning
the faith in Christ.
25 And as he reasoned of righ-
teousness, temperance, and judg-
ment to come, Felix trembled, and
answered, Go thy way for this time;
when I have a convenient season, I
will call for thee.
26 He hoped also that money
should have been given him of Paul,
that he might loose him: where-
fore he sent for him the oftener, and
communed with him.
27 But after two years Porcius Fes-
tus came into Felix' room: and Felix,
willing to shew the Jews a pleasure,
left Paul bound.

Paul Appeals to Caesar

25 Now when Festus was come
into the province, after three
days he ascended from Caesarea to
Jerusalem.
2 Then the high priest and the
chief of the Jews informed him
against Paul, and besought him,
3 And desired favour against him,
that he would send for him to Jeru-
salem, laying wait in the way to kill
him.
4 But Festus answered, that Paul
should be kept at Caesarea, and that
he himself would depart shortly
thither.
5 Let them therefore, said he,
which among you are able, go down
with *me,* and accuse this man, if
there be any wickedness in him.
6 And when he had tarried among
them more than ten days, he went

down unto Caesarea; and the next day sitting on the judgment seat commanded Paul to be brought.

7 And when he was come, the Jews which came down from Jerusalem stood round about, and laid many and grievous complaints against Paul, which they could not prove.

8 While he answered for himself, Neither against the law of the Jews, neither against the temple, nor yet against Caesar, have I offended any thing at all.

9 But Festus, willing to do the Jews a pleasure, answered Paul, and said, Wilt thou go up to Jerusalem, and there be judged of these things before me?

10 Then said Paul, I stand at Caesar's judgment seat, where I ought to be judged: to the Jews have I done no wrong, as thou very well knowest.

11 For if I be an offender, or have committed any thing worthy of death, I refuse not to die: but if there be none of these things whereof these accuse me, no man may deliver me unto them. I appeal unto Caesar.

12 Then Festus, when he had conferred with the council, answered, Hast thou appealed unto Caesar? unto Caesar shalt thou go.

King Agrippa Visits Festus

13 And after certain days king Agrippa and Bernice came unto Caesarea to salute Festus.

14 And when they had been there many days, Festus declared Paul's cause unto the king, saying, There is a certain man left in bonds by Felix:

15 About whom, when I was at Jerusalem, the chief priests and the elders of the Jews informed *me,* desiring *to have* judgment against him.

16 To whom I answered, It is not the manner of the Romans to deliver any man to die, before that he which is accused have the accusers face to face, and have licence to answer for himself concerning the crime laid against him.

17 Therefore, when they were come hither, without any delay on the morrow I sat on the judgment seat, and commanded the man to be brought forth.

18 Against whom when the accusers stood up, they brought none accusation of such things as I supposed:

19 But had certain questions against him of their own superstition, and of one Jesus, which was dead, whom Paul affirmed to be alive.

20 And because I doubted of such manner of questions, I asked *him* whether he would go to Jerusalem, and there be judged of these matters.

21 But when Paul had appealed to be reserved unto the hearing of Augustus, I commanded him to be kept till I might send him to Caesar.

22 Then Agrippa said unto Festus, I would also hear the man myself. To morrow, said he, thou shalt hear him.

Festus Orders a Hearing

23 And on the morrow, when Agrippa was come, and Bernice, with great pomp, and was entered into the place of hearing, with the chief captains, and principal men of the city, at Festus' commandment Paul was brought forth.

24 And Festus said, King Agrippa, and all men which are here present with us, ye see this man, about whom all the multitude of the Jews have dealt with me, both at Jerusalem, and *also* here, crying that he ought not to live any longer.

25 But when I found that he had committed nothing worthy of death, and that he himself hath appealed to Augustus, I have determined to send him.

26 Of whom I have no certain
thing to write unto my lord. Where-
fore I have brought him forth be-
fore you, and specially before thee,
O king Agrippa, that, after examina-
tion had, I might have somewhat to
write.
27 For it seemeth to me unrea-
sonable to send a prisoner, and not
withal to signify the crimes *laid*
against him.

Paul Appears Before Agrippa

26 Then Agrippa said unto Paul,
Thou art permitted to speak
for thyself. Then Paul stretched
forth the hand, and answered for
himself:
2 I think myself happy, king
Agrippa, because I shall answer for
myself this day before thee touching
all the things whereof I am accused
of the Jews:
3 Especially *because I know* thee to
be expert in all customs and ques-
tions which are among the Jews:
wherefore I beseech thee to hear
me patiently.
4 My manner of life from my
youth, which was at the first among
mine own nation at Jerusalem,
know all the Jews;
5 Which knew me from the be-
ginning, if they would testify, that
after the most straitest sect of our
religion I lived a Pharisee.
6 And now I stand and am judged
for the hope of the promise made of
God unto our fathers:
7 Unto which *promise* our twelve
tribes, instantly serving *God* day
and night, hope to come. For which
hope's sake, king Agrippa, I am ac-
cused of the Jews.
8 Why should it be thought a thing
incredible with you, that God should
raise the dead?
9 I verily thought with myself, that
I ought to do many things contrary
to the name of Jesus of Nazareth.
10 Which thing I also did in Jeru-
salem: and many of the saints did I
shut up in prison, having received
authority from the chief priests; and
when they were put to death, I gave
my voice against *them.*
11 And I punished them oft in ev-
ery synagogue, and compelled *them*
to blaspheme; and being exceed-
ingly mad against them, I perse-
cuted *them* even unto strange cities.

Paul Describes His Conversion

12 Whereupon as I went to Da-
mascus with authority and com-
mission from the chief priests,
13 At midday, O king, I saw in the
way a light from heaven, above
the brightness of the sun, shining
round about me and them which
journeyed with me.
14 And when we were all fallen to
the earth, I heard a voice speaking
unto me, and saying in the Hebrew
tongue, Saul, Saul, why persecutest
thou me? *it is* hard for thee to kick
against the pricks.
15 And I said, Who art thou, Lord?
And he said, I am Jesus whom thou
persecutest.
16 But rise, and stand upon thy
feet: for I have appeared unto thee
for this purpose, to make thee a
minister and a witness both of these
things which thou hast seen, and
of those things in the which I will
appear unto thee;
17 Delivering thee from the peo-
ple, and *from* the Gentiles, unto
whom now I send thee,
18 To open their eyes, *and* to turn
them from darkness to light, and
from the power of Satan unto God,
that they may receive forgiveness of
sins, and inheritance among them
which are sanctified by faith that is
in me.
19 Whereupon, O king Agrippa, I
was not disobedient unto the heav-
enly vision:
20 But shewed first unto them of
Damascus, and at Jerusalem, and

throughout all the coasts of Judaea,
and *then* to the Gentiles, that they
should repent and turn to God, and
do works meet for repentance.
21 For these causes the Jews
caught me in the temple, and went
about to kill *me*.
22 Having therefore obtained help
of God, I continue unto this day,
witnessing both to small and great,
saying none other things than those
which the prophets and Moses did
say should come:
23 That Christ should suffer, *and*
that he should be the first that
should rise from the dead, and
should shew light unto the people,
and to the Gentiles.

Almost Persuaded

24 And as he thus spake for him-
self, Festus said with a loud voice,
Paul, thou art beside thyself; much
learning doth make thee mad.
25 But he said, I am not mad, most
noble Festus; but speak forth the
words of truth and soberness.
26 For the king knoweth of these
things, before whom also I speak
freely: for I am persuaded that none
of these things are hidden from him;
for this thing was not done in a cor-
ner.
27 King Agrippa, believest thou
the prophets? I know that thou be-
lievest.
28 Then Agrippa said unto Paul,
Almost thou persuadest me to be a
Christian.
29 And Paul said, I would to God,
that not only thou, but also all that
hear me this day, were both almost,
and altogether such as I am, except
these bonds.
30 And when he had thus spoken,
the king rose up, and the governor,
and Bernice, and they that sat with
them:
31 And when they were gone
aside, they talked between them-
selves, saying, This man doeth
nothing worthy of death or of
bonds.
32 Then said Agrippa unto Festus,
This man might have been set at
liberty, if he had not appealed unto
Caesar.

Paul Sent to Rome

27 And when it was determined
that we should sail into It-
aly, they delivered Paul and certain
other prisoners unto *one* named Jul-
ius, a centurion of Augustus' band.
2 And entering into a ship of Adra-
myttium, we launched, meaning to
sail by the coasts of Asia; *one* Aristar-
chus, a Macedonian of Thessalonica,
being with us.
3 And the next *day* we touched
at Sidon. And Julius courteously
entreated Paul, and gave *him* lib-
erty to go unto his friends to refresh
himself.
4 And when we had launched from
thence, we sailed under Cyprus, be-
cause the winds were contrary.
5 And when we had sailed over
the sea of Cilicia and Pamphylia,
we came to Myra, *a city* of Lycia.
6 And there the centurion found a
ship of Alexandria sailing into Italy;
and he put us therein.
7 And when we had sailed slowly
many days, and scarce were come
over against Cnidus, the wind not
suffering us, we sailed under Crete,
over against Salmone;
8 And, hardly passing it, came
unto a place which is called The fair
havens; nigh whereunto was the city
of Lasea.
9 Now when much time was
spent, and when sailing was now
dangerous, because the fast was
now already past, Paul admonished
them,
10 And said unto them, Sirs, I per-
ceive that this voyage will be with
hurt and much damage, not only of
the lading and ship, but also of our
lives.

11 Nevertheless the centurion be-
lieved the master and the owner of
the ship, more than those things
which were spoken by Paul.
12 And because the haven was not
commodious to winter in, the more
part advised to depart thence also,
if by any means they might attain
to Phenice, *and there* to winter;
which is an haven of Crete, and lieth
toward the south west and north
west.

A Storm Arises

13 And when the south wind blew
softly, supposing that they had ob-
tained *their* purpose, loosing *thence,*
they sailed close by Crete.
14 But not long after there arose
against it a tempestuous wind,
called Euroclydon.
15 And when the ship was caught,
and could not bear up into the wind,
we let *her* drive.
16 And running under a certain
island which is called Clauda, we
had much work to come by the boat:
17 Which when they had taken up,
they used helps, undergirding the
ship; and, fearing lest they should
fall into the quicksands, strake sail,
and so were driven.
18 And we being exceedingly
tossed with a tempest, the next *day*
they lightened the ship;
19 And the third *day* we cast out
with our own hands the tackling of
the ship.
20 And when neither sun nor
stars in many days appeared, and
no small tempest lay on *us,* all hope
that we should be saved was then
taken away.
21 But after long abstinence Paul
stood forth in the midst of them,
and said, Sirs, ye should have heark-
ened unto me, and not have loosed
from Crete, and to have gained this
harm and loss.
22 And now I exhort you to be of
good cheer: for there shall be no loss
of *any man's* life among you, but of
the ship.
23 For there stood by me this night
the angel of God, whose I am, and
whom I serve,
24 Saying, Fear not, Paul; thou
must be brought before Caesar: and,
lo, God hath given thee all them that
sail with thee.
25 Wherefore, sirs, be of good
cheer: for I believe God, that it shall
be even as it was told me.
26 Howbeit we must be cast upon
a certain island.

The Shipwreck

27 But when the fourteenth night
was come, as we were driven up and
down in Adria, about midnight the
shipmen deemed that they drew
near to some country;
28 And sounded, and found *it*
twenty fathoms: and when they had
gone a little further, they sounded
again, and found *it* fifteen fathoms.
29 Then fearing lest we should
have fallen upon rocks, they cast
four anchors out of the stern, and
wished for the day.
30 And as the shipmen were about
to flee out of the ship, when they
had let down the boat into the sea,
under colour as though they would
have cast anchors out of the fore-
ship,
31 Paul said to the centurion and
to the soldiers, Except these abide
in the ship, ye cannot be saved.
32 Then the soldiers cut off the
ropes of the boat, and let her fall off.
33 And while the day was com-
ing on, Paul besought *them* all to
take meat, saying, This day is the
fourteenth day that ye have tarried
and continued fasting, having taken
nothing.
34 Wherefore I pray you to take
some meat: for this is for your
health: for there shall not an hair
fall from the head of any of you.
35 And when he had thus spoken,

he took bread, and gave thanks to God in presence of them all: and when he had broken *it,* he began to eat.

36 Then were they all of good cheer, and they also took *some* meat.

37 And we were in all in the ship two hundred threescore and sixteen souls.

38 And when they had eaten enough, they lightened the ship, and cast out the wheat into the sea.

39 And when it was day, they knew not the land: but they discovered a certain creek with a shore, into the which they were minded, if it were possible, to thrust in the ship.

40 And when they had taken up the anchors, they committed *themselves* unto the sea, and loosed the rudder bands, and hoised up the mainsail to the wind, and made toward shore.

41 And falling into a place where two seas met, they ran the ship aground; and the forepart stuck fast, and remained unmoveable, but the hinder part was broken with the violence of the waves.

42 And the soldiers' counsel was to kill the prisoners, lest any of them should swim out, and escape.

43 But the centurion, willing to save Paul, kept them from *their* purpose; and commanded that they which could swim should cast *themselves* first *into the sea,* and get to land:

44 And the rest, some on boards, and some on *broken pieces* of the ship. And so it came to pass, that they escaped all safe to land.

Paul's Healing Ministry on Melita

28 And when they were escaped, then they knew that the island was called Melita.

2 And the barbarous people shewed us no little kindness: for they kindled a fire, and received us every one, because of the present rain, and because of the cold.

3 And when Paul had gathered a bundle of sticks, and laid *them* on the fire, there came a viper out of the heat, and fastened on his hand.

4 And when the barbarians saw the *venomous* beast hang on his hand, they said among themselves, No doubt this man is a murderer, whom, though he hath escaped the sea, yet vengeance suffereth not to live.

5 And he shook off the beast into the fire, and felt no harm.

6 Howbeit they looked when he should have swollen, or fallen down dead suddenly: but after they had looked a great while, and saw no harm come to him, they changed their minds, and said that he was a god.

7 In the same quarters were possessions of the chief man of the island, whose name was Publius; who received us, and lodged us three days courteously.

8 And it came to pass, that the father of Publius lay sick of a fever and of a bloody flux: to whom Paul entered in, and prayed, and laid his hands on him, and healed him.

9 So when this was done, others also, which had diseases in the island, came, and were healed:

10 Who also honoured us with many honours; and when we departed, they laded *us* with such things as were necessary.

Paul Arrives at Rome

11 And after three months we departed in a ship of Alexandria, which had wintered in the isle, whose sign was Castor and Pollux.

12 And landing at Syracuse, we tarried *there* three days.

13 And from thence we fetched a compass, and came to Rhegium: and after one day the south wind blew, and we came the next day to Puteoli:

14 Where we found brethren, and were desired to tarry with them seven days: and so we went toward Rome.

15 And from thence, when the brethren heard of us, they came to meet us as far as Appii forum, and The three taverns: whom when Paul saw, he thanked God, and took courage.

16 And when we came to Rome, the centurion delivered the prisoners to the captain of the guard: but Paul was suffered to dwell by himself with a soldier that kept him.

Paul Speaks to the Jews

17 And it came to pass, that after three days Paul called the chief of the Jews together: and when they were come together, he said unto them, Men *and* brethren, though I have committed nothing against the people, or customs of our fathers, yet was I delivered prisoner from Jerusalem into the hands of the Romans.

18 Who, when they had examined me, would have let *me* go, because there was no cause of death in me.

19 But when the Jews spake against *it,* I was constrained to appeal unto Caesar; not that I had ought to accuse my nation of.

20 For this cause therefore have I called for you, to see *you,* and to speak with *you:* because that for the hope of Israel I am bound with this chain.

21 And they said unto him, We neither received letters out of Judaea concerning thee, neither any of the brethren that came shewed or spake any harm of thee.

22 But we desire to hear of thee what thou thinkest: for as concerning this sect, we know that every where it is spoken against.

23 And when they had appointed him a day, there came many to him into *his* lodging; to whom he expounded and testified the kingdom of God, persuading them concerning Jesus, both out of the law of Moses, and *out of* the prophets, from morning till evening.

Some Believe and Some Do Not

24 And some believed the things which were spoken, and some believed not.

25 And when they agreed not among themselves, they departed, after that Paul had spoken one word, Well spake the Holy Ghost by Esaias the prophet unto our fathers,

26 Saying, Go unto this people, and say, Hearing ye shall hear, and shall not understand; and seeing ye shall see, and not perceive:

27 For the heart of this people is waxed gross, and their ears are dull of hearing, and their eyes have they closed; lest they should see with *their* eyes, and hear with *their* ears, and understand with *their* heart, and should be converted, and I should heal them.

28 Be it known therefore unto you, that the salvation of God is sent unto the Gentiles, and *that* they will hear it.

29 And when he had said these words, the Jews departed, and had great reasoning among themselves.

30 And Paul dwelt two whole years in his own hired house, and received all that came in unto him,

31 Preaching the kingdom of God, and teaching those things which concern the Lord Jesus Christ, with all confidence, no man forbidding him.

The Epistle of Paul the Apostle to the
ROMANS

Paul's Salutation

Paul, a servant of Jesus Christ,
called *to be* an apostle, separated
unto the gospel of God,
2 (Which he had promised afore
by his prophets in the holy scrip-
tures,)
3 Concerning his Son Jesus Christ
our Lord, which was made of the
seed of David according to the flesh;
4 And declared *to be* the Son of
God with power, according to the
spirit of holiness, by the resurrec-
tion from the dead:
5 By whom we have received grace
and apostleship, for obedience to
the faith among all nations, for his
name:
6 Among whom are ye also the
called of Jesus Christ:
7 To all that be in Rome, beloved
of God, called *to be* saints: Grace to
you and peace from God our Father,
and the Lord Jesus Christ.

Paul Longs to Visit Rome

8 First, I thank my God through
Jesus Christ for you all, that your
faith is spoken of throughout the
whole world.
9 For God is my witness, whom I
serve with my spirit in the gospel
of his Son, that without ceasing I
make mention of you always in my
prayers;
10 Making request, if by any means
now at length I might have a pros-
perous journey by the will of God to
come unto you.
11 For I long to see you, that I may
impart unto you some spiritual gift,
to the end ye may be established;
12 That is, that I may be comforted
together with you by the mutual
faith both of you and me.
13 Now I would not have you ig-
norant, brethren, that oftentimes
I purposed to come unto you, (but
was let hitherto,) that I might have
some fruit among you also, even as
among other Gentiles.
14 I am debtor both to the Greeks,
and to the Barbarians; both to the
wise, and to the unwise.
15 So, as much as in me is, I am
ready to preach the gospel to you
that are at Rome also.

The Just Shall Live by Faith

16 For I am not ashamed of the
gospel of Christ: for it is the power
of God unto salvation to every one
that believeth; to the Jew first, and
also to the Greek.
17 For therein is the righteousness
of God revealed from faith to faith:
as it is written, The just shall live by
faith.

God's Wrath Against Ungodliness

18 For the wrath of God is revealed
from heaven against all ungodliness
and unrighteousness of men, who
hold the truth in unrighteousness;
19 Because that which may be
known of God is manifest in them;
for God hath shewed *it* unto them.
20 For the invisible things of him
from the creation of the world are

clearly seen, being understood by
the things that are made, *even* his
eternal power and Godhead; so that
they are without excuse:
21 Because that, when they knew
God, they glorified *him* not as God,
neither were thankful; but became
vain in their imaginations, and their
foolish heart was darkened.
22 Professing themselves to be
wise, they became fools,
23 And changed the glory of the
uncorruptible God into an image
made like to corruptible man, and
to birds, and fourfooted beasts, and
creeping things.
24 Wherefore God also gave them
up to uncleanness through the lusts
of their own hearts, to dishonour
their own bodies between them-
selves:
25 Who changed the truth of
God into a lie, and worshipped and
served the creature more than the
Creator, who is blessed for ever.
Amen.
26 For this cause God gave them
up unto vile affections: for even
their women did change the nat-
ural use into that which is against
nature:
27 And likewise also the men,
leaving the natural use of the
woman, burned in their lust one
toward another; men with men
working that which is unseemly,
and receiving in themselves that
recompence of their error which
was meet.
28 And even as they did not like
to retain God in *their* knowledge,
God gave them over to a reprobate
mind, to do those things which are
not convenient;
29 Being filled with all unrigh-
teousness, fornication, wickedness,
covetousness, maliciousness; full of
envy, murder, debate, deceit, malig-
nity; whisperers,
30 Backbiters, haters of God, de-
spiteful, proud, boasters, inventors
of evil things, disobedient to par-
ents,
31 Without understanding, cov-
enantbreakers, without natural
affection, implacable, unmerciful:
32 Who knowing the judgment of
God, that they which commit such
things are worthy of death, not only
do the same, but have pleasure in
them that do them.

God's Righteous Judgment

2 Therefore thou art inexcusable,
O man, whosoever thou art that
judgest: for wherein thou judgest
another, thou condemnest thyself;
for thou that judgest doest the same
things.
2 But we are sure that the judg-
ment of God is according to truth
against them which commit such
things.
3 And thinkest thou this, O man,
that judgest them which do such
things, and doest the same, that
thou shalt escape the judgment of
God?
4 Or despisest thou the riches of
his goodness and forbearance and
longsuffering; not knowing that
the goodness of God leadeth thee
to repentance?
5 But after thy hardness and im-
penitent heart treasurest up unto
thyself wrath against the day of
wrath and revelation of the righ-
teous judgment of God;
6 Who will render to every man
according to his deeds:
7 To them who by patient contin-
uance in well doing seek for glory
and honour and immortality, eternal
life:
8 But unto them that are conten-
tious, and do not obey the truth, but
obey unrighteousness, indignation
and wrath,
9 Tribulation and anguish, upon
every soul of man that doeth evil, of
the Jew first, and also of the Gentile;
10 But glory, honour, and peace, to

every man that worketh good, to the Jew first, and also to the Gentile:

11 For there is no respect of persons with God.

12 For as many as have sinned without law shall also perish without law: and as many as have sinned in the law shall be judged by the law;

13 (For not the hearers of the law *are* just before God, but the doers of the law shall be justified.

14 For when the Gentiles, which have not the law, do by nature the things contained in the law, these, having not the law, are a law unto themselves:

15 Which shew the work of the law written in their hearts, their conscience also bearing witness, and *their* thoughts the mean while accusing or else excusing one another;)

16 In the day when God shall judge the secrets of men by Jesus Christ according to my gospel.

Cautions Against Hypocrisy

17 Behold, thou art called a Jew, and restest in the law, and makest thy boast of God,

18 And knowest *his* will, and approvest the things that are more excellent, being instructed out of the law;

19 And art confident that thou thyself art a guide of the blind, a light of them which are in darkness,

20 An instructor of the foolish, a teacher of babes, which hast the form of knowledge and of the truth in the law.

21 Thou therefore which teachest another, teachest thou not thyself? thou that preachest a man should not steal, dost thou steal?

22 Thou that sayest a man should not commit adultery, dost thou commit adultery? thou that abhorrest idols, dost thou commit sacrilege?

23 Thou that makest thy boast of the law, through breaking the law dishonourest thou God?

24 For the name of God is blasphemed among the Gentiles through you, as it is written.

25 For circumcision verily profiteth, if thou keep the law: but if thou be a breaker of the law, thy circumcision is made uncircumcision.

26 Therefore if the uncircumcision keep the righteousness of the law, shall not his uncircumcision be counted for circumcision?

27 And shall not uncircumcision which is by nature, if it fulfil the law, judge thee, who by the letter and circumcision dost transgress the law?

28 For he is not a Jew, which is one outwardly; neither *is that* circumcision, which is outward in the flesh:

29 But he *is* a Jew, which is one inwardly; and circumcision *is that* of the heart, in the spirit, *and* not in the letter; whose praise *is* not of men, but of God.

God Is Faithful and Just

3 What advantage then hath the Jew? or what profit *is there* of circumcision?

2 Much every way: chiefly, because that unto them were committed the oracles of God.

3 For what if some did not believe? shall their unbelief make the faith of God without effect?

4 God forbid: yea, let God be true, but every man a liar; as it is written, That thou mightest be justified in thy sayings, and mightest overcome when thou art judged.

5 But if our unrighteousness commend the righteousness of God, what shall we say? *Is* God unrighteous who taketh vengeance? (I speak as a man)

6 God forbid: for then how shall God judge the world?

7 For if the truth of God hath more

abounded through my lie unto his
glory; why yet am I also judged as
a sinner?
8 And not *rather,* (as we be slan-
derously reported, and as some af-
firm that we say,) Let us do evil, that
good may come? whose damnation
is just.

No One Is Righteous

9 What then? are we better *than
they?* No, in no wise: for we have be-
fore proved both Jews and Gentiles,
that they are all under sin;
10 As it is written, There is none
righteous, no, not one:
11 There is none that understand-
eth, there is none that seeketh after
God.
12 They are all gone out of the way,
they are together become unprofit-
able; there is none that doeth good,
no, not one.
13 Their throat *is* an open sepul-
chre; with their tongues they have
used deceit; the poison of asps *is*
under their lips:
14 Whose mouth *is* full of cursing
and bitterness:
15 Their feet *are* swift to shed
blood:
16 Destruction and misery *are* in
their ways:
17 And the way of peace have they
not known:
18 There is no fear of God before
their eyes.
19 Now we know that what things
soever the law saith, it saith to them
who are under the law: that every
mouth may be stopped, and all the
world may become guilty before
God.
20 Therefore by the deeds of the
law there shall no flesh be justified
in his sight: for by the law *is* the
knowledge of sin.

God's Righteousness by Faith

21 But now the righteousness of
God without the law is manifested,
being witnessed by the law and the
prophets;
22 Even the righteousness of God
which is by faith of Jesus Christ unto
all and upon all them that believe:
for there is no difference:
23 For all have sinned, and come
short of the glory of God;
24 Being justified freely by his
grace through the redemption that
is in Christ Jesus:
25 Whom God hath set forth *to be*
a propitiation through faith in his
blood, to declare his righteousness
for the remission of sins that are
past, through the forbearance of
God;
26 To declare, *I say,* at this time
his righteousness: that he might be
just, and the justifier of him which
believeth in Jesus.
27 Where *is* boasting then? It is
excluded. By what law? of works?
Nay: but by the law of faith.
28 Therefore we conclude that a
man is justified by faith without the
deeds of the law.
29 *Is he* the God of the Jews only?
is he not also of the Gentiles? Yes, of
the Gentiles also:
30 Seeing *it is* one God, which shall
justify the circumcision by faith, and
uncircumcision through faith.
31 Do we then make void the law
through faith? God forbid: yea, we
establish the law.

Justification Through Faith

4 What shall we say then that
Abraham our father, as pertain-
ing to the flesh, hath found?
2 For if Abraham were justified by
works, he hath *whereof* to glory; but
not before God.
3 For what saith the scripture?
Abraham believed God, and it was
counted unto him for righteousness.
4 Now to him that worketh is the
reward not reckoned of grace, but
of debt.
5 But to him that worketh not,

but believeth on him that justifieth
the ungodly, his faith is counted for
righteousness.
6 Even as David also describeth
the blessedness of the man, unto
whom God imputeth righteousness
without works,
7 *Saying,* Blessed *are* they whose
iniquities are forgiven, and whose
sins are covered.
8 Blessed *is* the man to whom the
Lord will not impute sin.
9 *Cometh* this blessedness then
upon the circumcision *only,* or upon
the uncircumcision also? for we say
that faith was reckoned to Abraham
for righteousness.
10 How was it then reckoned?
when he was in circumcision, or in
uncircumcision? Not in circumci-
sion, but in uncircumcision.
11 And he received the sign of cir-
cumcision, a seal of the righteous-
ness of the faith which *he had yet*
being uncircumcised: that he might
be the father of all them that believe,
though they be not circumcised;
that righteousness might be im-
puted unto them also:
12 And the father of circumcision
to them who are not of the circum-
cision only, but who also walk in
the steps of that faith of our father
Abraham, which *he had* being *yet*
uncircumcised.

A Father of Many Nations

13 For the promise, that he should
be the heir of the world, *was* not to
Abraham, or to his seed, through the
law, but through the righteousness
of faith.
14 For if they which are of the law
be heirs, faith is made void, and the
promise made of none effect:
15 Because the law worketh wrath:
for where no law is, *there is* no trans-
gression.
16 Therefore *it is* of faith, that *it*
might be by grace; to the end the
promise might be sure to all the
seed; not to that only which is of
the law, but to that also which is
of the faith of Abraham; who is the
father of us all,
17 (As it is written, I have made
thee a father of many nations,) be-
fore him whom he believed, *even*
God, who quickeneth the dead, and
calleth those things which be not as
though they were.
18 Who against hope believed in
hope, that he might become the fa-
ther of many nations, according to
that which was spoken, So shall thy
seed be.
19 And being not weak in faith,
he considered not his own body
now dead, when he was about an
hundred years old, neither yet the
deadness of Sarah's womb:
20 He staggered not at the prom-
ise of God through unbelief; but
was strong in faith, giving glory to
God;
21 And being fully persuaded that,
what he had promised, he was able
also to perform.
22 And therefore it was imputed
to him for righteousness.
23 Now it was not written for his
sake alone, that it was imputed to
him;
24 But for us also, to whom it shall
be imputed, if we believe on him
that raised up Jesus our Lord from
the dead;
25 Who was delivered for our of-
fences, and was raised again for our
justification.

Justified by the Blood of Christ

5 Therefore being justified by
faith, we have peace with God
through our Lord Jesus Christ:
2 By whom also we have access
by faith into this grace wherein we
stand, and rejoice in hope of the
glory of God.
3 And not only *so,* but we glory
in tribulations also: knowing that

tribulation worketh patience;
4 And patience, experience; and
experience, hope:
5 And hope maketh not ashamed;
because the love of God is shed
abroad in our hearts by the Holy
Ghost which is given unto us.
6 For when we were yet without
strength, in due time Christ died for
the ungodly.
7 For scarcely for a righteous man
will one die: yet peradventure for a
good man some would even dare to
die.
8 But God commendeth his love
toward us, in that, while we were
yet sinners, Christ died for us.
9 Much more then, being now
justified by his blood, we shall be
saved from wrath through him.
10 For if, when we were enemies,
we were reconciled to God by the
death of his Son, much more, being
reconciled, we shall be saved by his
life.
11 And not only *so,* but we also
joy in God through our Lord Jesus
Christ, by whom we have now re-
ceived the atonement.

The Abundant Grace of Christ

12 Wherefore, as by one man sin
entered into the world, and death
by sin; and so death passed upon
all men, for that all have sinned:
13 (For until the law sin was in the
world: but sin is not imputed when
there is no law.
14 Nevertheless death reigned
from Adam to Moses, even over
them that had not sinned after the
similitude of Adam's transgression,
who is the figure of him that was to
come.
15 But not as the offence, so
also *is* the free gift. For if through
the offence of one many be dead,
much more the grace of God, and
the gift by grace, *which is* by one
man, Jesus Christ, hath abounded
unto many.
16 And not as *it was* by one that
sinned, *so is* the gift: for the judg-
ment *was* by one to condemnation,
but the free gift *is* of many offences
unto justification.
17 For if by one man's offence
death reigned by one; much more
they which receive abundance of
grace and of the gift of righteous-
ness shall reign in life by one, Jesus
Christ.)
18 Therefore as by the offence of
one *judgment came* upon all men to
condemnation; even so by the righ-
teousness of one *the free gift came*
upon all men unto justification of
life.
19 For as by one man's disobedi-
ence many were made sinners, so
by the obedience of one shall many
be made righteous.
20 Moreover the law entered,
that the offence might abound.
But where sin abounded, grace did
much more abound:
21 That as sin hath reigned unto
death, even so might grace reign
through righteousness unto eternal
life by Jesus Christ our Lord.

Walk in Newness of Life

6 What shall we say then? Shall
we continue in sin, that grace
may abound?
2 God forbid. How shall we, that
are dead to sin, live any longer
therein?
3 Know ye not, that so many of us
as were baptized into Jesus Christ
were baptized into his death?
4 Therefore we are buried with
him by baptism into death: that like
as Christ was raised up from the
dead by the glory of the Father, even
so we also should walk in newness
of life.
5 For if we have been planted to-
gether in the likeness of his death,
we shall be also *in the likeness* of *his*
resurrection:
6 Knowing this, that our old man

is crucified with *him,* that the body of sin might be destroyed, that henceforth we should not serve sin.

7 For he that is dead is freed from sin.

8 Now if we be dead with Christ, we believe that we shall also live with him:

9 Knowing that Christ being raised from the dead dieth no more; death hath no more dominion over him.

10 For in that he died, he died unto sin once: but in that he liveth, he liveth unto God.

11 Likewise reckon ye also yourselves to be dead indeed unto sin, but alive unto God through Jesus Christ our Lord.

12 Let not sin therefore reign in your mortal body, that ye should obey it in the lusts thereof.

13 Neither yield ye your members *as* instruments of unrighteousness unto sin: but yield yourselves unto God, as those that are alive from the dead, and your members *as* instruments of righteousness unto God.

14 For sin shall not have dominion over you: for ye are not under the law, but under grace.

Servants of Righteousness

15 What then? shall we sin, because we are not under the law, but under grace? God forbid.

16 Know ye not, that to whom ye yield yourselves servants to obey, his servants ye are to whom ye obey; whether of sin unto death, or of obedience unto righteousness?

17 But God be thanked, that ye were the servants of sin, but ye have obeyed from the heart that form of doctrine which was delivered you.

18 Being then made free from sin, ye became the servants of righteousness.

19 I speak after the manner of men because of the infirmity of your flesh: for as ye have yielded your members servants to uncleanness and to iniquity unto iniquity; even so now yield your members servants to righteousness unto holiness.

20 For when ye were the servants of sin, ye were free from righteousness.

21 What fruit had ye then in those things whereof ye are now ashamed? for the end of those things *is* death.

22 But now being made free from sin, and become servants to God, ye have your fruit unto holiness, and the end everlasting life.

23 For the wages of sin *is* death; but the gift of God *is* eternal life through Jesus Christ our Lord.

Deliverance from the Law

7 Know ye not, brethren, (for I speak to them that know the law,) how that the law hath dominion over a man as long as he liveth?

2 For the woman which hath an husband is bound by the law to *her* husband so long as he liveth; but if the husband be dead, she is loosed from the law of *her* husband.

3 So then if, while *her* husband liveth, she be married to another man, she shall be called an adulteress: but if her husband be dead, she is free from that law; so that she is no adulteress, though she be married to another man.

4 Wherefore, my brethren, ye also are become dead to the law by the body of Christ; that ye should be married to another, *even* to him who is raised from the dead, that we should bring forth fruit unto God.

5 For when we were in the flesh, the motions of sins, which were by the law, did work in our members to bring forth fruit unto death.

6 But now we are delivered from the law, that being dead wherein we were held; that we should serve in newness of spirit, and not *in* the oldness of the letter.

The Struggle Against Sin

7 What shall we say then? *Is* the law sin? God forbid. Nay, I had not known sin, but by the law: for I had not known lust, except the law had said, Thou shalt not covet.

8 But sin, taking occasion by the commandment, wrought in me all manner of concupiscence. For without the law sin *was* dead.

9 For I was alive without the law once: but when the commandment came, sin revived, and I died.

10 And the commandment, which *was ordained* to life, I found *to be* unto death.

11 For sin, taking occasion by the commandment, deceived me, and by it slew *me*.

12 Wherefore the law *is* holy, and the commandment holy, and just, and good.

13 Was then that which is good made death unto me? God forbid. But sin, that it might appear sin, working death in me by that which is good; that sin by the commandment might become exceeding sinful.

14 For we know that the law is spiritual: but I am carnal, sold under sin.

15 For that which I do I allow not: for what I would, that do I not; but what I hate, that do I.

16 If then I do that which I would not, I consent unto the law that *it is* good.

17 Now then it is no more I that do it, but sin that dwelleth in me.

18 For I know that in me (that is, in my flesh,) dwelleth no good thing: for to will is present with me; but *how* to perform that which is good I find not.

19 For the good that I would I do not: but the evil which I would not, that I do.

20 Now if I do that which I would not, it is no more I that do it, but sin that dwelleth in me.

21 I find then a law, that, when I would do good, evil is present with me.

22 For I delight in the law of God after the inward man:

23 But I see another law in my members, warring against the law of my mind, and bringing me into captivity to the law of sin which is in my members.

24 O wretched man that I am! who shall deliver me from the body of this death?

25 I thank God through Jesus Christ our Lord. So then with the mind I myself serve the law of God; but with the flesh the law of sin.

The Spirit of Life

8 *There is* therefore now no condemnation to them which are in Christ Jesus, who walk not after the flesh, but after the Spirit.

2 For the law of the Spirit of life in Christ Jesus hath made me free from the law of sin and death.

3 For what the law could not do, in that it was weak through the flesh, God sending his own Son in the likeness of sinful flesh, and for sin, condemned sin in the flesh:

4 That the righteousness of the law might be fulfilled in us, who walk not after the flesh, but after the Spirit.

5 For they that are after the flesh do mind the things of the flesh; but they that are after the Spirit the things of the Spirit.

6 For to be carnally minded *is* death; but to be spiritually minded *is* life and peace.

7 Because the carnal mind *is* enmity against God: for it is not subject to the law of God, neither indeed can be.

8 So then they that are in the flesh cannot please God.

9 But ye are not in the flesh, but in the Spirit, if so be that the Spirit of God dwell in you. Now if any man

have not the Spirit of Christ, he is none of his.

10 And if Christ *be* in you, the body *is* dead because of sin; but the Spirit *is* life because of righteousness.

11 But if the Spirit of him that raised up Jesus from the dead dwell in you, he that raised up Christ from the dead shall also quicken your mortal bodies by his Spirit that dwelleth in you.

Led by the Spirit

12 Therefore, brethren, we are debtors, not to the flesh, to live after the flesh.

13 For if ye live after the flesh, ye shall die: but if ye through the Spirit do mortify the deeds of the body, ye shall live.

14 For as many as are led by the Spirit of God, they are the sons of God.

15 For ye have not received the spirit of bondage again to fear; but ye have received the Spirit of adoption, whereby we cry, Abba, Father.

16 The Spirit itself beareth witness with our spirit, that we are the children of God:

17 And if children, then heirs; heirs of God, and joint-heirs with Christ; if so be that we suffer with *him,* that we may be also glorified together.

Anticipation of Glory

18 For I reckon that the sufferings of this present time *are* not worthy *to be compared* with the glory which shall be revealed in us.

19 For the earnest expectation of the creature waiteth for the manifestation of the sons of God.

20 For the creature was made subject to vanity, not willingly, but by reason of him who hath subjected *the same* in hope,

21 Because the creature itself also shall be delivered from the bondage of corruption into the glorious liberty of the children of God.

22 For we know that the whole creation groaneth and travaileth in pain together until now.

23 And not only *they,* but ourselves also, which have the firstfruits of the Spirit, even we ourselves groan within ourselves, waiting for the adoption, *to wit,* the redemption of our body.

24 For we are saved by hope: but hope that is seen is not hope: for what a man seeth, why doth he yet hope for?

25 But if we hope for that we see not, *then* do we with patience wait for *it.*

26 Likewise the Spirit also helpeth our infirmities: for we know not what we should pray for as we ought: but the Spirit itself maketh intercession for us with groanings which cannot be uttered.

27 And he that searcheth the hearts knoweth what *is* the mind of the Spirit, because he maketh intercession for the saints according to *the will of* God.

More than Conquerors

28 And we know that all things work together for good to them that love God, to them who are the called according to *his* purpose.

29 For whom he did foreknow, he also did predestinate *to be* conformed to the image of his Son, that he might be the firstborn among many brethren.

30 Moreover whom he did predestinate, them he also called: and whom he called, them he also justified: and whom he justified, them he also glorified.

31 What shall we then say to these things? If God *be* for us, who *can be* against us?

32 He that spared not his own Son, but delivered him up for us all, how shall he not with him also freely give us all things?

33 Who shall lay any thing to the

charge of God's elect? *It is* God that
justifieth.
34 Who *is* he that condemneth? *It*
is Christ that died, yea rather, that
is risen again, who is even at the
right hand of God, who also maketh
intercession for us.
35 Who shall separate us from the
love of Christ? *shall* tribulation, or
distress, or persecution, or famine,
or nakedness, or peril, or sword?
36 As it is written, For thy sake we
are killed all the day long; we are ac-
counted as sheep for the slaughter.
37 Nay, in all these things we are
more than conquerors through him
that loved us.
38 For I am persuaded, that nei-
ther death, nor life, nor angels,
nor principalities, nor powers, nor
things present, nor things to come,
39 Nor height, nor depth, nor any
other creature, shall be able to sep-
arate us from the love of God, which
is in Christ Jesus our Lord.

Paul's Burden for Israel

9 I say the truth in Christ, I lie not,
my conscience also bearing me
witness in the Holy Ghost,
2 That I have great heaviness and
continual sorrow in my heart.
3 For I could wish that myself were
accursed from Christ for my brethren,
my kinsmen according to the flesh:
4 Who are Israelites; to whom
pertaineth the adoption, and the
glory, and the covenants, and the
giving of the law, and the service *of*
God, and the promises;
5 Whose *are* the fathers, and of
whom as concerning the flesh Christ
came, who is over all, God blessed
for ever. Amen.
6 Not as though the word of God
hath taken none effect. For they *are*
not all Israel, which are of Israel:
7 Neither, because they are the
seed of Abraham, *are they* all chil-
dren: but, In Isaac shall thy seed be
called.
8 That is, They which are the chil-
dren of the flesh, these *are* not the
children of God: but the children of
the promise are counted for the seed.
9 For this *is* the word of promise,
At this time will I come, and Sarah
shall have a son.
10 And not only *this;* but when Re-
becca also had conceived by one,
even by our father Isaac;
11 (For *the children* being not yet
born, neither having done any good
or evil, that the purpose of God ac-
cording to election might stand, not
of works, but of him that calleth;)
12 It was said unto her, The elder
shall serve the younger.
13 As it is written, Jacob have I
loved, but Esau have I hated.

God Shows Mercy as He Wills

14 What shall we say then? *Is there*
unrighteousness with God? God for-
bid.
15 For he saith to Moses, I will
have mercy on whom I will have
mercy, and I will have compassion
on whom I will have compassion.
16 So then *it is* not of him that will-
eth, nor of him that runneth, but of
God that sheweth mercy.
17 For the scripture saith unto
Pharaoh, Even for this same pur-
pose have I raised thee up, that I
might shew my power in thee, and
that my name might be declared
throughout all the earth.
18 Therefore hath he mercy on
whom he will *have mercy,* and
whom he will he hardeneth.
19 Thou wilt say then unto me,
Why doth he yet find fault? For who
hath resisted his will?
20 Nay but, O man, who art thou
that repliest against God? Shall the
thing formed say to him that formed
it, Why hast thou made me thus?
21 Hath not the potter power over
the clay, of the same lump to make
one vessel unto honour, and another
unto dishonour?

22 *What* if God, willing to shew *his* wrath, and to make his power known, endured with much long-suffering the vessels of wrath fitted to destruction:

23 And that he might make known the riches of his glory on the vessels of mercy, which he had afore prepared unto glory,

24 Even us, whom he hath called, not of the Jews only, but also of the Gentiles?

25 As he saith also in Osee, I will call them my people, which were not my people; and her beloved, which was not beloved.

26 And it shall come to pass, *that* in the place where it was said unto them, Ye *are* not my people; there shall they be called the children of the living God.

27 Esaias also crieth concerning Israel, Though the number of the children of Israel be as the sand of the sea, a remnant shall be saved:

28 For he will finish the work, and cut *it* short in righteousness: because a short work will the Lord make upon the earth.

29 And as Esaias said before, Except the Lord of Sabaoth had left us a seed, we had been as Sodoma, and been made like unto Gomorrha.

Israel Stumbles

30 What shall we say then? That the Gentiles, which followed not after righteousness, have attained to righteousness, even the righteousness which is of faith.

31 But Israel, which followed after the law of righteousness, hath not attained to the law of righteousness.

32 Wherefore? Because *they sought it* not by faith, but as it were by the works of the law. For they stumbled at that stumblingstone;

33 As it is written, Behold, I lay in Sion a stumblingstone and rock of offence: and whosoever believeth on him shall not be ashamed.

Israel's Rejection of Christ

10 Brethren, my heart's desire and prayer to God for Israel is, that they might be saved.

2 For I bear them record that they have a zeal of God, but not according to knowledge.

3 For they being ignorant of God's righteousness, and going about to establish their own righteousness, have not submitted themselves unto the righteousness of God.

4 For Christ *is* the end of the law for righteousness to every one that believeth.

5 For Moses describeth the righteousness which is of the law, That the man which doeth those things shall live by them.

6 But the righteousness which is of faith speaketh on this wise, Say not in thine heart, Who shall ascend into heaven? (that is, to bring Christ down *from above:*)

7 Or, Who shall descend into the deep? (that is, to bring up Christ again from the dead.)

8 But what saith it? The word is nigh thee, *even* in thy mouth, and in thy heart: that is, the word of faith, which we preach;

9 That if thou shalt confess with thy mouth the Lord Jesus, and shalt believe in thine heart that God hath raised him from the dead, thou shalt be saved.

10 For with the heart man believeth unto righteousness; and with the mouth confession is made unto salvation.

11 For the scripture saith, Whosoever believeth on him shall not be ashamed.

12 For there is no difference between the Jew and the Greek: for the same Lord over all is rich unto all that call upon him.

13 For whosoever shall call upon the name of the Lord shall be saved.

Preaching to a Disobedient People

14 How then shall they call on him
in whom they have not believed?
and how shall they believe in him of
whom they have not heard? and how
shall they hear without a preacher?
15 And how shall they preach, except they be sent? as it is written,
How beautiful are the feet of them
that preach the gospel of peace, and
bring glad tidings of good things!
16 But they have not all obeyed
the gospel. For Esaias saith, Lord,
who hath believed our report?
17 So then faith *cometh* by hearing,
and hearing by the word of God.
18 But I say, Have they not heard?
Yes verily, their sound went into all
the earth, and their words unto the
ends of the world.
19 But I say, Did not Israel know?
First Moses saith, I will provoke
you to jealousy by *them that are*
no people, *and* by a foolish nation
I will anger you.
20 But Esaias is very bold, and
saith, I was found of them that
sought me not; I was made manifest
unto them that asked not after me.
21 But to Israel he saith, All day
long I have stretched forth my hands
unto a disobedient and gainsaying
people.

A Remnant Remains

11 I say then, Hath God cast away
his people? God forbid. For I
also am an Israelite, of the seed of
Abraham, *of* the tribe of Benjamin.
2 God hath not cast away his people which he foreknew. Wot ye not
what the scripture saith of Elias?
how he maketh intercession to God
against Israel, saying,
3 Lord, they have killed thy prophets, and digged down thine altars;
and I am left alone, and they seek
my life.
4 But what saith the answer of
God unto him? I have reserved to
myself seven thousand men, who
have not bowed the knee to *the image of* Baal.
5 Even so then at this present time
also there is a remnant according to
the election of grace.
6 And if by grace, then *is it* no
more of works: otherwise grace is
no more grace. But if *it be* of works,
then is it no more grace: otherwise
work is no more work.
7 What then? Israel hath not obtained that which he seeketh for;
but the election hath obtained it,
and the rest were blinded
8 (According as it is written, God
hath given them the spirit of slumber, eyes that they should not see,
and ears that they should not hear;)
unto this day.
9 And David saith, Let their table
be made a snare, and a trap, and a
stumblingblock, and a recompence
unto them:
10 Let their eyes be darkened, that
they may not see, and bow down
their back alway.

New Branches Graffed In

11 I say then, Have they stumbled
that they should fall? God forbid: but
rather through their fall salvation *is
come* unto the Gentiles, for to provoke them to jealousy.
12 Now if the fall of them *be* the
riches of the world, and the diminishing of them the riches of the Gentiles; how much more their fulness?
13 For I speak to you Gentiles, inasmuch as I am the apostle of the
Gentiles, I magnify mine office:
14 If by any means I may provoke
to emulation *them which are* my
flesh, and might save some of them.
15 For if the casting away of them
be the reconciling of the world, what
shall the receiving *of them be,* but
life from the dead?
16 For if the firstfruit *be* holy, the
lump *is* also *holy:* and if the root *be*
holy, so *are* the branches.

17 And if some of the branches be
broken off, and thou, being a wild
olive tree, wert graffed in among
them, and with them partakest of
the root and fatness of the olive tree;
18 Boast not against the branches.
But if thou boast, thou bearest not
the root, but the root thee.
19 Thou wilt say then, The
branches were broken off, that I
might be graffed in.
20 Well; because of unbelief they
were broken off, and thou standest
by faith. Be not highminded, but
fear:
21 For if God spared not the natural branches, *take heed* lest he also spare not thee.
22 Behold therefore the goodness
and severity of God: on them which
fell, severity; but toward thee, goodness, if thou continue in *his* goodness: otherwise thou also shalt be
cut off.
23 And they also, if they abide not
still in unbelief, shall be graffed in:
for God is able to graff them in again.
24 For if thou wert cut out of the
olive tree which is wild by nature,
and wert graffed contrary to nature
into a good olive tree: how much
more shall these, which be the natural *branches,* be graffed into their
own olive tree?

God's Covenant with Israel

25 For I would not, brethren, that
ye should be ignorant of this mystery, lest ye should be wise in your
own conceits; that blindness in part
is happened to Israel, until the fulness of the Gentiles be come in.
26 And so all Israel shall be saved:
as it is written, There shall come out
of Sion the Deliverer, and shall turn
away ungodliness from Jacob:
27 For this *is* my covenant unto
them, when I shall take away their
sins.
28 As concerning the gospel, *they
are* enemies for your sakes: but as
touching the election, *they are* beloved for the fathers' sakes.
29 For the gifts and calling of God
are without repentance.
30 For as ye in times past have not
believed God, yet have now obtained
mercy through their unbelief:
31 Even so have these also now
not believed, that through your
mercy they also may obtain mercy.
32 For God hath concluded them
all in unbelief, that he might have
mercy upon all.

Glory to God

33 O the depth of the riches both
of the wisdom and knowledge of
God! how unsearchable *are* his judgments, and his ways past finding
out!
34 For who hath known the mind
of the Lord? or who hath been his
counsellor?
35 Or who hath first given to him,
and it shall be recompensed unto
him again?
36 For of him, and through him,
and to him, *are* all things: to whom
be glory for ever. Amen.

The Perfect Will of God

12 I beseech you therefore, brethren, by the mercies of God,
that ye present your bodies a living
sacrifice, holy, acceptable unto God,
which is your reasonable service.
2 And be not conformed to this
world: but be ye transformed by
the renewing of your mind, that ye
may prove what *is* that good, and
acceptable, and perfect, will of God.
3 For I say, through the grace
given unto me, to every man that
is among you, not to think *of himself*
more highly than he ought to think;
but to think soberly, according as
God hath dealt to every man the
measure of faith.
4 For as we have many members
in one body, and all members have
not the same office:

5 So we, *being* many, are one body in Christ, and every one members one of another.

6 Having then gifts differing according to the grace that is given to us, whether prophecy, *let us prophesy* according to the proportion of faith;

7 Or ministry, *let us wait* on *our* ministering: or he that teacheth, on teaching;

8 Or he that exhorteth, on exhortation: he that giveth, *let him do it* with simplicity; he that ruleth, with diligence; he that sheweth mercy, with cheerfulness.

Overcome Evil with Good

9 *Let* love be without dissimulation. Abhor that which is evil; cleave to that which is good.

10 *Be* kindly affectioned one to another with brotherly love; in honour preferring one another;

11 Not slothful in business; fervent in spirit; serving the Lord;

12 Rejoicing in hope; patient in tribulation; continuing instant in prayer;

13 Distributing to the necessity of saints; given to hospitality.

14 Bless them which persecute you: bless, and curse not.

15 Rejoice with them that do rejoice, and weep with them that weep.

16 *Be* of the same mind one toward another. Mind not high things, but condescend to men of low estate. Be not wise in your own conceits.

17 Recompense to no man evil for evil. Provide things honest in the sight of all men.

18 If it be possible, as much as lieth in you, live peaceably with all men.

19 Dearly beloved, avenge not yourselves, but *rather* give place unto wrath: for it is written, Vengeance *is* mine; I will repay, saith the Lord.

20 Therefore if thine enemy hunger, feed him; if he thirst, give him drink: for in so doing thou shalt heap coals of fire on his head.

21 Be not overcome of evil, but overcome evil with good.

Be Subject to Higher Powers

13 Let every soul be subject unto the higher powers. For there is no power but of God: the powers that be are ordained of God.

2 Whosoever therefore resisteth the power, resisteth the ordinance of God: and they that resist shall receive to themselves damnation.

3 For rulers are not a terror to good works, but to the evil. Wilt thou then not be afraid of the power? do that which is good, and thou shalt have praise of the same:

4 For he is the minister of God to thee for good. But if thou do that which is evil, be afraid; for he beareth not the sword in vain: for he is the minister of God, a revenger to *execute* wrath upon him that doeth evil.

5 Wherefore *ye* must needs be subject, not only for wrath, but also for conscience sake.

6 For for this cause pay ye tribute also: for they are God's ministers, attending continually upon this very thing.

7 Render therefore to all their dues: tribute to whom tribute *is due;* custom to whom custom; fear to whom fear; honour to whom honour.

Love One Another

8 Owe no man any thing, but to love one another: for he that loveth another hath fulfilled the law.

9 For this, Thou shalt not commit adultery, Thou shalt not kill, Thou shalt not steal, Thou shalt not bear false witness, Thou shalt not covet; and if *there be* any other commandment, it is briefly comprehended in this saying, namely, Thou shalt love thy neighbour as thyself.

10 Love worketh no ill to his neigh-
bour: therefore love *is* the fulfilling
of the law.
11 And that, knowing the time,
that now *it is* high time to awake
out of sleep: for now *is* our salvation
nearer than when we believed.
12 The night is far spent, the day
is at hand: let us therefore cast off
the works of darkness, and let us
put on the armour of light.
13 Let us walk honestly, as in the
day; not in rioting and drunkenness,
not in chambering and wantonness,
not in strife and envying.
14 But put ye on the Lord Jesus
Christ, and make not provision for
the flesh, to *fulfil* the lusts *thereof.*

Christian Liberty

14 Him that is weak in the faith
receive ye, *but* not to doubtful
disputations.
2 For one believeth that he may
eat all things: another, who is weak,
eateth herbs.
3 Let not him that eateth despise
him that eateth not; and let not him
which eateth not judge him that
eateth: for God hath received him.
4 Who art thou that judgest an-
other man's servant? to his own
master he standeth or falleth. Yea,
he shall be holden up: for God is able
to make him stand.
5 One man esteemeth one day
above another: another esteemeth
every day *alike.* Let every man be
fully persuaded in his own mind.
6 He that regardeth the day, re-
gardeth *it* unto the Lord; and he that
regardeth not the day, to the Lord he
doth not regard *it.* He that eateth,
eateth to the Lord, for he giveth God
thanks; and he that eateth not, to
the Lord he eateth not, and giveth
God thanks.
7 For none of us liveth to himself,
and no man dieth to himself.
8 For whether we live, we live unto
the Lord; and whether we die, we
die unto the Lord: whether we live
therefore, or die, we are the Lord's.
9 For to this end Christ both died,
and rose, and revived, that he might
be Lord both of the dead and living.
10 But why dost thou judge thy
brother? or why dost thou set at
nought thy brother? for we shall all
stand before the judgment seat of
Christ.
11 For it is written, *As* I live, saith
the Lord, every knee shall bow to
me, and every tongue shall confess
to God.

We Are All Accountable

12 So then every one of us shall
give account of himself to God.
13 Let us not therefore judge one
another any more: but judge this
rather, that no man put a stumbling-
block or an occasion to fall in *his*
brother's way.
14 I know, and am persuaded by
the Lord Jesus, that *there is* nothing
unclean of itself: but to him that
esteemeth any thing to be unclean,
to him *it is* unclean.
15 But if thy brother be grieved
with *thy* meat, now walkest thou
not charitably. Destroy not him with
thy meat, for whom Christ died.
16 Let not then your good be evil
spoken of:
17 For the kingdom of God is not
meat and drink; but righteousness,
and peace, and joy in the Holy Ghost.
18 For he that in these things serv-
eth Christ *is* acceptable to God, and
approved of men.
19 Let us therefore follow after the
things which make for peace, and
things wherewith one may edify
another.
20 For meat destroy not the work
of God. All things indeed *are* pure;
but *it is* evil for that man who eateth
with offence.
21 *It is* good neither to eat flesh,
nor to drink wine, nor *any thing*
whereby thy brother stumbleth, or

is offended, or is made weak.
22 Hast thou faith? have *it* to thy-
self before God. Happy *is* he that
condemneth not himself in that
thing which he alloweth.
23 And he that doubteth is
damned if he eat, because *he eateth*
not of faith: for whatsoever *is* not of
faith is sin.

Be Likeminded

15 We then that are strong ought
to bear the infirmities of the
weak, and not to please ourselves.
2 Let every one of us please *his*
neighbour for *his* good to edifica-
tion.
3 For even Christ pleased not
himself; but, as it is written, The
reproaches of them that reproached
thee fell on me.
4 For whatsoever things were
written aforetime were written for
our learning, that we through pa-
tience and comfort of the scriptures
might have hope.
5 Now the God of patience and
consolation grant you to be like-
minded one toward another accord-
ing to Christ Jesus:

Glorify God Together

6 That ye may with one mind *and*
one mouth glorify God, even the
Father of our Lord Jesus Christ.
7 Wherefore receive ye one an-
other, as Christ also received us to
the glory of God.
8 Now I say that Jesus Christ was a
minister of the circumcision for the
truth of God, to confirm the prom-
ises *made* unto the fathers:
9 And that the Gentiles might glo-
rify God for *his* mercy; as it is writ-
ten, For this cause I will confess to
thee among the Gentiles, and sing
unto thy name.
10 And again he saith, Rejoice, ye
Gentiles, with his people.
11 And again, Praise the Lord, all ye
Gentiles; and laud him, all ye people.
12 And again, Esaias saith, There
shall be a root of Jesse, and he that
shall rise to reign over the Gentiles;
in him shall the Gentiles trust.
13 Now the God of hope fill you
with all joy and peace in believ-
ing, that ye may abound in hope,
through the power of the Holy
Ghost.

Paul Ministers to the Gentiles

14 And I myself also am persuaded
of you, my brethren, that ye also
are full of goodness, filled with all
knowledge, able also to admonish
one another.
15 Nevertheless, brethren, I have
written the more boldly unto you in
some sort, as putting you in mind,
because of the grace that is given to
me of God,
16 That I should be the minister
of Jesus Christ to the Gentiles, min-
istering the gospel of God, that the
offering up of the Gentiles might be
acceptable, being sanctified by the
Holy Ghost.
17 I have therefore whereof I may
glory through Jesus Christ in those
things which pertain to God.
18 For I will not dare to speak of
any of those things which Christ
hath not wrought by me, to make
the Gentiles obedient, by word and
deed,
19 Through mighty signs and won-
ders, by the power of the Spirit of
God; so that from Jerusalem, and
round about unto Illyricum, I have
fully preached the gospel of Christ.
20 Yea, so have I strived to preach
the gospel, not where Christ was
named, lest I should build upon
another man's foundation:
21 But as it is written, To whom
he was not spoken of, they shall see:
and they that have not heard shall
understand.
22 For which cause also I have
been much hindered from coming
to you.

Paul Desires to Visit Rome

23 But now having no more place
in these parts, and having a great
desire these many years to come
unto you;
24 Whensoever I take my journey
into Spain, I will come to you: for I
trust to see you in my journey, and
to be brought on my way thither-
ward by you, if first I be somewhat
filled with your *company.*
25 But now I go unto Jerusalem
to minister unto the saints.
26 For it hath pleased them of
Macedonia and Achaia to make a
certain contribution for the poor
saints which are at Jerusalem.
27 It hath pleased them verily;
and their debtors they are. For if the
Gentiles have been made partakers
of their spiritual things, their duty is
also to minister unto them in carnal
things.
28 When therefore I have per-
formed this, and have sealed to
them this fruit, I will come by you
into Spain.
29 And I am sure that, when I come
unto you, I shall come in the fulness
of the blessing of the gospel of Christ.
30 Now I beseech you, brethren,
for the Lord Jesus Christ's sake,
and for the love of the Spirit, that
ye strive together with me in *your*
prayers to God for me;
31 That I may be delivered from
them that do not believe in Judaea;
and that my service which *I have* for
Jerusalem may be accepted of the
saints;
32 That I may come unto you with
joy by the will of God, and may with
you be refreshed.
33 Now the God of peace *be* with
you all. Amen.

Paul's Greetings

16 I commend unto you Phebe
our sister, which is a servant
of the church which is at Cenchrea:
2 That ye receive her in the Lord,
as becometh saints, and that ye as-
sist her in whatsoever business she
hath need of you: for she hath been
a succourer of many, and of myself
also.
3 Greet Priscilla and Aquila my
helpers in Christ Jesus:
4 Who have for my life laid down
their own necks: unto whom not
only I give thanks, but also all the
churches of the Gentiles.
5 Likewise *greet* the church that
is in their house. Salute my wellbe-
loved Epaenetus, who is the first-
fruits of Achaia unto Christ.
6 Greet Mary, who bestowed much
labour on us.
7 Salute Andronicus and Junia, my
kinsmen, and my fellowprisoners,
who are of note among the apostles,
who also were in Christ before me.
8 Greet Amplias my beloved in the
Lord.
9 Salute Urbane, our helper in
Christ, and Stachys my beloved.
10 Salute Apelles approved in
Christ. Salute them which are of
Aristobulus' *household.*
11 Salute Herodion my kinsman.
Greet them that be of the *household*
of Narcissus, which are in the Lord.
12 Salute Tryphena and Tryphosa,
who labour in the Lord. Salute the
beloved Persis, which laboured
much in the Lord.
13 Salute Rufus chosen in the
Lord, and his mother and mine.
14 Salute Asyncritus, Phlegon,
Hermas, Patrobas, Hermes, and
the brethren which are with them.
15 Salute Philologus, and Julia, Ne-
reus, and his sister, and Olympas, and
all the saints which are with them.
16 Salute one another with an holy
kiss. The churches of Christ salute
you.

Avoid Them Who Cause Divisions

17 Now I beseech you, brethren,
mark them which cause divisions

and offences contrary to the doc-
trine which ye have learned; and
avoid them.
18 For they that are such serve not
our Lord Jesus Christ, but their own
belly; and by good words and fair
speeches deceive the hearts of the
simple.
19 For your obedience is come
abroad unto all *men*. I am glad
therefore on your behalf: but yet
I would have you wise unto that
which is good, and simple concern-
ing evil.
20 And the God of peace shall
bruise Satan under your feet shortly.
The grace of our Lord Jesus Christ
be with you. Amen.

Final Salutations

21 Timotheus my workfellow, and
Lucius, and Jason, and Sosipater,
my kinsmen, salute you.
22 I Tertius, who wrote *this* epis-
tle, salute you in the Lord.
23 Gaius mine host, and of the
whole church, saluteth you. Erastus
the chamberlain of the city saluteth
you, and Quartus a brother.
24 The grace of our Lord Jesus
Christ *be* with you all. Amen.

Glory to God Only Wise

25 Now to him that is of power to
stablish you according to my gospel,
and the preaching of Jesus Christ,
according to the revelation of the
mystery, which was kept secret
since the world began,
26 But now is made manifest, and
by the scriptures of the prophets,
according to the commandment of
the everlasting God, made known to
all nations for the obedience of faith:
27 To God only wise, *be* glory
through Jesus Christ for ever. Amen.

The First Epistle of Paul the Apostle to the CORINTHIANS

Grace and Peace

Paul, called *to be* an apostle of Jesus Christ through the will of God, and Sosthenes *our* brother,

2 Unto the church of God which is at Corinth, to them that are sanctified in Christ Jesus, called *to be* saints, with all that in every place call upon the name of Jesus Christ our Lord, both theirs and ours:

3 Grace *be* unto you, and peace, from God our Father, and *from* the Lord Jesus Christ.

Paul's Thankfulness

4 I thank my God always on your behalf, for the grace of God which is given you by Jesus Christ;

5 That in every thing ye are enriched by him, in all utterance, and *in* all knowledge;

6 Even as the testimony of Christ was confirmed in you:

7 So that ye come behind in no gift; waiting for the coming of our Lord Jesus Christ:

8 Who shall also confirm you unto the end, *that ye may be* blameless in the day of our Lord Jesus Christ.

9 God *is* faithful, by whom ye were called unto the fellowship of his Son Jesus Christ our Lord.

Contentions in the Church

10 Now I beseech you, brethren, by the name of our Lord Jesus Christ, that ye all speak the same thing, and *that* there be no divisions among you; but *that* ye be perfectly joined together in the same mind and in the same judgment.

11 For it hath been declared unto me of you, my brethren, by them *which are of the house* of Chloe, that there are contentions among you.

12 Now this I say, that every one of you saith, I am of Paul; and I of Apollos; and I of Cephas; and I of Christ.

13 Is Christ divided? was Paul crucified for you? or were ye baptized in the name of Paul?

14 I thank God that I baptized none of you, but Crispus and Gaius;

15 Lest any should say that I had baptized in mine own name.

16 And I baptized also the household of Stephanas: besides, I know not whether I baptized any other.

17 For Christ sent me not to baptize, but to preach the gospel: not with wisdom of words, lest the cross of Christ should be made of none effect.

The Foolishness of the World's Wisdom

18 For the preaching of the cross is to them that perish foolishness; but unto us which are saved it is the power of God.

19 For it is written, I will destroy the wisdom of the wise, and will bring to nothing the understanding of the prudent.

20 Where *is* the wise? where *is* the scribe? where *is* the disputer of this world? hath not God made foolish the wisdom of this world?

21 For after that in the wisdom of
God the world by wisdom knew not
God, it pleased God by the foolish-
ness of preaching to save them that
believe.
22 For the Jews require a sign, and
the Greeks seek after wisdom:
23 But we preach Christ crucified,
unto the Jews a stumblingblock, and
unto the Greeks foolishness;
24 But unto them which are called,
both Jews and Greeks, Christ the
power of God, and the wisdom of
God.
25 Because the foolishness of God
is wiser than men; and the weakness
of God is stronger than men.

Glory in the Lord

26 For ye see your calling, breth-
ren, how that not many wise men
after the flesh, not many mighty,
not many noble, *are called:*
27 But God hath chosen the fool-
ish things of the world to confound
the wise; and God hath chosen the
weak things of the world to con-
found the things which are mighty;
28 And base things of the world,
and things which are despised, hath
God chosen, *yea,* and things which
are not, to bring to nought things
that are:
29 That no flesh should glory in
his presence.
30 But of him are ye in Christ
Jesus, who of God is made unto us
wisdom, and righteousness, and
sanctification, and redemption:
31 That, according as it is written,
He that glorieth, let him glory in the
Lord.

Faith in God's Power

2 And I, brethren, when I came to
you, came not with excellency of
speech or of wisdom, declaring unto
you the testimony of God.
2 For I determined not to know
any thing among you, save Jesus
Christ, and him crucified.
3 And I was with you in weakness,
and in fear, and in much trembling.
4 And my speech and my preach-
ing *was* not with enticing words of
man's wisdom, but in demonstra-
tion of the Spirit and of power:
5 That your faith should not stand
in the wisdom of men, but in the
power of God.

The Wisdom of God

6 Howbeit we speak wisdom
among them that are perfect: yet
not the wisdom of this world, nor of
the princes of this world, that come
to nought:
7 But we speak the wisdom of God
in a mystery, *even* the hidden *wis-
dom,* which God ordained before
the world unto our glory:
8 Which none of the princes of this
world knew: for had they known *it,*
they would not have crucified the
Lord of glory.
9 But as it is written, Eye hath not
seen, nor ear heard, neither have
entered into the heart of man, the
things which God hath prepared for
them that love him.
10 But God hath revealed *them*
unto us by his Spirit: for the Spirit
searcheth all things, yea, the deep
things of God.
11 For what man knoweth the
things of a man, save the spirit of
man which is in him? even so the
things of God knoweth no man, but
the Spirit of God.
12 Now we have received, not the
spirit of the world, but the spirit
which is of God; that we might know
the things that are freely given to us
of God.
13 Which things also we speak, not
in the words which man's wisdom
teacheth, but which the Holy Ghost
teacheth; comparing spiritual things
with spiritual.
14 But the natural man receiveth
not the things of the Spirit of God:
for they are foolishness unto him:

neither can he know *them,* because they are spiritually discerned.

15 But he that is spiritual judgeth all things, yet he himself is judged of no man.

16 For who hath known the mind of the Lord, that he may instruct him? But we have the mind of Christ.

Labourers with God

3 And I, brethren, could not speak unto you as unto spiritual, but as unto carnal, *even* as unto babes in Christ.

2 I have fed you with milk, and not with meat: for hitherto ye were not able *to bear it,* neither yet now are ye able.

3 For ye are yet carnal: for whereas *there is* among you envying, and strife, and divisions, are ye not carnal, and walk as men?

4 For while one saith, I am of Paul; and another, I *am* of Apollos; are ye not carnal?

5 Who then is Paul, and who *is* Apollos, but ministers by whom ye believed, even as the Lord gave to every man?

6 I have planted, Apollos watered; but God gave the increase.

7 So then neither is he that planteth any thing, neither he that watereth; but God that giveth the increase.

8 Now he that planteth and he that watereth are one: and every man shall receive his own reward according to his own labour.

9 For we are labourers together with God: ye are God's husbandry, *ye are* God's building.

10 According to the grace of God which is given unto me, as a wise masterbuilder, I have laid the foundation, and another buildeth thereon. But let every man take heed how he buildeth thereupon.

11 For other foundation can no man lay than that is laid, which is Jesus Christ.

12 Now if any man build upon this foundation gold, silver, precious stones, wood, hay, stubble;

13 Every man's work shall be made manifest: for the day shall declare it, because it shall be revealed by fire; and the fire shall try every man's work of what sort it is.

14 If any man's work abide which he hath built thereupon, he shall receive a reward.

15 If any man's work shall be burned, he shall suffer loss: but he himself shall be saved; yet so as by fire.

The Temple of God

16 Know ye not that ye are the temple of God, and *that* the Spirit of God dwelleth in you?

17 If any man defile the temple of God, him shall God destroy; for the temple of God is holy, which *temple* ye are.

18 Let no man deceive himself. If any man among you seemeth to be wise in this world, let him become a fool, that he may be wise.

19 For the wisdom of this world is foolishness with God. For it is written, He taketh the wise in their own craftiness.

20 And again, The Lord knoweth the thoughts of the wise, that they are vain.

21 Therefore let no man glory in men. For all things are yours;

22 Whether Paul, or Apollos, or Cephas, or the world, or life, or death, or things present, or things to come; all are yours;

23 And ye are Christ's; and Christ *is* God's.

Ministers and Stewards

4 Let a man so account of us, as of the ministers of Christ, and stewards of the mysteries of God.

2 Moreover it is required in stewards, that a man be found faithful.

3 But with me it is a very small thing that I should be judged of you,

or of man's judgment: yea, I judge
not mine own self.
4 For I know nothing by myself;
yet am I not hereby justified: but
he that judgeth me is the Lord.
5 Therefore judge nothing before
the time, until the Lord come, who
both will bring to light the hidden
things of darkness, and will make
manifest the counsels of the hearts:
and then shall every man have
praise of God.
6 And these things, brethren, I
have in a figure transferred to my-
self and *to* Apollos for your sakes;
that ye might learn in us not to think
of men above that which is written,
that no one of you be puffed up for
one against another.
7 For who maketh thee to differ
from another? and what hast thou
that thou didst not receive? now
if thou didst receive *it,* why dost
thou glory, as if thou hadst not re-
ceived *it?*
8 Now ye are full, now ye are rich,
ye have reigned as kings without us:
and I would to God ye did reign, that
we also might reign with you.

Fools for Christ's Sake

9 For I think that God hath set
forth us the apostles last, as it were
appointed to death: for we are made
a spectacle unto the world, and to
angels, and to men.
10 We *are* fools for Christ's sake,
but ye *are* wise in Christ; we *are*
weak, but ye *are* strong; ye *are* hon-
ourable, but we *are* despised.
11 Even unto this present hour
we both hunger, and thirst, and are
naked, and are buffeted, and have
no certain dwellingplace;
12 And labour, working with our
own hands: being reviled, we bless;
being persecuted, we suffer it:
13 Being defamed, we intreat: we
are made as the filth of the world,
and are the offscouring of all things
unto this day.

Paul's Fatherly Guidance

14 I write not these things to
shame you, but as my beloved sons
I warn *you.*
15 For though ye have ten thou-
sand instructors in Christ, yet *have*
ye not many fathers: for in Christ
Jesus I have begotten you through
the gospel.
16 Wherefore I beseech you, be ye
followers of me.
17 For this cause have I sent unto
you Timotheus, who is my beloved
son, and faithful in the Lord, who
shall bring you into remembrance
of my ways which be in Christ, as I
teach every where in every church.
18 Now some are puffed up, as
though I would not come to you.
19 But I will come to you shortly,
if the Lord will, and will know, not
the speech of them which are puffed
up, but the power.
20 For the kingdom of God *is* not
in word, but in power.
21 What will ye? shall I come unto
you with a rod, or in love, and *in* the
spirit of meekness?

Fornication in the Church

5 It is reported commonly *that*
there is fornication among you,
and such fornication as is not so
much as named among the Gentiles,
that one should have his father's
wife.
2 And ye are puffed up, and have
not rather mourned, that he that
hath done this deed might be taken
away from among you.
3 For I verily, as absent in body,
but present in spirit, have judged
already, as though I were present,
concerning him that hath so done
this deed,
4 In the name of our Lord Jesus
Christ, when ye are gathered to-
gether, and my spirit, with the
power of our Lord Jesus Christ,
5 To deliver such an one unto
Satan for the destruction of the

flesh, that the spirit may be saved
in the day of the Lord Jesus.
6 Your glorying *is* not good. Know
ye not that a little leaven leaveneth
the whole lump?
7 Purge out therefore the old
leaven, that ye may be a new lump,
as ye are unleavened. For even Christ
our passover is sacrificed for us:
8 Therefore let us keep the feast,
not with old leaven, neither with the
leaven of malice and wickedness;
but with the unleavened *bread* of
sincerity and truth.

Put Away the Wicked

9 I wrote unto you in an epistle
not to company with fornicators:
10 Yet not altogether with the for-
nicators of this world, or with the
covetous, or extortioners, or with
idolaters; for then must ye needs
go out of the world.
11 But now I have written unto
you not to keep company, if any man
that is called a brother be a fornica-
tor, or covetous, or an idolater, or a
railer, or a drunkard, or an extor-
tioner; with such an one no not to
eat.
12 For what have I to do to judge
them also that are without? do not
ye judge them that are within?
13 But them that are without God
judgeth. Therefore put away from
among yourselves that wicked per-
son.

Judgment by the Saints

6 Dare any of you, having a mat-
ter against another, go to law
before the unjust, and not before
the saints?
2 Do ye not know that the saints
shall judge the world? and if the
world shall be judged by you, are
ye unworthy to judge the smallest
matters?
3 Know ye not that we shall judge
angels? how much more things that
pertain to this life?
4 If then ye have judgments of
things pertaining to this life, set
them to judge who are least es-
teemed in the church.
5 I speak to your shame. Is it so,
that there is not a wise man among
you? no, not one that shall be able
to judge between his brethren?
6 But brother goeth to law with
brother, and that before the unbe-
lievers.
7 Now therefore there is utterly a
fault among you, because ye go to
law one with another. Why do ye
not rather take wrong? why do ye
not rather *suffer yourselves to* be
defrauded?
8 Nay, ye do wrong, and defraud,
and that *your* brethren.
9 Know ye not that the unrigh-
teous shall not inherit the kingdom
of God? Be not deceived: neither
fornicators, nor idolaters, nor adul-
terers, nor effeminate, nor abusers
of themselves with mankind,
10 Nor thieves, nor covetous, nor
drunkards, nor revilers, nor extor-
tioners, shall inherit the kingdom
of God.
11 And such were some of you: but
ye are washed, but ye are sanctified,
but ye are justified in the name of
the Lord Jesus, and by the Spirit of
our God.

The Believer's Body a Temple

12 All things are lawful unto me,
but all things are not expedient: all
things are lawful for me, but I will
not be brought under the power of
any.
13 Meats for the belly, and the belly
for meats: but God shall destroy
both it and them. Now the body *is*
not for fornication, but for the Lord;
and the Lord for the body.
14 And God hath both raised up
the Lord, and will also raise up us
by his own power.
15 Know ye not that your bodies
are the members of Christ? shall I

then take the members of Christ, and make *them* the members of an harlot? God forbid.

16 What? know ye not that he which is joined to an harlot is one body? for two, saith he, shall be one flesh.

17 But he that is joined unto the Lord is one spirit.

18 Flee fornication. Every sin that a man doeth is without the body; but he that committeth fornication sinneth against his own body.

19 What? know ye not that your body is the temple of the Holy Ghost *which is* in you, which ye have of God, and ye are not your own?

20 For ye are bought with a price: therefore glorify God in your body, and in your spirit, which are God's.

Paul's Teachings on Marriage

7 Now concerning the things whereof ye wrote unto me: *It is* good for a man not to touch a woman.

2 Nevertheless, *to avoid* fornication, let every man have his own wife, and let every woman have her own husband.

3 Let the husband render unto the wife due benevolence: and likewise also the wife unto the husband.

4 The wife hath not power of her own body, but the husband: and likewise also the husband hath not power of his own body, but the wife.

5 Defraud ye not one the other, except *it be* with consent for a time, that ye may give yourselves to fasting and prayer; and come together again, that Satan tempt you not for your incontinency.

6 But I speak this by permission, *and* not of commandment.

7 For I would that all men were even as I myself. But every man hath his proper gift of God, one after this manner, and another after that.

8 I say therefore to the unmarried and widows, It is good for them if they abide even as I.

9 But if they cannot contain, let them marry: for it is better to marry than to burn.

Abide in the Same Calling

10 And unto the married I command, *yet* not I, but the Lord, Let not the wife depart from *her* husband:

11 But and if she depart, let her remain unmarried, or be reconciled to *her* husband: and let not the husband put away *his* wife.

12 But to the rest speak I, not the Lord: If any brother hath a wife that believeth not, and she be pleased to dwell with him, let him not put her away.

13 And the woman which hath an husband that believeth not, and if he be pleased to dwell with her, let her not leave him.

14 For the unbelieving husband is sanctified by the wife, and the unbelieving wife is sanctified by the husband: else were your children unclean; but now are they holy.

15 But if the unbelieving depart, let him depart. A brother or a sister is not under bondage in such *cases:* but God hath called us to peace.

16 For what knowest thou, O wife, whether thou shalt save *thy* husband? or how knowest thou, O man, whether thou shalt save *thy* wife?

17 But as God hath distributed to every man, as the Lord hath called every one, so let him walk. And so ordain I in all churches.

18 Is any man called being circumcised? let him not become uncircumcised. Is any called in uncircumcision? let him not be circumcised.

19 Circumcision is nothing, and uncircumcision is nothing, but the keeping of the commandments of God.

20 Let every man abide in the same calling wherein he was called.

21 Art thou called *being* a servant? care not for it: but if thou mayest be made free, use *it* rather.

22 For he that is called in the Lord, *being* a servant, is the Lord's freeman: likewise also he that is called, *being* free, is Christ's servant.

23 Ye are bought with a price; be not ye the servants of men.

24 Brethren, let every man, wherein he is called, therein abide with God.

Unmarried Men and Women

25 Now concerning virgins I have no commandment of the Lord: yet I give my judgment, as one that hath obtained mercy of the Lord to be faithful.

26 I suppose therefore that this is good for the present distress, *I say,* that *it is* good for a man so to be.

27 Art thou bound unto a wife? seek not to be loosed. Art thou loosed from a wife? seek not a wife.

28 But and if thou marry, thou hast not sinned; and if a virgin marry, she hath not sinned. Nevertheless such shall have trouble in the flesh: but I spare you.

29 But this I say, brethren, the time *is* short: it remaineth, that both they that have wives be as though they had none;

30 And they that weep, as though they wept not; and they that rejoice, as though they rejoiced not; and they that buy, as though they possessed not;

31 And they that use this world, as not abusing *it:* for the fashion of this world passeth away.

32 But I would have you without carefulness. He that is unmarried careth for the things that belong to the Lord, how he may please the Lord:

33 But he that is married careth for the things that are of the world, how he may please *his* wife.

34 There is difference *also* between a wife and a virgin. The unmarried woman careth for the things of the Lord, that she may be holy both in body and in spirit: but she that is married careth for the things of the world, how she may please *her* husband.

35 And this I speak for your own profit; not that I may cast a snare upon you, but for that which is comely, and that ye may attend upon the Lord without distraction.

36 But if any man think that he behaveth himself uncomely toward his virgin, if she pass the flower of *her* age, and need so require, let him do what he will, he sinneth not: let them marry.

37 Nevertheless he that standeth stedfast in his heart, having no necessity, but hath power over his own will, and hath so decreed in his heart that he will keep his virgin, doeth well.

38 So then he that giveth *her* in marriage doeth well; but he that giveth *her* not in marriage doeth better.

39 The wife is bound by the law as long as her husband liveth; but if her husband be dead, she is at liberty to be married to whom she will; only in the Lord.

40 But she is happier if she so abide, after my judgment: and I think also that I have the Spirit of God.

Food Sacrificed to Idols

8 Now as touching things offered unto idols, we know that we all have knowledge. Knowledge puffeth up, but charity edifieth.

2 And if any man think that he knoweth any thing, he knoweth nothing yet as he ought to know.

3 But if any man love God, the same is known of him.

4 As concerning therefore the eating of those things that are offered in sacrifice unto idols, we know that an idol *is* nothing in the world, and that *there is* none other God but one.

5 For though there be that are called gods, whether in heaven or

in earth, (as there be gods many,
and lords many,)
6 But to us *there is but* one God,
the Father, of whom *are* all things,
and we in him; and one Lord Jesus
Christ, by whom *are* all things, and
we by him.
7 Howbeit *there is* not in every
man that knowledge: for some with
conscience of the idol unto this hour
eat *it* as a thing offered unto an idol;
and their conscience being weak is
defiled.
8 But meat commendeth us not
to God: for neither, if we eat, are we
the better; neither, if we eat not, are
we the worse.
9 But take heed lest by any means
this liberty of yours become a stum-
blingblock to them that are weak.
10 For if any man see thee which
hast knowledge sit at meat in the
idol's temple, shall not the con-
science of him which is weak be
emboldened to eat those things
which are offered to idols;
11 And through thy knowledge
shall the weak brother perish, for
whom Christ died?
12 But when ye sin so against the
brethren, and wound their weak
conscience, ye sin against Christ.
13 Wherefore, if meat make my
brother to offend, I will eat no flesh
while the world standeth, lest I
make my brother to offend.

Apostles' Freedom and Power

9 Am I not an apostle? am I not
free? have I not seen Jesus
Christ our Lord? are not ye my work
in the Lord?
2 If I be not an apostle unto oth-
ers, yet doubtless I am to you: for
the seal of mine apostleship are ye
in the Lord.
3 Mine answer to them that do
examine me is this,
4 Have we not power to eat and
to drink?
5 Have we not power to lead about
a sister, a wife, as well as other apos-
tles, and *as* the brethren of the Lord,
and Cephas?
6 Or I only and Barnabas, have not
we power to forbear working?
7 Who goeth a warfare any time
at his own charges? who planteth a
vineyard, and eateth not of the fruit
thereof? or who feedeth a flock, and
eateth not of the milk of the flock?
8 Say I these things as a man? or
saith not the law the same also?
9 For it is written in the law of
Moses, Thou shalt not muzzle the
mouth of the ox that treadeth out
the corn. Doth God take care for
oxen?
10 Or saith he *it* altogether for
our sakes? For our sakes, no doubt,
this is written: that he that ploweth
should plow in hope; and that he
that thresheth in hope should be
partaker of his hope.
11 If we have sown unto you spir-
itual things, *is it* a great thing if we
shall reap your carnal things?
12 If others be partakers of *this*
power over you, *are* not we rather?
Nevertheless we have not used this
power; but suffer all things, lest we
should hinder the gospel of Christ.
13 Do ye not know that they which
minister about holy things live *of
the things* of the temple? and they
which wait at the altar are partakers
with the altar?
14 Even so hath the Lord ordained
that they which preach the gospel
should live of the gospel.
15 But I have used none of these
things: neither have I written these
things, that it should be so done
unto me: for *it were* better for me to
die, than that any man should make
my glorying void.
16 For though I preach the gospel,
I have nothing to glory of: for ne-
cessity is laid upon me; yea, woe is
unto me, if I preach not the gospel!
17 For if I do this thing willingly,
I have a reward: but if against my

will, a dispensation *of the gospel* is committed unto me.

18 What is my reward then? *Verily* that, when I preach the gospel, I may make the gospel of Christ without charge, that I abuse not my power in the gospel.

A Servant unto All

19 For though I be free from all *men,* yet have I made myself servant unto all, that I might gain the more.

20 And unto the Jews I became as a Jew, that I might gain the Jews; to them that are under the law, as under the law, that I might gain them that are under the law;

21 To them that are without law, as without law, (being not without law to God, but under the law to Christ,) that I might gain them that are without law.

22 To the weak became I as weak, that I might gain the weak: I am made all things to all *men,* that I might by all means save some.

23 And this I do for the gospel's sake, that I might be partaker thereof with *you.*

24 Know ye not that they which run in a race run all, but one receiveth the prize? So run, that ye may obtain.

25 And every man that striveth for the mastery is temperate in all things. Now they *do it* to obtain a corruptible crown; but we an incorruptible.

26 I therefore so run, not as uncertainly; so fight I, not as one that beateth the air:

27 But I keep under my body, and bring *it* into subjection: lest that by any means, when I have preached to others, I myself should be a castaway.

Israel's History as an Example

10 Moreover, brethren, I would not that ye should be ignorant, how that all our fathers were under the cloud, and all passed through the sea;

2 And were all baptized unto Moses in the cloud and in the sea;

3 And did all eat the same spiritual meat;

4 And did all drink the same spiritual drink: for they drank of that spiritual Rock that followed them: and that Rock was Christ.

5 But with many of them God was not well pleased: for they were overthrown in the wilderness.

6 Now these things were our examples, to the intent we should not lust after evil things, as they also lusted.

7 Neither be ye idolaters, as *were* some of them; as it is written, The people sat down to eat and drink, and rose up to play.

8 Neither let us commit fornication, as some of them committed, and fell in one day three and twenty thousand.

9 Neither let us tempt Christ, as some of them also tempted, and were destroyed of serpents.

10 Neither murmur ye, as some of them also murmured, and were destroyed of the destroyer.

11 Now all these things happened unto them for ensamples: and they are written for our admonition, upon whom the ends of the world are come.

12 Wherefore let him that thinketh he standeth take heed lest he fall.

13 There hath no temptation taken you but such as is common to man: but God *is* faithful, who will not suffer you to be tempted above that ye are able; but will with the temptation also make a way to escape, that ye may be able to bear *it.*

14 Wherefore, my dearly beloved, flee from idolatry.

15 I speak as to wise men; judge ye what I say.

16 The cup of blessing which we bless, is it not the communion of the

blood of Christ? The bread which we
break, is it not the communion of
the body of Christ?
17 For we *being* many are one
bread, *and* one body: for we are all
partakers of that one bread.
18 Behold Israel after the flesh: are
not they which eat of the sacrifices
partakers of the altar?
19 What say I then? that the idol is
any thing, or that which is offered
in sacrifice to idols is any thing?
20 But *I say,* that the things which
the Gentiles sacrifice, they sacri-
fice to devils, and not to God: and I
would not that ye should have fel-
lowship with devils.
21 Ye cannot drink the cup of the
Lord, and the cup of devils: ye can-
not be partakers of the Lord's table,
and of the table of devils.
22 Do we provoke the Lord to jeal-
ousy? are we stronger than he?

Do All to the Glory of God

23 All things are lawful for me,
but all things are not expedient:
all things are lawful for me, but all
things edify not.
24 Let no man seek his own, but
every man another's *wealth.*
25 Whatsoever is sold in the sham-
bles, *that* eat, asking no question for
conscience sake:
26 For the earth *is* the Lord's, and
the fulness thereof.
27 If any of them that believe not
bid you *to a feast,* and ye be disposed
to go; whatsoever is set before you,
eat, asking no question for con-
science sake.
28 But if any man say unto you,
This is offered in sacrifice unto idols,
eat not for his sake that shewed it,
and for conscience sake: for the
earth *is* the Lord's, and the fulness
thereof:
29 Conscience, I say, not thine
own, but of the other: for why is
my liberty judged of another *man's*
conscience?
30 For if I by grace be a partaker,
why am I evil spoken of for that for
which I give thanks?
31 Whether therefore ye eat, or
drink, or whatsoever ye do, do all
to the glory of God.
32 Give none offence, neither to
the Jews, nor to the Gentiles, nor
to the church of God:
33 Even as I please all *men* in all
things, not seeking mine own profit,
but the *profit* of many, that they may
be saved.

Proper Worship

11 Be ye followers of me, even as
I also *am* of Christ.
2 Now I praise you, brethren, that
ye remember me in all things, and
keep the ordinances, as I delivered
them to you.
3 But I would have you know, that
the head of every man is Christ; and
the head of the woman *is* the man;
and the head of Christ *is* God.
4 Every man praying or proph-
esying, having *his* head covered,
dishonoureth his head.
5 But every woman that prayeth
or prophesieth with *her* head un-
covered dishonoureth her head: for
that is even all one as if she were
shaven.
6 For if the woman be not covered,
let her also be shorn: but if it be a
shame for a woman to be shorn or
shaven, let her be covered.
7 For a man indeed ought not to
cover *his* head, forasmuch as he is
the image and glory of God: but the
woman is the glory of the man.
8 For the man is not of the woman;
but the woman of the man.
9 Neither was the man created for
the woman; but the woman for the
man.
10 For this cause ought the woman
to have power on *her* head because
of the angels.
11 Nevertheless neither is the
man without the woman, neither

the woman without the man, in the Lord.

12 For as the woman *is* of the man, even so *is* the man also by the woman; but all things of God.

13 Judge in yourselves: is it comely that a woman pray unto God uncovered?

14 Doth not even nature itself teach you, that, if a man have long hair, it is a shame unto him?

15 But if a woman have long hair, it is a glory to her: for *her* hair is given her for a covering.

16 But if any man seem to be contentious, we have no such custom, neither the churches of God.

Unworthy Communion

17 Now in this that I declare *unto you* I praise *you* not, that ye come together not for the better, but for the worse.

18 For first of all, when ye come together in the church, I hear that there be divisions among you; and I partly believe it.

19 For there must be also heresies among you, that they which are approved may be made manifest among you.

20 When ye come together therefore into one place, *this* is not to eat the Lord's supper.

21 For in eating every one taketh before *other* his own supper: and one is hungry, and another is drunken.

22 What? have ye not houses to eat and to drink in? or despise ye the church of God, and shame them that have not? What shall I say to you? shall I praise you in this? I praise *you* not.

The Lord's Supper

23 For I have received of the Lord that which also I delivered unto you, That the Lord Jesus the *same* night in which he was betrayed took bread:

24 And when he had given thanks, he brake *it*, and said, Take, eat: this is my body, which is broken for you: this do in remembrance of me.

25 After the same manner also *he took* the cup, when he had supped, saying, This cup is the new testament in my blood: this do ye, as oft as ye drink *it*, in remembrance of me.

26 For as often as ye eat this bread, and drink this cup, ye do shew the Lord's death till he come.

27 Wherefore whosoever shall eat this bread, and drink *this* cup of the Lord, unworthily, shall be guilty of the body and blood of the Lord.

28 But let a man examine himself, and so let him eat of *that* bread, and drink of *that* cup.

29 For he that eateth and drinketh unworthily, eateth and drinketh damnation to himself, not discerning the Lord's body.

30 For this cause many *are* weak and sickly among you, and many sleep.

31 For if we would judge ourselves, we should not be judged.

32 But when we are judged, we are chastened of the Lord, that we should not be condemned with the world.

33 Wherefore, my brethren, when ye come together to eat, tarry one for another.

34 And if any man hunger, let him eat at home; that ye come not together unto condemnation. And the rest will I set in order when I come.

The Diversities of Gifts

12 Now concerning spiritual *gifts*, brethren, I would not have you ignorant.

2 Ye know that ye were Gentiles, carried away unto these dumb idols, even as ye were led.

3 Wherefore I give you to understand, that no man speaking by the

Spirit of God calleth Jesus accursed: and *that* no man can say that Jesus is the Lord, but by the Holy Ghost.

4 Now there are diversities of gifts, but the same Spirit.

5 And there are differences of administrations, but the same Lord.

6 And there are diversities of operations, but it is the same God which worketh all in all.

7 But the manifestation of the Spirit is given to every man to profit withal.

8 For to one is given by the Spirit the word of wisdom; to another the word of knowledge by the same Spirit;

9 To another faith by the same Spirit; to another the gifts of healing by the same Spirit;

10 To another the working of miracles; to another prophecy; to another discerning of spirits; to another *divers* kinds of tongues; to another the interpretation of tongues:

11 But all these worketh that one and the selfsame Spirit, dividing to every man severally as he will.

The Body of Christ

12 For as the body is one, and hath many members, and all the members of that one body, being many, are one body: so also *is* Christ.

13 For by one Spirit are we all baptized into one body, whether *we be* Jews or Gentiles, whether *we be* bond or free; and have been all made to drink into one Spirit.

14 For the body is not one member, but many.

15 If the foot shall say, Because I am not the hand, I am not of the body; is it therefore not of the body?

16 And if the ear shall say, Because I am not the eye, I am not of the body; is it therefore not of the body?

17 If the whole body *were* an eye, where *were* the hearing? If the whole *were* hearing, where *were* the smelling?

18 But now hath God set the members every one of them in the body, as it hath pleased him.

19 And if they were all one member, where *were* the body?

20 But now *are they* many members, yet but one body.

21 And the eye cannot say unto the hand, I have no need of thee: nor again the head to the feet, I have no need of you.

22 Nay, much more those members of the body, which seem to be more feeble, are necessary:

23 And those *members* of the body, which we think to be less honourable, upon these we bestow more abundant honour; and our uncomely *parts* have more abundant comeliness.

24 For our comely *parts* have no need: but God hath tempered the body together, having given more abundant honour to that *part* which lacked:

25 That there should be no schism in the body; but *that* the members should have the same care one for another.

26 And whether one member suffer, all the members suffer with it; or one member be honoured, all the members rejoice with it.

27 Now ye are the body of Christ, and members in particular.

28 And God hath set some in the church, first apostles, secondarily prophets, thirdly teachers, after that miracles, then gifts of healings, helps, governments, diversities of tongues.

29 *Are* all apostles? *are* all prophets? *are* all teachers? *are* all workers of miracles?

30 Have all the gifts of healing? do all speak with tongues? do all interpret?

31 But covet earnestly the best gifts: and yet shew I unto you a more excellent way.

Charity Never Fails

13 Though I speak with the tongues of men and of angels, and have not charity, I am become *as* sounding brass, or a tinkling cymbal.

2 And though I have *the gift of* prophecy, and understand all mysteries, and all knowledge; and though I have all faith, so that I could remove mountains, and have not charity, I am nothing.

3 And though I bestow all my goods to feed *the poor,* and though I give my body to be burned, and have not charity, it profiteth me nothing.

4 Charity suffereth long, *and* is kind; charity envieth not; charity vaunteth not itself, is not puffed up,

5 Doth not behave itself unseemly, seeketh not her own, is not easily provoked, thinketh no evil;

6 Rejoiceth not in iniquity, but rejoiceth in the truth;

7 Beareth all things, believeth all things, hopeth all things, endureth all things.

8 Charity never faileth: but whether *there be* prophecies, they shall fail; whether *there be* tongues, they shall cease; whether *there be* knowledge, it shall vanish away.

9 For we know in part, and we prophesy in part.

10 But when that which is perfect is come, then that which is in part shall be done away.

Put Away Childish Things

11 When I was a child, I spake as a child, I understood as a child, I thought as a child: but when I became a man, I put away childish things.

12 For now we see through a glass, darkly; but then face to face: now I know in part; but then shall I know even as also I am known.

13 And now abideth faith, hope, charity, these three; but the greatest of these *is* charity.

The Gift of Tongues

14 Follow after charity, and desire spiritual *gifts,* but rather that ye may prophesy.

2 For he that speaketh in an *unknown* tongue speaketh not unto men, but unto God: for no man understandeth *him;* howbeit in the spirit he speaketh mysteries.

3 But he that prophesieth speaketh unto men *to* edification, and exhortation, and comfort.

4 He that speaketh in an *unknown* tongue edifieth himself; but he that prophesieth edifieth the church.

5 I would that ye all spake with tongues, but rather that ye prophesied: for greater *is* he that prophesieth than he that speaketh with tongues, except he interpret, that the church may receive edifying.

6 Now, brethren, if I come unto you speaking with tongues, what shall I profit you, except I shall speak to you either by revelation, or by knowledge, or by prophesying, or by doctrine?

7 And even things without life giving sound, whether pipe or harp, except they give a distinction in the sounds, how shall it be known what is piped or harped?

8 For if the trumpet give an uncertain sound, who shall prepare himself to the battle?

9 So likewise ye, except ye utter by the tongue words easy to be understood, how shall it be known what is spoken? for ye shall speak into the air.

10 There are, it may be, so many kinds of voices in the world, and none of them *is* without signification.

11 Therefore if I know not the meaning of the voice, I shall be unto him that speaketh a barbarian, and he that speaketh *shall be* a barbarian unto me.

12 Even so ye, forasmuch as ye are zealous of spiritual *gifts,* seek that

ye may excel to the edifying of the
church.

The Gift of Interpretation

13 Wherefore let him that speak-
eth in an *unknown* tongue pray that
he may interpret.
14 For if I pray in an *unknown*
tongue, my spirit prayeth, but my
understanding is unfruitful.
15 What is it then? I will pray with
the spirit, and I will pray with the
understanding also: I will sing with
the spirit, and I will sing with the
understanding also.
16 Else when thou shalt bless with
the spirit, how shall he that occupi-
eth the room of the unlearned say
Amen at thy giving of thanks, seeing
he understandeth not what thou
sayest?
17 For thou verily givest thanks
well, but the other is not edified.
18 I thank my God, I speak with
tongues more than ye all:
19 Yet in the church I had rather
speak five words with my under-
standing, that *by my voice* I might
teach others also, than ten thousand
words in an *unknown* tongue.
20 Brethren, be not children in
understanding: howbeit in malice
be ye children, but in understanding
be men.
21 In the law it is written, With
men of other tongues and other lips
will I speak unto this people; and
yet for all that will they not hear me,
saith the Lord.
22 Wherefore tongues are for
a sign, not to them that believe,
but to them that believe not: but
prophesying *serveth* not for them
that believe not, but for them which
believe.
23 If therefore the whole church
be come together into one place,
and all speak with tongues, and
there come in *those that are* un-
learned, or unbelievers, will they
not say that ye are mad?
24 But if all prophesy, and there
come in one that believeth not, or
one unlearned, he is convinced of
all, he is judged of all:
25 And thus are the secrets of his
heart made manifest; and so falling
down on *his* face he will worship
God, and report that God is in you
of a truth.

The Author of Peace

26 How is it then, brethren? when
ye come together, every one of you
hath a psalm, hath a doctrine, hath
a tongue, hath a revelation, hath
an interpretation. Let all things be
done unto edifying.
27 If any man speak in an *un-
known* tongue, *let it be* by two, or
at the most *by* three, and *that* by
course; and let one interpret.
28 But if there be no interpreter,
let him keep silence in the church;
and let him speak to himself, and to
God.
29 Let the prophets speak two or
three, and let the other judge.
30 If *any thing* be revealed to an-
other that sitteth by, let the first hold
his peace.
31 For ye may all prophesy one by
one, that all may learn, and all may
be comforted.
32 And the spirits of the prophets
are subject to the prophets.
33 For God is not *the author* of
confusion, but of peace, as in all
churches of the saints.
34 Let your women keep silence in
the churches: for it is not permitted
unto them to speak; but *they are
commanded* to be under obedience,
as also saith the law.
35 And if they will learn any thing,
let them ask their husbands at
home: for it is a shame for women
to speak in the church.
36 What? came the word of God
out from you? or came it unto you
only?
37 If any man think himself to

be a prophet, or spiritual, let him
acknowledge that the things that I
write unto you are the command-
ments of the Lord.
38 But if any man be ignorant, let
him be ignorant.
39 Wherefore, brethren, covet to
prophesy, and forbid not to speak
with tongues.
40 Let all things be done decently
and in order.

Witnesses of Christ's Resurrection

15 Moreover, brethren, I declare
unto you the gospel which I
preached unto you, which also
ye have received, and wherein ye
stand;
2 By which also ye are saved, if ye
keep in memory what I preached
unto you, unless ye have believed
in vain.
3 For I delivered unto you first of
all that which I also received, how
that Christ died for our sins accord-
ing to the scriptures;
4 And that he was buried, and that
he rose again the third day accord-
ing to the scriptures:
5 And that he was seen of Cephas,
then of the twelve:
6 After that, he was seen of above
five hundred brethren at once; of
whom the greater part remain unto
this present, but some are fallen
asleep.
7 After that, he was seen of James;
then of all the apostles.
8 And last of all he was seen of me
also, as of one born out of due time.
9 For I am the least of the apostles,
that am not meet to be called an
apostle, because I persecuted the
church of God.
10 But by the grace of God I am
what I am: and his grace which *was*
bestowed upon me was not in vain;
but I laboured more abundantly
than they all: yet not I, but the grace
of God which was with me.
11 Therefore whether *it were* I or
they, so we preach, and so ye be-
lieved.

The Resurrection Defended

12 Now if Christ be preached that
he rose from the dead, how say
some among you that there is no
resurrection of the dead?
13 But if there be no resurrection
of the dead, then is Christ not risen:
14 And if Christ be not risen, then
is our preaching vain, and your faith
is also vain.
15 Yea, and we are found false
witnesses of God; because we have
testified of God that he raised up
Christ: whom he raised not up, if
so be that the dead rise not.
16 For if the dead rise not, then is
not Christ raised:
17 And if Christ be not raised, your
faith *is* vain; ye are yet in your sins.
18 Then they also which are fallen
asleep in Christ are perished.
19 If in this life only we have hope
in Christ, we are of all men most
miserable.
20 But now is Christ risen from the
dead, *and* become the firstfruits of
them that slept.
21 For since by man *came* death,
by man *came* also the resurrection
of the dead.
22 For as in Adam all die, even so
in Christ shall all be made alive.
23 But every man in his own or-
der: Christ the firstfruits; afterward
they that are Christ's at his coming.
24 Then *cometh* the end, when he
shall have delivered up the kingdom
to God, even the Father; when he
shall have put down all rule and all
authority and power.
25 For he must reign, till he hath
put all enemies under his feet.
26 The last enemy *that* shall be
destroyed *is* death.
27 For he hath put all things under
his feet. But when he saith all things
are put under *him, it is* manifest

that he is excepted, which did put
all things under him.
28 And when all things shall be
subdued unto him, then shall the
Son also himself be subject unto
him that put all things under him,
that God may be all in all.
29 Else what shall they do which
are baptized for the dead, if the dead
rise not at all? why are they then
baptized for the dead?
30 And why stand we in jeopardy
every hour?
31 I protest by your rejoicing
which I have in Christ Jesus our
Lord, I die daily.
32 If after the manner of men I
have fought with beasts at Ephesus,
what advantageth it me, if the dead
rise not? let us eat and drink; for to
morrow we die.
33 Be not deceived: evil commu-
nications corrupt good manners.
34 Awake to righteousness, and
sin not; for some have not the
knowledge of God: I speak *this* to
your shame.

The Resurrection Body Explained

35 But some *man* will say, How are
the dead raised up? and with what
body do they come?
36 *Thou* fool, that which thou sow-
est is not quickened, except it die:
37 And that which thou sowest,
thou sowest not that body that shall
be, but bare grain, it may chance of
wheat, or of some other *grain:*
38 But God giveth it a body as it
hath pleased him, and to every seed
his own body.
39 All flesh *is* not the same flesh:
but *there is* one *kind of* flesh of men,
another flesh of beasts, another of
fishes, *and* another of birds.
40 *There are* also celestial bodies,
and bodies terrestrial: but the glory
of the celestial *is* one, and the *glory*
of the terrestrial *is* another.
41 *There is* one glory of the sun,
and another glory of the moon, and
another glory of the stars: for *one*
star differeth from *another* star in
glory.
42 So also *is* the resurrection of
the dead. It is sown in corruption;
it is raised in incorruption:
43 It is sown in dishonour; it is
raised in glory: it is sown in weak-
ness; it is raised in power:
44 It is sown a natural body; it is
raised a spiritual body. There is a
natural body, and there is a spiritual
body.
45 And so it is written, The first
man Adam was made a living soul;
the last Adam *was made* a quicken-
ing spirit.
46 Howbeit that *was* not first
which is spiritual, but that which
is natural; and afterward that which
is spiritual.
47 The first man *is* of the earth,
earthy: the second man *is* the Lord
from heaven.
48 As *is* the earthy, such *are* they
also that are earthy: and as *is* the
heavenly, such *are* they also that
are heavenly.
49 And as we have borne the im-
age of the earthy, we shall also bear
the image of the heavenly.
50 Now this I say, brethren, that
flesh and blood cannot inherit the
kingdom of God; neither doth cor-
ruption inherit incorruption.

Victory over Death

51 Behold, I shew you a mystery;
We shall not all sleep, but we shall
all be changed,
52 In a moment, in the twinkling
of an eye, at the last trump: for the
trumpet shall sound, and the dead
shall be raised incorruptible, and
we shall be changed.
53 For this corruptible must put
on incorruption, and this mortal
must put on immortality.
54 So when this corruptible shall
have put on incorruption, and this

mortal shall have put on immor-
tality, then shall be brought to pass
the saying that is written, Death is
swallowed up in victory.
55 O death, where *is* thy sting?
O grave, where *is* thy victory?
56 The sting of death *is* sin; and
the strength of sin *is* the law.
57 But thanks *be* to God, which
giveth us the victory through our
Lord Jesus Christ.
58 Therefore, my beloved breth-
ren, be ye stedfast, unmoveable,
always abounding in the work of
the Lord, forasmuch as ye know
that your labour is not in vain in
the Lord.

A Collection for the Saints

16 Now concerning the collection
for the saints, as I have given
order to the churches of Galatia,
even so do ye.
2 Upon the first *day* of the week
let every one of you lay by him in
store, as *God* hath prospered him,
that there be no gatherings when I
come.
3 And when I come, whomsoever
ye shall approve by *your* letters,
them will I send to bring your lib-
erality unto Jerusalem.
4 And if it be meet that I go also,
they shall go with me.

Stand Fast in the Faith

5 Now I will come unto you, when
I shall pass through Macedonia: for
I do pass through Macedonia.
6 And it may be that I will abide,
yea, and winter with you, that ye
may bring me on my journey whith-
ersoever I go.
7 For I will not see you now by the
way; but I trust to tarry a while with
you, if the Lord permit.
8 But I will tarry at Ephesus until
Pentecost.
9 For a great door and effectual
is opened unto me, and *there are*
many adversaries.
10 Now if Timotheus come, see
that he may be with you without
fear: for he worketh the work of the
Lord, as I also *do*.
11 Let no man therefore despise
him: but conduct him forth in peace,
that he may come unto me: for I look
for him with the brethren.
12 As touching *our* brother Apol-
los, I greatly desired him to come
unto you with the brethren: but his
will was not at all to come at this
time; but he will come when he shall
have convenient time.
13 Watch ye, stand fast in the faith,
quit you like men, be strong.
14 Let all your things be done with
charity.
15 I beseech you, brethren, (ye
know the house of Stephanas, that
it is the firstfruits of Achaia, and *that*
they have addicted themselves to
the ministry of the saints,)
16 That ye submit yourselves unto
such, and to every one that helpeth
with *us*, and laboureth.
17 I am glad of the coming of
Stephanas and Fortunatus and
Achaicus: for that which was lacking
on your part they have supplied.
18 For they have refreshed my
spirit and yours: therefore acknowl-
edge ye them that are such.

Paul Delivers Salutations

19 The churches of Asia salute you.
Aquila and Priscilla salute you much
in the Lord, with the church that is
in their house.
20 All the brethren greet you.
Greet ye one another with an holy
kiss.
21 The salutation of *me* Paul with
mine own hand.
22 If any man love not the Lord
Jesus Christ, let him be Anathema
Maranatha.
23 The grace of our Lord Jesus
Christ *be* with you.
24 My love *be* with you all in Christ
Jesus. Amen.

The Second Epistle of Paul the Apostle to the CORINTHIANS

Greeting

Paul, an apostle of Jesus Christ
by the will of God, and Timo-
thy *our* brother, unto the church of
God which is at Corinth, with all the
saints which are in all Achaia:
2 Grace *be* to you and peace from
God our Father, and *from* the Lord
Jesus Christ.

The Comfort of God

3 Blessed *be* God, even the Father
of our Lord Jesus Christ, the Father
of mercies, and the God of all com-
fort;
4 Who comforteth us in all our
tribulation, that we may be able
to comfort them which are in any
trouble, by the comfort wherewith
we ourselves are comforted of God.
5 For as the sufferings of Christ
abound in us, so our consolation
also aboundeth by Christ.
6 And whether we be afflicted, *it is*
for your consolation and salvation,
which is effectual in the enduring of
the same sufferings which we also
suffer: or whether we be comforted,
it is for your consolation and salva-
tion.
7 And our hope of you *is* stedfast,
knowing, that as ye are partakers of
the sufferings, so *shall ye be* also of
the consolation.

Deliverance from Suffering and Death

8 For we would not, brethren,
have you ignorant of our trouble
which came to us in Asia, that
we were pressed out of measure,
above strength, insomuch that we
despaired even of life:
9 But we had the sentence of
death in ourselves, that we should
not trust in ourselves, but in God
which raiseth the dead:
10 Who delivered us from so great
a death, and doth deliver: in whom
we trust that he will yet deliver *us;*
11 Ye also helping together by
prayer for us, that for the gift *be-
stowed* upon us by the means of
many persons thanks may be given
by many on our behalf.

Simplicity and Godly Sincerity

12 For our rejoicing is this, the
testimony of our conscience, that
in simplicity and godly sincerity,
not with fleshly wisdom, but by the
grace of God, we have had our con-
versation in the world, and more
abundantly to you-ward.
13 For we write none other things
unto you, than what ye read or ac-
knowledge; and I trust ye shall ac-
knowledge even to the end;
14 As also ye have acknowledged
us in part, that we are your rejoicing,
even as ye also *are* ours in the day
of the Lord Jesus.
15 And in this confidence I was
minded to come unto you before,
that ye might have a second ben-
efit;
16 And to pass by you into Mac-
edonia, and to come again out of
Macedonia unto you, and of you

to be brought on my way toward
Judaea.
17 When I therefore was thus
minded, did I use lightness? or the
things that I purpose, do I purpose
according to the flesh, that with me
there should be yea yea, and nay
nay?
18 But *as* God *is* true, our word
toward you was not yea and nay.
19 For the Son of God, Jesus Christ,
who was preached among you by
us, *even* by me and Silvanus and
Timotheus, was not yea and nay,
but in him was yea.
20 For all the promises of God in
him *are* yea, and in him Amen, unto
the glory of God by us.
21 Now he which stablisheth
us with you in Christ, and hath
anointed us, *is* God;
22 Who hath also sealed us, and
given the earnest of the Spirit in our
hearts.
23 Moreover I call God for a record
upon my soul, that to spare you I
came not as yet unto Corinth.
24 Not for that we have dominion
over your faith, but are helpers of
your joy: for by faith ye stand.

Paul's Love for the Corinthian Church

2 But I determined this with my-
self, that I would not come again
to you in heaviness.
2 For if I make you sorry, who
is he then that maketh me glad,
but the same which is made sorry
by me?
3 And I wrote this same unto you,
lest, when I came, I should have sor-
row from them of whom I ought to
rejoice; having confidence in you all,
that my joy is *the joy* of you all.
4 For out of much affliction and
anguish of heart I wrote unto you
with many tears; not that ye should
be grieved, but that ye might know
the love which I have more abun-
dantly unto you.

Forgiveness and Comfort

5 But if any have caused grief, he
hath not grieved me, but in part:
that I may not overcharge you all.
6 Sufficient to such a man *is* this
punishment, which *was inflicted* of
many.
7 So that contrariwise ye *ought*
rather to forgive *him,* and comfort
him, lest perhaps such a one should
be swallowed up with overmuch
sorrow.
8 Wherefore I beseech you that
ye would confirm *your* love toward
him.
9 For to this end also did I write,
that I might know the proof of
you, whether ye be obedient in all
things.
10 To whom ye forgive any thing,
I *forgive* also: for if I forgave any
thing, to whom I forgave *it,* for your
sakes *forgave I it* in the person of
Christ;
11 Lest Satan should get an advan-
tage of us: for we are not ignorant
of his devices.

The Savour of Life and Death

12 Furthermore, when I came to
Troas to *preach* Christ's gospel, and
a door was opened unto me of the
Lord,
13 I had no rest in my spirit, be-
cause I found not Titus my brother:
but taking my leave of them, I went
from thence into Macedonia.
14 Now thanks *be* unto God, which
always causeth us to triumph in
Christ, and maketh manifest the
savour of his knowledge by us in
every place.
15 For we are unto God a sweet
savour of Christ, in them that are
saved, and in them that perish:
16 To the one *we are* the savour of
death unto death; and to the other
the savour of life unto life. And who
is sufficient for these things?
17 For we are not as many, which
corrupt the word of God: but as of

sincerity, but as of God, in the sight
of God speak we in Christ.

Ministers of the New Testament

3 Do we begin again to commend
ourselves? or need we, as some
others, epistles of commendation
to you, or *letters* of commendation
from you?
2 Ye are our epistle written in our
hearts, known and read of all men:
3 *Forasmuch as ye are* manifestly
declared to be the epistle of Christ
ministered by us, written not with
ink, but with the Spirit of the living
God; not in tables of stone, but in
fleshy tables of the heart.
4 And such trust have we through
Christ to God-ward:
5 Not that we are sufficient of
ourselves to think any thing as of
ourselves; but our sufficiency *is* of
God;
6 Who also hath made us able
ministers of the new testament;
not of the letter, but of the spirit:
for the letter killeth, but the spirit
giveth life.

The Glory of the Lord

7 But if the ministration of death,
written *and* engraven in stones, was
glorious, so that the children of Is-
rael could not stedfastly behold the
face of Moses for the glory of his
countenance; which *glory* was to
be done away:
8 How shall not the ministration
of the spirit be rather glorious?
9 For if the ministration of con-
demnation *be* glory, much more
doth the ministration of righteous-
ness exceed in glory.
10 For even that which was made
glorious had no glory in this respect,
by reason of the glory that excelleth.
11 For if that which is done away
was glorious, much more that which
remaineth *is* glorious.
12 Seeing then that we have such
hope, we use great plainness of
speech:
13 And not as Moses, *which* put a
vail over his face, that the children
of Israel could not stedfastly look to
the end of that which is abolished:
14 But their minds were blinded:
for until this day remaineth the
same vail untaken away in the read-
ing of the old testament; which *vail*
is done away in Christ.
15 But even unto this day, when
Moses is read, the vail is upon their
heart.
16 Nevertheless when it shall turn
to the Lord, the vail shall be taken
away.
17 Now the Lord is that Spirit: and
where the Spirit of the Lord *is,* there
is liberty.
18 But we all, with open face be-
holding as in a glass the glory of the
Lord, are changed into the same
image from glory to glory, *even* as
by the Spirit of the Lord.

Preaching Christ Jesus the Lord

4 Therefore seeing we have this
ministry, as we have received
mercy, we faint not;
2 But have renounced the hidden
things of dishonesty, not walking in
craftiness, nor handling the word of
God deceitfully; but by manifesta-
tion of the truth commending our-
selves to every man's conscience in
the sight of God.
3 But if our gospel be hid, it is hid
to them that are lost:
4 In whom the god of this world
hath blinded the minds of them
which believe not, lest the light of
the glorious gospel of Christ, who
is the image of God, should shine
unto them.
5 For we preach not ourselves, but
Christ Jesus the Lord; and ourselves
your servants for Jesus' sake.
6 For God, who commanded the
light to shine out of darkness, hath

shined in our hearts, to *give* the light
of the knowledge of the glory of God
in the face of Jesus Christ.
7 But we have this treasure in
earthen vessels, that the excellency
of the power may be of God, and not
of us.

Cast Down but Not Destroyed

8 *We are* troubled on every side,
yet not distressed; *we are* perplexed,
but not in despair;
9 Persecuted, but not forsaken;
cast down, but not destroyed;
10 Always bearing about in the
body the dying of the Lord Jesus,
that the life also of Jesus might be
made manifest in our body.
11 For we which live are alway de-
livered unto death for Jesus' sake,
that the life also of Jesus might be
made manifest in our mortal flesh.
12 So then death worketh in us,
but life in you.
13 We having the same spirit of
faith, according as it is written, I
believed, and therefore have I spo-
ken; we also believe, and therefore
speak;
14 Knowing that he which raised
up the Lord Jesus shall raise up us
also by Jesus, and shall present *us*
with you.
15 For all things *are* for your sakes,
that the abundant grace might
through the thanksgiving of many
redound to the glory of God.
16 For which cause we faint not;
but though our outward man perish,
yet the inward *man* is renewed day
by day.
17 For our light affliction, which
is but for a moment, worketh for
us a far more exceeding *and* eternal
weight of glory;
18 While we look not at the things
which are seen, but at the things
which are not seen: for the things
which are seen *are* temporal; but
the things which are not seen *are*
eternal.

An Eternal Building in the Heavens

5 For we know that if our earthly
house of *this* tabernacle were
dissolved, we have a building of God,
an house not made with hands, eter-
nal in the heavens.
2 For in this we groan, earnestly
desiring to be clothed upon with
our house which is from heaven:
3 If so be that being clothed we
shall not be found naked.
4 For we that are in *this* tabernacle
do groan, being burdened: not for
that we would be unclothed, but
clothed upon, that mortality might
be swallowed up of life.
5 Now he that hath wrought us
for the selfsame thing *is* God, who
also hath given unto us the earnest
of the Spirit.
6 Therefore *we are* always confi-
dent, knowing that, whilst we are
at home in the body, we are absent
from the Lord:
7 (For we walk by faith, not by
sight:)
8 We are confident, *I say,* and
willing rather to be absent from
the body, and to be present with
the Lord.
9 Wherefore we labour, that,
whether present or absent, we may
be accepted of him.
10 For we must all appear before
the judgment seat of Christ; that
every one may receive the things
done in *his* body, according to that
he hath done, whether *it be* good or
bad.

The Constraining Love of Christ

11 Knowing therefore the terror
of the Lord, we persuade men; but
we are made manifest unto God;
and I trust also are made manifest
in your consciences.
12 For we commend not ourselves
again unto you, but give you occa-
sion to glory on our behalf, that ye

may have somewhat to *answer* them which glory in appearance, and not in heart.

13 For whether we be beside ourselves, *it is* to God: or whether we be sober, *it is* for your cause.

14 For the love of Christ constraineth us; because we thus judge, that if one died for all, then were all dead:

15 And *that* he died for all, that they which live should not henceforth live unto themselves, but unto him which died for them, and rose again.

16 Wherefore henceforth know we no man after the flesh: yea, though we have known Christ after the flesh, yet now henceforth know we *him* no more.

A New Creature in Christ

17 Therefore if any man *be* in Christ, *he is* a new creature: old things are passed away; behold, all things are become new.

18 And all things *are* of God, who hath reconciled us to himself by Jesus Christ, and hath given to us the ministry of reconciliation;

19 To wit, that God was in Christ, reconciling the world unto himself, not imputing their trespasses unto them; and hath committed unto us the word of reconciliation.

20 Now then we are ambassadors for Christ, as though God did beseech *you* by us: we pray *you* in Christ's stead, be ye reconciled to God.

21 For he hath made him *to be* sin for us, who knew no sin; that we might be made the righteousness of God in him.

The Day of Salvation

6 We then, *as* workers together *with him*, beseech *you* also that ye receive not the grace of God in vain.

2 (For he saith, I have heard thee in a time accepted, and in the day of salvation have I succoured thee: behold, now *is* the accepted time; behold, now *is* the day of salvation.)

Give No Offence in Any Thing

3 Giving no offence in any thing, that the ministry be not blamed:

4 But in all *things* approving ourselves as the ministers of God, in much patience, in afflictions, in necessities, in distresses,

5 In stripes, in imprisonments, in tumults, in labours, in watchings, in fastings;

6 By pureness, by knowledge, by longsuffering, by kindness, by the Holy Ghost, by love unfeigned,

7 By the word of truth, by the power of God, by the armour of righteousness on the right hand and on the left,

8 By honour and dishonour, by evil report and good report: as deceivers, and *yet* true;

9 As unknown, and *yet* well known; as dying, and, behold, we live; as chastened, and not killed;

10 As sorrowful, yet alway rejoicing; as poor, yet making many rich; as having nothing, and *yet* possessing all things.

11 O *ye* Corinthians, our mouth is open unto you, our heart is enlarged.

12 Ye are not straitened in us, but ye are straitened in your own bowels.

13 Now for a recompence in the same, (I speak as unto *my* children,) be ye also enlarged.

Be Not Unequally Yoked

14 Be ye not unequally yoked together with unbelievers: for what fellowship hath righteousness with unrighteousness? and what communion hath light with darkness?

15 And what concord hath Christ with Belial? or what part hath he that believeth with an infidel?

16 And what agreement hath the temple of God with idols? for ye are the temple of the living God; as God hath said, I will dwell in them, and walk in *them;* and I will be their God, and they shall be my people.

17 Wherefore come out from among them, and be ye separate, saith the Lord, and touch not the unclean *thing;* and I will receive you,

18 And will be a Father unto you, and ye shall be my sons and daughters, saith the Lord Almighty.

Joyful in Tribulation

7 Having therefore these promises, dearly beloved, let us cleanse ourselves from all filthiness of the flesh and spirit, perfecting holiness in the fear of God.

2 Receive us; we have wronged no man, we have corrupted no man, we have defrauded no man.

3 I speak not *this* to condemn *you:* for I have said before, that ye are in our hearts to die and live with *you.*

4 Great *is* my boldness of speech toward you, great *is* my glorying of you: I am filled with comfort, I am exceeding joyful in all our tribulation.

5 For, when we were come into Macedonia, our flesh had no rest, but we were troubled on every side; without *were* fightings, within *were* fears.

6 Nevertheless God, that comforteth those that are cast down, comforted us by the coming of Titus;

7 And not by his coming only, but by the consolation wherewith he was comforted in you, when he told us your earnest desire, your mourning, your fervent mind toward me; so that I rejoiced the more.

8 For though I made you sorry with a letter, I do not repent, though I did repent: for I perceive that the same epistle hath made you sorry, though *it were* but for a season.

Godly Sorrow

9 Now I rejoice, not that ye were made sorry, but that ye sorrowed to repentance: for ye were made sorry after a godly manner, that ye might receive damage by us in nothing.

10 For godly sorrow worketh repentance to salvation not to be repented of: but the sorrow of the world worketh death.

11 For behold this selfsame thing, that ye sorrowed after a godly sort, what carefulness it wrought in you, yea, *what* clearing of yourselves, yea, *what* indignation, yea, *what* fear, yea, *what* vehement desire, yea, *what* zeal, yea, *what* revenge! In all *things* ye have approved yourselves to be clear in this matter.

12 Wherefore, though I wrote unto you, *I did it* not for his cause that had done the wrong, nor for his cause that suffered wrong, but that our care for you in the sight of God might appear unto you.

13 Therefore we were comforted in your comfort: yea, and exceedingly the more joyed we for the joy of Titus, because his spirit was refreshed by you all.

14 For if I have boasted any thing to him of you, I am not ashamed; but as we spake all things to you in truth, even so our boasting, which *I made* before Titus, is found a truth.

15 And his inward affection is more abundant toward you, whilst he remembereth the obedience of you all, how with fear and trembling ye received him.

16 I rejoice therefore that I have confidence in you in all *things.*

Macedonians an Example of Giving

8 Moreover, brethren, we do you to wit of the grace of God bestowed on the churches of Macedonia;

2 How that in a great trial of affliction the abundance of their joy and their deep poverty abounded

unto the riches of their liberality.
3 For to *their* power, I bear record,
yea, and beyond *their* power *they
were* willing of themselves;
4 Praying us with much intreaty
that we would receive the gift, and
take upon us the fellowship of the
ministering to the saints.
5 And *this they did,* not as we
hoped, but first gave their own
selves to the Lord, and unto us by
the will of God.
6 Insomuch that we desired Titus,
that as he had begun, so he would
also finish in you the same grace
also.
7 Therefore, as ye abound in every
thing, in faith, and utterance, and
knowledge, and *in* all diligence, and
in your love to us, *see* that ye abound
in this grace also.
8 I speak not by commandment,
but by occasion of the forwardness
of others, and to prove the sincerity
of your love.
9 For ye know the grace of our
Lord Jesus Christ, that, though
he was rich, yet for your sakes he
became poor, that ye through his
poverty might be rich.
10 And herein I give *my* advice:
for this is expedient for you, who
have begun before, not only to do,
but also to be forward a year ago.
11 Now therefore perform the do-
ing *of it;* that as *there was* a readi-
ness to will, so *there may be* a per-
formance also out of that which ye
have.
12 For if there be first a willing
mind, *it is* accepted according to
that a man hath, *and* not according
to that he hath not.
13 For *I mean* not that other men
be eased, and ye burdened:
14 But by an equality, *that* now at
this time your abundance *may be
a supply* for their want, that their
abundance also may be *a supply*
for your want: that there may be
equality:
15 As it is written, He that *had
gathered* much had nothing over;
and he that *had gathered* little had
no lack.

*Titus's Love
for the Corinthian Church*

16 But thanks *be* to God, which
put the same earnest care into the
heart of Titus for you.
17 For indeed he accepted the ex-
hortation; but being more forward,
of his own accord he went unto you.
18 And we have sent with him the
brother, whose praise *is* in the gos-
pel throughout all the churches;
19 And not *that* only, but who was
also chosen of the churches to travel
with us with this grace, which is
administered by us to the glory of
the same Lord, and *declaration of*
your ready mind:
20 Avoiding this, that no man
should blame us in this abundance
which is administered by us:
21 Providing for honest things,
not only in the sight of the Lord,
but also in the sight of men.
22 And we have sent with them
our brother, whom we have of-
tentimes proved diligent in many
things, but now much more diligent,
upon the great confidence which *I
have* in you.
23 Whether *any do enquire* of
Titus, *he is* my partner and fel-
lowhelper concerning you: or our
brethren *be enquired of, they are*
the messengers of the churches,
and the glory of Christ.
24 Wherefore shew ye to them,
and before the churches, the proof
of your love, and of our boasting on
your behalf.

Ministry to the Saints

9 For as touching the ministering
to the saints, it is superfluous
for me to write to you:
2 For I know the forwardness of
your mind, for which I boast of you

to them of Macedonia, that Achaia
was ready a year ago; and your zeal
hath provoked very many.
3 Yet have I sent the brethren, lest
our boasting of you should be in vain
in this behalf; that, as I said, ye may
be ready:
4 Lest haply if they of Macedo-
nia come with me, and find you
unprepared, we (that we say not,
ye) should be ashamed in this same
confident boasting.

God Loves a Cheerful Giver

5 Therefore I thought it neces-
sary to exhort the brethren, that
they would go before unto you, and
make up beforehand your bounty,
whereof ye had notice before, that
the same might be ready, as *a matter
of* bounty, and not as *of* covetous-
ness.
6 But this *I say,* He which soweth
sparingly shall reap also sparingly;
and he which soweth bountifully
shall reap also bountifully.
7 Every man according as he pur-
poseth in his heart, *so let him give;*
not grudgingly, or of necessity: for
God loveth a cheerful giver.
8 And God *is* able to make all grace
abound toward you; that ye, always
having all sufficiency in all *things,*
may abound to every good work:
9 (As it is written, He hath dis-
persed abroad; he hath given to the
poor: his righteousness remaineth
for ever.
10 Now he that ministereth seed
to the sower both minister bread
for *your* food, and multiply your
seed sown, and increase the fruits
of your righteousness;)
11 Being enriched in every thing
to all bountifulness, which causeth
through us thanksgiving to God.
12 For the administration of this
service not only supplieth the want
of the saints, but is abundant also
by many thanksgivings unto God;
13 Whiles by the experiment of
this ministration they glorify God
for your professed subjection unto
the gospel of Christ, and for *your*
liberal distribution unto them, and
unto all *men;*
14 And by their prayer for you,
which long after you for the exceed-
ing grace of God in you.
15 Thanks *be* unto God for his un-
speakable gift.

Mighty Weapons of Warfare

10 Now I Paul myself beseech
you by the meekness and gen-
tleness of Christ, who in presence
am base among you, but being ab-
sent am bold toward you:
2 But I beseech *you,* that I may not
be bold when I am present with that
confidence, wherewith I think to be
bold against some, which think of
us as if we walked according to the
flesh.
3 For though we walk in the flesh,
we do not war after the flesh:
4 (For the weapons of our warfare
are not carnal, but mighty through
God to the pulling down of strong
holds;)
5 Casting down imaginations,
and every high thing that exalteth
itself against the knowledge of God,
and bringing into captivity every
thought to the obedience of Christ;
6 And having in a readiness to re-
venge all disobedience, when your
obedience is fulfilled.
7 Do ye look on things after the
outward appearance? If any man
trust to himself that he is Christ's,
let him of himself think this again,
that, as he *is* Christ's, even so *are*
we Christ's.
8 For though I should boast some-
what more of our authority, which
the Lord hath given us for edifica-
tion, and not for your destruction,
I should not be ashamed:
9 That I may not seem as if I would
terrify you by letters.
10 For *his* letters, say they, *are*

weighty and powerful; but *his* bodily presence *is* weak, and *his* speech contemptible.

11 Let such an one think this, that, such as we are in word by letters when we are absent, such *will we be* also in deed when we are present.

God's Rule of Measure

12 For we dare not make ourselves of the number, or compare ourselves with some that commend themselves: but they measuring themselves by themselves, and comparing themselves among themselves, are not wise.

13 But we will not boast of things without *our* measure, but according to the measure of the rule which God hath distributed to us, a measure to reach even unto you.

14 For we stretch not ourselves beyond *our measure,* as though we reached not unto you: for we are come as far as to you also in *preaching* the gospel of Christ:

15 Not boasting of things without *our* measure, *that is,* of other men's labours; but having hope, when your faith is increased, that we shall be enlarged by you according to our rule abundantly,

16 To preach the gospel in the *regions* beyond you, *and* not to boast in another man's line of things made ready to our hand.

17 But he that glorieth, let him glory in the Lord.

18 For not he that commendeth himself is approved, but whom the Lord commendeth.

Guard Against False Preaching

11 Would to God ye could bear with me a little in *my* folly: and indeed bear with me.

2 For I am jealous over you with godly jealousy: for I have espoused you to one husband, that I may present *you as* a chaste virgin to Christ.

3 But I fear, lest by any means, as the serpent beguiled Eve through his subtilty, so your minds should be corrupted from the simplicity that is in Christ.

4 For if he that cometh preacheth another Jesus, whom we have not preached, or *if* ye receive another spirit, which ye have not received, or another gospel, which ye have not accepted, ye might well bear with *him.*

5 For I suppose I was not a whit behind the very chiefest apostles.

6 But though *I be* rude in speech, yet not in knowledge; but we have been throughly made manifest among you in all things.

7 Have I committed an offence in abasing myself that ye might be exalted, because I have preached to you the gospel of God freely?

8 I robbed other churches, taking wages *of them,* to do you service.

9 And when I was present with you, and wanted, I was chargeable to no man: for that which was lacking to me the brethren which came from Macedonia supplied: and in all *things* I have kept myself from being burdensome unto you, and *so* will I keep *myself.*

10 As the truth of Christ is in me, no man shall stop me of this boasting in the regions of Achaia.

11 Wherefore? because I love you not? God knoweth.

12 But what I do, that I will do, that I may cut off occasion from them which desire occasion; that wherein they glory, they may be found even as we.

13 For such *are* false apostles, deceitful workers, transforming themselves into the apostles of Christ.

14 And no marvel; for Satan himself is transformed into an angel of light.

15 Therefore *it is* no great thing if his ministers also be transformed as the ministers of righteousness;

whose end shall be according to
their works.

Suffering for the Lord's Glory

16 I say again, Let no man think
me a fool; if otherwise, yet as a fool
receive me, that I may boast myself
a little.
17 That which I speak, I speak *it*
not after the Lord, but as it were
foolishly, in this confidence of
boasting.
18 Seeing that many glory after
the flesh, I will glory also.
19 For ye suffer fools gladly, seeing
ye *yourselves* are wise.
20 For ye suffer, if a man bring you
into bondage, if a man devour *you,*
if a man take *of you,* if a man exalt
himself, if a man smite you on the
face.
21 I speak as concerning reproach,
as though we had been weak. How-
beit whereinsoever any is bold, (I
speak foolishly,) I am bold also.
22 Are they Hebrews? so *am* I. Are
they Israelites? so *am* I. Are they the
seed of Abraham? so *am* I.
23 Are they ministers of Christ?
(I speak as a fool) I *am* more; in la-
bours more abundant, in stripes
above measure, in prisons more
frequent, in deaths oft.
24 Of the Jews five times received
I forty *stripes* save one.
25 Thrice was I beaten with rods,
once was I stoned, thrice I suffered
shipwreck, a night and a day I have
been in the deep;
26 *In* journeyings often, in perils
of waters, *in* perils of robbers, *in*
perils by *mine own* countrymen,
in perils by the heathen, *in* perils in
the city, *in* perils in the wilderness,
in perils in the sea, *in* perils among
false brethren;
27 In weariness and painfulness,
in watchings often, in hunger and
thirst, in fastings often, in cold and
nakedness.
28 Beside those things that are
without, that which cometh upon
me daily, the care of all the churches.
29 Who is weak, and I am not
weak? who is offended, and I burn
not?
30 If I must needs glory, I will
glory of the things which concern
mine infirmities.
31 The God and Father of our Lord
Jesus Christ, which is blessed for
evermore, knoweth that I lie not.
32 In Damascus the governor un-
der Aretas the king kept the city of
the Damascenes with a garrison,
desirous to apprehend me:
33 And through a window in a
basket was I let down by the wall,
and escaped his hands.

Paul's Vision of Paradise

12 It is not expedient for me
doubtless to glory. I will
come to visions and revelations of
the Lord.
2 I knew a man in Christ above
fourteen years ago, (whether in
the body, I cannot tell; or whether
out of the body, I cannot tell: God
knoweth;) such an one caught up
to the third heaven.
3 And I knew such a man,
(whether in the body, or out of the
body, I cannot tell: God knoweth;)
4 How that he was caught up into
paradise, and heard unspeakable
words, which it is not lawful for a
man to utter.
5 Of such an one will I glory: yet of
myself I will not glory, but in mine
infirmities.
6 For though I would desire to
glory, I shall not be a fool; for I will
say the truth: but *now* I forbear, lest
any man should think of me above
that which he seeth me *to be,* or *that*
he heareth of me.

Paul's Thorn in the Flesh

7 And lest I should be exalted
above measure through the abun-
dance of the revelations, there was

given to me a thorn in the flesh, the
messenger of Satan to buffet me, lest
I should be exalted above measure.
8 For this thing I besought the
Lord thrice, that it might depart
from me.
9 And he said unto me, My grace is
sufficient for thee: for my strength
is made perfect in weakness. Most
gladly therefore will I rather glory
in my infirmities, that the power of
Christ may rest upon me.
10 Therefore I take pleasure in
infirmities, in reproaches, in ne-
cessities, in persecutions, in dis-
tresses for Christ's sake: for when
I am weak, then am I strong.

The Signs of an Apostle

11 I am become a fool in glorying;
ye have compelled me: for I ought to
have been commended of you: for in
nothing am I behind the very chief-
est apostles, though I be nothing.
12 Truly the signs of an apostle
were wrought among you in all pa-
tience, in signs, and wonders, and
mighty deeds.
13 For what is it wherein ye were
inferior to other churches, except
it be that I myself was not burden-
some to you? forgive me this wrong.

Paul's Love for the Church

14 Behold, the third time I am
ready to come to you; and I will not
be burdensome to you: for I seek
not yours, but you: for the children
ought not to lay up for the parents,
but the parents for the children.
15 And I will very gladly spend and
be spent for you; though the more
abundantly I love you, the less I be
loved.
16 But be it so, I did not burden
you: nevertheless, being crafty, I
caught you with guile.
17 Did I make a gain of you by any
of them whom I sent unto you?
18 I desired Titus, and with *him*
I sent a brother. Did Titus make a
gain of you? walked we not in the
same spirit? *walked we* not in the
same steps?
19 Again, think ye that we excuse
ourselves unto you? we speak before
God in Christ: but *we do* all things,
dearly beloved, for your edifying.
20 For I fear, lest, when I come, I
shall not find you such as I would,
and *that* I shall be found unto you
such as ye would not: lest *there be*
debates, envyings, wraths, strifes,
backbitings, whisperings, swellings,
tumults:
21 *And* lest, when I come again,
my God will humble me among
you, and *that* I shall bewail many
which have sinned already, and have
not repented of the uncleanness
and fornication and lasciviousness
which they have committed.

Examine Yourselves

13 This *is* the third *time* I am
coming to you. In the mouth
of two or three witnesses shall every
word be established.
2 I told you before, and foretell
you, as if I were present, the sec-
ond time; and being absent now
I write to them which heretofore
have sinned, and to all other, that,
if I come again, I will not spare:
3 Since ye seek a proof of Christ
speaking in me, which to you-ward
is not weak, but is mighty in you.
4 For though he was crucified
through weakness, yet he liveth by
the power of God. For we also are
weak in him, but we shall live with
him by the power of God toward you.
5 Examine yourselves, whether
ye be in the faith; prove your own
selves. Know ye not your own
selves, how that Jesus Christ is in
you, except ye be reprobates?
6 But I trust that ye shall know
that we are not reprobates.
7 Now I pray to God that ye do no
evil; not that we should appear ap-
proved, but that ye should do that

which is honest, though we be as
reprobates.
8 For we can do nothing against
the truth, but for the truth.
9 For we are glad, when we are
weak, and ye are strong: and this
also we wish, *even* your perfection.
10 Therefore I write these things
being absent, lest being present I
should use sharpness, according
to the power which the Lord hath
given me to edification, and not to
destruction.

Live in Peace

11 Finally, brethren, farewell. Be
perfect, be of good comfort, be of
one mind, live in peace; and the
God of love and peace shall be with
you.
12 Greet one another with an holy
kiss.
13 All the saints salute you.
14 The grace of the Lord Jesus
Christ, and the love of God, and the
communion of the Holy Ghost, *be*
with you all. Amen.

The Epistle of Paul the Apostle to the GALATIANS

Salutation

Paul, an apostle, (not of men, neither by man, but by Jesus Christ, and God the Father, who raised him from the dead;)

2 And all the brethren which are with me, unto the churches of Galatia:

3 Grace *be* to you and peace from God the Father, and *from* our Lord Jesus Christ,

4 Who gave himself for our sins, that he might deliver us from this present evil world, according to the will of God and our Father:

5 To whom *be* glory for ever and ever. Amen.

Pervert Not the Gospel

6 I marvel that ye are so soon removed from him that called you into the grace of Christ unto another gospel:

7 Which is not another; but there be some that trouble you, and would pervert the gospel of Christ.

8 But though we, or an angel from heaven, preach any other gospel unto you than that which we have preached unto you, let him be accursed.

9 As we said before, so say I now again, If any *man* preach any other gospel unto you than that ye have received, let him be accursed.

10 For do I now persuade men, or God? or do I seek to please men? for if I yet pleased men, I should not be the servant of Christ.

The Revelation of Jesus Christ

11 But I certify you, brethren, that the gospel which was preached of me is not after man.

12 For I neither received it of man, neither was I taught *it,* but by the revelation of Jesus Christ.

13 For ye have heard of my conversation in time past in the Jews' religion, how that beyond measure I persecuted the church of God, and wasted it:

14 And profited in the Jews' religion above many my equals in mine own nation, being more exceedingly zealous of the traditions of my fathers.

15 But when it pleased God, who separated me from my mother's womb, and called *me* by his grace,

16 To reveal his Son in me, that I might preach him among the heathen; immediately I conferred not with flesh and blood:

17 Neither went I up to Jerusalem to them which were apostles before me; but I went into Arabia, and returned again unto Damascus.

18 Then after three years I went up to Jerusalem to see Peter, and abode with him fifteen days.

19 But other of the apostles saw I none, save James the Lord's brother.

20 Now the things which I write unto you, behold, before God, I lie not.

21 Afterwards I came into the regions of Syria and Cilicia;

22 And was unknown by face unto

the churches of Judaea which were in Christ:

23 But they had heard only, That he which persecuted us in times past now preacheth the faith which once he destroyed.

24 And they glorified God in me.

The Gospel of the Uncircumcision

2 Then fourteen years after I went up again to Jerusalem with Barnabas, and took Titus with *me* also.

2 And I went up by revelation, and communicated unto them that gospel which I preach among the Gentiles, but privately to them which were of reputation, lest by any means I should run, or had run, in vain.

3 But neither Titus, who was with me, being a Greek, was compelled to be circumcised:

4 And that because of false brethren unawares brought in, who came in privily to spy out our liberty which we have in Christ Jesus, that they might bring us into bondage:

5 To whom we gave place by subjection, no, not for an hour; that the truth of the gospel might continue with you.

6 But of these who seemed to be somewhat, (whatsoever they were, it maketh no matter to me: God accepteth no man's person:) for they who seemed *to be somewhat* in conference added nothing to me:

7 But contrariwise, when they saw that the gospel of the uncircumcision was committed unto me, as *the gospel* of the circumcision *was* unto Peter;

8 (For he that wrought effectually in Peter to the apostleship of the circumcision, the same was mighty in me toward the Gentiles:)

9 And when James, Cephas, and John, who seemed to be pillars, perceived the grace that was given unto me, they gave to me and Barnabas the right hands of fellowship; that we *should go* unto the heathen, and they unto the circumcision.

10 Only *they would* that we should remember the poor; the same which I also was forward to do.

Paul's Charge Against Peter

11 But when Peter was come to Antioch, I withstood him to the face, because he was to be blamed.

12 For before that certain came from James, he did eat with the Gentiles: but when they were come, he withdrew and separated himself, fearing them which were of the circumcision.

13 And the other Jews dissembled likewise with him; insomuch that Barnabas also was carried away with their dissimulation.

14 But when I saw that they walked not uprightly according to the truth of the gospel, I said unto Peter before *them* all, If thou, being a Jew, livest after the manner of Gentiles, and not as do the Jews, why compellest thou the Gentiles to live as do the Jews?

15 We *who are* Jews by nature, and not sinners of the Gentiles,

16 Knowing that a man is not justified by the works of the law, but by the faith of Jesus Christ, even we have believed in Jesus Christ, that we might be justified by the faith of Christ, and not by the works of the law: for by the works of the law shall no flesh be justified.

17 But if, while we seek to be justified by Christ, we ourselves also are found sinners, *is* therefore Christ the minister of sin? God forbid.

18 For if I build again the things which I destroyed, I make myself a transgressor.

19 For I through the law am dead to the law, that I might live unto God.

20 I am crucified with Christ: nevertheless I live; yet not I, but Christ

liveth in me: and the life which I
now live in the flesh I live by the
faith of the Son of God, who loved
me, and gave himself for me.
21 I do not frustrate the grace of
God: for if righteousness *come* by
the law, then Christ is dead in vain.

The Just Shall Live by Faith

3 O foolish Galatians, who hath
bewitched you, that ye should
not obey the truth, before whose
eyes Jesus Christ hath been evi-
dently set forth, crucified among
you?
2 This only would I learn of you,
Received ye the Spirit by the works
of the law, or by the hearing of faith?
3 Are ye so foolish? having begun
in the Spirit, are ye now made per-
fect by the flesh?
4 Have ye suffered so many things
in vain? if *it be* yet in vain.
5 He therefore that ministereth to
you the Spirit, and worketh mira-
cles among you, *doeth he it* by the
works of the law, or by the hearing
of faith?
6 Even as Abraham believed God,
and it was accounted to him for
righteousness.
7 Know ye therefore that they
which are of faith, the same are the
children of Abraham.
8 And the scripture, foreseeing
that God would justify the heathen
through faith, preached before the
gospel unto Abraham, *saying,* In
thee shall all nations be blessed.
9 So then they which be of faith
are blessed with faithful Abraham.
10 For as many as are of the works
of the law are under the curse: for it
is written, Cursed *is* every one that
continueth not in all things which
are written in the book of the law to
do them.
11 But that no man is justified by
the law in the sight of God, *it is* evi-
dent: for, The just shall live by faith.
12 And the law is not of faith: but,
The man that doeth them shall live
in them.
13 Christ hath redeemed us from
the curse of the law, being made a
curse for us: for it is written, Cursed
is every one that hangeth on a tree:
14 That the blessing of Abraham
might come on the Gentiles through
Jesus Christ; that we might receive
the promise of the Spirit through
faith.

The Covenant Confirmed in Christ

15 Brethren, I speak after the
manner of men; Though *it be* but
a man's covenant, yet *if it be* con-
firmed, no man disannulleth, or
addeth thereto.
16 Now to Abraham and his seed
were the promises made. He saith
not, And to seeds, as of many; but
as of one, And to thy seed, which is
Christ.
17 And this I say, *that* the cov-
enant, that was confirmed before
of God in Christ, the law, which was
four hundred and thirty years after,
cannot disannul, that it should make
the promise of none effect.
18 For if the inheritance *be* of the
law, *it is* no more of promise: but
God gave *it* to Abraham by promise.
19 Wherefore then *serveth* the law?
It was added because of transgres-
sions, till the seed should come to
whom the promise was made; *and it
was* ordained by angels in the hand
of a mediator.
20 Now a mediator is not *a medi-
ator* of one, but God is one.
21 *Is* the law then against the
promises of God? God forbid: for if
there had been a law given which
could have given life, verily righ-
teousness should have been by the
law.
22 But the scripture hath con-
cluded all under sin, that the prom-
ise by faith of Jesus Christ might be
given to them that believe.

23 But before faith came, we were
kept under the law, shut up unto
the faith which should afterwards
be revealed.
24 Wherefore the law was our
schoolmaster *to bring us* unto
Christ, that we might be justified
by faith.
25 But after that faith is come, we
are no longer under a schoolmaster.

One in Christ Jesus

26 For ye are all the children of
God by faith in Christ Jesus.
27 For as many of you as have
been baptized into Christ have put
on Christ.
28 There is neither Jew nor Greek,
there is neither bond nor free, there
is neither male nor female: for ye are
all one in Christ Jesus.
29 And if ye *be* Christ's, then are ye
Abraham's seed, and heirs according
to the promise.

The Heirs of God's Grace

4 Now I say, *That* the heir, as long
as he is a child, differeth noth-
ing from a servant, though he be
lord of all;
2 But is under tutors and gover-
nors until the time appointed of the
father.
3 Even so we, when we were chil-
dren, were in bondage under the
elements of the world:
4 But when the fulness of the time
was come, God sent forth his Son,
made of a woman, made under the
law,
5 To redeem them that were under
the law, that we might receive the
adoption of sons.
6 And because ye are sons, God
hath sent forth the Spirit of his Son
into your hearts, crying, Abba, Fa-
ther.
7 Wherefore thou art no more a
servant, but a son; and if a son, then
an heir of God through Christ.

Paul Urges Faithfulness

8 Howbeit then, when ye knew
not God, ye did service unto them
which by nature are no gods.
9 But now, after that ye have
known God, or rather are known of
God, how turn ye again to the weak
and beggarly elements, whereunto
ye desire again to be in bondage?
10 Ye observe days, and months,
and times, and years.
11 I am afraid of you, lest I have
bestowed upon you labour in vain.
12 Brethren, I beseech you, be as
I *am;* for I *am* as ye *are:* ye have not
injured me at all.
13 Ye know how through infirmity
of the flesh I preached the gospel
unto you at the first.
14 And my temptation which was
in my flesh ye despised not, nor re-
jected; but received me as an angel
of God, *even* as Christ Jesus.
15 Where is then the blessedness
ye spake of? for I bear you record,
that, if *it had been* possible, ye
would have plucked out your own
eyes, and have given them to me.
16 Am I therefore become your
enemy, because I tell you the truth?
17 They zealously affect you, *but*
not well; yea, they would exclude
you, that ye might affect them.
18 But *it is* good to be zealously
affected always in *a* good *thing,* and
not only when I am present with
you.
19 My little children, of whom I
travail in birth again until Christ be
formed in you,
20 I desire to be present with you
now, and to change my voice; for I
stand in doubt of you.
21 Tell me, ye that desire to be
under the law, do ye not hear the
law?

The Children of Promise

22 For it is written, that Abraham
had two sons, the one by a bond-
maid, the other by a freewoman.

23 But he *who was* of the bondwoman was born after the flesh; but he of the freewoman *was* by promise.

24 Which things are an allegory: for these are the two covenants; the one from the mount Sinai, which gendereth to bondage, which is Agar.

25 For this Agar is mount Sinai in Arabia, and answereth to Jerusalem which now is, and is in bondage with her children.

26 But Jerusalem which is above is free, which is the mother of us all.

27 For it is written, Rejoice, *thou* barren that bearest not; break forth and cry, thou that travailest not: for the desolate hath many more children than she which hath an husband.

28 Now we, brethren, as Isaac was, are the children of promise.

29 But as then he that was born after the flesh persecuted him *that was born* after the Spirit, even so *it is* now.

30 Nevertheless what saith the scripture? Cast out the bondwoman and her son: for the son of the bondwoman shall not be heir with the son of the freewoman.

31 So then, brethren, we are not children of the bondwoman, but of the free.

The Hope of Righteousness

5 Stand fast therefore in the liberty wherewith Christ hath made us free, and be not entangled again with the yoke of bondage.

2 Behold, I Paul say unto you, that if ye be circumcised, Christ shall profit you nothing.

3 For I testify again to every man that is circumcised, that he is a debtor to do the whole law.

4 Christ is become of no effect unto you, whosoever of you are justified by the law; ye are fallen from grace.

5 For we through the Spirit wait for the hope of righteousness by faith.

6 For in Jesus Christ neither circumcision availeth any thing, nor uncircumcision; but faith which worketh by love.

7 Ye did run well; who did hinder you that ye should not obey the truth?

8 This persuasion *cometh* not of him that calleth you.

9 A little leaven leaveneth the whole lump.

10 I have confidence in you through the Lord, that ye will be none otherwise minded: but he that troubleth you shall bear his judgment, whosoever he be.

11 And I, brethren, if I yet preach circumcision, why do I yet suffer persecution? then is the offence of the cross ceased.

12 I would they were even cut off which trouble you.

13 For, brethren, ye have been called unto liberty; only *use* not liberty for an occasion to the flesh, but by love serve one another.

14 For all the law is fulfilled in one word, *even* in this; Thou shalt love thy neighbour as thyself.

15 But if ye bite and devour one another, take heed that ye be not consumed one of another.

The Works of the Flesh

16 *This* I say then, Walk in the Spirit, and ye shall not fulfil the lust of the flesh.

17 For the flesh lusteth against the Spirit, and the Spirit against the flesh: and these are contrary the one to the other: so that ye cannot do the things that ye would.

18 But if ye be led of the Spirit, ye are not under the law.

19 Now the works of the flesh are manifest, which are *these;* Adultery, fornication, uncleanness, lasciviousness,

20 Idolatry, witchcraft, hatred,
variance, emulations, wrath, strife,
seditions, heresies,
21 Envyings, murders, drunken-
ness, revellings, and such like: of
the which I tell you before, as I have
also told *you* in time past, that they
which do such things shall not in-
herit the kingdom of God.

The Fruit of the Spirit

22 But the fruit of the Spirit is love,
joy, peace, longsuffering, gentle-
ness, goodness, faith,
23 Meekness, temperance: against
such there is no law.
24 And they that are Christ's have
crucified the flesh with the affec-
tions and lusts.
25 If we live in the Spirit, let us
also walk in the Spirit.
26 Let us not be desirous of vain
glory, provoking one another, en-
vying one another.

Bear One Another's Burdens

6 Brethren, if a man be overtaken
in a fault, ye which are spiritual,
restore such an one in the spirit of
meekness; considering thyself, lest
thou also be tempted.
2 Bear ye one another's burdens,
and so fulfil the law of Christ.
3 For if a man think himself to be
something, when he is nothing, he
deceiveth himself.
4 But let every man prove his
own work, and then shall he have
rejoicing in himself alone, and not
in another.
5 For every man shall bear his own
burden.
6 Let him that is taught in the
word communicate unto him that
teacheth in all good things.
7 Be not deceived; God is not
mocked: for whatsoever a man
soweth, that shall he also reap.
8 For he that soweth to his flesh
shall of the flesh reap corruption;
but he that soweth to the Spirit shall
of the Spirit reap life everlasting.
9 And let us not be weary in well
doing: for in due season we shall
reap, if we faint not.
10 As we have therefore oppor-
tunity, let us do good unto all *men*,
especially unto them who are of the
household of faith.

Crucified to the World

11 Ye see how large a letter I have
written unto you with mine own
hand.
12 As many as desire to make a fair
shew in the flesh, they constrain you
to be circumcised; only lest they
should suffer persecution for the
cross of Christ.
13 For neither they themselves
who are circumcised keep the law;
but desire to have you circumcised,
that they may glory in your flesh.
14 But God forbid that I should
glory, save in the cross of our Lord
Jesus Christ, by whom the world is
crucified unto me, and I unto the
world.
15 For in Christ Jesus neither cir-
cumcision availeth any thing, nor
uncircumcision, but a new creature.
16 And as many as walk according
to this rule, peace *be* on them, and
mercy, and upon the Israel of God.
17 From henceforth let no man
trouble me: for I bear in my body
the marks of the Lord Jesus.
18 Brethren, the grace of our Lord
Jesus Christ *be* with your spirit.
Amen.

The Epistle of Paul the Apostle to the

EPHESIANS

Salutation to the Saints

Paul, an apostle of Jesus Christ
by the will of God, to the saints
which are at Ephesus, and to the
faithful in Christ Jesus:
2 Grace *be* to you, and peace, from
God our Father, and *from* the Lord
Jesus Christ.

Redemption by Christ

3 Blessed *be* the God and Father
of our Lord Jesus Christ, who hath
blessed us with all spiritual bless-
ings in heavenly *places* in Christ:
4 According as he hath chosen us
in him before the foundation of the
world, that we should be holy and
without blame before him in love:
5 Having predestinated us unto
the adoption of children by Jesus
Christ to himself, according to the
good pleasure of his will,
6 To the praise of the glory of his
grace, wherein he hath made us ac-
cepted in the beloved.
7 In whom we have redemption
through his blood, the forgiveness
of sins, according to the riches of
his grace;
8 Wherein he hath abounded to-
ward us in all wisdom and prudence;
9 Having made known unto us
the mystery of his will, according
to his good pleasure which he hath
purposed in himself:
10 That in the dispensation of the
fulness of times he might gather
together in one all things in Christ,
both which are in heaven, and which
are on earth; *even* in him:
11 In whom also we have obtained
an inheritance, being predestinated
according to the purpose of him
who worketh all things after the
counsel of his own will:
12 That we should be to the praise
of his glory, who first trusted in
Christ.
13 In whom ye also *trusted,* after
that ye heard the word of truth,
the gospel of your salvation: in
whom also after that ye believed,
ye were sealed with that holy Spirit
of promise,
14 Which is the earnest of our in-
heritance until the redemption of
the purchased possession, unto the
praise of his glory.

Prayerful Thanksgiving

15 Wherefore I also, after I heard
of your faith in the Lord Jesus, and
love unto all the saints,
16 Cease not to give thanks for
you, making mention of you in my
prayers;
17 That the God of our Lord Jesus
Christ, the Father of glory, may give
unto you the spirit of wisdom and
revelation in the knowledge of him:
18 The eyes of your understand-
ing being enlightened; that ye may
know what is the hope of his calling,
and what the riches of the glory of
his inheritance in the saints,
19 And what *is* the exceeding
greatness of his power to us-ward
who believe, according to the work-
ing of his mighty power,
20 Which he wrought in Christ,

when he raised him from the dead,
and set *him* at his own right hand
in the heavenly *places,*
21 Far above all principality, and
power, and might, and dominion,
and every name that is named, not
only in this world, but also in that
which is to come:
22 And hath put all *things* under
his feet, and gave him *to be* the head
over all *things* to the church,
23 Which is his body, the fulness
of him that filleth all in all.

Saved by Grace

2 And you *hath he quickened,*
who were dead in trespasses
and sins;
2 Wherein in time past ye walked
according to the course of this world,
according to the prince of the power
of the air, the spirit that now work-
eth in the children of disobedience:
3 Among whom also we all had
our conversation in times past in
the lusts of our flesh, fulfilling the
desires of the flesh and of the mind;
and were by nature the children of
wrath, even as others.
4 But God, who is rich in mercy,
for his great love wherewith he
loved us,
5 Even when we were dead in sins,
hath quickened us together with
Christ, (by grace ye are saved;)
6 And hath raised *us* up together,
and made *us* sit together in heavenly
places in Christ Jesus:
7 That in the ages to come he
might shew the exceeding riches
of his grace in *his* kindness toward
us through Christ Jesus.
8 For by grace are ye saved
through faith; and that not of your-
selves: *it is* the gift of God:
9 Not of works, lest any man
should boast.
10 For we are his workmanship,
created in Christ Jesus unto good
works, which God hath before or-
dained that we should walk in them.

Reconciled unto Christ

11 Wherefore remember, that ye
being in time past Gentiles in the
flesh, who are called Uncircumcision
by that which is called the Circum-
cision in the flesh made by hands;
12 That at that time ye were
without Christ, being aliens from
the commonwealth of Israel, and
strangers from the covenants of
promise, having no hope, and with-
out God in the world:
13 But now in Christ Jesus ye who
sometimes were far off are made
nigh by the blood of Christ.

Christ Our Peace

14 For he is our peace, who hath
made both one, and hath broken
down the middle wall of partition
between us;
15 Having abolished in his flesh the
enmity, *even* the law of command-
ments *contained* in ordinances; for
to make in himself of twain one new
man, *so* making peace;
16 And that he might reconcile
both unto God in one body by the
cross, having slain the enmity
thereby:
17 And came and preached peace
to you which were afar off, and to
them that were nigh.
18 For through him we both have
access by one Spirit unto the Father.

Christ Our Cornerstone

19 Now therefore ye are no more
strangers and foreigners, but fel-
lowcitizens with the saints, and of
the household of God;
20 And are built upon the founda-
tion of the apostles and prophets,
Jesus Christ himself being the chief
corner *stone;*
21 In whom all the building fitly
framed together groweth unto an
holy temple in the Lord:
22 In whom ye also are builded
together for an habitation of God
through the Spirit.

The Mystery Made Known

3 For this cause I Paul, the prisoner of Jesus Christ for you Gentiles,

2 If ye have heard of the dispensation of the grace of God which is given me to you-ward:

3 How that by revelation he made known unto me the mystery; (as I wrote afore in few words,

4 Whereby, when ye read, ye may understand my knowledge in the mystery of Christ)

5 Which in other ages was not made known unto the sons of men, as it is now revealed unto his holy apostles and prophets by the Spirit;

6 That the Gentiles should be fellowheirs, and of the same body, and partakers of his promise in Christ by the gospel:

7 Whereof I was made a minister, according to the gift of the grace of God given unto me by the effectual working of his power.

The Unsearchable Riches of Christ

8 Unto me, who am less than the least of all saints, is this grace given, that I should preach among the Gentiles the unsearchable riches of Christ;

9 And to make all *men* see what *is* the fellowship of the mystery, which from the beginning of the world hath been hid in God, who created all things by Jesus Christ:

10 To the intent that now unto the principalities and powers in heavenly *places* might be known by the church the manifold wisdom of God,

11 According to the eternal purpose which he purposed in Christ Jesus our Lord:

12 In whom we have boldness and access with confidence by the faith of him.

13 Wherefore I desire that ye faint not at my tribulations for you, which is your glory.

Praying for the Ephesians

14 For this cause I bow my knees unto the Father of our Lord Jesus Christ,

15 Of whom the whole family in heaven and earth is named,

16 That he would grant you, according to the riches of his glory, to be strengthened with might by his Spirit in the inner man;

17 That Christ may dwell in your hearts by faith; that ye, being rooted and grounded in love,

18 May be able to comprehend with all saints what *is* the breadth, and length, and depth, and height;

19 And to know the love of Christ, which passeth knowledge, that ye might be filled with all the fulness of God.

20 Now unto him that is able to do exceeding abundantly above all that we ask or think, according to the power that worketh in us,

21 Unto him *be* glory in the church by Christ Jesus throughout all ages, world without end. Amen.

Keep the Unity of the Spirit

4 I therefore, the prisoner of the Lord, beseech you that ye walk worthy of the vocation wherewith ye are called,

2 With all lowliness and meekness, with longsuffering, forbearing one another in love;

3 Endeavouring to keep the unity of the Spirit in the bond of peace.

4 *There is* one body, and one Spirit, even as ye are called in one hope of your calling;

5 One Lord, one faith, one baptism,

6 One God and Father of all, who *is* above all, and through all, and in you all.

The Gifts of Christ

7 But unto every one of us is given grace according to the measure of the gift of Christ.

8 Wherefore he saith, When he ascended up on high, he led captivity captive, and gave gifts unto men.

9 (Now that he ascended, what is it but that he also descended first into the lower parts of the earth?

10 He that descended is the same also that ascended up far above all heavens, that he might fill all things.)

11 And he gave some, apostles; and some, prophets; and some, evangelists; and some, pastors and teachers;

12 For the perfecting of the saints, for the work of the ministry, for the edifying of the body of Christ:

13 Till we all come in the unity of the faith, and of the knowledge of the Son of God, unto a perfect man, unto the measure of the stature of the fulness of Christ:

14 That we *henceforth* be no more children, tossed to and fro, and carried about with every wind of doctrine, by the sleight of men, *and* cunning craftiness, whereby they lie in wait to deceive;

15 But speaking the truth in love, may grow up into him in all things, which is the head, *even* Christ:

16 From whom the whole body fitly joined together and compacted by that which every joint supplieth, according to the effectual working in the measure of every part, maketh increase of the body unto the edifying of itself in love.

Put on the New Man

17 This I say therefore, and testify in the Lord, that ye henceforth walk not as other Gentiles walk, in the vanity of their mind,

18 Having the understanding darkened, being alienated from the life of God through the ignorance that is in them, because of the blindness of their heart:

19 Who being past feeling have given themselves over unto lasciviousness, to work all uncleanness with greediness.

20 But ye have not so learned Christ;

21 If so be that ye have heard him, and have been taught by him, as the truth is in Jesus:

22 That ye put off concerning the former conversation the old man, which is corrupt according to the deceitful lusts;

23 And be renewed in the spirit of your mind;

24 And that ye put on the new man, which after God is created in righteousness and true holiness.

25 Wherefore putting away lying, speak every man truth with his neighbour: for we are members one of another.

26 Be ye angry, and sin not: let not the sun go down upon your wrath:

27 Neither give place to the devil.

28 Let him that stole steal no more: but rather let him labour, working with *his* hands the thing which is good, that he may have to give to him that needeth.

29 Let no corrupt communication proceed out of your mouth, but that which is good to the use of edifying, that it may minister grace unto the hearers.

30 And grieve not the holy Spirit of God, whereby ye are sealed unto the day of redemption.

31 Let all bitterness, and wrath, and anger, and clamour, and evil speaking, be put away from you, with all malice:

32 And be ye kind one to another, tenderhearted, forgiving one another, even as God for Christ's sake hath forgiven you.

Walk in Love

5 Be ye therefore followers of God, as dear children;

2 And walk in love, as Christ also hath loved us, and hath given him-

self for us an offering and a sacrifice
to God for a sweetsmelling savour.
3 But fornication, and all unclean-
ness, or covetousness, let it not be
once named among you, as becom-
eth saints;
4 Neither filthiness, nor foolish
talking, nor jesting, which are not
convenient: but rather giving of
thanks.
5 For this ye know, that no whore-
monger, nor unclean person, nor
covetous man, who is an idolater,
hath any inheritance in the kingdom
of Christ and of God.
6 Let no man deceive you with
vain words: for because of these
things cometh the wrath of God
upon the children of disobedience.
7 Be not ye therefore partakers
with them.

Walk as Children of Light

8 For ye were sometimes dark-
ness, but now *are ye* light in the
Lord: walk as children of light:
9 (For the fruit of the Spirit *is* in
all goodness and righteousness and
truth;)
10 Proving what is acceptable unto
the Lord.
11 And have no fellowship with
the unfruitful works of darkness,
but rather reprove *them*.
12 For it is a shame even to speak
of those things which are done of
them in secret.
13 But all things that are reproved
are made manifest by the light: for
whatsoever doth make manifest is
light.
14 Wherefore he saith, Awake thou
that sleepest, and arise from the
dead, and Christ shall give thee light.

Walk Not as Fools

15 See then that ye walk circum-
spectly, not as fools, but as wise,
16 Redeeming the time, because
the days are evil.
17 Wherefore be ye not unwise,
but understanding what the will of
the Lord *is*.
18 And be not drunk with wine,
wherein is excess; but be filled with
the Spirit;
19 Speaking to yourselves in
psalms and hymns and spiritual
songs, singing and making melody
in your heart to the Lord;
20 Giving thanks always for all
things unto God and the Father in
the name of our Lord Jesus Christ;
21 Submitting yourselves one to
another in the fear of God.

Instructions for Marriage

22 Wives, submit yourselves unto
your own husbands, as unto the
Lord.
23 For the husband is the head of
the wife, even as Christ is the head
of the church: and he is the saviour
of the body.
24 Therefore as the church is sub-
ject unto Christ, so *let* the wives *be*
to their own husbands in every
thing.
25 Husbands, love your wives,
even as Christ also loved the church,
and gave himself for it;
26 That he might sanctify and
cleanse it with the washing of water
by the word,
27 That he might present it to
himself a glorious church, not hav-
ing spot, or wrinkle, or any such
thing; but that it should be holy and
without blemish.
28 So ought men to love their
wives as their own bodies. He that
loveth his wife loveth himself.
29 For no man ever yet hated
his own flesh; but nourisheth and
cherisheth it, even as the Lord the
church:
30 For we are members of his
body, of his flesh, and of his bones.
31 For this cause shall a man leave
his father and mother, and shall be
joined unto his wife, and they two
shall be one flesh.

32 This is a great mystery: but I speak concerning Christ and the church.

33 Nevertheless let every one of you in particular so love his wife even as himself; and the wife *see* that she reverence *her* husband.

Instructions to Children

6 Children, obey your parents in the Lord: for this is right.

2 Honour thy father and mother; which is the first commandment with promise;

3 That it may be well with thee, and thou mayest live long on the earth.

4 And, ye fathers, provoke not your children to wrath: but bring them up in the nurture and admonition of the Lord.

Servants and Masters

5 Servants, be obedient to them that are *your* masters according to the flesh, with fear and trembling, in singleness of your heart, as unto Christ;

6 Not with eyeservice, as menpleasers; but as the servants of Christ, doing the will of God from the heart;

7 With good will doing service, as to the Lord, and not to men:

8 Knowing that whatsoever good thing any man doeth, the same shall he receive of the Lord, whether *he be* bond or free.

9 And, ye masters, do the same things unto them, forbearing threatening: knowing that your Master also is in heaven; neither is there respect of persons with him.

The Whole Armour of God

10 Finally, my brethren, be strong in the Lord, and in the power of his might.

11 Put on the whole armour of God, that ye may be able to stand against the wiles of the devil.

12 For we wrestle not against flesh and blood, but against principalities, against powers, against the rulers of the darkness of this world, against spiritual wickedness in high *places.*

13 Wherefore take unto you the whole armour of God, that ye may be able to withstand in the evil day, and having done all, to stand.

14 Stand therefore, having your loins girt about with truth, and having on the breastplate of righteousness;

15 And your feet shod with the preparation of the gospel of peace;

16 Above all, taking the shield of faith, wherewith ye shall be able to quench all the fiery darts of the wicked.

17 And take the helmet of salvation, and the sword of the Spirit, which is the word of God:

18 Praying always with all prayer and supplication in the Spirit, and watching thereunto with all perseverance and supplication for all saints;

19 And for me, that utterance may be given unto me, that I may open my mouth boldly, to make known the mystery of the gospel,

20 For which I am an ambassador in bonds: that therein I may speak boldly, as I ought to speak.

Final Greetings

21 But that ye also may know my affairs, *and* how I do, Tychicus, a beloved brother and faithful minister in the Lord, shall make known to you all things:

22 Whom I have sent unto you for the same purpose, that ye might know our affairs, and *that* he might comfort your hearts.

23 Peace *be* to the brethren, and love with faith, from God the Father and the Lord Jesus Christ.

24 Grace *be* with all them that love our Lord Jesus Christ in sincerity. Amen.

The Epistle of Paul the Apostle to the

PHILIPPIANS

Greetings

Paul and Timotheus, the ser-
vants of Jesus Christ, to all the
saints in Christ Jesus which are
at Philippi, with the bishops and
deacons:
2 Grace *be* unto you, and peace,
from God our Father, and *from* the
Lord Jesus Christ.
3 I thank my God upon every re-
membrance of you,
4 Always in every prayer of mine
for you all making request with joy,
5 For your fellowship in the gospel
from the first day until now;
6 Being confident of this very
thing, that he which hath begun a
good work in you will perform *it*
until the day of Jesus Christ:
7 Even as it is meet for me to think
this of you all, because I have you
in my heart; inasmuch as both in
my bonds, and in the defence and
confirmation of the gospel, ye all
are partakers of my grace.
8 For God is my record, how
greatly I long after you all in the
bowels of Jesus Christ.
9 And this I pray, that your love
may abound yet more and more in
knowledge and *in* all judgment;
10 That ye may approve things that
are excellent; that ye may be sincere
and without offence till the day of
Christ;
11 Being filled with the fruits of
righteousness, which are by Jesus
Christ, unto the glory and praise of
God.

Paul's Bonds in Christ

12 But I would ye should under-
stand, brethren, that the things
which happened unto me have fallen
out rather unto the furtherance of
the gospel;
13 So that my bonds in Christ are
manifest in all the palace, and in all
other *places;*
14 And many of the brethren in
the Lord, waxing confident by my
bonds, are much more bold to speak
the word without fear.
15 Some indeed preach Christ even
of envy and strife; and some also of
good will:
16 The one preach Christ of con-
tention, not sincerely, supposing to
add affliction to my bonds:
17 But the other of love, knowing
that I am set for the defence of the
gospel.
18 What then? notwithstanding,
every way, whether in pretence, or
in truth, Christ is preached; and I
therein do rejoice, yea, and will re-
joice.
19 For I know that this shall turn
to my salvation through your prayer,
and the supply of the Spirit of Jesus
Christ,

Christ Is Magnified Through Paul

20 According to my earnest expec-
tation and *my* hope, that in nothing
I shall be ashamed, but *that* with
all boldness, as always, *so* now
also Christ shall be magnified in

my body, whether *it be* by life, or by death.

21 For to me to live *is* Christ, and to die *is* gain.

22 But if I live in the flesh, this *is* the fruit of my labour: yet what I shall choose I wot not.

23 For I am in a strait betwixt two, having a desire to depart, and to be with Christ; which is far better:

24 Nevertheless to abide in the flesh *is* more needful for you.

25 And having this confidence, I know that I shall abide and continue with you all for your furtherance and joy of faith;

26 That your rejoicing may be more abundant in Jesus Christ for me by my coming to you again.

27 Only let your conversation be as it becometh the gospel of Christ: that whether I come and see you, or else be absent, I may hear of your affairs, that ye stand fast in one spirit, with one mind striving together for the faith of the gospel;

28 And in nothing terrified by your adversaries: which is to them an evident token of perdition, but to you of salvation, and that of God.

29 For unto you it is given in the behalf of Christ, not only to believe on him, but also to suffer for his sake;

30 Having the same conflict which ye saw in me, and now hear *to be* in me.

Be of One Accord and One Mind

2 If *there be* therefore any consolation in Christ, if any comfort of love, if any fellowship of the Spirit, if any bowels and mercies,

2 Fulfil ye my joy, that ye be likeminded, having the same love, *being* of one accord, of one mind.

3 *Let* nothing *be done* through strife or vainglory; but in lowliness of mind let each esteem other better than themselves.

4 Look not every man on his own things, but every man also on the things of others.

5 Let this mind be in you, which was also in Christ Jesus:

6 Who, being in the form of God, thought it not robbery to be equal with God:

7 But made himself of no reputation, and took upon him the form of a servant, and was made in the likeness of men:

8 And being found in fashion as a man, he humbled himself, and became obedient unto death, even the death of the cross.

9 Wherefore God also hath highly exalted him, and given him a name which is above every name:

10 That at the name of Jesus every knee should bow, of *things* in heaven, and *things* in earth, and *things* under the earth;

11 And *that* every tongue should confess that Jesus Christ *is* Lord, to the glory of God the Father.

Shine as Lights in the World

12 Wherefore, my beloved, as ye have always obeyed, not as in my presence only, but now much more in my absence, work out your own salvation with fear and trembling.

13 For it is God which worketh in you both to will and to do of *his* good pleasure.

14 Do all things without murmurings and disputings:

15 That ye may be blameless and harmless, the sons of God, without rebuke, in the midst of a crooked and perverse nation, among whom ye shine as lights in the world;

16 Holding forth the word of life; that I may rejoice in the day of Christ, that I have not run in vain, neither laboured in vain.

17 Yea, and if I be offered upon the sacrifice and service of your faith, I joy, and rejoice with you all.

18 For the same cause also do ye joy, and rejoice with me.

Timothy's Faithful Service

19 But I trust in the Lord Jesus to
send Timotheus shortly unto you,
that I also may be of good comfort,
when I know your state.
20 For I have no man likeminded,
who will naturally care for your
state.
21 For all seek their own, not the
things which are Jesus Christ's.
22 But ye know the proof of him,
that, as a son with the father, he
hath served with me in the gospel.
23 Him therefore I hope to send
presently, so soon as I shall see how
it will go with me.
24 But I trust in the Lord that I
also myself shall come shortly.

Epaphroditus's Service to Paul

25 Yet I supposed it necessary
to send to you Epaphroditus, my
brother, and companion in labour,
and fellowsoldier, but your mes-
senger, and he that ministered to
my wants.
26 For he longed after you all, and
was full of heaviness, because that
ye had heard that he had been sick.
27 For indeed he was sick nigh
unto death: but God had mercy on
him; and not on him only, but on
me also, lest I should have sorrow
upon sorrow.
28 I sent him therefore the more
carefully, that, when ye see him
again, ye may rejoice, and that I
may be the less sorrowful.
29 Receive him therefore in the
Lord with all gladness; and hold
such in reputation:
30 Because for the work of Christ
he was nigh unto death, not regard-
ing his life, to supply your lack of
service toward me.

That I May Win Christ

3 Finally, my brethren, rejoice
in the Lord. To write the same
things to you, to me indeed *is* not
grievous, but for you *it is* safe.
2 Beware of dogs, beware of evil
workers, beware of the concision.
3 For we are the circumcision,
which worship God in the spirit,
and rejoice in Christ Jesus, and have
no confidence in the flesh.
4 Though I might also have confi-
dence in the flesh. If any other man
thinketh that he hath whereof he
might trust in the flesh, I more:
5 Circumcised the eighth day, of
the stock of Israel, *of* the tribe of
Benjamin, an Hebrew of the He-
brews; as touching the law, a Phar-
isee;
6 Concerning zeal, persecuting the
church; touching the righteousness
which is in the law, blameless.
7 But what things were gain to
me, those I counted loss for Christ.
8 Yea doubtless, and I count all
things *but* loss for the excellency of
the knowledge of Christ Jesus my
Lord: for whom I have suffered the
loss of all things, and do count them
but dung, that I may win Christ,
9 And be found in him, not having
mine own righteousness, which is
of the law, but that which is through
the faith of Christ, the righteousness
which is of God by faith:
10 That I may know him, and the
power of his resurrection, and the
fellowship of his sufferings, being
made conformable unto his death;
11 If by any means I might attain
unto the resurrection of the dead.
12 Not as though I had already
attained, either were already per-
fect: but I follow after, if that I may
apprehend that for which also I am
apprehended of Christ Jesus.

The High Calling of God

13 Brethren, I count not myself
to have apprehended: but *this* one
thing *I do,* forgetting those things
which are behind, and reaching
forth unto those things which are
before,

14 I press toward the mark for the prize of the high calling of God in Christ Jesus.

15 Let us therefore, as many as be perfect, be thus minded: and if in any thing ye be otherwise minded, God shall reveal even this unto you.

16 Nevertheless, whereto we have already attained, let us walk by the same rule, let us mind the same thing.

17 Brethren, be followers together of me, and mark them which walk so as ye have us for an ensample.

18 (For many walk, of whom I have told you often, and now tell you even weeping, *that they are* the enemies of the cross of Christ:

19 Whose end *is* destruction, whose God *is their* belly, and *whose* glory *is* in their shame, who mind earthly things.)

20 For our conversation is in heaven; from whence also we look for the Saviour, the Lord Jesus Christ:

21 Who shall change our vile body, that it may be fashioned like unto his glorious body, according to the working whereby he is able even to subdue all things unto himself.

The God of Peace

4 Therefore, my brethren dearly beloved and longed for, my joy and crown, so stand fast in the Lord, *my* dearly beloved.

2 I beseech Euodias, and beseech Syntyche, that they be of the same mind in the Lord.

3 And I intreat thee also, true yokefellow, help those women which laboured with me in the gospel, with Clement also, and *with* other my fellowlabourers, whose names *are* in the book of life.

4 Rejoice in the Lord alway: *and* again I say, Rejoice.

5 Let your moderation be known unto all men. The Lord *is* at hand.

6 Be careful for nothing; but in every thing by prayer and supplication with thanksgiving let your requests be made known unto God.

7 And the peace of God, which passeth all understanding, shall keep your hearts and minds through Christ Jesus.

8 Finally, brethren, whatsoever things are true, whatsoever things *are* honest, whatsoever things *are* just, whatsoever things *are* pure, whatsoever things *are* lovely, whatsoever things *are* of good report; if *there be* any virtue, and if *there be* any praise, think on these things.

9 Those things, which ye have both learned, and received, and heard, and seen in me, do: and the God of peace shall be with you.

An Acceptable Sacrifice

10 But I rejoiced in the Lord greatly, that now at the last your care of me hath flourished again; wherein ye were also careful, but ye lacked opportunity.

11 Not that I speak in respect of want: for I have learned, in whatsoever state I am, *therewith* to be content.

12 I know both how to be abased, and I know how to abound: every where and in all things I am instructed both to be full and to be hungry, both to abound and to suffer need.

13 I can do all things through Christ which strengtheneth me.

14 Notwithstanding ye have well done, that ye did communicate with my affliction.

15 Now ye Philippians know also, that in the beginning of the gospel, when I departed from Macedonia, no church communicated with me as concerning giving and receiving, but ye only.

16 For even in Thessalonica ye sent once and again unto my necessity.

17 Not because I desire a gift: but

I desire fruit that may abound to
your account.
18 But I have all, and abound: I
am full, having received of Epaph-
roditus the things *which were sent*
from you, an odour of a sweet smell,
a sacrifice acceptable, wellpleasing
to God.
19 But my God shall supply all your
need according to his riches in glory
by Christ Jesus.
20 Now unto God and our Father
be glory for ever and ever. Amen.

A Salute to the Saints

21 Salute every saint in Christ
Jesus. The brethren which are with
me greet you.
22 All the saints salute you, chiefly
they that are of Caesar's household.
23 The grace of our Lord Jesus
Christ *be* with you all. Amen.

The Epistle of Paul the Apostle to the COLOSSIANS

Walk Worthy of the Lord

Paul, an apostle of Jesus Christ by
the will of God, and Timotheus
our brother,
2 To the saints and faithful breth-
ren in Christ which are at Colosse:
Grace *be* unto you, and peace, from
God our Father and the Lord Jesus
Christ.
3 We give thanks to God and the
Father of our Lord Jesus Christ,
praying always for you,
4 Since we heard of your faith in
Christ Jesus, and of the love *which*
ye have to all the saints,
5 For the hope which is laid up for
you in heaven, whereof ye heard
before in the word of the truth of
the gospel;
6 Which is come unto you, as *it is*
in all the world; and bringeth forth
fruit, as *it doth* also in you, since
the day ye heard *of it,* and knew the
grace of God in truth:
7 As ye also learned of Epaphras
our dear fellowservant, who is for
you a faithful minister of Christ;
8 Who also declared unto us your
love in the Spirit.
9 For this cause we also, since
the day we heard *it,* do not cease
to pray for you, and to desire that ye
might be filled with the knowledge
of his will in all wisdom and spiritual
understanding;
10 That ye might walk worthy of
the Lord unto all pleasing, being
fruitful in every good work, and in-
creasing in the knowledge of God;
11 Strengthened with all might, ac-
cording to his glorious power, unto
all patience and longsuffering with
joyfulness;
12 Giving thanks unto the Father,
which hath made us meet to be
partakers of the inheritance of the
saints in light:
13 Who hath delivered us from
the power of darkness, and hath
translated *us* into the kingdom of
his dear Son:
14 In whom we have redemption
through his blood, *even* the forgive-
ness of sins:

The Preeminence of Christ

15 Who is the image of the invisi-
ble God, the firstborn of every crea-
ture:
16 For by him were all things cre-
ated, that are in heaven, and that
are in earth, visible and invisible,
whether *they be* thrones, or domin-
ions, or principalities, or powers: all
things were created by him, and for
him:
17 And he is before all things, and
by him all things consist.
18 And he is the head of the body,
the church: who is the beginning,
the firstborn from the dead; that in
all *things* he might have the preem-
inence.
19 For it pleased *the Father* that in
him should all fulness dwell;
20 And, having made peace
through the blood of his cross, by
him to reconcile all things unto him-
self; by him, *I say,* whether *they be*
things in earth, or things in heaven.

Christ the Hope of Glory

21 And you, that were sometime
alienated and enemies in *your* mind
by wicked works, yet now hath he
reconciled
22 In the body of his flesh through
death, to present you holy and un-
blameable and unreproveable in his
sight:
23 If ye continue in the faith
grounded and settled, and *be* not
moved away from the hope of the
gospel, which ye have heard, *and*
which was preached to every crea-
ture which is under heaven; whereof
I Paul am made a minister;
24 Who now rejoice in my suffer-
ings for you, and fill up that which is
behind of the afflictions of Christ in
my flesh for his body's sake, which
is the church:
25 Whereof I am made a minister,
according to the dispensation of
God which is given to me for you,
to fulfil the word of God;
26 *Even* the mystery which hath
been hid from ages and from gen-
erations, but now is made manifest
to his saints:
27 To whom God would make
known what *is* the riches of the glory
of this mystery among the Gentiles;
which is Christ in you, the hope of
glory:
28 Whom we preach, warning ev-
ery man, and teaching every man
in all wisdom; that we may present
every man perfect in Christ Jesus:
29 Whereunto I also labour, striv-
ing according to his working, which
worketh in me mightily.

Present in the Spirit

2 For I would that ye knew what
great conflict I have for you,
and *for* them at Laodicea, and *for*
as many as have not seen my face
in the flesh;
2 That their hearts might be com-
forted, being knit together in love,
and unto all riches of the full assur-
ance of understanding, to the ac-
knowledgement of the mystery of
God, and of the Father, and of Christ;
3 In whom are hid all the treasures
of wisdom and knowledge.
4 And this I say, lest any man
should beguile you with enticing
words.
5 For though I be absent in the
flesh, yet am I with you in the spirit,
joying and beholding your order,
and the stedfastness of your faith
in Christ.

Rooted in Christ Jesus

6 As ye have therefore received
Christ Jesus the Lord, *so* walk ye in
him:
7 Rooted and built up in him, and
stablished in the faith, as ye have
been taught, abounding therein
with thanksgiving.
8 Beware lest any man spoil you
through philosophy and vain deceit,
after the tradition of men, after the
rudiments of the world, and not af-
ter Christ.
9 For in him dwelleth all the ful-
ness of the Godhead bodily.
10 And ye are complete in him,
which is the head of all principality
and power:
11 In whom also ye are circum-
cised with the circumcision made
without hands, in putting off the
body of the sins of the flesh by the
circumcision of Christ:
12 Buried with him in baptism,
wherein also ye are risen with *him*
through the faith of the operation
of God, who hath raised him from
the dead.

Dead to the World Yet Alive

13 And you, being dead in your
sins and the uncircumcision of your
flesh, hath he quickened together
with him, having forgiven you all
trespasses;
14 Blotting out the handwriting
of ordinances that was against us,

which was contrary to us, and took it out of the way, nailing it to his cross;
15 *And* having spoiled principalities and powers, he made a shew of them openly, triumphing over them in it.
16 Let no man therefore judge you in meat, or in drink, or in respect of an holyday, or of the new moon, or of the sabbath *days:*
17 Which are a shadow of things to come; but the body *is* of Christ.
18 Let no man beguile you of your reward in a voluntary humility and worshipping of angels, intruding into those things which he hath not seen, vainly puffed up by his fleshly mind,
19 And not holding the Head, from which all the body by joints and bands having nourishment ministered, and knit together, increaseth with the increase of God.
20 Wherefore if ye be dead with Christ from the rudiments of the world, why, as though living in the world, are ye subject to ordinances,
21 (Touch not; taste not; handle not;
22 Which all are to perish with the using;) after the commandments and doctrines of men?
23 Which things have indeed a shew of wisdom in will worship, and humility, and neglecting of the body; not in any honour to the satisfying of the flesh.

Seek the Things Which Are Above

3 If ye then be risen with Christ, seek those things which are above, where Christ sitteth on the right hand of God.
2 Set your affection on things above, not on things on the earth.
3 For ye are dead, and your life is hid with Christ in God.
4 When Christ, *who is* our life, shall appear, then shall ye also appear with him in glory.
5 Mortify therefore your members which are upon the earth; fornication, uncleanness, inordinate affection, evil concupiscence, and covetousness, which is idolatry:
6 For which things' sake the wrath of God cometh on the children of disobedience:
7 In the which ye also walked some time, when ye lived in them.
8 But now ye also put off all these; anger, wrath, malice, blasphemy, filthy communication out of your mouth.
9 Lie not one to another, seeing that ye have put off the old man with his deeds;

Put on the New Man

10 And have put on the new *man,* which is renewed in knowledge after the image of him that created him:
11 Where there is neither Greek nor Jew, circumcision nor uncircumcision, Barbarian, Scythian, bond *nor* free: but Christ *is* all, and in all.
12 Put on therefore, as the elect of God, holy and beloved, bowels of mercies, kindness, humbleness of mind, meekness, longsuffering;
13 Forbearing one another, and forgiving one another, if any man have a quarrel against any: even as Christ forgave you, so also *do* ye.
14 And above all these things *put on* charity, which is the bond of perfectness.
15 And let the peace of God rule in your hearts, to the which also ye are called in one body; and be ye thankful.
16 Let the word of Christ dwell in you richly in all wisdom; teaching and admonishing one another in psalms and hymns and spiritual songs, singing with grace in your hearts to the Lord.
17 And whatsoever ye do in word or deed, *do* all in the name of the

Lord Jesus, giving thanks to God and the Father by him.

Husbands and Wives

18 Wives, submit yourselves unto your own husbands, as it is fit in the Lord.

19 Husbands, love *your* wives, and be not bitter against them.

20 Children, obey *your* parents in all things: for this is well pleasing unto the Lord.

21 Fathers, provoke not your children *to anger,* lest they be discouraged.

22 Servants, obey in all things *your* masters according to the flesh; not with eyeservice, as menpleasers; but in singleness of heart, fearing God:

23 And whatsoever ye do, do *it* heartily, as to the Lord, and not unto men;

24 Knowing that of the Lord ye shall receive the reward of the inheritance: for ye serve the Lord Christ.

25 But he that doeth wrong shall receive for the wrong which he hath done: and there is no respect of persons.

Walk in Wisdom

4 Masters, give unto *your* servants that which is just and equal; knowing that ye also have a Master in heaven.

2 Continue in prayer, and watch in the same with thanksgiving;

3 Withal praying also for us, that God would open unto us a door of utterance, to speak the mystery of Christ, for which I am also in bonds:

4 That I may make it manifest, as I ought to speak.

5 Walk in wisdom toward them that are without, redeeming the time.

6 Let your speech *be* alway with grace, seasoned with salt, that ye may know how ye ought to answer every man.

Greetings from Believers

7 All my state shall Tychicus declare unto you, *who is* a beloved brother, and a faithful minister and fellowservant in the Lord:

8 Whom I have sent unto you for the same purpose, that he might know your estate, and comfort your hearts;

9 With Onesimus, a faithful and beloved brother, who is *one* of you. They shall make known unto you all things which *are done* here.

10 Aristarchus my fellowprisoner saluteth you, and Marcus, sister's son to Barnabas, (touching whom ye received commandments: if he come unto you, receive him;)

11 And Jesus, which is called Justus, who are of the circumcision. These only *are my* fellowworkers unto the kingdom of God, which have been a comfort unto me.

12 Epaphras, who is *one* of you, a servant of Christ, saluteth you, always labouring fervently for you in prayers, that ye may stand perfect and complete in all the will of God.

13 For I bear him record, that he hath a great zeal for you, and them *that are* in Laodicea, and them in Hierapolis.

14 Luke, the beloved physician, and Demas, greet you.

15 Salute the brethren which are in Laodicea, and Nymphas, and the church which is in his house.

Grace Be with You

16 And when this epistle is read among you, cause that it be read also in the church of the Laodiceans; and that ye likewise read the *epistle* from Laodicea.

17 And say to Archippus, Take heed to the ministry which thou hast received in the Lord, that thou fulfil it.

18 The salutation by the hand of me Paul. Remember my bonds. Grace *be* with you. Amen.

The First Epistle of Paul the Apostle to the THESSALONIANS

The Thessalonians' Work of Faith

Paul, and Silvanus, and Timotheus,
unto the church of the Thessalo-
nians *which is* in God the Father and
in the Lord Jesus Christ: Grace *be*
unto you, and peace, from God our
Father, and the Lord Jesus Christ.
2 We give thanks to God always
for you all, making mention of you
in our prayers;
3 Remembering without ceasing
your work of faith, and labour of
love, and patience of hope in our
Lord Jesus Christ, in the sight of
God and our Father;
4 Knowing, brethren beloved,
your election of God.
5 For our gospel came not unto
you in word only, but also in power,
and in the Holy Ghost, and in much
assurance; as ye know what manner
of men we were among you for your
sake.
6 And ye became followers of us,
and of the Lord, having received the
word in much affliction, with joy of
the Holy Ghost:
7 So that ye were ensamples to
all that believe in Macedonia and
Achaia.
8 For from you sounded out the
word of the Lord not only in Mac-
edonia and Achaia, but also in ev-
ery place your faith to God-ward is
spread abroad; so that we need not
to speak any thing.
9 For they themselves shew of us
what manner of entering in we had
unto you, and how ye turned to God
from idols to serve the living and
true God;
10 And to wait for his Son from
heaven, whom he raised from the
dead, *even* Jesus, which delivered
us from the wrath to come.

Paul Recalls His Conduct

2 For yourselves, brethren, know
our entrance in unto you, that
it was not in vain:
2 But even after that we had suf-
fered before, and were shamefully
entreated, as ye know, at Philippi,
we were bold in our God to speak
unto you the gospel of God with
much contention.
3 For our exhortation *was* not of
deceit, nor of uncleanness, nor in
guile:
4 But as we were allowed of God to
be put in trust with the gospel, even
so we speak; not as pleasing men,
but God, which trieth our hearts.
5 For neither at any time used we
flattering words, as ye know, nor a
cloke of covetousness; God *is* wit-
ness:
6 Nor of men sought we glory, nei-
ther of you, nor *yet* of others, when
we might have been burdensome,
as the apostles of Christ.
7 But we were gentle among you,
even as a nurse cherisheth her chil-
dren:
8 So being affectionately desirous
of you, we were willing to have im-
parted unto you, not the gospel of
God only, but also our own souls,
because ye were dear unto us.

9 For ye remember, brethren, our labour and travail: for labouring night and day, because we would not be chargeable unto any of you, we preached unto you the gospel of God.

10 Ye *are* witnesses, and God *also,* how holily and justly and unblameably we behaved ourselves among you that believe:

11 As ye know how we exhorted and comforted and charged every one of you, as a father *doth* his children,

12 That ye would walk worthy of God, who hath called you unto his kingdom and glory.

Paul's Glory and Joy

13 For this cause also thank we God without ceasing, because, when ye received the word of God which ye heard of us, ye received *it* not *as* the word of men, but as it is in truth, the word of God, which effectually worketh also in you that believe.

14 For ye, brethren, became followers of the churches of God which in Judaea are in Christ Jesus: for ye also have suffered like things of your own countrymen, even as they *have* of the Jews:

15 Who both killed the Lord Jesus, and their own prophets, and have persecuted us; and they please not God, and are contrary to all men:

16 Forbidding us to speak to the Gentiles that they might be saved, to fill up their sins alway: for the wrath is come upon them to the uttermost.

17 But we, brethren, being taken from you for a short time in presence, not in heart, endeavoured the more abundantly to see your face with great desire.

18 Wherefore we would have come unto you, even I Paul, once and again; but Satan hindered us.

19 For what *is* our hope, or joy, or crown of rejoicing? *Are* not even ye in the presence of our Lord Jesus Christ at his coming?

20 For ye are our glory and joy.

Timothy's Good Report

3 Wherefore when we could no longer forbear, we thought it good to be left at Athens alone;

2 And sent Timotheus, our brother, and minister of God, and our fellowlabourer in the gospel of Christ, to establish you, and to comfort you concerning your faith:

3 That no man should be moved by these afflictions: for yourselves know that we are appointed thereunto.

4 For verily, when we were with you, we told you before that we should suffer tribulation; even as it came to pass, and ye know.

5 For this cause, when I could no longer forbear, I sent to know your faith, lest by some means the tempter have tempted you, and our labour be in vain.

6 But now when Timotheus came from you unto us, and brought us good tidings of your faith and charity, and that ye have good remembrance of us always, desiring greatly to see us, as we also *to see* you:

Stand Fast in the Lord

7 Therefore, brethren, we were comforted over you in all our affliction and distress by your faith:

8 For now we live, if ye stand fast in the Lord.

9 For what thanks can we render to God again for you, for all the joy wherewith we joy for your sakes before our God;

10 Night and day praying exceedingly that we might see your face, and might perfect that which is lacking in your faith?

11 Now God himself and our Father, and our Lord Jesus Christ, direct our way unto you.

12 And the Lord make you to in-
crease and abound in love one to-
ward another, and toward all *men,*
even as we *do* toward you:
13 To the end he may stablish your
hearts unblameable in holiness be-
fore God, even our Father, at the
coming of our Lord Jesus Christ
with all his saints.

Called to Holiness

4 Furthermore then we beseech
you, brethren, and exhort *you*
by the Lord Jesus, that as ye have
received of us how ye ought to
walk and to please God, *so* ye would
abound more and more.
2 For ye know what command-
ments we gave you by the Lord
Jesus.
3 For this is the will of God, *even*
your sanctification, that ye should
abstain from fornication:
4 That every one of you should
know how to possess his vessel in
sanctification and honour;
5 Not in the lust of concupiscence,
even as the Gentiles which know not
God:
6 That no *man* go beyond and de-
fraud his brother in *any* matter: be-
cause that the Lord *is* the avenger of
all such, as we also have forewarned
you and testified.
7 For God hath not called us unto
uncleanness, but unto holiness.
8 He therefore that despiseth, de-
spiseth not man, but God, who hath
also given unto us his holy Spirit.
9 But as touching brotherly love
ye need not that I write unto you:
for ye yourselves are taught of God
to love one another.
10 And indeed ye do it toward all
the brethren which are in all Mac-
edonia: but we beseech you, breth-
ren, that ye increase more and more;
11 And that ye study to be quiet,
and to do your own business, and
to work with your own hands, as we
commanded you;
12 That ye may walk honestly to-
ward them that are without, and
that ye may have lack of nothing.

The Dead in Christ Shall Rise

13 But I would not have you to
be ignorant, brethren, concerning
them which are asleep, that ye sor-
row not, even as others which have
no hope.
14 For if we believe that Jesus died
and rose again, even so them also
which sleep in Jesus will God bring
with him.
15 For this we say unto you by the
word of the Lord, that we which are
alive *and* remain unto the coming
of the Lord shall not prevent them
which are asleep.
16 For the Lord himself shall de-
scend from heaven with a shout,
with the voice of the archangel, and
with the trump of God: and the dead
in Christ shall rise first:
17 Then we which are alive *and*
remain shall be caught up together
with them in the clouds, to meet the
Lord in the air: and so shall we ever
be with the Lord.
18 Wherefore comfort one another
with these words.

Concluding Exhortations

5 But of the times and the seasons,
brethren, ye have no need that
I write unto you.
2 For yourselves know perfectly
that the day of the Lord so cometh
as a thief in the night.
3 For when they shall say, Peace
and safety; then sudden destruction
cometh upon them, as travail upon
a woman with child; and they shall
not escape.
4 But ye, brethren, are not in dark-
ness, that that day should overtake
you as a thief.
5 Ye are all the children of light,
and the children of the day: we are
not of the night, nor of darkness.
6 Therefore let us not sleep, as

do others; but let us watch and be
sober.
7 For they that sleep sleep in the
night; and they that be drunken are
drunken in the night.
8 But let us, who are of the day, be
sober, putting on the breastplate of
faith and love; and for an helmet,
the hope of salvation.
9 For God hath not appointed us
to wrath, but to obtain salvation by
our Lord Jesus Christ,
10 Who died for us, that, whether
we wake or sleep, we should live
together with him.
11 Wherefore comfort yourselves
together, and edify one another,
even as also ye do.
12 And we beseech you, brethren,
to know them which labour among
you, and are over you in the Lord,
and admonish you;
13 And to esteem them very highly
in love for their work's sake. *And* be
at peace among yourselves.
14 Now we exhort you, brethren,
warn them that are unruly, com-
fort the feebleminded, support the
weak, be patient toward all *men.*
15 See that none render evil for evil
unto any *man;* but ever follow that
which is good, both among your-
selves, and to all *men.*
16 Rejoice evermore.
17 Pray without ceasing.
18 In every thing give thanks: for
this is the will of God in Christ Jesus
concerning you.
19 Quench not the Spirit.
20 Despise not prophesyings.
21 Prove all things; hold fast that
which is good.
22 Abstain from all appearance
of evil.
23 And the very God of peace
sanctify you wholly; and *I pray
God* your whole spirit and soul
and body be preserved blameless
unto the coming of our Lord Jesus
Christ.
24 Faithful *is* he that calleth you,
who also will do *it.*
25 Brethren, pray for us.
26 Greet all the brethren with an
holy kiss.
27 I charge you by the Lord that
this epistle be read unto all the holy
brethren.
28 The grace of our Lord Jesus
Christ *be* with you. Amen.

The Second Epistle of Paul the Apostle to the

THESSALONIANS

Patience and Faith in Persecutions

Paul, and Silvanus, and Timotheus, unto the church of the Thessalonians in God our Father and the Lord Jesus Christ:

2 Grace unto you, and peace, from God our Father and the Lord Jesus Christ.

3 We are bound to thank God always for you, brethren, as it is meet, because that your faith groweth exceedingly, and the charity of every one of you all toward each other aboundeth;

4 So that we ourselves glory in you in the churches of God for your patience and faith in all your persecutions and tribulations that ye endure:

5 *Which is* a manifest token of the righteous judgment of God, that ye may be counted worthy of the kingdom of God, for which ye also suffer:

6 Seeing *it is* a righteous thing with God to recompense tribulation to them that trouble you;

7 And to you who are troubled rest with us, when the Lord Jesus shall be revealed from heaven with his mighty angels,

8 In flaming fire taking vengeance on them that know not God, and that obey not the gospel of our Lord Jesus Christ:

9 Who shall be punished with everlasting destruction from the presence of the Lord, and from the glory of his power;

10 When he shall come to be glorified in his saints, and to be admired in all them that believe (because our testimony among you was believed) in that day.

Counted Worthy of God's Calling

11 Wherefore also we pray always for you, that our God would count you worthy of *this* calling, and fulfil all the good pleasure of *his* goodness, and the work of faith with power:

12 That the name of our Lord Jesus Christ may be glorified in you, and ye in him, according to the grace of our God and the Lord Jesus Christ.

The Mystery of Iniquity

2 Now we beseech you, brethren, by the coming of our Lord Jesus Christ, and *by* our gathering together unto him,

2 That ye be not soon shaken in mind, or be troubled, neither by spirit, nor by word, nor by letter as from us, as that the day of Christ is at hand.

3 Let no man deceive you by any means: for *that day shall not come,* except there come a falling away first, and that man of sin be revealed, the son of perdition;

4 Who opposeth and exalteth himself above all that is called God, or that is worshipped; so that he as God sitteth in the temple of God, shewing himself that he is God.

5 Remember ye not, that, when I
was yet with you, I told you these
things?
6 And now ye know what with-
holdeth that he might be revealed
in his time.
7 For the mystery of iniquity doth
already work: only he who now
letteth *will let,* until he be taken out
of the way.
8 And then shall that Wicked be
revealed, whom the Lord shall con-
sume with the spirit of his mouth,
and shall destroy with the bright-
ness of his coming:
9 *Even him,* whose coming is after
the working of Satan with all power
and signs and lying wonders,
10 And with all deceivableness of
unrighteousness in them that per-
ish; because they received not the
love of the truth, that they might be
saved.
11 And for this cause God shall
send them strong delusion, that
they should believe a lie:
12 That they all might be damned
who believed not the truth, but had
pleasure in unrighteousness.

Called to the Obtaining of Christ's Glory

13 But we are bound to give
thanks alway to God for you, breth-
ren beloved of the Lord, because
God hath from the beginning cho-
sen you to salvation through sanc-
tification of the Spirit and belief of
the truth:
14 Whereunto he called you by our
gospel, to the obtaining of the glory
of our Lord Jesus Christ.
15 Therefore, brethren, stand fast,
and hold the traditions which ye
have been taught, whether by word,
or our epistle.
16 Now our Lord Jesus Christ
himself, and God, even our Father,
which hath loved us, and hath given
us everlasting consolation and good
hope through grace,
17 Comfort your hearts, and stab-
lish you in every good word and
work.

The Lord Is Faithful

3 Finally, brethren, pray for us,
that the word of the Lord may
have *free* course, and be glorified,
even as *it is* with you:
2 And that we may be delivered
from unreasonable and wicked
men: for all *men* have not faith.
3 But the Lord is faithful, who shall
stablish you, and keep *you* from evil.
4 And we have confidence in the
Lord touching you, that ye both do
and will do the things which we
command you.
5 And the Lord direct your hearts
into the love of God, and into the
patient waiting for Christ.

Be Not Weary in Well Doing

6 Now we command you, breth-
ren, in the name of our Lord Jesus
Christ, that ye withdraw yourselves
from every brother that walketh dis-
orderly, and not after the tradition
which he received of us.
7 For yourselves know how ye
ought to follow us: for we behaved
not ourselves disorderly among you;
8 Neither did we eat any man's
bread for nought; but wrought with
labour and travail night and day,
that we might not be chargeable to
any of you:
9 Not because we have not power,
but to make ourselves an ensample
unto you to follow us.
10 For even when we were with
you, this we commanded you, that if
any would not work, neither should
he eat.
11 For we hear that there are some
which walk among you disorderly,
working not at all, but are busy-
bodies.
12 Now them that are such we
command and exhort by our Lord
Jesus Christ, that with quietness

they work, and eat their own bread.
13 But ye, brethren, be not weary
in well doing.
14 And if any man obey not our
word by this epistle, note that man,
and have no company with him, that
he may be ashamed.
15 Yet count *him* not as an enemy,
but admonish *him* as a brother.

Peace by All Means

16 Now the Lord of peace himself
give you peace always by all means.
The Lord *be* with you all.
17 The salutation of Paul with
mine own hand, which is the token
in every epistle: so I write.
18 The grace of our Lord Jesus
Christ be with you all. Amen.

The First Epistle of Paul the Apostle to
TIMOTHY

Greeting

Paul, an apostle of Jesus Christ
by the commandment of God
our Saviour, and Lord Jesus Christ,
which is our hope;
2 Unto Timothy, *my* own son in
the faith: Grace, mercy, *and* peace,
from God our Father and Jesus
Christ our Lord.

Teach No Other Doctrine

3 As I besought thee to abide still
at Ephesus, when I went into Mac-
edonia, that thou mightest charge
some that they teach no other doc-
trine,
4 Neither give heed to fables and
endless genealogies, which minister
questions, rather than godly edify-
ing which is in faith: *so do.*
5 Now the end of the command-
ment is charity out of a pure heart,
and *of* a good conscience, and *of*
faith unfeigned:
6 From which some having
swerved have turned aside unto
vain jangling;
7 Desiring to be teachers of the
law; understanding neither what
they say, nor whereof they affirm.
8 But we know that the law *is*
good, if a man use it lawfully;
9 Knowing this, that the law is not
made for a righteous man, but for
the lawless and disobedient, for the
ungodly and for sinners, for unholy
and profane, for murderers of fa-
thers and murderers of mothers,
for manslayers,
10 For whoremongers, for them
that defile themselves with man-
kind, for menstealers, for liars, for
perjured persons, and if there be
any other thing that is contrary to
sound doctrine;
11 According to the glorious gos-
pel of the blessed God, which was
committed to my trust.

God's Mercy Toward Paul

12 And I thank Christ Jesus our
Lord, who hath enabled me, for that
he counted me faithful, putting me
into the ministry;
13 Who was before a blasphemer,
and a persecutor, and injurious: but
I obtained mercy, because I did *it*
ignorantly in unbelief.
14 And the grace of our Lord was
exceeding abundant with faith and
love which is in Christ Jesus.
15 This *is* a faithful saying, and
worthy of all acceptation, that Christ
Jesus came into the world to save
sinners; of whom I am chief.
16 Howbeit for this cause I ob-
tained mercy, that in me first Jesus
Christ might shew forth all longsuf-
fering, for a pattern to them which
should hereafter believe on him to
life everlasting.
17 Now unto the King eternal, im-
mortal, invisible, the only wise God,
be honour and glory for ever and
ever. Amen.
18 This charge I commit unto
thee, son Timothy, according to the
prophecies which went before on
thee, that thou by them mightest
war a good warfare;

19 Holding faith, and a good conscience; which some having put away concerning faith have made shipwreck:

20 Of whom is Hymenaeus and Alexander; whom I have delivered unto Satan, that they may learn not to blaspheme.

Prayers for All Men

2 I exhort therefore, that, first of all, supplications, prayers, intercessions, *and* giving of thanks, be made for all men;

2 For kings, and *for* all that are in authority; that we may lead a quiet and peaceable life in all godliness and honesty.

3 For this *is* good and acceptable in the sight of God our Saviour;

4 Who will have all men to be saved, and to come unto the knowledge of the truth.

5 For *there is* one God, and one mediator between God and men, the man Christ Jesus;

6 Who gave himself a ransom for all, to be testified in due time.

7 Whereunto I am ordained a preacher, and an apostle, (I speak the truth in Christ, *and* lie not;) a teacher of the Gentiles in faith and verity.

8 I will therefore that men pray every where, lifting up holy hands, without wrath and doubting.

Women's Adornment and Behaviour

9 In like manner also, that women adorn themselves in modest apparel, with shamefacedness and sobriety; not with broided hair, or gold, or pearls, or costly array;

10 But (which becometh women professing godliness) with good works.

11 Let the woman learn in silence with all subjection.

12 But I suffer not a woman to teach, nor to usurp authority over the man, but to be in silence.

13 For Adam was first formed, then Eve.

14 And Adam was not deceived, but the woman being deceived was in the transgression.

15 Notwithstanding she shall be saved in childbearing, if they continue in faith and charity and holiness with sobriety.

Qualifications for Bishops

3 This *is* a true saying, If a man desire the office of a bishop, he desireth a good work.

2 A bishop then must be blameless, the husband of one wife, vigilant, sober, of good behaviour, given to hospitality, apt to teach;

3 Not given to wine, no striker, not greedy of filthy lucre; but patient, not a brawler, not covetous;

4 One that ruleth well his own house, having his children in subjection with all gravity;

5 (For if a man know not how to rule his own house, how shall he take care of the church of God?)

6 Not a novice, lest being lifted up with pride he fall into the condemnation of the devil.

7 Moreover he must have a good report of them which are without; lest he fall into reproach and the snare of the devil.

Qualifications for Deacons

8 Likewise *must* the deacons *be* grave, not doubletongued, not given to much wine, not greedy of filthy lucre;

9 Holding the mystery of the faith in a pure conscience.

10 And let these also first be proved; then let them use the office of a deacon, being *found* blameless.

11 Even so *must their* wives *be* grave, not slanderers, sober, faithful in all things.

12 Let the deacons be the husbands of one wife, ruling their chil-

dren and their own houses well.
13 For they that have used the
office of a deacon well purchase
to themselves a good degree, and
great boldness in the faith which is
in Christ Jesus.
14 These things write I unto thee,
hoping to come unto thee shortly:
15 But if I tarry long, that thou
mayest know how thou oughtest
to behave thyself in the house of
God, which is the church of the liv-
ing God, the pillar and ground of the
truth.
16 And without controversy great
is the mystery of godliness: God was
manifest in the flesh, justified in
the Spirit, seen of angels, preached
unto the Gentiles, believed on in the
world, received up into glory.

Paul's Warnings of False Teachers

4 Now the Spirit speaketh ex-
pressly, that in the latter times
some shall depart from the faith,
giving heed to seducing spirits, and
doctrines of devils;
2 Speaking lies in hypocrisy; hav-
ing their conscience seared with a
hot iron;
3 Forbidding to marry, *and com-*
manding to abstain from meats,
which God hath created to be re-
ceived with thanksgiving of them
which believe and know the truth.
4 For every creature of God *is*
good, and nothing to be refused, if
it be received with thanksgiving:
5 For it is sanctified by the word
of God and prayer.
6 If thou put the brethren in re-
membrance of these things, thou
shalt be a good minister of Jesus
Christ, nourished up in the words of
faith and of good doctrine, where-
unto thou hast attained.
7 But refuse profane and old
wives' fables, and exercise thyself
rather unto godliness.
8 For bodily exercise profiteth lit-
tle: but godliness is profitable unto
all things, having promise of the life
that now is, and of that which is to
come.
9 This *is* a faithful saying and wor-
thy of all acceptation.
10 For therefore we both labour
and suffer reproach, because we
trust in the living God, who is the
Saviour of all men, specially of those
that believe.
11 These things command and
teach.

Be an Example

12 Let no man despise thy youth;
but be thou an example of the be-
lievers, in word, in conversation, in
charity, in spirit, in faith, in purity.
13 Till I come, give attendance to
reading, to exhortation, to doctrine.
14 Neglect not the gift that is
in thee, which was given thee by
prophecy, with the laying on of the
hands of the presbytery.
15 Meditate upon these things;
give thyself wholly to them; that
thy profiting may appear to all.
16 Take heed unto thyself, and
unto the doctrine; continue in them:
for in doing this thou shalt both save
thyself, and them that hear thee.

Provisions for Widows

5 Rebuke not an elder, but intreat
him as a father; *and* the younger
men as brethren;
2 The elder women as mothers;
the younger as sisters, with all pu-
rity.
3 Honour widows that are widows
indeed.
4 But if any widow have children
or nephews, let them learn first to
shew piety at home, and to requite
their parents: for that is good and
acceptable before God.
5 Now she that is a widow indeed,
and desolate, trusteth in God, and
continueth in supplications and
prayers night and day.

6 But she that liveth in pleasure
is dead while she liveth.
7 And these things give in charge,
that they may be blameless.
8 But if any provide not for his
own, and specially for those of his
own house, he hath denied the faith,
and is worse than an infidel.
9 Let not a widow be taken into
the number under threescore years
old, having been the wife of one
man,
10 Well reported of for good works;
if she have brought up children, if
she have lodged strangers, if she
have washed the saints' feet, if she
have relieved the afflicted, if she
have diligently followed every good
work.

Counsel for Younger Widows

11 But the younger widows refuse:
for when they have begun to wax
wanton against Christ, they will
marry;
12 Having damnation, because
they have cast off their first faith.
13 And withal they learn *to be*
idle, wandering about from house
to house; and not only idle, but tat-
tlers also and busybodies, speaking
things which they ought not.
14 I will therefore that the
younger women marry, bear chil-
dren, guide the house, give none
occasion to the adversary to speak
reproachfully.
15 For some are already turned
aside after Satan.
16 If any man or woman that be-
lieveth have widows, let them re-
lieve them, and let not the church
be charged; that it may relieve them
that are widows indeed.

Honour the Elders

17 Let the elders that rule well be
counted worthy of double honour,
especially they who labour in the
word and doctrine.
18 For the scripture saith, Thou
shalt not muzzle the ox that tread-
eth out the corn. And, The labourer
is worthy of his reward.
19 Against an elder receive not an
accusation, but before two or three
witnesses.
20 Them that sin rebuke before
all, that others also may fear.
21 I charge *thee* before God, and
the Lord Jesus Christ, and the elect
angels, that thou observe these
things without preferring one be-
fore another, doing nothing by par-
tiality.
22 Lay hands suddenly on no man,
neither be partaker of other men's
sins: keep thyself pure.
23 Drink no longer water, but use
a little wine for thy stomach's sake
and thine often infirmities.
24 Some men's sins are open
beforehand, going before to judg-
ment; and some *men* they follow
after.
25 Likewise also the good works
of some are manifest beforehand;
and they that are otherwise cannot
be hid.

Honour Your Masters

6 Let as many servants as are un-
der the yoke count their own
masters worthy of all honour, that
the name of God and *his* doctrine
be not blasphemed.
2 And they that have believing
masters, let them not despise
them, because they are brethren;
but rather do *them* service, because
they are faithful and beloved, par-
takers of the benefit. These things
teach and exhort.
3 If any man teach otherwise, and
consent not to wholesome words,
even the words of our Lord Jesus
Christ, and to the doctrine which
is according to godliness;
4 He is proud, knowing nothing,
but doting about questions and
strifes of words, whereof cometh
envy, strife, railings, evil surmisings,

5 Perverse disputings of men of corrupt minds, and destitute of the truth, supposing that gain is godliness: from such withdraw thyself.

The Root of All Evil

6 But godliness with contentment is great gain.

7 For we brought nothing into *this* world, *and it is* certain we can carry nothing out.

8 And having food and raiment let us be therewith content.

9 But they that will be rich fall into temptation and a snare, and *into* many foolish and hurtful lusts, which drown men in destruction and perdition.

10 For the love of money is the root of all evil: which while some coveted after, they have erred from the faith, and pierced themselves through with many sorrows.

Fight the Good Fight of Faith

11 But thou, O man of God, flee these things; and follow after righteousness, godliness, faith, love, patience, meekness.

12 Fight the good fight of faith, lay hold on eternal life, whereunto thou art also called, and hast professed a good profession before many witnesses.

13 I give thee charge in the sight of God, who quickeneth all things, and *before* Christ Jesus, who before Pontius Pilate witnessed a good confession;

14 That thou keep *this* commandment without spot, unrebukeable, until the appearing of our Lord Jesus Christ:

15 Which in his times he shall shew, *who is* the blessed and only Potentate, the King of kings, and Lord of lords;

16 Who only hath immortality, dwelling in the light which no man can approach unto; whom no man hath seen, nor can see: to whom *be* honour and power everlasting. Amen.

Be Trustworthy

17 Charge them that are rich in this world, that they be not highminded, nor trust in uncertain riches, but in the living God, who giveth us richly all things to enjoy;

18 That they do good, that they be rich in good works, ready to distribute, willing to communicate;

19 Laying up in store for themselves a good foundation against the time to come, that they may lay hold on eternal life.

20 O Timothy, keep that which is committed to thy trust, avoiding profane *and* vain babblings, and oppositions of science falsely so called:

21 Which some professing have erred concerning the faith. Grace *be* with thee. Amen.

The Second Epistle of Paul to TIMOTHY

Timothy's Unfeigned Faith

Paul, an apostle of Jesus Christ by the will of God, according to the promise of life which is in Christ Jesus,

2 To Timothy, *my* dearly beloved son: Grace, mercy, *and* peace, from God the Father and Christ Jesus our Lord.

3 I thank God, whom I serve from *my* forefathers with pure conscience, that without ceasing I have remembrance of thee in my prayers night and day;

4 Greatly desiring to see thee, being mindful of thy tears, that I may be filled with joy;

5 When I call to remembrance the unfeigned faith that is in thee, which dwelt first in thy grandmother Lois, and thy mother Eunice; and I am persuaded that in thee also.

6 Wherefore I put thee in remembrance that thou stir up the gift of God, which is in thee by the putting on of my hands.

7 For God hath not given us the spirit of fear; but of power, and of love, and of a sound mind.

The Lord's Testimony

8 Be not thou therefore ashamed of the testimony of our Lord, nor of me his prisoner: but be thou partaker of the afflictions of the gospel according to the power of God;

9 Who hath saved us, and called *us* with an holy calling, not according to our works, but according to his own purpose and grace, which was given us in Christ Jesus before the world began,

10 But is now made manifest by the appearing of our Saviour Jesus Christ, who hath abolished death, and hath brought life and immortality to light through the gospel:

11 Whereunto I am appointed a preacher, and an apostle, and a teacher of the Gentiles.

12 For the which cause I also suffer these things: nevertheless I am not ashamed: for I know whom I have believed, and am persuaded that he is able to keep that which I have committed unto him against that day.

13 Hold fast the form of sound words, which thou hast heard of me, in faith and love which is in Christ Jesus.

14 That good thing which was committed unto thee keep by the Holy Ghost which dwelleth in us.

15 This thou knowest, that all they which are in Asia be turned away from me; of whom are Phygellus and Hermogenes.

16 The Lord give mercy unto the house of Onesiphorus; for he oft refreshed me, and was not ashamed of my chain:

17 But, when he was in Rome, he sought me out very diligently, and found *me*.

18 The Lord grant unto him that he may find mercy of the Lord in that day: and in how many things he ministered unto me at Ephesus, thou knowest very well.

Be Strong in the Grace of Christ

2 Thou therefore, my son, be strong in the grace that is in Christ Jesus.

2 And the things that thou hast heard of me among many witnesses, the same commit thou to faithful men, who shall be able to teach others also.

3 Thou therefore endure hardness, as a good soldier of Jesus Christ.

4 No man that warreth entangleth himself with the affairs of *this* life; that he may please him who hath chosen him to be a soldier.

5 And if a man also strive for masteries, *yet* is he not crowned, except he strive lawfully.

6 The husbandman that laboureth must be first partaker of the fruits.

7 Consider what I say; and the Lord give thee understanding in all things.

The Word of God Is Not Bound

8 Remember that Jesus Christ of the seed of David was raised from the dead according to my gospel:

9 Wherein I suffer trouble, as an evil doer, *even* unto bonds; but the word of God is not bound.

10 Therefore I endure all things for the elect's sakes, that they may also obtain the salvation which is in Christ Jesus with eternal glory.

11 *It is* a faithful saying: For if we be dead with *him*, we shall also live with *him:*

12 If we suffer, we shall also reign with *him:* if we deny *him*, he also will deny us:

13 If we believe not, *yet* he abideth faithful: he cannot deny himself.

Work for God's Approval

14 Of these things put *them* in remembrance, charging *them* before the Lord that they strive not about words to no profit, *but* to the subverting of the hearers.

15 Study to shew thyself approved unto God, a workman that needeth not to be ashamed, rightly dividing the word of truth.

16 But shun profane *and* vain babblings: for they will increase unto more ungodliness.

17 And their word will eat as doth a canker: of whom is Hymenaeus and Philetus;

18 Who concerning the truth have erred, saying that the resurrection is past already; and overthrow the faith of some.

19 Nevertheless the foundation of God standeth sure, having this seal, The Lord knoweth them that are his. And, Let every one that nameth the name of Christ depart from iniquity.

20 But in a great house there are not only vessels of gold and of silver, but also of wood and of earth; and some to honour, and some to dishonour.

21 If a man therefore purge himself from these, he shall be a vessel unto honour, sanctified, and meet for the master's use, *and* prepared unto every good work.

Flee Youthful Lusts

22 Flee also youthful lusts: but follow righteousness, faith, charity, peace, with them that call on the Lord out of a pure heart.

23 But foolish and unlearned questions avoid, knowing that they do gender strifes.

24 And the servant of the Lord must not strive; but be gentle unto all *men*, apt to teach, patient,

25 In meekness instructing those that oppose themselves; if God peradventure will give them repentance to the acknowledging of the truth;

26 And *that* they may recover themselves out of the snare of the devil, who are taken captive by him at his will.

Perilous Times Shall Come

3 This know also, that in the last
days perilous times shall come.
2 For men shall be lovers of their
own selves, covetous, boasters,
proud, blasphemers, disobedient
to parents, unthankful, unholy,
3 Without natural affection, truce-
breakers, false accusers, inconti-
nent, fierce, despisers of those that
are good,
4 Traitors, heady, highminded,
lovers of pleasures more than lovers
of God;
5 Having a form of godliness, but
denying the power thereof: from
such turn away.
6 For of this sort are they which
creep into houses, and lead cap-
tive silly women laden with sins,
led away with divers lusts,
7 Ever learning, and never able to
come to the knowledge of the truth.
8 Now as Jannes and Jambres
withstood Moses, so do these also
resist the truth: men of corrupt
minds, reprobate concerning the
faith.
9 But they shall proceed no fur-
ther: for their folly shall be manifest
unto all *men,* as theirs also was.

All Scripture Is Inspired

10 But thou hast fully known my
doctrine, manner of life, purpose,
faith, longsuffering, charity, pa-
tience,
11 Persecutions, afflictions, which
came unto me at Antioch, at Ico-
nium, at Lystra; what persecutions
I endured: but out of *them* all the
Lord delivered me.
12 Yea, and all that will live godly in
Christ Jesus shall suffer persecution.
13 But evil men and seducers shall
wax worse and worse, deceiving,
and being deceived.
14 But continue thou in the things
which thou hast learned and hast
been assured of, knowing of whom
thou hast learned *them;*
15 And that from a child thou hast
known the holy scriptures, which
are able to make thee wise unto
salvation through faith which is in
Christ Jesus.
16 All scripture *is* given by inspi-
ration of God, and *is* profitable for
doctrine, for reproof, for correction,
for instruction in righteousness:
17 That the man of God may be
perfect, throughly furnished unto
all good works.

Preach the Word

4 I charge *thee* therefore before
God, and the Lord Jesus Christ,
who shall judge the quick and the
dead at his appearing and his king-
dom;
2 Preach the word; be instant in
season, out of season; reprove, re-
buke, exhort with all longsuffering
and doctrine.
3 For the time will come when
they will not endure sound doctrine;
but after their own lusts shall they
heap to themselves teachers, having
itching ears;
4 And they shall turn away *their*
ears from the truth, and shall be
turned unto fables.
5 But watch thou in all things, en-
dure afflictions, do the work of an
evangelist, make full proof of thy
ministry.
6 For I am now ready to be offered,
and the time of my departure is at
hand.
7 I have fought a good fight, I have
finished *my* course, I have kept the
faith:
8 Henceforth there is laid up for
me a crown of righteousness, which
the Lord, the righteous judge, shall
give me at that day: and not to me
only, but unto all them also that love
his appearing.

Personal Requests

9 Do thy diligence to come shortly
unto me:

10 For Demas hath forsaken me, having loved this present world, and is departed unto Thessalonica; Crescens to Galatia, Titus unto Dalmatia.
11 Only Luke is with me. Take Mark, and bring him with thee: for he is profitable to me for the ministry.
12 And Tychicus have I sent to Ephesus.
13 The cloke that I left at Troas with Carpus, when thou comest, bring *with thee,* and the books, *but* especially the parchments.
14 Alexander the coppersmith did me much evil: the Lord reward him according to his works:
15 Of whom be thou ware also; for he hath greatly withstood our words.

The Lord Shall Deliver

16 At my first answer no man stood with me, but all *men* forsook me: *I pray God* that it may not be laid to their charge.
17 Notwithstanding the Lord stood with me, and strengthened me; that by me the preaching might be fully known, and *that* all the Gentiles might hear: and I was delivered out of the mouth of the lion.
18 And the Lord shall deliver me from every evil work, and will preserve *me* unto his heavenly kingdom: to whom *be* glory for ever and ever. Amen.
19 Salute Prisca and Aquila, and the household of Onesiphorus.
20 Erastus abode at Corinth: but Trophimus have I left at Miletum sick.
21 Do thy diligence to come before winter. Eubulus greeteth thee, and Pudens, and Linus, and Claudia, and all the brethren.
22 The Lord Jesus Christ *be* with thy spirit. Grace *be* with you. Amen.

The Epistle of Paul to

TITUS

Paul's Son in the Faith

Paul, a servant of God, and an apostle of Jesus Christ, according to the faith of God's elect, and the acknowledging of the truth which is after godliness;

2 In hope of eternal life, which God, that cannot lie, promised before the world began;

3 But hath in due times manifested his word through preaching, which is committed unto me according to the commandment of God our Saviour;

4 To Titus, *mine* own son after the common faith: Grace, mercy, *and* peace, from God the Father and the Lord Jesus Christ our Saviour.

Qualifications for Leaders

5 For this cause left I thee in Crete, that thou shouldest set in order the things that are wanting, and ordain elders in every city, as I had appointed thee:

6 If any be blameless, the husband of one wife, having faithful children not accused of riot or unruly.

7 For a bishop must be blameless, as the steward of God; not selfwilled, not soon angry, not given to wine, no striker, not given to filthy lucre;

8 But a lover of hospitality, a lover of good men, sober, just, holy, temperate;

9 Holding fast the faithful word as he hath been taught, that he may be able by sound doctrine both to exhort and to convince the gainsayers.

Rebuke the Vain Talkers

10 For there are many unruly and vain talkers and deceivers, specially they of the circumcision:

11 Whose mouths must be stopped, who subvert whole houses, teaching things which they ought not, for filthy lucre's sake.

12 One of themselves, *even* a prophet of their own, said, The Cretians *are* alway liars, evil beasts, slow bellies.

13 This witness is true. Wherefore rebuke them sharply, that they may be sound in the faith;

14 Not giving heed to Jewish fables, and commandments of men, that turn from the truth.

15 Unto the pure all things *are* pure: but unto them that are defiled and unbelieving *is* nothing pure; but even their mind and conscience is defiled.

16 They profess that they know God; but in works they deny *him,* being abominable, and disobedient, and unto every good work reprobate.

Teach Sound Doctrine

2 But speak thou the things which become sound doctrine:

2 That the aged men be sober, grave, temperate, sound in faith, in charity, in patience.

3 The aged women likewise, that *they be* in behaviour as becometh holiness, not false accusers, not given to much wine, teachers of good things;

4 That they may teach the young women to be sober, to love their husbands, to love their children,

5 *To be* discreet, chaste, keepers at home, good, obedient to their own husbands, that the word of God be not blasphemed.

6 Young men likewise exhort to be sober minded.

7 In all things shewing thyself a pattern of good works: in doctrine *shewing* uncorruptness, gravity, sincerity,

8 Sound speech, that cannot be condemned; that he that is of the contrary part may be ashamed, having no evil thing to say of you.

9 *Exhort* servants to be obedient unto their own masters, *and* to please *them* well in all *things;* not answering again;

10 Not purloining, but shewing all good fidelity; that they may adorn the doctrine of God our Saviour in all things.

Teachings of the Grace of God

11 For the grace of God that bringeth salvation hath appeared to all men,

12 Teaching us that, denying ungodliness and worldly lusts, we should live soberly, righteously, and godly, in this present world;

13 Looking for that blessed hope, and the glorious appearing of the great God and our Saviour Jesus Christ;

14 Who gave himself for us, that he might redeem us from all iniquity, and purify unto himself a peculiar people, zealous of good works.

15 These things speak, and exhort, and rebuke with all authority. Let no man despise thee.

Justified by God's Grace

3 Put them in mind to be subject to principalities and powers, to obey magistrates, to be ready to every good work,

2 To speak evil of no man, to be no brawlers, *but* gentle, shewing all meekness unto all men.

3 For we ourselves also were sometimes foolish, disobedient, deceived, serving divers lusts and pleasures, living in malice and envy, hateful, *and* hating one another.

4 But after that the kindness and love of God our Saviour toward man appeared,

5 Not by works of righteousness which we have done, but according to his mercy he saved us, by the washing of regeneration, and renewing of the Holy Ghost;

6 Which he shed on us abundantly through Jesus Christ our Saviour;

7 That being justified by his grace, we should be made heirs according to the hope of eternal life.

Maintain Good Works

8 *This is* a faithful saying, and these things I will that thou affirm constantly, that they which have believed in God might be careful to maintain good works. These things are good and profitable unto men.

9 But avoid foolish questions, and genealogies, and contentions, and strivings about the law; for they are unprofitable and vain.

10 A man that is an heretick after the first and second admonition reject;

11 Knowing that he that is such is subverted, and sinneth, being condemned of himself.

Closing Remarks

12 When I shall send Artemas unto thee, or Tychicus, be diligent to come unto me to Nicopolis: for I have determined there to winter.

13 Bring Zenas the lawyer and Apollos on their journey diligently, that nothing be wanting unto them.

14 And let ours also learn to maintain good works for necessary uses, that they be not unfruitful.

15 All that are with me salute thee. Greet them that love us in the faith. Grace *be* with you all. Amen.

The Epistle of Paul to PHILEMON

Philemon's Faith

Paul, a prisoner of Jesus Christ,
and Timothy *our* brother, unto
Philemon our dearly beloved, and
fellowlabourer,
2 And to *our* beloved Apphia, and
Archippus our fellowsoldier, and to
the church in thy house:
3 Grace to you, and peace, from
God our Father and the Lord Jesus
Christ.
4 I thank my God, making mention
of thee always in my prayers,
5 Hearing of thy love and faith,
which thou hast toward the Lord
Jesus, and toward all saints;
6 That the communication of thy
faith may become effectual by the
acknowledging of every good thing
which is in you in Christ Jesus.
7 For we have great joy and con-
solation in thy love, because the
bowels of the saints are refreshed
by thee, brother.

Paul's Intercession for Onesimus

8 Wherefore, though I might be
much bold in Christ to enjoin thee
that which is convenient,
9 Yet for love's sake I rather be-
seech *thee,* being such an one as
Paul the aged, and now also a pris-
oner of Jesus Christ.
10 I beseech thee for my son Ones-
imus, whom I have begotten in my
bonds:
11 Which in time past was to thee
unprofitable, but now profitable to
thee and to me:
12 Whom I have sent again: thou
therefore receive him, that is, mine
own bowels:
13 Whom I would have retained
with me, that in thy stead he might
have ministered unto me in the
bonds of the gospel:
14 But without thy mind would I
do nothing; that thy benefit should
not be as it were of necessity, but
willingly.
15 For perhaps he therefore de-
parted for a season, that thou
shouldest receive him for ever;
16 Not now as a servant, but above
a servant, a brother beloved, spe-
cially to me, but how much more
unto thee, both in the flesh, and in
the Lord?
17 If thou count me therefore a
partner, receive him as myself.
18 If he hath wronged thee, or
oweth *thee* ought, put that on mine
account;
19 I Paul have written *it* with mine
own hand, I will repay *it:* albeit I
do not say to thee how thou owest
unto me even thine own self be-
sides.

Paul Encourages Philemon's Obedience

20 Yea, brother, let me have joy of
thee in the Lord: refresh my bowels
in the Lord.
21 Having confidence in thy obe-
dience I wrote unto thee, knowing
that thou wilt also do more than I
say.
22 But withal prepare me also a
lodging: for I trust that through your
prayers I shall be given unto you.

23 There salute thee Epaphras,
my fellowprisoner in Christ Jesus;
24 Marcus, Aristarchus, Demas,
Lucas, my fellowlabourers.
25 The grace of our Lord Jesus
Christ *be* with your spirit. Amen.

The Epistle to the
HEBREWS

God's Son Better than Angels

God, who at sundry times and in
divers manners spake in time
past unto the fathers by the proph-
ets,
2 Hath in these last days spoken
unto us by *his* Son, whom he hath
appointed heir of all things, by
whom also he made the worlds;
3 Who being the brightness of *his*
glory, and the express image of his
person, and upholding all things by
the word of his power, when he had
by himself purged our sins, sat down
on the right hand of the Majesty on
high;
4 Being made so much better than
the angels, as he hath by inheritance
obtained a more excellent name
than they.
5 For unto which of the angels said
he at any time, Thou art my Son,
this day have I begotten thee? And
again, I will be to him a Father, and
he shall be to me a Son?
6 And again, when he bringeth in
the firstbegotten into the world, he
saith, And let all the angels of God
worship him.
7 And of the angels he saith, Who
maketh his angels spirits, and his
ministers a flame of fire.

A Sceptre of Righteousness

8 But unto the Son *he saith,* Thy
throne, O God, *is* for ever and ever:
a sceptre of righteousness *is* the
sceptre of thy kingdom.
9 Thou hast loved righteousness,
and hated iniquity; therefore God,
even thy God, hath anointed thee
with the oil of gladness above thy
fellows.
10 And, Thou, Lord, in the begin-
ning hast laid the foundation of the
earth; and the heavens are the works
of thine hands:
11 They shall perish; but thou re-
mainest; and they all shall wax old
as doth a garment;
12 And as a vesture shalt thou fold
them up, and they shall be changed:
but thou art the same, and thy years
shall not fail.
13 But to which of the angels said
he at any time, Sit on my right hand,
until I make thine enemies thy foot-
stool?
14 Are they not all ministering
spirits, sent forth to minister for
them who shall be heirs of salvation?

Give Earnest Heed
to Salvation

2 Therefore we ought to give the
more earnest heed to the things
which we have heard, lest at any
time we should let *them* slip.
2 For if the word spoken by angels
was stedfast, and every transgres-
sion and disobedience received a
just recompence of reward;
3 How shall we escape, if we ne-
glect so great salvation; which at
the first began to be spoken by the
Lord, and was confirmed unto us
by them that heard *him;*
4 God also bearing *them* witness,
both with signs and wonders, and
with divers miracles, and gifts of the
Holy Ghost, according to his own
will?

5 For unto the angels hath he not
put in subjection the world to come,
whereof we speak.
6 But one in a certain place testi-
fied, saying, What is man, that thou
art mindful of him? or the son of
man, that thou visitest him?
7 Thou madest him a little lower
than the angels; thou crownedst
him with glory and honour, and
didst set him over the works of thy
hands:
8 Thou hast put all things in sub-
jection under his feet. For in that
he put all in subjection under him,
he left nothing *that is* not put un-
der him. But now we see not yet all
things put under him.

A Crown of Glory and Honour

9 But we see Jesus, who was made
a little lower than the angels for the
suffering of death, crowned with
glory and honour; that he by the
grace of God should taste death for
every man.
10 For it became him, for whom
are all things, and by whom *are* all
things, in bringing many sons unto
glory, to make the captain of their
salvation perfect through sufferings.
11 For both he that sanctifieth
and they who are sanctified *are* all
of one: for which cause he is not
ashamed to call them brethren,
12 Saying, I will declare thy name
unto my brethren, in the midst of
the church will I sing praise unto
thee.
13 And again, I will put my trust
in him. And again, Behold I and the
children which God hath given me.

A Merciful High Priest

14 Forasmuch then as the children
are partakers of flesh and blood, he
also himself likewise took part of the
same; that through death he might
destroy him that had the power of
death, that is, the devil;
15 And deliver them who through
fear of death were all their lifetime
subject to bondage.
16 For verily he took not on *him
the nature of* angels; but he took on
him the seed of Abraham.
17 Wherefore in all things it be-
hoved him to be made like unto *his*
brethren, that he might be a merci-
ful and faithful high priest in things
pertaining to God, to make recon-
ciliation for the sins of the people.
18 For in that he himself hath suf-
fered being tempted, he is able to
succour them that are tempted.

The House of Christ

3 Wherefore, holy brethren, par-
takers of the heavenly calling,
consider the Apostle and High Priest
of our profession, Christ Jesus;
2 Who was faithful to him that
appointed him, as also Moses *was
faithful* in all his house.
3 For this *man* was counted wor-
thy of more glory than Moses, inas-
much as he who hath builded the
house hath more honour than the
house.
4 For every house is builded by
some *man;* but he that built all
things *is* God.
5 And Moses verily *was* faithful
in all his house, as a servant, for a
testimony of those things which
were to be spoken after;
6 But Christ as a son over his own
house; whose house are we, if we
hold fast the confidence and the
rejoicing of the hope firm unto the
end.

The Evil Heart of Unbelief

7 Wherefore (as the Holy Ghost
saith, To day if ye will hear his voice,
8 Harden not your hearts, as in the
provocation, in the day of tempta-
tion in the wilderness:
9 When your fathers tempted me,
proved me, and saw my works forty
years.
10 Wherefore I was grieved with

that generation, and said, They do
alway err in *their* heart; and they
have not known my ways.
11 So I sware in my wrath, They
shall not enter into my rest.)
12 Take heed, brethren, lest there
be in any of you an evil heart of un-
belief, in departing from the living
God.
13 But exhort one another daily,
while it is called To day; lest any of
you be hardened through the de-
ceitfulness of sin.
14 For we are made partakers of
Christ, if we hold the beginning of
our confidence stedfast unto the
end;
15 While it is said, To day if ye
will hear his voice, harden not your
hearts, as in the provocation.

The Unheeding Israelites

16 For some, when they had heard,
did provoke: howbeit not all that
came out of Egypt by Moses.
17 But with whom was he grieved
forty years? *was it* not with them
that had sinned, whose carcases
fell in the wilderness?
18 And to whom sware he that
they should not enter into his rest,
but to them that believed not?
19 So we see that they could not
enter in because of unbelief.

Labour to Enter God's Rest

4 Let us therefore fear, lest, a
promise being left *us* of enter-
ing into his rest, any of you should
seem to come short of it.
2 For unto us was the gospel
preached, as well as unto them: but
the word preached did not profit
them, not being mixed with faith
in them that heard *it.*
3 For we which have believed do
enter into rest, as he said, As I have
sworn in my wrath, if they shall en-
ter into my rest: although the works
were finished from the foundation
of the world.
4 For he spake in a certain place of
the seventh *day* on this wise, And
God did rest the seventh day from
all his works.
5 And in this *place* again, If they
shall enter into my rest.

Harden Not Your Hearts

6 Seeing therefore it remaineth
that some must enter therein, and
they to whom it was first preached
entered not in because of unbelief:
7 Again, he limiteth a certain
day, saying in David, To day, after
so long a time; as it is said, To day
if ye will hear his voice, harden not
your hearts.
8 For if Jesus had given them rest,
then would he not afterward have
spoken of another day.
9 There remaineth therefore a rest
to the people of God.
10 For he that is entered into his
rest, he also hath ceased from his
own works, as God *did* from his.
11 Let us labour therefore to enter
into that rest, lest any man fall after
the same example of unbelief.
12 For the word of God *is* quick,
and powerful, and sharper than any
twoedged sword, piercing even to
the dividing asunder of soul and
spirit, and of the joints and marrow,
and *is* a discerner of the thoughts
and intents of the heart.
13 Neither is there any creature
that is not manifest in his sight: but
all things *are* naked and opened
unto the eyes of him with whom
we have to do.

A Great High Priest

14 Seeing then that we have a great
high priest, that is passed into the
heavens, Jesus the Son of God, let
us hold fast *our* profession.
15 For we have not an high priest
which cannot be touched with the
feeling of our infirmities; but was
in all points tempted like as *we are,*
yet without sin.

16 Let us therefore come boldly
unto the throne of grace, that we
may obtain mercy, and find grace
to help in time of need.

The Priesthood of Jesus Christ

5 For every high priest taken from
among men is ordained for men
in things *pertaining* to God, that he
may offer both gifts and sacrifices
for sins:
2 Who can have compassion on
the ignorant, and on them that are
out of the way; for that he himself
also is compassed with infirmity.
3 And by reason hereof he ought,
as for the people, so also for himself,
to offer for sins.
4 And no man taketh this honour
unto himself, but he that is called of
God, as *was* Aaron.
5 So also Christ glorified not him-
self to be made an high priest; but
he that said unto him, Thou art my
Son, to day have I begotten thee.
6 As he saith also in another *place,*
Thou *art* a priest for ever after the
order of Melchisedec.
7 Who in the days of his flesh,
when he had offered up prayers and
supplications with strong crying
and tears unto him that was able
to save him from death, and was
heard in that he feared;
8 Though he were a Son, yet
learned he obedience by the things
which he suffered;
9 And being made perfect, he be-
came the author of eternal salvation
unto all them that obey him;
10 Called of God an high priest af-
ter the order of Melchisedec.

Milk and Strong Meat

11 Of whom we have many things
to say, and hard to be uttered, seeing
ye are dull of hearing.
12 For when for the time ye ought
to be teachers, ye have need that
one teach you again which *be* the
first principles of the oracles of God;
and are become such as have need
of milk, and not of strong meat.
13 For every one that useth milk *is*
unskilful in the word of righteous-
ness: for he is a babe.
14 But strong meat belongeth
to them that are of full age, *even*
those who by reason of use have
their senses exercised to discern
both good and evil.

Striving for Perfection

6 Therefore leaving the principles
of the doctrine of Christ, let us
go on unto perfection; not laying
again the foundation of repentance
from dead works, and of faith to-
ward God,
2 Of the doctrine of baptisms, and
of laying on of hands, and of resur-
rection of the dead, and of eternal
judgment.
3 And this will we do, if God per-
mit.
4 For *it is* impossible for those
who were once enlightened, and
have tasted of the heavenly gift, and
were made partakers of the Holy
Ghost,
5 And have tasted the good word
of God, and the powers of the world
to come,
6 If they shall fall away, to renew
them again unto repentance; seeing
they crucify to themselves the Son
of God afresh, and put *him* to an
open shame.
7 For the earth which drinketh in
the rain that cometh oft upon it, and
bringeth forth herbs meet for them
by whom it is dressed, receiveth
blessing from God:
8 But that which beareth thorns
and briers *is* rejected, and *is* nigh
unto cursing; whose end *is* to be
burned.
9 But, beloved, we are persuaded
better things of you, and things that
accompany salvation, though we
thus speak.
10 For God *is* not unrighteous to

forget your work and labour of love,
which ye have shewed toward his
name, in that ye have ministered
to the saints, and do minister.
11 And we desire that every one of
you do shew the same diligence to
the full assurance of hope unto the
end:
12 That ye be not slothful, but fol-
lowers of them who through faith
and patience inherit the promises.

The Promise of God

13 For when God made promise to
Abraham, because he could swear
by no greater, he sware by himself,
14 Saying, Surely blessing I will
bless thee, and multiplying I will
multiply thee.
15 And so, after he had patiently
endured, he obtained the promise.
16 For men verily swear by the
greater: and an oath for confirma-
tion *is* to them an end of all strife.
17 Wherein God, willing more
abundantly to shew unto the heirs
of promise the immutability of his
counsel, confirmed *it* by an oath:
18 That by two immutable things,
in which *it was* impossible for God
to lie, we might have a strong con-
solation, who have fled for refuge to
lay hold upon the hope set before us:
19 Which *hope* we have as an an-
chor of the soul, both sure and sted-
fast, and which entereth into that
within the veil;
20 Whither the forerunner is for
us entered, *even* Jesus, made an
high priest for ever after the order
of Melchisedec.

The King of Righteousness

7 For this Melchisedec, king of
Salem, priest of the most high
God, who met Abraham returning
from the slaughter of the kings, and
blessed him;
2 To whom also Abraham gave a
tenth part of all; first being by inter-
pretation King of righteousness, and
after that also King of Salem, which
is, King of peace;
3 Without father, without mother,
without descent, having neither
beginning of days, nor end of life;
but made like unto the Son of God;
abideth a priest continually.
4 Now consider how great this
man *was,* unto whom even the pa-
triarch Abraham gave the tenth of
the spoils.
5 And verily they that are of the
sons of Levi, who receive the office
of the priesthood, have a command-
ment to take tithes of the people
according to the law, that is, of their
brethren, though they come out of
the loins of Abraham:
6 But he whose descent is not
counted from them received tithes
of Abraham, and blessed him that
had the promises.
7 And without all contradiction
the less is blessed of the better.
8 And here men that die receive
tithes; but there he *receiveth them,*
of whom it is witnessed that he
liveth.
9 And as I may so say, Levi also,
who receiveth tithes, payed tithes
in Abraham.
10 For he was yet in the loins of his
father, when Melchisedec met him.

A Surety of a Better Testament

11 If therefore perfection were by
the Levitical priesthood, (for under
it the people received the law,) what
further need *was there* that another
priest should rise after the order of
Melchisedec, and not be called after
the order of Aaron?
12 For the priesthood being
changed, there is made of necessity
a change also of the law.
13 For he of whom these things are
spoken pertaineth to another tribe,
of which no man gave attendance
at the altar.
14 For *it is* evident that our Lord
sprang out of Juda; of which tribe

Moses spake nothing concerning priesthood.

15 And it is yet far more evident: for that after the similitude of Melchisedec there ariseth another priest,

16 Who is made, not after the law of a carnal commandment, but after the power of an endless life.

17 For he testifieth, Thou *art* a priest for ever after the order of Melchisedec.

18 For there is verily a disannulling of the commandment going before for the weakness and unprofitableness thereof.

19 For the law made nothing perfect, but the bringing in of a better hope *did;* by the which we draw nigh unto God.

20 And inasmuch as not without an oath *he was made priest:*

21 (For those priests were made without an oath; but this with an oath by him that said unto him, The Lord sware and will not repent, Thou *art* a priest for ever after the order of Melchisedec:)

22 By so much was Jesus made a surety of a better testament.

An Unchangeable Priesthood

23 And they truly were many priests, because they were not suffered to continue by reason of death:

24 But this *man,* because he continueth ever, hath an unchangeable priesthood.

25 Wherefore he is able also to save them to the uttermost that come unto God by him, seeing he ever liveth to make intercession for them.

26 For such an high priest became us, *who is* holy, harmless, undefiled, separate from sinners, and made higher than the heavens;

27 Who needeth not daily, as those high priests, to offer up sacrifice, first for his own sins, and then for the people's: for this he did once, when he offered up himself.

28 For the law maketh men high priests which have infirmity; but the word of the oath, which was since the law, *maketh* the Son, who is consecrated for evermore.

A More Excellent Ministry

8 Now of the things which we have spoken *this is* the sum: We have such an high priest, who is set on the right hand of the throne of the Majesty in the heavens;

2 A minister of the sanctuary, and of the true tabernacle, which the Lord pitched, and not man.

3 For every high priest is ordained to offer gifts and sacrifices: wherefore *it is* of necessity that this man have somewhat also to offer.

4 For if he were on earth, he should not be a priest, seeing that there are priests that offer gifts according to the law:

5 Who serve unto the example and shadow of heavenly things, as Moses was admonished of God when he was about to make the tabernacle: for, See, saith he, *that* thou make all things according to the pattern shewed to thee in the mount.

6 But now hath he obtained a more excellent ministry, by how much also he is the mediator of a better covenant, which was established upon better promises.

The Need for a New Covenant

7 For if that first *covenant* had been faultless, then should no place have been sought for the second.

8 For finding fault with them, he saith, Behold, the days come, saith the Lord, when I will make a new covenant with the house of Israel and with the house of Judah:

9 Not according to the covenant that I made with their fathers in the day when I took them by the hand to lead them out of the land of Egypt; because they continued not in my

covenant, and I regarded them not, saith the Lord.

Laws Written in Their Hearts

10 For this *is* the covenant that I will make with the house of Israel after those days, saith the Lord; I will put my laws into their mind, and write them in their hearts: and I will be to them a God, and they shall be to me a people:

11 And they shall not teach every man his neighbour, and every man his brother, saying, Know the Lord: for all shall know me, from the least to the greatest.

12 For I will be merciful to their unrighteousness, and their sins and their iniquities will I remember no more.

13 In that he saith, A new *covenant,* he hath made the first old. Now that which decayeth and waxeth old *is* ready to vanish away.

A Worldly Sanctuary

9 Then verily the first *covenant* had also ordinances of divine service, and a worldly sanctuary.

2 For there was a tabernacle made; the first, wherein *was* the candlestick, and the table, and the shewbread; which is called the sanctuary.

3 And after the second veil, the tabernacle which is called the Holiest of all;

4 Which had the golden censer, and the ark of the covenant overlaid round about with gold, wherein *was* the golden pot that had manna, and Aaron's rod that budded, and the tables of the covenant;

5 And over it the cherubims of glory shadowing the mercyseat; of which we cannot now speak particularly.

6 Now when these things were thus ordained, the priests went always into the first tabernacle, accomplishing the service *of God.*

7 But into the second *went* the high priest alone once every year, not without blood, which he offered for himself, and *for* the errors of the people:

8 The Holy Ghost this signifying, that the way into the holiest of all was not yet made manifest, while as the first tabernacle was yet standing:

9 Which *was* a figure for the time then present, in which were offered both gifts and sacrifices, that could not make him that did the service perfect, as pertaining to the conscience;

10 *Which stood* only in meats and drinks, and divers washings, and carnal ordinances, imposed *on them* until the time of reformation.

A More Perfect Tabernacle

11 But Christ being come an high priest of good things to come, by a greater and more perfect tabernacle, not made with hands, that is to say, not of this building;

12 Neither by the blood of goats and calves, but by his own blood he entered in once into the holy place, having obtained eternal redemption *for us.*

13 For if the blood of bulls and of goats, and the ashes of an heifer sprinkling the unclean, sanctifieth to the purifying of the flesh:

14 How much more shall the blood of Christ, who through the eternal Spirit offered himself without spot to God, purge your conscience from dead works to serve the living God?

The Mediator of the New Testament

15 And for this cause he is the mediator of the new testament, that by means of death, for the redemption of the transgressions *that were* under the first testament, they which are called might receive the promise of eternal inheritance.

16 For where a testament *is,* there must also of necessity be the death of the testator.

17 For a testament *is* of force after men are dead: otherwise it is of no strength at all while the testator liveth.

18 Whereupon neither the first *testament* was dedicated without blood.

The Blood of the Testament

19 For when Moses had spoken every precept to all the people according to the law, he took the blood of calves and of goats, with water, and scarlet wool, and hyssop, and sprinkled both the book, and all the people,

20 Saying, This *is* the blood of the testament which God hath enjoined unto you.

21 Moreover he sprinkled with blood both the tabernacle, and all the vessels of the ministry.

22 And almost all things are by the law purged with blood; and without shedding of blood is no remission.

23 *It was* therefore necessary that the patterns of things in the heavens should be purified with these; but the heavenly things themselves with better sacrifices than these.

24 For Christ is not entered into the holy places made with hands, *which are* the figures of the true; but into heaven itself, now to appear in the presence of God for us:

25 Nor yet that he should offer himself often, as the high priest entereth into the holy place every year with blood of others;

26 For then must he often have suffered since the foundation of the world: but now once in the end of the world hath he appeared to put away sin by the sacrifice of himself.

27 And as it is appointed unto men once to die, but after this the judgment:

28 So Christ was once offered to bear the sins of many; and unto them that look for him shall he appear the second time without sin unto salvation.

Christ the Perfect Sacrifice

10 For the law having a shadow of good things to come, *and* not the very image of the things, can never with those sacrifices which they offered year by year continually make the comers thereunto perfect.

2 For then would they not have ceased to be offered? because that the worshippers once purged should have had no more conscience of sins.

3 But in those *sacrifices there is* a remembrance again *made* of sins every year.

4 For *it is* not possible that the blood of bulls and of goats should take away sins.

5 Wherefore when he cometh into the world, he saith, Sacrifice and offering thou wouldest not, but a body hast thou prepared me:

6 In burnt offerings and *sacrifices* for sin thou hast had no pleasure.

7 Then said I, Lo, I come (in the volume of the book it is written of me,) to do thy will, O God.

8 Above when he said, Sacrifice and offering and burnt offerings and *offering* for sin thou wouldest not, neither hadst pleasure *therein;* which are offered by the law;

9 Then said he, Lo, I come to do thy will, O God. He taketh away the first, that he may establish the second.

10 By the which will we are sanctified through the offering of the body of Jesus Christ once *for all.*

11 And every priest standeth daily ministering and offering oftentimes the same sacrifices, which can never take away sins:

12 But this man, after he had offered one sacrifice for sins for ever,

sat down on the right hand of God;
13 From henceforth expecting till
his enemies be made his footstool.
14 For by one offering he hath
perfected for ever them that are
sanctified.
15 *Whereof* the Holy Ghost also is
a witness to us: for after that he had
said before,
16 This *is* the covenant that I will
make with them after those days,
saith the Lord, I will put my laws
into their hearts, and in their minds
will I write them;
17 And their sins and iniquities
will I remember no more.
18 Now where remission of these
is, there is no more offering for sin.

Hold Fast the Faith

19 Having therefore, brethren,
boldness to enter into the holiest
by the blood of Jesus,
20 By a new and living way, which
he hath consecrated for us, through
the veil, that is to say, his flesh;
21 And *having* an high priest over
the house of God;
22 Let us draw near with a true
heart in full assurance of faith, hav-
ing our hearts sprinkled from an evil
conscience, and our bodies washed
with pure water.
23 Let us hold fast the profession
of *our* faith without wavering; (for
he *is* faithful that promised;)
24 And let us consider one another
to provoke unto love and to good
works:
25 Not forsaking the assembling of
ourselves together, as the manner of
some *is;* but exhorting *one another:*
and so much the more, as ye see the
day approaching.

Punishment for Wilful Sin

26 For if we sin wilfully after that
we have received the knowledge of
the truth, there remaineth no more
sacrifice for sins,
27 But a certain fearful looking for
of judgment and fiery indignation,
which shall devour the adversaries.
28 He that despised Moses' law
died without mercy under two or
three witnesses:
29 Of how much sorer pun-
ishment, suppose ye, shall he be
thought worthy, who hath trodden
under foot the Son of God, and hath
counted the blood of the covenant,
wherewith he was sanctified, an
unholy thing, and hath done despite
unto the Spirit of grace?
30 For we know him that hath
said, Vengeance *belongeth* unto me,
I will recompense, saith the Lord.
And again, The Lord shall judge his
people.
31 *It is* a fearful thing to fall into
the hands of the living God.

A Call to Remember the Former Days

32 But call to remembrance the
former days, in which, after ye were
illuminated, ye endured a great fight
of afflictions;
33 Partly, whilst ye were made
a gazingstock both by reproaches
and afflictions; and partly, whilst ye
became companions of them that
were so used.
34 For ye had compassion of me
in my bonds, and took joyfully the
spoiling of your goods, knowing in
yourselves that ye have in heaven a
better and an enduring substance.
35 Cast not away therefore your
confidence, which hath great rec-
ompence of reward.
36 For ye have need of patience,
that, after ye have done the will of
God, ye might receive the promise.
37 For yet a little while, and he
that shall come will come, and will
not tarry.
38 Now the just shall live by faith:
but if *any man* draw back, my soul
shall have no pleasure in him.
39 But we are not of them who
draw back unto perdition; but of

them that believe to the saving of
the soul.

Faith Before the Flood

11 Now faith is the substance of
things hoped for, the evidence
of things not seen.
2 For by it the elders obtained a
good report.
3 Through faith we understand
that the worlds were framed by the
word of God, so that things which
are seen were not made of things
which do appear.
4 By faith Abel offered unto God a
more excellent sacrifice than Cain,
by which he obtained witness that
he was righteous, God testifying of
his gifts: and by it he being dead yet
speaketh.
5 By faith Enoch was translated
that he should not see death; and
was not found, because God had
translated him: for before his trans-
lation he had this testimony, that he
pleased God.
6 But without faith *it is* impossible
to please *him:* for he that cometh
to God must believe that he is, and
that he is a rewarder of them that
diligently seek him.
7 By faith Noah, being warned of
God of things not seen as yet, moved
with fear, prepared an ark to the
saving of his house; by the which he
condemned the world, and became
heir of the righteousness which is
by faith.

The Faith of the Patriarchs

8 By faith Abraham, when he was
called to go out into a place which
he should after receive for an inheri-
tance, obeyed; and he went out, not
knowing whither he went.
9 By faith he sojourned in the land
of promise, as *in* a strange country,
dwelling in tabernacles with Isaac
and Jacob, the heirs with him of the
same promise:
10 For he looked for a city which
hath foundations, whose builder
and maker *is* God.
11 Through faith also Sara her-
self received strength to conceive
seed, and was delivered of a child
when she was past age, because
she judged him faithful who had
promised.
12 Therefore sprang there even
of one, and him as good as dead,
so many as the stars of the sky in
multitude, and as the sand which
is by the sea shore innumerable.
13 These all died in faith, not hav-
ing received the promises, but hav-
ing seen them afar off, and were
persuaded of *them,* and embraced
them, and confessed that they were
strangers and pilgrims on the earth.
14 For they that say such things
declare plainly that they seek a
country.
15 And truly, if they had been
mindful of that *country* from
whence they came out, they might
have had opportunity to have re-
turned.
16 But now they desire a better
country, that is, an heavenly: where-
fore God is not ashamed to be called
their God: for he hath prepared for
them a city.
17 By faith Abraham, when he was
tried, offered up Isaac: and he that
had received the promises offered
up his only begotten *son,*
18 Of whom it was said, That in
Isaac shall thy seed be called:
19 Accounting that God *was* able
to raise *him* up, even from the dead;
from whence also he received him
in a figure.
20 By faith Isaac blessed Jacob
and Esau concerning things to
come.
21 By faith Jacob, when he was
a dying, blessed both the sons of
Joseph; and worshipped, *leaning*
upon the top of his staff.
22 By faith Joseph, when he died,
made mention of the departing of

the children of Israel; and gave commandment concerning his bones.

Moses and Other Faithful Servants

23 By faith Moses, when he was born, was hid three months of his parents, because they saw *he was* a proper child; and they were not afraid of the king's commandment.
24 By faith Moses, when he was come to years, refused to be called the son of Pharaoh's daughter;
25 Choosing rather to suffer affliction with the people of God, than to enjoy the pleasures of sin for a season;
26 Esteeming the reproach of Christ greater riches than the treasures in Egypt: for he had respect unto the recompence of the reward.
27 By faith he forsook Egypt, not fearing the wrath of the king: for he endured, as seeing him who is invisible.
28 Through faith he kept the passover, and the sprinkling of blood, lest he that destroyed the firstborn should touch them.
29 By faith they passed through the Red sea as by dry *land:* which the Egyptians assaying to do were drowned.
30 By faith the walls of Jericho fell down, after they were compassed about seven days.
31 By faith the harlot Rahab perished not with them that believed not, when she had received the spies with peace.
32 And what shall I more say? for the time would fail me to tell *of* Gedeon, and *of* Barak, and *of* Samson, and *of* Jephthae; *of* David also, and Samuel, and *of* the prophets:
33 Who through faith subdued kingdoms, wrought righteousness, obtained promises, stopped the mouths of lions,
34 Quenched the violence of fire, escaped the edge of the sword, out of weakness were made strong, waxed valiant in fight, turned to flight the armies of the aliens.
35 Women received their dead raised to life again: and others were tortured, not accepting deliverance; that they might obtain a better resurrection:
36 And others had trial of *cruel* mockings and scourgings, yea, moreover of bonds and imprisonment:
37 They were stoned, they were sawn asunder, were tempted, were slain with the sword: they wandered about in sheepskins and goatskins; being destitute, afflicted, tormented;
38 (Of whom the world was not worthy:) they wandered in deserts, and *in* mountains, and *in* dens and caves of the earth.
39 And these all, having obtained a good report through faith, received not the promise:
40 God having provided some better thing for us, that they without us should not be made perfect.

The Author and Finisher of Our Faith

12 Wherefore seeing we also are compassed about with so great a cloud of witnesses, let us lay aside every weight, and the sin which doth so easily beset *us,* and let us run with patience the race that is set before us,
2 Looking unto Jesus the author and finisher of *our* faith; who for the joy that was set before him endured the cross, despising the shame, and is set down at the right hand of the throne of God.
3 For consider him that endured such contradiction of sinners against himself, lest ye be wearied and faint in your minds.
4 Ye have not yet resisted unto blood, striving against sin.
5 And ye have forgotten the ex-

hortation which speaketh unto you
as unto children, My son, despise
not thou the chastening of the Lord,
nor faint when thou art rebuked of
him:
6 For whom the Lord loveth he
chasteneth, and scourgeth every
son whom he receiveth.

Endure Chastening

7 If ye endure chastening, God
dealeth with you as with sons; for
what son is he whom the father
chasteneth not?
8 But if ye be without chastise-
ment, whereof all are partakers,
then are ye bastards, and not sons.
9 Furthermore we have had fa-
thers of our flesh which corrected
us, and we gave *them* reverence:
shall we not much rather be in sub-
jection unto the Father of spirits,
and live?
10 For they verily for a few days
chastened *us* after their own plea-
sure; but he for *our* profit, that *we*
might be partakers of his holiness.
11 Now no chastening for the
present seemeth to be joyous, but
grievous: nevertheless afterward it
yieldeth the peaceable fruit of righ-
teousness unto them which are ex-
ercised thereby.
12 Wherefore lift up the hands
which hang down, and the feeble
knees;
13 And make straight paths for
your feet, lest that which is lame
be turned out of the way; but let it
rather be healed.

Peace with All Men

14 Follow peace with all *men,* and
holiness, without which no man
shall see the Lord:
15 Looking diligently lest any man
fail of the grace of God; lest any root
of bitterness springing up trouble
you, and thereby many be defiled;
16 Lest there *be* any fornicator, or
profane person, as Esau, who for
one morsel of meat sold his birth-
right.
17 For ye know how that after-
ward, when he would have inherited
the blessing, he was rejected: for
he found no place of repentance,
though he sought it carefully with
tears.

Not the Terrible Mountain

18 For ye are not come unto the
mount that might be touched, and
that burned with fire, nor unto
blackness, and darkness, and tem-
pest,
19 And the sound of a trumpet,
and the voice of words; which *voice*
they that heard intreated that the
word should not be spoken to them
any more:
20 (For they could not endure that
which was commanded, And if so
much as a beast touch the moun-
tain, it shall be stoned, or thrust
through with a dart:
21 And so terrible was the sight,
that Moses said, I exceedingly fear
and quake:)

The City of the Living God

22 But ye are come unto mount
Sion, and unto the city of the living
God, the heavenly Jerusalem, and to
an innumerable company of angels,
23 To the general assembly and
church of the firstborn, which are
written in heaven, and to God the
Judge of all, and to the spirits of just
men made perfect,
24 And to Jesus the mediator of
the new covenant, and to the blood
of sprinkling, that speaketh better
things than *that of* Abel.

The Unmoveable Kingdom

25 See that ye refuse not him that
speaketh. For if they escaped not
who refused him that spake on
earth, much more *shall not* we *es-
cape,* if we turn away from him that
speaketh from heaven:

26 Whose voice then shook the earth: but now he hath promised, saying, Yet once more I shake not the earth only, but also heaven.

27 And this *word,* Yet once more, signifieth the removing of those things that are shaken, as of things that are made, that those things which cannot be shaken may remain.

28 Wherefore we receiving a kingdom which cannot be moved, let us have grace, whereby we may serve God acceptably with reverence and godly fear:

29 For our God *is* a consuming fire.

The Lord Is My Helper

13 Let brotherly love continue.

2 Be not forgetful to entertain strangers: for thereby some have entertained angels unawares.

3 Remember them that are in bonds, as bound with them; *and* them which suffer adversity, as being yourselves also in the body.

4 Marriage *is* honourable in all, and the bed undefiled: but whoremongers and adulterers God will judge.

5 *Let your* conversation *be* without covetousness; *and be* content with such things as ye have: for he hath said, I will never leave thee, nor forsake thee.

6 So that we may boldly say, The Lord *is* my helper, and I will not fear what man shall do unto me.

7 Remember them which have the rule over you, who have spoken unto you the word of God: whose faith follow, considering the end of *their* conversation.

8 Jesus Christ the same yesterday, and to day, and for ever.

Beware of Strange Doctrines

9 Be not carried about with divers and strange doctrines. For *it is* a good thing that the heart be established with grace; not with meats, which have not profited them that have been occupied therein.

10 We have an altar, whereof they have no right to eat which serve the tabernacle.

11 For the bodies of those beasts, whose blood is brought into the sanctuary by the high priest for sin, are burned without the camp.

12 Wherefore Jesus also, that he might sanctify the people with his own blood, suffered without the gate.

13 Let us go forth therefore unto him without the camp, bearing his reproach.

14 For here have we no continuing city, but we seek one to come.

15 By him therefore let us offer the sacrifice of praise to God continually, that is, the fruit of *our* lips giving thanks to his name.

16 But to do good and to communicate forget not: for with such sacrifices God is well pleased.

Obey Your Rulers

17 Obey them that have the rule over you, and submit yourselves: for they watch for your souls, as they that must give account, that they may do it with joy, and not with grief: for that *is* unprofitable for you.

18 Pray for us: for we trust we have a good conscience, in all things willing to live honestly.

19 But I beseech *you* the rather to do this, that I may be restored to you the sooner.

20 Now the God of peace, that brought again from the dead our Lord Jesus, that great shepherd of the sheep, through the blood of the everlasting covenant,

21 Make you perfect in every good work to do his will, working in you that which is wellpleasing in his sight, through Jesus Christ; to whom *be* glory for ever and ever. Amen.

Closing Words

22 And I beseech you, brethren,
suffer the word of exhortation: for
I have written a letter unto you in
few words.
23 Know ye that *our* brother Tim-
othy is set at liberty; with whom, if
he come shortly, I will see you.
24 Salute all them that have the
rule over you, and all the saints.
They of Italy salute you.
25 Grace *be* with you all. Amen.

The General Epistle of
JAMES

Greetings to the Twelve Tribes

James, a servant of God and of the
Lord Jesus Christ, to the twelve
tribes which are scattered abroad,
greeting.

Trials Make Patience

2 My brethren, count it all joy
when ye fall into divers tempta-
tions;
3 Knowing *this,* that the trying of
your faith worketh patience.
4 But let patience have *her* perfect
work, that ye may be perfect and
entire, wanting nothing.
5 If any of you lack wisdom, let
him ask of God, that giveth to all
men liberally, and upbraideth not;
and it shall be given him.
6 But let him ask in faith, nothing
wavering. For he that wavereth is
like a wave of the sea driven with
the wind and tossed.
7 For let not that man think that
he shall receive any thing of the
Lord.
8 A double minded man *is* unsta-
ble in all his ways.
9 Let the brother of low degree
rejoice in that he is exalted:
10 But the rich, in that he is made
low: because as the flower of the
grass he shall pass away.
11 For the sun is no sooner risen
with a burning heat, but it withereth
the grass, and the flower thereof
falleth, and the grace of the fashion
of it perisheth: so also shall the rich
man fade away in his ways.
12 Blessed *is* the man that en-
dureth temptation: for when he is
tried, he shall receive the crown of
life, which the Lord hath promised
to them that love him.
13 Let no man say when he is
tempted, I am tempted of God: for
God cannot be tempted with evil,
neither tempteth he any man:
14 But every man is tempted,
when he is drawn away of his own
lust, and enticed.
15 Then when lust hath conceived,
it bringeth forth sin: and sin, when
it is finished, bringeth forth death.
16 Do not err, my beloved breth-
ren.
17 Every good gift and every per-
fect gift is from above, and cometh
down from the Father of lights, with
whom is no variableness, neither
shadow of turning.
18 Of his own will begat he us with
the word of truth, that we should be
a kind of firstfruits of his creatures.

Hearers and Doers of the Word

19 Wherefore, my beloved breth-
ren, let every man be swift to hear,
slow to speak, slow to wrath:
20 For the wrath of man worketh
not the righteousness of God.
21 Wherefore lay apart all filthi-
ness and superfluity of naughtiness,
and receive with meekness the en-
grafted word, which is able to save
your souls.
22 But be ye doers of the word,
and not hearers only, deceiving your
own selves.
23 For if any be a hearer of the
word, and not a doer, he is like unto

a man beholding his natural face in a glass:

24 For he beholdeth himself, and goeth his way, and straightway forgetteth what manner of man he was.

25 But whoso looketh into the perfect law of liberty, and continueth *therein,* he being not a forgetful hearer, but a doer of the work, this man shall be blessed in his deed.

26 If any man among you seem to be religious, and bridleth not his tongue, but deceiveth his own heart, this man's religion *is* vain.

27 Pure religion and undefiled before God and the Father is this, To visit the fatherless and widows in their affliction, *and* to keep himself unspotted from the world.

Favouritism Condemned

2 My brethren, have not the faith of our Lord Jesus Christ, *the Lord* of glory, with respect of persons.

2 For if there come unto your assembly a man with a gold ring, in goodly apparel, and there come in also a poor man in vile raiment;

3 And ye have respect to him that weareth the gay clothing, and say unto him, Sit thou here in a good place; and say to the poor, Stand thou there, or sit here under my footstool:

4 Are ye not then partial in yourselves, and are become judges of evil thoughts?

5 Hearken, my beloved brethren, Hath not God chosen the poor of this world rich in faith, and heirs of the kingdom which he hath promised to them that love him?

6 But ye have despised the poor. Do not rich men oppress you, and draw you before the judgment seats?

7 Do not they blaspheme that worthy name by the which ye are called?

8 If ye fulfil the royal law according to the scripture, Thou shalt love thy neighbour as thyself, ye do well:

9 But if ye have respect to persons, ye commit sin, and are convinced of the law as transgressors.

10 For whosoever shall keep the whole law, and yet offend in one *point,* he is guilty of all.

11 For he that said, Do not commit adultery, said also, Do not kill. Now if thou commit no adultery, yet if thou kill, thou art become a transgressor of the law.

12 So speak ye, and so do, as they that shall be judged by the law of liberty.

13 For he shall have judgment without mercy, that hath shewed no mercy; and mercy rejoiceth against judgment.

Faith Without Works

14 What *doth it* profit, my brethren, though a man say he hath faith, and have not works? can faith save him?

15 If a brother or sister be naked, and destitute of daily food,

16 And one of you say unto them, Depart in peace, be *ye* warmed and filled; notwithstanding ye give them not those things which are needful to the body; what *doth it* profit?

17 Even so faith, if it hath not works, is dead, being alone.

18 Yea, a man may say, Thou hast faith, and I have works: shew me thy faith without thy works, and I will shew thee my faith by my works.

19 Thou believest that there is one God; thou doest well: the devils also believe, and tremble.

20 But wilt thou know, O vain man, that faith without works is dead?

21 Was not Abraham our father justified by works, when he had offered Isaac his son upon the altar?

22 Seest thou how faith wrought with his works, and by works was faith made perfect?

23 And the scripture was fulfilled
which saith, Abraham believed God,
and it was imputed unto him for
righteousness: and he was called
the Friend of God.
24 Ye see then how that by works
a man is justified, and not by faith
only.
25 Likewise also was not Rahab
the harlot justified by works, when
she had received the messengers,
and had sent *them* out another way?
26 For as the body without the
spirit is dead, so faith without works
is dead also.

The Unruly Tongue

3 My brethren, be not many mas-
ters, knowing that we shall re-
ceive the greater condemnation.
2 For in many things we offend
all. If any man offend not in word,
the same *is* a perfect man, *and* able
also to bridle the whole body.
3 Behold, we put bits in the horses'
mouths, that they may obey us; and
we turn about their whole body.
4 Behold also the ships, which
though *they be* so great, and *are*
driven of fierce winds, yet are they
turned about with a very small
helm, whithersoever the governor
listeth.
5 Even so the tongue is a little
member, and boasteth great things.
Behold, how great a matter a little
fire kindleth!
6 And the tongue *is* a fire, a world
of iniquity: so is the tongue among
our members, that it defileth the
whole body, and setteth on fire the
course of nature; and it is set on fire
of hell.
7 For every kind of beasts, and of
birds, and of serpents, and of things
in the sea, is tamed, and hath been
tamed of mankind:
8 But the tongue can no man
tame; *it is* an unruly evil, full of
deadly poison.
9 Therewith bless we God, even
the Father; and therewith curse we
men, which are made after the si-
militude of God.
10 Out of the same mouth pro-
ceedeth blessing and cursing. My
brethren, these things ought not
so to be.
11 Doth a fountain send forth at
the same place sweet *water* and
bitter?
12 Can the fig tree, my brethren,
bear olive berries? either a vine, figs?
so *can* no fountain both yield salt
water and fresh.

Earthly and Heavenly Wisdom

13 Who *is* a wise man and endued
with knowledge among you? let him
shew out of a good conversation his
works with meekness of wisdom.
14 But if ye have bitter envying
and strife in your hearts, glory not,
and lie not against the truth.
15 This wisdom descendeth not
from above, but *is* earthly, sensual,
devilish.
16 For where envying and strife
is, there *is* confusion and every evil
work.
17 But the wisdom that is from
above is first pure, then peaceable,
gentle, *and* easy to be intreated, full
of mercy and good fruits, without
partiality, and without hypocrisy.
18 And the fruit of righteousness
is sown in peace of them that make
peace.

Draw Near to God

4 From whence *come* wars and
fightings among you? *come they*
not hence, *even* of your lusts that
war in your members?
2 Ye lust, and have not: ye kill, and
desire to have, and cannot obtain:
ye fight and war, yet ye have not,
because ye ask not.
3 Ye ask, and receive not, because
ye ask amiss, that ye may consume
it upon your lusts.

4 Ye adulterers and adulteresses, know ye not that the friendship of the world is enmity with God? whosoever therefore will be a friend of the world is the enemy of God.

5 Do ye think that the scripture saith in vain, The spirit that dwelleth in us lusteth to envy?

6 But he giveth more grace. Wherefore he saith, God resisteth the proud, but giveth grace unto the humble.

7 Submit yourselves therefore to God. Resist the devil, and he will flee from you.

8 Draw nigh to God, and he will draw nigh to you. Cleanse *your* hands, *ye* sinners; and purify *your* hearts, *ye* double minded.

9 Be afflicted, and mourn, and weep: let your laughter be turned to mourning, and *your* joy to heaviness.

10 Humble yourselves in the sight of the Lord, and he shall lift you up.

11 Speak not evil one of another, brethren. He that speaketh evil of *his* brother, and judgeth his brother, speaketh evil of the law, and judgeth the law: but if thou judge the law, thou art not a doer of the law, but a judge.

12 There is one lawgiver, who is able to save and to destroy: who art thou that judgest another?

Rejoicing in Boastings Is Evil

13 Go to now, ye that say, To day or to morrow we will go into such a city, and continue there a year, and buy and sell, and get gain:

14 Whereas ye know not what *shall be* on the morrow. For what *is* your life? It is even a vapour, that appeareth for a little time, and then vanisheth away.

15 For that ye *ought* to say, If the Lord will, we shall live, and do this, or that.

16 But now ye rejoice in your boastings: all such rejoicing is evil.

17 Therefore to him that knoweth to do good, and doeth *it* not, to him it is sin.

Rich Oppressors Rebuked

5 Go to now, *ye* rich men, weep and howl for your miseries that shall come upon *you.*

2 Your riches are corrupted, and your garments are motheaten.

3 Your gold and silver is cankered; and the rust of them shall be a witness against you, and shall eat your flesh as it were fire. Ye have heaped treasure together for the last days.

4 Behold, the hire of the labourers who have reaped down your fields, which is of you kept back by fraud, crieth: and the cries of them which have reaped are entered into the ears of the Lord of sabaoth.

5 Ye have lived in pleasure on the earth, and been wanton; ye have nourished your hearts, as in a day of slaughter.

6 Ye have condemned *and* killed the just; *and* he doth not resist you.

The Value of Patience and Prayer

7 Be patient therefore, brethren, unto the coming of the Lord. Behold, the husbandman waiteth for the precious fruit of the earth, and hath long patience for it, until he receive the early and latter rain.

8 Be ye also patient; stablish your hearts: for the coming of the Lord draweth nigh.

9 Grudge not one against another, brethren, lest ye be condemned: behold, the judge standeth before the door.

10 Take, my brethren, the prophets, who have spoken in the name of the Lord, for an example of suffering affliction, and of patience.

11 Behold, we count them happy which endure. Ye have heard of the patience of Job, and have seen the

end of the Lord; that the Lord is very
pitiful, and of tender mercy.
12 But above all things, my breth-
ren, swear not, neither by heaven,
neither by the earth, neither by any
other oath: but let your yea be yea;
and *your* nay, nay; lest ye fall into
condemnation.
13 Is any among you afflicted? let
him pray. Is any merry? let him sing
psalms.
14 Is any sick among you? let him
call for the elders of the church; and
let them pray over him, anointing
him with oil in the name of the Lord:
15 And the prayer of faith shall
save the sick, and the Lord shall
raise him up; and if he have com-
mitted sins, they shall be forgiven
him.
16 Confess *your* faults one to an-
other, and pray one for another,
that ye may be healed. The effectual
fervent prayer of a righteous man
availeth much.
17 Elias was a man subject to like
passions as we are, and he prayed
earnestly that it might not rain: and
it rained not on the earth by the
space of three years and six months.
18 And he prayed again, and the
heaven gave rain, and the earth
brought forth her fruit.
19 Brethren, if any of you do err
from the truth, and one convert him;
20 Let him know, that he which
converteth the sinner from the error
of his way shall save a soul from
death, and shall hide a multitude
of sins.

The First Epistle General of
PETER

Salutation to Scattered Strangers

Peter, an apostle of Jesus Christ, to
the strangers scattered through-
out Pontus, Galatia, Cappadocia,
Asia, and Bithynia,
2 Elect according to the fore-
knowledge of God the Father,
through sanctification of the Spirit,
unto obedience and sprinkling of
the blood of Jesus Christ: Grace unto
you, and peace, be multiplied.

An Incorruptible Inheritance

3 Blessed *be* the God and Father
of our Lord Jesus Christ, which ac-
cording to his abundant mercy hath
begotten us again unto a lively hope
by the resurrection of Jesus Christ
from the dead,
4 To an inheritance incorruptible,
and undefiled, and that fadeth not
away, reserved in heaven for you,
5 Who are kept by the power of
God through faith unto salvation
ready to be revealed in the last time.
6 Wherein ye greatly rejoice,
though now for a season, if need be,
ye are in heaviness through mani-
fold temptations:
7 That the trial of your faith, be-
ing much more precious than of
gold that perisheth, though it be
tried with fire, might be found unto
praise and honour and glory at the
appearing of Jesus Christ:
8 Whom having not seen, ye love;
in whom, though now ye see *him*
not, yet believing, ye rejoice with
joy unspeakable and full of glory:
9 Receiving the end of your faith,
even the salvation of *your* souls.
10 Of which salvation the prophets
have enquired and searched dili-
gently, who prophesied of the grace
that should come unto you:
11 Searching what, or what manner
of time the Spirit of Christ which was
in them did signify, when it testified
beforehand the sufferings of Christ,
and the glory that should follow.
12 Unto whom it was revealed,
that not unto themselves, but unto
us they did minister the things,
which are now reported unto you by
them that have preached the gospel
unto you with the Holy Ghost sent
down from heaven; which things
the angels desire to look into.

Without Spot or Blemish

13 Wherefore gird up the loins of
your mind, be sober, and hope to
the end for the grace that is to be
brought unto you at the revelation
of Jesus Christ;
14 As obedient children, not fash-
ioning yourselves according to the
former lusts in your ignorance:
15 But as he which hath called you
is holy, so be ye holy in all manner
of conversation;
16 Because it is written, Be ye holy;
for I am holy.
17 And if ye call on the Father, who
without respect of persons judgeth
according to every man's work, pass
the time of your sojourning *here* in
fear:
18 Forasmuch as ye know that ye
were not redeemed with corrupt-
ible things, *as* silver and gold, from

your vain conversation *received* by
tradition from your fathers;
19 But with the precious blood of
Christ, as of a lamb without blemish
and without spot:
20 Who verily was foreordained
before the foundation of the world,
but was manifest in these last times
for you,
21 Who by him do believe in God,
that raised him up from the dead,
and gave him glory; that your faith
and hope might be in God.

The Word of the Lord Endures Forever

22 Seeing ye have purified your
souls in obeying the truth through
the Spirit unto unfeigned love of
the brethren, *see that ye* love one
another with a pure heart fervently:
23 Being born again, not of cor-
ruptible seed, but of incorruptible,
by the word of God, which liveth
and abideth for ever.
24 For all flesh *is* as grass, and all
the glory of man as the flower of
grass. The grass withereth, and the
flower thereof falleth away:
25 But the word of the Lord en-
dureth for ever. And this is the word
which by the gospel is preached
unto you.

Lay Aside All Evil

2 Wherefore laying aside all
malice, and all guile, and hy-
pocrisies, and envies, and all evil
speakings,
2 As newborn babes, desire the
sincere milk of the word, that ye
may grow thereby:
3 If so be ye have tasted that the
Lord is gracious.

An Holy Priesthood

4 To whom coming, *as unto* a liv-
ing stone, disallowed indeed of men,
but chosen of God, *and* precious,
5 Ye also, as lively stones, are built
up a spiritual house, an holy priest-
hood, to offer up spiritual sacrifices,
acceptable to God by Jesus Christ.
6 Wherefore also it is contained in
the scripture, Behold, I lay in Sion a
chief corner stone, elect, precious:
and he that believeth on him shall
not be confounded.
7 Unto you therefore which be-
lieve *he is* precious: but unto them
which be disobedient, the stone
which the builders disallowed, the
same is made the head of the corner,
8 And a stone of stumbling, and a
rock of offence, *even to them* which
stumble at the word, being disobe-
dient: whereunto also they were
appointed.
9 But ye *are* a chosen generation,
a royal priesthood, an holy nation, a
peculiar people; that ye should shew
forth the praises of him who hath
called you out of darkness into his
marvellous light:
10 Which in time past *were* not a
people, but *are* now the people of
God: which had not obtained mercy,
but now have obtained mercy.
11 Dearly beloved, I beseech *you*
as strangers and pilgrims, abstain
from fleshly lusts, which war against
the soul;
12 Having your conversation
honest among the Gentiles: that,
whereas they speak against you as
evildoers, they may by *your* good
works, which they shall behold, glo-
rify God in the day of visitation.

Submission to Rulers

13 Submit yourselves to every
ordinance of man for the Lord's
sake: whether it be to the king, as
supreme;
14 Or unto governors, as unto
them that are sent by him for the
punishment of evildoers, and for
the praise of them that do well.
15 For so is the will of God, that
with well doing ye may put to si-
lence the ignorance of foolish men:
16 As free, and not using *your*

liberty for a cloak of maliciousness,
but as the servants of God.
17 Honour all *men*. Love the
brotherhood. Fear God. Honour the
king.
18 Servants, *be* subject to *your*
masters with all fear; not only to
the good and gentle, but also to the
froward.
19 For this *is* thankworthy, if a man
for conscience toward God endure
grief, suffering wrongfully.
20 For what glory *is it*, if, when
ye be buffeted for your faults, ye
shall take it patiently? but if, when
ye do well, and suffer *for it*, ye take
it patiently, this *is* acceptable with
God.
21 For even hereunto were ye
called: because Christ also suffered
for us, leaving us an example, that
ye should follow his steps:
22 Who did no sin, neither was
guile found in his mouth:
23 Who, when he was reviled, re-
viled not again; when he suffered,
he threatened not; but committed
himself to him that judgeth righ-
teously:
24 Who his own self bare our sins
in his own body on the tree, that we,
being dead to sins, should live unto
righteousness: by whose stripes ye
were healed.
25 For ye were as sheep going
astray; but are now returned unto
the Shepherd and Bishop of your
souls.

Subjection in Marriage

3 Likewise, ye wives, *be* in sub-
jection to your own husbands;
that, if any obey not the word, they
also may without the word be won
by the conversation of the wives;
2 While they behold your chaste
conversation *coupled* with fear.
3 Whose adorning let it not be that
outward *adorning* of plaiting the
hair, and of wearing of gold, or of
putting on of apparel;
4 But *let it be* the hidden man
of the heart, in that which is not
corruptible, *even the ornament* of
a meek and quiet spirit, which is in
the sight of God of great price.
5 For after this manner in the old
time the holy women also, who
trusted in God, adorned themselves,
being in subjection unto their own
husbands:
6 Even as Sara obeyed Abraham,
calling him lord: whose daughters
ye are, as long as ye do well, and are
not afraid with any amazement.
7 Likewise, ye husbands, dwell
with *them* according to knowledge,
giving honour unto the wife, as unto
the weaker vessel, and as being heirs
together of the grace of life; that
your prayers be not hindered.

Inheritance of a Blessing

8 Finally, *be ye* all of one mind,
having compassion one of another,
love as brethren, *be* pitiful, *be* cour-
teous:
9 Not rendering evil for evil, or
railing for railing: but contrariwise
blessing; knowing that ye are there-
unto called, that ye should inherit a
blessing.
10 For he that will love life, and
see good days, let him refrain his
tongue from evil, and his lips that
they speak no guile:
11 Let him eschew evil, and do
good; let him seek peace, and en-
sue it.
12 For the eyes of the Lord *are* over
the righteous, and his ears *are open*
unto their prayers: but the face of
the Lord *is* against them that do evil.
13 And who *is* he that will harm
you, if ye be followers of that which
is good?
14 But and if ye suffer for righ-
teousness' sake, happy *are ye:* and
be not afraid of their terror, neither
be troubled;
15 But sanctify the Lord God in
your hearts: and *be* ready always

to *give* an answer to every man that
asketh you a reason of the hope that
is in you with meekness and fear:
16 Having a good conscience; that,
whereas they speak evil of you, as
of evildoers, they may be ashamed
that falsely accuse your good con-
versation in Christ.
17 For *it is* better, if the will of God
be so, that ye suffer for well doing,
than for evil doing.
18 For Christ also hath once suf-
fered for sins, the just for the unjust,
that he might bring us to God, being
put to death in the flesh, but quick-
ened by the Spirit:
19 By which also he went and
preached unto the spirits in prison;
20 Which sometime were dis-
obedient, when once the longsuf-
fering of God waited in the days of
Noah, while the ark was a prepar-
ing, wherein few, that is, eight souls
were saved by water.
21 The like figure whereunto *even*
baptism doth also now save us (not
the putting away of the filth of the
flesh, but the answer of a good con-
science toward God,) by the resur-
rection of Jesus Christ:
22 Who is gone into heaven, and
is on the right hand of God; angels
and authorities and powers being
made subject unto him.

Charity Among Yourselves

4 Forasmuch then as Christ hath
suffered for us in the flesh, arm
yourselves likewise with the same
mind: for he that hath suffered in
the flesh hath ceased from sin;
2 That he no longer should live the
rest of *his* time in the flesh to the
lusts of men, but to the will of God.
3 For the time past of *our* life may
suffice us to have wrought the will
of the Gentiles, when we walked
in lasciviousness, lusts, excess of
wine, revellings, banquetings, and
abominable idolatries:
4 Wherein they think it strange
that ye run not with *them* to the
same excess of riot, speaking evil
of *you:*
5 Who shall give account to him
that is ready to judge the quick and
the dead.
6 For for this cause was the gospel
preached also to them that are dead,
that they might be judged according
to men in the flesh, but live accord-
ing to God in the spirit.
7 But the end of all things is at
hand: be ye therefore sober, and
watch unto prayer.
8 And above all things have fer-
vent charity among yourselves: for
charity shall cover the multitude of
sins.
9 Use hospitality one to another
without grudging.
10 As every man hath received the
gift, *even so* minister the same one
to another, as good stewards of the
manifold grace of God.
11 If any man speak, *let him speak*
as the oracles of God; if any man
minister, *let him do it* as of the abil-
ity which God giveth: that God in
all things may be glorified through
Jesus Christ, to whom be praise and
dominion for ever and ever. Amen.

Partakers of Christ's Sufferings

12 Beloved, think it not strange
concerning the fiery trial which is
to try you, as though some strange
thing happened unto you:
13 But rejoice, inasmuch as ye are
partakers of Christ's sufferings; that,
when his glory shall be revealed, ye
may be glad also with exceeding joy.
14 If ye be reproached for the name
of Christ, happy *are ye;* for the spirit
of glory and of God resteth upon
you: on their part he is evil spoken
of, but on your part he is glorified.
15 But let none of you suffer as
a murderer, or *as* a thief, or *as* an
evildoer, or as a busybody in other
men's matters.

16 Yet if *any man suffer* as a Chris-
tian, let him not be ashamed; but let
him glorify God on this behalf.
17 For the time *is come* that judg-
ment must begin at the house of
God: and if *it* first *begin* at us, what
shall the end *be* of them that obey
not the gospel of God?
18 And if the righteous scarcely be
saved, where shall the ungodly and
the sinner appear?
19 Wherefore let them that suffer
according to the will of God commit
the keeping of their souls *to him* in
well doing, as unto a faithful Creator.

Be Subject One to Another

5 The elders which are among you
I exhort, who am also an elder,
and a witness of the sufferings of
Christ, and also a partaker of the
glory that shall be revealed:
2 Feed the flock of God which is
among you, taking the oversight
thereof, not by constraint, but will-
ingly; not for filthy lucre, but of a
ready mind;
3 Neither as being lords over *God's*
heritage, but being ensamples to the
flock.
4 And when the chief Shepherd
shall appear, ye shall receive a crown
of glory that fadeth not away.
5 Likewise, ye younger, submit
yourselves unto the elder. Yea, all
of you be subject one to another,
and be clothed with humility: for
God resisteth the proud, and giveth
grace to the humble.
6 Humble yourselves therefore
under the mighty hand of God, that
he may exalt you in due time:
7 Casting all your care upon him;
for he careth for you.
8 Be sober, be vigilant; because
your adversary the devil, as a roaring
lion, walketh about, seeking whom
he may devour:
9 Whom resist stedfast in the
faith, knowing that the same af-
flictions are accomplished in your
brethren that are in the world.
10 But the God of all grace, who
hath called us unto his eternal glory
by Christ Jesus, after that ye have
suffered a while, make you perfect,
stablish, strengthen, settle *you.*
11 To him *be* glory and dominion
for ever and ever. Amen.

Peace in Jesus Christ

12 By Silvanus, a faithful brother
unto you, as I suppose, I have writ-
ten briefly, exhorting, and testifying
that this is the true grace of God
wherein ye stand.
13 The *church that is* at Babylon,
elected together with *you,* saluteth
you; and *so doth* Marcus my son.
14 Greet ye one another with a kiss
of charity. Peace *be* with you all that
are in Christ Jesus. Amen.

The Second Epistle General of
PETER

Grace and Peace

Simon Peter, a servant and an apostle of Jesus Christ, to them that have obtained like precious faith with us through the righteousness of God and our Saviour Jesus Christ:

2 Grace and peace be multiplied unto you through the knowledge of God, and of Jesus our Lord,

Fruitful in the Knowledge of Christ

3 According as his divine power hath given unto us all things that *pertain* unto life and godliness, through the knowledge of him that hath called us to glory and virtue:

4 Whereby are given unto us exceeding great and precious promises: that by these ye might be partakers of the divine nature, having escaped the corruption that is in the world through lust.

5 And beside this, giving all diligence, add to your faith virtue; and to virtue knowledge;

6 And to knowledge temperance; and to temperance patience; and to patience godliness;

7 And to godliness brotherly kindness; and to brotherly kindness charity.

8 For if these things be in you, and abound, they make *you that ye shall* neither *be* barren nor unfruitful in the knowledge of our Lord Jesus Christ.

9 But he that lacketh these things is blind, and cannot see afar off, and hath forgotten that he was purged from his old sins.

10 Wherefore the rather, brethren, give diligence to make your calling and election sure: for if ye do these things, ye shall never fall:

11 For so an entrance shall be ministered unto you abundantly into the everlasting kingdom of our Lord and Saviour Jesus Christ.

Eyewitnesses of His Majesty

12 Wherefore I will not be negligent to put you always in remembrance of these things, though ye know *them,* and be established in the present truth.

13 Yea, I think it meet, as long as I am in this tabernacle, to stir you up by putting *you* in remembrance;

14 Knowing that shortly I must put off *this* my tabernacle, even as our Lord Jesus Christ hath shewed me.

15 Moreover I will endeavour that ye may be able after my decease to have these things always in remembrance.

16 For we have not followed cunningly devised fables, when we made known unto you the power and coming of our Lord Jesus Christ, but were eyewitnesses of his majesty.

17 For he received from God the Father honour and glory, when there came such a voice to him from the excellent glory, This is my beloved Son, in whom I am well pleased.

18 And this voice which came from heaven we heard, when we were with him in the holy mount.

19 We have also a more sure word of prophecy; whereunto ye do well

that ye take heed, as unto a light that
shineth in a dark place, until the day
dawn, and the day star arise in your
hearts:
20 Knowing this first, that no
prophecy of the scripture is of any
private interpretation.
21 For the prophecy came not
in old time by the will of man: but
holy men of God spake *as they were*
moved by the Holy Ghost.

Destruction for False Teachers

2 But there were false prophets
also among the people, even as
there shall be false teachers among
you, who privily shall bring in dam-
nable heresies, even denying the
Lord that bought them, and bring
upon themselves swift destruction.
2 And many shall follow their per-
nicious ways; by reason of whom
the way of truth shall be evil spo-
ken of.
3 And through covetousness shall
they with feigned words make mer-
chandise of you: whose judgment
now of a long time lingereth not,
and their damnation slumbereth
not.
4 For if God spared not the angels
that sinned, but cast *them* down to
hell, and delivered *them* into chains
of darkness, to be reserved unto
judgment;
5 And spared not the old world,
but saved Noah the eighth *person,* a
preacher of righteousness, bringing
in the flood upon the world of the
ungodly;
6 And turning the cities of Sodom
and Gomorrha into ashes con-
demned *them* with an overthrow,
making *them* an ensample unto
those that after should live ungodly;
7 And delivered just Lot, vexed
with the filthy conversation of the
wicked:
8 (For that righteous man dwell-
ing among them, in seeing and
hearing, vexed *his* righteous soul
from day to day with *their* unlawful
deeds;)
9 The Lord knoweth how to de-
liver the godly out of temptations,
and to reserve the unjust unto the
day of judgment to be punished:
10 But chiefly them that walk after
the flesh in the lust of uncleanness,
and despise government. Presump-
tuous *are they,* selfwilled, they are
not afraid to speak evil of dignities.
11 Whereas angels, which are
greater in power and might, bring
not railing accusation against them
before the Lord.
12 But these, as natural brute
beasts, made to be taken and de-
stroyed, speak evil of the things that
they understand not; and shall ut-
terly perish in their own corruption;
13 And shall receive the reward of
unrighteousness, *as* they that count
it pleasure to riot in the day time.
Spots *they are* and blemishes, sport-
ing themselves with their own de-
ceivings while they feast with you;
14 Having eyes full of adultery,
and that cannot cease from sin;
beguiling unstable souls: an heart
they have exercised with covetous
practices; cursed children:
15 Which have forsaken the right
way, and are gone astray, follow-
ing the way of Balaam *the son* of
Bosor, who loved the wages of un-
righteousness;
16 But was rebuked for his iniq-
uity: the dumb ass speaking with
man's voice forbad the madness of
the prophet.
17 These are wells without water,
clouds that are carried with a tem-
pest; to whom the mist of darkness
is reserved for ever.
18 For when they speak great
swelling *words* of vanity, they al-
lure through the lusts of the flesh,
through much wantonness, those
that were clean escaped from them
who live in error.

19 While they promise them liberty, they themselves are the servants of corruption: for of whom a man is overcome, of the same is he brought in bondage.

20 For if after they have escaped the pollutions of the world through the knowledge of the Lord and Saviour Jesus Christ, they are again entangled therein, and overcome, the latter end is worse with them than the beginning.

21 For it had been better for them not to have known the way of righteousness, than, after they have known *it,* to turn from the holy commandment delivered unto them.

22 But it is happened unto them according to the true proverb, The dog *is* turned to his own vomit again; and the sow that was washed to her wallowing in the mire.

Unwilling for Any to Perish

3 This second epistle, beloved, I now write unto you; in *both* which I stir up your pure minds by way of remembrance:

2 That ye may be mindful of the words which were spoken before by the holy prophets, and of the commandment of us the apostles of the Lord and Saviour:

3 Knowing this first, that there shall come in the last days scoffers, walking after their own lusts,

4 And saying, Where is the promise of his coming? for since the fathers fell asleep, all things continue as *they were* from the beginning of the creation.

5 For this they willingly are ignorant of, that by the word of God the heavens were of old, and the earth standing out of the water and in the water:

6 Whereby the world that then was, being overflowed with water, perished:

7 But the heavens and the earth, which are now, by the same word are kept in store, reserved unto fire against the day of judgment and perdition of ungodly men.

8 But, beloved, be not ignorant of this one thing, that one day *is* with the Lord as a thousand years, and a thousand years as one day.

9 The Lord is not slack concerning his promise, as some men count slackness; but is longsuffering to us-ward, not willing that any should perish, but that all should come to repentance.

10 But the day of the Lord will come as a thief in the night; in the which the heavens shall pass away with a great noise, and the elements shall melt with fervent heat, the earth also and the works that are therein shall be burned up.

11 *Seeing* then *that* all these things shall be dissolved, what manner *of persons* ought ye to be in *all* holy conversation and godliness,

12 Looking for and hasting unto the coming of the day of God, wherein the heavens being on fire shall be dissolved, and the elements shall melt with fervent heat?

13 Nevertheless we, according to his promise, look for new heavens and a new earth, wherein dwelleth righteousness.

14 Wherefore, beloved, seeing that ye look for such things, be diligent that ye may be found of him in peace, without spot, and blameless.

Grow in Grace

15 And account *that* the longsuffering of our Lord *is* salvation; even as our beloved brother Paul also according to the wisdom given unto him hath written unto you;

16 As also in all *his* epistles, speaking in them of these things; in which are some things hard to be understood, which they that are

unlearned and unstable wrest, as
they do also the other scriptures,
unto their own destruction.
17 Ye therefore, beloved, seeing ye
know *these things* before, beware
lest ye also, being led away with the
error of the wicked, fall from your
own stedfastness.
18 But grow in grace, and *in* the
knowledge of our Lord and Saviour
Jesus Christ. To him *be* glory both
now and for ever. Amen.

The First Epistle General of
JOHN

Be Full of Joy

That which was from the be-
ginning, which we have heard,
which we have seen with our eyes,
which we have looked upon, and our
hands have handled, of the Word
of life;
2 (For the life was manifested, and
we have seen *it,* and bear witness,
and shew unto you that eternal life,
which was with the Father, and was
manifested unto us;)
3 That which we have seen and
heard declare we unto you, that
ye also may have fellowship with
us: and truly our fellowship *is* with
the Father, and with his Son Jesus
Christ.
4 And these things write we unto
you, that your joy may be full.

Walk in the Light

5 This then is the message which
we have heard of him, and declare
unto you, that God is light, and in
him is no darkness at all.
6 If we say that we have fellowship
with him, and walk in darkness, we
lie, and do not the truth:
7 But if we walk in the light, as he
is in the light, we have fellowship
one with another, and the blood of
Jesus Christ his Son cleanseth us
from all sin.
8 If we say that we have no sin, we
deceive ourselves, and the truth is
not in us.
9 If we confess our sins, he is faith-
ful and just to forgive us *our* sins,
and to cleanse us from all unrigh-
teousness.
10 If we say that we have not
sinned, we make him a liar, and his
word is not in us.

Our Advocate with the Father

2 My little children, these things
write I unto you, that ye sin not.
And if any man sin, we have an ad-
vocate with the Father, Jesus Christ
the righteous:
2 And he is the propitiation for our
sins: and not for ours only, but also
for *the sins of* the whole world.
3 And hereby we do know that we
know him, if we keep his command-
ments.
4 He that saith, I know him, and
keepeth not his commandments, is
a liar, and the truth is not in him.
5 But whoso keepeth his word,
in him verily is the love of God per-
fected: hereby know we that we are
in him.
6 He that saith he abideth in him
ought himself also so to walk, even
as he walked.
7 Brethren, I write no new com-
mandment unto you, but an old
commandment which ye had from
the beginning. The old command-
ment is the word which ye have
heard from the beginning.
8 Again, a new commandment I
write unto you, which thing is true
in him and in you: because the dark-
ness is past, and the true light now
shineth.
9 He that saith he is in the light,
and hateth his brother, is in dark-
ness even until now.
10 He that loveth his brother abid-

eth in the light, and there is none occasion of stumbling in him.

11 But he that hateth his brother is in darkness, and walketh in darkness, and knoweth not whither he goeth, because that darkness hath blinded his eyes.

12 I write unto you, little children, because your sins are forgiven you for his name's sake.

13 I write unto you, fathers, because ye have known him *that is* from the beginning. I write unto you, young men, because ye have overcome the wicked one. I write unto you, little children, because ye have known the Father.

14 I have written unto you, fathers, because ye have known him *that is* from the beginning. I have written unto you, young men, because ye are strong, and the word of God abideth in you, and ye have overcome the wicked one.

Love the Father, Not the World

15 Love not the world, neither the things *that are* in the world. If any man love the world, the love of the Father is not in him.

16 For all that *is* in the world, the lust of the flesh, and the lust of the eyes, and the pride of life, is not of the Father, but is of the world.

17 And the world passeth away, and the lust thereof: but he that doeth the will of God abideth for ever.

Beware of Antichrists

18 Little children, it is the last time: and as ye have heard that antichrist shall come, even now are there many antichrists; whereby we know that it is the last time.

19 They went out from us, but they were not of us; for if they had been of us, they would *no doubt* have continued with us: but *they went out,* that they might be made manifest that they were not all of us.

20 But ye have an unction from the Holy One, and ye know all things.

21 I have not written unto you because ye know not the truth, but because ye know it, and that no lie is of the truth.

22 Who is a liar but he that denieth that Jesus is the Christ? He is antichrist, that denieth the Father and the Son.

23 Whosoever denieth the Son, the same hath not the Father: *[but] he that acknowledgeth the Son hath the Father also.*

Abide in Christ

24 Let that therefore abide in you, which ye have heard from the beginning. If that which ye have heard from the beginning shall remain in you, ye also shall continue in the Son, and in the Father.

25 And this is the promise that he hath promised us, *even* eternal life.

26 These *things* have I written unto you concerning them that seduce you.

27 But the anointing which ye have received of him abideth in you, and ye need not that any man teach you: but as the same anointing teacheth you of all things, and is truth, and is no lie, and even as it hath taught you, ye shall abide in him.

28 And now, little children, abide in him; that, when he shall appear, we may have confidence, and not be ashamed before him at his coming.

29 If ye know that he is righteous, ye know that every one that doeth righteousness is born of him.

Let No Man Deceive You

3 Behold, what manner of love the Father hath bestowed upon us, that we should be called the sons of God: therefore the world knoweth us not, because it knew him not.

2 Beloved, now are we the sons of God, and it doth not yet appear what

we shall be: but we know that, when
he shall appear, we shall be like him;
for we shall see him as he is.
3 And every man that hath this
hope in him purifieth himself, even
as he is pure.
4 Whosoever committeth sin
transgresseth also the law: for sin
is the transgression of the law.
5 And ye know that he was mani-
fested to take away our sins; and in
him is no sin.
6 Whosoever abideth in him sin-
neth not: whosoever sinneth hath
not seen him, neither known him.
7 Little children, let no man de-
ceive you: he that doeth righteous-
ness is righteous, even as he is righ-
teous.
8 He that committeth sin is of the
devil; for the devil sinneth from the
beginning. For this purpose the Son
of God was manifested, that he
might destroy the works of the devil.
9 Whosoever is born of God doth
not commit sin; for his seed re-
maineth in him: and he cannot sin,
because he is born of God.
10 In this the children of God are
manifest, and the children of the
devil: whosoever doeth not righ-
teousness is not of God, neither he
that loveth not his brother.

Love in Deed and in Truth

11 For this is the message that ye
heard from the beginning, that we
should love one another.
12 Not as Cain, *who* was of that
wicked one, and slew his brother.
And wherefore slew he him? Be-
cause his own works were evil, and
his brother's righteous.
13 Marvel not, my brethren, if the
world hate you.
14 We know that we have passed
from death unto life, because we
love the brethren. He that loveth
not *his* brother abideth in death.
15 Whosoever hateth his brother
is a murderer: and ye know that no
murderer hath eternal life abiding
in him.
16 Hereby perceive we the love *of*
God, because he laid down his life
for us: and we ought to lay down
our lives for the brethren.
17 But whoso hath this world's
good, and seeth his brother have
need, and shutteth up his bowels *of*
compassion from him, how dwelleth
the love of God in him?
18 My little children, let us not love
in word, neither in tongue; but in
deed and in truth.
19 And hereby we know that we
are of the truth, and shall assure
our hearts before him.
20 For if our heart condemn us,
God is greater than our heart, and
knoweth all things.
21 Beloved, if our heart condemn
us not, *then* have we confidence to-
ward God.
22 And whatsoever we ask, we
receive of him, because we keep
his commandments, and do those
things that are pleasing in his sight.
23 And this is his commandment,
That we should believe on the name
of his Son Jesus Christ, and love one
another, as he gave us command-
ment.
24 And he that keepeth his com-
mandments dwelleth in him, and he
in him. And hereby we know that he
abideth in us, by the Spirit which he
hath given us.

Be Sure the Spirits Are of God

4 Beloved, believe not every spirit,
but try the spirits whether they
are of God: because many false
prophets are gone out into the
world.
2 Hereby know ye the Spirit of
God: Every spirit that confesseth
that Jesus Christ is come in the flesh
is of God:
3 And every spirit that confesseth
not that Jesus Christ is come in the
flesh is not of God: and this is that

spirit of antichrist, whereof ye have
heard that it should come; and even
now already is it in the world.
4 Ye are of God, little children,
and have overcome them: because
greater is he that is in you, than he
that is in the world.
5 They are of the world: therefore
speak they of the world, and the
world heareth them.
6 We are of God: he that knoweth
God heareth us; he that is not of God
heareth not us. Hereby know we the
spirit of truth, and the spirit of error.

Love One Another

7 Beloved, let us love one another:
for love is of God; and every one that
loveth is born of God, and knoweth
God.
8 He that loveth not knoweth not
God; for God is love.
9 In this was manifested the love
of God toward us, because that God
sent his only begotten Son into the
world, that we might live through
him.
10 Herein is love, not that we loved
God, but that he loved us, and sent
his Son *to be* the propitiation for our
sins.
11 Beloved, if God so loved us, we
ought also to love one another.
12 No man hath seen God at any
time. If we love one another, God
dwelleth in us, and his love is per-
fected in us.
13 Hereby know we that we dwell
in him, and he in us, because he hath
given us of his Spirit.
14 And we have seen and do testify
that the Father sent the Son *to be*
the Saviour of the world.
15 Whosoever shall confess that
Jesus is the Son of God, God dwell-
eth in him, and he in God.
16 And we have known and be-
lieved the love that God hath to us.
God is love; and he that dwelleth
in love dwelleth in God, and God in
him.
17 Herein is our love made perfect,
that we may have boldness in the
day of judgment: because as he is,
so are we in this world.
18 There is no fear in love; but per-
fect love casteth out fear: because
fear hath torment. He that feareth
is not made perfect in love.
19 We love him, because he first
loved us.
20 If a man say, I love God, and
hateth his brother, he is a liar: for
he that loveth not his brother whom
he hath seen, how can he love God
whom he hath not seen?
21 And this commandment have
we from him, That he who loveth
God love his brother also.

Love God and Keep His Commandments

5 Whosoever believeth that Jesus
is the Christ is born of God: and
every one that loveth him that begat
loveth him also that is begotten of
him.
2 By this we know that we love the
children of God, when we love God,
and keep his commandments.
3 For this is the love of God, that
we keep his commandments: and
his commandments are not griev-
ous.
4 For whatsoever is born of God
overcometh the world: and this is
the victory that overcometh the
world, *even* our faith.
5 Who is he that overcometh the
world, but he that believeth that
Jesus is the Son of God?
6 This is he that came by water
and blood, *even* Jesus Christ; not by
water only, but by water and blood.
And it is the Spirit that beareth wit-
ness, because the Spirit is truth.
7 For there are three that bear
record in heaven, the Father, the
Word, and the Holy Ghost: and these
three are one.
8 And there are three that bear
witness in earth, the Spirit, and

the water, and the blood: and these three agree in one.

9 If we receive the witness of men, the witness of God is greater: for this is the witness of God which he hath testified of his Son.

10 He that believeth on the Son of God hath the witness in himself: he that believeth not God hath made him a liar; because he believeth not the record that God gave of his Son.

11 And this is the record, that God hath given to us eternal life, and this life is in his Son.

12 He that hath the Son hath life; *and* he that hath not the Son of God hath not life.

We Know God Hears Us

13 These things have I written unto you that believe on the name of the Son of God; that ye may know that ye have eternal life, and that ye may believe on the name of the Son of God.

14 And this is the confidence that we have in him, that, if we ask any thing according to his will, he heareth us:

15 And if we know that he hear us, whatsoever we ask, we know that we have the petitions that we desired of him.

16 If any man see his brother sin a sin *which is* not unto death, he shall ask, and he shall give him life for them that sin not unto death. There is a sin unto death: I do not say that he shall pray for it.

17 All unrighteousness is sin: and there is a sin not unto death.

18 We know that whosoever is born of God sinneth not; but he that is begotten of God keepeth himself, and that wicked one toucheth him not.

19 *And* we know that we are of God, and the whole world lieth in wickedness.

20 And we know that the Son of God is come, and hath given us an understanding, that we may know him that is true, and we are in him that is true, *even* in his Son Jesus Christ. This is the true God, and eternal life.

21 Little children, keep yourselves from idols. Amen.

The Second Epistle of
JOHN

The Elect Lady and Her Children

The elder unto the elect lady and
her children, whom I love in the
truth; and not I only, but also all they
that have known the truth;
2 For the truth's sake, which
dwelleth in us, and shall be with
us for ever.
3 Grace be with you, mercy, *and*
peace, from God the Father, and
from the Lord Jesus Christ, the Son
of the Father, in truth and love.
4 I rejoiced greatly that I found
of thy children walking in truth, as
we have received a commandment
from the Father.
5 And now I beseech thee, lady,
not as though I wrote a new com-
mandment unto thee, but that
which we had from the beginning,
that we love one another.
6 And this is love, that we walk
after his commandments. This is
the commandment, That, as ye have
heard from the beginning, ye should
walk in it.
7 For many deceivers are entered
into the world, who confess not
that Jesus Christ is come in the
flesh. This is a deceiver and an anti-
christ.
8 Look to yourselves, that we lose
not those things which we have
wrought, but that we receive a full
reward.

Abide in the Doctrine of Christ

9 Whosoever transgresseth, and
abideth not in the doctrine of Christ,
hath not God. He that abideth in the
doctrine of Christ, he hath both the
Father and the Son.
10 If there come any unto you, and
bring not this doctrine, receive him
not into *your* house, neither bid him
God speed:
11 For he that biddeth him God
speed is partaker of his evil deeds.
12 Having many things to write
unto you, I would not *write* with
paper and ink: but I trust to come
unto you, and speak face to face,
that our joy may be full.
13 The children of thy elect sister
greet thee. Amen.

The Third Epistle of
JOHN

Greeting

The elder unto the wellbeloved
Gaius, whom I love in the truth.
2 Beloved, I wish above all things
that thou mayest prosper and be in
health, even as thy soul prospereth.
3 For I rejoiced greatly, when the
brethren came and testified of the
truth that is in thee, even as thou
walkest in the truth.
4 I have no greater joy than to hear
that my children walk in truth.

Gaius's Generosity Commended

5 Beloved, thou doest faithfully
whatsoever thou doest to the breth-
ren, and to strangers;
6 Which have borne witness of thy
charity before the church: whom if
thou bring forward on their journey
after a godly sort, thou shalt do well:
7 Because that for his name's sake
they went forth, taking nothing of
the Gentiles.
8 We therefore ought to receive
such, that we might be fellowhelp-
ers to the truth.
9 I wrote unto the church: but
Diotrephes, who loveth to have
the preeminence among them, re-
ceiveth us not.
10 Wherefore, if I come, I will re-
member his deeds which he doeth,
prating against us with malicious
words: and not content therewith,
neither doth he himself receive the
brethren, and forbiddeth them that
would, and casteth *them* out of the
church.
11 Beloved, follow not that which
is evil, but that which is good. He
that doeth good is of God: but he
that doeth evil hath not seen God.
12 Demetrius hath good report
of all *men,* and of the truth itself:
yea, and we *also* bear record; and
ye know that our record is true.
13 I had many things to write, but
I will not with ink and pen write
unto thee:
14 But I trust I shall shortly see
thee, and we shall speak face to
face. Peace *be* to thee. *Our* friends
salute thee. Greet the friends by
name.

The General Epistle of
JUDE

Loved by God the Father

Jude, the servant of Jesus Christ, and brother of James, to them that are sanctified by God the Father, and preserved in Jesus Christ, *and* called:

2 Mercy unto you, and peace, and love, be multiplied.

Earnest Contention for the Faith

3 Beloved, when I gave all diligence to write unto you of the common salvation, it was needful for me to write unto you, and exhort *you* that ye should earnestly contend for the faith which was once delivered unto the saints.

4 For there are certain men crept in unawares, who were before of old ordained to this condemnation, ungodly men, turning the grace of our God into lasciviousness, and denying the only Lord God, and our Lord Jesus Christ.

5 I will therefore put you in remembrance, though ye once knew this, how that the Lord, having saved the people out of the land of Egypt, afterward destroyed them that believed not.

6 And the angels which kept not their first estate, but left their own habitation, he hath reserved in everlasting chains under darkness unto the judgment of the great day.

7 Even as Sodom and Gomorrha, and the cities about them in like manner, giving themselves over to fornication, and going after strange flesh, are set forth for an example, suffering the vengeance of eternal fire.

8 Likewise also these *filthy* dreamers defile the flesh, despise dominion, and speak evil of dignities.

9 Yet Michael the archangel, when contending with the devil he disputed about the body of Moses, durst not bring against him a railing accusation, but said, The Lord rebuke thee.

10 But these speak evil of those things which they know not: but what they know naturally, as brute beasts, in those things they corrupt themselves.

11 Woe unto them! for they have gone in the way of Cain, and ran greedily after the error of Balaam for reward, and perished in the gainsaying of Core.

12 These are spots in your feasts of charity, when they feast with you, feeding themselves without fear: clouds *they are* without water, carried about of winds; trees whose fruit withereth, without fruit, twice dead, plucked up by the roots;

13 Raging waves of the sea, foaming out their own shame; wandering stars, to whom is reserved the blackness of darkness for ever.

14 And Enoch also, the seventh from Adam, prophesied of these, saying, Behold, the Lord cometh with ten thousands of his saints,

15 To execute judgment upon all, and to convince all that are ungodly among them of all their ungodly deeds which they have ungodly

committed, and of all their hard *speeches* which ungodly sinners have spoken against him.

16 These are murmurers, complainers, walking after their own lusts; and their mouth speaketh great swelling *words,* having men's persons in admiration because of advantage.

Keep Yourselves in God's Love

17 But, beloved, remember ye the words which were spoken before of the apostles of our Lord Jesus Christ;

18 How that they told you there should be mockers in the last time, who should walk after their own ungodly lusts.

19 These be they who separate themselves, sensual, having not the Spirit.

20 But ye, beloved, building up yourselves on your most holy faith, praying in the Holy Ghost,

21 Keep yourselves in the love of God, looking for the mercy of our Lord Jesus Christ unto eternal life.

22 And of some have compassion, making a difference:

23 And others save with fear, pulling *them* out of the fire; hating even the garment spotted by the flesh.

24 Now unto him that is able to keep you from falling, and to present *you* faultless before the presence of his glory with exceeding joy,

25 To the only wise God our Saviour, *be* glory and majesty, dominion and power, both now and ever. Amen.

The
REVELATION
of Jesus Christ

Greeting to the Seven Churches

The Revelation of Jesus Christ,
which God gave unto him, to
shew unto his servants things which
must shortly come to pass; and he
sent and signified *it* by his angel
unto his servant John:
2 Who bare record of the word of
God, and of the testimony of Jesus
Christ, and of all things that he saw.
3 Blessed *is* he that readeth, and
they that hear the words of this
prophecy, and keep those things
which are written therein: for the
time *is* at hand.
4 JOHN to the seven churches
which are in Asia: Grace *be* unto you,
and peace, from him which is, and
which was, and which is to come;
and from the seven Spirits which
are before his throne;
5 And from Jesus Christ, *who is*
the faithful witness, *and* the first
begotten of the dead, and the prince
of the kings of the earth. Unto him
that loved us, and washed us from
our sins in his own blood,
6 And hath made us kings and
priests unto God and his Father; to
him *be* glory and dominion for ever
and ever. Amen.
7 Behold, he cometh with clouds;
and every eye shall see him, and
they *also* which pierced him: and
all kindreds of the earth shall wail
because of him. Even so, Amen.
8 I am Alpha and Omega, the be-
ginning and the ending, saith the
Lord, which is, and which was, and
which is to come, the Almighty.

The Alpha and Omega

9 I John, who also am your
brother, and companion in tribu-
lation, and in the kingdom and pa-
tience of Jesus Christ, was in the isle
that is called Patmos, for the word of
God, and for the testimony of Jesus
Christ.
10 I was in the Spirit on the Lord's
day, and heard behind me a great
voice, as of a trumpet,
11 Saying, I am Alpha and Omega,
the first and the last: and, What thou
seest, write in a book, and send *it*
unto the seven churches which are
in Asia; unto Ephesus, and unto
Smyrna, and unto Pergamos, and
unto Thyatira, and unto Sardis, and
unto Philadelphia, and unto Laodi-
cea.

The First and the Last

12 And I turned to see the voice
that spake with me. And being
turned, I saw seven golden candle-
sticks;
13 And in the midst of the seven
candlesticks *one* like unto the Son of
man, clothed with a garment down
to the foot, and girt about the paps
with a golden girdle.
14 His head and *his* hairs *were*
white like wool, as white as snow;
and his eyes *were* as a flame of fire;
15 And his feet like unto fine brass,
as if they burned in a furnace; and

his voice as the sound of many wa-
ters.
16 And he had in his right hand
seven stars: and out of his mouth
went a sharp twoedged sword: and
his countenance *was* as the sun
shineth in his strength.
17 And when I saw him, I fell at
his feet as dead. And he laid his
right hand upon me, saying unto
me, Fear not; I am the first and the
last:
18 I *am* he that liveth, and was
dead; and, behold, I am alive for
evermore, Amen; and have the keys
of hell and of death.
19 Write the things which thou
hast seen, and the things which are,
and the things which shall be here-
after;
20 The mystery of the seven stars
which thou sawest in my right hand,
and the seven golden candlesticks.
The seven stars are the angels of
the seven churches: and the seven
candlesticks which thou sawest are
the seven churches.

The Church in Ephesus

2 Unto the angel of the church
of Ephesus write; These things
saith he that holdeth the seven stars
in his right hand, who walketh in
the midst of the seven golden can-
dlesticks;
2 I know thy works, and thy la-
bour, and thy patience, and how
thou canst not bear them which are
evil: and thou hast tried them which
say they are apostles, and are not,
and hast found them liars:
3 And hast borne, and hast pa-
tience, and for my name's sake hast
laboured, and hast not fainted.
4 Nevertheless I have *somewhat*
against thee, because thou hast left
thy first love.
5 Remember therefore from
whence thou art fallen, and repent,
and do the first works; or else I will
come unto thee quickly, and will
remove thy candlestick out of his
place, except thou repent.
6 But this thou hast, that thou hat-
est the deeds of the Nicolaitanes,
which I also hate.
7 He that hath an ear, let him
hear what the Spirit saith unto the
churches; To him that overcometh
will I give to eat of the tree of life,
which is in the midst of the paradise
of God.

The Church in Smyrna

8 And unto the angel of the church
in Smyrna write; These things saith
the first and the last, which was
dead, and is alive;
9 I know thy works, and tribu-
lation, and poverty, (but thou art
rich) and *I know* the blasphemy of
them which say they are Jews, and
are not, but *are* the synagogue of
Satan.
10 Fear none of those things which
thou shalt suffer: behold, the devil
shall cast *some* of you into prison,
that ye may be tried; and ye shall
have tribulation ten days: be thou
faithful unto death, and I will give
thee a crown of life.
11 He that hath an ear, let him
hear what the Spirit saith unto the
churches; He that overcometh shall
not be hurt of the second death.

The Church in Pergamos

12 And to the angel of the church in
Pergamos write; These things saith
he which hath the sharp sword with
two edges;
13 I know thy works, and where
thou dwellest, *even* where Satan's
seat *is:* and thou holdest fast my
name, and hast not denied my faith,
even in those days wherein Anti-
pas *was* my faithful martyr, who
was slain among you, where Satan
dwelleth.
14 But I have a few things against
thee, because thou hast there them
that hold the doctrine of Balaam,

who taught Balac to cast a stum-
blingblock before the children of
Israel, to eat things sacrificed unto
idols, and to commit fornication.
15 So hast thou also them that
hold the doctrine of the Nicolai-
tanes, which thing I hate.
16 Repent; or else I will come
unto thee quickly, and will fight
against them with the sword of
my mouth.
17 He that hath an ear, let him
hear what the Spirit saith unto the
churches; To him that overcom-
eth will I give to eat of the hidden
manna, and will give him a white
stone, and in the stone a new name
written, which no man knoweth
saving he that receiveth *it*.

The Church in Thyatira

18 And unto the angel of the
church in Thyatira write; These
things saith the Son of God, who
hath his eyes like unto a flame of
fire, and his feet *are* like fine brass;
19 I know thy works, and charity,
and service, and faith, and thy pa-
tience, and thy works; and the last
to be more than the first.
20 Notwithstanding I have a few
things against thee, because thou
sufferest that woman Jezebel, which
calleth herself a prophetess, to teach
and to seduce my servants to com-
mit fornication, and to eat things
sacrificed unto idols.
21 And I gave her space to repent
of her fornication; and she repented
not.
22 Behold, I will cast her into a
bed, and them that commit adul-
tery with her into great tribulation,
except they repent of their deeds.
23 And I will kill her children with
death; and all the churches shall
know that I am he which searcheth
the reins and hearts: and I will give
unto every one of you according to
your works.
24 But unto you I say, and unto
the rest in Thyatira, as many as have
not this doctrine, and which have
not known the depths of Satan, as
they speak; I will put upon you none
other burden.
25 But that which ye have *already*
hold fast till I come.
26 And he that overcometh, and
keepeth my works unto the end,
to him will I give power over the
nations:
27 And he shall rule them with a
rod of iron; as the vessels of a potter
shall they be broken to shivers: even
as I received of my Father.
28 And I will give him the morning
star.
29 He that hath an ear, let him
hear what the Spirit saith unto the
churches.

The Church in Sardis

3 And unto the angel of the church
in Sardis write; These things
saith he that hath the seven Spirits
of God, and the seven stars; I know
thy works, that thou hast a name
that thou livest, and art dead.
2 Be watchful, and strengthen the
things which remain, that are ready
to die: for I have not found thy works
perfect before God.
3 Remember therefore how thou
hast received and heard, and hold
fast, and repent. If therefore thou
shalt not watch, I will come on thee
as a thief, and thou shalt not know
what hour I will come upon thee.
4 Thou hast a few names even in
Sardis which have not defiled their
garments; and they shall walk with
me in white: for they are worthy.
5 He that overcometh, the same
shall be clothed in white raiment;
and I will not blot out his name out
of the book of life, but I will confess
his name before my Father, and be-
fore his angels.
6 He that hath an ear, let him
hear what the Spirit saith unto the
churches.

The Church in Philadelphia

7 And to the angel of the church
in Philadelphia write; These things
saith he that is holy, he that is true,
he that hath the key of David, he that
openeth, and no man shutteth; and
shutteth, and no man openeth;
8 I know thy works: behold, I have
set before thee an open door, and no
man can shut it: for thou hast a little
strength, and hast kept my word,
and hast not denied my name.
9 Behold, I will make them of the
synagogue of Satan, which say they
are Jews, and are not, but do lie;
behold, I will make them to come
and worship before thy feet, and to
know that I have loved thee.
10 Because thou hast kept the word
of my patience, I also will keep thee
from the hour of temptation, which
shall come upon all the world, to try
them that dwell upon the earth.
11 Behold, I come quickly: hold
that fast which thou hast, that no
man take thy crown.
12 Him that overcometh will I
make a pillar in the temple of my
God, and he shall go no more out:
and I will write upon him the name
of my God, and the name of the city
of my God, *which is* new Jerusalem,
which cometh down out of heaven
from my God: and *I will write upon
him* my new name.
13 He that hath an ear, let him
hear what the Spirit saith unto the
churches.

The Church in Laodicea

14 And unto the angel of the
church of the Laodiceans write;
These things saith the Amen, the
faithful and true witness, the be-
ginning of the creation of God;
15 I know thy works, that thou art
neither cold nor hot: I would thou
wert cold or hot.
16 So then because thou art luke-
warm, and neither cold nor hot, I
will spue thee out of my mouth.
17 Because thou sayest, I am rich,
and increased with goods, and have
need of nothing; and knowest not
that thou art wretched, and misera-
ble, and poor, and blind, and naked:
18 I counsel thee to buy of me gold
tried in the fire, that thou mayest
be rich; and white raiment, that
thou mayest be clothed, and *that*
the shame of thy nakedness do not
appear; and anoint thine eyes with
eyesalve, that thou mayest see.
19 As many as I love, I rebuke and
chasten: be zealous therefore, and
repent.
20 Behold, I stand at the door, and
knock: if any man hear my voice,
and open the door, I will come in
to him, and will sup with him, and
he with me.
21 To him that overcometh will I
grant to sit with me in my throne,
even as I also overcame, and am set
down with my Father in his throne.
22 He that hath an ear, let him
hear what the Spirit saith unto the
churches.

The Throne Set in Heaven

4 After this I looked, and, behold, a
door *was* opened in heaven: and
the first voice which I heard *was* as it
were of a trumpet talking with me;
which said, Come up hither, and I
will shew thee things which must
be hereafter.
2 And immediately I was in the
spirit: and, behold, a throne was
set in heaven, and *one* sat on the
throne.
3 And he that sat was to look upon
like a jasper and a sardine stone: and
there was a rainbow round about the
throne, in sight like unto an emerald.
4 And round about the throne
were four and twenty seats: and
upon the seats I saw four and
twenty elders sitting, clothed in
white raiment; and they had on
their heads crowns of gold.
5 And out of the throne proceeded

lightnings and thunderings and
voices: and *there were* seven lamps
of fire burning before the throne,
which are the seven Spirits of God.
6 And before the throne *there was*
a sea of glass like unto crystal: and in
the midst of the throne, and round
about the throne, *were* four beasts
full of eyes before and behind.
7 And the first beast *was* like a
lion, and the second beast like a calf,
and the third beast had a face as a
man, and the fourth beast *was* like
a flying eagle.
8 And the four beasts had each
of them six wings about *him;* and
they were full of eyes within: and
they rest not day and night, saying,
Holy, holy, holy, Lord God Almighty,
which was, and is, and is to come.
9 And when those beasts give
glory and honour and thanks to him
that sat on the throne, who liveth
for ever and ever,
10 The four and twenty elders fall
down before him that sat on the
throne, and worship him that liveth
for ever and ever, and cast their
crowns before the throne, saying,
11 Thou art worthy, O Lord, to re-
ceive glory and honour and power:
for thou hast created all things, and
for thy pleasure they are and were
created.

The Book Sealed with Seven Seals

5 And I saw in the right hand
of him that sat on the throne
a book written within and on the
backside, sealed with seven seals.
2 And I saw a strong angel pro-
claiming with a loud voice, Who is
worthy to open the book, and to
loose the seals thereof?
3 And no man in heaven, nor in
earth, neither under the earth, was
able to open the book, neither to
look thereon.
4 And I wept much, because no
man was found worthy to open and
to read the book, neither to look
thereon.
5 And one of the elders saith unto
me, Weep not: behold, the Lion of
the tribe of Juda, the Root of David,
hath prevailed to open the book, and
to loose the seven seals thereof.
6 And I beheld, and, lo, in the
midst of the throne and of the four
beasts, and in the midst of the el-
ders, stood a Lamb as it had been
slain, having seven horns and seven
eyes, which are the seven Spirits of
God sent forth into all the earth.
7 And he came and took the book
out of the right hand of him that sat
upon the throne.
8 And when he had taken the
book, the four beasts and four *and*
twenty elders fell down before the
Lamb, having every one of them
harps, and golden vials full of
odours, which are the prayers of
saints.
9 And they sung a new song, say-
ing, Thou art worthy to take the
book, and to open the seals thereof:
for thou wast slain, and hast re-
deemed us to God by thy blood out
of every kindred, and tongue, and
people, and nation;
10 And hast made us unto our God
kings and priests: and we shall reign
on the earth.

Worthy Is the Lamb

11 And I beheld, and I heard the
voice of many angels round about
the throne and the beasts and the
elders: and the number of them was
ten thousand times ten thousand,
and thousands of thousands;
12 Saying with a loud voice, Wor-
thy is the Lamb that was slain to
receive power, and riches, and wis-
dom, and strength, and honour, and
glory, and blessing.
13 And every creature which is in
heaven, and on the earth, and un-
der the earth, and such as are in the
sea, and all that are in them, heard

I saying, Blessing, and honour, and
glory, and power, *be* unto him that
sitteth upon the throne, and unto
the Lamb for ever and ever.
14 And the four beasts said, Amen.
And the four *and* twenty elders fell
down and worshipped him that
liveth for ever and ever.

The First Seal Opened

6 And I saw when the Lamb
opened one of the seals, and I
heard, as it were the noise of thun-
der, one of the four beasts saying,
Come and see.
2 And I saw, and behold a white
horse: and he that sat on him had a
bow; and a crown was given unto
him: and he went forth conquering,
and to conquer.

The Second Seal Opened

3 And when he had opened the
second seal, I heard the second
beast say, Come and see.
4 And there went out another
horse *that was* red: and *power* was
given to him that sat thereon to take
peace from the earth, and that they
should kill one another: and there
was given unto him a great sword.

The Third Seal Opened

5 And when he had opened the
third seal, I heard the third beast
say, Come and see. And I beheld,
and lo a black horse; and he that sat
on him had a pair of balances in his
hand.
6 And I heard a voice in the midst
of the four beasts say, A measure of
wheat for a penny, and three mea-
sures of barley for a penny; and *see*
thou hurt not the oil and the wine.

The Fourth Seal Opened

7 And when he had opened the
fourth seal, I heard the voice of the
fourth beast say, Come and see.
8 And I looked, and behold a pale
horse: and his name that sat on him
was Death, and Hell followed with
him. And power was given unto
them over the fourth part of the
earth, to kill with sword, and with
hunger, and with death, and with
the beasts of the earth.

The Fifth Seal Opened

9 And when he had opened the
fifth seal, I saw under the altar the
souls of them that were slain for the
word of God, and for the testimony
which they held:
10 And they cried with a loud
voice, saying, How long, O Lord,
holy and true, dost thou not judge
and avenge our blood on them that
dwell on the earth?
11 And white robes were given
unto every one of them; and it was
said unto them, that they should
rest yet for a little season, until their
fellowservants also and their breth-
ren, that should be killed as they
were, should be fulfilled.

The Sixth Seal Opened

12 And I beheld when he had
opened the sixth seal, and, lo, there
was a great earthquake; and the sun
became black as sackcloth of hair,
and the moon became as blood;
13 And the stars of heaven fell
unto the earth, even as a fig tree
casteth her untimely figs, when she
is shaken of a mighty wind.
14 And the heaven departed as a
scroll when it is rolled together; and
every mountain and island were
moved out of their places.
15 And the kings of the earth, and
the great men, and the rich men, and
the chief captains, and the mighty
men, and every bondman, and every
free man, hid themselves in the dens
and in the rocks of the mountains;
16 And said to the mountains and
rocks, Fall on us, and hide us from
the face of him that sitteth on the
throne, and from the wrath of the
Lamb:

17 For the great day of his wrath
is come; and who shall be able to
stand?

Twelve Thousand Sealed from Each Tribe

7 And after these things I saw four
angels standing on the four cor-
ners of the earth, holding the four
winds of the earth, that the wind
should not blow on the earth, nor
on the sea, nor on any tree.
2 And I saw another angel ascend-
ing from the east, having the seal
of the living God: and he cried with
a loud voice to the four angels, to
whom it was given to hurt the earth
and the sea,
3 Saying, Hurt not the earth, nei-
ther the sea, nor the trees, till we
have sealed the servants of our God
in their foreheads.
4 And I heard the number of them
which were sealed: *and there were*
sealed an hundred *and* forty *and*
four thousand of all the tribes of the
children of Israel.
5 Of the tribe of Juda *were* sealed
twelve thousand. Of the tribe of
Reuben *were* sealed twelve thou-
sand. Of the tribe of Gad *were* sealed
twelve thousand.
6 Of the tribe of Aser *were* sealed
twelve thousand. Of the tribe of
Nephthalim *were* sealed twelve
thousand. Of the tribe of Manasses
were sealed twelve thousand.
7 Of the tribe of Simeon *were*
sealed twelve thousand. Of the tribe
of Levi *were* sealed twelve thousand.
Of the tribe of Issachar *were* sealed
twelve thousand.
8 Of the tribe of Zabulon *were*
sealed twelve thousand. Of the tribe
of Joseph *were* sealed twelve thou-
sand. Of the tribe of Benjamin *were*
sealed twelve thousand.

A Multitude in White Robes

9 After this I beheld, and, lo, a
great multitude, which no man
could number, of all nations, and
kindreds, and people, and tongues,
stood before the throne, and before
the Lamb, clothed with white robes,
and palms in their hands;
10 And cried with a loud voice,
saying, Salvation to our God which
sitteth upon the throne, and unto
the Lamb.
11 And all the angels stood round
about the throne, and *about* the
elders and the four beasts, and fell
before the throne on their faces, and
worshipped God,
12 Saying, Amen: Blessing, and
glory, and wisdom, and thanks-
giving, and honour, and power, and
might, *be* unto our God for ever and
ever. Amen.
13 And one of the elders answered,
saying unto me, What are these
which are arrayed in white robes?
and whence came they?
14 And I said unto him, Sir, thou
knowest. And he said to me, These
are they which came out of great
tribulation, and have washed their
robes, and made them white in the
blood of the Lamb.
15 Therefore are they before the
throne of God, and serve him day
and night in his temple: and he that
sitteth on the throne shall dwell
among them.
16 They shall hunger no more, nei-
ther thirst any more; neither shall
the sun light on them, nor any heat.
17 For the Lamb which is in the
midst of the throne shall feed them,
and shall lead them unto living
fountains of waters: and God shall
wipe away all tears from their eyes.

The Seventh Seal Opened

8 And when he had opened the
seventh seal, there was silence
in heaven about the space of half
an hour.
2 And I saw the seven angels
which stood before God; and to
them were given seven trumpets.

An Angel Offers Incense

3 And another angel came and stood at the altar, having a golden censer; and there was given unto him much incense, that he should offer *it* with the prayers of all saints upon the golden altar which was before the throne.

4 And the smoke of the incense, *which came* with the prayers of the saints, ascended up before God out of the angel's hand.

5 And the angel took the censer, and filled it with fire of the altar, and cast *it* into the earth: and there were voices, and thunderings, and lightnings, and an earthquake.

6 And the seven angels which had the seven trumpets prepared themselves to sound.

The First Trumpet

7 The first angel sounded, and there followed hail and fire mingled with blood, and they were cast upon the earth: and the third part of trees was burnt up, and all green grass was burnt up.

The Second Trumpet

8 And the second angel sounded, and as it were a great mountain burning with fire was cast into the sea: and the third part of the sea became blood;

9 And the third part of the creatures which were in the sea, and had life, died; and the third part of the ships were destroyed.

The Third Trumpet

10 And the third angel sounded, and there fell a great star from heaven, burning as it were a lamp, and it fell upon the third part of the rivers, and upon the fountains of waters;

11 And the name of the star is called Wormwood: and the third part of the waters became wormwood; and many men died of the waters, because they were made bitter.

The Fourth Trumpet

12 And the fourth angel sounded, and the third part of the sun was smitten, and the third part of the moon, and the third part of the stars; so as the third part of them was darkened, and the day shone not for a third part of it, and the night likewise.

13 And I beheld, and heard an angel flying through the midst of heaven, saying with a loud voice, Woe, woe, woe, to the inhabiters of the earth by reason of the other voices of the trumpet of the three angels, which are yet to sound!

The Fifth Trumpet

9 And the fifth angel sounded, and I saw a star fall from heaven unto the earth: and to him was given the key of the bottomless pit.

2 And he opened the bottomless pit; and there arose a smoke out of the pit, as the smoke of a great furnace; and the sun and the air were darkened by reason of the smoke of the pit.

3 And there came out of the smoke locusts upon the earth: and unto them was given power, as the scorpions of the earth have power.

4 And it was commanded them that they should not hurt the grass of the earth, neither any green thing, neither any tree; but only those men which have not the seal of God in their foreheads.

5 And to them it was given that they should not kill them, but that they should be tormented five months: and their torment *was* as the torment of a scorpion, when he striketh a man.

6 And in those days shall men seek death, and shall not find it; and shall desire to die, and death shall flee from them.

7 And the shapes of the locusts
were like unto horses prepared unto
battle; and on their heads *were* as
it were crowns like gold, and their
faces *were* as the faces of men.
8 And they had hair as the hair of
women, and their teeth were as *the
teeth* of lions.
9 And they had breastplates, as it
were breastplates of iron; and the
sound of their wings *was* as the
sound of chariots of many horses
running to battle.
10 And they had tails like unto
scorpions, and there were stings
in their tails: and their power *was*
to hurt men five months.
11 And they had a king over them,
which is the angel of the bottom-
less pit, whose name in the Hebrew
tongue *is* Abaddon, but in the Greek
tongue hath *his* name Apollyon.
12 One woe is past; *and,* behold,
there come two woes more here-
after.

The Sixth Trumpet

13 And the sixth angel sounded,
and I heard a voice from the four
horns of the golden altar which is
before God,
14 Saying to the sixth angel which
had the trumpet, Loose the four an-
gels which are bound in the great
river Euphrates.
15 And the four angels were loosed,
which were prepared for an hour,
and a day, and a month, and a year,
for to slay the third part of men.
16 And the number of the army of
the horsemen *were* two hundred
thousand thousand: and I heard
the number of them.
17 And thus I saw the horses in the
vision, and them that sat on them,
having breastplates of fire, and of ja-
cinth, and brimstone: and the heads
of the horses *were* as the heads of
lions; and out of their mouths issued
fire and smoke and brimstone.
18 By these three was the third
part of men killed, by the fire, and
by the smoke, and by the brimstone,
which issued out of their mouths.
19 For their power is in their
mouth, and in their tails: for their
tails *were* like unto serpents, and
had heads, and with them they do
hurt.
20 And the rest of the men which
were not killed by these plagues yet
repented not of the works of their
hands, that they should not worship
devils, and idols of gold, and silver,
and brass, and stone, and of wood:
which neither can see, nor hear, nor
walk:
21 Neither repented they of their
murders, nor of their sorceries, nor
of their fornication, nor of their
thefts.

An Angel and Seven Thunders

10 And I saw another mighty an-
gel come down from heaven,
clothed with a cloud: and a rainbow
was upon his head, and his face *was*
as it were the sun, and his feet as
pillars of fire:
2 And he had in his hand a little
book open: and he set his right foot
upon the sea, and *his* left *foot* on the
earth,
3 And cried with a loud voice, as
when a lion roareth: and when he
had cried, seven thunders uttered
their voices.
4 And when the seven thunders
had uttered their voices, I was
about to write: and I heard a voice
from heaven saying unto me, Seal
up those things which the seven
thunders uttered, and write them
not.
5 And the angel which I saw stand
upon the sea and upon the earth
lifted up his hand to heaven,
6 And sware by him that liveth for
ever and ever, who created heaven,
and the things that therein are,
and the earth, and the things that
therein are, and the sea, and the

things which are therein, that there
should be time no longer:
7 But in the days of the voice of the
seventh angel, when he shall begin
to sound, the mystery of God should
be finished, as he hath declared to
his servants the prophets.

The Sweet and Bitter Book

8 And the voice which I heard
from heaven spake unto me again,
and said, Go *and* take the little book
which is open in the hand of the
angel which standeth upon the sea
and upon the earth.
9 And I went unto the angel, and
said unto him, Give me the little
book. And he said unto me, Take
it, and eat it up; and it shall make
thy belly bitter, but it shall be in thy
mouth sweet as honey.
10 And I took the little book out
of the angel's hand, and ate it up;
and it was in my mouth sweet as
honey: and as soon as I had eaten
it, my belly was bitter.
11 And he said unto me, Thou
must prophesy again before many
peoples, and nations, and tongues,
and kings.

The Prophecy of the Two Witnesses

11 And there was given me a reed
like unto a rod: and the angel
stood, saying, Rise, and measure
the temple of God, and the altar, and
them that worship therein.
2 But the court which is without
the temple leave out, and measure it
not; for it is given unto the Gentiles:
and the holy city shall they tread
under foot forty *and* two months.
3 And I will give *power* unto my
two witnesses, and they shall proph-
esy a thousand two hundred *and*
threescore days, clothed in sackcloth.
4 These are the two olive trees,
and the two candlesticks standing
before the God of the earth.
5 And if any man will hurt them,
fire proceedeth out of their mouth,
and devoureth their enemies: and
if any man will hurt them, he must
in this manner be killed.
6 These have power to shut
heaven, that it rain not in the days of
their prophecy: and have power over
waters to turn them to blood, and
to smite the earth with all plagues,
as often as they will.

The Beast of the Bottomless Pit

7 And when they shall have fin-
ished their testimony, the beast that
ascendeth out of the bottomless pit
shall make war against them, and
shall overcome them, and kill them.
8 And their dead bodies *shall*
lie in the street of the great city,
which spiritually is called Sodom
and Egypt, where also our Lord was
crucified.
9 And they of the people and kin-
dreds and tongues and nations shall
see their dead bodies three days and
an half, and shall not suffer their
dead bodies to be put in graves.
10 And they that dwell upon the
earth shall rejoice over them, and
make merry, and shall send gifts
one to another; because these two
prophets tormented them that
dwelt on the earth.
11 And after three days and an half
the Spirit of life from God entered
into them, and they stood upon
their feet; and great fear fell upon
them which saw them.
12 And they heard a great voice
from heaven saying unto them,
Come up hither. And they ascended
up to heaven in a cloud; and their
enemies beheld them.
13 And the same hour was there a
great earthquake, and the tenth part
of the city fell, and in the earthquake
were slain of men seven thousand:
and the remnant were affrighted,
and gave glory to the God of heaven.
14 The second woe is past; *and,* be-
hold, the third woe cometh quickly.

The Seventh Trumpet

15 And the seventh angel sounded; and there were great voices in heaven, saying, The kingdoms of this world are become *the kingdoms* of our Lord, and of his Christ; and he shall reign for ever and ever.

16 And the four and twenty elders, which sat before God on their seats, fell upon their faces, and worshipped God,

17 Saying, We give thee thanks, O Lord God Almighty, which art, and wast, and art to come; because thou hast taken to thee thy great power, and hast reigned.

18 And the nations were angry, and thy wrath is come, and the time of the dead, that they should be judged, and that thou shouldest give reward unto thy servants the prophets, and to the saints, and them that fear thy name, small and great; and shouldest destroy them which destroy the earth.

19 And the temple of God was opened in heaven, and there was seen in his temple the ark of his testament: and there were lightnings, and voices, and thunderings, and an earthquake, and great hail.

The Woman with Child

12 And there appeared a great wonder in heaven; a woman clothed with the sun, and the moon under her feet, and upon her head a crown of twelve stars:

2 And she being with child cried, travailing in birth, and pained to be delivered.

3 And there appeared another wonder in heaven; and behold a great red dragon, having seven heads and ten horns, and seven crowns upon his heads.

4 And his tail drew the third part of the stars of heaven, and did cast them to the earth: and the dragon stood before the woman which was ready to be delivered, for to devour her child as soon as it was born.

5 And she brought forth a man child, who was to rule all nations with a rod of iron: and her child was caught up unto God, and *to* his throne.

6 And the woman fled into the wilderness, where she hath a place prepared of God, that they should feed her there a thousand two hundred *and* threescore days.

War Against the Dragon

7 And there was war in heaven: Michael and his angels fought against the dragon; and the dragon fought and his angels,

8 And prevailed not; neither was their place found any more in heaven.

9 And the great dragon was cast out, that old serpent, called the Devil, and Satan, which deceiveth the whole world: he was cast out into the earth, and his angels were cast out with him.

10 And I heard a loud voice saying in heaven, Now is come salvation, and strength, and the kingdom of our God, and the power of his Christ: for the accuser of our brethren is cast down, which accused them before our God day and night.

11 And they overcame him by the blood of the Lamb, and by the word of their testimony; and they loved not their lives unto the death.

12 Therefore rejoice, *ye* heavens, and ye that dwell in them. Woe to the inhabiters of the earth and of the sea! for the devil is come down unto you, having great wrath, because he knoweth that he hath but a short time.

The Dragon's Persecution of the Woman

13 And when the dragon saw that he was cast unto the earth, he persecuted the woman which brought forth the man *child*.

14 And to the woman were given two wings of a great eagle, that she might fly into the wilderness, into her place, where she is nourished for a time, and times, and half a time, from the face of the serpent.

15 And the serpent cast out of his mouth water as a flood after the woman, that he might cause her to be carried away of the flood.

16 And the earth helped the woman, and the earth opened her mouth, and swallowed up the flood which the dragon cast out of his mouth.

17 And the dragon was wroth with the woman, and went to make war with the remnant of her seed, which keep the commandments of God, and have the testimony of Jesus Christ.

The Beast of the Sea

13 And I stood upon the sand of the sea, and saw a beast rise up out of the sea, having seven heads and ten horns, and upon his horns ten crowns, and upon his heads the name of blasphemy.

2 And the beast which I saw was like unto a leopard, and his feet were as *the feet* of a bear, and his mouth as the mouth of a lion: and the dragon gave him his power, and his seat, and great authority.

3 And I saw one of his heads as it were wounded to death; and his deadly wound was healed: and all the world wondered after the beast.

4 And they worshipped the dragon which gave power unto the beast: and they worshipped the beast, saying, Who *is* like unto the beast? who is able to make war with him?

5 And there was given unto him a mouth speaking great things and blasphemies; and power was given unto him to continue forty *and* two months.

6 And he opened his mouth in blasphemy against God, to blaspheme his name, and his tabernacle, and them that dwell in heaven.

7 And it was given unto him to make war with the saints, and to overcome them: and power was given him over all kindreds, and tongues, and nations.

8 And all that dwell upon the earth shall worship him, whose names are not written in the book of life of the Lamb slain from the foundation of the world.

9 If any man have an ear, let him hear.

10 He that leadeth into captivity shall go into captivity: he that killeth with the sword must be killed with the sword. Here is the patience and the faith of the saints.

The Beast of the Earth

11 And I beheld another beast coming up out of the earth; and he had two horns like a lamb, and he spake as a dragon.

12 And he exerciseth all the power of the first beast before him, and causeth the earth and them which dwell therein to worship the first beast, whose deadly wound was healed.

13 And he doeth great wonders, so that he maketh fire come down from heaven on the earth in the sight of men,

14 And deceiveth them that dwell on the earth by *the means of* those miracles which he had power to do in the sight of the beast; saying to them that dwell on the earth, that they should make an image to the beast, which had the wound by a sword, and did live.

15 And he had power to give life unto the image of the beast, that the image of the beast should both speak, and cause that as many as would not worship the image of the beast should be killed.

16 And he causeth all, both small

and great, rich and poor, free and
bond, to receive a mark in their right
hand, or in their foreheads:
17 And that no man might buy or
sell, save he that had the mark, or
the name of the beast, or the num-
ber of his name.
18 Here is wisdom. Let him that
hath understanding count the num-
ber of the beast: for it is the num-
ber of a man; and his number *is* Six
hundred threescore *and* six.

The Redeemed with the Lamb

14 And I looked, and, lo, a Lamb
stood on the mount Sion, and
with him an hundred forty *and* four
thousand, having his Father's name
written in their foreheads.
2 And I heard a voice from heaven,
as the voice of many waters, and as
the voice of a great thunder: and I
heard the voice of harpers harping
with their harps:
3 And they sung as it were a new
song before the throne, and before
the four beasts, and the elders: and
no man could learn that song but
the hundred *and* forty *and* four
thousand, which were redeemed
from the earth.
4 These are they which were not
defiled with women; for they are
virgins. These are they which follow
the Lamb whithersoever he goeth.
These were redeemed from among
men, *being* the firstfruits unto God
and to the Lamb.
5 And in their mouth was found
no guile: for they are without fault
before the throne of God.

The Angels' Messages

6 And I saw another angel fly in
the midst of heaven, having the
everlasting gospel to preach unto
them that dwell on the earth, and
to every nation, and kindred, and
tongue, and people,
7 Saying with a loud voice, Fear
God, and give glory to him; for the
hour of his judgment is come: and
worship him that made heaven, and
earth, and the sea, and the fountains
of waters.
8 And there followed another
angel, saying, Babylon is fallen, is
fallen, that great city, because she
made all nations drink of the wine
of the wrath of her fornication.
9 And the third angel followed
them, saying with a loud voice, If
any man worship the beast and his
image, and receive *his* mark in his
forehead, or in his hand,
10 The same shall drink of the
wine of the wrath of God, which is
poured out without mixture into
the cup of his indignation; and he
shall be tormented with fire and
brimstone in the presence of the
holy angels, and in the presence of
the Lamb:
11 And the smoke of their torment
ascendeth up for ever and ever: and
they have no rest day nor night, who
worship the beast and his image,
and whosoever receiveth the mark
of his name.
12 Here is the patience of the
saints: here *are* they that keep the
commandments of God, and the
faith of Jesus.
13 And I heard a voice from heaven
saying unto me, Write, Blessed *are*
the dead which die in the Lord from
henceforth: Yea, saith the Spirit, that
they may rest from their labours;
and their works do follow them.

The Ripe Harvest

14 And I looked, and behold a
white cloud, and upon the cloud
one sat like unto the Son of man,
having on his head a golden crown,
and in his hand a sharp sickle.
15 And another angel came out
of the temple, crying with a loud
voice to him that sat on the cloud,
Thrust in thy sickle, and reap: for
the time is come for thee to reap;
for the harvest of the earth is ripe.

16 And he that sat on the cloud
thrust in his sickle on the earth; and
the earth was reaped.
17 And another angel came out of
the temple which is in heaven, he
also having a sharp sickle.
18 And another angel came out
from the altar, which had power
over fire; and cried with a loud cry
to him that had the sharp sickle,
saying, Thrust in thy sharp sickle,
and gather the clusters of the vine
of the earth; for her grapes are fully
ripe.
19 And the angel thrust in his
sickle into the earth, and gathered
the vine of the earth, and cast *it* into
the great winepress of the wrath of
God.
20 And the winepress was trod-
den without the city, and blood
came out of the winepress, even
unto the horse bridles, by the space
of a thousand *and* six hundred fur-
longs.

The Seven Last Plagues

15 And I saw another sign in
heaven, great and marvellous,
seven angels having the seven last
plagues; for in them is filled up the
wrath of God.
2 And I saw as it were a sea of
glass mingled with fire: and them
that had gotten the victory over the
beast, and over his image, and over
his mark, *and* over the number of
his name, stand on the sea of glass,
having the harps of God.
3 And they sing the song of Moses
the servant of God, and the song of
the Lamb, saying, Great and mar-
vellous *are* thy works, Lord God Al-
mighty; just and true *are* thy ways,
thou King of saints.
4 Who shall not fear thee, O Lord,
and glorify thy name? for *thou* only
art holy: for all nations shall come
and worship before thee; for thy
judgments are made manifest.

The Tabernacle of the Testimony

5 And after that I looked, and,
behold, the temple of the taberna-
cle of the testimony in heaven was
opened:
6 And the seven angels came out
of the temple, having the seven
plagues, clothed in pure and white
linen, and having their breasts
girded with golden girdles.
7 And one of the four beasts gave
unto the seven angels seven golden
vials full of the wrath of God, who
liveth for ever and ever.
8 And the temple was filled with
smoke from the glory of God, and
from his power; and no man was
able to enter into the temple, till the
seven plagues of the seven angels
were fulfilled.

The Seven Vials of God's Wrath

16 And I heard a great voice out
of the temple saying to the
seven angels, Go your ways, and
pour out the vials of the wrath of
God upon the earth.

The First Vial

2 And the first went, and poured
out his vial upon the earth; and
there fell a noisome and grievous
sore upon the men which had the
mark of the beast, and *upon* them
which worshipped his image.

The Second Vial

3 And the second angel poured out
his vial upon the sea; and it became
as the blood of a dead *man:* and ev-
ery living soul died in the sea.

The Third Vial

4 And the third angel poured out
his vial upon the rivers and foun-
tains of waters; and they became
blood.
5 And I heard the angel of the
waters say, Thou art righteous,

O Lord, which art, and wast, and
shalt be, because thou hast judged
thus.
6 For they have shed the blood of
saints and prophets, and thou hast
given them blood to drink; for they
are worthy.
7 And I heard another out of the
altar say, Even so, Lord God Al-
mighty, true and righteous *are* thy
judgments.

The Fourth Vial

8 And the fourth angel poured out
his vial upon the sun; and power
was given unto him to scorch men
with fire.
9 And men were scorched with
great heat, and blasphemed the
name of God, which hath power over
these plagues: and they repented
not to give him glory.

The Fifth Vial

10 And the fifth angel poured out
his vial upon the seat of the beast;
and his kingdom was full of dark-
ness; and they gnawed their tongues
for pain,
11 And blasphemed the God of
heaven because of their pains and
their sores, and repented not of their
deeds.

The Sixth Vial

12 And the sixth angel poured out
his vial upon the great river Euphra-
tes; and the water thereof was dried
up, that the way of the kings of the
east might be prepared.
13 And I saw three unclean spirits
like frogs *come* out of the mouth of
the dragon, and out of the mouth
of the beast, and out of the mouth
of the false prophet.
14 For they are the spirits of devils,
working miracles, *which* go forth
unto the kings of the earth and of
the whole world, to gather them to
the battle of that great day of God
Almighty.
15 Behold, I come as a thief.
Blessed *is* he that watcheth, and
keepeth his garments, lest he walk
naked, and they see his shame.
16 And he gathered them together
into a place called in the Hebrew
tongue Armageddon.

The Seventh Vial

17 And the seventh angel poured
out his vial into the air; and there
came a great voice out of the temple
of heaven, from the throne, saying,
It is done.
18 And there were voices, and
thunders, and lightnings; and there
was a great earthquake, such as was
not since men were upon the earth,
so mighty an earthquake, *and* so
great.
19 And the great city was divided
into three parts, and the cities of
the nations fell: and great Babylon
came in remembrance before God,
to give unto her the cup of the wine
of the fierceness of his wrath.
20 And every island fled away, and
the mountains were not found.
21 And there fell upon men a great
hail out of heaven, *every stone* about
the weight of a talent: and men blas-
phemed God because of the plague
of the hail; for the plague thereof
was exceeding great.

The Woman
and the Scarlet Beast

17 And there came one of the
seven angels which had the
seven vials, and talked with me,
saying unto me, Come hither; I will
shew unto thee the judgment of
the great whore that sitteth upon
many waters:
2 With whom the kings of the
earth have committed fornication,
and the inhabitants of the earth
have been made drunk with the
wine of her fornication.
3 So he carried me away in the
spirit into the wilderness: and I saw

a woman sit upon a scarlet coloured
beast, full of names of blasphemy,
having seven heads and ten horns.
4 And the woman was arrayed
in purple and scarlet colour, and
decked with gold and precious
stones and pearls, having a golden
cup in her hand full of abomina-
tions and filthiness of her fornica-
tion:
5 And upon her forehead *was* a
name written, MYSTERY, BAB-
YLON THE GREAT, THE MOTHER
OF HARLOTS AND ABOMINATIONS
OF THE EARTH.
6 And I saw the woman drunken
with the blood of the saints, and
with the blood of the martyrs of
Jesus: and when I saw her, I won-
dered with great admiration.

The Mystery of the Woman and the Beast

7 And the angel said unto me,
Wherefore didst thou marvel? I will
tell thee the mystery of the woman,
and of the beast that carrieth her,
which hath the seven heads and ten
horns.
8 The beast that thou sawest was,
and is not; and shall ascend out of
the bottomless pit, and go into per-
dition: and they that dwell on the
earth shall wonder, whose names
were not written in the book of life
from the foundation of the world,
when they behold the beast that
was, and is not, and yet is.
9 And here *is* the mind which hath
wisdom. The seven heads are seven
mountains, on which the woman
sitteth.
10 And there are seven kings:
five are fallen, and one is, *and* the
other is not yet come; and when he
cometh, he must continue a short
space.
11 And the beast that was, and is
not, even he is the eighth, and is of
the seven, and goeth into perdition.
12 And the ten horns which thou
sawest are ten kings, which have
received no kingdom as yet; but re-
ceive power as kings one hour with
the beast.
13 These have one mind, and shall
give their power and strength unto
the beast.
14 These shall make war with the
Lamb, and the Lamb shall overcome
them: for he is Lord of lords, and
King of kings: and they that are
with him *are* called, and chosen,
and faithful.
15 And he saith unto me, The wa-
ters which thou sawest, where the
whore sitteth, are peoples, and mul-
titudes, and nations, and tongues.
16 And the ten horns which thou
sawest upon the beast, these shall
hate the whore, and shall make her
desolate and naked, and shall eat
her flesh, and burn her with fire.
17 For God hath put in their hearts
to fulfil his will, and to agree, and
give their kingdom unto the beast,
until the words of God shall be ful-
filled.
18 And the woman which thou
sawest is that great city, which
reigneth over the kings of the earth.

Babylon Is Fallen

18 And after these things I saw
another angel come down
from heaven, having great power;
and the earth was lightened with
his glory.
2 And he cried mightily with a
strong voice, saying, Babylon the
great is fallen, is fallen, and is be-
come the habitation of devils, and
the hold of every foul spirit, and a
cage of every unclean and hateful
bird.
3 For all nations have drunk of the
wine of the wrath of her fornication,
and the kings of the earth have com-
mitted fornication with her, and the
merchants of the earth are waxed
rich through the abundance of her
delicacies.

Babylon's Iniquities

4 And I heard another voice from
heaven, saying, Come out of her, my
people, that ye be not partakers of
her sins, and that ye receive not of
her plagues.
5 For her sins have reached unto
heaven, and God hath remembered
her iniquities.
6 Reward her even as she re-
warded you, and double unto her
double according to her works: in
the cup which she hath filled fill to
her double.
7 How much she hath glorified
herself, and lived deliciously, so
much torment and sorrow give
her: for she saith in her heart, I sit
a queen, and am no widow, and shall
see no sorrow.
8 Therefore shall her plagues
come in one day, death, and mourn-
ing, and famine; and she shall be
utterly burned with fire: for strong
is the Lord God who judgeth her.

Babylon's Destruction

9 And the kings of the earth, who
have committed fornication and
lived deliciously with her, shall be-
wail her, and lament for her, when
they shall see the smoke of her burn-
ing,
10 Standing afar off for the fear
of her torment, saying, Alas, alas
that great city Babylon, that mighty
city! for in one hour is thy judgment
come.
11 And the merchants of the earth
shall weep and mourn over her; for
no man buyeth their merchandise
any more:
12 The merchandise of gold, and
silver, and precious stones, and of
pearls, and fine linen, and purple,
and silk, and scarlet, and all thy-
ine wood, and all manner vessels
of ivory, and all manner vessels of
most precious wood, and of brass,
and iron, and marble,
13 And cinnamon, and odours,
and ointments, and frankincense,
and wine, and oil, and fine flour, and
wheat, and beasts, and sheep, and
horses, and chariots, and slaves,
and souls of men.
14 And the fruits that thy soul
lusted after are departed from thee,
and all things which were dainty and
goodly are departed from thee, and
thou shalt find them no more at all.
15 The merchants of these things,
which were made rich by her, shall
stand afar off for the fear of her tor-
ment, weeping and wailing,
16 And saying, Alas, alas that great
city, that was clothed in fine linen,
and purple, and scarlet, and decked
with gold, and precious stones, and
pearls!
17 For in one hour so great riches
is come to nought. And every ship-
master, and all the company in
ships, and sailors, and as many as
trade by sea, stood afar off,
18 And cried when they saw the
smoke of her burning, saying, What
city is like unto this great city!
19 And they cast dust on their
heads, and cried, weeping and
wailing, saying, Alas, alas that great
city, wherein were made rich all that
had ships in the sea by reason of her
costliness! for in one hour is she
made desolate.
20 Rejoice over her, *thou* heaven,
and *ye* holy apostles and prophets;
for God hath avenged you on her.

Babylon Will Be Thrown Down

21 And a mighty angel took up a
stone like a great millstone, and cast
it into the sea, saying, Thus with
violence shall that great city Bab-
ylon be thrown down, and shall be
found no more at all.
22 And the voice of harpers, and
musicians, and of pipers, and trum-
peters, shall be heard no more at all
in thee; and no craftsman, of what-
soever craft *he be,* shall be found

any more in thee; and the sound of
a millstone shall be heard no more
at all in thee;
23 And the light of a candle shall
shine no more at all in thee; and the
voice of the bridegroom and of the
bride shall be heard no more at all
in thee: for thy merchants were the
great men of the earth; for by thy
sorceries were all nations deceived.
24 And in her was found the blood
of prophets, and of saints, and of all
that were slain upon the earth.

The Judgment of the Great Whore

19 And after these things I heard
a great voice of much people
in heaven, saying, Alleluia; Salva-
tion, and glory, and honour, and
power, unto the Lord our God:
2 For true and righteous *are* his
judgments: for he hath judged the
great whore, which did corrupt the
earth with her fornication, and hath
avenged the blood of his servants at
her hand.
3 And again they said, Alleluia. And
her smoke rose up for ever and ever.

The Elders and the Four Beasts

4 And the four and twenty elders
and the four beasts fell down and
worshipped God that sat on the
throne, saying, Amen; Alleluia.
5 And a voice came out of the
throne, saying, Praise our God, all
ye his servants, and ye that fear him,
both small and great.
6 And I heard as it were the voice
of a great multitude, and as the voice
of many waters, and as the voice of
mighty thunderings, saying, Alle-
luia: for the Lord God omnipotent
reigneth.
7 Let us be glad and rejoice, and
give honour to him: for the marriage
of the Lamb is come, and his wife
hath made herself ready.
8 And to her was granted that she
should be arrayed in fine linen, clean
and white: for the fine linen is the
righteousness of saints.

The Marriage Supper of the Lamb

9 And he saith unto me, Write,
Blessed *are* they which are called
unto the marriage supper of the
Lamb. And he saith unto me, These
are the true sayings of God.
10 And I fell at his feet to worship
him. And he said unto me, See *thou*
do it not: I am thy fellowservant,
and of thy brethren that have the
testimony of Jesus: worship God: for
the testimony of Jesus is the spirit
of prophecy.

The Righteous Judge

11 And I saw heaven opened, and
behold a white horse; and he that
sat upon him *was* called Faithful
and True, and in righteousness he
doth judge and make war.
12 His eyes *were* as a flame of fire,
and on his head *were* many crowns;
and he had a name written, that no
man knew, but he himself.
13 And he *was* clothed with a ves-
ture dipped in blood: and his name
is called The Word of God.
14 And the armies *which were* in
heaven followed him upon white
horses, clothed in fine linen, white
and clean.
15 And out of his mouth goeth a
sharp sword, that with it he should
smite the nations: and he shall rule
them with a rod of iron: and he tread-
eth the winepress of the fierceness
and wrath of Almighty God.
16 And he hath on *his* vesture and
on his thigh a name written, KING
OF KINGS, AND LORD OF LORDS.
17 And I saw an angel standing in
the sun; and he cried with a loud
voice, saying to all the fowls that fly
in the midst of heaven, Come and
gather yourselves together unto the
supper of the great God;

18 That ye may eat the flesh of kings, and the flesh of captains, and the flesh of mighty men, and the flesh of horses, and of them that sit on them, and the flesh of all *men, both* free and bond, both small and great.

The Capture of the Beast

19 And I saw the beast, and the kings of the earth, and their armies, gathered together to make war against him that sat on the horse, and against his army.

20 And the beast was taken, and with him the false prophet that wrought miracles before him, with which he deceived them that had received the mark of the beast, and them that worshipped his image. These both were cast alive into a lake of fire burning with brimstone.

21 And the remnant were slain with the sword of him that sat upon the horse, which *sword* proceeded out of his mouth: and all the fowls were filled with their flesh.

Satan Bound for a Thousand Years

20 And I saw an angel come down from heaven, having the key of the bottomless pit and a great chain in his hand.

2 And he laid hold on the dragon, that old serpent, which is the Devil, and Satan, and bound him a thousand years,

3 And cast him into the bottomless pit, and shut him up, and set a seal upon him, that he should deceive the nations no more, till the thousand years should be fulfilled: and after that he must be loosed a little season.

4 And I saw thrones, and they sat upon them, and judgment was given unto them: and I *saw* the souls of them that were beheaded for the witness of Jesus, and for the word of God, and which had not worshipped the beast, neither his image, neither had received *his* mark upon their foreheads, or in their hands; and they lived and reigned with Christ a thousand years.

5 But the rest of the dead lived not again until the thousand years were finished. This *is* the first resurrection.

6 Blessed and holy *is* he that hath part in the first resurrection: on such the second death hath no power, but they shall be priests of God and of Christ, and shall reign with him a thousand years.

The Lake of Fire and Brimstone

7 And when the thousand years are expired, Satan shall be loosed out of his prison,

8 And shall go out to deceive the nations which are in the four quarters of the earth, Gog and Magog, to gather them together to battle: the number of whom *is* as the sand of the sea.

9 And they went up on the breadth of the earth, and compassed the camp of the saints about, and the beloved city: and fire came down from God out of heaven, and devoured them.

10 And the devil that deceived them was cast into the lake of fire and brimstone, where the beast and the false prophet *are,* and shall be tormented day and night for ever and ever.

The Book of Life

11 And I saw a great white throne, and him that sat on it, from whose face the earth and the heaven fled away; and there was found no place for them.

12 And I saw the dead, small and great, stand before God; and the books were opened: and another book was opened, which is *the book* of life: and the dead were judged out

of those things which were written in the books, according to their works.

13 And the sea gave up the dead which were in it; and death and hell delivered up the dead which were in them: and they were judged every man according to their works.

14 And death and hell were cast into the lake of fire. This is the second death.

15 And whosoever was not found written in the book of life was cast into the lake of fire.

A New Heaven and New Earth

21 And I saw a new heaven and a new earth: for the first heaven and the first earth were passed away; and there was no more sea.

2 And I John saw the holy city, new Jerusalem, coming down from God out of heaven, prepared as a bride adorned for her husband.

3 And I heard a great voice out of heaven saying, Behold, the tabernacle of God *is* with men, and he will dwell with them, and they shall be his people, and God himself shall be with them, *and be* their God.

4 And God shall wipe away all tears from their eyes; and there shall be no more death, neither sorrow, nor crying, neither shall there be any more pain: for the former things are passed away.

5 And he that sat upon the throne said, Behold, I make all things new. And he said unto me, Write: for these words are true and faithful.

The Fountain of Life

6 And he said unto me, It is done. I am Alpha and Omega, the beginning and the end. I will give unto him that is athirst of the fountain of the water of life freely.

7 He that overcometh shall inherit all things; and I will be his God, and he shall be my son.

8 But the fearful, and unbelieving, and the abominable, and murderers, and whoremongers, and sorcerers, and idolaters, and all liars, shall have their part in the lake which burneth with fire and brimstone: which is the second death.

9 And there came unto me one of the seven angels which had the seven vials full of the seven last plagues, and talked with me, saying, Come hither, I will shew thee the bride, the Lamb's wife.

10 And he carried me away in the spirit to a great and high mountain, and shewed me that great city, the holy Jerusalem, descending out of heaven from God,

11 Having the glory of God: and her light *was* like unto a stone most precious, even like a jasper stone, clear as crystal;

12 And had a wall great and high, *and* had twelve gates, and at the gates twelve angels, and names written thereon, which are *the names* of the twelve tribes of the children of Israel:

13 On the east three gates; on the north three gates; on the south three gates; and on the west three gates.

14 And the wall of the city had twelve foundations, and in them the names of the twelve apostles of the Lamb.

The Golden Reed

15 And he that talked with me had a golden reed to measure the city, and the gates thereof, and the wall thereof.

16 And the city lieth foursquare, and the length is as large as the breadth: and he measured the city with the reed, twelve thousand furlongs. The length and the breadth and the height of it are equal.

17 And he measured the wall thereof, an hundred *and* forty *and* four cubits, *according to* the measure of a man, that is, of the angel.

18 And the building of the wall of it was *of* jasper: and the city *was* pure gold, like unto clear glass.

19 And the foundations of the wall
of the city *were* garnished with all
manner of precious stones. The first
foundation *was* jasper; the second,
sapphire; the third, a chalcedony;
the fourth, an emerald;
20 The fifth, sardonyx; the sixth,
sardius; the seventh, chrysolyte; the
eighth, beryl; the ninth, a topaz; the
tenth, a chrysoprasus; the eleventh,
a jacinth; the twelfth, an amethyst.
21 And the twelve gates *were*
twelve pearls; every several gate
was of one pearl: and the street of
the city *was* pure gold, as it were
transparent glass.

The City's Light and Glory

22 And I saw no temple therein:
for the Lord God Almighty and the
Lamb are the temple of it.
23 And the city had no need of the
sun, neither of the moon, to shine in
it: for the glory of God did lighten it,
and the Lamb *is* the light thereof.
24 And the nations of them which
are saved shall walk in the light of it:
and the kings of the earth do bring
their glory and honour into it.
25 And the gates of it shall not be
shut at all by day: for there shall be
no night there.
26 And they shall bring the glory
and honour of the nations into it.
27 And there shall in no wise enter
into it any thing that defileth, nei-
ther *whatsoever* worketh abomina-
tion, or *maketh* a lie: but they which
are written in the Lamb's book of
life.

The Pure River of Life

22 And he shewed me a pure
river of water of life, clear as
crystal, proceeding out of the throne
of God and of the Lamb.
2 In the midst of the street of
it, and on either side of the river,
was there the tree of life, which
bare twelve *manner of* fruits, *and*
yielded her fruit every month: and
the leaves of the tree *were* for the
healing of the nations.
3 And there shall be no more
curse: but the throne of God and
of the Lamb shall be in it; and his
servants shall serve him:
4 And they shall see his face; and
his name *shall be* in their foreheads.
5 And there shall be no night
there; and they need no candle, nei-
ther light of the sun; for the Lord
God giveth them light: and they shall
reign for ever and ever.
6 And he said unto me, These say-
ings *are* faithful and true: and the
Lord God of the holy prophets sent
his angel to shew unto his servants
the things which must shortly be
done.

Jesus Will Come Quickly

7 Behold, I come quickly: blessed
is he that keepeth the sayings of the
prophecy of this book.
8 And I John saw these things, and
heard *them*. And when I had heard
and seen, I fell down to worship
before the feet of the angel which
shewed me these things.
9 Then saith he unto me, See *thou*
do it not: for I am thy fellowservant,
and of thy brethren the prophets,
and of them which keep the sayings
of this book: worship God.
10 And he saith unto me, Seal not
the sayings of the prophecy of this
book: for the time is at hand.
11 He that is unjust, let him be
unjust still: and he which is filthy,
let him be filthy still: and he that is
righteous, let him be righteous still:
and he that is holy, let him be holy
still.

The Bright and Morning Star

12 And, behold, I come quickly; and
my reward *is* with me, to give every
man according as his work shall be.
13 I am Alpha and Omega, the be-
ginning and the end, the first and
the last.

14 Blessed *are* they that do his
commandments, that they may have
right to the tree of life, and may enter
in through the gates into the city.
15 For without *are* dogs, and sor-
cerers, and whoremongers, and
murderers, and idolaters, and who-
soever loveth and maketh a lie.
16 I Jesus have sent mine angel
to testify unto you these things in
the churches. I am the root and the
offspring of David, *and* the bright
and morning star.
17 And the Spirit and the bride say,
Come. And let him that heareth say,
Come. And let him that is athirst
come. And whosoever will, let him
take the water of life freely.

Come, Lord Jesus

18 For I testify unto every man that
heareth the words of the prophecy
of this book, If any man shall add
unto these things, God shall add
unto him the plagues that are writ-
ten in this book:
19 And if any man shall take away
from the words of the book of this
prophecy, God shall take away his
part out of the book of life, and out
of the holy city, and *from* the things
which are written in this book.
20 He which testifieth these things
saith, Surely I come quickly. Amen.
Even so, come, Lord Jesus.
21 The grace of our Lord Jesus
Christ *be* with you all. Amen.